THE HUMAN RIGHTS FIELD OPERATION

The Human Rights Field Operation
Law, Theory and Practice

Edited by
MICHAEL O'FLAHERTY

629399002

Published by
Ashgate Publishing Limited
Gower House
Croft Road
Aldershot
Hampshire GU11 3HR
England

Ashgate Publishing Company
Suite 420
101 Cherry Street
Burlington, VT 05401-4405
USA

Ashgate website: http://www.ashgate.com

British Library Cataloguing in Publication Data
The human rights field operation : law, theory and practice
  1. United Nations 2. Humanitarian intervention
  3. Humanitarian intervention - Case studies 4. Human rights
  workers 5. Human rights workers - Case studies
  I. O'Flaherty, Michael, solicitor
  341.5'84

Library of Congress Cataloging-in-Publication Data
The human rights field operation : law, theory and practice / edited by Michael O'Flaherty.
    p. cm.
  Includes bibliographical references and index.
  ISBN-13: 978-0-7546-4936-6
  ISBN-13: 978-0-7546-4937-3 1. Human rights
field operations. 2. Humanitarian assistance. 3. Human rights
workers. 4. United Nations. I. O'Flaherty, Michael, solicitor.

  JC571.H865 2006
  341.5'84--dc22

                                                                    2006025017

ISBN 978 0 7546 4936 6 (HBK)
ISBN 978 0 7546 4937 3 (PBK)

Printed and bound in Great Britain by TJ International Ltd, Padstow, Cornwall.

JC
571
· H8528
2007

Contents

List of Figures

Notes on Contributors

Alain Aeschlimann, a Swiss national, is a lawyer by training. He joined the International Committee of the Red Cross (ICRC) in 1987. In the field, his assignments included long-term missions in Iraq, Angola and Peru before his heading ICRC operations in Iraq, Israel and the Palestinian Occupied and Autonomous Territories, and Ethiopia.

He was appointed Head of the Central Tracing Agency and Protection Division in mid-2003. He had earlier served at the ICRC Headquarters as Coordinator of Legal Advisors to the Operations and Deputy Head of Detention Division, then Central Tracing Agency and Protection Division.

He has written or contributed to several articles, including 'Reflections on a dissemination operation in Burundi', 'Declaration for Standards of Humanitarian Conduct: Appeal for a Minimum of Humanity in a Situation of Internal Violence' (IRRC August 1997), 'Protection of Detainees: ICRC Action Behind Bars' (IRRC, March 2005), 'Protection of IDPs: An ICRC View' (FMR October 2005).

Patrick Burgess is a barrister with extensive experience as a trial and appellate advocate in Australian courts. He has worked in Rwanda, Burundi, Zaire, Uganda, Yemen, India, Nepal, Indonesia and Timor Leste. He spent six continuous years working for United Nations (UN) missions in East Timor between 1999 and 2005. He was the senior humanitarian officer in the United Nations Assistance Mission in East Timor, a District Administrator in the period immediately following the intense conflict of 1999, and Director of Human Rights for the United Nations Transitional Administration in East Timor and United Nations Mission in East Timor missions, 1999–2002. From 2002–2005 he was Senior Advisor and Principal Legal Counsel for the East Timor Commission for Reception, Truth and Reconciliation. He is currently an international consultant in the fields of transitional justice, human rights and rule of law.

Nicholas Howen is Secretary-General of the International Commission of Jurists (ICJ). Immediately prior to assuming the office of Secretary-General of the ICJ in April 2004, he was based in Bangkok as the first Asia-Pacific Regional Representative for the Office of the United Nations High Commissioner for Human Rights (OHCHR). From 1998–2000 he led the Human Rights Division of the United Nations peacekeeping operation in Angola. During the 1990s he was chief legal counsel at Amnesty International for four years.

He has also worked as an international human rights law consultant, writing on international human rights issues and working with UN agencies, non-governmental organisations (NGOs) and development cooperation agencies. He is the co-founder and former co-director of the Tibet Information Network. He is an Australian international human rights lawyer and practised law as a solicitor in Sydney, Australia.

Todd Howland is currently the Director of the Robert F. Kennedy Memorial Center for Human Rights, an organisation that partners with human rights advocates around the world in pursuit of concrete human rights change. Previously, he was with OHCHR posted to Angola and Rwanda. He was Officer-in-Charge of the Human Rights Division of the United Nations Mission to Angola and the head of the Legal and Human Rights Promotion Unit of the UN Human Rights Field Operation for Rwanda. He also has worked with various NGOs, including the Carter Center in Ethiopia.

Karin Landgren has been the United Nations Children's Fund's (UNICEF) Chief of Child Protection since 1998, directing the agency's efforts to protect children from violence, exploitation and abuse. Prior to this, she spent nearly 20 years with the Office of the United Nations High Commissioner for Refugees (UNHCR), heading their office in Bosnia and Herzegovina during the war, as well as offices in Eritrea and Singapore. She was also UNHCR's Chief of Standards and Legal Advice. In the 1980s, she worked extensively with Afghan, Iranian and Vietnamese asylum seekers as Protection Officer for UNHCR in India and as Deputy Representative in the Philippines.

She has lectured and written on refugee protection, child protection and the protection of human rights in humanitarian crises. She is a Corresponding Editor of *International Legal Materials*. She holds degrees in International Relations (BSc) and International Law (LLM) from the London School of Economics. She is a Swedish national, and grew up in Japan.

Milburn Line worked a total of nine years with the United Nations Human Rights Verification Mission, managing a United States Agency for International Development-funded human rights project in Guatemala, and with the Organization for Security and Co-operation in Europe (OSCE) and Office of the High Representative in Bosnia and Herzegovina.

Annette Lyth has an LLM in international human rights and humanitarian law from the Raoul Wallenberg Institute in Sweden. She has worked for Amnesty International, the UN human rights field operation in Rwanda and the OSCE Mission to Kosovo. She was the Deputy Head of the Human Rights Department at OSCE/Office for Democratic Institutions and Human Rights for three years and is currently working with the United Nations Development Fund for Women as Governance, Peace and Security Programme Manager.

Liam Mahony is the Civilian Protection Analyst for the Centre for Humanitarian Dialogue. He is a pioneer in the theory and practice of international protection with unarmed presence. He began working in the mid-1980s in Guatemala, with Peace

Brigades International (PBI), offering international accompaniment to civil society activists threatened by death squads and military dictatorship. He subsequently helped to develop training frameworks for PBI's international protection, and co-founded PBI's field presence in Haiti. He co-authored: *Unarmed Bodyguards: International Accompaniment for the Protection of Human Rights*, a book analysing protective accompaniment and providing theoretical models for understanding its impact. He edited the *Kosovo Report* of the Independent International Commission on Kosovo (Oxford University Press, 2000). He has been Lecturer in Public and International Affairs at the Woodrow Wilson School, Princeton University, and was the series editor of the Tactical Notebook series of the New Tactics in Human Rights Project of the Center for Victims of Torture (www.newtactics.org). His recent consulting includes the Rockefeller Foundation, the World Council of Churches, Amnesty International, OHCHR and the World Food Programme.

David Marshall is Human Rights Officer: Transitional Justice, OHCHR. He is the former head of Legal Systems Monitoring Section, Human Rights Division, OSCE, Kosovo; former project director, Afghanistan, Department of Justice, Canada; former consultant to Amnesty International on US criminal justice issues; a member of the Bar of England and Wales, New York and US Supreme Court Bar; and holds the degrees of LLB Leeds, LLM Harvard.

Daniel Moeckli is working on a doctoral thesis on terrorism and human rights at the University of Nottingham, where he is also a Research Associate at the Human Rights Law Centre. He has previously worked for the Human Rights Institute of the International Bar Association, Amnesty International and the Supreme Court of the Canton of Bern (Switzerland). He holds a law degree from the University of Bern, an LLM from the London School of Economics and Politics and a Diploma in Human Rights Law from the European University Institute. He is a member of the Swiss Bar.

Manfred Nowak is Professor of Constitutional Law and Human Rights at the University of Vienna and Director of the Ludwig Boltzmann Institute of Human Rights. Since 1996, he has served as Judge at the Human Rights Chamber for Bosnia and Herzegovina, and, since 2000, as Chairperson of the European Master Programme on Human Rights and Democratization in Venice. From 1987 to 1989, he was Director of the Netherlands Institute of Human Rights at the University of Utrecht, and from 2002 to 2003 Visiting Professor at the University of Lund.

He was a member of the Austrian delegation to the UN Commission on Human Rights for many years, before he was appointed in 1993 as an expert member of the UN Working Group on Enforced and Involuntary Disappearances. During this term he also served as a United Nations expert on missing persons in the former Yugoslavia, and in 2001 he was appointed United Nations expert on legal issues relating to the drafting of a binding instrument on enforced disappearances. In December 2004, he was appointed United Nations Special Rapporteur on Torture.

He has published more than 350 books and articles in the fields of human rights, public law and politics. He holds an LLM from Columbia University in New York and a PhD from Vienna University.

Marco Odello, Lecturer in Law, University of Wales, Aberystwyth. He has worked with UNICEF-Italy, the International Institute of Humanitarian Law (San Remo), and the European Public Law Centre (Athens). He has taught international law, international organisations, comparative law and human rights in Peru, Venezuela and Mexico. He lectures at the Summer University of Human Rights (Geneva) and at the International Institute of Humanitarian Law. He is co-author of *La Convenzione Internazionale sui Diritti del Minore e l'Ordinamento Italiano* (Naples, ESI, 1994); Mazzarelli and Odello (eds), *L'insegnamento dei Diritti Umani* (Rome, EDIUN, 1999); and co-author of *Problemas Actuales del Derecho Público en Mexico* (Mexico DF, Porrua, 2004).

Michael O'Flaherty is Reader in Human Rights and Co-Director of the Human Rights Law Centre at the University of Nottingham. In 2004 he was elected to a four-year term as Member of the United Nations Human Rights Committee. Until 2003, he was a Senior Research Officer at UNICEF. Previous UN postings included coordination of the Asia and Pacific programmes at OHCHR, establishment of the UN human rights field operations in Sierra Leone and Bosnia and Herzegovina, Secretary of the UN Committee on the Elimination of Racial Discrimination and UN human rights advisor for implementation of the Dayton Peace Agreement. From 2000 to 2002 he chaired the UN task force on human rights and humanitarian action.

He is a Visiting Professor at the Sant'Anna School of Advanced Studies (Pisa), Fellow of Kingston University and has served as an advisor to, among others, OHCHR, UNICEF, the UN Office for the Coordination of Humanitarian Affairs, the Council of Europe, the European Union and the Special Court for Sierra Leone. He is a member of a number of journal editorial boards and NGO advisory committees as well as the Council of the European Inter-University Centre for Human Rights and Democratisation. He holds degrees in law (BCL: UCD, Dublin), theology and philosophy (BPh, STB: PUG, Rome), international relations (MA, MPhil: Amsterdam) and is a Solicitor of the Irish Courts.

William G. O'Neill is a lawyer specialising in international human rights, humanitarian and refugee law. He chaired a UN Task Force on Developing Rule of Law Strategies in Peace Operations and was Senior Advisor on Human Rights in the UN Mission in Kosovo. He was Chief of the UN Human Rights Field Operation in Rwanda and directed the Legal Department of the UN/Organization of American States International Civilian Mission in Haiti. He has investigated mass killings in Afghanistan for OHCHR and conducted assessments of the High Commissioner's Office in Abkhazia/Georgia and of the OSCE's Human Rights Department in Bosnia-Herzegovina. He trained the UN human rights officers in Darfur, Sudan in early 2005. His work in Sierra Leone focused on how the Special Court can contribute to broad-based legal reform, and in Burundi, Cape Verde, Nepal and Mauritania, on developing and implementing national human rights action plans. He has created and delivered training courses on peace operations for military, police, humanitarian and human rights officers and contributed chapters to the United Nations *Manual on Peacekeeping*. The question of how to integrate human rights in development work has become a recent focus of his work. He has published widely on rule of law issues, peacekeeping and human rights.

Bertrand G. Ramcharan is Chancellor of the University of Guyana and Distinguished Visiting Fellow at the Human Rights Law Centre of the University of Nottingham. He was Deputy United Nations High Commissioner for Human Rights from 1998 to 2003 and Acting High Commissioner in 2003–2004. He is a Barrister-at-Law of Lincoln's Inn and has Masters and Doctorate degrees in Law from the London School of Economics and Political Science, earned the Diploma in International Law of The Hague Academy of International Law, a Diploma in Air and Space Law and a Diploma in International Affairs from the University of London. He has previously been Director of Studies at the Research Centre of The Hague Academy of International Law. He served as Director of the International Conference on the Former Yugoslavia between 1992 and 1996. Earlier, he was for five years the Head of the UN secretary-general's speechwriting team and wrote the first draft of *Agenda for Peace*. He was a Director in the Department of Political Affairs from 1996–1998, dealing with African issues. He has taught at various universities and is the author of several books, including *A United Nations High Commissioner in Defence of Human Rights* (2005).

Susanne Ringgaard-Pedersen has worked on human rights and humanitarian law issues for OSCE in missions in Kosovo and the former Yugoslav Republic of Macedonia, the OSCE Secretariat in Vienna and the OSCE Office for Democratic Institutions and Human Rights in Warsaw. Other experience includes human rights field work in Cambodia and Sri Lanka. She currently works with the OHCHR field operation in Nepal. She has a BA in international studies from Western Maryland College and an MA degree in international human rights and humanitarian law from the Raoul Wallenberg Institute, Lund University, Sweden.

Maria Stavropoulou (JD Athens, LLM University College London, LLM Harvard Law School) has served at the United Nations Centre for Human Rights from 1993 to 1996 and has since worked with UNHCR. Since 1990 her area of work has been the human rights of refugees and internally displaced persons.

Kevin Turner is Research Fellow and Project Officer at the University of Nottingham Human Rights Law Centre. He has worked previously with the US Senate, the Center for Creative Problem Solving and the Joan B. Kroc Institute for Peace & Justice, and has published in media outlets on international humanitarian law, human rights law and peace processes. He holds degrees in government and politics (George Mason

University, BA), peace and justice studies (University of San Diego, MA) and human rights law (University of Nottingham, LLM).

George Ulrich is, since 2003, Secretary-General of the European Inter-University Centre for Human Rights and Democratisation, where he served previously for three years as the Academic Coordinator and Acting Programme Director of the E.MA programme. Prior to this, he was Senior Researcher at the Danish Centre for Human Rights and Research Fellow at the University of Copenhagen's Institute of Anthropology. He has published widely on issues of ethics and human rights, and lectured throughout Europe and Africa. He holds a Cand.Mag. degree in social anthropology and history of ideas from Aarhus University and an MA and PhD in philosophy from the University of Toronto.

Nigel D. White is Professor of International Law at the University of Sheffield. He is author of *Keeping the Peace* (1997), *The UN System* (2002) and *The Law of International Organisations* (2005). He has edited and co-edited *Collective Security Law* (2004), *The UN, Human Rights and Post-conflict Situations* (2005) and *International Conflict and Security Law* (2005). He is co-editor of the *Journal of Conflict and Security Law* (volume 11 in 2006).

Acknowledgements

I express my appreciation to all of the authors for delivering their texts within tight deadlines, notwithstanding their many other commitments. The anonymous reviewers nominated by Ashgate should also be thanked for making comments that were of great assistance in finalising the book. I am grateful to the European Inter-University Centre for Human Rights and Democratisation for hosting a meeting of the authors at its premises in Venice and for the generous financing of editorial assistance. Appreciation is due to my colleagues at the University of Nottingham Human Rights Law Centre, especially my Co-Director, Professor David Harris and the Centre's Coordinator, Dr James Harrison, as well as the 2005–2006 LLM students who participated in a module I teach on the law and practice of human rights field operations. I owe a great debt of gratitude to those human rights field officers with whom I have served and from whom I have learned so much. I am particularly grateful for the editorial assistance of Kevin Turner, ably supported by Emilie Hunter.

Michael O'Flaherty
April 2006

Chapter 1

Human Rights Field Operations: An Introductory Analysis

Michael O'Flaherty

The Human Rights Field Operation: Law, Theory and Practice seeks to take stock of the development of human rights field operations of the United Nations (UN) and other intergovernmental organisations and to make a substantial contribution to the debate and understanding with regard to the sector's underlying doctrine. The volume, unprecedented in its scope, addresses the range of aspects of the nature, role and activities of field operations. It draws together the reflections of academics, policy makers and field practitioners and its analysis is located within the context of applicable normative frameworks, assessment of former and current practice and examination of complementary and analogous experiences.

For purposes of the examination, the term 'human rights field operation' refers primarily to those types of civilian field missions that are either deployed or supported by the Office of the United Nations High Commissioner for Human Rights (OHCHR), as well as analogous missions of organisations such as the Organization for Security and Co-operation in Europe (OSCE). Accordingly, the volume addresses issues of relevance to standalone OHCHR 'field presences' and the civilian human rights components of UN peace missions. The focus of attention is on operations in armed conflict or post-conflict situations. The volume does not include in its primary focus the work of UN agencies, funds and programmes, the International Committee of the Red Cross (ICRC) and non-governmental organisations (NGOs). Instead, all of these categories of actors are reflected on as sources of 'lessons learned' and in terms of the forms of partnership that field operations need to sustain. This framework takes account of the distinct and acute needs that have been identified within the sector of field operations associated with OHCHR (and the similar missions of other intergovernmental bodies) and allows for the type of focused approach that is capable of generating solid theoretical, policy and practice-related guidance.

It would be unhelpful, nevertheless, to maintain a rigid insistence on definitions and distinctions. The sector is in such a state of flux and the partnership requirements are so extensive that almost every chapter is required to address and reflect on the roles and activities of multiple actors with human rights responsibilities. In any case, and taking account of the significance of 'right-based approaches' and of human rights 'mainstreaming', any form of narrow niche-focused writing would be anachronistic.

With a view to the location of the volume in the context of the development and current state-of-play of human rights field operations, it is useful, at the outset, to undertake an historical and functional analysis.

Historical Review

Issues of human rights and armed conflict interact in multiple ways.[1] The origins of conflict frequently coincide with patterns of human rights abuse – such as the systemic oppression of minorities or of other vulnerable groups. With conflict underway, the assault on human rights is evident. In the first place there is the direct targeting of civilians. Account needs also to be taken of the impact on people of the destruction of human and economic infrastructure and capital and of a slide into humanitarian crisis. Efforts to resolve conflict can also cause the denial of human rights. Peace agreements may trade off human rights protection for some other goal, such as when they institutionalise arrangements that either reflect existing patterns of discrimination or create new ones. Peace processes can also exacerbate victimisation by failing to address past patterns of abuse, above all when they fail to tackle issues of justice and of redress for victims. Conversely, the value of peace and reconstruction processes integrating attention to human rights is increasingly acknowledged – with the development of strong human rights institutions and the general promotion of a 'human rights culture' perceived to be central to the consolidation of peace.[2]

In recognition of the interaction of human rights, armed conflict, peace and reconstruction, the UN increasingly deploys human rights field operations to conflict and post-conflict environments.[3] The UN's involvement in general conflict-related civilian field activities is longstanding. For instance, as early as

[1]   See B. Ramcharan, 'Human Rights and Conflict Resolution', *Human Rights Law Review* vol. 4, no. 1 (2004); D. Carment and A. Schnabel, *Conflict Prevention: Path to Peace or Grand Illusion* (Tokyo: United Nations University, 2003); H. Thoolen, 'Early Warning and Prevention', in G. Alfredsson *et al.* (eds), *International Human Rights Monitoring Mechanisms: Essays in Honour of Jakob Th. Moller* (The Hague: Martinus Nijhoff, 2001), p. 301; L. Mahony, 'Unarmed Monitoring and Human Rights Field Presences: Civilian Protection and Conflict Protection', *The Journal of Humanitarian Assistance* (2003), http://www.jha.ac/articles/a122.htm; E. Lutz *et al.*, 'Human Rights and Conflict Resolution from the Practitioners' Perspective', *The Fletcher Forum of World Affairs* vol. 27, no. 1 (2003); J. Saunders, *Bridging Human Rights and Conflict Prevention: A Dialogue between Critical Communities*, Carnegie Council on Ethics and International Affairs, at http://www.cceia.org/viewMedia.php/prmTemplateID/1/prmID/161; M. O'Flaherty, 'Sierra Leone's Peace Process: The Role of the Human Rights Community', *Human Rights Quarterly* vol. 26, no. 1 (2004); M. O'Flaherty, 'Future Protection of Human Rights in Post-Conflict Societies: The Role of the United Nations', *Human Rights Law Review* vol. 3, no. 1 (2003).

[2]   O'Flaherty, 'Future Protection of Human Rights'.

[3]   For an overview of current UN programmes see OHCHR, *Annual Appeal 2005* (Geneva: OHCHR, 2005) at http://www.unhchr.ch/pdf/appeal2005.pdf; See also http://www.unhchr.ch/html/menu2/5/field.htm.

1978, in Namibia, its mission was responsible for election monitoring, development of electoral legislation, repatriation of refuges and release of political prisoners.[4] However, the practice of deploying specifically mandated human rights field teams only began in 1991.[5] It had its origins in the surge of optimism regarding its capacity as a peace-builder which emerged with the end of the Cold War. The first specifically human rights-mandated mission, was tasked with monitoring the implementation of the San Jose peace agreement in El Salvador.[6] In 1992 the UN established a mission to oversee the political transition in Cambodia, again with a human rights component.[7] 1993 saw the establishment, jointly by the UN and the Organization of American States (OAS), of the first exclusively human rights-focused mission, in Haiti.[8] Another dedicated human rights mission was established by the UN for Guatemala in 1994.[9]

All of these first missions were realised within the framework of the UN's political programming. They were established under the authority of, or otherwise in close consultations with, the Security Council or, less frequently, the General Assembly, headquartered in New York, and without the involvement of the organisation's human rights component, then called the Centre for Human Rights and located in Geneva. The Centre, though, was itself starting to undertake the deployment of human rights monitors in the former Yugoslavia in support of the Commission on Human Right's

---

[4]   See Security Council resolution 431 (1978), UN Doc. S/RES/431 (1978) and Security Council resolution 435 (1978), UN Doc. S/RES/435 (1978).

[5]   See M. Katayanagi, *Human Rights Functions of United Nations Peacekeeping Operations* (The Hague: Kluwer Law International, 2002); B. G. Ramcharan, *The United Nations High Commissioner for Human Rights: The Challenges of International Protection*, International Studies in Human Rights vol. 71 (The Hague: Kluwer Law International, 2002).

[6]   The United Nations Observer Mission in El Salvador (ONUSAL). See R. Brody, 'The United Nations and Human Rights in El Salvador's "Negotiated Revolution"', *Harvard Human Rights Journal* vol. 8 (1995), 153; D. García-Sayán, 'The Experience of ONUSAL in El Salvador', and T. Whitfield, 'Staying the Course in El Salvador', in A. Henkin (ed.), *Honoring Human Rights* (The Hague: Kluwer Law International, 2000).

[7]   The United Nations Transitional Authority in Cambodia (UNTAC). See D. McNamara, 'UN Human Rights Activities in Cambodia: An Evaluation', and B. Adams, 'UN Human Rights Work in Cambodia: Efforts to Preserve the Jewel in the Peacekeeping Crown', in *Honoring Human Rights*; M. Kirby, 'Human Rights, the United Nations and Cambodia', *Australian Quarterly* vol. 67, no. 4 (1995), 26.

[8]   The OAS/UN International Civilian Mission in Haiti (MICIVIH). See W. G. O'Neill, 'Human Rights Monitoring versus Political Expediency: The Experience of the OAS/UN Mission in Haiti', *Harvard Human Rights Journal* vol. 8 (1995), 101; W. G. O'Neill, 'Gaining Compliance without Force: Human Rights Field Operations', in S. Chesterman (ed.), *Civilians in War* (Boulder: Lynne Reinner, 2001); I. Martin, 'Paper versus Steel: the First Phase of the International Civilian Mission in Haiti', and C. Granderson, 'Institutionalizing Peace: The Haiti Experience', in *Honoring Human Rights*.

[9]   The United Nations Human Rights Verification Mission in Guatemala (MINUGUA). See L. Franco and J. Kotler, 'Combining Institution Building and Human Rights Verification in Guatemala: The Challenge of Buying in Without Selling Out', in *Honoring Human Rights*.

special rapporteur for that region[10] and, in 1993, had assumed responsibility to take over the UN human rights programme in Cambodia upon the closure of the United Nations Transitional Authority in Cambodia (UNTAC). In 1994, in response to the Rwanda genocide and under the guidance of the newly appointed first UN high commissioner for human rights,[11] the Centre established a mission[12] which, by late 1995 comprised 130 international staff.[13] 1995 also saw the deployment by the Centre of human rights monitors in Burundi. These missions were launched notwithstanding the Centre's lack of relevant experience and infrastructure and were funded by voluntary contributions rather than, as was the case for the New York-led operations, from the regular UN budget.[14]

By the mid-1990s,[15] commentators were drawing attention to a number of concerns regarding the development of human rights field operations. These included: (a) the need to ensure that human rights be addressed in the design and operation of all New York-led peace missions rather than the handful that have been mentioned here; (b) how best to involve the Geneva-based high commissioner for human rights and the Centre in the guidance of these missions; (c) the unsustainability of the Geneva-led voluntarily funded operations; (d) how best to balance the monitoring functions of such missions with the delivery of capacity building technical cooperation; and (e) the extent to which regional organisations could or would mount human rights field operations.

---

[10] A similar scheme was envisaged to support the mandate of the special rapporteur on Iraq but deployment to that country was not feasible.

[11] The post was established by UN General Assembly resolution 141 (1993), UN Doc. A/RES/48/141 (1993). See Ramcharan, *The United Nations High Commissioner for Human Rights*.

[12] Human Rights Field Operation for Rwanda (HRFOR)

[13] See W. Clarance, 'The Human Rights Field Operation in Rwanda: Protective Practice Evolves on the Ground', *International Peacekeeping* vol. 2, no. 3 (1995); I. Martin, 'After Genocide: The UN Human Rights Field Operation in Rwanda', in *Honoring Human Rights*; T. Howland, 'Mirage, Magic or Mixed Bag? The United Nations High Commissioner for Human Rights' Field Operation in Rwanda', *Human Rights Quarterly* vol. 21, no. 1 (1999).

[14] With the single exception of the Cambodia office the core costs of which are met from the UN regular budget.

[15] See the papers presented at meetings in 1995 and 1998 contained in *Honoring Human Rights*; D. García-Sayán, 'Human Rights and Peacekeeping Operations', *University of Richmond Law Review* vol. 29, no. 1 (1994); D. Little, 'Protecting Human Rights During and After Conflicts: The Role of the United Nations', *Tulsa Journal of Comparative and International Law* vol. 4, no. 1 (1996); W. Clarance, 'Field Strategy for the Protection of Human Rights', *International Journal of Refugee Law* vol. 9, no. 2 (1997); I. Martin, 'Human Rights Monitoring and Institution-Building in Post-Conflict Societies: The Role of Human Rights Field Operations', paper delivered to USAID Conference, 'Promoting Democracy, Human Rights and Reintegration', October 30–31, 1997, on file with the present author, and I. Martin, 'A New Frontier: The Early Experience and Future of International Human Rights Field Operations', *Netherlands Quarterly of Human Rights* vol. 16, no. 2 (1998). See also O'Neill, 'Gaining Compliance without Force'.

These concerns came to be addressed within the context of a general move to operationalise the notion of human rights as a cross-cutting responsibility in all the work areas of the UN – a concept that was articulated by the secretary-general in his 1996 UN Reform Programme.[16] In the first place, the Centre for Human Rights (from 1998 renamed OHCHR) adopted a policy of seeking, as far as possible, to insert human rights components in New York-led missions rather than itself mounting entire operations. New York departments, for their part, grew increasingly willing to insert human rights components as integral parts of peacekeeping and, to a lesser extent, peacemaking operations. It was in this context that human rights programmes were located in UN missions such as those for Georgia,[17] Liberia,[18] Angola,[19] Sierra Leone,[20] Guinea-Bissau, Democratic Republic of Congo[21] and Ethiopia and Eritrea.[22] Those UN missions which assumed transitional authority, such as in Kosovo[23] and East Timor,[24] also included human rights components.

---

[16] Report of the Secretary-General, Renewing the United Nations: A Programme for Reform, UN Doc. A/51/950 (1997).

[17] The United Nations Observer Mission in Georgia (UNOMIG). The human rights component of this mission is jointly staffed by UN and OSCE human rights officers.

[18] The United Nations Observer Mission in Liberia (UNOMIL). See B. Nowrojee, 'Joining Forces: United Nations and Regional Peacekeeping – Lessons from Liberia', *Harvard Human Rights Journal* vol. 8 (1995), p. 129; and A. Clapham and F. Martin, 'Smaller Missions Bigger Problems', in *Honoring Human Rights*.

[19] The United Nations Verification Mission III and the United Nations Observer Mission in Angola, (UNAVEM III and UNOMA). See chapter 16 by T. Howland in the present volume.

[20] The United Nations Observer Mission in Sierra Leone and the United Nations Assistance Mission in Sierra Leone (UNOMSIL and UNAMSIL). See O'Flaherty, 'Sierra Leone's Peace Process'; Centre for Humanitarian Dialogue, *Politics and Humanitarianism, Coherence in Crisis?* (Geneva: 2003), chapter 5.

[21] The United Nations Organisation Mission in the Democratic Republic of the Congo (MONUC). See Centre for Humanitarian Dialogue, *Politics and Humanitarianism, Coherence in Crisis?*

[22] The United Nations Mission in Ethiopia and Eritrea (UNMEE).

[23] The United Nations Mission in Kosovo (UNMIK). See W. Betts *et al.*, 'The Post-Conflict Transitional Administration of Kosovo and the Lessons Learned in Efforts to Establish a Judiciary and Rule of Law', *Michigan Journal of International Law* vol. 22, no. 3 (2001); H. Strohmeyer, 'Collapse and Reconstruction of a Judicial System: The United Nations Missions in Kosovo and East Timor', *American Journal of International Law* vol. 95, no. 1 (2001); H. Strohmeyer, 'Making Multilateral Interventions Work: The UN and the Creation of Transitional Justice Systems in Kosovo and East Timor', *Fletcher Forum of World Affairs* vol. 25, no. 2 (2001), 107; D. Marshall and S. Inglis, 'The Disempowerment of Human Rights-Based Justice in the United Nations Mission in Kosovo', *Harvard Human Rights Journal* vol. 16 (2003), 95.

[24] The United Nations Transitional Administration in East Timor (UNTAET). See Strohmeyer, 'Making Multilateral Interventions Work: The UN and the Creation of Transitional Justice Systems in Kosovo and East Timor'; D. Criswell, 'Durable Consent and a Strong Transitional Peacekeeping Plan: The Success of UNTAET in Light of the Lessons Learned in Cambodia', *Pacific Rim Law and Policy Journal* vol. 2, no. 3 (2002); B. Kondoch, 'The

Within a number of missions, components were also established outside the human rights programme but with a clear overlap of interest – such as for promotion of rule of law, protection of the rights of the child and addressing gender considerations. Civilian police components also assumed clear human rights-related responsibilities – as illustrated by the establishment of a policing mission in post-conflict Bosnia and Herzegovina with a predominantly human rights-related mandate.[25]

During the period there continued to be cases of OHCHR establishing its own missions, such as in Colombia, Democratic Republic of Congo and Burundi. These missions have their origins in such considerations as specific initiatives of the UN Commission on Human Rights or of intended work areas, such as human rights technical cooperation, which were not then seen as related to the competencies of the New York departments or for which OHCHR project funding would be required. Sometimes OHCHR programmes were established side by side with the human rights operations of peace missions, as in the case of the OHCHR programme in Sierra Leone, which supported that country's truth and reconciliation commission.

The development of a doctrine and methodology regarding human rights field operations received a stimulus in 2000 with publication of the 'Report of the Panel on United Nations Peace Operations'[26] (the 'Brahimi Report'), which undertook a thorough review of the UN peace and security activities. The report emphasised the need for mission wide team approaches to upholding the rule of law and respect for human rights.[27] It also described the human rights component of a peace operation as 'indeed critical to effective peace-building'[28] and observed that the operations should engage in both human rights monitoring and capacity building. Management models were proposed whereby OHCHR would be a participant throughout the design and oversight of future UN peace operations.[29] The publication of the report coincided with the finalisation of a memorandum of understanding (MOU) between OHCHR and the Department of Peacekeeping Operations (DPKO) which established a formal relationship between them for the design and operation of peacekeeping missions. There is no such MOU with Department of Political Affairs – apparently due to the desire of the latter to maintain the flexibility of the currently informal arrangements.

United Nations Administration of East Timor', *Journal of Conflict and Security Law* vol. 6, no. 2 (2001).

[25] The United Nations International Police Task Force (IPTF). See O'Flaherty, 'International Human Rights Operations in Bosnia and Herzegovina', in *Honoring Human Rights*; and O'Flaherty and Gisvold (eds), *Post-war Protection of Human Rights in Bosnia and Herzegovina*, (The Hague: Martinus Nijhoff, 1998).

[26] Report of the Panel on United Nations Peace Operations, UN Doc. A/55/305 S/2000/809 (2000).

[27] *Ibid.*, at 47.

[28] *Ibid.*, at 41.

[29] *Ibid.*, at 244.

The report's proposals were first tested in 2002, with the design, under Brahimi's leadership, of a new UN 'integrated mission' in Afghanistan.[30] In this case, OHCHR supported a mission design that 'mainstreamed' the human rights monitoring function and ensured a human rights capacity-building programme by means of a project to be funded by OHCHR. This design gave cause for comment[31] because the mainstreaming of the monitoring function resulted in the absence from the mission of a dedicated human rights monitoring unit. Subsequent integrated missions, such as those for Iraq,[32] Liberia[33] and Côte d'Ivoire,[34] have reverted to a model of including specific human rights units within the missions,[35] with the Côte d'Ivoire mission also innovatively giving access to the UN regular budget for the undertaking of capacity-building activities.[36]

The human rights mainstreaming process received further impetus with the 2002 report of the secretary-general, 'Strengthening of the United Nations: An Agenda for Further Change'.[37] In this context, OHCHR, under then-High Commissioner Mary Robinson, described its own field role as being primarily that of supporting human rights actions of other parts of the UN system and it reaffirmed its commitment to integrated post-Brahimi peace missions.[38] Side by side with its support to the human rights components of peace missions it also commenced the deployment of human rights experts to serve as advisers within UN country teams, including in such conflict-affected countries as Sri Lanka and Nepal.[39] In 2003, as a further development of this idea, a UN country-team level human rights capacity-building operation was established in Angola following the departure of the peace mission – with a similar operation also proposed for eventual deployment in Timor Leste.[40]

The years 2004–2006 witnessed a raised level of academic and policy-level attention to the state of UN human rights field operations. In early 2004, the present author published a paper that sought to identify the parameters of human rights

---

[30] The United Nations Assistance Mission in Afghanistan (UNAMA).

[31] See O'Flaherty, 'Future Protection of Human Rights'; Centre for Humanitarian Dialogue, *Politics and Humanitarianism, Coherence in Crisis?*.

[32] The United Nations Assistance Mission for Iraq (UNAMI).

[33] The United Nations Mission in Liberia (UNMIL).

[34] The United Nations Operation in Côte d'Ivoire (UNOCI).

[35] With regard the Iraq, human rights was first integrated in UN programming in 2002 by means of secondment of OHCHR staff to the Office of the UN Humanitarian Coordinator for Iraq (UNOHCI), See OHCHR, *Annual Appeal 2004* (Geneva: OHCHR, 2004) p. 53.

[36] OHCHR, 'Africa region', Quarterly Reports of Field Offices, March 2004, available at http://www.unhchr.ch/html/menu2/5/africa-mar04.doc.

[37] Report of the Secretary-General, Strengthening of the United Nations: An Agenda for Further Change, UN Doc. A/57/387 (2002).

[38] B. G. Ramcharan, Acting High Commissioner for Human Rights, 'The Future Directions of Human Rights Field Presences', Address at the Annual Meeting of OHCHR Field Presences, 17 November 2003, http://www.unhchr.ch.

[39] See OHCHR, 'Asian and Pacific region', Quarterly Reports of Field Offices, March 2004, at http://www.unhchr.ch/html/menu2/5/asia-mar04.doc, p. 5.

[40] OHCHR, *Annual Appeal 2004*, pp. 32–33.

field work and the principal challenges to be addressed.[41] The paper recommended that the high commissioner stimulate a comprehensive review of the sector with a view to enhanced performance of field operations and their widespread deployment on the basis of need rather than any other political consideration. It was suggested that for this to be accomplished it would be necessary to go beyond the catalytic model, described above, and to significantly augment OHCHR's resources. In May 2005, further to a request contained in the secretary-general's report, 'In Larger Freedom: Towards Development, Security and Human Rights for All',[42] the then recently appointed High Commissioner Louise Arbour, published a *Plan of Action* for OHCHR.[43] In this she stated that her office would become more present on the ground 'in a sustained manner' and that her preference was for 'stand-alone' OHCHR offices rather than for the catalytic approach.[44] The *Plan of Action* also proposed what would amount to the largest restructuring and expansion of resources in the short history of that office. The new enthusiasm of OHCHR for the establishment of its own field operations was anticipated in the first months of 2005 by the opening of offices in two conflict-affected countries, neither of which was considered likely to host a UN peace-mission, Uganda and Nepal.[45] In each case, the high commissioner negotiated with the government in question a sturdy mandate for human rights monitoring and capacity building.

Given the extent to which human rights field work is implemented by means of the insertion of human rights components in peace missions, the lack of attention to such operations in the *Plan of Action* is striking, dealt with in just two brief and vague paragraphs.[46] This treatment may reflect what was then a growing disenchantment with the integrated-mission model among human rights policy makers: it is noteworthy that during 2004–2005, voices could increasingly be heard suggesting that such missions unacceptably subordinated human rights to political considerations and that their human rights components lacked the necessary autonomy and resources.[47] Similar views had also been expressed at an expert consultation meeting on human rights field presences, held at OHCHR in November 2004.[48]

A number of these concerns were addressed by the UN secretary-general by means of decisions that constitute important clarifications on policy, albeit that at

---

[41]   M. O'Flaherty, 'Human Rights Monitoring and Armed Conflict, Challenges for the UN', *Disarmament Forum* no. 3 (2004). See also, M. O'Flaherty, 'We are Failing the Victims of War', in B. G. Ramcharan (ed.), *Human Rights Protection in the Field* (Leiden: Martinus Nijhof, 2006).

[42]   Report of the Secretary-General, In Larger Freedom: Towards Development, Security and Human Rights for All, UN Doc. A/59/2005 (2005), at 145.

[43]   The United Nations High Commissioner for Human Rights, *The OHCHR Plan of Action: Protection and Empowerment* (Geneva: OHCHR, 2005).

[44]   *Ibid.*, p. 15.

[45]   See http://www.ohchr.org/english/countries/field/index.htm.

[46]   The United Nations High Commissioner for Human Rights, *The OHCHR Plan of Action*, p. 16.

[47]   See OHCHR, 'Internal Review on Human Rights and Integrated Missions: Responses from Heads of Human Rights Components' (18 July 2005), on file with the present author.

[48]   Available at http://www.humanrightsprofessionals.org.

the time of writing this chapter it is impossible to assess their impact for practice. Decision No. 2005/24, 'Human Rights in Integrated Missions' (26 October, 2005)[49] forthrightly reasserts the role and status of the human rights components within integrated missions: '(a) All UN entities have a responsibility to ensure that human rights are promoted and protected through and within their operations in the field; (b) A commitment to human rights and the ability to give the necessary prominence to human rights should be important factors in the election of SRSGs/DRSGs, and in the monitoring of their performance, as well as that of the mission; (c) OHCHR, as "lead agency" on human rights issues, has a central role to play through the provision of expertise, guidance and support to human rights components. These components should discharge core human rights functions and help mainstream human rights across all mission activities; and, (d) Separate public reporting by the mission and/ or the High Commissioner on issues of human rights concern should be routine'. Subsequently, in January 2006, the secretary-general issued a note, 'Guidance on Integrated Missions',[50] which reiterated the elements of the decision and observed that, '[h]uman rights are a cross-cutting concern for both the mission and the UN country team and they need to be fully integrated into peace operations. The SRSG will uphold human rights law in the implementation of the mission's mandate ... [a]s representative of the High Commissioner for Human Rights, the head of the human rights component should be a full member of the expanded UN Country Team'.

A survey of UN approaches to the human rights needs of conflict and post-conflict societies must also take account of the manner in which a number of UN agencies, including the United Nations Children's Fund (UNICEF),[51] the United Nations Development Programme (UNDP),[52] and the Office of the United Nations High Commissioner for Refugees (UNHCR),[53] have already gone some distance in integrating human rights approaches in their work. These increasingly system-wide developments demand new partnership configurations and present other challenges for human rights field operations.

Beyond the context of UN operations there have been some regional intergovernmental initiatives – in 1993 with OAS involvement in Haiti and, more recently, in Europe where OSCE deployed human rights missions in Bosnia and Herzegovina, Kosovo and elsewhere, sometimes in collaboration with the UN and other international organisations.[54] Since then, developments at the regional level have included the inauguration of dedicated training programmes by such regional

---

[49] On file with the present author.

[50] On file with the present author.

[51] UNICEF, *Children Affected by Armed Conflict: UNICEF Actions,* (New York: UNICEF, 2002).

[52] UNDP, *Integrating Human Rights with Sustainable Human Development* (New York: UNDP, 1998).

[53] UNHCR, An Agenda for Protection, UN Doc. A/AC.96/965/Add.1 (2002).

[54] See O'Flaherty and Gisvold (eds), *Post-war Protection of Human Rights in Bosnia and Herzegovina*; and the materials listed at footnote 23 regarding Kosovo.

organisations as the European Union and OSCE and the first deployment of human rights field staff by the African Union, in the Darfur region of Sudan.[55]

A number of peace missions have also been assembled by specific clusters of interested states,[56] such as the Temporary International Presence in Hebron, the Sri Lanka Monitoring Mission and the Joint Monitoring Mission in the Nuba Mountains, Sudan. Similarly, a number of NGO-led peace missions have been deployed, including operations of Peace Brigades International (PBI) in Colombia, Indonesia and Mexico, the Non-Violent Peace Force in Sri Lanka and the World Council of Churches' Ecumenical Accompaniment Project in Palestine and Israel.[57] These operations, while not tending to have explicit human rights mandates, do have objectives such as civilian protection which are consistent therewith.

The Functions of Human Rights Field Operations

All of the functions of civilian human rights field operations are closely related to each other. One can, however, distinguish specific work areas, which may, depending on specific mandates, be found in the human rights programmes of human rights field operations: monitoring, reporting, advocacy and intervention, human rights capacity building, supporting rights-related work of humanitarian and development actors, participation in peace processes and support to programmes of transitional justice, and human rights sensitisation within UN operations. Still another function, participation in UN governance of transitional territories, though much discussed,[58] is rarely applicable.

Monitoring

Monitoring provides the basis for all other human rights work of a mission since programming of any kind needs to be based on reliable information. Monitoring may also contain within it a preventive function in that the very presence of monitors can deter human rights violations.[59] The implementation of a monitoring mandate can prove extremely challenging. In terms of the nature of the mandate, such issues arise as the identification of whom to monitor. Should both government and non-

---

[55]   See, African Union, Overview of AU's Efforts to Address the Conflict in the Darfur Region of the Sudan, AU Doc. CONF/P/2(1), (May 2005).

[56]   See L. Mahony, 'Unarmed Monitoring and Human Rights Field Presences'; and L. Mahony, 'Promoting Unarmed Monitoring: Thinking Long-term', January 5, 2004, informally distributed essay on file with the present author.

[57]   *Ibid.*

[58]   See, *inter alia*, the materials regarding Kosovo and East Timor at footnotes 23 and 24. See also, A. Henkin (ed.), *Honoring Human Rights under International Mandates: Lessons from Bosnia, Kosovo and East Timor* (Washington, DC: Aspen Institute, 2003).

[59]   See Mahony, 'Unarmed Monitoring and Human Rights Field Presences'; and Mahony, 'Promoting Unarmed Monitoring: Thinking Long-term'.

state armed groups be monitored, how can monitoring be even-handed when the mission has varying levels of access across a given country, and should peacekeepers themselves be subject to monitoring? What rights should be monitored – what is the role of a mission in terms of the monitoring of economic, social and cultural rights? When and how should it monitor the implementation of international humanitarian law? How should the monitoring be undertaken – should it seek to establish personal responsibility for actions and collect court-ready evidence or instead simply map out patterns of human rights abuse. When is it appropriate to monitor individual cases – are these cases the actual object of the monitoring exercise or are they instead intended to serve as illustrations of broader phenomena – or is this even a valid distinction? When should past situations be monitored/recorded and when should the focus be on contemporary abuses?

Turning to monitoring capacities, the issue arises of how to monitor a situation with the typically modest human rights team of a mission. What can be done when the mission lacks the requisite skills to monitor certain phenomena – for instance economic rights, sexual abuse or the rights of the child? How can monitoring be done in a manner that does not expose victims, witnesses, monitors to harm or jeopardise programmes and operations?

Missions, on a case-by-case basis, seek to respond to questions such as these. They are hampered by a lack of agreed or shared doctrine. OHCHR did produce a human rights monitoring manual in 2001 but this, while containing much that is of value, does not chart a route through many of the complex challenges a mission will confront in practice.[60]

Reporting

Good information is useless unless it gets to where it is needed. The UN has had difficulties in addressing this truism. At the time of writing there is still not a standard model for human rights reporting and, instead, each field operation adopts its own style and approach[61] – not always a bad thing but inevitably at odds with the development of system-wide methodologies. Turning to the transmittal of reports, many field operations have encountered the problem that insufficient human rights information or excessively redacted information is transmitted to headquarters.[62] The identity of recipients of internal information has caused some controversy and the practice of copying reports to the high commissioner for human rights, now more or less in place, took a number of years to evolve. There remains uncertainty regarding when and how to share internal reports with UN member states, including at the level of the Security Council. The issue also arises at the local level in terms of

---

[60]   OHCHR, *Training Manual on Human Rights Monitoring* (Geneva: OHCHR, 2001).

[61]   Although elements of standardisation of publicly issued reports are emerging in the context of an OHCHR effort to place regular information regarding its field operations on its website. See http://www.unhchr.ch/html/menu2/5/field.htm.

[62]   See, for instance, O'Flaherty, 'Sierra Leone's Peace Process'.

what information to share with the government and with diplomats and which parts of government and which diplomats to share it with.[63] Regarding public reporting, and notwithstanding the UN decision of 2005 in its favour (referred to above), there is the question of how much data to put in the public domain, taking account not least of such prosaic considerations as the current restrictions on the length of UN reports.[64] More importantly, the UN still lacks the sort of public information programme that can ensure that reports generate timely media attention. Instead, it is often the case that NGOs are credited with the exposure of human rights situations that the UN may have already been reporting on for some time – not in itself a problem but nevertheless diminishing perceptions of the UN's engagement with these situations.

Advocacy and Intervention

Forms of advocacy and intervention have always been integral to UN human rights operations and have taken multiple forms, from quiet diplomacy to forceful condemnations. They have been undertaken at local, national and international levels. They have been targeted directly to perpetrators and also to other actors who can bring pressure to bear. Here again, there remains a lack of systems and methodologies. It is rare, for instance, that a mission will have intervened or done advocacy on the basis of a carefully worked out power and vulnerability analysis of a given location/situation. Sometimes intervention may be directed to quick resolution in a manner that undermines long-term capacities – such as when judicial solutions are bypassed or military actors are asked to deal with situations best left to the police. And the issue again arises of how to deal with individual cases – how can the field operation be both compassionate in the face of individual suffering and retain capacity and resources to address all parts of its mandate? For instance, within a peace mission it will not always be clear who should undertake a specific intervention – whether it should be the mission head, the human rights component, the police or military elements or otherwise. It may even be the case that multiple or inconsistent interventions may be undertaken by mission elements unfamiliar with each other's initiatives. Sometimes, a field operation will want to involve another actor in an advocacy/intervention. This will be the case, for instance, when it draws situations to the attention of UN special rapporteurs or treaty bodies[65] – a practice that has seen a welcome growth in recent years – or when it encourages the direct engagement of the UN secretary-general.[66] But it is not always clear when and how

---

    [63]   *Ibid.*

    [64]   A problem which may be overcome by means of the innovative OHCHR practice of publishing regular web-based informal reports of its field operations. See footnotes 36 and 39.

    [65]   See M. O'Flaherty, 'Treaty Bodies Responding to States of Emergency', in J. Crawford and P. Alston, (eds), *The Future of UN Human Rights Treaty Monitoring*, (Cambridge: Cambridge University Press, 2000), pp. 443–444.

    [66]   See generally O'Flaherty, 'Future Protection of Human Rights'.

to deal with actors outside the field operation – when, for instance, is it appropriate to refer matters to national human rights institutions and to NGOs? Finally, the UN, like many NGOs, does not have systems in place to specifically evaluate the effectiveness of its advocacy and intervention.

Human Rights Capacity Building

As has been already noted, commentators have drawn attention to the need for the UN to undertake human rights capacity building side by side with its monitoring and reporting activities. A number of hurdles have had to be, and are still being, negotiated.[67] One of these has been the view that it is not possible to undertake capacity building in times of conflict. This perception is at odds with experience and overlooks the manner in which elements of civil society may remain vigorous even in moments of turmoil and be keen to receive training and other support. The perception also overlooks the many instances of programming in such contexts.[68] A converse problem is the perception that in post-conflict scenarios the monitoring, reporting and advocacy/intervention functions can be terminated and replaced by exclusively technical cooperation activities – it may be that this understanding is informing the current UN tendency, described above, to address the human rights needs of certain conflict and post-conflict situations by deployment of advisors within UN country teams.[69]

Capacity building has been hampered by the lack of resources within regular UN-budget-funded peace missions. Instead, the field operations' human rights programmes had either to rely on OHCHR to devise voluntarily funded projects or had themselves to enter into complicated and fragile relationships with local donors and service providers.[70]

A further challenge is that of the relationship between human rights capacity building and broader development and humanitarian programming.[71] Until recently the former was considered to be somewhat distinct, focusing on a limited range of activities such as human rights education and development of standard operating procedures for key professions and sectors including police, lawyers, judiciary and NGOs. This is no longer tenable in light of new perceptions of human rights as cross-cutting all humanitarian and development sectors and of the related impossibility of viewing 'human rights activities' as discrete and divisible from other programming areas. There clearly remains a role for the specialisations that the human rights

---

[67] *Ibid.*

[68] See the papers at footnotes 19, 20, 24 and 25.

[69] The approach is described in Ramcharan, footnote 38. It is commented on by Mahony, 'Promoting Unarmed Monitoring'.

[70] See chapter 16 by T. Howland in the present volume.

[71] See the various papers at http://www.unhchr.ch/development/approaches.html; O'Flaherty, 'Future Protection of Human Rights'; U. Jonsson, *Human Rights Approach to Development Programming* (New York: UNICEF, 2004).

programmes can bring to the humanitarian and development tables – but within the context of new and broad partnerships.

Engaging with Humanitarian and Development Partners

The theoretical links between human rights and humanitarian and development programming have not yet been matched by widespread patterns of partnership between human rights teams and their counterparts in the UN agencies and elsewhere. Instead there remains considerable mutual mistrust and a lack of understanding of the tangible forms the partnerships might take.[72] Humanitarian and development actors occasionally fear that engagement with the human rights people might bring them into conflict with authorities and have a negative impact for their programmes. They sometimes also fail to see the added value that human rights bring to their work. Human rights people frequently lack an understanding of humanitarian and development action or of the links with their own work. Both communities have for a long time been without tools to help them in bridging the sectors. Fortunately this situation is beginning to change. The experiences in a number of countries of partnerships between peace missions and UN agencies have been written up[73] and tools are becoming available. These include human rights related elements of the guidelines for the humanitarian consolidated appeal process (CAP)[74] and the Common Country Assessment/United Nations Development Assistance Framework (CCA/UNDAF)[75] as well as human rights guidelines for UN resident coordinators[76] and for UN humanitarian coordinators.[77]

Support to Peace Processes and for Transitional Justice

On a broad level of analysis, everything the human rights field operations do may be seen as contributing to conflict resolution and the establishment of sustainable peace.[78] They have also assumed more specific peace-related tasks, such as provision of advice to peace negotiations and oversight of implementation of elements of peace

---

[72]   See J. Darcy, 'Human Rights and Humanitarian Action: A Review of the Issues', paper delivered to a workshop on human rights and humanitarian action convened by OHCHR, UNICEF and International Council of Voluntary Agencies, Geneva, April 2004, at http://www.odi.org.uk/rights/Publications/HPGBackgroundPaperforIASC.pdf.

[73]   See, in particular, Inter-Agency Standing Committee (IASC), *Growing the Sheltering Tree* (New York: UNICEF, 2002).

[74]   The various guidelines can be found at http://www.humanitarianinfo.org/iasc/publications.asp.

[75]   The various guidelines can be found at http://www.undg.org/recent.cfm.

[76]   *Ibid.*

[77]   The initial draft was undertaken by the present author at the request of OHCHR. The final version is pending UN publication.

[78]   See O'Flaherty, 'Sierra Leone's Peace Process'.

settlements and agreements.[79] Practice has developed in a somewhat *ad hoc* manner,[80] although it has benefited from significant recent research attention.[81] Broad guidance to UN peace negotiators regarding their human rights-related responsibilities[82] has not always been matched by the presence in negotiation teams of human rights specialists. Peace agreements themselves sometimes address and sometimes ignore issues of human rights. Those which address human rights sometimes do so in a controversial or eccentric manner.[83] The agreements in certain cases invest human rights actors, including in peace missions, with specific monitoring and other roles – they do not always identify where the resources and capacities will come from to carry out these roles. In still other cases the human rights actors assume such implementation and supervisory roles in situations where the peace agreements have failed to address the issue.[84]

In one area of peace-related activity, that of transitional justice, considerable progress is being made in clarifying doctrine and practice to guide human rights missions.[85] The principle now seems to be established that the UN will not countenance impunity for perpetrators of war crimes and crimes against humanity and a range of tools and lessons learned are emerging to guide UN action across the spectrum of transitional justice.[86] Much has been learned from the UN experience in former Yugoslavia, Rwanda, East Timor and Sierra Leone.[87] In 2006, OHCHR published a set of guidelines intended to assist field personnel address such issues as the relationship between judicial processes and non-judicial accountability and on how to address the needs and rights of victims.[88] But there is still a long way to go.

---

[79]　See C. Bell, *Peace Agreements and Human Rights*, (Oxford: Oxford University Press, 2000).

[80]　See Lutz, *et al.*, 'Human Rights and Conflict Resolution from the Practitioners' Perspective'.

[81]　International Council on Human Rights Policy, *Negotiating Justice? Human Rights and Peace Agreements*, (Versoix, 2006), which assesses and draws conclusions form practice in Cambodia, El Salvador, Mozambique, Bosnia and Herzegovina, Guatemala, Northern Ireland, Sierra Leone and Burundi. See also, H. Hannum, 'Human Rights in Conflict Resolution: The Role of the Office of the High Commissioner for Human Rights in UN Peacemaking and Peacebuilding', *Human Rights Quarterly* vol. 28, no. 1 (2006).

[82]　I. Martin, 'Justice and Reconciliation: Responsibilities and Dilemmas of Peace Makers and Peace-Builders', paper delivered to Aspen Institute meeting, 'The Legacy of Abuse – Justice and Reconciliation in a New Landscape', November 2000, on file with the present author.

[83]　See footnote 1 and Bell, *Peace Agreements.*

[84]　*Ibid.*

[85]　See O'Flaherty, 'Future Protection of Human Rights'.

[86]　See OHCHR, *Rule-of-Law Tools for Post-Conflict States* (New York and Geneva: UN, 2006).

[87]　See the various materials and links available at http://www.ictj.org/research.

[88]　See OHCHR, *Annual Appeal 2004*, p. 106. See also, Mô Bleeker (ed.), *Dealing with the Past and Transitional Justice: Creating Conditions for Peace, Human Rights and the Rule of Law*, Dealing with the Past – Series (Bern, 2006).

The UN is not consistent in its approach – there are situations, such as in Afghanistan, where it has been exceptionally timid in addressing transitional justice.[89] There remain elements of doctrine and methodology that are unclear – such as regarding how to ensure that processes are locally owned and not seen as international impositions. There is the reality that a sincere *de jure* rejection of impunity may only very rarely convert into a *de facto* prosecution of all key perpetrators. Difficult issues of the relationship between judicial and non-judicial procedures remain to be resolved.[90] There is uncertainty regarding the nature of justice for victims or at least regarding how to ensure it.[91] Problems also arise of the manner whereby human rights field operations may cooperate with international criminal tribunals. During 2005, at the Special Court for Sierra Leone, the issue arose of the extent to which a human rights field officer may give evidence while declining to disclose confidential sources.[92] In that case, where the present author was the (former) human rights field officer in question, an Appeals Chamber eventually ruled that the sources need not be disclosed.[93]

In-mission Sensitisation

The role of the human rights unit of a peace mission in sensitising other mission personnel regarding human rights is one of those functions that is generally assumed but only occasionally reflected specifically in a mission mandate. It tends to have a dual nature. In the first place, it concerns the raising of awareness throughout a mission of the human rights implications of mission activities, as well as concerning the standards that mission personnel should abide by – no small task given the nature of peace operations and the scandals reported through the 1990s.[94] General issues of human rights tend to be addressed as well as such specific topics as child protection and the avoidance of any form of sexual abuse.[95] Secondly, human rights

---

[89]   See for instance the criticisms levelled by the human rights NGO, Human Rights Watch: http://hrw.org/english/docs/2003/12/31/afghan6991.htm.

[90]   See W. Schabas, 'The Relationship Between Truth Commissions and International Courts: The Case of Sierra Leone', *Human Rights Quarterly* vol. 25, no. 4 (2003).

[91]   For a recent discussion of the range of issues see Redress, *The International Criminal Court's Trust Fund for Victims*, available at http://www.redress.org.

[92]   See Anonymous, 'The Sierra Leone Special Court: Undermining Possibilities for Partnerships between Human Rights and Humanitarian Operations', *Humanitarian Exchange* no. 33 (March 2006).

[93]   Decision on Prosecution Appeal against Decision on Oral Application for Witness TF1-150 to Testify without being Compelled to Answer Questions on Grounds of Confidentiality, SCSL-04-16-AR73 (18290-18332), 26 May 2006.

[94]   See, for instance, the materials accessible at http://www.globalpolicy.org/security/peacekpg/general, and at http://www.reliefweb.int/w/rwb.nsf/0/2fcd11349cbcccdd85256b6e007d2765?OpenDocument.

[95]   The latter having received considerable attention in 2002 following allegations of sexual abuse by humanitarian workers in West Africa. See UNHCR and Save the Children-

sensitisation is often undertaken with a view to building monitoring, reporting and other partnerships – very important in the context of missions which, typically, will have considerably more police and military observer personnel than human rights officers. In-mission sensitisation has taken on new significance in light of the Brahimi Report's emphasis on the mission-wide responsibility to promote human rights, and resources have been invested in the development of manuals and training materials for the various mission components. For instance, the UN has recently developed a training module on human rights for senior mission management.[96] Such achievements notwithstanding, challenges remain as to how best to train military and police personnel who rotate in and out of missions very frequently and how to achieve the balance between training undertaken before and during deployment. The UN has also yet to identify how best to assist military peace operations that are not under its direct authority, such as in the case of deployment of a regional peacekeeping force side by side with a UN civilian mission, as was the case in Sierra Leone until 1999.

Participation in UN Governance of Transitional Territories

All of the functions discussed above apply equally in the case of UN missions that have governance roles on a territory. The governmental function does however generate additional issues for a field operation, analogous to those relevant for the human rights promotion and protection responsibilities of any state and concerning issues of both law and practice. In the first instance, the question arises of the determination of the applicable human rights law, whether comprising just the treaties otherwise ratified with regard to the affected territory (as well as customary law) or embracing all possible universal and regional human rights instruments. At the level of practice, the matter of how human rights activities are managed is of great concern: whether through a discrete programme or mainstreamed across the organs of UN governance or by means of some variant of these options. In terms of actual work areas, the field operation has to address such issues as the human rights vetting of UN sponsored legislative instruments and the monitoring of their implementation, as well as the establishment and oversight of human rights compliant institutions of state. The UN's experience in such locations as East Timor and Kosovo has helped clarify the range of issues and has generated many lessons. These have been extensively addressed in the literature and, taking account of the *sui generis* nature of UN governance and its extreme rarity in practice, the matter is not explored further here.[97]

UK, *Note for Implementing and Operational Partners by UNHCR and Save the Children-UK on Sexual Violence & Exploitation*, 2002 available at http://www.reliefweb.int/w/rwb.nsf/vID/6010F9ED3C651C93C1256B6D00560FCA?OpenDocument, and which is now the subject of a UN Secretary-General's Bulletin, Special Measures for Protection from Sexual Abuse and Sexual Exploitation, UN Doc. ST/SGB/2003/13 (2003).

[96]   On file with the present author.

[97]   See footnote 58.

Introduction to the Present Volume

Taking account of the youth of the human rights field operations sector and its somewhat accidental historical development, this volume is intended as a preliminary contribution to the articulation of an underlying doctrine. While it does address the various functions as categorised above, with a number of the chapters revisiting these from the particular point of view and expertise of the respective author, the volume seeks to go beyond functions to more fundamental considerations of theory, principle and cross-cutting concerns. It is this approach that has determined the book's structure.

Following this chapter's context-setting historical and functional analysis, the volume addresses what are the more or less universally[98] recognised ultimate purposes of human rights field work – the protection of the human rights of affected populations (Nicholas Howen). Howen begins with reference to High Commissioner Louise Arbour's sturdy affirmation of the centrality of protection, 'human rights protection must be recognised as the first and foremost priority of OHCHR as it is the basis for all human rights work: capacity-building, technical assistance and mainstreaming are of little or no value … if the basic fundamental of protection is not secured'.[99] Howen tends to support the approach to protection that was developed within the context of a series of ICRC workshops, whereby a protection activity is defined as any activity that, 'prevents or puts a stop to a specific pattern of abuse and/or alleviates its immediate effects (responsive action); restores people's dignity and ensures adequate living conditions through reparation, restitution and rehabilitation (remedial action); fosters an environment conducive to respect for the rights of individuals in accordance with the relevant bodies of law (environment-building)'.[100] This definition has the merit of locating human rights capacity building within a protection framework, thereby undermining any proposition that the two categories of activity may be seen as distinct or capable of competition *inter se*. Elsewhere, the present author has come to a similar conclusion whereby he suggested that human rights capacity building may best be categorised as a form of activity aimed at 'future-protection'.[101] With regard to the actual content of protection strategies, Howen draws to our attention the recent fascinating research of Liam Mahony.[102] Mahony suggests that, at its heart, protection comprises, 'persuasive human rights diplomacy'. He proposes a systematic model of protection-related actions that which will be of considerable value for practitioners, albeit it seems only lightly to touch on the capacity-building aspect of protection.

---

[98]   See, for example, L. Arbour, 'Protecting Human Rights: Charting the Way Forward', 2004 OHCHR Heads of Field Presences Meeting, at http://www.unhchr.ch/huricane/huricane.nsf/view01/24D3F8500C54D4DEC1256F550036A9E1?opendocument.

[99]   N. Howen, chapter 2 in the present volume, p. 31.

[100] *Ibid.*, p. 36.

[101] See O'Flaherty, 'Future Protection of Human Rights'.

[102] Howen, chapter 2 in the present volume, p. 40.

Howen's analysis provides a foundation and hermeneutic for an examination of the bodies of law that do, or which should, guide the activities of field operations (Nigel White and Marco Odello).[103] Concentrating on the UN, White and Odello consider both the legal justification for the establishment of field operations and the legal framework in which they operate. Concerning the former, they refer to the significance of the application of the doctrine of implied powers as well as the role of state consent and the enforcement powers under chapters VI and VII of the UN Charter.[104] With regard to the legal framework for field operations they observe the myriad confusing legal options that must be confronted. They suggest that a highly pragmatic approach be adopted whereby legal obligations are prioritised on the basis of the actual situation on the ground. This is surely correct and certainly correlates with practice.[105] It does though raise interesting issues regarding the process of prioritisation. Why, for instance, does the protection and promotion of economic and social right tend to be perceived as of secondary urgency in a post-conflict or emergency situation?[106] This particular prioritisation is sometimes at odds with the demands of victims[107] and it may also be inconsistent with the principle of the indivisibility of human rights – a principle that is as relevant to the actual nature of the enjoyment of human rights as it is to legal theory.[108] On the subject of the obligations upon field operations, White and Odello argue that, 'the UN is the beneficiary of rights but is also subject to duties on the international plane, primarily the fundamental principles of public international law including human rights law. In addition, the framework of human rights treaties sponsored by the UN and deriving from the General Assembly's UDHR in 1948 must form part of the constitutional law of the UN and be binding on it in that sense'.[109] The implications of this position for the UN in general and for field operations in particular are startling, proposing a comprehensive legal framework that puts human rights at its centre. One of the implications concerns the matter of personal and organisational accountability for human rights violations perpetrated by UN personnel. White and Odello offer a preliminary review of the issues, observing that accountability must have legal, political and administrative components, and they suggest that the topic is in need

---

[103] N. D. White and M. Odello, chapter 3 in the present volume, p. 47–67.

[104] Charter of the United Nations, 59 Stat. 1031, T.S. 993, 3 Bevans 1153, (entered into force Oct. 24, 1945).

[105] See chapters 14 by P. Burgess, 15 by the present author, 16 by T. Howland and 17 by M. Line in the present volume.

[106] White and Odello, chapter 3 in the present volume, p. 59.

[107] As indicated to the present author on numerous occasions, most recently when interviewing Iraqi civilians in 2005, all of whom argued that the most pressing human rights needs in their country concerned the rights to work and to education.

[108] See, M. O'Flaherty, 'Towards the Integration of United Nations Human Rights Treaty Body Recommendations – the Rights Based Approach Model', in M. A. Baderin and R. McCorquodale (eds), *Economic, Social and Cultural Rights in Action* (Oxford: Oxford University Press, forthcoming).

[109] White and Odello, chapter 3 in the present volume, p. 66.

of considerable further reflection. In general, White and Odello's chapter leaves the reader with a strong sense of the extent to which there remains a gap within the UN between law and practice.

Law can only provide an element of the normative framework for human rights field work. It is also essential to undertake an examination of the ethics applicable to the sector. Little work has been undertaken in this regard and the relevant chapter of the present volume is intended as an opening contribution (George Ulrich). As with the previous chapter, Ulrich distinguishes considerations regarding the establishment and the activities of human rights field operations. On the moral imperative to set up an operation he suggests the relevance of the work of the philosopher, Hans Jonas and the 'growing acknowledgement of moral relations across great distances in time and space'.[110] Turning to the activities of an operation and the responsibility of individual human rights field officers, he observes and argues convincingly against a tendency to equate applicable human rights standards with an ethical code. As a contribution to a debate on the content of such a code, Ulrich proposes five areas of principal ethical concern: harm/protection, communication, justice, collaboration and compliance with institutional objectives and standards. This categorisation raises a number of interesting issues. For instance, it relegates the matter of compliance with institutional standards to be just one among the categories notwithstanding that, 'more than half of the 12 articles of the 1999 OHCHR Code of Conduct are devoted to issues of compliance with organisational aims, policies and procedures and projecting an image of professionalism on behalf of the organisation'.[111] The categorisation also serves to highlight various aspects of, 'the obligation to conduct one's work in a spirit of respectful interaction with local counterparts'.[112] On these and many other issues, the chapter by Ulrich launches a novel and important debate which, he argues, must be conducted among 'practicing members of the profession ... Only thus can a would-be formal code of ethical conduct come to serve as a source of identification, pride and true guidance for human rights professionals'.[113]

Still another aspect of the normative environment for a field operation is that of the nature of its establishment and of its specific mandate. Issues such as these are considered in a chapter that also examines how some situations of human rights abuse attract international field operations, whereas others do not, and whereby there have evolved a multiplicity of mandate models (Daniel Moeckli and Manfred Nowak). Moeckli and Nowak undertake a comprehensive review of the establishment of human rights field operations by the UN and regional organisations, noting the vast diversity and many anomalies as well as the very low incidence of operations established with a view to the prevention of human rights abuses. They argue that the inconsistent practice is a function of a number of considerations. In the first place it relates to the degree of pressure that states are willing to apply towards a

---

[110] G. Ulrich, chapter 4 in the present volume, p. 69.

[111] *Ibid.*, p. 84.

[112] *Ibid.*, p. 81.

[113] *Ibid.*, p. 85.

country where abuses are occurring, a consideration that is governed by geopolitical concerns. Then the manner by which such pressure is negotiated through the institutional decision-making process will be of great significance, in as much as such processes are largely unregulated and are calibrated towards the production of *ad hoc* outputs. Moeckli and Nowak also observe the relevance in terms of mission mandate of financial considerations, such as, for instance, with regard to whether an operation is established in a manner whereby it can rely on the regular UN budget or must be supported instead by voluntary contributions. Moeckli and Nowak argue that the operation of considerations such as these, with the resultant inconsistencies, raise issues of compliance by the UN with its human rights legal obligations. They also suggest that they undermine the organisation's legitimacy. Among the chapter's conclusions is the aspiration that the newly-established Human Rights Council might be capable of bringing order into the sector. They argue that, '[T]he transfer of main responsibilities concerning the establishment and guidance of human rights field missions to the Human Rights Council could constitute an important contribution to the urgently required development' of a more coherent deployment policy'.[114] This is an interesting proposal, although it may be that the transfer of such a role to the Human Rights Council might exacerbate rather than diminish the impact of politics for decision making. Other implications of the suggestion, which would need consideration, include its impact for the hard won human rights activism of the Security Council and for the autonomous mandate of the high commissioner for human rights.

Human rights field operations exist within the context of broader international and local programmes of support to affected societies. As such, they require to insert themselves into complex partnerships and to ensure that they achieve their own human rights objectives within such mediated environments. Four chapters of the present volume address the principal contemporary contexts for partnership in post-conflict and emergency situations: peace (Bertrand Ramcharan), security (William O'Neill), justice (David Marshall), and humanitarianism (the present author). In each case, the author explores the relationship between human rights and the stated topic, assesses the partnership implications, reviews the state of theory and practice and reflects on some of the principal controversies.

Ramcharan examines the role of a human rights field operation in the phases of conflict prevention, peace negotiation, peace implementation and peace consolidation. It is his thesis that concern for human rights at all these stages will contribute to the establishment of durable peace, a proposition he defends with reference to instances of UN practice, many of which have not before been in the public domain. For instance, he provides a fascinating account of the efforts, sometimes successful, to put human rights at the centre of the Yugoslav peace process. He also locates and assesses more recent experience in countries such as Côte d'Ivoire, Afghanistan and Iraq. Ramcharan concludes by publishing, for the first time, a set of 1998 UN

---

[114] D. Moeckli and M. Nowak, chapter 5 in the present volume, p. 104.

policy recommendations on the integration of human rights in UN peace-related activities.[115] These still read as timely and pertinent.

O'Neill identifies partnership with security forces as, 'essential to the overall success of the human rights field operation, whether it is part of a multidimensional peacekeeping operation or is a standalone mission working with local security forces'.[116] The possibilities for partnership are primarily within the framework of a field operation's programmes for monitoring/reporting, training and institution building. In each case, O'Neill assesses actual field practice, identifying good or promising approaches and, in a number of cases, providing the first published assessment of their utility. For instance, he analyses the partnership between the UN mission in Sudan and the regional peacekeeping force, concluding that, 'Darfur provides cutting-edge opportunities to build on (human rights field operation) collaboration in a dangerous and demanding environment. Some in the human rights and especially in the humanitarian community criticise a creeping "politicisation" or "militarisation" of humanitarian assistance or human rights work. Darfur shows, however, that striking the right balance between cooperation and "independence" is possible; while the risks are there, the rewards from a healthy collaboration between the international security sector and (human rights field operation) are potentially enormous and worth the risk'.[117] He also discusses the need to match training efforts for local security forces with efforts to undertake institutional capacity building and, in this context, addresses the novel efforts for transitional reform of the security sectors in Bosnia and Herzegovina and the then East Timor.

O'Neill's discussion of the reform of the security sector introduces reflection on transitional justice in general, the topic addressed by Marshall. Marshall's starting point is an admission that, notwithstanding UN field operation's increasing involvement in providing assistance to transitional justice mechanisms, its 'knowledge and know-how remains in its infancy'. It is in this context that his presentation and analysis of new UN 'transitional justice tools' is of particular interest. The tools, for mapping of the justice sector; for design of prosecutorial initiatives; for vetting and institutional reform of justice-related actors; for the monitoring of legal systems and for the establishment of truth seeking mechanisms, represent a welcome initiative to learn from field experience and develop standardised core methodologies. Marshall undertakes a critical examination of truth seeking, drawing attention to the shortcomings of discussions of truth seeking that focus on process while overlooking such fundamental matters of substance as whether truth telling can actually lead to reconciliation. His comparative study of the post-conflict phases in Sierra Leone (where there was a truth commission) and Mozambique (where no such institution was established) is telling, indicative of a need for transitional justice frameworks to embrace traditional local healing and coping mechanisms. Concerning Mozambique, he suggests that, '[t]he healing and restoration of harmony is effective because it takes

---

[115] B. G. Ramcharan, chapter 6 in the present volume, pp. 121–123.

[116] W. G. O'Neill, chapter 7 in the present volume, p. 125.

[117] *Ibid.*, p. 134.

place within a wider context of family, community and the spirit world, consistent with cultural beliefs about self and health'. He draws similar conclusions for Sierra Leone, thereby locating the achievements of that country's Truth and Reconciliation Commission within a larger context of an array of healing and reconciliation actions. Marshall's analysis has clear implications for human rights field operations in terms of their need to engage vigorously and respectfully with the local communities which they serve. In a manner consistent with the ethical analysis by Ulrich, he concludes, '[w]hat is essential is that UN field operations, in a thoughtful and deliberative manner, develop a rich understanding of local reconciliation processes and traditions since truth-seeking initiatives considered a success in one context may not be suitable in another. Moreover, the field operation must proactively seek practical, flexible solutions that respond to what victims themselves desire, acknowledge the potential contributions of indigenous healing traditions, and maintain pressure for implementation of recommendations to remedy victims suffering and the societal conditions which fed the conflict' (see D. Marshall, present volume, p.157).

In the chapter on partnership with the humanitarian community, the present author reviews the period since the adoption of humanitarianism's '*magna carta*',[118] UN General Assembly resolution 46/182 of 1991. He charts the unsteady progress in theory and practice that has made such partnership possible, paying particular attention to the significance of the rise of what is commonly termed, 'new humanitarianism'. He assesses the manner whereby the debate on the relationship of humanitarianism and human rights has concentrated on issues of protection and, until recently, overlooked implications of human rights for the delivery of humanitarian assistance. In this context the present author explores the significance for humanitarian programming of the debate on right-based approaches to development (RBAD) and, particularly, one model thereof which he describes as the 'UN school of RBAD'. More generally, reflecting on contemporary concerns, he suggests that advocates of the view that human rights serves to politicise and therefore undermine humanitarian activity are misguided: '[I]t is inconceivable to consider any human rights or humanitarian action that will not have consequences for a given political situation. It is not this unavoidable aspect of the actions which is at issue, but rather the challenge of ensuring that the actions are consistently implemented on the basis of the applicable laws and principles'. The present author concludes the chapter with a set of recommendations that might form the basis for partnership between the two sectors in the field and observes that such partnership is possible across the entire spectrum of the work areas of the human rights field operation.

Human rights field operations have much to learn for the undertaking of protection work by UN agencies, funds and programmes, the International Committee of the Red Cross (ICRC) and NGOs. chapters on UNICEF (Karin Landgren), UNHCR (Maria Stavropoulou), ICRC (Alain Aeschlimann) and one major NGO, PBI (Liam Mahony), take stock of this experience and its possible implications for human rights field operations.

---

[118] M. O'Flaherty, chapter 9 in the present volume, p. 160.

Landgren reviews the short but remarkable development of UNICEF's work for the promotion and protection of the rights of the child whereby, 'from 2002, UNICEF identified child protection and emergency responses as agency priorities, adopting organising frameworks for both to promote a more systematised approach'.[119] She considers such milestones as the role of UNICEF in inducing rebel forces in South Sudan to commit to implementation of the Convention on the Rights of the Child[120] and the process surrounding the preparation and implementation of the Machel report on child soldiers. She assesses the evolution of UNICEF's child protection methodologies, paying particular attention to its 'protective environment approach' and its 'core commitments in emergencies'. Notably, and echoing the discussion of issues of protection/capacity building by the present author, Howen *et al*, she observes how the protective environment approach, 'expressed protection in terms of the broad factors that determine whether or not children are likely to be protected, including the existence of appropriate legislation and its implementation, the prevailing customs and attitudes, and the availability of essential services'.[121] Landgren demonstrates the manner whereby UNICEF seeks to continuously adapt to ever-changing protection environments. For instance, she describes its leadership in the response to disclosures of widespread sexual abuse of children by UN personnel, its novel tools for the engagement of children with transitional justice mechanisms and its efforts to develop systematised monitoring and reporting mechanisms. Overall, and notwithstanding the specificity of the UNICEF mandate and the global scale of its operations, the chapter shows the extent to which that agency has much to teach the deployers of human rights field operations. Landgren describes an institutional culture that continuously listens to and learns from the field and then models its programmes and methods around key protection concerns. She conveys the importance placed by UNICEF in the systematisation of methodologies. Her account makes clear the importance of such policy and methodological approaches having the full support of all levels of policy and decision makers. Finally, she indicates the need for policy and protection methods to remain under continuing review.

The great merit of the chapter on UNHCR by Stavropoulou is to demonstrate the extent to which its protection work mirrors the work of more general human rights field operations in terms of function and form, albeit with UNHCR's narrower client base and its mandate to seek durable protection solutions for refugees. The categories of protection activity are all familiar: monitoring, reporting, advocacy and intervention, dealing with individual cases, capacity building and, even, empowerment of local civil society. Stavropoulou assesses the various methodologies that have been introduced, such as that for the assessment of the protection environment, and she takes note of the high degree of specialisation expected of protection personnel – all of which may suggest directions to be taken as human rights field work seeks

---

[119] K. Landgren, chapter 10 in the present volume, p. 184.

[120] Convention on the Rights of the Child, adopted 20 Nov. 1989, G.A. res. 44/25, UN GAOR, 44th Sess., Supp. No. 49, UN Doc. A/44/49 (1989) (entered into force 2 Sept. 1990).

[121] K. Landgren, chapter 10 in the present volume, p. 191.

to better professionalise itself. The final section of the chapter also has much to suggest for human rights operations – the analysis of some UNHCR organisational challenges, such as for accountability of the organisation and on the need to sustain an institutional culture of learning and of support for personnel, are instructional for organisations deploying human rights field personnel.

Aeschlimann begins his chapter on ICRC with the view that 'consultation between [organisations active in the field] is an ethical, legal and operational necessity, imposed by people's right to enjoy maximum protection. Being mainly field oriented with a longstanding experience in protection and a clear mandate, ICRC strongly wishes to be part of this dialogue, as an integral element of the global protection framework'.[122] The chapter may be seen as a contribution to that dialogue. Aeschlimann revisits the ICRC-sponsored process of reflection on the nature of protection work, applying it to contemporary issues for the field and examines the extent to which protection needs can only be addressed with a framework of complementary organisational approaches. The need for complementarity is reinforced when account is taken of the challenges for ICRC's protection work, all of which resonate for human rights field operations: security constraints, ensuring the quality of information and analysis, legal characterisation of situations and the evaluation of the effectiveness of protection activities. Observing that ICRC and human rights field operations have already interacted to varying degrees in some 25 locations, Aeschlimann proposes that complementarity, which may be established between them, should be 'on the basis of the qualification of the situation concerned, the need to have an independent and neutral intermediary involved, respective mandates and capacities, the areas and types of respective activities, the ways of action, the period and duration of intervention and the body of law concerned'.[123] He develops his point with a presentation of what ICRC considers to be features of human rights field operations that may complement ICRC's approach. These go to such matters as expertise in human rights law, regular use of public communications, links with human rights systems and mechanisms, close relations with UN member states and efforts to uphold the rule of law. He makes reference to instances of effective cooperation in such locations as Nepal, Liberia, Colombia and Rwanda. The chapter concludes with the admonition that future possibilities for cooperation between ICRC and field operations will require to take account of, 'how human rights field operations develop, how much predictability can exist and how the best possible complementarity can be worked out at general and local levels'.[124]

Assessment of the work of field operations of international human rights NGOs is rendered difficult by virtue of the rarity of such deployments on the part of the major organisations as well as the extreme diversity of organisational types and approaches. Accordingly, the chapter on NGO experience focuses on the experience of just one organisation, PBI. The assessment of its methods

---

[122] A. Aeschlimann, chapter 12 in the present volume, p. 223.

[123] *Ibid.*, p. 239.

[124] *Ibid.*, p. 241.

allows for the identification of multiple good practices. Mahony concentrates on an examination of PBI's strategy of 'unarmed international accompaniment ... the physical accompaniment by international personnel of activists, organisations or communities who are threatened with politically-motivated attacks' (see L. Mahony, chapter 13, p.243). Accompaniment contains elements of human rights protection and capacity building, '[t]his accompaniment service has three simultaneous and mutually reinforcing impacts. The international presence protects threatened activists ... encourages civil society activism ... [and] ... strengthens the international movement for peace and human rights' (see L. Mahony, chapter 13, p. 243–244). As presented by Mahony, accompaniment benefits from an elaborated theoretical framework, whereby its application is calibrated to best address local circumstances. Much of this framework can have a more general application for the design and implementation of a wide range of protection approaches. The chapter benefits from reference to practice in a number of states, some of which, such as Indonesia and Sri Lanka, are not normally considered in the context of review of human rights field operations. Mahony also draws attention to the importance that PBI places in careful selection and training of its personnel, with the latter notably focusing more on competencies/values than on skills, '[v]olunteers go through a series of exercises and role-plays to help them visualise the challenge they are considering and to help trainers gauge their preparedness. These trainings consider such criteria as commitment to non-violence and human rights, capacity for intensive political analysis, understanding of the country of the project, cautious judgement, patience and humility, ability to work in a team under high stress and more' (see L. Mahony, chapter 13, p. 256).

The present volume does not contain an extensive section devoted to an examination of specific human rights field operations. Much such analysis is instead to be found within the thematic chapters. In addition, a wide range of case studies has been published elsewhere, notably in a series of volumes by the Aspen Institute.[125] Those case studies that have been included here have been chosen on the basis that they complement the other chapters and ensure adequate examination of important themes, such as the role of human rights field operations within a peace process and the undertaking of human rights monitoring, reporting and capacity building. The country situations/field operations examined are, East Timor (Patrick Burgess), Sierra Leone (the present author), Angola (Todd Howland) and Bosnia and Herzegovina/Guatemala (Milburn Line). The latter three chapters first appeared elsewhere. There is also a chapter on the field operations of OSCE (Susanne Ringgaard-Pedersen and Annette Lyth). The chapter is included in order to take account of the distinct practice of that organisation and the method is one of a review of its general practice rather than an examination of any particular operation.

Burgess' chapter on East Timor constitutes a survey of the lifespan of a highly complex mission, which at one time or another had to engage with a wide range of challenges and concerns, including with regard to transitional justice, monitoring and capacity building. Notwithstanding that the UN mission had governmental authority, much of its experience is directly relevant for other field operations, for instance

---

[125] See footnote 15, as well as Henkin (ed.), *Honoring Human Rights under International Mandates*.

regarding relations with local human rights civil society, strategies for recruitment and training of national staff. The experience of the human rights team in negotiating operational space within a complex UN mission is also generally pertinent as is the manner in which the East Timor operation managed to maintain relations with the UN's political and human rights centres. Burgess concludes his chapter with specific recommendations for mission planning, design of mandate, recruitment of personnel and management support.

Many of the issues raised by Burgess are also addressed by the present author, in the context of a very different operating environment, in the chapter on Sierra Leone. This chapter concentrates on the conflict and immediate post-conflict periods and addresses the manner in which a field operation must operate within the framework of complex partnerships, comprising local and international civil society, government, the humanitarian and conflict resolution communities and others. It demonstrates how Sierra Leone can be considered a case study for the engagement of human rights actors with all phases of a peace process, including preparations for peace, peace negotiations and implementation of a peace agreement. In this context, the chapter also examines strategies for human rights monitoring, reporting and advocacy/intervention, as well as the possibilities for human rights capacity building in times of emergency.

While Howland also addresses a range of post-conflict related issues in his chapter on Angola, his primary focus is on the subject of human rights capacity building. He observes that, 'it is difficult to imagine how sustainable improvement in the human rights situation can be achieved in Angola without a quantitative and qualitative change in the institutions needed to protect human rights' (see chapter 16, p. 332) and assesses the UN's experience in developing measurable indicators for success of capacity building efforts as well as in assisting the Angola government and civil society to create 'useful measures for keeping their "fingers on the pulse" of the current human rights situation and determining the extent to which human rights interventions are positively impacting the situation' (see chapter 16, p. 333). He explores in some detail the challenges that the UN operation faced in funding its work and its innovative responses, ranging from partnership with NGOs to establishment of trust funds. He concludes with a favourable assessment of the impact of the operation and of its contribution to the attainment of peace.

The chapter by Line addresses a number of points pertinent to human rights field operations but in the more general context of the deployment of broader peace-related operations in post-conflict situations. His approach is comparative, with an analysis of the experiences in Bosnia and Herzegovina and Guatemala, situations which he considers analogous in terms of the typology of conflict and peace process. He undertakes an interesting analysis of such phenomena as a typical failure to place, consistently, coherently and effectively, human rights considerations at the heart of mission design. He draws particular attention to the importance for a field operation of a strategic planning process, the imperative need for comprehensive organisational accountability and the importance of ensuring local 'ownership' (see chapter 17, p. 349) of reform of the justice sector – all points that resonate with other chapters in this volume and are reinforced by means of his comparative examination of the two country situations.

The chapter on the practice of OSCE draws attention to that body's leadership in insisting on a link between issues of security and human rights, an understanding that stimulated and informed an extensive range of political commitments and operational initiatives. Ringgaard-Pedersen and Lyth identify how this process generated an agreement between states, 'that pluralistic democracy based on law is the only system of government suitable to guarantee human rights'. This is the context for the human rights work of OSCE field operations, mandated to, 'assist host governments in solving specific problems and in meeting their commitments ... [a]ll OSCE missions implicitly have a human rights mandate, but one that is an integrated part of a broad mission mandate encompassing all ... dimensions of the OSCE security concept'. Notwithstanding the array of jurisdictional and policy approaches that may distinguish an OSCE field operation from those of the UN, the chapter demonstrates the extent to which they address similar work areas and challenges. There is also a useful survey of the OSCE experience for the development of methodologies and training tools. The chapter concludes with reference to a number of challenges that OSCE must confront, some of which – such as those regarding small-scale operations – are generically relevant for the missions of all organisations. In another conclusion with broad resonance, the authors observe that, '[t]he strength of OSCE human rights field work has historically been within the core mandate functions, such as human rights monitoring, conducted in the context of early warning, conflict prevention, conflict management and post-conflict rehabilitation. The challenge lies in maintaining this aspect of OSCE field work while conducting technical assistance for rule of law development and human rights capacity-building projects where appropriate'.

The final chapter of the volume is a compendium of published materials on field operations deployed since 1991 (Kevin Turner). It draws attention to a striking disparity of academic and other expert attention to specific field operations, with some, such as in the former Yugoslavia, subject to extensive commentary and others, for instance many operations in Africa, seemingly entirely overlooked. This chapter is augmented by a select bibliography drawing together all references to hardcopy publications that have been cited in the volume.

Conclusions

As this volume demonstrates, much has been achieved in the short history of intergovernmental human rights field work. Dozens of UN and regional operations have been deployed and have been administered by many hundreds of dedicated personnel. These programmes have evolved into multifaceted operations which more or less keep pace with changing perceptions of the nature of conflict and of the relevance of international human rights law for its resolution. Notwithstanding these achievements there are a number of challenges that require attention.[126]

---

[126] Some of the ideas that follow have been stimulated by ideas in Mahony, 'Unarmed Monitoring and Human Rights Field Presences'; and Mahony, 'Promoting Unarmed Monitoring: Thinking Long-term'.

The first challenge is that of the comprehensive professionalisation of the sector through the clarification of overarching principles, goals and methods – to describe the core 'doctrine' of human rights field work.[127] The present situation is very far from this point. Yes there is the underlying body of international human rights law. Certainly there are some components of an operational doctrine in place. There are even some helpful 'best practice' reviews of certain practices and field operations[128] and a number of discrete methodological tools have been devised. However, there remain vast gaps – entire work areas where no guidance is available and the field operation is obliged to proceed in a trial and error process of experimentation. As a corollary to the lack of guidance there is a dearth of performance indicators whereby field work can be properly evaluated and whereby field operation designers, managers and personnel may be held accountable.[129]

That we should be so little advanced in terms of the articulation of a doctrine is perhaps not surprising given the youth of the sector – good practice can only emerge from a phase of case-specific experimentation. Such a phase though will prove to be wasteful and harmful if it is not matched by an ongoing and system-wide assessment of good and bad practice, whereby overarching practice principles may emerge. It is high time for existing achievements and efforts to be placed in the context of a much more ambitious scheme – in essence, to map out a new professional sector and, in so doing, to identify and describe the human rights field officer, clarify the human rights role of other actors in the context of mainstreamed approaches to human rights work and propose models for the forms of partnership required. This exercise requires addressing UN practice, the experience of human rights operations of regional organisations and that of NGOs and others as relevant. And it needs to be an ongoing process that takes account of changing circumstances and undertakes continuous review of whatever tools and guidance may be produced. Professionalisation of the sector has to be matched by consistent application in practice of human rights approaches regardless of the nature or the location of a given armed conflict.

This volume draws on the expertise of its authors to make a substantial but necessarily tentative contribution to the development of the required understanding and doctrine. While intended to clarify elements of the principles underlying human rights field work as well as of their practice implications, it is accepted that at least some of the findings are provisional and that sustained inter-disciplinary study will continue to be required across the range of issues. Multiple examples of such areas have been identified already in this chapter and are discussed throughout the

---

[127] For a useful and apposite discussion of the nature of professionalism and the requirements for development of the profession of humanitarianism see P. Walker, 'What does it Mean to be a Professional Humanitarian', *The Journal of Humanitarian Assistance*, January 2004, at http://www.jha.ac/articles/a127.htm.

[128] DPKO has established a best practices unit. See http://www.un.org/Depts/dpko/lessons/.

[129] See the interesting discussion of performance indicators in O'Neill, 'Gaining Compliance without Force'.

volume. For instance, many of the contributions are informed by an underlying assumption that all field work is ultimately concerned with human rights protection. This requires further examination so that the frequently perceived tension between protection and capacity building can be resolved in both practice and theory. Another overarching consideration, that of field work being intended to ensure sustainable 'empowerment' of local actors, requires much deeper exploration. The editor and a number of the authors, as well as others, are engaged in such reflection within the framework of a research project, 'Consolidating the Profession: The Human Rights Field Officer', the proceedings and findings of which may be found at www. humanrightsprofessionals.org. Readers are invited to visit that site.[130]

More generally, the addressing of the challenges will require action from myriad actors at the political, technical and educational levels, nationally, regionally and internationally. It will only succeed if it is strongly and coherently led in a manner that integrates attention to the political/policy and the technical/programmatic aspects. The role of the UN high commissioner for human rights is compelling, vested as she is with the overarching responsibility to promote human rights approaches across the UN system and to be a voice of principle and guidance on human rights for all parts of the international community. Only the high commissioner has the status, authority and comprehensive mandate to articulate the vision and guide the action that will be required.[131] In her *Plan of Action* of 2005, High Commissioner Arbour has shown herself willing to address that challenge. It may confidently be predicted that, on her watch, the human rights field sector is poised for significant development.

---

[130] See, also, 'Annex VII, Consolidating the Profession: The Human Rights Field Officer', in B. G. Ramcharan (ed.), *Human Rights Protection in the Field*, (Leiden: Martinus Nijhof, 2006).

[131] See Ramcharan, *The United Nations High Commissioner for Human Rights.*

Chapter 2

The Fundamental Protection Function of the Human Rights Field Operation

Nicholas Howen

[H]uman rights protection must be recognized as the first and foremost priority of [the Office of the High Commissioner for Human Rights], as it is the basis for all human rights work: capacity building, technical assistance and mainstreaming are of little or no value … if the basic fundamental of protection is not secured. Human rights protection also lies at the heart of OHCHR's mandate …

(Louise Arbour, United Nations High Commissioner for Human Rights[1])

Introduction

The word 'protection' is one of the most frequently used and misused words in the field of human rights. A recent Google search of the website of the Office of the United Nations High Commissioner for Human Rights (OHCHR) found 65,100 references to the word 'protection'. It appears in the title of human rights treaties, in names of human rights bodies, in the title of the *Action Plan* launched by the high commissioner for human rights,[2] in United Nations (UN) human rights resolutions on countries and themes, and in recommendations made by human rights treaty bodies. Using the word protection can convey a comforting but perhaps misleading image of proactive actions and an environment of safety and security.

This chapter looks specifically at the meaning and role of human rights protection within the work of in-country UN human rights field operations supported by OHCHR – whether standalone OHCHR presences or human rights components of peace operations. The chapter describes how OHCHR is increasingly accepting that

---

[1]   'Protecting Human Rights: Charting the Way Forward', Speech by Louise Arbour, United Nations High Commissioner for Human Rights, at the 2004 Heads of Field Presences Meeting, 22 November 2004, Geneva, Switzerland.

[2]   See The High Commissioner for Human Rights, *The OHCHR Plan of Action: Protection and Empowerment* (Geneva: OHCHR, 2005). The plan has been endorsed by UN member states approving through the General Assembly a remarkable addition of nearly a hundred posts in OHCHR to implement the plan.

protection is a core and distinctive part of its mandate and identity, including in the field, although OHCHR is still buffeted by intense political pressures and cross-currents pushing in different directions – towards increased and reduced human rights protection in the field. Because of these political pressures, it is necessary to have a working understanding of what is protection. At its core is action to prevent or end specific human rights violations suffered by victims and carried out by perpetrators. While the present author agrees that capacity building activities are essential in a field operation and can create an environment in which rights will be protected, especially if the protection perspective is built into the projects, some governments still use 'technical assistance' to blunt and avoid tougher accountability measures and direct protection activities. The chapter then explores what protection means in practice for human rights field operations – complex and interrelated actions revolving around human rights diplomacy, which aims to increase the consequences of carrying out human rights abuses and decrease the risks for civil society and officials to defend human rights.

Removing the Ambiguity: The Central Role of Protection in OHCHR Field Operations

Despite the international political currents trying to chase protection work into the shadows, OHCHR is increasingly accepting and asserting with more confidence that protection is a fundamental function of OHCHR and of its field operations.

Several UN agencies in the field carry out human rights capacity building, promotion and education activities (especially the United Nations Development Programme, the United Nations Children's Fund [UNICEF] and the United Nations Development Fund for Women); some expressly protect particular groups (the Office of the United Nations High Commissioner for Refugees [UNHCR] for refugees, UNICEF for children, the Joint United Nations Programme on HIV/AIDs for those living with HIV/AIDS); some provide or coordinate humanitarian assistance which in many cases directly or indirectly protects people from human rights violations (such as the United Nations Office for the Coordination of Humanitarian Affairs, the World Food Programme, UNICEF, UNHCR). OHCHR, however, is the only UN agency in the field that has an express mandate to *protect* people from all types of *human rights violations* – civil, cultural, economic, political and social. This is clear from the December 1993 General Assembly resolution establishing the post of high commissioner for human rights, which expressly gave this official 'principal responsibility' to 'protect the effective enjoyment by all' of all human rights and to coordinate human rights '… protection activities throughout the UN system'.[3]

At key moments past high commissioners have claimed this role; for example, when the first High Commissioner Ayala Lasso swiftly deployed the first significant standalone presence to Rwanda and then four years later when the Rwandan

---

3   General Assembly resolution 48/141 (1993), UN Doc. A/RES/48/141 (1993), at 4.

government ended the operation because Mary Robinson insisted it must include protection functions.

However, no OHCHR standalone operation was set up for almost nine years after the establishment of the field operation in Colombia in 1996. This absence opened the door to much debate about the mandate, identity and 'comparative advantage' of OHCHR. It was unclear whether or not OHCHR had retreated from the idea of playing a significant protection role through standalone presences – or just whether the politics were not right to establish such operations (although OHCHR did continue to staff human rights components of peace operations in the same period).

The ambiguity was swept away when the current High Commissioner, Louise Arbour, accepted and actively facilitated the proposal to deploy a standalone OHCHR human rights field operation in the midst of the armed conflict in Nepal. The agreement, signed by the government of Nepal with OHCHR in April 2005, has a far-reaching mandate with all the express references to protection functions it needs to give legitimacy and strength to protection activities in a country where gross and systematic violations are being committed by both the government and rebel Communist Party of Nepal (Maoist).[4]

The current high commissioner has been robust in drawing on the General Assembly resolution and, as a matter of policy, putting to an end any lingering controversy about whether or not OHCHR can and should carry out protection activities as a core and unavoidable part of its mandate. When the General Assembly mandate is linked to the decision by the high commissioner to expand in-country and regional presences,[5] it is clear that OHCHR has laid out as policy that its protection mandate will increasingly be put into practice in the field, through OHCHR staff.

After Nepal, the protection approach was consolidated further when the high commissioner agreed in June 2005 to deploy human rights field officers in districts in Uganda, primarily to help provide emergency protection to people living in conflict-affected areas of northern Uganda. 2005 also saw the agreement to set up an OHCHR standalone operation in Guatemala, following the departure of the UN Verification Mission, with a mandate that includes monitoring elements as well as capacity building.[6]

The debate has shifted from a discussion about *whether*, to *how* OHCHR should carry out protection functions in the field. How much and what sort of protection work a human rights field operation carries out will depend on the words of the mandate of the operation,[7] the extent to which it could be interpreted expansively and the extent to which such activities are needed in the country. Even technical assistance or capacity building projects that have no express protection mandate

---

[4]   See http://nepal.ohchr.org/.

[5]   The United Nations High Commissioner for Human Rights, *The OHCHR Plan of Action.*

[6]   See OHCHR, *High Commissioner's Strategic Management Plan 2006-2007* (Geneva: OHCHR, 2006), pp. 57–58.

[7]   For a discussion of the factors influencing the nature of the mandate, see chapter 5 by D. Moeckli and M. Nowak in the present volume.

cannot be divorced from the protection perspective (see *Building Protection into Capacity Building*, below).

OHCHR presences operate in a country within the broader UN system. In many cases development (and sometimes humanitarian) agencies unfamiliar with a human rights approach to problems in a country are apprehensive that a too bold human rights protection role by the UN will jeopardise access to, and relations with, a government. However, in the present author's experience, other UN agencies often welcome and even request OHCHR to be present to address – often difficult – human rights issues that they are unwilling or ill-equipped to tackle.

The comprehensive nature of its mandate gives OHCHR an important comparative advantage in relation to other UN agencies. However, in comparison to most other UN agencies it is also grossly under-funded and still in the very early stages of developing the necessary policies, standard methods of work and training to ensure it can consistently exercise its role professionally, reflecting both human rights expertise and sophisticated political judgment. There is still a need, for example, for the emerging OHCHR policy approach to be grounded in clear methodological ground rules or doctrine – as has been done by the International Committee of the Red Cross (ICRC) – by which every government will know that an agreement establishing an OHCHR presence will necessarily include certain core functions and methods of work, including both protection and capacity building.

Apart from standalone presences, it is also now accepted practice for human rights components of UN peace operations to have mandates with express protection functions. The 'Report of the Panel on United Nations Peace Operations'[8] (the 'Brahimi Report') reaffirmed that human rights components of peace operations are essential and that they should do both human rights monitoring and capacity building. After a hiccup when the first post-Brahimi Report peace operation in Afghanistan created a human rights component with only capacity building functions, subsequent components in Iraq,[9] Liberia[10] and Côte d'Ivoire,[11] have all had some elements of protection functions expressly referred to in their mandates.

The Politics of Protection: Pressures to Reduce or Increase Human Rights Protection

Whether or not a particular field operation is given an adequate protection mandate and whether it has enough political space to exercise it, will always depend largely on the unique local and international political situation. In the case of Colombia in 1996 and Nepal in 2005, there was intense political pressure on the governments over systematic human rights violations, an effective international non-governmental organisation (NGO) coalition and support from key states that had influence over the governments. Both governments acquiesced to an OHCHR

---

[8]   Report of the Panel on United Nations Peace Operations, UN Doc. A/55/305-S/2000/809 (2000).
[9]   See Security Council resolution 1546 (2004), UN Doc. S/RES/1564 (2004), at 7.
[10] See Security Council resolution 1509 (2003), UN Doc. S/RES/1509 (2003), at 3.
[11] See Security Council resolution 1528 (2004), UN Doc. S/RES/1528 (2004), at 6.

field operation rather than risk having the United Nations Commission on Human Rights appoint a special rapporteur to investigate human rights violations and report back to the Commission. Both operations were given effective mandates.

Nevertheless, conflicting global political pressures and currents also influence the rise and decline of protection mandates in the field. The fierce controversies in 2005 and 2006 over the new UN Human Rights Council to replace the Commission on Human Rights, revealed the attempts by a number of states to weaken the ability of the UN to scrutinise the human rights record of states and, by extension, to avoid the deployment of human rights operations that would carry out human rights protection work. They argued that the main purpose of any Council should be to help provide human rights capacity building and other technical assistance at the request of a government, that it should no longer adopt resolutions on individual countries (which has been an important way to increase support for deployment of a field operation). Although these proposals were rejected, they reflect some of the pressures to limit protection and emphasise promotion and technical assistance.

At the same time, wide media coverage of massive violations of human rights such as in Darfur in Sudan, fuels calls for emergency protection measures (although media coverage and sustained NGO advocacy have consistently failed to generate enough support for a international presence in Chechnya, given Russia's status as a permanent member of the Security Council). In a significant policy breakthrough, the UN Millennium Summit in September 2005 agreed that, as a last resort, the international community has a responsibility to use, under Chapter VII enforcement powers to protect populations from genocide, war crimes, ethnic cleansing and crimes against humanity.[12] While this implies military intervention, it brings in its wake recognition of use of a wide range of protective measures, including human rights protection strategies.

Protection: Preventing/Ending Abuse and Ensuring Reparation

There is no consensus among different human rights and humanitarian organisations on the definition of protection. Some very broad definitions identify an all-encompassing and long-term concept of protection, often described as activities aimed at the implementation of full respect for the rights of the individual. While this is no doubt correct, it is too abstract and broad to be of use in an operational setting and to help decide whether any particular activity is sufficiently connected with, and contributes to, protection.

In its common sense meaning, 'protection' conveys the idea of preventing or ending harm or injury,[13] usually suffered by someone, from a particular source. In human rights terms this conjures up images of helping victims and stopping

---

[12]   2005 World Summit Outcome, 15 September 2005, UN Doc. A/60/L.1 (2005), at 138–139.

[13]   The *Collins English Dictionary* defines 'protect' as 'to defend from trouble, harm, attack, etc.' (London: Harper Collins, 1999), p. 1240.

perpetrators, of preventing or stopping the impact on people of deliberate or negligent acts or omissions by, or on behalf of, governments or armed opposition groups: acts that amount to carrying out, ordering or acquiescing in human rights violations.

In other words, at its core, human rights protection in field operations must include action that seeks to prevent, stop or provide remedies and reparation for specific violations of human rights that are suffered by particular individuals (in some cases as members of a group) and that are carried out by perpetrators, whether known or unidentified. There is immediacy to this work[14] and different types of protection activities are considered below.

Relationship between Protection and Capacity Building

A controversy within OHCHR, and more broadly within the United Nations, has often been the extent to which capacity building, promotion and human rights education activities should also be considered as protection work and a sufficient response to serious human rights violations.

Between 1996 and 2000, the ICRC convened a series of workshops involving human rights and humanitarian organisations, to develop a common understanding of the meaning and approaches to protecting civilians in conflicts. These workshops came closer than any other process to agreeing a definition of protection in conflict situations. The ICRC 'egg' protection framework brought into one description the different elements of protection activities – responsive action, remedial action and environment-building – in a way that conveyed there was not meant to be any hierarchy of activities, that each depended in some way on the others and all could be carried out simultaneously. The 'egg' framework defined a protection activity as any activity which:

> prevents or puts a stop to a specific pattern of abuse and/or alleviates its immediate effects (responsive action); restores people's dignity and ensures adequate living conditions through reparation, restitution and rehabilitation (remedial action); fosters an environment conducive to respect for the rights of individuals in accordance with the relevant bodies of law (environment-building).[15]

This definition includes the core concept of responding and remedying abuses and also includes the broader capacity building perspective. Leaders of UN human

---

[14] See also chapter 12 by A. Aeschlimann in the present volume, in which he says that, within the ICRC, protection *stricto senso* encompasses 'activities aimed at preventing and/or putting an end to and/or avoiding the recurrence of the violations of the obligations of the authorities/armed carriers or the rights of individuals in accordance with the letter and spirit of IHL and other fundamental protective norms in situations of violence'. Such protection work is contrasted with assistance activities that are aimed mainly at giving aid to cover material, physical or psychological needs of victims and other affected persons.

[15] ICRC, *Strengthening Protection in War: A Search for Professional Standards* (Geneva: ICRC, 2001), p. 20.

rights operations recognised a decade ago that human rights field operations should not only carry out immediate protection work, but also leave a legacy of longer-term institution-building, legal reform and human rights education[16] – often called 'technical assistance', although the present author prefers the term 'capacity building'.[17] Victims and potential victims will be better protected if effective national laws and institutions are established or strengthened that are able and willing to protect – whether an independent judiciary alert to its role as a protector of human rights, an effective national human rights institution, a responsive bureaucracy aware of its human rights duties, a vibrant media and a civil society able to advocate and influence laws, policies and behaviour. Rights are also more likely to be protected if a culture of human rights, of preventive action and of accountability pervades a country, through human rights education, public debate and effective training of government officials.

Some environment-building activities are quite immediate, encouraging reformers in a government to defend human rights-friendly policies, and stimulating debate in a country about human rights abuses. However, complex capacity building projects usually need a long time before their effects are felt. It is of little comfort to tell a victim that the UN is protecting them from abuse by helping to set up a national human rights institution. Clearly both the immediate and long-term activities are necessary, but they play very different roles.

This relationship between protection and capacity building is significant because of the political pressures by some governments on the UN to do less work that acknowledges and responds to often serious patterns of human rights violations and to do more 'technical assistance', often seen as less confrontational and carried out only at the request of the government. Where the human rights violations are deliberately carried out by, or on behalf of, the government, or there is a lack of political will to end the violations, putting money into 'technical assistance' is at best ineffectual. Practitioners often say that one well-targeted conviction of a senior military officer responsible for torture or extrajudicial executions is worth a thousand human rights training sessions. Certainly, at worst, technical assistance masks the real reasons for the violations and can be used by the government to shield it from tougher scrutiny and action. Where there *is* a minimum level of political will, building the capacity of national institutions like the police, the justice system or ministries can indeed lead to the violations being addressed and leaves a vital long-term impact of the field presence.

The further one moves along the protection continuum towards capacity building, the greater is the political risk that a government or the UN itself, will use the existence of such assistance as an excuse to avoid accountability in international human rights political bodies and to reject tougher protection activities on the ground. The tension will always exist, but can be minimised if responsive and remedial

---

[16] D. García-Sayán, 'The Experience of ONUSAL in El Salvador', in A. Henkin (ed.), *Honoring Human Rights* (The Hague: Kluwer Law International, 2000).

[17] The present author prefers the phrase 'capacity building' to 'technical assistance' because it indicates more clearly the long-term purpose and active nature of the endeavour.

actions are also taking place and if capacity building projects build in an inherent protection perspective.

Building Protection into Capacity Building

The human rights field practitioners writing in the 1990s emphasised the 'most important operational lesson',[18] that there is a vital 'intimate and supportive relationship'[19] between the sharp end of protecting human rights on the one hand, including transparent and public monitoring and reporting, and the long-term creation and capacity building of local state and non-governmental institutions on the other.

Investigating, documenting and analysing human rights violations shows patterns that need to be changed and points to the causes of human rights violations. This diagnostic should shape the objectives of capacity building projects: provide baseline data, as well as some of the benchmarks and indicators of change. Continuous monitoring during the life of the project and in post-project evaluations helps to measure its impact and the continuing political will of the authorities and acts a self-correcting mechanism. In many cases it will be possible to raise continuing patterns of violations with the authorities during the project, as part of the operation's protection activities and to provide feedback to refine the project.

The clear policy of the high commissioner for human rights, reflected in the quote at the head of the present chapter, should settle once and for all any residual controversy over the relationship between protection and capacity building projects. A human rights field operation will need to use delicate diplomatic skills to resist requests from a government for capacity building projects or to discuss openly with authorities how projects should be shaped by the diagnostic provided by the UN's protection activities. A nimble and astute human rights field officer will also be able to use the close relationships developed with a government from within a long-term capacity building project to encourage more immediate remedial responses by a government to human rights violations. Nevertheless, there is a natural tension between the pressures for silence that often comes with access to the workings of government, and the need for more robust and swift protection action to address ongoing human rights violations.

Which Rights?

What rights do human rights field operations protect? By definition, the starting point for human rights field operations are the rights guaranteed in *human rights instruments* – the human rights treaties ratified by the country,[20] customary

---

[18]   T. Hammarberg and P. Gavigan, 'Introduction', in A. Henkin (ed.), *Honoring Human Rights – From Peace to Justice: Recommendations to the International Community* (Washington, DC: Aspen Institute, 1998), p. 19.

[19]   *Ibid.*, p. 29.

[20]   The starting point is the Universal Declaration of Human Rights and what are considered by OHCHR as the seven core international human rights treaties (on civil and political rights, on economic, social and cultural rights, against torture and other ill-treatment,

international law that applies in all countries regardless of which treaties have been ratified, and a large range of authoritative but non-binding guidelines and principles that often contain detailed standards of use to field operations. In situations of armed conflict, international humanitarian law, or the laws of war, especially the four Geneva Conventions of 1949,[21] will also apply alongside human rights law. In some situations, the 1951 Convention and Protocol Relating to the Status of Refugees [22] will be relevant, but probably rarely, as this falls more squarely in the mandate of the UN high commissioner for refugees.[23]

In contrast, some other UN agencies have a much broader concept of the harm from which they seek to protect. UNICEF, for example, protects children from harm that would not normally be considered violations of human rights, such as being separated from caregivers and disability.[24]

However broad or narrow are the rights being protected, it is important for human rights field officers to understand the standards that will be applied by the field operation. This allows the officer to assess what acts or omissions raise human rights concerns and which do not. Field operations are still relatively weak in applying standards relating to economic, social and cultural rights and developing methodologies as sophisticated as those used for civil and political rights protection work.

What is Protection in Practice?

Protection activities are often seen as mysterious and unfathomable or reduced to simple notions of 'monitoring and reporting'. In reality, protection relies on a web of complex human relationships between human rights field officers and potential or actual perpetrators and potential or actual victims, as well as with civil society organisations, the diplomatic community, the courts, UN agencies and other national and international actors. It is closer to diplomacy than enforcement, although activating the law and justice systems are essential parts of a protection strategy. It offers incentives and brings pressure to bear on perpetrators and their superiors.

---

on racial discrimination, on child rights, on non-discrimination against women and on migrant workers) but also encompasses a significant body of international human rights standards that are not found in legally binding treaties, but amount to authoritative recommendations adopted by the UN General Assembly, in documents that often include phrases such as 'Principles' or 'Guidelines' of 'Declaration'.

[21] Geneva Convention for the Amelioration of the Condition of the Wounded and Sick in Armed Forces in the Field of August 12, 1949, 75 UNTS (1950), 31; Geneva Convention for the Amelioration of the Condition of Wounded, Sick and Shipwrecked Members of Armed Forces at Sea of August 12, 1949, 75 UNTS (1950), 85; Geneva Convention Relative to the Treatment of Prisoners of War of August 12, 1949, 75 UNTS (1950), 135; Geneva Convention Relative to the Protection of Civilian Persons in Time of War of August 12, 1949, 75 UNTS (1950), 286.

[22] Convention Relating to the Status of Refugees, signed 28 July 1951, 189 UNTS 150 (entered into force 22 April 1954); Protocol Relating to the Status of Refugees, 606 UNTS 267 (entered into force 4 Oct. 1967).

[23] See chapter 11 by M. Stavropoulou in the present volume.

[24] See chapter 10 by K. Landgren in the present volume.

It seeks to bolster the political will of government or armed group leaders to give orders, create procedures and structures to prevent and stop human rights violations. It seeks to create safe political space for authorities to do the right thing and for civil society to assert their rights. It encourages the reformers in government or armed groups and encourages those in civil society who are ready to defend rights. Although a field operation will sometimes physically give refuge to a person facing abuse, in the vast majority of cases, protection is about persuading authorities to act in line with their human rights responsibilities.

A remarkable study and manual[25] by the Centre for Humanitarian Dialogue (the 'HDC study'), based on detailed field research into nine missions, has demystified how governmental or non-governmental, unarmed field presences in conflict zones can protect civilians. The study shows how both abusers and civil society constantly make decisions, by trial and error, based on a series of calculations and recalculations, informed by accurate or mistaken intelligence, perceptions or misperceptions, about the likely cost or consequences of their decisions – a decision by a soldier to kill civilians or a decision by a non-governmental organisation to investigate an arbitrary detention or a decision by a reformer in government to oppose a policy to forcibly displace a large population. A field mission can influence these decisions through constant interaction at every level, especially if it is complemented by effective action at the international level to hold states and armed groups accountable. It can move the border between what are seen as the acceptable and unacceptable consequences of decisions. It can increase the real or perceived political space for civil society to defend rights safely. It can decrease the real or perceived space for perpetrators to violate human rights. Staff in all the field missions studied in the HDC study reaffirmed that abusers *are* far more sensitive to pressure than is often assumed, that the question is rather how sensitive they are, what kinds of pressure to apply and what strategies to use.

Protection strategies and activities can be broken down into a number of identifiable methods or activities,[26] although they may be carried out both simultaneously and sequentially.

- A foundation for all protection work is extensive and sophisticated *gathering of intelligence and information*, not only to *verify* the truth about alleged human rights violations and their causes, but also about command and control structures of civilian and military structures and the web of formal decision-making and informal power and influence, which will be the targets of protection diplomacy and advocacy. It is especially important to identify individuals and institutions that are open to acting to stop or prevent violations,

---

[25] L. Mahony, Proactive *Presence: Field strategies for civilian protection* (Geneva: Centre for Humanitarian Dialogue, 2006); see also chapter 13 by L. Mahony in the present volume.

[26] The following list draws from the HDC study as well as the present author's own experiences and those of different field operations with which the author is familiar.

as no government or armed group is monolithic.

- Based on an *analysis* of the information, the mission will develop *strategies to influence* authorities at every level and those who have influence on the decision-makers. This requires a sophisticated understanding of governance structures and power relations, the reasons why individuals take certain decisions and incentives and disincentives that can be applied.
- A deliberate and *visible presence* itself is a method of protection, which requires a large enough staff, offices placed in provincial locations, a strategy of being constantly on the move, and visiting locations outside of large cities and towns.
- *Investigating and verifying* allegations of human rights violations is both an end in itself and a tool for further action. Even the process of investigation increases the pressure on perpetrators, more so if there are possible further consequences, such as referral to a court or sustained public exposure and cumulative pressure for international action against a government or armed group. The results of human rights investigations are the building blocks for the constant dialogue with authorities on individual cases and patterns, identifying the systemic problems that need a dose of immediate political will and/or openness to capacity building. The operation in Nepal has shown how relatively few, but well-targeted, special investigations into a selected number of many serious incidents that occur can have a significant impact, especially if an operation does not have, or will never have, sufficient staff to be effectively present in the countryside.
- At the heart of protection is *persuasive human rights diplomacy*, exploiting the myriad day-to-day conversations and communications at local, regional and national levels, with deliberate and constant messages and discussions, based on the information gathered, the analysis and strategy developed, seeking to raise the cost of abusing rights and lower the cost of protecting rights, in individual cases and in relations to broader patterns.
- The HDC study speaks about '*encouragement*' – using presence to help people overcome fears about acting to protect their own and others' rights, supporting organisations that can do more to protect, and helping to legitimise and tackle the stigma and isolation often facing civil society groups in polarised political climates. Encouragement includes helping reformers in the government or an armed group to influence decisions that will create change from within.
- While in most missions the volume of behind-the-scenes advocacy is far greater than its public face, *public advocacy*, including *writing* and *publicly releasing statements and reports*, is an essential method of human rights protection. Public advocacy will sometimes incur the wrath of authorities and can invite retaliation, from refusing to cooperate or give access, to attempts to end the mission's mandate and even putting the lives of staff or contacts in danger. A public advocacy strategy must be carefully managed, when and how reports and statements are published and how they are used to multiply the effect of the mission's human rights diplomacy, provide analysis and recommendations

that others can take up and generate greater pressure for change. The public reporting of missions is often one of the few sources of objective information in a sea of disinformation and polarised political opinions. It can encourage reformers, legitimise the human rights work of civil society and stimulate debate about the human rights future of a country.

- Strategies to use the formal *justice system* can complement the diplomacy of human rights protection, depending on the mandate of an operation, including directly referring cases to legal authorities for possible prosecution, providing victims with legal assistance or supporting lawyers to seek remedies such as *habeas corpus*. Missions will often monitor and encourage the judiciary, if still operating, proactively to protect rights. A major cause of serious human rights violations is impunity of perpetrators and a significant element of an operation's advocacy is often directed at persuading authorities to bring perpetrators to justice.

- A human rights operation is able to exploit its character as an impartial international presence to bring together actors who are often isolated from each other or mutually distrusting – a *convening and bridging* function.[27] The operation can create bridges between civil society, government authorities, embassies, UN agencies and international NGOs and experts not in-country. By seeking similar human rights commitments from both sides, or formally through tools such as human rights accords, an operation can not only impact the human rights situation but also have potential impact on the political climate and relations between a government and an armed group.

- OHCHR is uniquely able to activate and help others in-country to activate *UN human rights bodies and mechanisms*. An urgent communication or a country visit by an expert special rapporteur or working group[28] of the Human Rights Council can add incrementally to pressure to stop abuses, can encourage and legitimise civil society and can give resonance at the international level to the findings of the mission on the ground, thereby increasing the likelihood of the authorities being scrutinised both locally and in international political bodies. The UN human rights treaty bodies can sometimes also play a role in increasing pressure for change if they are able to consider a report from the government or request specific urgent information.

This is a complex range of strategies, requiring a field operation and individual human rights field officers to exercise sophisticated, subtle, multidisciplinary skills and knowledge. The current moves to professionalise the work of human rights field

---

[27] See L. Mahony, *Proactive Presence: Field strategies for civilian protection.*

[28] There are currently 28 special rapporteurs, special representatives, independent experts and working groups covering a wide range of themes, from arbitrary detention, torture and extrajudicial executions, to freedom of expression, human rights defenders, religious intolerance and the internally displaced. Many of these experts are able to issue urgent humanitarian appeals on individual cases and/or carry out on-site visits.

officers[29] are essential if operations are to avoid serious mistakes and be able to fulfil the potential of protection.

What is the impact of human rights protection strategies and does it justify the considerable financial and human investment required? There is, of course, anecdotal evidence on both sides, of lives saved but also of failure. The HDC study concluded that every mission it examined had some positive incremental impact on civilian safety and that 'although causality is nearly impossible to ever prove in these settings, this evidence suggests that an international presence moderates or diminishes abusive behaviour, but cannot by itself reverse systematically abusive strategies that result from deeper conflict dynamics'.[30] Over time, as a field operation demonstrates credibility and authority and increasingly understands the subtleties of the political situation and levers of power and influence, it can exploit the full potential of the range of protection strategies.

While human rights field operations can and do save lives and protect people from harm, there has so far been little study of how they can also do harm, increasing the risks people face or influencing in negative ways the political, economic and social environments in which they operate. In contrast, prompted by experiences in Somalia, Rwanda and Bosnia and Herzegovina in the 1990s, the humanitarian community has gone through a period of intense reflection on how to avoid the negative impacts of humanitarian assistance.[31]

There has also been little open policy discussion of the ethical dilemmas created by carrying out protection through the use of dialogue and diplomacy. Field operations are not just investigating and documenting violations and pointing out human rights or humanitarian law obligations. They are, in effect, 'negotiating' with their interlocutors. Human rights field officers will often face difficult trade-offs between insisting that the best global human rights safeguards must be put in place, and encouraging or acquiescing in a step that is short of the human rights standards, to achieve at least a modicum of protection. What compromises are acceptable? For whom does a human rights field officer speak? For example, should a human rights field officer insist that no civilian should ever be detained by the military in a remote region even if there is no functioning or secure police station? Is it acceptable to encourage or acquiesce in the military creating a detention centre in military barracks with full access to outside monitors? Responses will require a complex balancing of principle and pragmatism, understanding the human rights 'bottom line' and in some cases encouraging immediate achievable action while working for the ultimate human rights goal. Again, humanitarian workers openly discuss strategies to deal with the fact that they are often

---

[29]   See http://www.humanrightsprofessionals.org.

[30]   See L. Mahony, *Proactive Presence: Field strategies for civilian protection.*

[31]   See for example, M. B. Anderson, *Do No Harm: How Aid can Support Peace – or War* (Boulder: Lynne Rienner, 1999).

'between a rock and a hard place',[32] caught between the international obligations authorities should respect and the practical limits of negotiations.

An Adequate Protection Mandate

In light of what protection means in practice, the mandate of a human rights field operation, which will always be negotiated in some form with the government and in some cases with armed groups if there is an armed conflict, should contain the following powers and functions and commitments by the government (and where relevant any armed group):

- express reference to the international law and standards (usually international human rights and humanitarian law treaties) that the authorities are committed to implementing and that the operation will use as its human rights legal reference point;
- freedom of movement throughout the country and no restrictions on deploying human rights field officers temporarily or for longer periods throughout the country and opening sub-offices;
- unrestricted access to any site or institution, including any place of detention, whether civilian or military;
- unrestricted access to civilian and military authorities;
- where relevant, an operation should have a similar right of access to, and contact with, any armed group;
- a commitment by the authorities to interact with the operation, swiftly to take responsive and remedial action necessary to comply with the country's human rights obligations, including investigating and prosecuting those responsible for violations and taking other responsive or remedial measures;
- to be able to provide advice, not only to the executive branch, but also to the judiciary and the legislature;
- to investigate and verify allegations of human rights violations;
- to interview anyone freely and in private, including detainees and prisoners;
- to receive information from any individual, group or other source and to keep the information and the source confidential and if necessary to take steps to protect the authors of information it receives, as well as victims and witnesses to facts alleged;
- a commitment by the authorities that no one in contact with the operation will face reprisals:
- an unrestricted right to issue public statements and reports and to have contact with the media, and the right to report to the UN high commissioner for human rights and whichever political bodies are appropriate;

---

[32] D. Mancini-Griffoli and A. Picot, *Humanitarian Negotiation: A Handbook for Securing Access, Assistance and Protection for Civilians in Armed Conflict* (Geneva: Centre for Humanitarian Dialogue, 2004), p. 26 and generally pp. 24–31.

- to hold meetings freely anywhere in the territory;
- freedom to develop working relationships with civil society;
- to propose necessary capacity building projects appropriate in light of the protection needs;
- a commitment by the government (and if relevant any armed group) to ensure the security of the operation and all international and national staff, with the right of the mission also to make its own security arrangements;
- appropriate immunities and privileges for national staff as well as international staff.

With a clear and detailed negotiated mandate, wise recruitment, better training and professionalisation of human rights field officers, a strengthened capacity in OHCHR to manage field operations, and political and financial support from member states and the UN system for field-based protection functions, human rights field operations will have an opportunity to show how their protection work can have a significant immediate and long-term impact on the human rights situation in a country.

Chapter 3

The Legal Base for Human Rights Field Operations

Nigel D. White and Marco Odello

Introduction

Since the end of the Second World War, human rights have been included on the international agenda. International norms, standards and monitoring mechanisms, including international courts, have been developed.[1] Within the United Nations (UN) and the Organization of American States (OAS), political and more independent mechanisms, such as human rights commissions, committees of experts and special rapporteurs, have developed a wide series of procedures for the supervision of human rights application. The Organization for Security and Co-operation in Europe (OSCE) has developed institutions such as the Office for Democratic Institutions and Human Rights (ODIHR), the High Commissioner on National Minorities and the Representative on Freedom of the Media. Mechanisms include the Vienna and Moscow inter-state procedures for dealing with human rights violations in all OSCE countries.

Some of these mechanisms included the possibility of a country visit, such as in the case of special rapporteurs of the UN Commission on Human Rights, the Inter-American Commission on Human Rights and the OSCE High Commissioner on National Minorities.

With the end of the Cold War, international human rights action undertaken by international institutions has developed new aspects. One of these aspects is generally identified as human rights field operations. Such operations are not foreseen by constitutive documents of international organisations, but they have become common practice since the early 1990s, and they have sometimes been a part of a much wider operation to temporarily administer territories.[2] All these actions are to be based on the respect of international human rights standards and norms, as

---

[1] See generally, A. F. Bayefsky, *The UN Human Rights Treaty System: Universality at the Crossroads* (The Hague: Kluwer Law International, 2001); H. J. Steiner and P. Alston, *International Human Rights in Context: Law, Politics, Morals: Text and Materials*, 2nd edn (Oxford: Oxford University Press, 2000); D. F. Forsythe, 'The United Nations and Human Rights', *Political Science Quarterly* vol. 100 (1985), 249–269.

[2] See S. Chesterman, *You, the People: The United Nations, Transitional Administration, and State Building* (Oxford: Oxford University Press, 2005), pp. 1–11, 48–99.

this is one of the main purposes of the UN and other international organisations. Protection and promotion of human rights are matters of international concern. The 1993 Vienna Conference on Human Rights[3] stressed the importance of international cooperation in the field of human rights,[4] decided on the creation of the Office of the United Nations High Commissioner for Human Rights (OHCHR),[5] and mentioned the importance of human rights components in peacekeeping operations.[6] As Kofi Annan expressed at the beginning of his mandate, 'the priority now is to translate ... norms and standards into national legislation and national practices, thus bringing about real change in peoples' lives. The UN, in partnership with governments and civil society, is poised to play a crucial role in this endeavor'.[7] These policy statements have been followed by the development of field operations that include a wide component of human rights protection and implementation.

The present chapter focuses on UN missions. The analysis of the legal justification and the legal framework governing those missions, with particular focus on post-conflict operations, will be the main purpose of the chapter. As human rights missions are not clearly defined and foreseen in any international legal document, it is necessary to look at several legal sources that can justify their existence. This would imply the analysis of primary norms, mainly constitutional documents, but also with reference to both institutional and state practice that can provide both legal justifications and regulations for field missions.

The chapter will be divided into two main parts. The first part will look at the legal justification and will focus on UN operations. The second part will define the legal framework regulating human rights field operations with particular reference to post-conflict situations.

Legal Basis

The legal justification for actions by international organisations can be founded on a number of different bases. They include treaty law, customary law, decisions adopted by organs of international organisations, international agreements between states and international organisations, implied, inherent powers and institutional law developed by the practice of international organisations (as derived from relevant treaty law).

Treaties are based on the consent of states. They provide the legal regulation of inter-state action and international obligations. International organisations, such as the UN and OAS are based on treaties, usually identified as the constitutional charters

---

[3]   Vienna, 14–25 June 1993.

[4]   World Conference on Human Rights, Vienna Declaration and Programme of Action, UN Doc. A/CONF.157/23 (1993), at 4.

[5]   *Ibid.*, at 17–18.

[6]   *Ibid.*, at 97.

[7]   K. Annan, 'Strengthening United Nations Action in the Field of Human Rights: Prospects and Priorities', *Harvard Human Rights Journal* vol. 10 (1997), 1–2.

of each institution. Once the organisation is established, it has a certain capacity to act in international relations. This is what has been defined as international legal personality.[8] International personality provides organisations with powers and legal capacity, as defined in their respective charters, and permits the organisation to act in conformity with, and for the aims and purposes defined in, the constitutive treaty.

Consent can be expressed also by states both within and outside international institutions. In the first case, organs of the organisation can express their will through different procedures usually defined in the constitutional charter. They express the will of the organisation. In this context, their legal justification is based on the original will of states that established the organisation and it is a consequence of the international legal personality of the organisation, as an independent legal person. In the second case, states freely enter into agreements either with other states or with international organisations.

Customary law, based on state practice, is also relevant as part of the development of international regulations concerning states' action and obligations. State practice can therefore develop new norms and general principles, while practice within each organisation can develop new institutional legal rules that better specify the usually broad and general terms provided by constitutional treaties.

Institutional developments also include the possibility to add new mechanisms and tasks based on the development of the mandate provided in constitutional documents. The aims and purposes of international organisations sometimes include broad goals that need further specification. In the case of the UN, the reform process that started in 1997[9] led in 2002 to the 'Action 2' Initiative based on the report of the secretary-general, entitled 'Strengthening of the United Nations: An Agenda for Further Change'.[10] The report affirmed that 'the promotion and protection of human rights is a bedrock requirement for the realization of the Charter's vision of a just and peaceful world'.[11]

The first mission including human rights components developed by the UN was the one established in El Salvador in 1991. In 1992, the UN Transitional Administration in Cambodia also included a human rights component. In 1993, the UN established the mission in Guatemala (MINUGUA). In 1992 the OAS established an International Civilian Mission in Haiti, later included in a wider joint UN/OAS human rights mission (MICIVIH).[12] The UN also established joint

---

[8] See N. D. White, *The Law of International Organisations*, Melland Schill Studies in International Law, 2nd edn (Manchester: Manchester University Press, 2005), chapter 3; C. F. Amerasinghe, *Principles of the Institutional Law of International Organizations*, 2nd edn (Cambridge: Cambridge University Press, 2005), chapter 3.

[9] Report of the Secretary-General, Renewing the United Nations: A Programme for Reform, UN Doc. A/51/950 (1997).

[10] Report of the Secretary-General, Strengthening of the United Nations: An Agenda for Further Change, UN Doc. A/57/387 (2002).

[11] *Ibid.*, at 45.

[12] See I. Martin, 'A New Frontier: The Early Experience and Future of International Human Rights Field Operations', *Netherlands Quarterly of Human Rights* vol. 16 (1998),

missions with OSCE in Abkhazia, Georgia[13] and in the Balkans.[14] These are new tools that provide a more active and pervasive action by international institutions for the promotion and implementation of human rights in specific countries.

In this section, the UN system will be addressed, with some reference to OAS and OSCE. The analysis will focus on several legal aspects that can be identified in the law related to field missions as developed by the organs of the institution.

The UN Charter

The UN is based on its constitutive Charter.[15] Reference to human rights is made in the preamble, in Articles 1(3), 13 and 55, as part of the general aims and purposes of the organisation. Apart from this general mandate, the UN has developed a broad legal system of human rights norms, starting with the 1948 Universal Declaration on Human Rights[16] (UDHR), including a wide number of international treaties. It has created a complex network of institutions, organs and legal rules, which represent the legal background for the international protection and promotion of human rights.

The legal powers of the organisation are vested in its organs. The Security Council, the General Assembly and the secretary-general are principal organs that have developed their own practice in the field of missions. Subsidiary organs, deriving their powers from the main organs and from the UN Charter, such as the Commission on Human Rights, and institutions like OHCHR, are also relevant for the identification of powers that can be derived both from the Charter and from the consent of states, or from the practice of those organs.

The powers of UN organs are expressly defined in the Charter. But their powers also may be implied or inherent to pursue the aims of the organisation.[17] The concept of implied powers was clearly established by the International Court of Justice in the *Reparation* case,[18] and more recently reaffirmed by the International Tribunal for the Former Yugoslavia in the *Tadic* case.[19] These powers can justify the expanded action of the UN, based on the aims and purposes of the organisation, especially when they

---

121–139.

[13]   A Human Rights Office in Abkhazia, Georgia (HROAG) was established on 10 December 1996 following Security Council Resolution 1077 (1996) of 22 October 1996. In this case, the office is jointly staffed by OHCHR and the OSCE, in accordance with a memorandum of understanding signed between the two organisations on 29 April 1997. The human rights office forms part of the DPKO United Nations Observer Mission in Georgia (UNOMIG), under the authority of the Head of Mission of UNOMIG.

[14]   See chapter 1 by M. O'Flaherty in the present volume.

[15]   Charter of the United Nations, 59 Stat. 1031, T.S. 993, 3 Bevans 1153, entered into force Oct. 24, 1945.

[16]   General Assembly resolution 217 A (III) (1948).

[17]   See White, *The Law of International Organisations*, chapter 3.

[18]   *Reparation for Injuries Suffered in the Service of the United Nations*, Advisory Opinion of 11 April 1949, [1949] ICJ Reports 1949, at 174.

[19]   *Prosecutor v. Tadic*, Decision on the Defence Motion for Interlocutory Appeal on Jurisdiction, Case No. IT-94-1, 2 October 1995.

are endorsed by declarations adopted in international conferences, such as the 1993 Vienna Conference mentioned before.

Even more general provisions are foreseen by the OAS Charter,[20] where reference is made to the importance of promotion of peace and security in the hemisphere, through democracy and eradication of extreme poverty (Article 2). Social justice and social security are considered the base for lasting peace (Article 3(j)). Specific institutions in the Inter-American system include the Inter-American Commission and Court for Human Rights.

OSCE operates in a more difficult context, as it is not based on an international treaty. The 1975 Helsinki Final Act[21] included human rights in the wide concept of international security, and provided a specific area of international cooperation, called the human dimension, where human rights play a central role. The basis for OSCE activity was not considered to be founded on international legal norms, but on political and moral obligations. Nevertheless, OSCE has developed several institutions and international standards that provide for action in the field of human rights, including country missions.[22]

Consent

Consent is the most traditional way to establish obligations and agreements in international law among states and with international organisations. Initial human rights missions were deployed in post-conflict countries. They were based on peace agreements between the parties to the conflict. They also foresaw the leading role of the UN missions in the supervision of the application of those agreements, including actions for the development of human rights protection and related institutions.

The mission in El Salvador (ONUSAL) was based on the San José Agreement on Human Rights[23] signed by the government of El Salvador and the Frente Farabundo Martí de Liberación Nacional (FMLN). On 20 May 1991, the Security Council adopted resolution 693 (1991), which established ONUSAL to monitor all the agreements between the Salvadoran government and the FMLN.

Similar background gave origin to the United Nations Transitional Authority in Cambodia (UNTAC). Based on the 1991 Paris peace agreements,[24] the mission was established by Security Council resolution 745 (1992). The United Nations

---

[20] Charter of the Organization of American States, OAS, Treaty Series, Nos. 1-C and 61 (entered into force 13 December 1951).

[21] The Final Act of the Conference on Security and Cooperation in Europe, 1 August 1975, ILM vol. 14, 1292.

[22] See generally, M. Bothe, N. Ronzitti and A. Rosas (eds), *The OSCE in the Maintenance of Peace and Security* (The Hague: Kluwer Law International, 1997).

[23] Signed on 26 July 1990. See I. Kircher, 'The Human Rights Work of the United Nations Observer Mission in El Salvador', *Netherlands Quarterly of Human Rights* vol. 10 (1992), 303.

[24] See S. R. Ratner, 'The Cambodia Settlement Agreements', *American Journal of International Law* vol. 87 (1993), 1–41.

Operation in Mozambique (ONUMOZ) established by Security Council resolution 797 (1993) was based on an invitation by the parties to the conflict to monitor the General Peace Agreement signed on 4 October 1992. More recent examples include the 1999 missions in East Timor[25] and in Kosovo.[26]

These missions are the result of the agreements among the parties to the conflict, who also agreed to invite the UN to supervise and implement some aspects of the agreement. The legal justification of these kinds of mission is therefore based on the consent of the parties, and the acceptance of the UN to be involved in the post-conflict process as an independent international actor to the agreement and/or as a supervisory and implementing body.

Office of the United Nations High Commissioner for Human Rights

A similar legal justification, based on the consent of the parties, can be also identified in the case of field missions established by OHCHR. The mandate of OHCHR derives from Articles 1, 13 and 55 of the UN Charter, the 1993 Vienna Declaration and Programme of Action, and General Assembly resolution 48/141 of 20 December 1993, by which the Assembly established the post of United Nations High Commissioner for Human Rights. The Office of the United Nations High Commissioner for Human Rights and the Centre for Human Rights were consolidated into a single Office of the United Nations High Commissioner for Human Rights on 15 September 1997.[27]

Two other types of field missions developed by OHCHR are based on (1) memorandums of understanding with the host state, or with international institutions, and (2) on the base of decisions of the Commission on Human Rights. In this section, the first type of mission will be addressed. Decisions of the Commission on Human Rights will be addressed later when dealing with this body.

Memorandum of Understanding

OHCHR has established field presences in the form of permanent offices with the agreement of host countries. They represent forms of country branches of OHCHR and are regulated by reciprocal agreements between OHCHR and the host governments under the form of technical cooperation of OHCHR. Examples include Palestine, Mexico and more recently Uganda, Nepal and Guatemala.

The Southern Africa Regional Office was established by a memorandum of understanding between United Nations Development Programme (UNDP) and OHCHR in 1998, as part of an overall strategy aimed at supporting UNDP Country

---

[25]   Agreement, between Indonesia and Portugal on the Question of East Timor (the General Agreement), UN Doc. A/53/951 S/1999/513 (1999).

[26]   See Agreement on Human Rights, Annex 6 to General Framework Agreement for Peace in Bosnia and Herzegovina, Attachment to UN Doc. A/50/790-S/1995/999 (1995).

[27]   Report of the Secretary-General, Renewing the United Nations: A Programme for Reform, UN Doc. A/51/950 (1997), at 79.

Offices.[28] A similar agreement was established with the UN Economic and Social Commission for Western Asia (ESCWA). In June 2001, a memorandum of intent (MOI), specifying the terms of the future collaboration between OHCHR and ESCWA, was signed by the high commissioner and the executive secretary of ESCWA. The MOI foresaw the appointment of a regional representative for the Arab region to be located within ESCWA in Beirut.[29]

The mentioned examples show that OHCHR can establish its missions with the consent of the host state alone, or with other international institutions. These missions are based on the will of international institutions and states, expressed through the traditional means of an agreement between or among the parties.

The Security Council and Chapters VI and VII of the UN Charter

The Security Council has broad powers derived from Chapters VI and VII of the Charter. These powers are related to the maintenance of international peace and security. Due to the link between promotion and respect of human rights and peace, the powers of the Security Council in dealing with human rights can be justified under the broad mandate of the UN for the maintenance of international peace and security. Actions are also identified in both mentioned Chapters, even if they are expressed in very broad terms. For instance, under Article 36 of Chapter VI, 'The Security Council may, at any stage of a dispute …, recommend appropriate procedures or methods of adjustment'.

In this context, peacekeeping operations were developed since the 1950s as part of the implied powers of the UN for the maintenance of international peace. Peacekeeping missions were not foreseen in any constitutional treaty or international agreement. For this reason they were also identified as 'chapter VI and a half' missions.[30] Initially formed mainly by international military forces for the control of ceasefire and as buffer forces between conflicting parties, they have gradually also included civilian components in conflict and post-conflict situations.

An early example of non-military activities within a peacekeeping mission can be found in the United Nations Transition Assistance Group in Namibia (UNTAG) established in 1978. UNTAG's mission included monitoring elections, developing electoral legislation, repatriation of refugees and release of political prisoners detained by South Africa. The mission was based on Security Council resolutions that defined the mandate of the special representative for Namibia,[31] and

---

[28]   The sub-regional project RAF/02/AH/19 (Regional Programme Office for Southern Africa) is a joint project of OHCHR and UNDP managed by the UN Office of Geneva (UNOG) and UNDP. The project started on 1 August 2002.

[29]   In February 2002, the Regional Representative Office for the Arab Region started its work in Beirut.

[30]   A term used by UN Secretary-General Dag Hammarskjold, see K. Annan, 'UN Peacekeeping Operations and Cooperation with NATO', *NATO Review* vol. 5 (1993), 3–7.

[31]   See Security Council resolution 431 (1978), UN Doc. S/RES/431 (1978).

the establishment of the UNTAG.[32] Other initial experiences include missions in El Salvador and Cambodia. Civilian human rights components of the Department of Peacekeeping Operations (DPKO) include: Burundi; Central African Republic; Democratic Republic of Congo; Eritrea/Ethiopia; Iraq; Afghanistan; Timor Leste; Georgia/Abkhazia; Tajikistan; Haiti. They are based on Security Council and General Assembly decisions and resolutions.[33]

Most peacekeeping operations conducted until the end of the Cold War were mainly military missions in post-conflict situations, but their mandate was mainly overseeing a ceasefire, not re-building a state. This traditional tool was further developed within the UN. Therefore, different types or generations of peacekeeping operations have been envisaged.[34] Involvement of peacekeeping operations in the human rights field gained momentum at the end of the Cold War. This new vision was found in the secretary-general's 'Agenda for Peace' of 1992.[35] This stressed the importance of dealing with the causes of conflict, the possibility of addressing them, and also providing support for the institutional building of post-conflict societies. Promotion and protection of human rights were central to this new vision of peacekeeping missions. This idea was expressed by the fact that 'peace-keeping requires that civilian political officers, human rights monitors, electoral officials, refugee and humanitarian aid specialists and police play as central a role as the military'.[36] This new task was identified as post-conflict peacebuilding.[37]

Under Articles 41 and 42 of Chapter VII the Security Council may decide on non-forcible and forcible measures to be employed to give effect to its decisions. These kind of Chapter VII measures were adopted, for instance, when the Security Council decided to intervene in Somalia in 1992. No peace agreements were previously negotiated among the parties and no government was in power in Somalia. The Security Council, acting under Chapter VII of the Charter, adopted resolution 794 (3 December 1992) to establish a secure environment for humanitarian assistance to the civilian population. The mission in Somalia cannot be regarded as a successful example, but it shows that the Security Council, under Chapter VII of the Charter, can establish international missions to promote human rights in a specific country without host-state consent, if the missions are considered appropriate for the maintenance of international peace and security.

Missions under Chapter VII are based on the acceptance by UN member states of the UN Charter mandate. They are used as a possible alternative to the consent

---

[32]   See Security Council resolution 435 (1978), UN Doc. S/RES/435 (1978).

[33]   See chapter 19 by K. Turner in the present volume.

[34]   See R. S. Lee, 'United Nations Peacekeeping: Development and Prospects', *Cornell International Law Journal* vol. 28 (1995), 619.

[35]   Report of the Secretary-General, An Agenda for Peace: Preventive Diplomacy, Peacemaking and Peace-keeping, UN Doc. A/47/277 S/24111 (1992). The report of the secretary-general is not a legal document, but it provides the political and institutional background for further developments.

[36]   *Ibid.*, at 52.

[37]   *Ibid.*, at chapter VI.

mentioned before. In some cases (Kosovo and East Timor), both Chapter VII[38] and consent[39] have been used. It might be considered redundant from the legal point of view using both legal bases. Actually, both legal bases may appear as contradictory, due to the fact that Chapter VII implies enforcement measures without the consent of the concerned state(s). However, owing to the complex and turbulent nature of post-conflict situations, they might provide international strength and alternative options to establish international missions in very fluid and unstable conditions.

UN General Assembly and Commission on Human Rights

The General Assembly has a wide competence, including in the areas of security and human rights.[40] Compared with the Security Council, the General Assembly cannot adopt mandatory decisions regarding UN member states, except in budgetary matters. Nevertheless, being the most representative body of the international community, it provides a high level of both legitimacy and authority to its decisions.

Recommendations adopted by the General Assembly may have several effects. They may be considered as 'soft law', which expresses the will of states in some specific areas, and therefore they may become relevant for the development of new customary law. They also can lead to future 'hard-law' documents in the form of treaty law. In general terms, the legislative power of the General Assembly can extend to any area covered by the UN Charter, and therefore to the field of human rights as well.

The Economic and Social Council (ECOSOC), under Article 68 of the UN Charter, has the power to 'set up Commissions in the economic and social field and for the promotion of human rights'. One of these organs is the Commission on Human Rights (CHR). CHR is the main intergovernmental body addressing human rights issues within the UN. It has the power to discuss issues related to human rights and also to nominate special rapporteurs and independent experts to deal with country situations and thematic mandates. In both cases, experts elected by CHR can be involved in human rights missions to investigate human rights violations. As a consequence of the information collected by experts, it may be the case that the CHR adopts resolutions concerning the establishment of field missions. This happened in the case of East Timor, where the CHR requested several special rapporteurs 'to carry out missions to East Timor and report on their findings to the Commission at its fifty-sixth session and, on an interim basis, to the General Assembly at its fifty-fourth session'.[41] Similar action was taken in the case of Rwanda, when a special rapporteur

---

[38]   See Security Council resolution 1244 (1999), UN Doc. S/RES/1244 (1999) (Kosovo) and Security Council resolution 1272 (1999), UN Doc. S/RES/1272 (1999) (East Timor).

[39]   See Security Council resolution 1236 (1999), UN Doc. S/RES/1236 (1999) (East Timor) and Letter Dated 99/06/07 from the Permanent Representative of Germany to the United Nations Addressed to the President of the Security Council UN Doc. S/1999/649 (1999) (Kosovo).

[40]   See Articles 10 and 11, UN Charter.

[41]   UN Commission on Human Rights, Situation of human rights in East Timor, resolution 1999/S-4/1, UN Doc. E/CN.4/1999/167/Add.1, E/1999/23/Add.1 (1999), at 7.

was created by CHR and OHCHR was requested to provide a team 'of human rights field officers acting in close cooperation with UNAMIR and other United Nations agencies and programmes operating in Rwanda'.[42] Some missions are established under the auspices of CHR but are carried out by other institutions, such as the case of OHCHR missions in Cambodia,[43] and in Democratic Republic of Congo.[44] In some cases, CHR acted after recommendations adopted by the General Assembly, as in the case of Sudan.[45]

The legal justification of these missions in based on the mandate of CHR as a subsidiary body of ECOSOC. CHR has the mandate to promote international human rights as enshrined in the UN Charter. To this end, CHR can adopt decisions and resolutions that call upon states to take action for the promotion of international human rights. Country missions and special rapporteurs are among the most useful tools that can be deployed by CHR to implement human rights in specific countries. Their legal justification is based on the powers derived from the UN Charter and from the mandate of the body as a subsidiary organ of ECOSOC, which is one of the main UN organs dealing with the protection and promotion of human rights.

The Legal Framework

While the first part of the present chapter considered the constitutional, more generally legal, basis for the establishment of human rights field missions, this part considers the legal framework that shapes their operation. Parallels between the legal basis and the legal framework are self evident. In a nutshell, human rights field missions are governed by the primary law of the Charter, the constitutional law of the organisation (for instance the Universal Declaration on Human Rights), basic rules of customary international law, and the secondary law of the mandate, along with the internal rules of the organisation.[46] In addition, the role of the domestic law of the country in which the mission is placed must be considered. However, rather than detailing the components that make up the international and national legal framework governing a human rights field presence, this part takes the issue further by placing them within a particular type of situation in which a human rights field officer is often present – the post-conflict situation. The discussion will enable the reader to consider the complexities of the law in a practical environment, and should illustrate how the

---

[42] UN Commission on Human Rights, The situation of human rights in Rwanda, resolution S-3/1, Report of the Commission on Human Rights on its Third Special Session, UN Doc. E/CN.4/S-3/4 (1994), at 23.

[43] UN Doc. E/CN.4/1993/6, 1993. For an analysis of its actions see CHR, Report of the Secretary-General, Role and Achievements of the Office of the United Nations High Commissioner for Human Rights in Assisting the Government and People of Cambodia in the Promotion and Protection of Human Rights, UN Doc. E/CN.4/2005/111 (2004).

[44] OHCHR opened an office in 1996, after the adoption of CHR resolution 1995/69.

[45] General Assembly resolution 51/112 (1997), Situation of Human Rights in the Sudan, UN Doc. A/RES/51/112 (1997).

[46] On internal rules see generally Amerasinghe, *Principles*, pp. 323–327.

basic legal principles may generally be the same whatever the type of operation or situation, although the practical application of these frameworks may differ.

A human rights field presence in a post-conflict situation, normally as part of a peacekeeping or peace support operation, will find itself in a difficult situation. Concern for law may seem to the field officer to simply consist of the promotion of the protection of human rights in a most basic way. The wider issue of the legal framework governing their activities is not of immediate concern. However, by promoting and protecting human rights, the field officer is already creating a legal framework for the immediate environment, collectively the country, and arguably for himself or herself as well. Human rights are framed as laws, internationally, and, often in post-conflict situations, nationally as well. Moreover, they are not standalone provisions but are part of a whole raft of international, domestic and possibly regional laws. In order to decipher which laws are applicable and to whom they apply, we must trace the development of the rule of law in a post-conflict situation.

Post-Conflict Context

The development of the rule of law is put in sharp relief in the case of a country or society that has emerged from a civil war that was in many instances externally fuelled. Normally, after exhaustion has set in or the military situation dramatically changes, a peace agreement results in a cessation of hostilities and a promise for a more peaceful future. Assuming that the agreement sticks, there has been a move from the conflict stage to a post-conflict or post-settlement situation.[47]

In these circumstances, although the term is often used in a pejorative way, 'state-building' involves crucial issues of law. State-building can conjure up a vision of neo-colonial liberal internationalist intervention,[48] and there can be no avoiding the fact that it is quite usual to have a high level of outside involvement because the country is so desperate and destroyed that a future can only be achieved with such help. It is a crucial issue of our times, although one beyond the remit of the present chapter, as to whether state-building with the help of international organisations produces a more peaceful and just society than one engineered by outside states,[49] although the norm, even today is for mixed intervention – by organisations and other non-state actors (mainly NGOs) and states.

There are a myriad of legal issues involved in the post-conflict stage – issues of international, constitutional, criminal and property law to name but a few. However, if we focus on the field officer's main concern, that of human rights, a number of

---

[47]   N. D. White, 'Towards a Strategy for Human Rights Protection in Post-conflict Situations', in N. D. White and D. Klaasen (eds), *The UN, Human Rights and Post-conflict Situations* (Manchester: Manchester University Press, 2005), p. 466.

[48]   See generally T. Evans, 'Human Rights and the Empire of Civil Society', in *The UN, Human Rights and Post-conflict Situations*, p. 177.

[49]   See generally R. Wilde, 'From Danzig to East Timor and Beyond: The Role of International Territorial Administration', *American Journal of International Law* vol. 95 (2001), 583.

crucial issues can be mentioned that will form the framework of the organisation's and its agents' activities, including the human rights content of the peace agreement, the human rights obligations of the parties as well as the organisation, and the human rights to be guaranteed in the immediate period and then in the medium and longer terms.

Although there have been many forms and instances of post-conflict rebuilding, the answers to these questions have not necessarily been clarified by practice. Tensions abound in human rights promotion and protection in post-conflict situations – between human rights and the achievement of an immediate peace, between building for the future and accounting for the past, between different generations of human rights, and ultimately between law and politics. This analysis will focus on the human rights choices as providing a focus to the legal framework within which human rights officers operate, before going on to detail the obligations on the different actors including the UN and its officers.

The Peace Agreement

The peace agreement generally establishes a political process though it might make a general reference to human rights.[50] Its primary purpose is to stop the conflict and put in place a peace process that might lead, for example, to the establishment of an interim government or an international administration. Following from the discussion contained in the first part of the present chapter, the legal basis of the post-conflict process as well as the international presence is the consent of the country represented by the former warring faction leaders who sign internationally brokered peace accords. Exceptionally, the sovereignty of the state is bypassed, or consent is supplemented, perhaps overridden, by the Security Council using Chapter VII of the UN Charter, presumably Article 41,[51] which has been used as something of an open cheque to introduce a number of non-forcible measures, amongst them international criminal tribunals and territorial administrations. In Kosovo after the North Atlantic Treaty Organization (NATO) military intervention of 1999, the Security Council established a post-conflict administration by a Security Council resolution adopted under Chapter VII.[52] The resolution obliges the UN Administration (UNMIK) to protect and promote human rights. This is detailed by an early example of UNMIK governance in the form of a regulation that stated that the UDHR, European Convention on Human Rights (ECHR), International Covenant on Civil and Political Rights (ICCPR), Convention on the Elimination of Racial Discrimination (CERD), Convention on the Elimination of All forms of Discrimination against Women (CEDAW), Convention on the Rights of the Child

---

[50]   See generally C. Bell, *Peace Agreements and Human Rights* (Oxford: Oxford University Press, 2000).

[51]   M. J. Matheson, 'United Nations Governance of Postconflict Societies', *American Journal of International Law* vol. 95 (2001), 83.

[52]   Security Council resolution 1244 (1999), UN Doc. S/RES/1244 (1999).

(CRC), and European Conventions on Minorities apply to Kosovo.[53] Tellingly, the regulation does not mention the International Covenant on Economic, Social and Cultural Rights (ICESCR).[54]

Security Council-imposed administrations are the exception to the normal peace accords agreed to by the factions within a war-torn country. But even in the normal situation the legal basis of the post-conflict rebuilding process is tenuous. The precise legal status of peace accords is unclear, indeed it could be argued that the accords are of a political nature only, given that in international treaty law at least only state signatories or other international legal persons such as the UN that sign the agreement are bound.[55] The primary stakeholders, the factions, are non-state actors whose legal status is unclear. It is unlikely that they have any recognised status in domestic law since they may well be responsible within the peace process for starting a new legal system (albeit one that by choice is largely based on the system that existed before the accords). In international law the status of such non-state actors is unclear, and hence there is uncertainty over whether the peace accords can produce any legal obligations. Although traditionally belligerents or insurgents can conclude valid agreements,[56] such actors are much more narrowly defined than would appear from everyday usage of the terms.[57] The more relevant view is expressed by Christine Bell:

> Negotiated peace agreements are often of dubious legal status. While reading as legal documents, and using the language of obligation captured in treaty-like language and conventions, the mix of state and non-state actors – many of whom cannot be argued to be subjects of international law – who typically sign peace agreements mean that their international and domestic legal status is questionable.[58]

---

[53] See UNMIK/REG/2001/9, 15 May 2001. See European Convention on Human Rights, Convention for the Protection of Human Rights and Fundamental Freedoms, 213 UNTS 222 (entered into force Sept. 3, 1953); International Covenant on Civil and Political Rights, adopted 19 Dec. 1966, G.A. res. 2200 (XXI), UN GAOR, 21st Sess., Supp. No. 16, UN Doc. A/6316 (1966), 999 UNTS 171 (entered into force 23 Mar. 1976); International Convention on the Elimination of All Forms of Racial Discrimination, adopted 21 Dec. 1965, 660 UNTS 195 (entered into force 4 Jan. 1969); Convention on the Elimination of All Forms of Discrimination against Women, G.A. res. 34/180, 34 UN GAOR Supp. (No. 46) at 193, UN Doc. A/34/46, (entered into force Sept. 3, 1981); Convention on the Rights of the Child, adopted 20 Nov. 1989, G.A. res. 44/25, UN GAOR, 44th Sess., Supp. No. 49, UN Doc. A/44/49 (1989) (entered into force 2 Sept. 1990).

[54] International Covenant on Economic, Social and Cultural Rights, adopted 19 Dec. 1966, G.A. res. 2200 (XXI), UN GAOR, 21st Sess., Supp. No. 16, UN Doc. A/6316 (1966), 993 UNTS 3 (entered into force 3 Jan. 1976).

[55] A. Aust, *Modern Treaty Law and Practice* (Cambridge: Cambridge University Press, 2000), p. 47.

[56] I. Brownlie, *Principles of Public International Law*, 6th edn (Oxford: Oxford University Press, 2003), p. 63.

[57] H. Lauterpacht, *Oppenheim's International Law*, 6th edn (London: Longman, 1940), pp. 197–202.

[58] C. Bell, 'Peace Agreements and Human Rights: Implications for the UN', in *The UN, Human Rights and Post-conflict Situations*, p. 243.

At best it could be argued that the factions have limited international legal personality if they are treated as such by the international community.[59] On this basis there may be at best an assumption that if such factions are parties to an internationally negotiated treaty such as the Paris Peace Accords of 1991 governing the peace process in Cambodia,[60] then they are subject to the obligations contained therein. Whether this argument applies to a peace accord such as the Good Friday Agreement of 10 April 1998, which was signed by the political parties in Northern Ireland and the British and Irish governments, is debatable.[61]

As well as setting in place a peaceful political process, and despite their tenuous legal status, peace accords do begin to establish the legal framework for the rebuilding of the country. Human rights choices are crucial in building this framework. According to Christine Bell:

> The typical peace blueprint involves a central deal on democratic access to power (including minority rights where relevant), with a human rights framework including measures such as bills of rights, constitutional courts, human rights commissions, reforms of policing and criminal justice, and mechanisms to address past human rights violations.[62]

However, there is considerable flexibility within these parameters, first of all with political balances to be achieved between group and individual rights, and, secondly, in the way the laws are framed, which gives a tremendous amount of leeway in how human rights are protected.[63]

It is usually a part of any peace agreement, especially one brokered by the UN, that the post-conflict state becomes a party to the main UN conventions – ICCPR, ICESCR, CEDAW, CRC, CERD, Convention Against Torture[64] and relevant regional treaties.[65] For instance, in the case of Afghanistan after the United States

---

[59]   Lauterpacht, *Oppenheim's International Law*, p. 173. See further G. de Beco, 'Compliance with International Humanitarian Law by Non-State Actors', *Journal of International Law of Peace and Armed Conflict* vol. 18 (2005), 190, who argues that while international humanitarian law is binding on insurgent groups, international human rights law is not. On the indirect regulation of non-state actors by international human rights law see H. J. Steiner, 'International Protection of Human Rights', in M. Evans (ed.), *International Law* (Oxford: Oxford University Press, 2003), pp. 776–777. For further discussion on humanitarian law and non-state actors see L. Moir, *The Law of Internal Armed Conflicts* (Cambridge: Cambridge University Press, 2002), pp. 52–58.

[60]   Note by the Secretary-General on Cambodia, UN Doc. S/23179 (1991).

[61]   For background see Bell, *Peace Agreements*, pp. 54–65, 172–176.

[62]   *Ibid.*, p. 1.

[63]   Bell, 'Peace Agreements', in *The UN, Human Rights and Post-conflict Situations*, pp. 246–249.

[64]   Convention Against Torture and Other Cruel, Inhuman or Degrading Treatment or Punishment, G.A. res. 39/46, [annex, 39 UN GAOR Supp. (No. 51) at 197, UN Doc. A/39/51 (1984)] (entered into force June 26, 1987).

[65]   J. Cerone, 'Reasonable Measures in Unreasonable Circumstances: A Legal Responsibility Framework for Human Rights Violations in Post-Conflict Territories under

(US) military intervention had removed the Taliban regime in 2001, the remaining parties signed the Bonn Agreement on Provisional Arrangements in Afghanistan Pending the Re-Establishment of Permanent Government Institutions in December 2001.[66] This made clear the interim authorities' obligation to act in accordance with the basic provisions contained in the human rights instruments to which Afghanistan was a party (Afghanistan joined the ICCPR and ICESCR in 1983). The Agreement also established a Judicial Commission to 'rebuild the domestic justice system in accordance with Islamic principles, international standards, the rule of law and Afghan legal traditions'. It also established a Human Rights Commission to monitor and investigate human rights abuses. An Afghan constitution was agreed in January 2004.[67] Article 6 provides that 'the state shall be obligated to create a prosperous and progressive society based on social justice, preservation of dignity, protection of human rights, realization of democracy, attainment of national unity as well as equality between all peoples ...'; while Article 7 declares that 'the state shall observe the United Nations Charter, inter-state agreements, as well as international treaties to which Afghanistan has joined, and the Universal Declaration on Human Rights ...'. Chapter 2 of the constitution includes a list of rights to be protected which covers civil/political and economic/social/cultural rights, while Article 58 establishes a Human Rights Commission to monitor and protect. Elections were held in Afghanistan on 9 October 2004, ten months after the constitution had been agreed by the parties.

The Transitional Period

The immediate period after the formal ending of hostilities is normally turbulent, with a lower level of violence than during the conflict, but certainly not a time of peace.[68] In this period, a human rights field officer will again be concerned with issues of priorities and therefore choice. While in the peace agreement phase, choices about human rights were made on the basis of politics, in the immediate post-accords period, choices are dictated by issues of immediacy and priority. What human rights should be guaranteed in this period, given the practical impossibility of guaranteeing all?

Although it is extremely unlikely that the interim authorities in a post-conflict state would wish to declare a state of emergency (for reasons of credibility), it can be argued that the legal framework of a state of emergency can provide guidance by way of analogy to the precarious situation often found in the immediate post-accord

---

UN Administration', in *The UN, Human Rights and Post-conflict Situations*, p. 42.

   [66]   http://www.afghangovernment.com/AfghanAgreementBonn.htm.

   [67]   http://www.afghangovernment.com/2004constitution.htm.

   [68]   Bell, 'Peace Agreements', in *The UN, Human Rights and Post-conflict Situations*, p. 246.

phase.[69] The state of emergency provision in the ICCPR provides information on non-derogable rights. These are arguably the rights that must be guaranteed above all others when in a state of emergency 'which threatens the life of the nation' or its equivalent. The non-derogable rights are: the right to life; freedom from torture or other cruel treatment; freedom from slavery and servitude; the right not to be imprisoned because of an inability to perform a contractual obligation; freedom from retrospective criminal laws; the right to recognition before the law; and the right to freedom of thought, conscience or religion.[70] Furthermore, any measures derogating from other human rights must not involve 'discrimination solely on the ground of race, colour, sex, language, religion or social origin'.[71]

Of course the situation in a state of emergency may well differ in some ways from the immediate post-conflict situation. The country declaring a state of emergency may well have a developed infrastructure providing the population with the necessities of life – food, water and shelter. In contrast, a post-conflict state will invariably not be able to do this and so it is contended that the basic framework of rights to be protected in the immediate stage flow from the basic right to life in the ICCPR, and include basic economic rights found in the ICESCR – the rights to food water and shelter as found in Article 11 of that treaty. Furthermore, the proper protection of the right to life in the immediate post-conflict period will involve the merging of human rights with security issues. This necessitates the quick establishment, with international assistance, of an effective police and criminal justice system that is human rights compliant, to ensure the security of the population from continuing violence.[72]

The recognition of a limited human rights framework being applicable to the society and actors (including human rights field officers) in the immediate post-conflict period does not undermine the universality of human rights. It is not being argued here that other human rights are inapplicable, but that immediate protection should be given to a fully developed right to life. State or UN action should not violate other human rights (and indeed they must ensure that the country's existing laws and institutions are human rights compliant), but positive measures to protect other rights may have to occur after the core is secured by the establishment of

---

[69]   See M. Kelly, 'The UN, Security and Human Rights: Achieving a Winning Balance', in *The UN, Human Rights and Post-conflict Situations*, p. 118. See generally, J. Oraa, *Human Rights in States of Emergency* (Oxford: Clarendon, 1999). See also on the applicability of international humanitarian law in post-conflict situations C. Campbell, 'Peace and the Laws of War: The Role of International Humanitarian Law in the Post-conflict Environment', *International Review of the Red Cross* vol. 839 (2000), 627.

[70]   Article 4(2) International Covenant on Civil and Political Rights.

[71]   Article 4(1) International Covenant on Civil and Political Rights.

[72]   Such a system may well have to investigate past atrocities in order to secure a society fully based on the rule. The issue of accountability for past atrocities is beyond the remit of the present chapter. See generally R. Cryer, 'Post-Conflict Accountability: A Matter of Judgement, Practice or Principle', in *The UN, Human Rights and Post-conflict Situations*, p. 267.

effective police and judicial services, and the basic provision of food, security and shelter. This reflects the practical realities of preserving life and security in order to achieve an acceptable level of peace and order before a better life can be achieved.

Elections and Democracy

A transition from the emergency-like situation to a more stable society where full human rights protection is achieved under the rule of law may well take many years. Although the UN and other international actors have put great weight on elections as marking a move from post-conflict to peace, they are unlikely to achieve this, especially if they simply consolidate the former warring factions in power. This is most likely when the period before elections is relatively short, given that a longer period may well facilitate the establishment of more 'civilian' political parties. However, the longer the wait for elections the greater the danger of the interim authorities (backed by outside actors) losing legitimacy with the population. Issues of legitimacy also surround the question of when a new constitution should be adopted – before or after elections. Differing views are to be found on this as reflected in the difference between the Afghan situation, in which the constitution was adopted before elections were held, and the case of Iraq after the US and United Kingdom (UK) invasion of 2003, when elections were held in January 2005 and a constitution was still being debated in August 2005.

In terms of human rights choices, the elections period could be said to be favouring civil and political rights – the right to vote and to participate in the political life of the country as reflected in Article 25 of the ICCPR. However, as with the necessity of protecting the right to life,[73] it can be argued that it is necessary to protect and uphold another fundamental right found in both Covenants (Article 1) – the right to self-determination, in both its political and economic aspects. Economically this means that, at a minimum, the interim authorities and then the elected government must have control over the country's natural resources.[74] In its political aspect, David Harris has identified both an external and an internal dimension. Externally there is 'a rule of international law by which the political future of a colonial or similar non-independent territory should be determined in accordance with the wishes of its inhabitants, within the limits of the principle of *uti possidetis*'. The internal dimension 'may require governments generally to have a democratic base, and that minorities be allowed political autonomy'.[75] Clearly though, elections should not be

---

[73] The fundamental importance of the protection of the person to the establishment of a society is made clear in Hart's seminal exposition of the establishment of law and a legal system – H. L. A. Hart, *The Concept of Law* (Oxford: Clarendon Press, 1961), pp. 89, 189–195.

[74] See A. Orakhelashvili, 'The Post-War Settlement in Iraq: The UN Security Council Resolution 1483 (2003) and General International Law', *Journal of Conflict and Security Law* vol. 8 (2003), 307.

[75] D. J. Harris, *Cases and Materials on International Law*, 6th edn (London: Sweet and Maxwell, 2004), p. 112.

predicated on producing a particular type of government, rather they should produce a system of government based on respect for the rule of law and human rights (civil and political and economic, social and cultural). This recognises democracy not as part of an imported liberal ideology but as 'the political framework in which human rights can best be safeguarded'.[76]

Development and Economic, Social and Cultural Rights

After elections, if stability is achieved, development issues come more to the fore. In terms of the developing legal framework, the attainment of economic, social and cultural rights, beyond those necessary to secure the right to life, is more of a medium and long-term goal in post-conflict situations. In essence, this represents a practical application of the qualified and progressive obligation contained in Article 2 of the ICESCR:

> Each State Party to the present Covenant undertakes to take steps, individually and through international assistance and co-operation, especially economic and technical, to the maximum of its available resources, with a view to achieving progressively the full realisation of the rights recognised in the present Covenant by all appropriate means…

A post-conflict state can attract high levels of economic and technical assistance from states and organisations such as the European Union in Bosnia and Kosovo. UN assistance moves from DPKO, the World Food Programme, the United Nations Children's Fund, the United Nations Office for the Coordination of Humanitarian Affairs, and the Office of the United Nations High Commissioner for Refugees in the post-conflict and elections phases, to UNDP and the International Bank for Reconstruction and Development (IBRD) in the development phase. OHCHR officers should be present throughout all stages of UN assistance to ensure that the various types of human rights are being implemented with an understanding that the protection of human rights is incremental not segmental. It will be argued that all international organisations' activities are required to be human rights compliant by international institutional law, but also often by their own guidelines and codes of practice.[77]

Human Rights Obligations

Although the priorities of both the government and international actors may change over the different periods after the peace accords have been signed, this is not to say that the human rights obligations on these actors vary. Difficult choices can be justified but only against the background of recognising the applicability of all

---

[76]   B. Boutros-Ghali, 'Human Rights: The Common Language of Humanity', *World Conference on Human Rights: The Vienna Declaration and Programme of Action* (New York: United Nations, 1993), p. 17.

[77]   On the International Monetary Fund and the IBRD see N. D. White, *The UN System: Toward International Justice* (Boulder: Lynne Rienner, 2002), pp. 268–285.

human rights. In terms of the ongoing obligation to protect and promote human rights in the post-conflict situation, the government (provisional then elected) is under a duty like any other state party to the main treaties and under customary law. Furthermore, the government must take reasonable and effective steps to respond to human rights violations by the remnants of any armed group.[78]

In addition to monitoring government compliance with its obligations, human rights field officers must also be careful to monitor the activities of other states present with the consent of the government or acting under an international mandate. The obligations of the international covenants and any relevant regional human rights treaties will be applicable to those third states, if that state is exercising 'effective control' of an area in the post-conflict state.[79]

As regards the obligations on the UN and other international organisations, their agents and officers, there is of course the formal problem that, unlike states (both the post-conflict state and third states), organisations are not party to the human rights treaties. There are several strong arguments to the effect that organisations are bound by human rights laws despite the lack of signature on the major treaties. This signifies that the obligation as regards human rights is not simply to promote their protection within countries,[80] but that the UN and its agents are themselves subject to the same legal framework they are promoting. This rule of law approach is especially applicable if the UN is acting in a governmental way within a country or territory as with Kosovo and East Timor in 1999, or is otherwise in effective control, by analogy with the law applicable to states acting extra-territorially.

As a recognised international legal person,[81] the UN is the beneficiary of rights but is also subject to duties on the international plane, primarily the fundamental principles of public international law including human rights law.[82] In addition, the framework of human rights treaties sponsored by the UN and deriving from the

---

[78] Cerone, 'Reasonable Measures in Unreasonable Circumstances'. On the issue of human rights being applicable to non-state actors see generally P. Alston (ed.), *Non-State Actors and Human Rights* (Oxford: Oxford University Press, 2005).

[79] For ECHR see *Loizidou v Turkey*, Preliminary Objections (ECHR Series A 310), [1995]. See however, *Bankovic v Belgium*, Decision of 12 December 2001 (ECHR 2001-XII 333), at 9. See the English case of *R (Al-Skeini and others) v Secretary of State for Defence*, 14 December 2004. For ICCPR and ICESCR see *Legal Consequences of the Construction of a Wall in the Occupied Palestinian Territory*, Advisory Opinion of 9 July 2004 [2004], ICJ Reports 2004, 184, at 43, paras. 111–112.

[80] Article 55(c) UN Charter.

[81] *Reparation for Injuries Suffered in the Service of the United Nations*, Advisory Opinion of 11 April 1949, [1949] ICJ Reports 1949, at 174.

[82] P. Sands and P. Klein, *Bowett's Law of International Institutions*, 5th edn (London: Sweet and Maxwell, 2001), pp. 458–459. Also, by creating an international organisation, states cannot avoid their own human rights or other international legal responsibilities – see *Matthews v UK*, Judgment of 18 February 1999 [1999] (ECHR 1999-I 251), at 32.

Assembly's UDHR in 1948 must form part of the constitutional law of the UN and be binding on it in that sense, as well as the members of the UN.[83]

Of course in many cases where there is a human rights presence in a country, whether post-conflict or not, the UN is not in effective control. Post-conflict territorial administrations are very much the exception. At lower levels of UN involvement the obligation on officers to act in a human rights compliant way remains, but the responsibility to protect the human rights of citizens falls primarily on the government. In the case of peacekeepers falling within a peace support operation, there may be a responsibility to protect people within their mandate, although this still remains unclear after its tentative introduction in the Brahimi report.[84]

Conclusion

Having considered the legal source of human rights field operations, then examined, using the post-conflict situation in which the UN increasingly finds itself, the legal framework that is applicable to the government and to the UN and its agents, it is necessary to conclude by considering briefly the issue of accountability for human rights abuses. To increase the level of effective application of the legal framework it is necessary to develop effective mechanisms of accountability – legal, political and administrative.[85]

The full development of this topic remains for a separate study; it is only intended here to mention some of the legal mechanisms of accountability within the context of post-conflict situations. In such situations there is a need to develop proper systems of accountability for both states and international organisations. In the case of abuse of prisoners in Iraq by certain prison guards from the US and the UK, accountability was through national military disciplinary systems.[86] In the case of sexual abuse of civilians by certain UN peacekeepers in the Democratic Republic of the Congo, a less legal method of accountability occurred through the investigation of the abuses by the UN.[87] Both of these methods of accountability leave a great deal to be desired. There is also the possibility of investigation and prosecution of such offences in the future by the International Criminal Court, although this is again unlikely. The role of the national courts of the host state remains to be developed, though these courts are stymied to a large extent by a combination of the provisions of the status

---

[83]   White, *UN System*, pp. 14–17.

[84]   Report of the Panel on United Nations Operations, UN Doc. A/55/305-S/2000/809 (2000), at 49–50. See S. Wills, 'Military Interventions on Behalf of Vulnerable Populations', *Journal of Conflict and Security Law* vol. 9 (2004), 387.

[85]   See generally White, *The Law of International Organisations*, chapter 7.

[86]   US authorities took action against nine military personnel from Abu Ghraib prison for abuse committed in October and November 2003. In February 2005, a British military tribunal convicted three British soldiers for abuse of Iraqi civilians in May 2003.

[87]   See Office of Internal Oversight Services, Report on Investigation into Allegations of Sexual Exploitation/abuse in MONUC, UN Doc. A/59/661 (2005).

of forces agreement, which normally obliges the host state to leave such matters to the sending state,[88] and the general privileges and immunities of the UN.[89] However, the immunity of the UN's agents from prosecution is only meant to be a functional one,[90] and furthermore does not excuse the responsibility and liability of the UN for human rights abuses.[91]

---

[88] See Model Status-of-Forces Agreement for Peacekeeping Operations, UN Doc. A/45/594 (1990), at 3, 15, 24–28, 40–49.

[89] UN Convention on Privileges and Immunities, 1 UNTS 15, 13 February 1946.

[90] Article 105 UN Charter. See generally A. Reinisch, *International Organizations before National Courts* (Cambridge: Cambridge University Press, 2000).

[91] See International Court of Justice Opinion in *Difference Relating to Immunity from Legal Process of a Special Rapporteur of the Commission on Human Rights*, ICJ Rep. 1999, 62 at 88–89.

Chapter 4

Towards an Ethical Base for the Work of Human Rights Field Operations

George Ulrich

The question concerning an ethical base for human rights field operations can be taken in two senses: what is the ethical justification for setting up human rights operations in the first place, and, more concretely, what are the ethical issues, problems, and challenges arising in conjunction with organising and working for a human rights operation?

The answer to the former question turns on a widespread sense of obligation on the part of the international community to protect human rights everywhere and, when violations escalate beyond a certain threshold, to intervene in order to stop violence against civilian populations and assist in rebuilding social structures and human rights protection mechanisms that may have atrophied or been destroyed.[1] This to a certain extent entails a readiness to bypass principles of state sovereignty in the name of a greater moral cause,[2] which in turn reflects a perception of global interrelatedness – of humanity inhabiting a finite sphere with limited resources and many shared vulnerabilities – that despite entrenched divisions is becoming increasingly predominant in our everyday lives. The justification of the international community intervening across national or communal boundaries further links with a growing acknowledgement of moral relations across great distances in time and space. As demonstrated by the German moral philosopher Hans Jonas in the 1970s and 1980s,[3] such a notion was alien to classical moral philosophy but has taken on crucial significance in a contemporary setting in view of developments in technology and communication. Conceptually, Jonas seeks to elucidate the new ethical challenges confronting humanity by according primacy to a principle of *responsibility* which, in contrast to principles such as recognition, virtue or care, extends beyond immediate

---

[1]   This sense of ethical obligation has a legal foundation in *preamble* and Article 1, Charter of the United Nations, 59 Stat. 1031, T.S. 993, 3 Bevans 1153, entered into force Oct. 24, 1945.

[2]   As is described in chapter 5 by D. Moeckli and M. Nowak in the present volume, most international human rights field operations are established with the consent of the host states, yet it must be recognised that this is often obtained under some degree of duress.

[3]   See H. Jonas, *The Imperative of Responsibility: In Search of an Ethics for the Technological Age*, H. Jonas and D. Herr (trans.) (Chicago: University of Chicago Press, 1984).

inter-subjective encounters and relations within one's immediate community. In this sense, one might suggest that the underlying ethical rationale of international human rights field missions is to face up to the responsibilities of an interrelated global society characterised by deep disparities of power and wealth and intermittently confronted with eruptions of massive violations of human rights. Human rights field operations at best realise this ethical calling in a partial manner.

It is not the present author's intention to examine this theme further in the present context, except in so far as a perception of global responsibility also serves as a moral impetus for individual human rights workers to devote their professional lives to this vocation. The focus of this chapter is on the ethical complications and challenges linked with working as a human rights professional in post-conflict (or analogous) situations.

To work as a human rights professional naturally implies an ethical commitment, however this is conceptualised. It is a line of work that is chosen out of a dedication to do good for one's fellow human beings or to stand up for social justice. However, as with other professions that are borne of a commitment to a good cause (such as the medical profession, humanitarian work and development cooperation), the fact of being so committed does not mean that all that one does in one's professional capacity, even with the best of intentions, is necessarily for the good.[4] Nor is the profession as such exempt from ethical accountability. Quite the contrary; the maxim guiding medical ethics that the tremendous capacity of medical professionals to do good is matched by a corresponding capacity to do harm, and that therefore this line of work is particularly ethically charged,[5] has some application to human rights professionals as well. Not only does the emerging human rights profession entail risks of directly or indirectly exposing individuals or groups to harm, also the very fact of interacting with people in exceptionally vulnerable and exposed circumstances requires a heightened level of sensitivity. This too defines a relation that would in most circumstances be perceived to be ethically charged.

As human rights field work becomes consolidated as a profession, it is paramount that the community of human rights professionals follows the lead of other analogous professions[6] and seeks to establish minimum ethical standards as well as a system of basic monitoring and accountability. Education and ethical awareness-raising in turn become indispensable tools in fostering compliance with established norms and, in so doing, in contributing to the formation of a shared sense of professional identity. Promoting professional ethics is also a matter of fostering analytical skills, thus enabling professionals to identify and negotiate the conflicting pulls in genuinely complex situations.

---

[4]   See D. Rieff, *A Bed for the Night* (London: Vintage, 2002), by way of an example.

[5]   See General Assembly of World Medical Association, Declaration of Geneva (1948), adopted by the General Assembly of World Medical Association at Geneva, Switzerland, September 1948 and World Medical Association, International Code of Medical Ethics, *World Medical Association Bulletin* vol. 1, no. 3 (1949), 109, 111.

[6]   Various points of reference from analogous professions are available at http://www.humanrightsprofessionals.org/index.php?option=com_content&task=view&id=51&Itemid=106.

The underlying aim in focusing attention on professional ethics must always be to empower practitioners and in so doing to raise the standards of professional conduct. The work of the human rights field officer (HRFO) is in fact highly complicated, as well as personally and ethically challenging, in ways that are not well described. While working under sometimes extreme conditions, the prevailing tendency is that altogether too much is left to the personal judgment and conscience of the individual practitioner, who thus may experience recurrent doubts and disillusionment – in some ways the flip side of the strong personal commitment and dedication that motivates HRFOs.[7]

Currently, the only international ethical standard that directly addresses HRFOs is an internal 'Code of Conduct' of the Office of the United Nations High Commissioner for Human Rights (OHCHR) adopted in 1999.[8] An OHCHR *Training Manual on Human Rights Monitoring* from 2001 devotes a full chapter to a review of ethical complications and norms relevant to human rights field operations and in this connection makes reference to a range of other United Nations documents establishing standards of professional ethics, notably in the field of peacekeeping and humanitarian assistance.[9] Such references include:

* the 'Report on Standards of Conduct in the International Civil Service' by the International Civil Service Advisory Board (1954);[10]
* the Convention on the Safety of United Nations and Associated Personnel adopted by the UN General Assembly 1994;[11]
* the UN 'Staff Rules Applicable to Service of a Limited Duration' issued in 1994;[12]
* the United Nations Civilian Police 'Code of Conduct' contained in the *Standard Administrative Procedures* of 1992;[13]
* the 'General Guidelines for Peace-keeping Operations' issued by the UN Department of Peacekeeping Operations (DPKO) in 1995;[14] and
* 'Ten Rules: Code of Personal Conduct for Blue Helmets' issued by DPKO in 1997.[15]

---

[7] See 'Survey of the Profession' at http://www.humanrightsprofessionals.org/.

[8] OHCHR, 'Code of Conduct for OHCHR staff', Directive No. 2 (1999).

[9] OHCHR, 'Norms Applicable to UN Human Rights Officers and Other Staff', *Training Manual on Human Rights Monitoring* (Geneva: OHCHR, 2001), pp. 449–464 .

[10] Available at http://www.ficsa.org/document/WEB%20Field/standards.pdf.

[11] Convention on the Safety of United Nations and Associated Personnel, G.A. res 49/59, 49 UN GAOR Supp. (No. 49), at 299, UN Doc. A/49/49 (1994).

[12] United Nations, Staff Rules, Rules 301.1 to 312.6 Governing Appointments for Service of a Limited Duration, UN Doc. ST/SGB/Staff Rules/3/Rev.5 (1994), (revising UN Doc. ST/SGB/Staff Rules/3/Rev.4 (1987)).

[13] United Nations Field Operations Division, 'Notes for the Guidance of Military Observers and Police Monitors', *Standard Administrative Procedures* (1992).

[14] DPKO, *General Guidelines for Peace-keeping Operations* (New York: United Nations, 1995).

[15] Available at http://www.un.org/Depts/dpko/training/tes_publications/books/peacekeeping_training/pocket_cards/ten_in.pdf.

Numerous other relevant references and sources of possible inspiration could be added, such as:

- the *Disaster Management Ethics* module of the United Nations Disaster Management Training Programme;[16]
- the *WHO Ethical and Safety Recommendations for Interviewing Trafficked Women* of 2003;[17]
- the United Nations Children's Fund 'Ethical guidelines – Principles for ethical reporting on children';[18] and, notably,
- the 'Code of Conduct for The International Red Cross and Red Crescent Movement and NGOs in Disaster Relief' adopted by the International Federation of Red Cross and Red Crescent Societies (1994).[19]

However, given this proliferation of ethics standards designed for parallel disciplines and covering situations of relevance to work in the field of human rights, it is clear that more can be done to describe the characteristic ethical dilemmas and challenges confronting HRFOs and to codify essential standards of conduct. Such a process can be assumed to form an integral part of the general consolidation of professional identity, which is an underlying theme of the present volume. In this regard, it is taken for granted that inspiration will be drawn from all of the abovementioned ethical codes and guidelines as well as from standards developed within other disciplines.[20]

What is particularly important in articulating authoritative ethical guidelines for an emerging profession, and subsequently in adapting such guidelines to a given concrete context, is that members of the profession are closely consulted and involved in the process.[21] This not only helps to ensure the pertinence and applicability of the established norms but also contributes to a shared sense of ownership and professional pride, which is of paramount importance if ethical standards are to have an impact in practice. If professional ethical standards are codified in a formal manner as an official code of conduct, it is essential that this avoids the character of being formulaic, paternalistic and dictated from the outside. This too is best attained by ensuring a vibrant process of consultation and ongoing adaptation.

---

[16] United Nations Development Programme, *Disaster Management Ethics*, Disaster Management Training Programme, 1st edn (United Nations, Department of Humanitarian Affairs,1997), available at http://www.undmtp.org/english/ethics/ethics.pdf.

[17] C. Zimmerman and C. Watts, *WHO Ethical and Safety Recommendations for Interviewing Trafficked Women* (Geneva: World Health Organization, London School of Hygiene and Tropical Medicine, Daphne Programme of the European Commission, 2003), available at http://www.who.int/entity/gender/documents/en/final%20recommendations%20 23%20oct.pdf.

[18] See http://www.unicef.org/media/media_tools_guidelines.html.

[19] See http://www.ifrc.org/publicat/conduct/.

[20] The two most important examples are the medical profession and humanitarian assistance, but many other professions – e.g. the legal profession, journalism, and social work – have also established codes of conduct that can be taken as inspiration for the ethics of human rights field work.

[21] See C. MacDonald, 'Guidance for Writing a Code of Ethics', at http://www.ethicsweb. ca/codes/coe3.htm.

The present chapter aims to contribute to such a process of internal articulation of ethical standards for human rights field professionals by outlining three main areas of consideration. The first section identifies key aspects of the work of HRFOs that are ethically charged or in other ways can be assumed to have ethical implications; the second section establishes a normative framework by proposing a general typology of issues of ethical concern (of relevance, notably, to professional ethics); and the third section seeks, in view of the previous two sections, to map specific ethical challenges and norms related to the work of the human rights professional. It is taken for granted that such a mapping is provisional and will need to be expanded and improved through a process of extensive consultation with experienced HRFOs.

Characteristic Features of the Work of the Human Rights Field Officer

Most human rights field operations are set in conflict or post-conflict areas or in societies of transition in which international organisations in various ways assist in facilitating compliance with recognised standards of human rights and democracy. Another characteristic area of employment for HRFOs is to contribute specialised expertise within broader missions, such as, for example, delegations of national or international organisations to third countries; not all of the observations in the following pertain fully to this category of field officers.

The threshold for the international community to establish a human rights field operation is generally high,[22] and the work of field officers in such situations is accordingly shaped by intense tensions and sensitivities. The context in which the HRFOs operates is typically one of egregious violence and violation of human rights on a massive scale, deep-seated patterns of discrimination, hatred and mistrust, and numerous forms of societal distortion, armament of civilians – sometimes even children, organised crime, paramilitary political organisation, etc.[23] The immediate purpose of the international mission is then to ensure some measure of stability and prevent renewed or continued violence, but looking beyond the immediate situation it is also to contribute to the rebuilding of basic societal structures and protection mechanisms, to facilitate the return of people and restoration of property, to re-establish communal relations and functioning democratic processes, and to support, if at all possible, a process of individual and collective healing, as can be facilitated both by judicial trials and by various truth and reconciliation mechanisms. Or the challenge may consist in building new social structures and relations from the ashes of what has been destroyed.[24] To work in such a context means to intervene in situations of heightened sensitivities due to the persisting risks of a re-escalation of violence, to the complexity of the relations involved

---

[22]   See chapter 5 by D. Moeckli and M. Nowak in the present volume.

[23]   See generally A. Henkin (ed.), *Honoring Human Rights* (The Hague: Kluwer Law International, 2000) and S. Chesterman (ed.), *Civilians in War* (Boulder: Lynne Rienner, 2001).

[24]   *Ibid.*

and to the lingering effects of recent suffering and loss. This obviously places high ethical demands on the HRFO.

Viewed in a geopolitical perspective, it is often the case that human rights field operations take place in contexts of marginalisation or even estrangement from the majority of regional and international integrative mechanisms in the economic, cultural and political spheres.[25] Indeed, such marginalisation may be found to be a contributing factor to the conflict situation that gave rise to the mission in the first place. It goes hand in hand with a lack of internal institutional controls and a general situation of social distortion which sometimes, in fact, is reinforced by the efforts of the international community suddenly to put surrogate structures into place.[26] Populations living in such areas experience a characteristic mix of deep-seated frustration with – and at the same time very high, perhaps exaggerated – expectations of the international community.[27] HRFOs and other internationals on the ground, who in effect are charged with compensating for the general neglect of the conflict or social transition area in question, often bear the brunt of such ambivalent sentiments. The overall distortion of the social environment adds to the ethical complexity of the work of the human rights professional in numerous ways.

A third, related aspect of international field operations is a tendency to assign an exceptional level of responsibility to individuals working on such missions. HRFOs are thus often assigned responsibilities beyond their ordinary capacity or at a level that they would only attain in their home environments through a gradual process of advancements, subject to ongoing tests and controls. Some rise to this challenge, others perform less well, but the general pattern at any rate produces imbalances and strained relations between locals and internationals, which also add a dimension of ethical complexity to the work of the HRFO.[28]

Thus, to recapitulate, characteristic features of the work of the human rights field officer of relevance to the following considerations include:

- HFROs work in environments characterised by deep social divisions, entrenched patterns of discrimination and mistrust, and for this reason heightened volatility and vulnerability. This is particularly true of post-conflict situations but also albeit to a lesser extent of many transitional societies.

---

[25] For example in Haiti, See I. Martin, 'Paper versus Steel: The First Phase of the International Civilian Mission in Haiti,' in *Honoring Human Rights*, pp. 73–117.

[26] As in Cambodia, Kosovo and elsewhere, see B. Adams, 'UN Human Rights Work in Cambodia: Efforts to Preserve the Jewel in the Peacekeeping Crown'; in *Honoring Human Rights*, pp. 345–382; M. Brand, 'Effective Human Rights Protection When the UN Becomes the State', in N. D. White and D. Klaasen (eds), *The UN, Human Rights and Post-conflict Situations* (Manchester: Manchester University Press, 2005), pp. 347–375; and R. Wilde, 'International Territorial Administration and Human Rights', in *The UN, Human Rights and Post-conflict Situations*, pp. 149–173.

[27] See, for example, chapter 14 by P. Burgess in the present volume.

[28] *Ibid.*, also, the OHCHR *Training Manual on Human Rights Monitoring* makes a related observation in noting that 'UN personnel are *sometimes viewed as leading a privileged lifestyle in the field*', p. 450 (emphasis in the original).

- The social and psychological context in which HRFOs operate is typically marked by raw sensitivities due to recent experience of suffering and traumatisation.
- The work of the HRFO often unfolds in areas that are marginalised from internationally integrative mechanisms and in other regards neglected by the international community. Such marginalisation produces relations of social distortion and at the same time confronts HRFOs with escalated, perhaps unrealistic expectations.
- International personnel working in conflict or post-conflict situations, including HRFOs, are often assigned responsibilities beyond their ordinary capacity or at a level that they would only attain in their home environments through a gradual process of advancements, subject to ongoing institutional controls.

Normative Framework: General Overview of Areas of Ethical Concern

The next step of the argument consists of examining the values and general moral commitments guiding professional conduct. It will be found that this question can also be framed in terms of an inquiry into how we conceptualise the realm of ethics in a broad sense. What types of issues are perceived to be ethically significant, and is there a shared perception of this not only among professionals themselves (often representing many diverse cultural and religious backgrounds) but also with the communities within which field operations are carried out? Experience shows that it is often more fruitful, especially when working in a cross-cultural context, to seek to develop a common conceptual language and typology of ethical issues – in essence, what is ethics about? – than immediately to seek to articulate specific binding norms.[29]

An obvious point of departure would be to establish that human rights professionals are fundamentally responsible for upholding standards of human rights in their own personal and professional conduct. This, indeed, serves as the first principle of the 'Code of Conduct' issued by OHCHR in 1999[30] and is repeated in the opening paragraphs of the OHCHR *Training Manual on Human Rights Monitoring*.[31] The present author would argue, however, that the normative framework enshrined by human rights needs to be complemented by expressly ethical standards of professional conduct, for whereas the commitment to human rights is beyond dispute

---

[29]   It should be noted that the considerations presented in the following are to a large extent based on the present author's direct experience of working with ethical problems and relations pertaining to the field of overseas medical research and to international development cooperation.

[30]   [Staff of the OHCHR shall:] 'Promote the advancement and observance of all human rights as defined by international instruments, and base all actions, statements, analysis and work on these standards.' OHCHR, 'Code of Conduct for OHCHR staff', para. 1.

[31]   OHCHR, 'Norms Applicable to UN Human Rights Officers and Other Staff', in *Training Manual on Human Rights Monitoring*, p. 450.

for human rights professionals and indeed does have important applications with respect to individual conduct,[32] it is nevertheless not sufficiently determinate to serve the current purpose. A primary reason for this is that the horizontal implications of human rights norms have not been well explored, in particular when it comes to individual human relations and reciprocal obligations. There is thus a conceptual gap between the level at which human rights norms are articulated and the actual issues confronting professionals on the ground. This gap can no doubt be narrowed, but to do so one would need to re-articulate the main issues in terms of the language of ethics. A further consideration pointing in the same direction is that many of the ethical issues arising in the context of professional conduct fail to reach the level of a human rights concern, yet they nevertheless remain pertinent and demand candid attention. To fail to accord such attention risks legitimating field professionals in perceiving themselves to be beyond reproach in mundane interpersonal matters because they work for a greater cause.

In view of the ethical experience of other comparable disciplines, most notably the medical profession, the present author proposes that the pertinent standards of professional conduct can, to a large extent, even if perhaps not exhaustively, be articulated with reference to a limited number of basic normative considerations and commitments.[33] It is specifically proposed that there are five main types of ethical issues that confront HRFOs. These are:[34]

A. harm/protection issues (about *what* one does to others, how one's actions and decisions affect others, directly or indirectly, physically, materially or psychologically, immediately or in the longer term, etc.);
B. communication issues (about *how* one relates to others; about respect for dignity, recognition of competence, reciprocity);

---

[32]   It is, for example, ethically objectionable as well as incompatible with human rights if employees of international organisations contribute to creating a market for prostitution in situations that are known to involve organised trafficking of women.

[33]   Various basic approaches have been advanced in this regard. Bernard Gert, among others, has developed a rule-based approach to medical ethics, whereas Tom Beauchamp and James Childress are associated with a principle-based approach. See, respectively, B. Gert, *Morality: A New Justification of the Moral Rules* (Oxford: Oxford University Press, 1988); or B. Gert, C. M. Cluver and K. D. Clouser, *Bioethics: A Return to Fundamentals* (Oxford: Oxford University Press, 1997); and T. L. Beauchamp and J. F. Childress, *Principles of Biomedical Ethics*, 5th edn (Oxford: Oxford University Press, 2001). The present author's own approach as presented in the following, which is partially inspired by both schools of thought, is described in further detail in G. Ulrich, *Globally Speaking: Report on the Ethics of Research in Developing Countries* (report prepared for Danida, Copenhagen, 1998); and G. Ulrich, 'Optimum Ethical Standards,' in *Acta Tropica* vol. 78, supp. 1, pp 1–126 (Elsevier, January 2001).

[34]   Elements of each of these issues are confronted in the various field operations reviewed in Henkin, *Honoring Human Rights*.

C. justice issues (about distribution of available scarce resources and goods, about redressing wrongs);
D. collaboration issues (about fairness in the negotiation of vested interests);
E. issues of compliance with institutional objectives and standards.

The essential ethical commitments deriving from each of these main areas of consideration will be briefly elaborated below and will subsequently serve as parameters for mapping ethical issues of specific concern to human rights professionals.

The commitment to *protecting vulnerable subjects from exposure to harm* is widely recognised as the foremost principle of professional ethics.[35] In a narrow sense it can be understood as an obligation to refrain from perpetrating or exposing others to harm – what in technical terms is known as the principle of *non-maleficence*.[36] In this case the human rights professional him- or herself, or by extension the institution for which he or she works, is viewed as a potential cause of harm (be this physical, mental or material harm; harm caused by acts of commission or acts of omission; harm perpetrated direct by the professional unit or indirectly by others, etc.) and the corresponding ethical obligation consists in not promulgating such harm.[37] As articulated, the ethical norm is proportional to the agency of the professional to whom it is addressed and therefore assumes the character of an absolute norm. However, the commitment to protecting vulnerable subjects from exposure to harm can also, in a wider sense, be interpreted as a matter of positively alleviating or reducing the risk of harm perpetrated by others. Analytically speaking this would fall under the general principle of doing good for others – *beneficence* – which in comparison with non-maleficence is less clear and determinate. Here the objective exceeds the agency of the professional to whom the norm is addressed (there is always more good to be done than any single agent is capable of doing) and the ethical obligation in question must therefore be viewed as relative to the capacities of the actors involved. The optimal ethical outcome will similarly, in most cases, only be an imperfect approximation of a greater objective (e.g. to end violence and alleviate suffering on a mass scale) which no individual or single institution can be responsible for bringing about.

A second important normative commitment has to do with treating one's fellow human beings with *dignity* and ensuring *reciprocity* and respect in interpersonal and in many cases also intercultural relations. This concerns not what one does *to* and *for*

---

[35] Within the medical profession, the principle *primum non nocerere* is thus widely perceived to date as far back as the Hippocratic Oath; it does not in fact appear explicitly in this ancient text, yet it has throughout the ages served as a cornerstone of medical ethics.

[36] A main source of this and related key principles of contemporary medical ethics is Beauchamp and Childress, *Principles of Biomedical Ethics*.

[37] Noteworthy here is the 'Do No Harm' approached champion by Mary B. Anderson and adopted by many humanitarian organisations. See M. B. Anderson, *Do No Harm: Supporting Local Capacities for Peace Through Aid* (Cambridge: Local Capacities for Peace Project, Collaborative for Development Action, 1996).

others, but the quality of *how* one interacts. Taken in a broad sense, the ethical issues in question can therefore be characterised as *communication issues*. They are not given nearly as much attention in the literature on professional ethics as the issues related to the protection of the exposed human being against harm,[38] yet they are of fundamental importance to a cross-cultural understanding of what ethics is about. Breaches of expectations of respectful communicative interaction, i.e. misrecognition of dignity and discursive competence, may in fact be perceived to be more offensive than inflictions of physical or material harm, and may in addition contribute to the formation of a context in which serious human rights violations are liable to occur.[39] As communicative interaction by its very nature unfolds in dispersed and unregulated settings, it is not always easy to clearly articulate, much less monitor, the specific operative norms, but their presence and gravity are continuously manifested by explicit and implicit reactions of the protagonists involved.

A third normative commitment, which must be regarded as integrally related to the work of the HRFO and in fact provides an underlying impetus for such work, is *to advance social justice* (e.g. in the distribution of scarce resources and goods), *redress structural and systemic wrong* and *contribute to the greater social good*. Like the commitment to alleviating or providing protection against harm, this too can be regarded as an application of the principle of beneficence, yet many ethical theorists would rather refer the ethical commitment in question to a principle of *justice* so as to accentuate the entitlement of victims of systemic wrong to some form of remedy rather than merely treat this as a matter of optional benevolence. Either way, the norm again exceeds the scope of individual agency and therefore only permits imperfect approximations, yet nevertheless has decisive consequences for individual action. It typically does not provide concrete guidance for action but rather confronts the ethical agent with a persistent need to determine how to comport oneself vis-à-vis injustice, not just in the abstract but in concrete manifestations unfolding before one's very eyes.

A fourth normative commitment consists of ensuring respectful and fair interaction with peers and other parties working in the same area. This may be styled the *ethics of collaboration* and has to do with negotiating vested interests associated with professional activity (e.g. career interests). It would be misguided to regard vested interests as such as inherently dubious. To the contrary, they provide a basic stimulus for professionalism and can work in constructive synergy with broader ethical and practical objectives. But it is, obviously, also possible that the interests of collaborators who are differently positioned in a given institutional framework

---

[38]   An interesting exception is found in the 1999 'Code of Ethics' of the US National Association of Social Workers. In comparison with other codes of professional ethics, this document is unusually elaborate but at the same time concise and rich in content, in particular on issues having to do with respect, competence, dignity and worth of the person. See http://www.naswdc.org/pubs/code/code.asp.

[39]   For an insightful discussion of the consequences of misrecognition, see R. Rorty, 'Human Rights, Rationality, and Sentimentality' in S. Shute and S. Hurley (eds), *On Human Rights: The Oxford Amnesty Lectures 1993* (New York: Basic Books, 1993).

and working relationship may come into conflict with one another.[40] There is then an ethical responsibility for the parties involved, or for the underlying institution, to ensure a balanced and fair resolution of the given conflict of interests, first of all because this is intrinsically right but also because it contributes to positive working relationships. Further to this, it becomes a matter of ethical concern if the pursuit of private interests comes to skew or override other considerations of an ethical nature. A case in point would be if scarce resources are being deployed in a less than optimal fashion due to certain private interests, or if certain risks of harm to vulnerable persons would be found to ensue from the pursuit of such interests. A common feature of all such cases of abuse of office is that the private interests that are unduly given priority are at the same time kept hidden. It is precisely for this reason that it is essential within the framework of professional ethics to bring vested interests out into the open and to define the manner of negotiating vested interests among peers and within an institutional framework as a matter of fundamental ethical concern.

A fifth indispensable dimension of professional ethics has to do with *respecting the standards of professionalism of the discipline and/or institutions with which one is associated.* For medical professionals this means pledging an oath to scrupulously practice one's craft in accordance with established procedures and on the basis of the most advanced knowledge of the profession, and for scientific researchers it means an obligation to carry out one's work in a manner consistent with scientific honesty and integrity.[41] For human rights professionals, similarly, it will become necessary to establish basic standards of professionalism (ethical and otherwise) which reflect the self-image of the discipline as well as the primary objectives, policies and public interests of the main international institutions and organisations undertaking human rights field operations.

HRFO Ethical Issues: Mapping of Specific Issues in Need of Closer Examination

Harm and Protection Issues

Given the sensitivity of the underlying context, it is particularly important to delimit the ethical responsibility of the HRFO with regard to harm and protection in a realistic fashion. This requires both conceptual and experience-based analysis. Whereas few HRFOs are likely to find themselves in a situation of directly perpetrating physical harm, they may in various ways expose individuals and groups to harm perpetrated by others, and they may through their actions or inactions be a cause of anguish and

---

[40]   Examples from human rights field operations include East Timor, see chapter 14 by P. Burgess in the present volume, and Afghanistan, see, International Policy Institute, *A Case for Change: A Review of Peace Operations* (King's College London, 2003).

[41]   Compare examples from these and other fields at http://www.ethicsweb.ca/resources/.

mental harm or, in some cases, of material loss or disadvantage.[42] Issues of indirect physical harm may arise, for example, in connection with the handling of sensitive data obtained through testimonies or interviews and in connection with protecting the identity of people who through their involvement with a human rights operation may become exposed to ongoing threats of violence. Mental harm is a fundamental concern in any interaction with recently traumatised people;[43] this confronts HRFOs with a particularly high level of responsibility, which they may not in fact be well equipped to handle, yet which are impossible to avoid given the general context. Issues of contributing to material harm and reinforcing inequities typically come up in connection with the ambiguous process of rebuilding damaged social structures, forging new structures, restoring property to its previous owners, certifying new property claims and realignments, etc.[44] The nature of rapid social dislocation and transformation is such that there may be no measures that are uncontroversially equitable, yet inaction is not an acceptable option either. This overall area of analysis is as of yet remarkably undeveloped and will require explicit attention in any future process of ethical standard setting for HRFOs.[45]

Dignity, Reciprocity and Respect

The imperative to treat recipients of assistance with dignity and respect and, when appropriate or possible, to engage in relations of communicative reciprocity, is rather more diffuse and indeterminate than the injunction against perpetrating harm, yet in ethical terms it is no less important. Issues of dignity and respect are particularly delicate in contexts of suffering and need. They are addressed in the International Committee of the Red Cross (ICRC) 'Code of Conduct'[46] as a key point of concern arising from widespread apprehension about international humanitarian organisations exploiting the imagery of suffering for purposes of campaigning, fundraising and institutional profiling, or in order to provoke a public reaction to natural and human disasters, which otherwise all too often tend to be treated with indifference and apathy. Unfortunately, the conditions of the international media culture, or media driven political culture, are such that the very imperative of generating an adequate and

---

[42] Although this is most likely to occur through *inaction*, particularly when HRFOs are obstructed by institutional or other impediments, note K. L. Cain, 'The Rape of Dinah: Human Rights, Civil War in Liberia, and Evil Triumphant', *Human Rights Quarterly* vol. 21, no. 2 (1999), 265–307; other scenarios could be envisaged.

[43] The literature is voluminous, but most pertinent here is the UN Disaster Management Training Programme's *Disaster Management Ethics*, see pp. 23–34.

[44] These issues are consistent throughout the various field operations discussed in Henkin, *Honoring Human Rights*, see especially M. O'Flaherty, 'International Human Rights Operations in Bosnia and Herzegovina', in *Honoring Human Rights*, pp. 234–240.

[45] An application of the principle of non-maleficence appears in the OHCHR 'Code of Conduct for OHCHR Staff' in para. 11, but the principle is not particularly prominent in this code. Surprisingly, it does not appear at all in the 1994 ICRC 'Code of Conduct'.

[46] See ICRC, 'Code of Conduct', paras 5, 6, and 10.

timely international response to human disasters places the organisations involved in a potential conflict with the dignity of ostensible beneficiaries of aid. This may in various ways apply to the field of human rights interventions as well, and the human rights community can no doubt learn from the lessons of the field of humanitarian intervention as drawn through a difficult process of self-scrutiny in the 1990s.[47]

The obligation to conduct one's work in a spirit of respectful interaction with local counterparts also of course applies to the daily work of the HRFO. This requires a general sensitivity to cultural differences, as is incumbent upon any professional working in an international setting. It is, however, complicated by the fact that the very same cultural differences may be a factor in the underlying conflict situation, yet this is precisely an added reason why the quality of communicative interaction centred around cultural issues are often of central importance in determining the overall success of a human rights mission.[48]

The need for a firm and conscious commitment to respect for the dignity and discursive competence of local counterparts and recipients of assistance is, furthermore, rendered complicated, and for that reason important, by the general tendency for overseas human rights professionals to assume responsibilities and functions that are disproportionate to what they would likely be assigned in their home environment. This requires a certain spirit of humility which, unfortunately, is not always salient among representatives of the international community working in post-conflict areas, and which stands in danger of eroding in situations where optimism about effecting positive change gives way to sentiments of disillusionment and cynicism. However, in so far as the ultimate aim of any international field operation, and perhaps in particular operations dedicated to the promotion and protection of human rights, is to build effective local capacity for the future,[49] an ethos of recognising and reinforcing existing competencies must be taken as a primary obligation of any HRFO. An ethical codex should address this in explicit terms.

---

[47] A provocative, yet informative account of this experience is found in A. De Waal, *Famine Crimes: Politics & the Disaster Relief Industry in Africa* (Oxford: James Currey, 1997). Generally speaking, it is clear that the multiple failures of international interventions in the Great Lakes Region during the 1990s, and most notably the Rwanda genocide, served as a defining moment for the codification of international standards for disaster relief. The *Sphere Project*, sponsored by the Red Cross and Red Crescent movement and launched in 1997, is the most tangible and elaborate outcome of this process, see http://www.sphereproject.org/.

[48] The 1993 mission to Haiti provides one example of this, see W. G. O'Neill, 'Gaining Compliance without Force: Human Rights Field Operations', in *Civilians in War*, pp. 102–112.

[49] Compare ICRC 'Code of Conduct', para. 6. See also M. O'Flaherty, 'Human Rights Monitoring and Armed Conflict: Challenges for the UN', *Disarmament Forum* vol. 3 (2004), 50–55.

Beneficence and Justice

The general ethical injunction to promote social justice and contribute to a greater good at the system level – and at the individual level, albeit on a more modest scale – has numerous obvious applications to the work of human right field officers. [50] In fact, as we have seen in the opening paragraphs of the present chapter, it is closely linked with the very vocation of the profession and the underlying rationale for establishing international human rights operations in the first place. However, the application of the principle is highly complicated in practice, both because it addresses interventions at a level where individual actors can only effect change to a limited extent, and because it implicates the moral agent in potential conflicts of interest.

A primary aim of the work of a HRFO is to contribute to laying the ground for a rebuilding of society, in other words for the creation of a post-conflict social order founded on institutional checks and balances and respect for human rights.[51] At the same time, HRFOs may typically become involved in advocacy issues on behalf of victims of human rights abuses in the past.[52] This risks exposing the HRFO, or the operation in general, to suspicions of partiality in relation to local conflicts, and as existing inequities are liable to become reinforced, sometimes realigned, during periods of transition, there rests a particularly heavy onus on individual professionals working for such a mission to transcend personal sympathies and antipathies and to dedicate one's best efforts to a forging of constructive prospective relations. This type of impartiality is not easy to achieve, and is perhaps rendered all the more difficult given the general escalation of personal responsibility in a situation characterised by distorted social relations, raw sensibilities and a lack of functioning institutional mechanisms.

Ethics of Collaboration

The complex negotiation of hierarchical and vertical relations, authority dynamics, career ambitions, salary expectations, agenda setting, claims to recognition, entitlements and frictions that can be summarised by the phrase *the ethics of collaboration* presents complications within any professional context.[53] Due to the salience of personally-vested interests, it is often particularly sensitive and difficult

---

[50]   The *humanitarian imperative* emphatically asserted in the 1990s by the ICRC and numerous other international organisations marks a notable example of according central status to the principle of beneficence in humanitarian field operations. No analogous imperative has been articulated for the human rights field (in many ways considerably more diverse), but conceivably this could be accomplished.

[51]   M. O'Flaherty, 'Future Protection of Human Rights in Post-conflict Societies: The Role of the UN', in *The UN, Human Rights and Post-conflict Situations*, pp. 380–383.

[52]   *Ibid.*

[53]   However, surprisingly few ethics codes address it explicitly. A noteworthy exception is the 'Code of Ethics' of the US National Association of Social Workers.

to broach in a candid and open fashion, yet a failure to do so is likely to have a negative impact on the success of the given mission and may lead to breaches of ethics in other regards. Vested personal interests should not be regarded as inherently suspect or compromising, even in contexts of alleviating suffering and redressing massive systemic injustices. To do so would imply constituting human rights field work as a form of charity. Not only is this unlikely to be conducive to fostering an ethos of professionalism, it furthermore stands in danger of placing recipients of assistance in a position of moral indebtedness that runs counter to the very concept of international human rights. It is therefore important that vested interests should be recognised as an integral part of any professional activity and should be openly addressed as such. When properly framed, vested interests can be harnessed to further the broader objectives of a given sphere of activity and can even serve to reinforce compliance with ethical standards. However, serious problems arise when particular private interests are accorded undue priority in comparison with other interests and objectives, and when the pursuit of personal gain leads individual professionals or groups to compromise on essential ethical concerns. Such behaviour is, due to its compound effect and the connotations of misuse of office, spontaneously recognised as a particularly pernicious form of unethical conduct. It is probably not uncommon, but usually occurs in obscure ways that are difficult to expose and that may in fact be shielded by a general reluctance to candidly confront complicated collaboration relations and issues of vested interests.

The central importance of the theme of collaboration as a basic parameter of professional ethics is reinforced by the consideration that international HRFOs working in post-conflict contexts, as are characteristic of human rights field operations, carry an obligation to contribute to capacity building among local colleagues and staff.[54] Since the presence of the international community in a given area is always assumed to be transitory, a concomitant aim of any activity must always be to help build a local professional community that is capable of managing the same functions and tasks in the future.[55] However, while this obligation is widely recognised, the transitory presence of international professional staff may sometimes lead to the opposite consequence, namely that individual short term gains are pursued at the expense of longer term structural objectives.[56] This and related ethical complications require further attention and analysis.

---

[54] See chapter 14 by P. Burgess in the present volume, as well O'Flaherty, 'Future Protection of Human Rights in Post-conflict Societies', in *The UN, Human Rights and Post-conflict Situations*.

[55] Cambodian and East Timor provide successful examples of UN work in this area. See D. McNamara, 'UN Human Rights Activities in Cambodia: An Evaluation', in *Honoring Human Rights*, pp. 47–72, and chapter 14 by P. Burgess in the present volume.

[56] As in Angola, Liberia and Malawi for example, see A. Clapham and F. Martin, 'Smaller Missions Bigger Problems', in *Honoring Human Rights*, pp. 289–317.

Professionalism and Organisational Loyalty

The ethical obligation to conduct oneself in compliance with the objectives and explicit policies of the organisation for which one works in a certain sense encompasses and re-introduces all of the ethical obligations described above, for it is probable that any case of (serious) ethical misconduct will compromise the ability of the organisation to realise its main objectives.[57] Beyond immediate questions of conduct, it is important that international actors in the field are seen to operate efficiently and fairly and to make optimal use of available scarce resources. What is at stake is, on the one hand, the good reputation and hence efficacy of the given organisation or mission and, on the other hand, the general receptivity of the environment in which the mission is situated to input and interventions by external actors. By analogy, it is widely recognised that unethical practices in medical science compromise not only the validity and outcome of the specific trial in question but they also 'spoil the field' in which the research is conducted for future related or comparable research activities. Since professionals working in various capacities on international missions in immediate post-conflict situations often constitute a primary and particularly visible group of international actors, the level of ethical standards and professionalism they are seen to maintain has far-reaching consequences for subsequent developments in the area. It is thus telling that more than half of the 12 Articles contained in the 1999 OHCHR 'Code of Conduct' are devoted to issues of compliance with organisational aims, policies and procedures and projecting an image of professionalism on behalf of the organisation.[58] Virtually all other ethics codes and documents applicable to operations of the international community in conflict and post-conflict situations accord a similar prominent status to this level of ethical consideration.[59]

The issues of corporate image and *esprit de corps* once again point to problems having to do with demoralisation and disillusionment. Whereas such reactions can be seen as a natural reaction to objective stress and distorted power dynamics, in other words an understandable reaction to work in extreme circumstances, they are, beyond a certain threshold, incompatible with necessary standards of professionalism that must be assumed in any human rights field mission. Any public articulation of misgivings about a given international human rights operation should therefore be very carefully considered, yet it is by the same token important that operations establish internal structures for the communication and processing of accumulated frustrations and concerns. Such measures are arguably essential to the cultivation of an ethos of professionalism.

---

[57]   It would, conversely, make sense to posit a set of ethical obligations of the employing organisation vis-à-vis its professional staff, notably staff members working under difficult and exposed circumstances such as HRFOs. This does not generally form part of professional ethics guidelines or codes of conduct (where the focus is typically on the conduct of individual practitioners) but could well be taken up in connection with defining ethical standards for human rights professionals and might be included in any future consultation procedure.

[58]   See OHCHR, 'Code of Conduct for OHCHR staff', paras 3, 4, 5, 6, 8, 9, 10, 12.

[59]   The various codes are available at http://www.humanrightsprofessionals.org/index. php?option=com_content&task=view&id=51&Itemid=106.

Concluding Remarks

It is common within professional environments to encounter scepticism about formal ethical standards and procedures. One source of such scepticism is a perception that codifying ethical norms does little to enhance ethical conduct on the ground. Another related source of scepticism is mistrust of the competence and integrity of ethics experts and implementing agencies. In effect, formalised ethics is suspected of functioning as a mere substitute for genuine ethical practice, and moreover one that lends itself to being co-opted for ulterior purposes.

In response to concerns of this nature, it must be freely acknowledged that no ethics code will supply a ready solution to the many concrete ambiguities and difficulties attending professional conduct in highly charged and complicated situations. Nor can the fact of instituting a formal framework of professional ethics substitute the need for HRFOs to individually assume responsibility for their conduct. Indeed, the sense of personal ethical commitment and pride in one's professional integrity is an invaluable resource in any professional context that can never be replaced by external, formal norms and procedures. However, this does not justify disregarding such formal norms and procedures or dismissing their utility and validity. For HRFOs and other professionals to place such a high level of trust in their personal ethical integrity that they feel justified in dismissing the utility and validity of public accountability structures is at best an expression of naivety, at worst a denial of the real ethical problems attending professional conduct – which, incidentally, aside from being a slippery slope, is an attitude utterly incompatible with the promotion of a culture of human rights.

The real question is not whether to adopt formal ethical guidelines and review procedures but rather how to ensure their pertinence and relevance through a firm contextualisation in concrete field practice. What is fundamentally required, therefore, is a vibrant process of consultation among experienced professionals. This is needed both during an initial phase of norm-setting and institution-building and subsequently, when general ethical standards and procedures are to be operationalised in practice. It should be noted that what is envisaged here is not unlike the process of contextualisation and adaptation that is needed in order to ensure the local relevance of universal human rights norms.

The primary aim of this chapter has been to galvanise such a process of internal consultation within the emerging community of human rights professionals and professional organisations. Any specific normative prescriptions contained in the chapter are only provisional – provisional not because the author is uncertain about the proposed scheme of analysis but rather because it is offered as a framework of interpretation that remains to be 'filled in' based on concrete experience. This can only be accomplished in a meaningful way by practicing members of the profession. Only thus can a would-be formal code of ethical conduct come to serve as a source of identification, pride and true guidance for human rights professionals.

Chapter 5

The Deployment of Human Rights Field Operations: Policy, Politics and Practice

Daniel Moeckli and Manfred Nowak[1]

Introduction

Different international and regional organisations have established presences that are covered by the term 'human rights field operation' – as defined in chapter 1 of the present volume – in various parts of the world. These presences differ widely in numerous important respects, including with regard to the selection of the host countries, the size of the operations, their operational structures and their mandates. In places such as Bosnia and Herzegovina or Kosovo, a plethora of international and regional organisations have set up substantial operations that carry out a wide array of human rights-related activities. The same organisations have deployed only very small human rights field missions, often consisting of a handful of officers and with very limited mandates, to other war-torn countries such as Liberia or Sri Lanka. In still other regions affected by armed conflict, including Chechnya and Northern Ireland, no form of international human rights presence has ever been established. The purpose of this chapter is to shed some light on this inconsistent, selective deployment policy and the reasons behind it as well as to explore the fundamental problems it poses.

The first section of the chapter gives an overview of the different forms and types of human rights field operations that the various parts of the United Nations (UN), as well as several regional organisations, normally deploy. As just stated, there are considerable inconsistencies in the deployment practice of these organisations, and the second section sets out the most important of them. The third section demonstrates that these inconsistencies are caused by numerous factors influencing the deployment decision, and which are not necessarily related to the actual needs on the ground. The fourth section argues that extreme forms of inconsistency between different human rights field operations raise – both from a legal and a 'strategic' point of view – fundamental concerns. The concluding section points to possible ways of achieving a more coherent deployment policy.

---

[1] The authors are grateful to James Green for his valuable research assistance.

The Different Forms of Deployment

The leading organisation in the deployment of human rights field operations is clearly the UN, which established its first such mission in 1991, followed by numerous other, often widely varying, types of human rights field presences. Several regional organisations have, however, also set up substantial field missions carrying out important human rights-related functions.

United Nations

Although human rights-related field operations deployed by the UN may take many different forms, a main distinction can be drawn between, on the one hand, human rights components of peacekeeping or political missions (directed by the respective departments based in New York) and, on the other, presences established under the auspices of the Office of the United Nations High Commissioner for Human Rights (OHCHR) (based in Geneva).

Human Rights Components of Peace Operations (New York-led)   UN peace operations are normally established under the authority of the Security Council, which, accordingly, will usually also broadly define the human rights-related functions of these operations. In theory, the General Assembly also has the power to create peace missions, including human rights components, but it has used this power only sparingly. Responsibilities concerning the executive direction and command of peacekeeping forces are commonly delegated to the secretary-general who will, at times, also instigate an operation himself. The actual management of peace operations is carried out by the United Nations Department of Political Affairs (DPA) and the Department of Peacekeeping Operations (DPKO), which often cooperate with OHCHR as far as human rights-related issues are concerned.

The first UN human rights field presences were established within the context of so-called second-generation or multidimensional peace operations, i.e. operations that were assigned, in addition to the traditional monitoring of ceasefires, various peacebuilding tasks, but which were still based on the principles of consent of the conflicting parties and the non-use of force. The very first UN mission with an explicit human rights component was the UN Observer Mission in El Salvador (ONUSAL), set up by the Security Council in 1991 to verify implementation of the San José Agreement, including the human rights commitments contained therein.[2] Further early UN operations with human rights components include those established by

---

[2]   Security Council resolution 693 (1991), UN Doc. S/RES/693 (1991). See D. García-Sayán, 'The Experience of ONUSAL in El Salvador' in A. Henkin (ed.), *Honoring Human Rights and Keeping the Peace – Lessons from El Salvador, Cambodia, and Haiti* (Washington, DC: Aspen Institute, 1995), pp. 31–56; R. Brody, 'The United Nations and Human Rights in El Salvador's "Negotiated Revolution"', *Harvard Human Rights Journal* vol. 8 (1995), 153–178.

the Security Council in Cambodia (UNTAC, 1992)[3] and by the General Assembly in Haiti (MICIVIH, 1993)[4] and Guatemala (MINUGUA, 1994).[5] The purely civilian mission in Haiti was the first operation whose principal function was the protection and promotion of human rights, and was unique in being a joint mission between the UN and a regional organisation, the Organization of American States (OAS). Following the example of these first human rights-related missions, later multidimensional peace operations of the UN have regularly incorporated human rights components.

Human rights presences have also been included within a number of so-called third-generation peace operations, i.e. operations that are not based on the consent of the parties to the conflict but on the Security Council's Chapter VII powers and are thus authorised to take enforcement action. One of the first such operations, UN Operation in Somalia II (UNOSOM II), included a small human rights unit,[6] as did the later UN Mission in Sierra Leone (UNAMSIL).[7] In other instances of peace enforcement, notably the UN Protection Force (UNPROFOR) in the former Yugoslavia and UN Assistance Mission for Rwanda (UNAMIR), human rights functions were, on the other hand, entrusted to entities operating independently from the peacekeeping forces.[8]

Human rights functions are also an important part of fourth-generation peace operations or international transitional administrations. The UN Transitional Administration in Eastern Slavonia, Baranja and Western Sirmium (UNTAES), established by the Security Council in 1996 following an agreement between the Croatian government and the local Croatian Serb authorities, was explicitly mandated with monitoring the parties' compliance with 'the highest standards of human rights and fundamental freedoms',[9] and a dedicated human rights unit was created for this

---

[3]   See Security Council resolution 745 (1992), UN Doc. S/RES/745 (1992). See D. McNamara, 'UN Human Rights Activities in Cambodia: An Evaluation' in *Honoring Human Rights and Keeping the Peace*, pp. 57–81; B. Adams, 'UN Human Rights Work in Cambodia: Efforts to Preserve the Jewel in the Peacekeeping Crown' in A. Henkin (ed.), *Honoring Human Rights – From Peace to Justice: Recommendations to the International Community* (Washington, DC: Aspen Institute, 1998), pp. 189–226.

[4]   See I. Martin, 'Paper versus Steel: The First Phase of the International Civilian Mission in Haiti' in *Honoring Human Rights and Keeping the Peace*, pp. 83–127; W. G. O'Neill, 'Human Rights Monitoring vs. Political Expediency: The Experience of the OAS/U.N. Mission in Haiti', *Harvard Human Rights Journal* vol. 8 (1995), 101–128.

[5]   General Assembly resolution 48/267 (1994), UN Doc. A/RES/48/267 (1994). See L. Franco and J. Kotler, 'Combining Institution Building and Human Rights Verification in Guatemala: The Challenge of Buying In Without Selling Out' in *Honoring Human Rights – From Peace to Justice*, pp. 39–70.

[6]   A. Clapham and M. Henry, 'Peacekeeping and Human Rights in Africa and Europe' in *Honoring Human Rights – From Peace to Justice*, p. 149.

[7]   M. O'Flaherty, 'Sierra Leone's Peace Process: The Role of the Human Rights Community', *Human Rights Quarterly* vol. 26, no. 1 (2004), 29–62.

[8]   Primarily to the Centre for Human Rights, see the following section.

[9]   See Security Council resolution 1037 (1996), UN Doc. S/RES/1037 (1996). See M. Katayanagi, *Human Rights Functions of United Nations Peacekeeping Operations* (The

purpose. Similarly, the UN Interim Administration Mission in Kosovo (UNMIK), set up in 1999, was given as one of its main responsibilities the protection and promotion of human rights;[10] the Organization for Security and Co-operation in Europe (OSCE) has assumed the lead role in the implementation of this responsibility. In contrast, the Security Council resolution establishing the UN Transitional Administration in East Timor (UNTAET),[11] passed only a few months after the comparable resolution establishing UNMIK, did not include an explicit general human rights mandate.[12] Nevertheless, human rights standards were embedded in all of UNTAET's activities,[13] and a specialised human rights unit was set up.

Some of the more recent UN peace missions have adopted a new management model, put forward in the 'Report of the Panel on United Nations Peace Operations' ('Brahimi Report'),[14] of subsuming the whole range of different actors engaged in the country concerned within an overall strategic framework. Although OHCHR participates in the design of such 'integrated missions', these do not necessarily include a specific human rights monitoring unit. Rather, the human rights-related functions are 'mainstreamed', i.e. the mission must ensure that all its activities integrate the promotion and protection of human rights. The model operation applying such an integrated approach is the UN Assistance Mission in Afghanistan (UNAMA). Similar recent peace operations, such as those in Iraq (UNAMI) and Sudan (UNMIS), on the other hand, do include dedicated human rights sections.[15]

OHCHR field operations and offices (Geneva-led)   Since 1993, the UN's human rights component in Geneva (then called Centre for Human Rights) has also become increasingly active in setting up field presences, often at the urging of the UN Commission on Human Rights. These Geneva-led initiatives may take a number of different forms, including the deployment of standalone field missions with monitoring functions, the setting up of technical cooperation presences, the insertion of human rights advisers in UN country teams and the establishment of regional offices.

Geneva-led field operations are normally based on a memorandum of understanding (MOU) signed with the government concerned and/or in keeping with resolutions of the Commission on Human Rights. Typically, they have a 'mixed mandate' to both

---

Hague: Martinus Nijhoff, 2002), pp. 191–193.

[10]   See Security Council resolution 1244 (1999), UN Doc. S/RES/1244 (1999); UNMIK Regulation No. 1999/24, 12 December 1999. See W. G. O'Neill, *Kosovo: An Unfinished Peace* (Boulder: Lynne Rienner, 2001).

[11]   See chapter 14 by P. Burgess in the present volume for a detailed discussion of this mission.

[12]   See Security Council resolution 1272 (1999), UN Doc. S/RES/1272 (1999).

[13]   See UNTAET Regulation No. 1999/1.

[14]   Report of the Panel on United Nations Peace Operations, UN Doc. A/55/305-S/2000/809 (2000).

[15]   On UNAMI see http://www.uniraq.org/aboutus/HR.asp and on UNMIS see http://www.unmis.org/english/humanrights.htm.

monitor the human rights situation and provide technical assistance. The origins of this kind of operation can be traced back to 1993, when the Centre for Human Rights deployed a number of human rights field officers to the former Yugoslavia to support the work of the Commission's special rapporteur for that region.[16] In the following year, in response to the genocide in Rwanda, the Commission mandated a special rapporteur on Rwanda and requested the high commissioner to support him with a field presence.[17] The resulting Human Rights Field Operation in Rwanda (HRFOR) was the first large human rights field operation responsible to the Geneva-based human rights system rather than the departments in New York, operating independently from the parallel peacekeeping operation (UNAMIR) and comprising more than 100 field officers.[18] Thereafter, missions whose mandate included the monitoring of the human rights situation were deployed to numerous further countries. At the time of writing, OHCHR has such standalone field operations in Bosnia and Herzegovina, Burundi, Cambodia, Colombia, the Democratic Republic of Congo, Serbia and Montenegro and, since 2005, in Guatemala, Nepal and Uganda.[19]

Over the past several years, OHCHR has also established technical cooperation presences in several countries. These presences have no explicit monitoring mandate, and the respective capacity-building projects are carried out at the request of the governments concerned. The earliest example of a technical cooperation presence is the office in Cambodia which, following UNTAC's withdrawal in 1993, was established at the request of the Commission on Human Rights;[20] this particular presence was later also assigned monitoring and protection functions. At present, OHCHR has staff posted in around 15 countries, including Mexico, the Occupied Palestinian Territories, Mongolia and Yemen, to help implement technical cooperation activities.[21]

In addition, OHCHR has, in recent years, started to deploy human rights experts to serve as advisers within UN country teams in countries such as Angola, Sri Lanka and, most recently, Togo.[22]

---

[16]   See M. Nowak, 'Lessons for the International Human Rights Regime from the Yugoslav Experience' in *Collected Courses of the Academy of European Law*, vol. VIII/2 (The Hague: Kluwer Law International, 2000), pp. 141–208; R. Wieruszewski, 'Case Study on the Former Yugoslavia: The International Mechanisms, Their Efficiency and Failures' in A. Bloed, L. Leicht, M. Nowak and A. Rosas (eds.), *Monitoring Human Rights in Europe: Comparing International Procedures and Mechanisms* (Dordrecht: Martinus Nijhoff, 1993), pp. 285–317.

[17]   See Commission on Human Rights, UN Doc. E/CN. 4/S-3/SR.2 (1994), at 76.

[18]   For assessments of this mission, see I. Martin, 'After Genocide: The UN Human Rights Field Operation in Rwanda' in *Honoring Human Rights – From Peace to Justice*, pp. 97–132; T. Howland, 'Mirage, Magic, or Mixed Bag? The United Nations High Commissioner for Human Rights' Field Operation in Rwanda', *Human Rights Quarterly* vol. 21, no. 1 (1999).

[19]   See the regularly updated field presences website of the OHCHR at http://www.ohchr. org/english/countries/field/index.htm.

[20]   Commission on Human Rights resolution 1993/6, UN Doc. E/CN.4/1993/6 (1993).

[21]   OHCHR, *Annual Appeal 2005*, pp. 33 and 67–68.

[22]   *Ibid.*, p. 33.

Finally, since it does not have the capacity to be present in all countries, OHCHR has opened seven regional and sub-regional offices (in Addis Ababa, Almaty, Bangkok, Beirut, Pretoria, Santiago and Yaoundé) which are responsible for a range of technical cooperation and promotional activities in their regions as well as for facilitating and encouraging the mainstreaming of human rights within the UN system.[23]

Regional Organisations

The two regional organisations that have been most active in the deployment of human rights field operations are OAS, which played a crucial role in the 1993 joint mission to Haiti, and, especially in more recent years, OSCE.[24]

OAS was the first organisation to establish a human rights field presence in Haiti, with a small team of human rights observers deployed in September 1992. From February 1993, this presence was integrated into the larger joint UN-OAS International Civilian Mission (MICIVIH), which was, as explained before, the first exclusively human rights-focused mission. OAS made a substantial contribution of around 100 field staff to this unique human rights operation.

Since the early 1990s, OSCE has started to establish long-term missions in the crisis regions of the Balkans, the Caucasus, Central Asia and the Baltic states, in some cases in close cooperation with the UN, the Commonwealth of Independent States (CIS) and other organisations.[25] Long-term missions, which often fulfil important human rights functions, are commonly deployed by the organisation's Permanent Council, with the consent of the host country. The size of OSCE presences varies considerably, ranging from small liaison offices in Central Asia to missions with several hundred officers in the Balkans. The organisation's longest-serving field operation is the Spillover Monitor Mission to Skopje,[26] originally established in 1992 to help prevent the tension in the former Yugoslavia from spreading to Macedonia. In Bosnia and Herzegovina, the OSCE presence, established under the Dayton Peace Accords of 1995,[27] has assumed the lead role among the numerous entities operating in that country in matters relating to the protection and promotion of human rights.[28]

---

[23]   *Ibid.*, p. 67.

[24]   On OSCE practice see chapter 18 by S. Ringgaard-Pedersen and A. Lyth in the present volume.

[25]   A. Rosas and T. Lahelma, 'OSCE Long-Term Missions' in M. Bothe, N. Ronzitti and A. Rosas (eds), *The OSCE in the Maintenance of Peace and Security: Conflict Prevention, Crisis Management and Peaceful Settlement of Disputes* (The Hague: Kluwer Law International, 1997), pp. 167–190.

[26]   See Articles of Understanding Concerning CSCE Spillover Monitor Mission to Skopje, at http://www.osce.org/documents/mms/1992/09/520_en.pdf.

[27]   See Agreement on Human Rights, Annex 6 to General Framework Agreement for Peace in Bosnia and Herzegovina, Attachment to UN Doc. A/50/790-S/1995/999 (1995).

[28]   M. O'Flaherty, 'International Human Rights Operations in Bosnia and Herzegovina' in M. O'Flaherty and G. Gisvold (eds), *Post-War Protection of Human Rights in Bosnia and*

The overall mission currently has approximately 800 staff members, of whom 150 work in the human rights department. Similarly, OSCE is the main organisation responsible for human rights and democratisation in Kosovo. Its mission there, set up in 1999, is OSCE's largest operation to date, with an overall staff of around 1300.[29] Other substantial OSCE missions with a human rights mandate exist in Croatia[30] and Serbia and Montenegro.[31] Its smaller field presences include offices in Albania, the Central Asian republics and the Caucasus, including a small human rights office in Abkhazia, Georgia, which is staffed jointly with the UN.[32]

The Council of Europe (CoE) has been operating a small field office in Sarajevo since 1996. Besides supporting CoE's efforts to contribute to the implementation of the human rights elements of the Dayton Agreement, this office who also tasked with assisting Bosnia and Herzegovina to meet the criteria for accession to the CoE.[33]

Numerous other regional organisations have established field presences that have important human rights aspects but not necessarily an explicit human rights mandate.

For example, the first peacekeeping operation undertaken by the African Union (AU), the African Mission in Burundi (AMIB, 2003), although not based on an express human rights mandate, did assume certain human rights-related functions in preparing the ground for national elections. Similarly, AU's recent mission to the Darfur region of Sudan (AMIS, 2004), established on the basis of the Humanitarian Ceasefire Agreement on the Darfur Conflict of April 2004, has taken over a number of human rights protection activities. In particular, its mandate includes not only monitoring compliance with the ceasefire agreement, but also assisting in the process of confidence building between the parties as well as contributing to a secure environment for the delivery of humanitarian relief and the return of displaced persons to their homes.[34] In contrast, the Economic Community of West African States (ECOWAS) has largely failed to integrate human rights protection into its field operations in Liberia (1990 and 2003), Sierra Leone (1998), Guinea Bissau

---

Herzegovina, (The Hague: Martinus Nijhoff, 1998), pp. 71–105; Nowak, 'Lessons for the International Human Rights Regime from the Yugoslav Experience', in *Collected Courses of the Academy of European Law*.

[29] Permanent Council Decision No. 305, OSCE Doc. PC.DEC/305 (1999).

[30] Permanent Council Decision No. 112, OSCE Doc. PC.DEC/112 (1996).

[31] Establishment of the OSCE Mission to the Federal Republic of Yugoslavia, Decision No. 401 of 11 January 2001 adopted by the Permanent Council of the Organization for Security and Co-operation in Europe, OSCE Doc. PC.DEC/401 (2001).

[32] For an overview, see the OSCE's field operations website at http://www.osce.org/about/13510.html.

[33] See the website of the office at http://www.coe.ba and M. Nowak, 'Is Bosnia and Herzegovina Ready For Membership in the Council of Europe?', *Human Rights Law Journal* vol. 20 (1999), 285.

[34] AU Peace and Security Council, Communiqué of the Seventeenth Meeting, 20 October 2004, AU Doc. PSC/PR/Comm. (XVII). For an overview of AMIS's activities, see African Union, 'Overview of AU's Efforts to Address the Conflict in the Darfur Region of the Sudan', 26 May 2005, AU Doc. CONF/PLG/2(I).

(1998) and Côte d'Ivoire (2002). On the contrary, ECOWAS forces themselves have been accused of human rights abuses.[35]

Peacekeeping forces deployed to Abkhazia, Georgia, by the CIS, in practice mostly dominated by Russian forces, cooperate closely with the human rights presence established there by UN and OSCE; the multinational peacekeeping force operating in the South Ossetian region of Georgia, in turn, is monitored by OSCE.

The European Union (EU), finally, is maintaining a mission with a wide-ranging monitoring mandate in the western Balkans (EU Monitoring Mission, EUMM),[36] a military operation in Bosnia and Herzegovina tasked with ensuring compliance with the Dayton Agreement (EU Force in Bosnia and Herzegovina, EUFOR),[37] as well as missions designed to establish policing arrangements according to the rule of law in Bosnia and Herzegovina (EUPM)[38] and the former Yugoslav Republic of Macedonia (EUPOL PROXIMA).[39] Most recently, in 2005, it launched an integrated rule of law mission for Iraq (EUJUST LEX), consisting of a training programme for judges, investigating magistrates, police and penitentiary officers.[40]

Inconsistencies in the Deployment Practice

As the short overview above demonstrates, different organisations – or different parts of the same organisation – have deployed widely divergent forms of human rights field operations to various parts of the world. Although some of the inconsistencies in the deployment of field missions can be explained with the different situations in the respective host countries, in many cases objective reasons are not readily apparent. This section points to the most important of these inconsistencies, relating to the selection of the countries where field presences have been established, the timing of the deployment, the size of the operations, their operational structure and their mandate.

The choice of the locations where human rights field operations have been sent to is clearly not always explicable with the gravity of the given situation. Whereas, as explained above, operations have been deployed to numerous countries affected by armed conflict, in other conflict or post-conflict situations with similarly high levels of human rights violations, an international field operation has never been

---

[35] See, for example, Human Rights Watch, *Waging War to Keep the Peace: The ECOMOG Intervention and Human Rights*, Human Rights Watch Report vol. 5, issue 6 (June 1993).

[36] Council Joint Action 2002/921/CFSP, 25 November 2002, L 321/51. The EUMM is a successor of the ECMM (European Community Monitoring Mission), which operated from 1999–2000.

[37] Council Joint Action 2004/570/CFSP, 12 July 2004, L 252/10 and Council Decision 2004/803/CFSP, 25 November 2004, L 353/21.

[38] Council Joint Action 2002/210/CFSP, 11 March 2002, L 70/1; EU Annual Report on Human Rights 2002, p. 40; EU Annual Report on Human Rights 2004, p. 39.

[39] Council Joint Action 2003/681/CFSP, 29 September 2003, L 249/66; EU Annual Report on Human Rights 2004, p. 39.

[40] Council Joint Action 2005/190/CFSP, 7 March 2005, L 62/37.

established. Probably the most obvious case in point is the Chechen Republic. Even though the armed conflict in Chechnya has been raging for years, with serious human rights abuses committed by both sides, there has never been, apart from the small and now closed OSCE Assistance Group to Chechnya, an international human rights field presence. Similarly, despite the decades-long conflict in Northern Ireland, an international field operation has never been established in that region.

Furthermore, there are significant differences as far as the timing of the deployment of human rights field operations is concerned. Only in very few cases have such missions been sent to crisis regions to prevent the outbreak of a full-scale armed conflict. OSCE's Spillover Monitor Mission to Skopje, its first mission to Kosovo in 1992 and the establishment of the OHCHR office in Burundi in 1995 belong to the rare examples of such 'preventive deployment'. More often, however, field operations have been deployed in situations where an armed conflict had already been going on for some time (for example in El Salvador and Cambodia), in many cases at a very late stage of the conflict in question (for example in the Darfur region of Sudan). Finally, a large number of human rights operations were only established once the most serious atrocities in a conflict had already been committed. Most notably, the OHCHR field operation in Rwanda (HRFOR) was only set up in August 1994 – four months after the genocide had been unleashed.

The discrepancies in the size of the various field presences established so far are equally striking. In some war-torn countries such as, for instance, Sri Lanka, the international human rights presence has been limited to a single human rights adviser placed on the UN country team. In stark contrast, in locations such as Bosnia and Herzegovina or Kosovo, a myriad of different entities have established (often very substantial) operations that carry out a range of human rights-related functions.[41] Even missions that fall within the same category of human rights field presence vary considerably in terms of their size, and it is often hard to detect objective reasons for these differences. Some of the UN peace missions, such as MICIVIH in Haiti with around 200 observers[42] and MINUGUA in Guatemala with up to 450 staff members,[43] included very strong human rights components. Other peace operations in countries affected by severe armed conflicts, such as the UN Observer Mission in Liberia (UNOMIL),[44] UNOSOM II in Somalia[45] or UNAMSIL in Sierra Leone,[46] however, had only very small human rights units, in the case of UNOMIL, for instance, consisting of three officers. Similarly, OHCHR's technical cooperation projects range from the substantial Cambodia office (which at one stage had a staff

---

[41]   See also Nowak, 'Lessons for the International Human Rights Regime from the Yugoslav Experience'.

[42]   Martin, 'Paper versus Steel' in *Honoring Human Rights – From Peace to Justice*, p. 91.

[43]   See Franco and Kotler, 'Combining Institution Building and Human Rights Verification in Guatemala', in *Honoring Human Rights – From Peace to Justice*, p. 46.

[44]   A. Clapham and F. Martin, 'Smaller Missions Bigger Problems' in *Honoring Human Rights – From Peace to Justice*, p. 136.

[45]   Clapham and Henry, 'Peacekeeping and Human Rights in Africa and Europe' in *Honoring Human Rights and Keeping the Peace*, p. 150.

[46]   O'Flaherty, 'Sierra Leone's Peace Process', 39.

of around 60)[47] and a web of 40 part-time experts and consultants in the Occupied Palestinian Territories to (now closed) one-person operations in Malawi and Liberia[48] and an envisaged two-person office in Somalia.[49] The same inconsistencies can be observed in the case of regional organisations. Some of OSCE's large field missions in the Balkans, for example, include human rights components with over 100 staff members, whereas its presence in the conflict region of Abkhazia, Georgia, is limited to a single officer.

As pointed out in the previous section, the organisational structure of field operations may take a variety of forms. In some countries, human rights field presences are integral parts of peace operations established by the Security Council or the General Assembly; in others, they have been deployed by OHCHR or regional organisations – in some cases (such as in Rwanda and Yugoslavia) alongside already existing UN peacekeeping operations. Human rights components of peace operations may be directed by either DPA (as in El Salvador or Guatemala) or DPKO (as in Cambodia or Sierra Leone), often in collaboration with OHCHR, while OHCHR manages its own field presences. Only rarely do these differences in the organisational arrangements of missions seem to reflect specific needs on the ground.

Finally, the mandates of field operations may vary widely with regard to the human rights guarantees they encompass, the functions the missions have to fulfil as well as the powers with which they are entrusted. Thus, the peace agreement underlying a given mission may not refer to human rights guarantees at all, as was the case in Liberia with the 1993 Cotonou Agreement.[50] In contrast, other peace agreements contain long and detailed lists of human rights standards, compliance with which is to be monitored by the international mission concerned; the 1995 Dayton Agreement, for example, includes a list of 16 international instruments whose guarantees the parties agree to ensure.[51] Even where human rights are explicitly referred to, however, not all standards are always afforded the same status. The mandate of MICIVIH, for example, was based on the International Covenant on Civil and Political Rights[52] and the American Convention on Human Rights,[53] with explicit priority given to 'the right to life, personal safety and security, freedom

---

[47]   Adams, 'UN Human Rights Work in Cambodia', in *Honoring Human Rights – From Peace to Justice*, p. 195.

[48]   Clapham and Martin, 'Smaller Missions Bigger Problems', in *Honoring Human Rights – From Peace to Justice*, p. 155..

[49]   OHCHR, *Annual Appeal 2005*, p. 72.

[50]   The agreement, signed by the three Liberian parties on 25 July 1993 is available at http://www.usip.org/library/pa/liberia/liberia_07251993.html. See also the corresponding Security Council resolution 866, UN Doc. S/RES/866 (1993).

[51]   General Framework Agreement for Peace in Bosnia and Herzegovina. On the application of these standards, see *Human Rights Chamber for Bosnia and Herzegovina; Digest: Decisions on Admissibility and Merits 1996-2002* (Kehl: Engel, 2003).

[52]   International Covenant on Civil and Political Rights, adopted 19 Dec. 1966, G.A. res. 2200 (XXI), UN GAOR, 21st Sess., Supp. No. 16, UN Doc. A/6316 (1966), 999 UNTS 171 (entered into force 23 Mar. 1976).

[53]   American Convention on Human Rights, 'Pact of San José, Costa Rica', adopted 22 Nov. 1969 OAS Treaty Series, no. 36 (entered into force 18 July 1978).

of expression and freedom of association';[54] despite the catastrophic economic and social situation in Haiti, no reference to economic and social rights was made. The aforementioned list of the Dayton Agreement, on the other hand, also includes instruments such as the International Covenant on Economic, Social and Cultural Rights[55] and the Convention on the Protection of the Rights of All Migrant Workers and Members of Their Families.[56]

As far as the functions of human rights presences are concerned, they may be defined very summarily, as in the original mandate of the OSCE Mission in Kosovo, which simply describes them as 'monitoring, protection and promotion of human rights.'[57] Or the mandate may be very broad and detailed, as in the case of HRFOR in Rwanda, which was tasked with investigating past human rights violations, monitoring the ongoing human rights situation, helping re-establish confidence and rebuild civic society, implementing programmes of technical cooperation and further functions.[58] Or it may, finally, be limited to tasks relating to a specific technical cooperation project.

The same holds true for the powers a mission is granted to carry out its mandate. In the case of El Salvador, for example, the San José Agreement contained a long and detailed list of ONUSAL's powers, including verifying the observance of human rights, receiving communications, visiting any place freely, interviewing any person freely, collecting information, using the media etc.[59] In Haiti, MICIVIH had equally substantial powers.[60] In contrast, in other cases, such as that of UNTAES in Croatia, the specific powers of the mission have not been spelled out at all.

These inconsistencies relating to different aspects of the deployment of international human rights field operations may ultimately result in variable levels of human rights protection afforded to different countries, which are unrelated to the gravity of the situation in these countries. As will be demonstrated later, this inconsistent deployment practice raises a number of fundamental concerns. First, however, the reasons for this incoherence need to be explored.

---

[54]   Terms of Reference for MICIVIH, reprinted in Martin, 'Paper versus Steel', in *Honoring Human Rights and Keeping the Peace*, p. 123.

[55]   International Covenant on Economic, Social and Cultural Rights, adopted 19 Dec. 1966, G.A. res. 2200 (XXI), UN GAOR, 21st Sess., Supp. No. 16, UN Doc. A/6316 (1966), 993 UNTS 3 (entered into force 3 Jan. 1976).

[56]   Convention on the Protection of the Rights of All Migrant Workers and Members of Their Families, adopted 18 Dec. 1990, G.A. res. 45/158, Supp. No. 49A (1990), UN GAOR, 45th Sess., UN Doc. A/RES/45/158 (1990) (entered into force 1 July 2003).

[57]   Permanent Council Decision No. 305, OSCE Doc. PC.DEC/305 (1999).

[58]   Martin, 'After Genocide' in *Honoring Human Rights – From Peace to Justice*, p. 101.

[59]   Agreement on Human Rights, Annex to UN Doc. A/44/971-S/21541 (1990), at 14.

[60]   See Terms of Reference for MICIVIH, Martin, 'Paper versus Steel', in *Honoring Human Rights and Keeping the Peace*, pp. 123–127.

Factors Influencing the Deployment

A complex web of different, often conflicting, interests of various actors influence the decision of international or regional organisations as to whether to establish a human rights field operation in any given country. Equally, where such a mission is in fact deployed, the timing of its deployment, its size and its mandate depend on numerous factors that do not necessarily relate to the requirements on the ground. These factors will obviously vary depending on the deploying entity and the concrete circumstances; this section tries to point to the most important generic elements influencing the deployment decision.

Human rights field operations of international or regional organisations are, like any intervention from outside, generally not welcomed by states; they are seen as an infringement of state sovereignty and as an acknowledgment of the occurrence of human rights violations within the country concerned. Yet at the same time, they depend – at least as long as they are not deployed within the context of a mission authorised by the Security Council under Chapter VII of the UN Charter – on the consent of the host state. As a consequence, the deployment of a field presence will often hinge on whether a given government can be pressured into accepting it and thus, ultimately, on the political strength of that state; a government might agree to a mission in order to prevent an official condemnation by the UN Commission on Human Rights or some other action by the international community or a group of states. Similarly, the exact terms of reference of a mission, normally laid down in a MOU negotiated between the deploying entity and the government concerned, will depend, among other factors, on that government's bargaining power. The matter is further complicated in situations of internal armed conflict where the mandate of a field operation will normally be based on a peace agreement between the different parties to the conflict. In this case, the level of human rights protection built into the agreement, as well as the functions and powers of the mission, can be shaped not only by the government in power but also by the other parties to the conflict.

It is thus crucial how much pressure outside actors are willing to bring to bear on a government (and, in the case of an internal armed conflict, on the other parties involved) to accept a human rights field operation and its terms. This, in turn, may depend on factors such as the prevailing international power relations, the geopolitical interests at stake and the political situation within powerful states that may exert such pressure. The deployment of the international civilian mission to Haiti, for example, was closely linked to a shift in United States policy after President Bill Clinton's election.[61] Also of importance is, of course, what the 'international community' actually perceives as a crisis situation and as the appropriate response to that situation. As shown in the recent Darfur crisis, this perception can change over time, and an international mission with a human rights mandate may be established only as a last resort. On the other hand, however, the deployment of a human rights field operation may also serve as a convenient alternative to other, more resolute, forms of action against states.

---

[61]   O'Neill, 'Human Rights Monitoring vs. Political Expediency', 104.

Where international political pressure to deploy a human rights field operation does exist, a further central issue is how this pressure is translated into action within the specific decision-making framework of an international or regional organisation. Neither the UN Security Council nor OHCHR nor the relevant bodies of regional organisations base their deployment decisions on a set of standardised criteria. Instead, they use an approach that is *ad hoc* in nature and thus highly susceptible to be influenced by political considerations of the day. The most politicised decision-making process is that of the Security Council, where any one of the veto powers can block, for whatever reason, the deployment of a mission. This explains the lack of a UN field mission in places such as Chechnya. Where the Security Council does set up a peace mission, the human rights dimensions of its mandate are determined through the same politicised process. In addition, the size of a possible human rights unit may hinge on the overall strength of the mission, which, in turn, may be contingent on the willingness of member states to contribute personnel. Yet also deployment decisions of OHCHR often depend, due to the required consent of the host state, on the generation of political pressure by other states in fora such as the Commission on Human Rights.

Political considerations may also be behind some of the differences in the operational structures of human rights field operations. For example, powerful states may prefer organisational arrangements whereby they can exert a certain degree of bilateral influence. This is one of the reasons why OSCE, rather than UN, was entrusted with central human rights functions in Bosnia and Herzegovina and Kosovo. OSCE, unlike the UN and other organisations, acts as a loose association of participating states and primarily relies on staff seconded by various governments. This kind of structure gives the larger participating states more leverage than operations with staff recruited directly through UN but is hardly conducive to the coherence of the field operation concerned.[62]

The availability of sufficient and stable funding for a human rights field operation, as well as the specific sources of that funding, is another crucial factor. In the case of the UN, human rights components of Security Council-mandated peace operations are funded through the special peacekeeping budgets, those mandated by the General Assembly through the regular UN budget, while funding for OHCHR missions comes either from its regular budget or voluntary contributions.[63] Funding through a peacekeeping budget obviously reinforces the dependency of any human rights mandate on the goodwill of the Security Council members, while funding through the regular UN budget means that operations may be affected by general budget constraints or cuts. Particularly problematic, however, is OHCHR's dependence on voluntary contributions to finance its operations, making a coherent long-term policy of deploying and planning missions difficult. This problem is compounded

---

[62] M. Nowak, *Introduction to the International Human Rights Regime* (Leiden: Martinus Nijhoff, 2003), p. 229.

[63] See I. Martin, 'A New Frontier: The Early Experience and Future of International Human Rights Field Operations', *Netherlands Quarterly of Human Rights* vol. 16, no. 2 (1998), 134.

by the fact that some donors earmark their contributions to specific projects,[64] which may lead to a situation whereby some operations rely on the backing from a small group of states. Ultimately, this may reinforce political selectivity in the deployment practice.

Finally, the pre-existing presence of other organisations or agencies on the ground may have a considerable influence on the deployment decision. The fact that certain intergovernmental or non-governmental organisations are already operating in a given region may create additional political pressure on other actors to also become involved. This may result in the concentration of activities in certain areas, leading to problems of coordination or even inter-agency tensions.

To sum up, decisions to deploy a human rights field operation are influenced by numerous elements that are not necessarily related to the actual needs on the ground; dependence on these different factors results in the inconsistencies listed in the previous section. As the following section demonstrates, these inconsistencies in the deployment practice are problematic for several reasons.

Problems Raised by Inconsistencies in Deployment

Human rights field operations are, to a certain degree, always *ad hoc* enterprises: they must inevitably be tailored to the specific actual requirements on the ground as well as the wider political context. There will only ever be a realistic prospect for the establishment of a human rights field operation if different political factors are taken into account, and it would be naïve to believe that such operations can somehow operate outside of the given power structures. From this perspective, it is nothing but normal that many operations have little in common. Nevertheless, extreme forms of inconsistency between different international field operations that cannot be explained by the different situations in the respective host countries do raise fundamental concerns, firstly, from a legal point of view and, secondly, from a 'strategic' point of view.

From a legal point of view, such inconsistencies may be problematic if they imply a failure on the part of international or regional organisations to provide, in certain cases, a minimum level of human rights protection. That *states* are bound by a positive obligation to ensure respect for human rights in all situations, and thus to take reasonable steps to prevent, and respond to, human rights violations, is part of the established jurisprudence of the major international human rights bodies.[65] The case is more difficult to make for international or regional organisations, since

---

[64]   See OHCHR, *Annual Appeal 2005*, p. 18.

[65]   See in particular Inter-American Court of Human Rights, *Velasquez Rodriguez* case, judgment of 29 July 1988, Inter-Am.Ct.H.R. (Ser. C) No. 4 (1988); for the UN Human Rights Committee, see, for example, General Comment No. 31, paras 6–8; General Comment No. 6; *Delgado Paéz v. Colombia*, Communication No. 195/1985, UN Doc. CCPR/C/39/D/195/1985 (1985), esp. at 5.5–5.6; for the European Court of Human Rights, see, for instance, *Osman v. United Kingdom* EHRR vol. 29 (1998), 245.

they are generally not parties to any of the human rights treaties. Nevertheless, a number of reasons support the position that intergovernmental organisations also must comply with international human rights standards.[66] First of all, it seems clear that intergovernmental organisations with an international legal personality, such as the UN, are at least bound by those elements of human rights law that have become part of customary international law.[67] An even more far-reaching obligation of intergovernmental organisations to also respect the wider and more detailed standards contained in the leading human rights instruments can be based on the following grounds. First, it can be argued that the member states of an intergovernmental organisation delegate their responsibilities under international human rights law to the organisation. Second, the constitutional roots of international organisations are in international law, and it would, therefore, be illogical if superiority over international law could be pleaded on their behalf. Third, abstention of international organisations from becoming parties to international human rights treaties cannot be interpreted as a desire not to be bound, since they are generally not accepted as parties to multilateral treaties. And fourth, the inherent nature of human rights implies that they are automatically part of the legal framework applicable to those with power to affect their enjoyment, including intergovernmental organisations.[68]

In the specific case of the UN, an additional argument can be adduced: the UN's constituent legal instrument, the Charter,[69] explicitly provides, in its Articles 1(3) and 55, that one of the organisation's purposes is the promotion and protection of human rights; the content of these provisions has been reinforced by the practice of both the member states and the UN's organs, suggesting that the UN is accountable for human rights.[70] Importantly, although the Charter is generally predicated on a large amount of discretion for the Security Council, especially when acting under Chapter VII, even this organ is expressly bound by Article 24 of the Charter to act in accordance with the purposes of the UN, including human rights.

Thus, there is a strong case that international and regional organisations are subject to international human rights standards and are, therefore, bound not only to respect but also to ensure respect for these standards. As a consequence, they

---

[66]   For a comprehensive discussion of the question as to the applicability of international law to international organisations, see, for example, H. G. Schermers and N. M. Blokker, *International Institutional Law: Unity within Diversity*, 4th edn (Leiden, Martinus Nijhoff, 2003), §§1572–1581; for the specific case of international human rights law, see, for example, K. Kenny, 'UN Accountability for its Human Rights Impact: Implementation Through Participation', in N. D. White and D. Klaasen (eds), *The UN, Human Rights and Post-conflict Situations* (Manchester: Manchester University Press, 2005), pp. 438–462.

[67]   See Schermers and Blokker, *International Institutional Law: Unity within Diversity*, §1579; P. Sands and P. Klein, *Bowett's Law of International Institutions*, 5th edn (London: Sweet & Maxwell, 2001), §14–037.

[68]   Schermers and Blokker, *International Institutional Law: Unity within Diversity*, §1574; Kenny, 'UN Accountability for its Human Rights Impact', pp. 440–441.

[69]   Charter of the United Nations, entered into force 24 October 1945.

[70]   Kenny, 'UN Accountability for its Human Rights Impact', pp. 441–446.

must take, in all their activities, including in the planning of field operations,[71] human rights guarantees into account and ensure at least a minimum level of human rights protection in all situations. From this perspective, it is deeply problematic if an organisation such as the UN fails to include a specific and strong human rights mandate or a robust human rights component in some of its peace operations; this is all the more true if the same organisation has proved in other situations that it has, in fact, the capabilities to do so. Finally, it is worth noting that in extreme cases of human rights abuses, such as genocide or crimes against humanity, the positive obligation to ensure respect for human rights might even be seen as implying a responsibility on the part of the UN, more specifically the Security Council, to authorise *military* intervention as a last resort: The International Commission on Intervention and State Sovereignty and, more recently, both the High-level Panel on Threats, Challenges and Change and the UN secretary-general have endorsed what they have described as an 'emerging norm that there is a collective responsibility to protect', exercisable by the Security Council.[72] In sum, inconsistencies in the deployment practice of international or regional organisations may be contrary to their obligations under human rights law if they imply a failure on their part to take reasonable steps to ensure a minimum level of human rights protection in all situations.

In addition to these legal problems, inconsistencies in the deployment of human rights field operations that are not based on objective reasons relating to the needs on the ground also raise fundamental concerns from a 'strategic' point of view. First of all, it is crucial for the success of any field operation that it is seen as legitimate by all actors involved, both those at the international level and those in the host country, including the conflicting parties and civil society. This legitimacy, in turn, depends to a large extent on a consistent overall deployment practice: The perception that human rights field operations are established according to double standards may seriously affect their credibility. Second, experience shows that, in order to be effective, human rights field operations must be grounded in clear and realistic mandates.[73] Yet such mandates can only be developed within the framework of a broader political strategy on the part of the international community that is consistent and transparent. Third, an incoherent deployment policy makes the systematic evaluation and constant improvement of field operations difficult, if not impossible. Deploying organisations can only develop performance indicators, lessons learned, best practices, overarching methodologies and system-wide training

---

[71]   That an obligation to ensure respect for human rights exists already at the planning stage has been established, for example, by the European Court of Human Rights in *McCann v. United Kingdom*, EHRR vol. 21 (1995), 97.

[72]   Report of the International Commission on Intervention and State Sovereignty, *The Responsibility to Protect*, (Ottawa: International Development Research Centre, 2001); Report of the High-level Panel on Threats, Challenges and Change, A More Secure World: Our Shared Responsibility, UN Doc. A/59/565, (2004); Report of the Secretary-General, In Larger Freedom: Towards Development, Security and Human Rights for All, UN Doc. A/59/2005 (2005).

[73]   For peace operations in general, see Brahimi Report, at 56–64.

approaches and, more generally, build up a relevant institutional memory if they operate according to transparent and consistent principles.

Conclusion

Fifteen years after the establishment of the first human rights field mission, as various international and regional organisations have acquired wide experience with different forms of operations, there is no longer a reason to rely on hasty *ad hoc* arrangements for their deployment. Rather, as demonstrated in the previous section, several reasons necessitate a more coherent policy on the deployment of human rights field presences.

The need to address existing inconsistencies is, in fact, now being increasingly acknowledged by important deploying entities. Within the UN, the advent of the concept of 'mainstreaming' human rights, including in the organisation's peace and security activities, is clear evidence of this development.[74] Similarly, the UN has recognised that there is a need for better coordination between the different bodies involved in decisions concerning the deployment of field missions. Accordingly, OHCHR and DPKO concluded in 1999 a MOU to strengthen their cooperation,[75] and the Security Council now increasingly invites the high commissioner to brief it on peace and security matters.[76] Finally, the recent proposal of the High-level Panel on Threats, Challenges and Change, endorsed by the secretary-general, to create an intergovernmental Peacebuilding Commission, as well as a Peacebuilding Support Office within the Secretariat, can be seen as a further attempt to achieve more consistency in the establishment of peace missions: as the secretary-general has pointed out, such a commission could encourage coherent decision-making on peacebuilding by member states and the different parts of the UN[77] as well as contribute to regularising best practice.[78]

All these recent developments represent important and encouraging steps towards a more coherent deployment policy within the UN. Yet, as the secretary-general has

---

[74]   See for example the Brahimi report, which highlights 'the essential importance of the United Nations system adhering to and promoting international human rights instruments and standards and international humanitarian law in all aspects of its peace and security activities', *ibid.*, at 1. At the field level, this is reflected by the recent trend towards integrated missions. See E. B. Eide, A. T. Kaspersen, R. Kent, K. Von Hippel, *Report on Integrated Missions: Practical Perspectives and Recommendations*, Independent Study for the Expanded UN ECHA Core Group, (May 2005).

[75]   Memorandum of Understanding between the OHCHR and the DPKO, 5 November 1999, available at http://www.unhchr.ch/html/menu2/4/mou_dpko.htm.

[76]   Report of the Secretary-General, In Larger Freedom: Towards Development, Security and Human Rights for All, at 144.

[77]   Report of the Secretary-General, In Larger Freedom: Towards Development, Security and Human Rights for All: Addendum: Peacebuilding Commission, UN Doc. A/59/2005/Add.2 (2005), at 6.

[78]   *Ibid.*, at 19.

also made clear, even more concrete action is needed to improve coordination and cooperation in this field, for example the increased involvement of OHCHR in the decision-making processes of the Security Council and of the proposed Peacebuilding Commission.[79] A further possibility of 'mainstreaming' the relevant decision-making processes of deploying entities such as the UN would be the elaboration of a set of objective and transparent criteria as a basis for all deployment decisions. The adoption of such guidelines would go a long way towards ensuring that human rights field missions are deployed according to the actual needs on the ground rather than political short-term considerations.

Finally, the replacement of the Commission on Human Rights with the Human Rights Council presents an opportunity for an even more far-reaching reform of the current deployment processes and policies. As the Human Rights Council is a standing body, able to meet regularly and at any time,[80] it should be able to react quickly to imminent crises; this – coupled, of course, with its human rights expertise – may make it a suitable entity to be involved in the deployment of human rights field missions. Thus, the transfer of main responsibilities concerning the establishment and guidance of human rights field missions to the Human Rights Council could constitute an important contribution to the urgently required development of a more coherent deployment policy.

---

[79]   Report of the Secretary-General, In Larger Freedom: Towards Development, Security and Human Rights for All, at 144 and 146.

[80]   See General Assembly resolution 60/25/, UN.Doc A/RES/60/25/ (2006) and Report of the Secretary-General, In Larger Freedom: Towards Development, Security and Human Rights for All: Addendum: Human Rights Council, UN Doc. A/59/2005/Add.1, (2005), at 4.

Chapter 6

The Human Rights Field Operation in Partnership for Peace

Bertrand G. Ramcharan

Introduction

Increasing emphasis is being placed on human rights protection in the field. We are, the plea goes, 'failing the victims of war'.[1] The protection needs in conflicts are indeed formidable. The challenge is a basic but difficult one: we must do our utmost to protect non-combatants: civilians, children, women, the elderly as well as act to help ameliorate unnecessary suffering on the part of combatants.

The International Committee of the Red Cross has sought to uphold the principle of humanity and other principles of international humanitarian law for a century and a half now. Other humanitarian and human rights organisations have also sought to contribute to the quest for protection.[2] More recently, the United Nations (UN) high commissioner for human rights has joined the efforts to help protect the victims of conflict.[3]

The chapters in the present volume are dedicated to methods of protection in the field. The present author has also explored this terrain in a volume assembled on human rights protection in the field.[4] The present chapter is concerned with the role of human rights field operations in conflict prevention, peace negotiations, peace implementation and peace consolidation. The outlines of this topic were traced by this author in a set of principles worked out as chair of a Task Force for the UN Executive Committee on Peace and Security and endorsed by the Executive Committee in November, 1998. The reader's attention is drawn to the principles worked out on the role of human rights generally in conflict prevention, peacemaking, peacekeeping and peacebuilding, which are reproduced at the end of this chapter. The focus of the chapter is on the role, specifically, of human rights field operations. It is based on the

---

[1]   See M. O'Flaherty, 'We Are Failing the Victims of War', in B. G. Ramcharan (ed.), *Human Rights Protection in the Field*, International Studies in Human Rights vol. 87 (Leiden: Martinus Nijhoff, 2006), pp. 41–57.

[2]   See for example chapter 13 by L. Mahony in the present volume.

[3]   See on this, B. G. Ramcharan, 'The UN High Commissioner for Human Rights and International Humanitarian Law', Occasional Paper Series No. 3, Program on Humanitarian Policy and Conflict Research, Harvard University (Spring 2005).

[4]   Ramcharan (ed.), *Human Rights Protection in the Field*.

experiences of the author with conflict prevention, peacemaking and peacekeeping, and on contacts with human rights field operations when serving in the Office of United Nations High Commissioner for Human Rights (OHCHR).

The Prevention of Conflicts and Gross Violations of Human Rights

That there is a preventive role for human rights field operations is undeniable. The present author has outlined elsewhere, based on their practice, the preventive roles of human rights field operations in Bosnia, Cambodia, and Colombia.[5] We are concerned here, however, more with conflict prevention as such. The questions that arise for consideration are: what is there in practice that might give us some leads in the future when it comes to the role of human rights field operations in the prevention of conflicts? And what are the policy objectives that should guide the human rights movement in the future? We shall take these two questions together as they are closely connected.

In a recent work, the present author reviewed the role of human rights in risk analysis and set out a list of human rights questions that need to be taken into account in making an analysis of the risks of conflict in any particular situation. The central argument was that human rights concerns must be at the heart of risk analysis.[6] Janelle Diller, in a work for the Minnesota Advocates for Human Rights, focused on the role that human rights organisations can play in conflict prevention.[7] We must here narrow this down to the specific role that human rights field operations can play in this context.

Attention is drawn to the dispatch of UN observers to watch over mass action by the African National Congress (ANC) in South Africa in 1992.[8] That was definitely a case of international observers being called upon to play a role in the prevention of conflict. Briefly stated, President F.W. de Klerk and ANC leader Nelson Mandela feared that the ANC-led campaign throughout South Africa to demonstrate their support among the South African people could provoke reactions on the part of the supporters of other parties. They requested then Secretary-General Boutros Boutros-Ghali to send UN observers to monitor the mass action campaign.[9] Ten UN officers were sent on a few days notice and helped contain the situation by their presence.[10]

---

[5]   See B. G. Ramcharan, The Protection Methods of Human Rights Field Offices, in Ramcharan (ed.), *Human Rights Protection in the Field*, chapter 9.

[6]   See B. G. Ramcharan, 'The Human Rights Dimension: Human Rights and Risk Analysis' in B. G. Ramcharan (ed.), *Conflict Prevention in Practice: Essays in Honour of James Sutterlin* (Leiden: Martinus Nijhoff, 2005), chapter 17.

[7]   On file with present author.

[8]   Report of the Secretary-General on the Question of South Africa, UN Doc. S/24389 (1992).

[9]   *Ibid.*, at 61.

[10]   See Security Council resolution 772 (1992), UN Doc. S/RES/772 (1992); See also B. G. Ramcharan, 'Internal Conflict Prevention: Observing Mass Action in South Africa

They were followed by a UN observation mission that monitored the situation in the country for the next two years in the run up to, and during, the historic elections that led to the independence of South Africa.[11]

In these two instances, observers were sent by the UN secretary-general. Today, however, they could also have been sent by the UN high commissioner for human rights, the Organization for Security and Co-operation in Europe (OSCE) high commissioner on national minorities,[12] or by an organisation such as the Carter Center.[13] This raises a fundamental policy question: how can one arrange to have human rights observers in preventive mode in more situations? When one is speaking of the role of human rights field operations the most important thing must surely be to use them to prevent conflicts and gross violations of human rights. As a matter of logic and of policy, the emphasis needs to be on prevention. How might this be achieved?

Some years ago, the late Prince Saddrudin Aga Khan, the former UN High commissioner for refugees, launched the idea of the establishment of a corps of humanitarian observers.[14] There is much discussion these days about the idea of establishing a rapid reaction force. The human rights movement must explore a human rights variant of this idea: the establishment of a corps of human rights observers.

This leads us to the question: what is there to date in the experience of human rights field operations that might help us take forward the concepts of risk assessment or the preventive deployment of human rights observers or peacekeepers? We discuss each of these in turn.

Risk Assessment by Human Rights Field Operations

If a field operation could assess and detect the risks in time, this might allow the possibility of preventive action to head off those risks, to the extent possible. One could advance the argument that every human rights field operation should, at the inception of its operations, engage in a comprehensive risk assessment of potential gross violations of human rights that might be prevented or whose prevention might help prevent the eruption or escalation of conflict.

The prevention of genocide, war crimes or crimes against humanity would require particular attention since these are international crimes under the statute of

---

(1992)', in *Conflict Prevention in Practice*, chapter 9.

[11]   See A. King, 'Internal Conflict Prevention: The UN Observer Mission to South Africa (UNOMSA) 1992', in *Conflict Prevention in Practice*, chapter 10.

[12]   For more on the OSCE high commissioner for minority's work in this area see http://www.osce.org/hcnm/13023.html.

[13]   See http://cartercenter.org/peaceprograms/program10.htm, see also L. Mahony, 'Unarmed Monitoring and Human Rights Field Presence: Civilian Protection and Conflict Prevention', *The Journal of Humanitarian Assistance* (2003), at http://www.jha.ac/articles/a122.htm.

[14]   Sadruddin Aga Khan, United Nations Study on Human Rights and Mass Exodus, UN Doc. E/CN.4/1503 (1981).

the International Criminal Court.[15] The secretary-general of the UN has established the position of special adviser on the prevention of genocide and there have been recent calls for intensified cooperation between this office-holder and OHCHR.[16] It would seem elementary that where there is cause for concern, a human rights field operation, through the high commissioner, should be in close touch with the office of the special adviser.

Where warranted, time and attention should be devoted to the preparation of a careful assessment of the risks, which might even be published if this would be appropriate in the circumstances. This brings to mind the assessment of the human rights experience of Mexico done at the invitation of the government of that country. A field operation of OHCHR did a comprehensive analysis of the historical and current dimensions of human rights in Mexico and proceeded to make valuable recommendations on strategies for the future protection of human rights. It emphasised the protection of indigenous peoples and strengthening the role of the courts in the protection of human rights. Based on the recommendations of this study, which were accepted by the Mexican government, a plan of action is currently under implementation for the strengthening of human rights in Mexico.[17] This was truly an innovative role for a human rights field operation.

Fact-finding

Fact-finding by a human rights field operation and the rapid publication of its report can have an important role in prevention.[18] The fact-finding reports done by the human rights component of the UN peacekeeping operations in the Democratic Republic of the Congo, together with the human rights field operation of OHCHR provide good examples[19] of such operations even if their preventive effect, in the situation prevailing in that country, might have been less than desirable. Stated summarily, in the face of evidence of massacres on different occasions, these field operations mounted investigations that led to the production of extensive reports documenting criminal violations of human rights by members of armed forces engaged in combat in different parts of the country.[20] The present author had occasion to present some

---

[15]   Rome Statute of the International Criminal Court, UN Doc. A/Conf.183/9 (1998) UNTS 90 (entered into force 1 July 2002).

[16]   See Commission on Human Rights, Summary Record of the 45th Meeting, UN Doc. E/CN.4/2005/SR.45 (2005), at 78.

[17]   See http://mexico.ohchr.org/.

[18]   See B. G. Ramcharan (ed.), *International Law and Fact-Finding in the Field of Human Rights*, International Studies in Human Rights vol. 2 (Leiden: Martinus Nijhoff, 1982).

[19]   See, for example, Third Special Report of the Secretary-General on the United Nations Organization Mission in the Democratic Republic of the Congo, UN Doc. S/2004/650 (2004), at Annex I.

[20]   *Ibid.*

of these reports to the Security Council when performing the functions of UN acting high commissioner for human rights.[21]

Preventive Deployment of Observers

The very *raison d'être* of a human rights field operation is to have a preventive influence on the situation in question. There may, however, be occasions in which the mounting of an *ad hoc* observer presence is called for, going beyond what was envisaged at the time of the establishment of the operation with a view to heading off gross violations of human rights or the outbreak, eruption or resumption of conflict due to underlying human rights root causes. It is in situations such as these that a corps of readily available human rights or humanitarian observers might be helpful. There are governmental and non-governmental programmes dedicated to training such observers so that they might be in readiness if called upon. The Swiss government has an annual training programme[22] and the Canadian non-governmental organisation, CANADEM,[23] also maintains a roster of trained personnel who might be called upon at short notice.

Preventive Deployment of Peacekeepers

Situations may arise in which the preventive deployment of observers would not be enough and it might be necessary to deploy peacekeepers to head off gross violations of human rights. This is not an easy proposition, since a lot would depend on the availability of peacekeepers, the assessment of the force commander on the ground, the assessment of the Department of Peacekeeping Operations (DPKO), and the attitudes of members of the Security Council.

We are here interested, however, in the role of the human rights field operation in question. Its responsibility in a situation where it considers the preventive deployment of peacekeepers warranted would include: providing its assessment to the head of mission and the high commissioner and, with the support of the high commissioner, pressing for the deployment of peacekeepers in the situation concerned. Time is of the essence in such situations and all concerned would need to act with the utmost dispatch.

Peace Negotiations

Moving from the sphere of conflict prevention to the sphere of peace negotiations, the question that presents itself for examination is how human rights field operations

---

[21]   See, B. G. Ramcharan, *A UN High Commissioner in Defence of Human Rights: No License to Kill or Torture* (Leiden: Martinus Nijhoff, 2005).

[22]   The 'Swiss Expert Pool for Civilian Peacekeeping' and its training programme are described further at http://www.eda.admin.ch/sub_expool/e/home/train.html.

[23]   See http://www.canadem.ca/.

might contribute to the efforts of peacemakers. One could approach this question in different contexts: first, there is a conflict, peace negotiators are designated, and they urge the deployment of human rights field officers to help them assess the facts on the ground that might assist the peace mediators in their tasks of negotiating a settlement to the conflict. Or it might be decided to establish a human rights field operation to monitor the situation of human rights while peacemaking goes on. Or it might be decided as part of the overall peace process to deploy human rights field officers to document atrocities with a view to the prosecution of alleged perpetrators. Or human rights components of UN peace operations might be functioning in theatres of concern to peacemakers, likewise for standalone field operations of OHCHR. We take each of these contexts in turn.

Human Rights Field Operations in the Peacemaking Phase

Many times, peace negotiators have to work with parties who present different versions of the facts on the ground, particularly with regard to conflict lines or the human rights or humanitarian situation. In the Yugoslav peace negotiations, the co-chairmen of the International Conference on the Former Yugoslavia decided on different occasions to deploy on the ground specially-trained staff who could interact with the parties and help the negotiators assess the situation on the ground.[24] This was a delicate matter, involving personnel with the requisite security training. At the same time, the Office of the United Nations High Commissioner for Refugees (UNHCR) had staff on the ground in different trouble spots and their reports were invaluable in allowing the peace negotiators to understand what was happening when it came to issues of human rights. UN Civilian Police already deployed as part of the UN Protection Force (UNPROFOR) provided, throughout, invaluable information, including on massacres such as that which took place in the Medak Pocket.[25]

Sometimes, the monitoring of sanctions might be the issue. The International Conference on the Former Yugoslavia established and ran an International Monitoring Mission that lasted nearly three years and had, at one stage, some 500 personnel.[26] The issue was one of human rights because sanctions had been imposed by Serbia on the Bosnian Serbs and their implementation was crucial to getting the Bosnian Serbs to give up their brutal practices of targeting civilians deliberately.[27]

---

[24] See B. G. Ramcharan (ed.), *The International Conference on the Former Yugoslavia*, Official Papers, 2 vols (Leiden: Martinus Nijhoff, 1997).

[25] See, for example, Report of the Secretary-General to the Security Council Pursuant to Security Council Resolution 871 (1993), UN Doc. S/26828 (1993), at 14.

[26] See Office of the High Representative and EU Special Representative, *1st Report of the High Representative for Implementation of the Bosnian Peace Agreement to the Secretary-General of the United Nations*, 14 March 1996, at http://www.ohr.int/other-doc/hr-reports/default.asp?content_id=3661#1.0.

[27] Note the periodic reports of the Special Rapporteur of the Commission on Human Rights on the Situation of Human Rights in the Territory of the Former Yugoslavia, Tadeusz Mazowiecki, UN Docs E/CN.4/1992/S-1/9 (1992); E/CN.4/1992/S-1/10 (1992); A/47/666-

How the UN/European Union (EU) negotiators, Thorvald Stoltenberg and Lord Owen came to establish what become known as the 'ICFY Mission' that monitored sanctions against the Bosnian Serbs is relatively unknown but holds many lessons for the future deployment of monitors by peacemakers.[28] The background was that the Bosnian Serb leadership had peeled itself off from the leadership in Belgrade when it came to the negotiation of a settlement of the conflict in Bosnia and Herzegovina. In the process, the Bosnian Serb military was behaving more and more in a criminal manner, leading countries of the North Atlantic Treaty Organization (NATO) alliance to threaten Belgrade with bombing raids unless it brought the Bosnian Serb leadership to book.[29]

Under pressure from NATO countries, Slobodan Milošević, then president of the Federal Republic of Yugoslavia, instituted economic sanctions against the Bosnian Serbs: fuel and goods would no longer be permitted to move from Serbia across the Drina River to Bosnian Serb territory.[30] This did not satisfy the NATO leadership. They called for international monitoring of the sanctions. President Milošević (and probably the Serbian people) was not prepared to countenance the idea of international monitors on Serbian territory.

Thorvald Stoltenberg and Lord Owen met President Milošević frequently to explore the options for peace and to help defuse dangerous situations. The year was 1993 and the international community was still in quest of peaceful solutions to the conflicts in the former Yugoslavia.[31] During a meeting with Thorvald Stoltenberg and Lord Owen, which the present author attended, President Milošević intimated that he would look favourably upon the deployment of humanitarian personnel, by humanitarian organisations, to witness the implementation of sanctions against the Bosnian Serbs across the Drina River.

This was a faint opening. That very evening, Thorvald Stoltenberg, a former foreign minister of Norway, called his friends, the foreign ministers of Denmark,

---

S/24809 (1992); E/CN.4/1993/50 (1993); E/CN.4/1994/3 (1993); E/CN.4/1994/4 (1993); E/CN.4/1994/6 (1993); E/CN.4/1994/8 (1993); E/CN.4/1994/47 (1993); E/CN.4/1994/110 (1994); E/CN.4/1995/4 (1994); E/CN.4/1995/10 (1994); A/49/641-S/1994/1252 (1994); E/CN.4/1995/54 (1994); E/CN.4/1995/57 (1995); E/CN.4/1996/3 (1995); E/CN.4/1996/6 (1995).

[28] See B. Boutros-Ghali, Letter dated 19 September 1994 from the Secretary-General addressed to the President of the Security Council, UN Doc. S/1994/1074 (1994).

[29] See S. L. Burg and P. S. Shoup *The War in Bosnia Herzegovina: Ethnic Conflict and International Intervention* (London: M. E. Sharpe, 2000) pp. 287–291, and NATO, 'Bringing Peace and Stability to the Balkans', NATO Briefing, (February 2005), p. 6, at http://www.nato.int/docu/briefing/balkans-e.pdf.

[30] S. P. Ramet, *Balkan Babel: The Disintegration of Yugoslavia from the Death of Tito to Ethnic War*, 2nd edn (Boulder: Westview, 1996), p. 250; see also Government of Norway, Ministry of Foreign Affairs, 'Norway and the Conflict in the former Yugoslavia' (1995), available at http://odin.dep.no/odin/english/p30008168/foreign/032005-990438/dok-bn.html.

[31] See S. L. Woodward, *Balkan Tragedy: Chaos and Dissolution after the Cold War* (Washington, DC: Brookings, 1995), pp. 273–332.

Finland, Norway and Sweden, with a request: would they consider providing, each, ten humanitarian personnel from humanitarian organisations and give a start-up contribution of $100,000 for a humanitarian operation to witness the sanctions on the Drina? They all replied positively, either on the spot, or within 24 hours.[32]

As director of the International Conference on the Former Yugoslavia, the present author worked personally on the establishment of this mission and watched over its operations substantively and managerially during its existence.[33] It was an extraordinary effort on the part of all involved and it shows what can be achieved with a sense of daring and innovation: two Norwegian humanitarian operatives came from Oslo with DM100,000 in a suitcase and proceeded to Belgrade. There they secured office space in a hotel, began to acquire a fleet of vehicles, purchased fuel on the black-market in Belgrade and laid the ground-work for an operation that would last three years and at one stage would have dozens of international monitors on the ground and hundreds of locals supporting them.

Stoltenberg and Owen designated Brigadier-General Bo Pellnas as head of the mission and he was later succeeded by Finnish General Tauno Nieminen. Both served the international community with great distinction. The mission was financed through contributions from a coalition of countries participating in the International Conference on the Former Yugoslavia. Stoltenberg and Owen insisted from the outset on flexibility for the mission. The UN director of administration in Geneva was dead set against this and it fell to the present author to set up a system, audited by Price Waterhouse, as it then was, outside of the UN framework. Price Waterhouse audited the mission regularly to ensure that it was above board in all respects, issuing several audit reports certifying the financial soundness of the mission administration.

The task of the mission, in this instance, was to monitor the application of sanctions imposed by Belgrade against Pale and it did this professionally. The precedent, however, is one that could be used, as needed, on specifically human rights tasks where required. The ICFY Mission showed that the mediators, on their own authority, could establish and operate for a period of three years a mission of hundreds of personnel, operating in a framework of accountability outside of the UN administrative rigidity, and render credible reports to the negotiators and the international community. The precedent is one that offers much to peace negotiators wishing to establish or use *ad hoc* international human rights field operations in situations of concern.

Peacemakers Moved by Considerations of Justice

The second scenario we might consider is if peace negotiators decide to establish a human rights monitoring operation in the midst of a conflict because justice and human rights imperatives demand it. Such a case occurred in the course of peacemaking in the former Yugoslavia.

---

[32]   Government of Norway, 'Norway and the Conflict in the former Yugoslavia'.

[33]   See Ramcharan (ed.), *The International Conference on the Former Yugoslavia*.

While Cyrus Vance and Lord Owen, and later Thorvald Stoltenberg and Lord Owen were leading the negotiations to try to bring peace to the former Yugoslavia, beginning in September 1992, wrenching reports continued to be received of gross violations of human rights, particularly by Bosnian Serbs and Croats against Bosnian Muslims (Bosniacs).[34] The Special Rapporteur of the UN Commission on Human Rights, Tadeusz Mazowiecki, led the efforts to document and expose these violations.[35] He was a man of conscience and he did his utmost to bring to the attention of the international community the need for stronger action to protect the human rights of the Bosniacs. In the end he would resign in protest against the failure of the international community to take stronger action.

The international negotiators, Vance and Owen, were, without a doubt, pained by the atrocities being reported and they repeatedly sought to use their influence on Radovan Karadzic and President Milošević, and also on President Tudjman, to stop the violations. This did not have much effect. The violations continued.

Vance and Owen, and then Stoltenberg and Owen, considered that the way to bring the violations to an end would be to negotiate a peace agreement and their energy was focused on this goal, above all. All three did their utmost to advance the human rights agenda but they never pressed this to the point of breaking off the negotiations. Vance personally led the search for justice for the victims of the massacres at Vukovar hospital; Stoltenberg, who doubled for a year as negotiator and special representative of the secretary-general (SRSG) in charge of all peacekeeping troops in the former Yugoslavia, provided the troops that guarded the mass-grave site at Ovčara near Vukovar, where the victims of the hospital massacre were buried, and Owen led the quest for the UN Human Rights Committee to call for reports from all the successor republics in the former Yugoslavia and for the establishment of processes within the Council of Europe to deal with human rights issues in the former Yugoslavia.[36]

On top of all of this, the Vance–Owen peace proposals, and later those of Stoltenberg–Owen, contained some of the most extensive human rights provisions of any peace agreements to date. It was these proposals that were built upon at Dayton in the human rights provisions of the Dayton Peace Agreement.[37] The present author

---

[34]   See, for example, Letter dated 13 August 1992 from the Chairman of the forty-fourth session of the Sub-Commission on Prevention of Discrimination and Protection of Minorities addressed to the Chairman of the Commission on Human Rights UN Doc. E/CN.4/Sub.2/1992/52 (1992), at 2.

[35]   See footnote 27 in the present chapter for the special rapporteur's reports.

[36]   See M. O'Flaherty, 'Treaty bodies responding to states of emergency: The case of Bosnia and Herzegovina', in P. Alston and J. Crawford (eds), *Treaty Bodies Responding to Emergencies* (Cambridge: Cambridge University Press, 2000), pp. 439–460.

[37]   See General Framework Agreement for Peace in Bosnia and Herzegovina, Attachment to UN Doc. A/50/790-S/1995/999 (1995). For a discussion of the human rights implications of the Dayton Peace Accords see W. Benedek, H. Alefsen, M. O'Flaherty and E. Sarajlija (eds), *Human Rights in Bosnia and Herzegovina after Dayton: From Theory to Practice* (Dordrecht: Martinus Nijhoff, 1996); M. O'Flaherty and G. Gisvold (eds), *Post War Protection of Human Rights in Bosnia and Herzegovina* (The Hague: Martinus Nijhoff, 1998); Z. Pajic,

was involved in the process of passing over to the organisers of the Dayton peace conference the key papers on human rights and related issues.[38]

This is written as a matter of historical record but it cannot be claimed that enough was done to defend human rights in the situation prevailing at the time. This is a matter for historians to reflect upon.[39] What we are particularly interested in here is the idea advanced by Vance and Owen, as part of the Vance–Owen peace plan, to establish an international human rights operation even as the peace negotiations proceeded. This was part of the Vance–Owen plan and it was continued and embellished in the Stoltenberg–Owen plans. How did we reach this idea?

As the reports of the atrocities continued to reach Vance and Owen in the autumn of 1992, the present author felt obliged to advise them that it was important that they be seen to be addressing the issue of human rights head on. Otherwise, they would come under sharp criticism from the human rights community. Heeding advice, Vance and Owen, in one of their reports to the Security Council, included an annex on the human rights contribution of the negotiators.[40]

At the request of Vance and Owen, the present author organised in New York, in the spring of 1993, a meeting of the leaders of several human rights non-governmental organizations (NGOs) to discuss the idea of the establishment of an international human rights monitoring mission in Bosnia and Herzegovina. We discussed with them the idea of human rights monitoring in the midst of a conflict. The participants in this meeting were split – there were those who strongly advocated the establishment of a monitoring mission, and there were those who equally strongly argued that it could not be done.

Notwithstanding the fact that the participants at the meeting were evenly divided on the idea, we went forward with it and included in the peace plan blueprints for the establishment of an international human rights monitoring mission and the designation of ombudspersons in Bosnia and Herzegovina. The blueprint provided for the establishment of a human rights monitoring mission headed by a human rights personality of renown. It also provided for the appointment of an ombudsperson for each of the three 'peoples' of Bosnia and Herzegovina.[41]

At one stage, when we thought that implementation of the idea for the establishment of an international human rights monitoring mission could go forward even as progress stalled on the conclusion of a peace agreement, the present author

---

'A Critical Appraisal of Human Rights Provisions of the Dayton Constitution of Bosnia and Herzegovina', *Human Rights Quarterly* vol. 20, no. 1 (1998), 125; and J. Sloan, 'The Dayton Peace Agreement: Human Rights Guarantees and their Implementation', *European Journal of International Law* vol. 7 (1996), 207.

[38]   See Ramcharan (ed.), *The International Conference on the Former Yugoslavia.*

[39]   See, in particular, Anonymous, 'Human Rights in Peace Negotiations', *Human Rights Quarterly* vol. 18, no. 2 (1996), 249–258; and reply by F. D. Gaer, 'UN-Anonymous: Reflections on Human Rights in Peace Negotiations', *Human Rights Quarterly* vol. 19, no. 1 (1997), 1–8.

[40]   See also Report of the Secretary General on the International Conference on the Former Yugoslavia, UN Doc. S/24795 (1992), at 63–66.

[41]   See B. Boutros-Ghali, Letter dated 6 August 1993 from the Secretary-General addressed to the President of the Security Council, UN Doc. S/26260 (1993), at Annex D.

approached on behalf of Stoltenberg and Owen a leading western international human rights lawyer now serving as a judge on the International Court of Justice to head the mission. He, gracious as always, was keen to accept, but was undergoing medical treatment and had to decline.

In the end, the Stoltenberg–Owen peace efforts were taken over by those of the 'Contact Group'[42] established by the United States and steered by Richard Holbrook and it fell to the Dayton peace conference to work out human rights proposals to be implemented following the conclusion of the Dayton peace accords. These included placing on the ground a large stabilisation force and the establishment of a Human Rights Chamber the majority of whose judges came from abroad. The prosecutor of the International Criminal Tribunal for the Former Yugoslavia would also become involved in investigating and following up on allegations of genocide, war crimes and crimes against humanity.[43]

Even though it did not materialise in the end, the blueprint for an international human rights monitoring mission, in the midst of a conflict, was an important precedent that could be considered by peacemakers, as appropriate, in future situations elsewhere.

Gathering Information about International Crimes alongside Peacemaking Efforts

The third scenario we need to consider is one in which, while peace negotiations are underway, it is decided to establish a fact-finding field mission to document allegations of war crimes and crimes against humanity. Again, the former Yugoslavia provides an example.

The decision to establish a Commission of Experts to gather information on possible international crimes being committed in the conflicts in the former Yugoslavia was taken by the UN Security Council.[44] It had the full support of Vance and Owen from the very beginning. Although some accounts insinuate otherwise, these accounts are unfounded and unfortunate.

Shortly after the members of the Commission assembled in Geneva, Vance requested the present author to arrange a meeting with the chairman, Professor Fritz Kalshoven of the Netherlands. It was a cordial meeting during which Vance raised with Kalshoven his determination to do everything he could to support investigations into the massacre that had taken place at Vukovar hospital.

When reports came in of a mass grave site at Ovčara, near Vukovar, Vance requested contact with Physicians for Human Rights for them to do a forensic

---

[42]   Woodward, *Balkan Tragedy*, pp. 314–315.
[43]   See Security Council resolution 808 (1993), UN Doc. S/RES/808 (1993); and Report of the Secretary-General Pursuant to Paragraph 2 of Security Council Resolution 808, UN Doc. S/25704 (1993), at 85.
[44]   See Security Council resolution 780 (1992), UN Doc. S/RES/780 (1992).

examination of the site.[45] This was coordinated by the present author, using the good offices of a friend in a human rights NGO, who facilitated the contacts. In order for Physicians for Human Rights to proceed with the forensic examination they needed the imprimatur of the Commission of Experts. Again Professor Kalshoven was contacted who readily agreed that Physicians for Human Rights could act under the auspices of the Commission of Experts. Vance had also written to Special Rapporteur Mazowiecki asking him to give his auspices to the forensic investigation.

This is how the first forensic examination of a mass grave site in the former Yugoslavia began. It stemmed from a direct initiative from the UN peace negotiator, Cyrus Vance. By the time the examination actually got under way Vance had moved on and been succeeded by Thorvald Stoltenberg. After the Vance–Owen plan was signed by the parties in Athens in April 1993, Secretary-General Boutros Boutros-Ghali designated Stoltenberg as special representative in charge of all UN operations in the former Yugoslavia. Boutros-Ghali thought that the implementation stage had been reached but, unfortunately, within a week of signing the accords in Athens, the Bosnian Serbs repudiated their signature and Stoltenberg went on, for a year, to double as special representative and as negotiator.

As special representative, Stoltenberg was in charge of the peacekeeping troops, the largest force ever assembled in the history of the UN. The present author doubled as director of the International Conference of the Former Yugoslavia and as director of the Office of the Special Representative.[46] The latter capacity permitted continued involvement in efforts regarding the mass grave site at Ovčara, as well as in efforts to get the peacekeeping troops to play a role on human rights issues.

The examination of the mass-grave site at Ovčara required painstaking work over several months. After the site had been opened up it was important to guard it so as to maintain its integrity and to prevent it from being tampered with. At Stoltenberg's request, the present author contacted the UN force commander to ask him to provide troops to guard the site. This he did. As the forensic examination proceeded, it would require the emplacement of troops at the site over several months. In the circumstances prevailing at the time, with the pressures on the troops, it took the direct involvement of Stoltenberg to secure that the troops would stay to guard the site.[47]

This was, admittedly, a situation in which the roles of peacemaker had been combined with that of peacekeeper and Stoltenberg therefore had considerable leverage on the force. It does bear out, however, that the direct involvement of the peacemaker can, and in this instance did, play an important role in furthering

---

[45]   For an account of the work of Physicians for Human Rights, see 'Testimony of Eric Stover, Executive Director, Physicians for Human Rights, January 25, 1993, before the U.S. Commission on Security and Cooperation in Europe', available at http://www.phrusa.org/research/forensics/bosnia/forwar.html.

[46]   See Ramcharan (ed.), *The International Conference on the Former Yugoslavia*.

[47]   See Physicians for Human Rights, 'Testimony of Eric Stover'.

the process of gathering information into possible international crimes committed during a conflict.

Stoltenberg, the negotiator and special representative, also played a decisive part in bringing about a human rights role for UN peacekeepers in the midst of a conflict – the first time this had ever been done in-conflict. How this came about is a story little known.

Professor Torkel Opsahl, a member of the Commission of Experts gathering information into possible crimes in the former Yugoslavia, was a fellow Norwegian and a good friend of Stoltenberg. He had served brilliantly as a member of the European Commission on Human Rights. The present author had been fortunate to have him as director of studies when participating in the Research Centre of The Hague Academy of International Law, and we had done a UN mission together to visit prisoner of war camps in Iran and Iraq during the war between those two countries.

Opsahl, a man of principle, was outraged by the atrocities being committed in the former Yugoslavia and he conveyed his views forcefully to Stoltenberg. When Stoltenberg became the special representative in charge of the forces, he requested the present author, as director of his office, to look into what might be done by the peacekeepers on the human rights front.

It will be remembered that the force had been established initially as a protection force and carried the name UNPROFOR.[48] The concept envisaged that it would be placed around the Serb enclaves in Croatia with the idea that there would be protection through presence. The main role in human rights-related issues was played by the Civilian Police (CIVPOL) but this was, again, largely a role of protection through presence.[49] In neither instance was it an active protection role.

The UN peacekeeping doctrine at the time did not envisage an active human rights protection role for UN peacekeepers and DPKO was far from having made the intellectual or policy leap into the notion that peacekeeping troops could play a role on human rights matters.[50] The cable traffic in the early days of the force bear this out and shall be re-visited on another occasion.

This prevailing culture came out very much in the present author's meetings with the force commander, deputy force commander and other senior peacekeeping personnel when we met to discuss the issue of a human rights role for the peacekeepers. The first meeting was in May 1993, with the deputy force commander and other senior leaders at the force headquarters in Zagreb. It was a cooperative and constructive meeting. The deputy force commander explained that peacekeeping forces had never been called upon to gather information and report on atrocities

---

[48] UN Doc. S/23620 (1992).

[49] See Report of the Secretary-General Pursuant to Security Council Resolution 721 (1991),UN Doc. S/23280 (1991), at Annex III.

[50] This came in 2000, with publication of the 'Brahimi Report'; see also Report of the Secretary General on the Protection of Civilians in Armed Conflict, UN Doc. S/2001/331 (2000).

committed by the parties among whom they were stationed. If it became known that they were doing this it would make their relations with the parties on the ground difficult. Moreover, across the former Yugoslavia, the force, though cumulatively large, was thinly distributed on the ground.

The present author, in turn, explained that we were dealing with a situation that had not arisen before. The forces were on the ground and serious violations of human rights were taking place in their midst. Members of the international community were harsh in their criticism and the situation we were in was untenable. We had to be seen as attentive to the human rights issues involved.

The deputy force commander was a gentleman and he clearly absorbed the arguments even though he maintained his position for the time being. The present author sought to make the case for the forces to at least report on what they were aware of, confidentially, understanding the discomfort of the peacekeeping leaders over the idea that they might report on violations and that this would become known to the parties on the ground. They were thinking about the fact that they had to operate among the parties and they were, at the end of the day, vulnerable, being so thinly spread out. Nevertheless, the case for reporting was pressed at least.

The leaders clearly showed goodwill. They reflected on the discussions. In the end there was a softening of their position on reporting, even if there was not an immediate change. After Yasushi Akashi took over as special representative following Stoltenberg's request to Boutros-Ghali that he be relieved of the position so that he could concentrate on the negotiations,[51] a unit was established in the Office of the Special Representative of the Secretary-General to gather information on violations of human rights and to report thereon to the special representative.[52] Thus it was that the first human rights component was established in a UN peacekeeping force operating prior to the conclusion of a peace agreement. It was a small step, but an important one. It began with the insistence of a peacemaker-peacekeeper, Thorvald Stoltenberg.

Admittedly, here also, the peacemaker was in a strong position because he doubled as special representative and therefore had considerably more leverage. But there are ways for the peacemaker to exert influence on people of goodwill in charge of peacekeeping forces. A peace negotiator who comes to the conclusion that there is need for human rights monitoring on the ground, even while peace negotiations are carried on, can and should exert such influence.

Peace Implementation

In the peace implementation phase, the blueprint for peace has hopefully been traced. Sometimes, it may require further elaboration on matters of details. A human rights field operation can have a vital role to play on what we would consider human

---

[51]   See B. Boutros-Ghali, Letter dated 1 January 1993 from the Secretary-General addressed to the President of the Security Council, UN Doc. S/26838 (1993).

[52]   See Report of the Secretary-General Pursuant to Resolution 908 (1994), UN Doc. S/1994/1067 (1994), at 21 and 49.

rights pressure points in either scenario. Let us take the situation in Côte d'Ivoire into consideration. In December 2002, the present author undertook a field mission to this war-torn country and submitted a report, through the secretary-general, to the Security Council.[53] As could be seen from that report, there were, and remain, several human rights pressure points in that situation that called for urgent attention.[54] A human rights field operation could contribute in a major way to addressing these pressure points.

In the first place, there was the issue of hate propaganda through the print and electronic media.[55] While this lasted, the chances for peace were slender. A human rights field operation could make this an urgent issue to be addressed in the peace process. Then there was the issue of the rights of expatriates who had lived for a long time in the country, as well as the rights of their children, for example with regard to the right to own land and to vote.[56] Côte d'Ivoire required urgent intercession on these pre-eminently human rights issues. A human rights field operation could make a crucial contribution to the search for peace. Thirdly, it was the present author's assessment that the establishment of a national human rights commission could help take the country forward on the basis of human rights principles. The establishment of a national commission had been dragging on for a long time. A human rights field operation could make this a key priority issue, working out a blueprint with the parties and helping to launch the commission.

Besides these pressure point issues, there are the classical issues that call for the attention of a field operation, such as human rights monitoring, promotion and protection. These are the topics of different chapters of the present volume and we shall not go into them here.[57] The concept of human rights pressure points is the one that is the most crucial when it comes to the role of a human rights field operation in peace implementation. Related to this is the issue of human rights reporting. It is essential that a human rights field operation provide regular, objective reports, on the human rights situation on the ground so that organs such as the Security Council can put pressure on the parties to abide by their obligations under the peace agreement.

Peace Consolidation

Finally, there is the issue of peace consolidation. In this phase, human rights field operations, while continuing to have human rights pressure points in view, must be endeavouring to help the country put down the foundations for an effective national human rights protection system. This requires attention to the integration of

---

[53] Re-printed in Ramcharan, *A UN High Commissioner in Defence of Human Rights*, pp. 374–395.

[54] See the report by Human Rights Watch, *Trapped between Two Wars: Violence against Civilians in Western Côte d'Ivoire*, Human Rights Watch Report vol. 15, no. 14(A) (August 2003).

[55] *Ibid.*, 12–14.

[56] *Ibid.*, 6–7.

[57] For an overview, see chapter 1 by M. O'Flaherty in the present volume.

international human rights norms in the constitutional and legislative provisions, the role of the courts in the application of human rights norms, human rights education, monitoring the situation of vulnerable groups and the establishment and operation of national human rights institutions, such as a national human rights commission.

Where a human rights field operation chooses to place the emphasis might vary from country to country. In the nature of things, it might require considerable time and resources to address all these issues. It must be important to place emphasis on the role of the courts, the role of a national human rights commission and human rights education. These are huge challenges, even for peace-time governments.

In Afghanistan, following the Bonn Agreement,[58] OHCHR rightly placed emphasis on the establishment and operation of a national human rights commission.[59] A human rights adviser to the special representative of the secretary-general also placed emphasis on the role of the national commission. OHCHR also sought to provide advice and assistance in the drafting of the human rights provisions of the constitution.[60]

In Iraq, OHCHR also sought to provide assistance on the human rights provisions of the constitution and to the Human Rights Ministry,[61] while having in its sights the establishment of a national commission on human rights. As the then acting high commissioner for human rights the present author met with the Iraqi Minister of Human Rights and did whatever could be done to support the establishment of a national human rights commission. It must be said that difficulties had to be overcome with the leadership of the Executive Office of the Secretary-General, who advised taking a hands-off position on relations with the ministry. The present author, however, chose to use personal judgment. Whatever political considerations there were, it must have been wise to provide advice and assistance on the establishment of a national human rights commission. The present author also called for such a commission in the special report issued on the situation of human rights in Iraq in June 2004.[62]

---

[58]   See Agreement on Provisional Arrangements in Afghanistan Pending Re-establishment of Permanent Government Institutions', UN Doc. S/2001/1154 (2001).

[59]   See the report by the Special Rapporteur on the Situation of Human Rights in Afghanistan, Kamal Hossain, UN Doc. E/CN.4/2002/43 (2002), at 47. For a brief historical overview see http://www.unama-afg.org/about/_hr/Human_Rights.htm.

[60]   OHCHR's work in Afghanistan is outlined at http://www.ohchr.org/english/countries/af/index.htm.

[61]   See the *Aide Mémoire* reprinted in Ramcharan, *A UN High Commissioner in Defence of Human Rights*, pp. 109–113.

[62]   B. G. Ramcharan, Report of the United Nations High Commissioner for Human Rights and Follow up to the World Conference on Human Rights: The Present Situation of Human Rights in Iraq, UN Doc. E/CN.4/2005/4 (2004), at 155–159.

Conclusion

To conclude this chapter, we would recapitulate the following policy recommendations.

At its outset, a human rights field operation should undertake a comprehensive risk assessment of potential situations of gross violations of human rights or the eruption of conflict and share these with the special representative of the secretary-general, the high commissioner for human rights, and if applicable, the special adviser on the prevention of genocide.

The human rights field operation should be ready to undertake, or arrange for, fact-finding missions into situations of concern. It should also have in its sights the possible need for the dispatch of *ad hoc* teams of observers or peacekeepers for preventive purposes.

If a human rights field operation is in existence as peacemaking operations are carried out, it should, through the high commissioner for human rights, provide to the peacemakers its assessment of human rights issues that it considers the peacemakers should pay particular attention to. This can be of great assistance to the peacemakers and help foster attitudes on their part that are more understanding and supportive of human rights concerns.

A human rights field operation, operational in the peacekeeping phase should make its assessments and recommendations available to the special representative of the secretary-general and the force commander on an ongoing basis, particularly as regards the risks of outbreaks of gross violations of human rights, recommendations about how they may be prevented, and, where called for, recommendations for the rapid dispatch of *ad hoc* human rights observers or peacekeepers.

At the peace consolidation phase, a human rights field operation, while keeping in mind the various considerations previously adduced, should have in its sights constantly, the emplacement and enhancement in the country of an adequate and effective national protection system.

In conclusion, we reproduce below the 'Principles for the Integration of Human Rights into United Nations Activities for Conflict Prevention, Peacemaking, Peacekeeping and Peacebuilding' drawn up by a Task Force of the Executive Committee on Peace and Security which the present author chaired in 1998. These *Principles* were endorsed by the Executive Committee in November 1998. It would be timely to re-visit them and to see how they relate to the evolving activities of human rights field operations and to what extent, indeed, those human rights field operations are living up to the principles!

Principles for the Integration of Human Rights into United Nations Activities for Conflict Prevention, Peacemaking, Peacekeeping and Peacebuilding[63]

(Endorsed by the Executive Committee on Peace and Security)

---

[63]   Copy on file with present author.

I. Conflict Prevention

It is important for the conflict prevention activities of the UN that human rights concerns figure in the analyses of situations and that coordinated preventive action be undertaken on the basis of the shared analysis, as human rights violations are often part of the underlying causes of a crisis and often reflect structural deficiencies, and gross and systematic human rights abuses are usually indicators of emerging situations. With this in mind, systematic exchange of relevant and timely information becomes essential.

The Department of Political Affairs, in presenting analyses to the Secretary-General in respect of issues or situations requiring preventive action, should invite the contribution of the OHCHR in preparing such analyses and should incorporate recommendations of the High Commissioner in submissions to the Secretary-General or the Security Council. The OHCHR should, whenever it considers it advisable, bring to the attention of DPA issues or situations for consideration about possible preventive action by the Secretary-General or the Security Council.

The OHCHR has an important role to play in conflict prevention by offering human rights technical assistance and cooperation, or sending human rights monitors, observers, or advisers.

II. Peacemaking

The promotion and respect for human rights are core components of peace negotiations and peacemaking exercises. To this end, every effort should be made to promote the integration of human rights in peace negotiations and agreements.

OHCHR, in cooperation with DPA, should develop materials and capacity that could be drawn upon by peace negotiators in drafting human rights provisions of peace agreements. OHCHR should likewise develop model agreements for human rights field presences that could be drawn upon by peace negotiators. OHCHR should offer to advise on, support and/or monitor, the implementation of the human rights components of the peace agreement.

III. Peacekeeping/Human Rights Missions/Humanitarian Action

The High Commissioner for Human Rights should be integrally involved in the design of human rights components of human rights missions managed by DPKO or DPA, and in the selection of their personnel. OHCHR should provide them with substantive guidance on human rights issues, and their heads should report, in parallel (through the SRSG), to the High Commissioner. Guidelines should be developed between OHCHR, DPKO, and DPA for the reporting by human rights components or advisers within peacekeeping or political missions.

Humanitarian emergency responses need to take into account human rights violations that may be at the root of crises and should strive for respect for international human rights norms.

IV. Peacebuilding

In his reform programme, the Secretary-General designated DPA as the focal point for post-conflict peacebuilding work, to ensure that UN efforts in countries that are emerging from crises are fully integrated. It is essential that all participating institutions in the Executive Committee on Peace and Security work closely to ensure that human rights concerns are fully integrated in this process.

Peacebuilding activities should include the development of institutional capacity for good governance and the protection and promotion of human rights. UNDP, in close cooperation with UNHCR, should be available for an active role in the development of such programmes. OHCHR should be integrally involved in, and be supportive of, the effective coordination by the Resident Coordinator of the in-country UN system and of international support, and should promote the integration of human rights in the work of other UN agencies and other international institutions, such as the World Bank. Any OHCHR presence should, wherever possible, be placed within the 'UN House'.

Chapter 7

The Human Rights Field Operation in Partnership for Security

William G. O'Neill

Introduction

Among the many partners human rights field officers (HRFOs) need to have, none present more novel challenges and exciting opportunities than does the security sector. For human rights professionals, people in uniform – the military, police, prison officials, border guards – will be essential to the overall success of the human rights field operation, whether it is part of a multidimensional peacekeeping operation or is a standalone mission working with local security forces.

This chapter will describe the different partners in the security sector that HRFOs will have to work with. It will then analyse how HRFOs can best operate with the security sector to address immediate human rights violations, drawing on examples from several United Nations (UN) and Organization for Security and Co-operation in Europe (OSCE) human rights field operations. Building respect for human rights and changing the ethos of local security forces who have traditionally been among the greatest abusers is a huge challenge; how to instil sustainable attitudes, procedures and practices among the military, police and corrections officers prevents future violations and this chapter will offer some case studies illustrating successful approaches. Finally, the chapter will offer a short list of recommendations – practical, pragmatic and concrete – to maximise the chances of success.

Security Sector: Who are the Possible Partners?

For HRFOs working in a complex, multifaceted peacekeeping operation, the number of people in uniform can be both overwhelming and baffling. Many HRFOs have never worked closely with military or police before; in fact, for many the security sector was the 'enemy', the one responsible for grave human rights violations and the target of public reporting by groups like Amnesty International and Human Rights Watch.[1] The peacekeeping landscape is different. HRFOs' relationship with their

---

[1]   In the UN/Organization of American States (OAS) International Civilian Mission in Haiti, several HRFOs from Argentina at first could not work with police and military from

peacekeeping counterparts in the international security forces must try to collaborate, cooperate and communicate without becoming too close or overly identified with one's uniformed peacekeeping colleagues. HRFOs also need to identify ways to improve the behaviour of the national and local security forces, while keeping a necessary arms-length distance to allow for objective and rigorous assessments of their conduct. This dual balancing act – close enough to gain confidence, access and influence versus not getting too close so that the HRFOs lose perspective or judgment – is one of the hardest parts of working with the security sector as a partner.[2]

UN peacekeeping operations, some in Europe sponsored by the OSCE or European Union (EU), and increasingly in Africa where the African Union (AU) has deployed soldiers and police to Burundi and Sudan, usually have international representatives of the security sector. Among the most important for the HRFO are the following.

Military Forces

'Blue Helmets' in UN parlance – these are often the largest single component of any peacekeeping operation. They come as formed units from their militaries, usually at the battalion level (800–1000 troops). These soldiers are armed and have varying mandates concerning their ability to use force. In most recent UN operations (Sierra Leone, Liberia, Côte d'Ivoire, Sudan, Haiti and Democratic Republic of the Congo [DRC]) UN soldiers have had authorisation based on Chapter VII of the UN Charter to intervene to protect civilians from immediate harm.[3] UN troops often are deployed all over the country and have superior logistical, transport and communication capacities compared to everyone else, especially the HRFO.

Military Observers

These are usually unarmed soldiers from various nations; unlike the Blue Helmets, they come as individuals and not in formed units and they are unarmed. In most

---

their country deployed as peacekeepers to Haiti because Argentine security forces had killed and tortured some of their relatives during Argentina's 'Dirty War' 20 years before.

2   Unfortunately, HRFOs may also have to monitor and report on violations committed by international military peacekeepers. In some missions, UN peacekeepers have sexually exploited and abused women and children. See Report by the Secretary-General's Adviser on Sexual Exploitation and Abuse, Prince Zeid Al-Hussein, UN Doc. A/59/710 (2005). So have civilians working for the UN in Kosovo, Bosnia, Sierra Leone, Democratic Republic of the Congo and Liberia.

3   Charter of the United Nations, 59 Stat. 1031, T.S. 993, 3 Bevans 1153 (entered into force Oct. 24, 1945). See Sierra Leone: Security Council resolution 1181 (1998), UN Doc. S/RES/1181 (1998); Liberia: Security Council resolution 1509 (2003), UN Doc. S/RES/1509 (2003); Côte d'Ivoire: Security Council resolution 1479 (2003), UN Doc. S/RES/1479 (2003); Sudan: Security Council resolution 1564 (2004), UN Doc. S/RES/1564 (2004); Haiti: Security Council resolution 1542 (2004), UN Doc. S/RES/1542 (2004); DRC: Security Council resolution 1493 (2003), UN Doc. S/RES/1493 (2003).

cases they observe and report on ceasefire violations or on adherence by parties to a truce or peace agreement. They too usually have excellent means of transport, communications and supplies. The AU has sent military observers to Darfur, a rare example of the use of observers outside the UN.

International Civilian Police

These are a growing part of UN peacekeeping operations, and are also used by the EU in Bosnia and Herzegovina, Albania and Macedonia. The AU has also sent civilian police officers to Darfur to work alongside the AU peacekeepers and military observers. In UN parlance they are known as 'CIVPOL'; the international civilian police have had varying mandates. Some CIVPOL have been armed and have full executive authority, which means they have the power to arrest and detain nationals (East Timor, Kosovo). Other operations have granted CIVPOL non-executive authority which means they are not armed and can only observe, report and recommend. International civilian police usually deploy as individuals; however, there is a growing use of sending specialised formed units of police to UN operations. Crowd control police units from Pakistan, Bangladesh and Jordan, for example, work in Haiti as part of UN CIVPOL, while specialised *gendarmerie* units from France, Spain, Portugal and Italy have worked in the Balkans both under UN and EU auspices.

Corrections Officers

Sometimes in uniform, sometimes not, prison experts are a relatively new and growing part of modern peace operations. The necessity of reforming penal systems dawned on policymakers only recently, so HRFOs need to understand how to work with these experts to protect human rights that were, and remain, at risk in detention centres and prisons. Corrections officers take on everything from rebuilding prisons to setting up systems to register detainees, feeding, clothing and providing medical care, to training prison guards and administrators.

Host country security forces will also be important partners or counterparts for HRFOs. The armed forces, police forces (municipal, state or federal), prison guards and administrators, border and customs officers, intelligence services, specialised protection units for various ministries, all these local uniformed bodies will often be the object of HRFO monitoring, investigations, reporting and reform efforts.

In most post-conflict contexts, HRFOs will also have to monitor, report and intervene with insurgent forces. These non-state actors present particular challenges to the HRFO, not least of which is access and influence. Contacting rebel groups in Burundi, the Maoists in Nepal, the *Fuerzas Armadas Revolucionarias de Colombia* and *Ejército de Liberación Nacional* rebels and right-wing paramilitary groups in Colombia, or insurgents and militias in Darfur is hard, trying to change their behaviour to respect human rights and humanitarian law is even harder.[4]

---

[4]   See M. Zahar, 'Protégés, Clients, Cannon Fodder: Civil Militia Relations in Internal Conflicts', in S. Chesterman (ed.), *Civilians in War* (Boulder: Lynne Rienner, 2001),

International military and police can help HRFOs in various ways, including introducing them to local security sector counterparts and providing basic information on their structure, deployment and senior personnel. The international military in particular can be the key intermediary for access to insurgent forces who are often in isolated areas with strictly controlled access and high security risks. Blue helmets, CIVPOL and UN Military Observers (UNMOs) may also have intelligence on national security forces, which could help HRFOs avoid danger and provide insights on internal command and control questions, the latter being crucial for human rights investigations, establishing accountability and influencing the lower ranks.

Where there is no international security presence in the country, as is the case for Colombia, Cambodia, Nepal, the Central African Republic, Angola and, in the past, Haiti, Guatemala, El Salvador and Rwanda, HRFOs are on their own. They will have to forge their own working relationships with and information about national security institutions and insurgent or paramilitary groups.

In all cases, HRFOs will have to construct programmes and relationships aimed at fundamental reform of rotten security institutions responsible for systematic violations of human rights. How have HRFOs tried to do this and how can one judge whether they were successful?

HRFOs have chosen three strategies to advance respect for human rights in their work with the security sector:[5]

- using monitoring, investigating and reporting human rights issues to influence the operations and behaviour of security sector partners;[6]
- training security forces to observe human rights standards and to punish those who violate these standards;[7] and
- building the institutional capacity of the security sector to improve the quality of personnel and systems to maximise respect for human rights, root out bias and corruption, and entrench these changes so that they outlive the presence of HRFOs.[8]

---

pp. 43–65; and P. Gassmann, 'Colombia: Persuading Belligerents to Comply with International Norms', in *Civilians in War*, pp. 67–92.

[5]   See M. O'Flaherty, 'Future Protection of Human Rights in Post-conflict Societies: The Role of the UN', in N. D. White and D. Klaasen (eds), *The UN, Human Rights and Post-conflict Situations* (Manchester: Manchester University Press, 2005), pp. 379–403, as well as the various case studies collected in A. Henkin (ed.), *Honoring Human Rights* (The Hague: Kluwer Law International, 2000).

[6]   See, generally, the materials identified at footnote 6.

[7]   For example in Haiti, Rwanda, Bosnia and Herzegovina, Angola and Sierra Leone, see W. G. O'Neill, 'Gaining Compliance without Force: The Human Rights Field Operation', in *Civilians in War*, pp. 111–118.

[8]   *Ibid.*; and C. Granderson, 'Institutionalizing Peace: The Haiti Experience', in *Honoring Human Rights*, pp. 383–412.

Monitoring, Investigating and Reporting

Rwanda

The United Nations Human Rights Field Operation in Rwanda (HRFOR) in 1995–98 had to try to work constructively with a military that had just successfully ended genocide when the world community failed to step in.[9] The Rwandan Patriotic Army (RPA) was strong, unified and well-led. They did not welcome criticism or even suggestions from anyone, least of all civilians from the very institution that they viewed had failed Rwanda in its greatest moment of need: the UN.

Yet the RPA-led government was committing serious human rights violations, not on the scale or gravity of genocide,[10] but worrying nonetheless. HRFOR human rights officers worked alone in this period.[11] The UN military peacekeepers and a weak and ineffectual CIVPOL group left Rwanda by early 1996. So HRFOs would have to identify a way to curb military excesses while fighting continued in north-west Rwanda where genocidal forces continued to attack from sanctuaries in the Democratic Republic of the Congo.

HRFOR realised that the only way to influence the RPA was to have solid information on their activities, especially on the way they used force in situations of alleged combat. The mission needed facts gathered in precisely the most dangerous parts of Rwanda, coupled with a sound knowledge of the laws of armed conflict.

Wielding HRFOR reports, both internal and public, as a wedge, HRFOs sought more meetings with officials to discuss human rights concerns. The number and quality of these substantive meetings gradually increased as the RPA realised the accuracy of the HRFOs' information. During these meetings, HRFOR would offer the RPA assistance to address the problem uncovered in the inquiries. For example, after a study showing that prison guards had adopted a shoot-to-kill policy for prisoners trying to escape, the mission leadership pointed out to senior military officers and the chief military prosecutor that international norms prohibit the use of deadly force except when lives are immediately in danger. HRFOs distributed copies of the relevant articles of the Geneva Conventions and Protocols[12] and the UN Basic

---

[9]　On HRFOR see I. Martin, 'After Genocide: The UN Human Rights Field Operation in Rwanda', in *Honoring Human Rights*.

[10]　See Report on the Situation of Human Rights in Rwanda submitted by Mr. René Degni-Ségui, Special Rapporteur, under paragraph 20 of resolution S-3/1 of 25 May 1994, UN Doc. E/CN.4/1996/7 (1995), at 56.

[11]　Report of the High Commissioner for Human Rights on the Activities of the Human Rights Field Operation in Rwanda submitted Pursuant to General Assembly Resolution 50/200, UN Doc. E/CN.4/1996/111 (1996), at 10–32.

[12]　Geneva Convention for the Amelioration of the Condition of the Wounded and Sick in Armed Forces in the Field of August 12, 1949, 75 UNTS (1950), 31; Geneva Convention for the Amelioration of the Condition of Wounded, Sick and Shipwrecked Members of Armed Forces at Sea of August 12, 1949, 75 UNTS (1950), 85; Geneva Convention Relative to the Treatment of Prisoners of War of August 12, 1949, 75 UNTS (1950), 135; Geneva Convention Relative

Principles on the Use of Force and Firearms by Law Enforcement Officials[13] in English and French. After some resistance, the Rwandese military agreed to change its policy and the number of such shootings dropped dramatically. HRFOR provided training for prison guards and the military on human rights and the use of force and the rights of detainees.[14]

Another example concerned the indiscriminate use of force by Rwanda's army in its fight against Hutu extremists in the northwest. Violence intensified in 1997,[15] resulting in several large massacres; many women, children and the elderly were killed. The RPA insisted they had been caught in the 'cross-fire' between the militias and the RPA. When HRFOs visited the sites to interview survivors, however, they often found no evidence of a battle. All signs indicated that the shooting was from one direction only: the RPA's. Despite several meetings with senior officers, no progress occurred on the issue. HRFOR felt compelled to document the most severe cases and to issue a public report in the face of such resistance and denial. Following the public report, although angry, senior RPA officers agreed that some 'excesses' might have occurred. The chief military prosecutor launched investigations and arrested several RPA officers.[16] The prosecutor also asked HRFOR for assistance in training his staff in investigating violations of the Geneva Conventions and in training senior RPA officers in the provisions of the Conventions and Protocols. HRFOR legal officers assisted the military prosecutor, trained his staff and attended trials to monitor their fairness. Several RPA commanding officers were convicted and given long prison sentences for violating the laws of war.

Abkhazia/Georgia

The UN and OSCE have had a joint human rights operation in the breakaway section of Abkhazia in the Republic of Georgia since the end of the civil war there in the early 1990s.[17] The office has four HRFOs allotted but frequently it is not fully staffed. Meanwhile, anywhere from 100–140 UN unarmed military observers are based in Abkhazia to monitor the ceasefire agreement and related issues, especially along the tense and heavily armed 'border' between Abkhazia and Georgia proper.

---

to the Protection of Civilian Persons in Time of War of August 12, 1949, 75 UNTS (1950), 286; Protocol Additional to the Geneva Conventions of 12 August 1949, and Relating to the Protection of Victims of International Armed Conflicts (Protocol I), 1125 UNTS (1979), 3.

13 Basic Principles on the Use of Force and Firearms by Law Enforcement Officials adopted by the Eighth United Nations Congress on the Prevention of Crime and the Treatment of Offenders, Havana, Cuba, 27 August to 7 September 1990.

14 *Ibid.*, at 8–9.

15 See Report of the High Commissioner for Human Rights on the Activities of the Human Rights Field Operation in Rwanda, UN Doc. E/CN.4/1998/61 (1998), at 10–32.

16 *Ibid.*

17 See A. Clapham and F. Martin, 'Smaller Missions Bigger Problems', in *Honoring Human Rights*, pp. 289–317 and the OSCE mission website at http://www.osce.org/georgia/16294.html.

Since Abkhazia is heavily mined and large sectors are inaccessible, HRFOs have had great difficulty gathering reliable information on the human rights situation. With only four people, they must develop other sources with access.

The UNMOs visit every sector of Abkazia. They have helicopters and land-mine resistant vehicles. While on assignment in Abkhazia in 1997, the present author reviewed UNMO daily situation reports (Sit Reps). The Sit Reps had an entry for information on the human rights situation, yet all the Sit Reps had 'NTR' or 'nothing to report' on human rights. The HRFOs knew in general terms that human rights abuses were rife but could neither get the details nor confirmation because they could not travel to interview witnesses or examine the scene.

The present author approached the Bangladeshi general heading the UNMO contingent and explained the situation to him. He readily agreed that the HRFOs should brief the UNMOs on human rights, what constitutes a violation, which rights are most at risk in Abkhazia and how to gather the most relevant details in a quick interview. HRFOs and the author briefed the UNMOs who said they would seek this type of information on their visits. Almost immediately the UNMO Sit Reps, which they shared with HRFOs, contained a wealth of information on discrimination against non-Abkhaz, tensions in the schools over language issues, harsh detentions in police lock-ups and illegal activities by government-sponsored militias. No more 'nothing to report' when it came to human rights.

HRFOs alone could never have gotten this information. The UN/OSCE operation was able to 'leverage' 120 eyes, ears and brains to extend its reach well beyond the three or four people on its staff. Later, HRFOs were able to accompany UNMOs on some of their visits. This allowed the HRFOs to get the information directly, but because so many people gather when they see HRFOs, staff cannot 'provide the local people willing to communicate what they know and feel with the level of confidentiality called for'.[18] This is a significant trade-off whenever HRFOs try to involve international security personnel, or any other sector, in fact-finding, follow-up and reporting. HRFOs' effective reach and access increases while confidentiality and control of the information decreases. This trade-off is usually worth it, but HRFOs should be aware of the possible negative consequences.

Kosovo

The United Nations Mission in Kosovo established a Joint Task Force on Minorities as soon as it began operations in the summer of 1999.[19] The Task Force had representatives from the North Atlantic Treaty Organization forces or Kosovo Force (KFOR), the UN CIVPOL, the OSCE Human Rights Department, the International

---

[18] L. Zaharieva, 'Abkhazia', *Human Rights*, No. 1/1999 (A quarterly review of OHCHR) (Geneva: OHCHR), 26.

[19] On Kosovo see W. G. O'Neill, *Kosovo: An Unfinished Peace* (Boulder: Lynne Rienner, 2002); and M. Brand, 'Effective Human Rights Protection when the UN Becomes the State: Lessons from UNMIK', in *The UN, Human Rights and Post-conflict Situations*, pp. 347–375.

Committee of the Red Cross, the United Nations Children's Fund (UNICEF), the Office of the United Nations High Commissioner for Refugees and the Human Rights Office of the special representative of the secretary-general (SRSG). Their job was to identify dangers to the non-Albanian minorities following the withdrawal of Serbian forces and to identify how best to protect the remaining Serbs, Roma, Slavic Muslims, Turks and Gorani from human rights violations.

The Task Force soon identified a serious problem in the Zupa Valley northeast of Prizren town in the fall of 1999. Men and women, predominantly Serb, but also including Muslim Slavs, most of whom were over 65 years old, were targeted in several villages in the valley by young Albanian thugs. KFOR sent patrols to these villages which were greatly appreciated but insufficient. The Task Force decided to send the SRSG's human rights advisor along with OSCE human rights officers to the Zupa Valley to gather first-hand information and report back to the Task Force with a recommended plan of action.[20]

The Task Force team visited several of the villages in early October 1999,[21] meeting several elderly Serb women and men who were completely terrified, and with good reason. Several had recently been severely beaten. One woman's face was still swollen badly and she had black and blue marks on her neck, ten days after the beating. A 96 year old man was beaten to death in one of the villages on 15 September; his body was found in his house with his hands tied behind his back and a strap tied across his mouth. Everyone begged for more KFOR protection. They feared for their lives. In some cases the alleged perpetrators were arrested, but were later released and were seen again in the area soon after. The Albanian-dominated judiciary refused to prosecute Albanians who had allegedly attacked Serbs or other minorities.

The Joint Task Force team met a German KFOR patrol and the soldiers said they wanted to do more to protect the villagers. So far, they could only patrol occasionally and everyone knew that the perpetrators of these crimes and human rights violations only waited for the patrols to leave and they then returned to terrorise, beat, kill and steal.

Following this visit, the team reported its findings to the entire Task Force who in turn recommended that the SRSG ask the KFOR Commander to install a permanent check-point on the one road leading to and from the villages in the Zupa Valley. The KFOR representative on the Task Force agreed to approach his superiors in the KFOR Commander's office to reinforce the request. The KFOR Commander agreed and ordered the Turkish contingent in Prizren to erect a checkpoint on the road. German KFOR increased their mobile patrols and varied the timing to make them unpredictable. The attacks in the Zupa Valley stopped. HRFOs' information, analysis and advocacy helped lead to decisive action by international military counterparts that increased human rights protection in a volatile setting.

---

[20]   This account draws on O'Neill, *Kosovo: An Unfinished Peace*, pp. 70–72.

[21]   See Report of the High Commissioner for Human Rights on the Situation of Human Rights in Kosovo, Federal Republic of Yugoslavia, UN Doc. E/CN.4/2000/10 (1999), at 90–128.

Darfur

Sudan's western region of Darfur presents one of the most compelling and complex human rights challenges of the 21st century.[22] Up to 400,000 people have been killed from the conflict or famine and disease generated by the war. Over 2,000,000 have been forced to flee their homes and farmland by the Sudanese armed forces and the militias that they arm and support. In response to such a huge human rights catastrophe in an area the size of France with no roads and limited logistics, the UN mustered eight HRFOs in August 2004 and sent them to Darfur with limited support, logistics and information.[23]

Similar to the situation described in Abkhazia, the HRFOs are not alone; the AU deployed about 3000 personnel by mid-2005. These included military observers, soldiers to protect them, and some international police. This force, known as the African Mission in Sudan (AMIS), has a limited mandate: to monitor, investigate and report on ceasefire violations primarily. It can also help civilians who are under imminent threat and in the immediate vicinity, consistent with AMIS's capacity, which is limited.[24]

The UN's HRFOs' capacity was even more limited. The eight observers' mobility was restricted, as was their access. Burning and looting of villages, rape, torture and illegal arrests occurred throughout Darfur but the HRFOs had difficulty confirming and providing details. They had few vehicles, no language assistants and Darfur's daunting geography prevented quick verification of violations. The Sudanese government's refusal to cooperate exacerbated the problems.

Even the AMIS troops do not have enough people, helicopters, planes, vehicles or computers; their communications and logistics are not up to the task.[25] But compared to the UN HRFOs, they are a powerful behemoth. Fortunately, many AMIS troops have unofficially shared their information with human rights and humanitarian officers, including horrific photographs documenting abuses almost as they occurred or immediately after.[26] Troops in AMIS from Rwanda have publicly stated that they

---

[22] See Report of the Special Rapporteur on the Human Rights Situation in the Sudan, Sima Samar, UN Doc. E/CN.4/2006/111 (2006); *Report of the International Commission of Inquiry on Darfur to the United Nations Secretary-General* (Geneva: OHCHR, 2005); and W. G. O'Neill and V. Cassis, *Protecting Two Million Displaced: The Successes and the Shortcomings of the African Union in Darfur*, Occasional Paper (The Brookings Institution-University of Bern Project on Internal Displacement, November 2005).

[23] Their number has grown to over 50 since June 2005 and support from the OHCHR and the United Nations Mission in Sudan peacekeeping operation has also increased.

[24] See African Union, Conclusions of the Third Meeting of the Military Staff Committee held on 25 April 2005, at Addis Ababa, Ethiopia (2005), at 1–3.

[25] For an extensive analysis of the AU's shortcomings, see Crisis Group, *The AU's Mission in Darfur: Bridging the Gaps*, Africa Briefing No. 28 (Nairobi/Brussels: Crisis Group, 2005).

[26] N. D. Kristof, 'The American Witness', *The New York Times*, 2 March 2005, A-19.

will not simply stand by and watch civilians be massacred as happened in their country under the eyes of helpless UN peacekeepers in 1994.[27]

HRFOs have established solid working relationships in each of Darfur's three states with AMIS. Regular meetings are held, information exchanged and analysed, and even coordinated approaches to the government designed. AMIS has designated liaison officers to work with the UN HRFOs and others concerned, such as UNHCR protection officers and United Nations Development Programme's (UNDP) rule of law officers. HRFOs are working with the AMIS CIVPOL to develop common strategies on investigating and prosecuting rape and sexual violence, which is rampant in Darfur.[28]

The United Nations Mission in Sudan (UNMIS) and AMIS reached an agreement in July 2005 under which AMIS provides transportation and escorts to UN human rights observers in high risk areas where the observers otherwise would never be able to go. These are precisely the spots where serious human rights violations occur and the need for monitoring and investigation the greatest. AMIS and the human rights observers have also agreed to share information and AMIS troops have received human rights training from the UN HRFOs.[29]

Darfur provides cutting edge opportunities to build on HRFO-security forces collaboration in a dangerous and demanding environment. Some in the human rights and especially in the humanitarian community criticise a creeping 'politicisation' or 'militarisation' of humanitarian assistance or human rights work.[30] Darfur shows, however, that striking the right balance between cooperation and 'independence' is possible; while the risks are there, the rewards from a healthy collaboration between the international security sector and HRFOs are potentially enormous and worth the risk.

Training

Examples of HRFOs' efforts to train both international and national security forces abound. It is the most common approach to forging a partnership between human rights and soldiers, police and corrections.

---

[27]   E. Wax, 'In Darfur, Rwandan Soldiers Relive their Past', *The Washington Post*, 28 September, 2004, A-20, who quotes a Rwandan soldier: 'Every night you go to sleep thinking, "I could do more. We could do more with a better mandate"'.

[28]   S. Sengupta, 'Unrelenting Attacks on Women in West Sudan Provoke an International Outcry', *The New York Times*, 26 October 2004, A-10. In one case, the AMIS soldiers went to the scene of a reported gang rape and found caked blood on the ground.

[29]   Monthly Report of the Secretary-General on Darfur, UN Doc. S/2005/523 (2005), at 14.

[30]   N. de Torrente, 'Politicized Humanitarianism', *Harvard Human Rights Journal* vol. 17 (2004), 1; for a response see P. O'Brian, 'Politicized Humanitarianism: A Response to Nicolas de Torrente', *Harvard Human Rights Journal* vol. 17 (2004), 31. See also G. Loescher, 'Threatened are the Peacemakers', *Notre Dame Magazine* (Spring 2005), available at www.nd.edu/~ndmag/sp2005/loescher.html.

Haiti

HRFOs working in the UN/OAS International Civilian Mission in Haiti (MICIVIH) worked with their UN CIVPOL colleagues to create a curriculum for the new National Police School that incorporated human rights in every subject. Human rights was not isolated and treated as a peripheral issue but permeated every aspect of policing. HRFOs stationed all over Haiti then monitored the performance of the newly-deployed Haitian National Police (HNP) after they had finished their training to provide feedback to their superiors and to their academy so that issues that presented continuing challenges received more attention and time.[31] The curriculum was updated based on 'real-world feedback' from HRFOs and continually tested as HNP officers worked their beats.

Guatemala

The United Nations Mission in Guatemala (MINUGUA) incorporated human rights standards in all subject areas of police training, e.g. arrests, detention, investigations, interrogations, use of force, crowd control. They did not relegate human rights to a peripheral area seen as 'optional' for police work. Domestic violence training received special attention because it pervades the country. Many police believed that this is a 'private matter' not requiring police intervention.[32]

MINUGUA also invited representatives of civil society to participate in the police training, something tried before successfully in Haiti. It is vital for both the police and the people they are meant to serve and protect – especially in situations where the police have done everything but serve and protect – to work together early to establish mutual trust. Having community leaders come to the police academy to speak to the trainees, participate in role-plays and training exercises, and just mingle at breaks and over lunch helps to change the culture and mentality in an institution that had brutalised the population for decades.

MINUGUA's police training included academic experts in criminology, anthropology and related disciplines who designed and delivered the training. This is another excellent initiative; often the UN overlooks local academic research and expertise which could strengthen police training and performance.[33]

---

[31] W. G. O'Neill, 'Human Rights Monitoring versus Political Expediency: The Experience of the OAS/UN Mission in Haiti', *Harvard Human Rights Journal* vol. 8 (1995), 101–128.

[32] See Report of the Independent Expert, Mrs Mónica Pinto, on the Situation of Human Rights in Guatemala, UN Doc. E/CN.4/1996/15 (1995), at 117.

[33] W. G. O'Neill, 'Human Rights and Police Reform: A HURIST Document', (July 2004), 29–32. HURIST is a joint program of UNDP and OHCHR.

Institution-building

Training in human rights is necessary but not sufficient to reform security forces. More effort and money need to be directed toward strengthening the army, police and penal systems as institutions. Promoting and awarding integrity and good performance, transparency in all hiring and firing decisions, accountability for the budget, using modern methods of administration, management and procurement, and creating an effective oversight body to deter, root out and punish misconduct are essential to lasting reform. HRFOs have addressed systemic problems in national security forces and embedded systems that will perpetuate reform long after the last international HRFOs or UN Blue Helmet leaves.[34]

East Timor

The local police force no longer existed by the time the United Nations Transitional Administration in East Timor (UNTAET) assumed responsibility for governing in October 1999; they fled following the scorched earth campaign of the Indonesian military and their East Timorese militias after the referendum on autonomy in August 1999.[35] The UN had to create a new police force from scratch. The UN established the new Timor Lorosa'e Police Service (TLPS) on 10 August 2001.[36]

UN HRFOs along with colleagues from UNDP and UNICEF realised that more than human rights training would be needed to build an effective, rights-respecting police force. They focused on building capacity in human resources management, finances (including accounting and oversight mechanisms to fight corruption), logistics, management (emphasising accountability, disciplinary procedures and operating policies/codes of conduct), community relations and on-the-job mentoring.[37] This holistic approach underscores the links among basic police skills development, standard setting, administrative/logistic support, integrity and discipline.

HRFOs helped to create standard operating procedures in sensitive areas where the potential for human rights abuse is great; for example, arrest, detention, use of force, domestic or gender-based violence, juveniles in trouble with the law and child abuse cases. HRFOs worked closely with CIVPOL in developing these procedures and a code of conduct.[38]

---

[34]   See the case studies collected in Henkin (ed.), *Honoring Human Rights*.

[35]   I. Martin, *Self-Determination in East Timor: The United Nations, the Ballot and International Intervention* (Boulder: Lynne Rienner, 2001).

[36]   UNTAET Regulation 2001/22 of 10 August 2001on the establishment of the East Timor Police Service.

[37]   For an analysis of UNTAET's police reform and institutional work, see International Policy Institute, *A Case for Change: A Review of Peace Operations* (King's College London, 2003), pp. 235–240.

[38]   'Report of the United Nations High Commissioner for Human Rights, Situation of Human Rights in Timor-Leste, UN Doc. E/CN.4/2003/37 (2003), at 19.

Giving police the skills to obtain the information they need to arrest or detain a suspect without violating his/her rights fulfils the multiple goals of providing effective policing, observing the rights of the suspect and providing care and support to the victim.[39] Interviewing techniques that do not rely on beating confessions from the suspect, as well as forensics, legal wire-tapping, using informants and examining financial records are crucial to developing a police force that respects rights and protects people.

Bosnia and Herzegovina

In addition to the typical training, awareness raising and community outreach efforts, HRFOs in the United Nations Mission in Bosnia and Herzegovina (UNMIBH), along with officers in the International Police Task Force (IPTF), launched several innovative reform initiatives.[40] UNMIBH established independent police commissioners in the ten cantons of the Federation and in the Republika Srpska to address the problem of political interference that had plagued policing and had led to human rights abuses, low morale, corruption and discriminatory law enforcement, which in turn exacerbated poor public confidence in the police. This attention to promoting professionalism and merit is a crucial element in police reform and has rarely received such prominence in UN security sector initiatives.

UNMIBH realised in 1999 when it began serious implementation of its mandate that sustainable police reform in such an ethnically polarised and politicised society could not succeed through training alone or even through intensive international oversight, co-location of international police with local police or on-the-job mentoring.[41]

UNMIBH focused on investigating the background of every police officer, checking for past criminal records, war-time experience, whether the officer was illegally occupying property, completion of IPTF training, citizenship and verifying educational credentials. If all was satisfied, the officer was 'certified'. A data-bank containing and categorising this information was created and cross-checked, creating a vital baseline. The goal was to signal to Bosnian society that the new police would possess a high standard of competence and integrity.

The main authors of this approach highlighted what they call the 'integrity deficit' as a fundamental challenge to effective public security sector reform in Bosnia and Herzegovina and probably in most other post-conflict societies. They noted that while knowledge about human rights and basic police skills is often deficient:

---

[39] There does not have to be a trade-off between effective policing that prevents and solves crime and respectful policing that honours human rights. See R. C. Davis and P. Mateu-Gelabert, *Respectful and Effective Policing: Two Examples in the South Bronx* (New York: Vera Institute of Justice, 1999), p. 20.

[40] M. O'Flaherty, 'International Human Rights Operations in Bosnia and Herzegovina,' in M. O'Flaherty and G. Gisvold (eds) *Post-War Protection of Human Rights in Bosnia and Herzegovina*, International Studies in Human Rights vol. 53 (The Hague: Kluwer Law International, 1998), pp. 71–105.

[41] *Ibid.*, pp. 91–92.

The lack of individual and organisational integrity is, however, generally more serious and detrimental. Frequently, these institutions 'know their job' but use their capacity for unlawful purposes. Addressing this lack of integrity represents a key challenge in the transition process. Only institutions with minimum levels of individual and organisational integrity will ensure accountability for past violations, respect human rights in the present, and protect human rights in the future.[42]

HRFOs and IPTF colleagues created a 'Capacity and Integrity Framework' with two operational tools, the 'Personnel Registry' and the 'Organisational Audit', which allowed UNMIBH 'to assess the capacity and integrity of both the organisation and personnel of public institutions, set realistic and achievable objectives, and measure progress achieved'.[43] These tools became the basis for UNMIBH's security sector implementation plan, which was later adapted for use in East Timor by the United Nations Mission in East Timor. It is a simple yet compelling tool to gauge reform of any public institution, but especially security bodies such as the police and the military.

The Personnel Registry 'provides decision-makers with the necessary baseline data and statistics on key factors such as personnel strength of public institutions, educational and professional standards, decision-making structures, professional conduct and conflict-era background'.[44] This information identifies training needs, establishes oversight mechanisms to strengthen accountability and also creates an objective and transparent personnel management structure that rewards professionalism while reducing the scope for political interference, ethnic favouritism or other outside pressures that undermine the integrity of security forces. A baseline of key data gathered by this Registry allows for reliable measurement of any progress or regression.

Haiti

'Creating effective disciplinary systems within the police should be a first-order priority'.[45] This is true for all security forces in any post-conflict setting. Effective, transparent and fair accountability mechanisms, both internal and external, will help ensure discipline and secure public trust. Impunity for the security forces has been a major problem in many post-conflict countries where the military, police and other state security literally got away with murder, torture, rape and extortion.

Misconduct by the new or reformed security forces will devastate reform. The population will see that the forces are just like the old, not worthy of their trust or support, and a dangerous dynamic will quickly develop. This was initially the case with the United Nations mission in El Salvador (ONUSAL) and the reform

---

[42]   A. Mayer-Rieckh, *Emerging Methodologies in Transitional Institution Building and Peacebuilding: Project Overview* (September 2002) (on file with the present author).

[43]   *Ibid.*

[44]   *Ibid.*

[45]   D. Bayley, *Democratizing the Police Abroad: What To Do and How To Do It* (Washington, DC: National Institute of Justice, 2001), p. 40.

effort suffered.[46] In Haiti, however, MICIVIH HRFOs and UN CIVPOL devoted substantial resources and time to create a strong, independent, competent and transparent Inspector General's Office (IG) for the new Haitian National Police. An energetic inspector general of the HNP in 1994–1995 disciplined, suspended and even turned over for prosecution misbehaving and abusive police officers.[47] This was literally revolutionary in Haiti and sent a clear signal to both the police and the population: impunity is over; you can lose your job and even go to jail if you violate the law or police code of ethics.

The public needs to know and have confidence in the complaint procedure; if a police officer or soldier engages in misconduct or criminal acts, a citizen can file a complaint and be sure that it will be acted on and not forgotten. HRFOs and CIVPOL in Haiti supported the HNP in conducting a public information campaign describing the process of how citizens can file a complaint for police misconduct. The inspector general issued public reports and issued regular press releases describing the allegations, the nature of the police abuse alleged and the names and ranks of the officers involved.[48] For a while in the mid-1990s, the Inspector General's Office of the HNP gave a weekly press conference, announcing the number of complaints made against the police, action taken – including the referral of serious cases for criminal prosecution, and an update on the status of earlier cases. This openness encouraged the population to work with the police, to provide information, tips, identify suspects and prevent crime. It allowed for community-based policing where before the police were the prime suspect in rights violations.

Oversight control mechanisms serve important purposes in addition to assessing behaviour and punishing misconduct. They assist in 'analyzing and changing the regulatory and management systems and practices of the police to refine their capabilities and improve their performance, both in effectiveness and ethics'.[49] Internal disciplinary mechanisms, if fair and objective, encourage good behaviour since they directly influence an officer's career. Performance assessments go into personnel files which then affect promotions, transfers, raises, assignments, opportunities for further training and skills enhancement.

---

[46]   D. García-Sayán, 'The Experience of ONUSAL in El Salvador', in *Honoring Human Rights*, pp. 21–45.

[47]   Research has shown that as a tool to promote change and better police practices, criminal prosecutions are blunt and have a limited deterrent effect. Prosecutions are cumbersome, expensive, backward looking and often dismissed by other police officers as frivolous and politically motivated. P. Chevigny, *The Edge of the Knife: Police Violence in the Americas* (New York: The New Press, 1995), p. 101.

[48]   Washington Office on Latin America and the National Coalition for Haitian Rights, *Can Haiti's Police Reforms Be Sustained?* (1998) available at http://www.wola.org/publications/pub_security_country_haiti_police_reforms_sustained_jan98.pdf.

[49]   R. Neild, *Internal Controls and Disciplinary Units: Themes and Debates in Public Security Reform: A manual for Civil Society* (Washington, DC: Washington Office on Latin America, 1998), p. 1.

Selected Good Practices

- HRFOs should establish a good working relationship with international military and police peacekeepers. Simple protocols on information sharing should be agreed.
- HRFOs should be ready to offer training, documents and advice on human rights and humanitarian law to international and national security forces.
- Training must be practical and participatory, based on real cases and involve problem-solving and teamwork. Rote memorisation and theoretical lectures do not work. Formal training should always be followed and supplemented by on-the-job mentoring, preferably by international counterparts who themselves have specialised expertise for this task.
- HRFOs should also collaborate more systematically with colleagues in UNICEF, UNDP, United Nations Development Fund for Women, UNHCR and other UN agencies who are incorporating human rights increasingly into their work. United, these UN civilian agencies and HRFOs can leverage their reach and influence with international security sector counterparts and with local military and police.
- HRFOs and their international security sector colleagues should collaborate more with local academics, universities, research centres and think tanks who have expertise on local security forces – their structures, command and control systems, ethnic/racial/religious composition, traditions, culture and biases.
- Local human rights experts should always be included in the design and delivery of training for both international and national security forces.
- Training, however, is not enough. HRFOs should insist on linking training with accountability and performance. HRFOs should monitor to determine whether training the police, military or corrections officers leads to better protection of human rights.
- HRFOs should emphasise the importance of having an independent, fair and transparent oversight body for all security forces. This is a first-order priority.
- Changing the culture and mentality of national security forces is a long-term project. One way to accelerate the process is to pay more attention to the integrity and competence of those entering or serving in the military, police or prison systems. HRFOs and international security partners should use the 'Capacity and Integrity Framework' developed by UNMIBH in Bosnia and Herzegovina.
- HRFOs need to invest more time and energy into developing the security services as well-run institutions. They need sound personnel practices, financial controls, modern management, administration, procurement and logistics. HRFOs too often have ignored these areas and reform efforts have withered quickly once they left.
- HRFOs' reports should be public as a rule, not the exception. The reports are an important part of any advocacy campaign to improve security sector behaviour and to hold violators accountable.

Chapter 8

The Human Rights Field Operation in Partnership for Transitional Justice

David Marshall[1]

Introduction

States emerging from conflict face pressing needs to address past gross human rights abuses, dysfunctional laws and institutions and a chronic lack of capacity. For many post-conflict states, the United Nations (UN) has been the key partner – in particular, the human rights field operations, be it standalone offices or human rights components to UN peacekeeping missions.[2] Although such operations have been at the centre of assisting emerging states in justice sector reform for many years, from legal systems monitoring to the provision of technical assistance for key justice actors, the years since 2000 have seen a remarkable development in the field of transitional justice, with states requesting assistance to prosecute gross human rights abuses, reform substantive provisions of domestic criminal legislation, assist in the creation of truth and reconciliation commissions (TRCs), reparations policies, reconciliation processes and vetting of public actors within the criminal justice system. The request for UN assistance has resulted in the need to develop expertise in areas not traditionally within the realm of the human rights field operations.

In the report of the secretary-general to the Security Council on the rule of law and transitional justice in conflict and post-conflict societies, the secretary-general articulated a common language of justice for the UN.[3] Although the concept of transitional justice has been part of the human rights lexicon for many years, it was defined in the report of the secretary-general as comprising 'the full range of processes and mechanisms associated with a society's attempts to come to terms with the legacy of large-scale past abuses, in order to ensure accountability, serve justice and achieve reconciliation'.[4] The definition identified such processes and

---

[1]   The author would like to acknowledge the research done for this chapter by Ann Nee.
[2]   See chapter 14 by P. Burgess in the present volume.
[3]   Report of the Secretary-General, The Rule of Law and Transitional Justice in Conflict and Post-Conflict Societies, UN Doc. S/2004/616 (2004).
[4]   *Ibid.*, at 8.

mechanisms to include prosecutions, reparations, truth-seeking, institutional reform, vetting and dismissals. In addition, the report emphasised that, in the context of transitional justice, strategies must be 'holistic, incorporating integrated attention to individual prosecutions, reparations, truth-seeking, institutional reform, vetting and dismissals, or an appropriately conceived combination thereof'.[5]

Background: Transitional Justice and United Nations Field Operations

In field operations, UN expertise on transitional justice issues can be found within the Office of the United Nations High Commissioner for Human Rights (OHCHR) field operations, and human rights and rule of law components of peacekeeping missions (e.g. Burundi,[6] Democratic Republic of the Congo,[7] Liberia[8] and Sierra Leone[9]). To date, however, most transitional justice-related issues are within the domain of the human rights component of peacekeeping missions, and rule of law components also have much to offer in the context of judicial reform issues, such as vetting. Elsewhere, other UN agencies, funds and programmes also engage in transitional justice-related activities. For example, in Côte d'Ivoire, transitional justice issues are solely within the domain of the rule of law component of the UN operation.[10] In Bosnia and Herzegovina, public consultations on the creation of a truth commission have been undertaken by the United Nations Development Programme (UNDP).[11]

As the UN focal point for coordinating system-wide attention for human rights, democracy and the rule of law, the OHCHR began, in 2003, to develop sustainable, long-term institutional capacity within UN field operations to respond to the demands in this area. To this end, OHCHR launched a project to enhance its capacity to provide effective and meaningful policy advice in the area of transitional justice. The project's primary outputs are five policy tools that will provide practical guidance to field operations and transitional administrations in critical transitional justice and rule of law-related areas.

The five tools are intended to outline the basic principles involved in addressing key transitional justice areas. They are meant to provide field operations and transitional administrations with the fundamental information required to effectively target interventions in these areas in line with international human rights standards

---

[5]   *Ibid.*, at 26.

[6]   United Nations Operation in Burundi, see http://www.un.org/depts/dpko/missions/onub/.

[7]   United Nations Organization Mission in the Democratic Republic of the Congo, see http://www.monuc.org/Home.aspx?lang=en.

[8]   United Nations Mission in Liberia, see http://www.unmil.org/.

[9]   United Nations Assistance Mission in Sierra Leone, see http://www.un.org/Depts/dpko/missions/unamsil/.

[10]   United Nations Operation in Côte d'Ivoire, see http://www.un.org/depts/dpko/missions/unoci/.

[11]   See http://www.undp.ba/.

and best practices. The tools should enhance efforts to ensure that human rights field operations have the means necessary to implement coordinated and system-wide responses in developing fair and effective justice systems in post-conflict states. They are the following:[12]

- *A mapping of the justice sector and some key related institutions* This tool specifically addresses the issue of mapping the justice sector and some key related institutions and is intended to assist UN field staff in understanding how the justice sector actually worked in the state prior to and during the conflict, and how it should function if the rule of law is to take root. It provides an overview of the key institutions, related entities or mechanisms, and identifies priorities such as the linkages between core institutions and the utility of oversight bodies.
- *Basic considerations on prosecutions initiatives* This tool sets out basic considerations on prosecution initiatives, and is intended to assist UN field staff when advising on approaches to addressing the challenges of prosecuting perpetrators of crimes such as genocide, crimes against humanity and war crimes. The focus of this guidance is mainly on the strategic and technical challenges that these prosecutions face domestically, and sets out the principal considerations that should be applied to all prosecutorial initiatives: the need for a clear political commitment to accountability; the need for a clear strategy; the need to ensure that initiatives are endowed with the necessary capacity and technical ability to investigate and prosecute the crimes in question; the need to pay particular attention to victims; and the need to have a clear understanding of the relevant law and an appreciation of trial management skills, as well as a strong commitment to due process.
- *An operational framework for vetting and institutional reform of justice-related actors* This tool is intended to assist UN field staff in advising on approaches to addressing the challenges of institutional and personnel reform in post-conflict states through the creation of vetting processes that exclude from public institutions persons who lack integrity. The tool is divided into three sections: the concept of vetting in the context of institutional reform and transitional justice; the political conditions of post-conflict or post-authoritarian reform, identifying the sources of a personnel reform mandate, recommending priorities in transitional personnel reform, and proposing the development of a public consultation and information strategy; and the operational guidelines themselves.
- *Legal systems monitoring methodology* This tool addresses human rights monitoring of the justice system through the creation of a more practical methodology and is intended to reflect a comprehensive overview of the

---

[12] OHCHR, *Rule-of-Law Tools for Post-conflict States* (New York and Geneva: United Nations, 2006).

principles, techniques and approaches involved in legal systems monitoring, principles that have been primarily garnered from previous experience and lessons learned from the UN, the Organization for Security and Co-operation in Europe and non-governmental (NGO) legal systems monitoring programmes. The objective of this tool is to provide a framework for developing a monitoring programme to analyse institutions and the justice system as a whole from which good practices can be reinforced and bad practices or deficiencies addressed.

• *Basic principles and approaches to truth commissions* This tool sets out basic principles and approaches to truth commissions and is intended to assist UN and other policymakers in advising on the development of truth-seeking mechanisms. The principles used in this tool have been primarily garnered from previous experience and lessons learned in the implementation of these techniques and mechanisms in UN field missions, including those in Sierra Leone and Timor-Leste.

Truth-seeking Mechanisms

This chapter now turns to a detailed examination of the most challenging and least-documented aspects of transitional justice: truth-seeking mechanisms. The intention is to examine closely some of the underlying beliefs and assumptions that lie at the heart of the work of truth commissions in particular, and truth-seeking frameworks in general. The focus is on issues of society, of goals and of process that have immediate significance for the work of human rights field operations.

The development of important policy tools notwithstanding, it will be essential that field operations, in a thoughtful and deliberative manner, develop a rich understanding of local reconciliation processes and traditions since truth-seeking initiatives considered a success in one context may be not be suitable in another. Public truth-telling as the necessary and exclusive route to reconciliation may not be the best approach at the community level. To maximise opportunity for success, any existing local reintegration and reconciliation processes and traditions should be sought out and carefully evaluated for conflict or convergence with new intended initiatives. Importantly, UN field operations will need to draw on resources beyond the legal and human rights fields to include regional experts in anthropology, history, psychology and social science.

Let us take stock of the context. Following the creation of truth commissions in Latin America and South Africa, a new burgeoning industry has emerged in post-conflict states, supported by the international community that supports the seemingly rapid establishment of a TRC.[13] Truth commissions have been established in over

---

[13] The terms 'truth commission', 'truth and reconciliation commission', TRC', and 'commission' are used alternately in the present chapter to represent this concept. For texts addressing the reconciliatory potential of truth commissions, see for example M. Minow, 'The Hope for Healing: What Can Truth Commissions Do?', in R. I. Robert and D. Thompson (eds), *Truth V. Justice: The Morality of Truth Commissions* (eds), (Princeton: Princeton University

25 countries,[14] and continue to be proposed in a wide variety of contexts in places such as Burundi and Afghanistan. These are official, temporary, non-judicial fact-finding bodies that investigate patterns of abuses of human rights or humanitarian law, usually committed over a number of years, with the intention of discovering, clarifying and formally acknowledging past abuses. A truth commission aims to respond to the needs of victims, contributing to justice and accountability and making recommendations that will prevent future conflict. The operating assumption is that truth commissions and their model of reconciliation through truth-telling are universally beneficial.

Many analyses of TRCs have centred on *process* – e.g. incorporating a start-up phase in a commission's mandate, providing victim and witness services, transparent selection of commissioners, record keeping and report writing.[15] These address important lessons learned in the practical implementation of truth commissions and are critical for ensuring the greatest possible success where establishment of such a mechanism has been decided.

Frameworks for conceptualising the *purposes and aims* of truth commissions have also come to the forefront in the past decade. Martha Minow has identified the following as principal aims of truth commissions: to overcome denial and gain public acknowledgement; to build an historical record; to end and prevent violence; to strengthen democracy and respect for human rights; to promote reconciliation; to promote psychological healing; to restore dignity to individuals; to punish and exclude perpetrators; and, to make these efforts complementary.[16] Priscilla Hayner has distilled a list of five basic goals: to clarify and acknowledge the truth; to respond to the needs and interests of victims; to contribute to justice and accountability; to outline institutional responsibility and recommended reforms; and to promote reconciliation and reduce tensions resulting from past violence.[17]

With their short durations and expedited timelines, it is impractical to expect that commissions can directly reconcile opposing sides or victims and perpetrators. Indeed, harbouring such goals can set a commission up for failure by forcing it to diffuse its focus and resources and foster unrealistic expectations for victims. In addition, there have been calls for commissions to more critically consider the different levels on which reconciliation can operate – e.g. personal versus national – in order to better understand their goals and target their efforts.

Press, 2002); and P. B. Hayner, *Unspeakable Truths: Confronting State Terror and Atrocity* (New York: Routledge, 2001).

[14] See the United States Institute of Peace's list of truth commissions at http://www.usip.org/library/truth.html#tc.

[15] See, OHCHR, *Rule-of-Law Tools for Post-Conflict States: Truth Commissions*, available at http://www.ohchr.org/english/about/publications/docs/ruleoflaw-TruthCommissions_en.pdf.

[16] Minow, 'The Hope for Healing', in *Truth V. Justice: The Morality of Truth Commissions*, p. 253.

[17] Hayner, *Unspeakable Truths*, p. 24.

Debate is also taking place on the tensions between truth commissions and other transitional or development goals.[18] For instance, is there necessarily a trade-off between peace on the one hand and truth and justice on the other, or a trade-off even between truth and justice? What sequencing should be taken for truth commissions and prosecutions? What power do TRCs hold to offer amnesties in the interests of truth or justice under international law? Could resources spent on commissions have been better invested in infrastructure reconstruction and poverty reduction programmes that would work to rectify the socio-economic causes and consequences of human rights abuses? These questions also bear on the issue of relative prioritisation of truth and reconciliation.

This issue has been particularly heated in the context of Timor-Leste, when, in March 2005, notwithstanding the creation of a truth and reconciliation commission, the governments of Indonesia and Timor-Leste issued a joint declaration establishing a Commission of Truth and Friendship 'aimed at dealing with matters pertaining to the events of 1999'.[19] The terms of reference stated that the two governments 'have opted to seek truth and promote friendship as a new and unique approach rather than the prosecutorial strategy'.[20] In addition, the terms of reference conclude that 'reconciliation has actually taken place'.[21] The UN Commission of Experts to Review the Prosecution of Serious Violations of Human Rights in Timor-Leste (then East Timor) in 1999, established in 2005, expressed serious reservations about the joint commission concluding that the terms of reference contradict international and domestic law, and offer no mechanisms for addressing serious crimes.[22]

Only recently have substantive questions about the basic assumptions of the truth commission model begun to be seriously re-examined in empirical case studies. Does truth telling actually lead to reconciliation? Can mechanisms other than truth-telling better promote reconciliation in a given context? How deeply can local traditions be incorporated before a truth commission becomes a reconciliation commission, and is this desirable? Some argue that truth is painful and may disturb the *status quo* and enflame tensions temporarily, but that it is necessary for true reconciliation.[23] Others claim that unitary objective truth may not always be possible and so forcing a society to try to create one without popular support can impede real reconciliation.[24]

Answering such questions is complicated by the lack of accepted indicators for measuring the outcomes of a truth commission, as well as by the myriad divergent goals generally assigned to one. How can reconciliation be measured? Is it a low level of inter-ethnic conflict in a community, a high percentage of victims who say they have forgiven their abusers, progress in changing underlying factors that gave rise to

---

[18]   See for example *ibid.*, chapters 7 and 13.

[19]   Joint Declaration, 9 March 2005 establishing the Commission of Truth and Friendship Indonesia – Timor-Leste. Terms of Reference can be found at www.ctf-ri-tl.org.

[20]   *Ibid.*, para. 10.

[21]   *Ibid.*, para. 7.

[22]   See Report to the Secretary-General of the Commission of Experts to Review the Prosecution of Serious Violations of Human Rights in Timor-Leste (then East Timor) in 1999, Annex II to UN Doc. S/2005/458 (2005), at 335.

[23]   Hayner, *Unspeakable Truths*, p. 133.

[24]   *Ibid.*, pp. 190–191.

the conflict? And in what time period is measurement of reconciliation meaningful? Citizens' short-term perceptions of the effectiveness of a truth commission may be heavily influenced by factors not directly under the control of the commission, such as continuing economic deprivation, failure by the government to implement recommendations, and blatant impunity for high-level perpetrators. Too close a proximity to the conflict itself could prevent any genuine assessment. Longer-term evaluations of truth commissions can be even harder to ascertain however, as it is impossible to compare the current conditions with what would have existed without a truth commission, or to determine the relative weight of government policies, a truth commission or other factors on the attitudes of victims.

A Diagnostic for Truth

One scientific basis for the healing power of truth-telling mechanisms arises from studies by psychologists of Americans soldiers following the war in Vietnam.[25] From these observations, psychologists developed treatments for a group of symptoms collectively called post-traumatic stress disorder (PTSD). Under this rubric, victims must relive their traumas through telling them, in order to place the trauma within the context of their lives, neutralise it, and be able to move beyond it.[26] With the recent increase in international and Western involvement in victim services in post-conflict situations, the language and methodology of PTSD have been imported to cultural and political contexts very different from their roots, prompting important inquiries into their universality.

Psychologists studying PTSD have identified three base assumptions relevant to its portability: that it pre-supposes a strong individualist approach to human life, in which society is 'understood to be a collection of separate individuals' who have the power to independently control and alter their mental condition; that psychiatric symptoms have the same significance across cultures and that the collection of symptoms identified in the West as constituting PTSD is a meaningful classification elsewhere; and that the underlying disorder and response to trauma must be the same in all cultures. From this, it is inferred that Western forms of therapy will be effective in non-Western societies.[27]

Recent Experiences

Modern challenges to these assumptions argue that constructions of self, individuality and agency are in fact historically and culturally variable, despite seeming self-evident and universal to those brought up within a particular tradition.[28] These

---

[25] P. J. Bracken and C. Petty (eds), *Rethinking the Trauma of War* (New York: Free Association Books, 1998), p. 4.

[26] P. J. Bracken, 'Hidden Agendas: Deconstructing Post Traumatic Stress Disorder,' in *Rethinking the Trauma of War*, pp. 45, 49.

[27] *Ibid.*, pp. 40–41.

[28] *Ibid.*, p. 51.

differences, however, frame the context within which individuals and communities respond to violence and attempt to recover from it.[29] In societies where war has been present for many years, local communities have often developed healing mechanisms incorporating their beliefs in culture, tradition, religion and mythology. When efforts to respond to trauma are based on culturally foreign concepts, and particularly when they counter or appear to discount traditional approaches, effective indigenous practices of healing may be unravelled, to the detriment of the victims and their communities.[30]

Questions have been raised even in South Africa over the comparative benefits and drawbacks for individual victims appearing before the commission. A study of victims who testified before South Africa's TRC found that 60% felt worse after doing so.[31] Recent experiences in countries such as Mozambique and Sierra Leone have led to a further re-evaluation of the universality of truth-telling mechanisms as a prerequisite for reconciliation, or as the best path to reconciliation.

In long-lasting conflicts, such as the 15-year civil war in Mozambique, a large number of civilians, including youths, lived all or nearly all of their lives in war, preventing effective formal education or civilian community socialisation. To 'reintegrate' such youths into a peaceful community of adherence to social norms is more than a matter of truth-telling – there is a deeper 'crisis of moral values'.[32] The single-minded focus of psychiatric trauma recovery has also come under criticism in child soldier demobilisation efforts because it crowds out attention to these underlying social conditions, including lack of education, training and job opportunities, and to the need for social rehabilitation.[33]

In Mozambique, where there was no formal truth commission, Alcinda Honwana has described the impact of local conceptions of self on approaches to healing.[34] In traditional Mozambican society, ill health, including mental health, transcends the control of an individual, and can be subject to intervention by the family, the community and the spirits of the dead.[35] Similarly, there is a belief in 'social pollution', where perpetrators of killings in the war become polluted, and thereby become potential pathways for spirits of the dead to enter and cause afflictions on themselves, their

---

[29] *Ibid.*, p. 55.

[30] R. Shaw, *Rethinking Truth and Reconciliation Commissions: Lessons from Sierra Leone*, United States Institute of Peace, Special Report No. 130 (February 2005), p. 12.

[31] Shaw, *Rethinking Truth and Reconciliation Commissions*, p. 7, citing a study by the Trauma Center for Victims of Violence and Torture in Cape Town, as reported by the *New York Times* in 1997.

[32] A. Honwana, 'Innocent & Guilty: Child-Soldiers as Interstitial and Tactical Agents', in A. Honwana and F. De Boeck (eds), *Makers and Breakers: Children and Youth in Postcolonial Africa* (Trenton, NJ: Africa World Press, Inc., 2005), p. 36.

[33] K. Peters and P. Richards, 'Fighting with Eyes Open: Youth Combatants Talking About War in Sierra Leone,' in *Rethinking the Trauma of War*.

[34] A. Honwana, 'Healing and Social Reintegration in Mozambique and Angola', in E. Skaar, S. Gloppen and A. Suhrke (eds), *Roads to Reconciliation* (Lanham: Lexington Books, 2005).

[35] *Ibid.*, p. 86.

families and even their communities.[36] Cleansing or 'rehumanisation' processes held by traditional healers are thus essential to protect the community and reintegrate those involved in the war.[37] Since many Mozambicans also believe that talking about past trauma can open the door for malevolent humans and spiritual forces to return, these rituals may not include verbalisation of the trauma, but rather emphasise the symbolic putting aside of traumatic experiences and the creation of a ritual change in status from lawlessness to social conformance.[38] Studies have shown that, in these societies, talk therapy does not appear to help victims as much as healing rituals.[39] This healing and restoration of harmony is effective because it takes place within a wider context of family, community and the spirit world, consistent with cultural beliefs about self and health.

These beliefs are most prevalent in rural areas, which were the hardest hit by the war, but are nevertheless still consonant in urban areas.[40] The refusal to speak about the war and past abuses was pervasive across classes, and any truth mechanism was emphatically rejected.[41] Hayner in fact suggests that one possible reason for Mozambique's rapid, widespread reconciliation following the ceasefire, and in the absence of a truth mechanism, was the enduring strength of traditional mechanisms for healing.[42]

In Sierra Leone, Rosalind Shaw has reported on the tension for many victims between the truth-telling emphasised by the TRC and the established community healing and re-integration processes derived from the widespread practice of 'social forgetting'. She distinguishes social forgetting from individual forgetting in that, while individuals may discuss the war privately, there is a communal refusal to do so publicly because of the belief that doing so could call back the violence both physically and spiritually, and worsen social tensions. In the north of Sierra Leone,

---

[36] *Ibid.*, p. 92.

[37] Hayner, *Unspeakable Truths*, pp. 192–193.

[38] For example, Honwana described a healing ritual for an ex-child soldier in Mozambique. The child, dressed in his rebel clothing, entered a small grass hut and undressed, after which the hut was set on fire. An adult relative then assisted the child in getting out of the hut, which was left to burn down with the child's rebel clothing and any other effects from the rebel camp. After the sacrifice of a chicken, the child inhaled smoke from herbal remedies and bathed in water treated with medicine. These symbolised separation from the past and cleansing of the body, allowing the child to return to the community and regain his place within it. Honwana, 'Healing and Social Reintegration', in *Roads to Reconciliation*, pp. 87, 95–96.

[39] Hayner, *Unspeakable Truths*, p. 193. Reports have also suggested that symptoms of PTSD have disappeared after these rituals. Honwana, 'Healing and Social Reintegration', in *Roads to Reconciliation*, p. 97.

[40] Honwana lists as factors the 'closeness of the individual or the family to their cultural roots, the availability of healthcare alternatives, as well as religious and political affiliations' as important to individuals' choice of healing. In Mozambique, people travel amongst traditional healers, hospitals, and religious figures for various types of healing contexts. *Ibid.*, pp. 86, 92–93.

[41] Hayner, *Unspeakable Truths*, pp. 189–190.

[42] *Ibid.*, p. 192.

for instance, social forgetting has been a cornerstone for ongoing community reintegration and healing for ex-combatants, including child ex-combatants. Rituals were performed to 'cool the heart' of child ex-combatants by restoring their links with god, the ancestors, family and community in group rituals and ceremonies. Maintaining a 'cool heart' involved transforming social identity, the relationship of the person within the community. Many communities in Sierra Leone were not interested in a detailed accounting of past acts so much as behavioural evidence of genuine remorse, as signs of the internal transformation and renunciation of past violence that would be required to reintegrate peacefully and maintain future moral relationships. After such rituals, community members were discouraged from talking publicly about the war, asking ex-combatants about past acts, or even labelling them as ex-combatants.[43]

This prioritisation of remorse by the community could also be seen in the proceedings of some of the truth commission hearings. For instance, in one northern town, the process seemed geared towards psychologically preparing perpetrators and the community to participate in a reconciliation ceremony planned for the last day. Questioning from commissioners elicited little detail of abuses, and perpetrators mostly accepted responsibility only as members of rebel forces that committed atrocities. Questioning seemed instead to serve the symbolic purpose of re-establishing community law over perpetrators, as they submitted themselves to its authority, scrutiny and disapprobation. Commissioners repeatedly reminded perpetrators and the audience of the ceremony to come, and that apology and remorse would be expected. The final reconciliation ceremony included the paramount chief and community elders, as well as a representative from the government and the inter-religious council. In this way, it appeared to invoke spiritual powers as well as the physical, emphasising the holistic inter-relational nature of reconciliation in Sierra Leone through remorse, acceptance and reintegration. In the end, despite the fact that little truth was revealed, as would be required in the Western tradition, the apologies of the last day appeared to be accepted by the community because of their evident sincerity.[44]

In Sierra Leone, there were instances reported of communities acting in concert to refuse to give statements to the TRC, or to give partial statements only, in order to protect child ex-combatants, their neighbours and their communities.[45] This was partially due to the conflict between the stated resolve of the TRC that reconciliation was only to be achieved through truth. The belief in social forgetting by many in Sierra Leone led them to reject the TRC, but this tension prevented either from having full effect.

---

[43]   See Shaw, *Rethinking Truth and Reconciliation Commissions: Lessons from Sierra Leone.*

[44]   This description is taken from Tim Kelsall's observations of a hearing in Magburaka Town, Tonkolili District, Northern Province in July 2003. See T. Kelsall, 'Truth, Lies, Ritual: Preliminary Reflections on the Truth and Reconciliation Commission in Sierra Leone,' *Human Rights Quarterly* vol. 27, no. 2 (2005), 361–391.

[45]   Shaw, *Rethinking Truth and Reconciliation Commissions*, pp. 8–9.

While there have been calls for more culturally-adaptive approaches in transitional justice generally, this critique is particularly germane for truth commissions. TRCs are the most directly and broadly participatory justice mechanism and the mechanism with the most far-reaching, explicit cultural goals: truth, reconciliation and long-term readjustment of social relations. To maximise opportunity for success, any existing local reintegration and reconciliation processes and traditions should be sought out and carefully evaluated for conflict or convergence with new intended initiatives.

Conducting the broad-based inquiries necessary for such evaluation can admittedly be difficult in post-conflict situations: security is poor, infrastructure demolished, traditional social structures torn apart, populations have been displaced, there is widespread fear of further violence and a general distrust of foreign intervention. The international community may also have further concerns in the compatibility of some traditional practices with human rights norms in terms of gender equality, due process and protection of minority rights; and with interference in a state's right to decide the balance between sanction of traditional hierarchies and respect for its own power structures. There could also be variances between reconciliation traditions in ethnically diverse societies, and varying needs and preferences within a society based on rural and urban settings. Local NGOs may speak the international language of reconciliation, instead of supporting the traditional approaches victims would prefer. There is a need to draw on resources beyond the legal and human rights fields to include regional experts in anthropology, history, psychology and social science as well.

Further complicating matters, in post-conflict situations there are often other reasons, besides tradition, that could make victims reluctant to testify. These could include fears of a breakdown in the peace process; fear by witnesses of retribution, if perpetrators are still armed or in positions of power; fear by perpetrators of prosecution; distrust of state bodies after years of oppression; shame over acts or failures to act; and disbelief in the possibility of accountability for perpetrators. Overcoming some of these fears may legitimately be part of the role of a TRC effort. How can international decision-makers weigh these real concerns against the purported benefits of a truth-seeking mechanism? How can they choose when they should override victims' indicated preferences in the interests of pursuing longer-term healing and reconciliation, without crossing the line into cultural imperialism?

A look at other similarities between the cases of Sierra Leone and Mozambique could help frame such policy discussions on TRCs. These factors could be placed under two categories: the character of human rights violations and of perpetrators; and the ability of the state to follow through on a commission and on alternatives to a commission.

Character of Human Rights Violations

State Sponsorship and Secrecy

Truth-seeking mechanisms were first developed and may continue to be more urgently demanded by victims where past human rights abuses were mainly perpetrated by the state apparatus or had a strong aspect of official denial, such as for disappearances or practices of torture in detention. This has often been the case in regime changes and transitions from authoritarian to more democratic forms of government, such as in South Africa and several Latin American nations. In these situations, victims and family members seek truth, in the form of information about those missing, and official, public acknowledgment of systematic state-sanctioned abuse. An *ad hoc* body with a special mandate is often required in order to compel government and military officials who have important information, but who are ordinarily protected by the system, to reveal top-level involvement.

Truth-seeking mechanisms are increasingly being applied in post-conflict situations, however, where the state may no longer be the sole or most egregious source of human rights violations. In such cases of state failure and widespread militia- or rebel-driven atrocity against the society at large, the abuses are often widely known and nearly universally experienced, as either victim or perpetrator. This may point to a need to recast some of the stated fundamental motives of a TRC. While a convergent history is still crucial, including the acknowledgment that all sides were involved in perpetrating human rights abuses, the need or desire of victims to tell their experiences publicly and to have them officially acknowledged may be lessened. In contrast, their need to develop a sense of security in their homes and communities against a repetition of attacks from the ranks of returned ex-combatants may be urgent as they now must live again in the same villages and towns. Fostering reintegration and reconciliation at the community level may legitimately be the priority of the victims and, therefore, should be a high priority in the design of a TRC mechanism.

Victim–Perpetrator Distinction

Victim demand for accountability and shaming of perpetrators through public truth mechanisms may also vary, based on how clearly the lines between victim and perpetrator can be drawn, and how closely related the two groups are. In transitions from authoritarian regimes, it can be easier to draw a broad line between victim groups and perpetrator groups, between civilians or minorities on one side and the state or the military on the other.[46] There may also be a sense that certain groups

---

[46]   Of course there will always be crossovers such as collaborators; activists for change in positions of power; armed guerrilla groups fighting against the government; or cases where, as a result of suffering human rights violations, victims may turn to terrorist acts to destabilise the government, as suggested by Minow.

profited through the systematic abuse and exploitation of other groups, such as in South Africa, and that the profiteers should therefore be publicly exposed and shamed. In post-conflict states when genocide was present or when atrocities were perpetrated on the basis of ethnic or religious divisions, such as in the former Yugoslavia, Rwanda, Burundi, or as alleged in Sudan, a broad line can similarly be drawn between abuser and abused on each side. Furthermore, in such cases, there is often state intent and planning, which, as discussed above, can drive demand for public truth-telling.

Where two (or more) opposing histories exist in such situations, they must foremost be publicly exposed, analysed, understood and reconciled in order to diffuse the potential for future recurrence of violence. Vast gulfs in understanding of historical events and context, reinforced through teaching of future generations, could make reconciliation impossible between readily distinguishable groups, who may often also live separately. Also in such cases, public processes of truth-seeking and the finding of a common understanding of history would be a logical priority, with the hope that such a process of political reconciliation would then make possible future individual reconciliation.

In Sierra Leone and Mozambique, however, the worst human rights abuses unleashed on civilians resembled more closely decentralised crimes of opportunity and impunity, rather than crimes by the state. In the case of Mozambique, they were instigated by foreign states rather than driven from within.[47] Victims and low-level perpetrators on both sides came from the same villages and the same families; ethnic or religious lines could not be clearly drawn.[48] Children were abducted, abused, drugged and coerced into carrying out violent attacks.[49] In some cases, they were ordered to kill their own family members, or to participate in attacks on their own villages in order to prevent them from returning home.[50] Young women were encouraged by their families to be 'wives' of rebel soldiers in order to secure protection from other soldiers and to preserve the family property.[51]

How justly could guilt and shame be assigned to perpetrators and collaborators who themselves were victims? What purpose would public stigma serve when all

---

[47] In Mozambique, for instance, Renamo, the main rebel group, was formed by Rhodesia (now Zimbabwe), which sought to undermine Mozambique's non-white government, and was then supported by South Africa, which considered it as the African National Congress' base of operations. When foreign support for Renamo ended, a ceasefire was soon declared. Hayner, *Unspeakable Truths*, p. 188.

[48] Hayner writes that it was 'not uncommon for siblings to be fighting on opposite sides of the war'. *Ibid.*, pp. 188–189.

[49] See for example Honwana, 'Innocent & Guilty', *Makers and Breakers: Children and Youth in Postcolonial Africa*, p. 41, for Mozambique.

[50] In Mozambique, for instance, this was a strategy employed by the Renamo rebel forces. See *ibid.*, p. 42.

[51] Utas addresses the issue of women during the war in Liberia, but also tells of the many Sierra Leonean girls brought by rebels to Liberia and who still remain, with no social ties or means. M. Utas, 'Agency of Victims: Young Women in the Liberian Civil War', in *Makers and Breakers, Children and Youth in Postcolonial Africa*, p. 58.

families and groups would be stained with it? Can a meaningful truth be distilled from a long, complex chaotic war without easy dividing lines to separate the parties and explain their motivations, as in Mozambique? Could such exposure be genuinely restorative or merely retributive and divisive? Where resistance to a commission is high, its assumptions and design should be reviewed for possible ways to improve its effectiveness for victims. When perpetrators are so closely intertwined with victims, and the lines between them so blurred, broad but genuine remorse and apology for the unspoken and unspeakable volumes of abuses during the war, combined with symbolism drawn from a shared background, may be the most effective catalyst for healing for victims and the most powerful route to reconciliation.

State Capabilities

Even without questioning the basic assumptions of truth-telling as a healing and reconciliation mechanism, the choice of design for a truth commission response in modern post-conflict situations should consider the capacity of the state to follow through on victim support, alternatives to commissions and commission recommendations.

The psychiatric model to address PTSD through truth-telling is a longer-term undertaking. Usually, the process of re-exposing trauma and neutralising it requires more time than that which a truth commission can provide. Re-opening painful memories without follow-up can re-traumatise victims, breaking through the coping mechanisms that they have developed and leaving them confused or even incapacitated.[52] In truth commissions, this psychological shock may be further aggravated by the practical necessity for victims to enter immediately into details of past trauma during statement-taking, without benefit of the recommended gradual, preparatory approach.[53] This issue cannot be resolved merely by an additional mandate to offer victims counselling or referrals – in some post-conflict states the capacity simply does not exist to provide mental health services to all those affected by the war.[54] Victims would depend on their communities and any local support groups to help them recover from re-traumatisation. Such groups may not be versed in Western-influenced recovery strategies, however, and may on the contrary have widely different traditions, including the 'social forgetting' described above. This lack of health service capacity could be a factor in the choice of mechanism for truth commissions.

One positive correlation found in South Africa, in contrast, was that where new information on specific abuses was uncovered, such as after amnesty hearings and in cases investigated by the commission, victims seemed to find a beneficial sense of closure.[55] Even in Sierra Leone, where little detail of abuses was revealed, far more

---

[52] Hayner, *Unspeakable Truths*, pp. 141–143.
[53] *Ibid.*, p. 139.
[54] *Ibid.*, p. 146.
[55] *Ibid.*, p. 140.

community members attended hearings when the few perpetrators were testifying as opposed to victim testimony,[56] as if it were sufficient to watch the struggle for reassertion of community order over the perpetrators and to seek key signs of remorse. In this sense, truth commissions may be more beneficial for victims when they can engage more people who are beyond the ability of victims to compel – the government, the military and other powerful perpetrators.

However, it can be difficult to drive perpetrators to submit to a truth commission without either a credible threat of prosecutions or a credible possibility of community reconciliation following testimony. South Africa, for instance, was able to use a combination of amnesty for testimony and a judiciary capable of prosecuting crimes under apartheid to motivate military officers to testify.[57] In Timor-Leste, the opposite tactic was chosen, in order to promote the return of the many Timorese who had fled and to facilitate reconciliation amongst citizens in the small, newly-created nation.[58] The mandate of the Timor-Leste truth commission (CAVR) allowed perpetrators of non-serious criminal offences to seek immunity from prosecution by disclosing all acts and undergoing an individualised Community Reconciliation Process (CRP), which could consist of community service, reparation, public apology or some other act of contrition. This resulted in an unusual mixture of standard truth commission mechanisms and flexible community-based measures that was generally considered successful in both of its aims.[59]

Finally, the political will and ability of the government to follow through on recommendations from truth commissions may be considered in design of a TRC. It has been conjectured that many witnesses only testify before the commission with the hope of receiving some compensation.[60] Others may seek justice against perpetrators, follow-up on their individual cases, or some other tangible change in their lives. If the government cannot fulfil these expectations, victims could lose faith in the new political system, or threats of armed violence could break out anew.[61]

---

[56]   Kelsall, 'Truth, Lies, Ritual', 370.

[57]   Amnesty International and Human Rights Watch, *Truth and Justice: Unfinished Business in South Africa* (13 February 2003).

[58]   The Community Reconciliation Process has received mixed reviews; see for example, Judicial System Monitoring Programme, *Unfulfilled Expectations: Community Views on CAVR's Community Reconciliation Process*, (August 2004), available at http://www.jsmp. minihub.org/Reports/jsmpreports/CAVR_Reports/cavr_report_2004_e.pdf.

[59]   By the end of CAVR's field operations in May 2004, 216 community reconciliation events had been held, involving 1,403 deponents. While most of the community reconciliation hearings consisted of apology and an undertaking not to repeat the acts, other examples included symbolic payments, contributions to a communal meal, restitution of stolen livestock and property, community clean-up and monetary contributions and labour for reconstruction projects. See *Final Report of the Commission for Reception, Truth and Reconciliation in East Timor*, available at http://www.ictj.org/cavr.report.asp.

[60]   Shaw, *Rethinking Truth and Reconciliation Commissions*, p. 8.

[61]   For example, when ex-community militia members in Guatemala did not receive pension checks from the government, they began holding mass demonstrations. J. Replogle,

Thus, a limited ability to carry out recommendations should also be considered in designing and advertising a commission.

Conclusion

That public truth-telling as the necessary and exclusive route to reconciliation may not be the best approach at the community level does not mean that efforts to provide a legitimate national history of the conflict and accompanying independent recommendations for reparations would not be beneficial. It is important to have truth commissions. In addition to the benefits and aims of TRCs listed at the outset, TRCs during transition can serve to counter popular myths of key events that have emerged, before they become so engrained as to be indisputable. Periods of transition, during the initial resurgence of hope after peace and before a new government has consolidated its power and the international community has lost interest, can also be an opportune time for change – for example in addressing gender violence issues – and commission reports calling attention to historical problem areas can be used as powerful leverage.

Having a well-developed foundation for recommending reparation programmes, in the form of a truth commission report, as early as possible during a transition can also help the government begin to consolidate the peace dividend and address the underlying causes of conflict. Governments cannot ignore the need for broader measures that will change the socio-economic situation of victims and perpetrators alike in order to form a lasting peace. This issue is addressed most directly by reparation in the form of education and job training for those harmed by the war and by investment in development.

If a truth commission is desirable but factors militate against establishment of a full public truth-telling mechanism such as used in South Africa, a spectrum of modifications can be made to the standard model. Different stated aims of the commission and different approaches could make achievement of national political reconciliation more compatible with community-level reconciliation in given situations. One model could be based on the Timor-Leste experience, with community-based reconciliation processes run under the auspices of the truth commission, but carried out at a local level and incorporating apologies with symbolic and real restitution. Another model could be the adaptation of an historical commission charged with assembling an integrated, common history and recommendations for reparation, and with no explicit mandate for reconciliation. Without an official, unified national approach to reconciliation, there is a risk that reconciliation efforts might not be pursued in some areas at all; however, in situations similar to those of Sierra Leone and Mozambique, indigenous rituals developed by the communities themselves could then be supported rather than interrupted. A third compromise model could consist of a flexible central truth commission, but with

---

'Paramilitaries demand payment', *Latinamerica Press*, 5 July 2005.

adaptive reconciliation and reparation mechanisms deployed in different areas of the country, such as large, lengthy public hearings in urban centres and community-based traditional ceremonies in rural areas.

Ultimately, it is for the field operation to not lose sight of the complexity of its task of providing advice on transitional justice. The UN is now equipped with five valuable transitional justice tools. These will be of great assistance. They will not and cannot substitute for profound understanding of local culture based on a wide and ongoing process of respectful listening.

In the end, the changes envisioned for the approach of the international community to design of post-conflict truth commissions do not have to be sweeping to improve coordination between national and local healing and reconciliation. What is essential is that UN field operations, in a thoughtful and deliberative manner, develop a rich understanding of local reconciliation processes and traditions since truth-seeking initiatives considered a success in one context may be not be suitable in another. Moreover, the field operation must proactively seek practical, flexible solutions that respond to what victims themselves desire, acknowledge the potential contributions of indigenous healing traditions, and maintain pressure for implementation of recommendations to remedy victim suffering and the societal conditions that fed the conflict.

Chapter 9

The Human Rights Field Operation in Partnership for Humanitarian Relief and Reconstruction

Michael O'Flaherty[1]

Introduction

Humanitarianism can be described as, 'the vocation of helping people when they most desperately need help, when they have lost or stand at risk of losing everything they have, including their lives'.[2] Almost invariably, a major life-threatening crisis, whether 'natural' or man-made, will attract a response from humanitarian actors, be they of the national authorities, the United Nations (UN), non-governmental organisations (NGOs) or otherwise, who will deploy specialist staff across the affected regions as quickly and as widely as possible.[3] Given the humanitarian preoccupation with the welfare of humanity, it might appear that possibilities are rife for partnership with human rights actors, including human rights field operations. The merits can seem to be obvious.[4] For field operations, for instance, humanitarian teams will probably be in the field ahead of them and in greater numbers, and their

[1]   The author would like to express appreciation to a great and inspiring humanitarian, Monique Nagelkerke. The author thanks Kevin Turner for his research assistance, James Harrison who commented on drafts of the chapter, and the friends and colleagues with whom he served as a member of the United Nations Inter-Agency Standing Committee Task Force on Human Rights and Humanitarian Action (2000–2002).

[2]   D. Rieff, *A Bed for the Night* (London: Vintage, 2002), p. 27.

[3]   For a succinct overview of the range of humanitarian actors see, T. G. Weiss, *Military-Civilian Interaction: Humanitarian Crises and the Responsibility to Protect*, 2nd edn, chapter 1, 'Armed Forces and Humanitarian Action, Past and Present' (Lanham: Rowman and Littlefield, 2005). See also A. Stoddard, 'Humanitarian NGOs: Challenges and Trends', in J. Macrae and A. Harmer (eds), *Humanitarian Assistance and the "Global War on Terror": A Review of the Trends and Issues*, Humanitarian Policy Group Report no. 14 (London: Overseas Development Institute, July 2003).

[4]   See M. O'Flaherty, 'Future Protection of Human Rights in Post-conflict Societies', in N. D. White and D. Klaasen (eds), *The UN, Human Rights and Post-conflict Situations* (Manchester: Manchester University Press, 2005), pp. 379–403. See also chapter 1 by M. O'Flaherty in the present volume.

cooperation can greatly augment local human rights monitoring and reporting capacity. For the humanitarian actors, the partnerships could serve, among other things, the goal of addressing the root causes of the crisis.

Just such a natural or synergistic relationship is assumed by some commentators as a starting point for reflection on the relationship between the two bodies of principle and of operations.[5] However, there are many other academic and policy-level authors who query the validity or appropriateness of the relationship at all or who suggest strict limits for operational cooperation.[6] There may also be found those who relate human rights to just some, rather than all, aspects of humanitarianism, for instance to the work of 'protection' rather than 'assistance',[7] while still others would outright reject even the validity of such categorisations.[8] In the context of such a maelstrom of diverse and sometimes conflicting views, it is not surprising that practice in the field is inconsistent – with intergovernmental and non-governmental humanitarian and human rights actors operating an array of distinct models.

This chapter seeks to take stock of the confused (or confusing) situation. The chosen method is an historic one addressing the short period, some 14 years, since the emergence of discourse regarding the relationship between human rights and humanitarian action. Reflection is focused chronologically, commencing with an assessment of the situation in 1991, followed by a review of developments during the subsequent ten years and concluding with an examination of the situation in 2005. From the analysis it also becomes possible to identify some basic principles to underlie the partnerships between humanitarian and human rights field operations.

Historical Review 1: The Situation as of 1991

UN General Assembly resolution 46/182 (1991), 'Strengthening of the coordination of humanitarian emergency assistance of the United Nations', adopted in 1991,[9] has been described as a humanitarian *magna carta*.[10] An examination of its elements can thus provide something of a snapshot of the state of humanitarian thinking as of 1991. The resolution provided a conceptual and organisational framework for UN humanitarian action. The guiding principles were articulated: including the 'cardinal

---

    5   A. Donini, 'The Forest and the Trees: The Evolving Nature of Coordination', in *The Humanitarian Decade* vol. 2 (New York: United Nations Office for the Coordination of Humanitarian Affairs (OCHA), 2004), pp. 127–141.

    6   N. de Torrente, 'Humanitarian Action under Attack: Reflections on the Iraq War', *Harvard Human Rights Journal* vol. 17 (2004).

    7   H. Slim and L. E. Eguren, *Humanitarian Protection* (Pilot Version) (London: Active Learning Network for Accountability and Performance in Humanitarian Action, March 2004), pp. 6–7.

    8   P. Walker, 'What Does it Mean to be a Professional Humanitarian', *The Journal of Humanitarian Assistance* (January 2004), http://www.jha.ac/articles/a127.htm.

    9   General Assembly Resolution 46/182 (1991), UN Doc. A/RES/46/182 (1991).

    10   K. Oshima, UN Emergency Relief Coordinator, address to Panel Discussion on the 10th anniversary of General Assembly resolution 46/182, 17 July 2002, reported in *The Humanitarian Decade* vol. 1 (New York: OCHA, 2004), pp. 3–6.

importance' of the provision of assistance to 'victims of natural disaster and other emergencies' and the need to provide assistance in accordance with the principles of humanity, neutrality and impartiality. The relative roles of states and humanitarian actors were located: while recognising that the 'primary responsibility' for provision of assistance falls on the affected state, international humanitarian assistance 'should' be provided with the consent of the affected country and 'in principle' on the basis of an appeal by that country. The resolution identified 'a clear relationship between emergency, rehabilitation and development', with the focus very much on natural disasters. Coordination structures were established and it was stated that the UN should coordinate well and work closely with the International Committee of the Red Cross (ICRC), the League of Red Cross and Red Crescent Societies as well as relevant non-governmental organisations.

The adoption of resolution 46/182 was an acknowledgement, in the optimistic post-Cold War mood, of the potential for good to be found in multilateral action.[11] The optimism of the time perhaps also helps explain the focus on natural disasters and the absence of any specific reference to conflict-related humanitarian emergencies, notwithstanding the long train of such situations that the UN had had to address in previous decades.[12] With its attention on natural disasters, it proposed a continuum model of emergency prediction, assistance, recovery and development – reflecting an understanding which, even then, was seen as ill-suited to addressing such man-made disasters as conflict-related displacement and the suffering precipitated by the collapse of states.[13] Notably, the resolution also referred just to the delivery of 'assistance' rather than also to such services as protection or advocacy. While this may seem consonant with the focus of attention on natural disasters it is also entirely consistent with much humanitarian practice of the time, which had no difficulty in severing notions of assistance and protection and indeed of entirely ignoring the latter.[14] The consistency is also reflected in the manner in which the resolution, by means of the citation of such guiding principles as the humanitarian imperative, humanity, neutrality and impartiality, associated its humanitarian policy with the traditions of the Red Cross movement.

The resolution makes no reference whatsoever to human rights. This is particularly notable given that contemporary international human rights law had specific provisions on the matter of humanitarian assistance. The International Covenant on Economic, Social and Cultural Rights,[15] at Article 2(1), states that, 'Each party to the present Covenant undertakes to take steps individually and through *international assistance*

---

[11]   See E. Tsui and T. Myint-U, 'The Institutional Response: Creating the Framework in Response to New Challenges', in *The Humanitarian Decade* vol. 2, pp. 1–14.

[12]   *Ibid.*

[13]   See M. Bowden, 'Natural disasters and the Millennium Goals', in *The Humanitarian Decade* vol. 2, pp. 206–211.

[14]   See L. Minear, *Helping People in an Age of Conflict: Toward a New Professionalism in U.S. Voluntary Humanitarian Assistance* (Washington, DC: Interaction, 1988).

[15]   International Covenant on Economic, Social and Cultural Rights, adopted 19 Dec. 1966, G.A. res. 2200 (XXI), UN GAOR, 21st Sess., Supp. No. 16, UN Doc. A/6316 (1966), 993 UNTS 3 (entered into force 3 Jan. 1976).

and cooperation (present author's italics), especially economic and technical, to the maximum of its available resources, with a view to achieving progressively the full realisation of the rights recognised in the present Covenant…'. At Article 11(2), the Covenant stipulates that, in recognition of 'the fundamental rights of everyone to be free from hunger', states parties, 'shall take, individually and through international cooperation, the measures, including specific programmes, which are needed'. In 1990, the international technical cooperation elements of the Covenant, particularly as they pertained to the work of various UN agencies, had been the subject of a commentary (a 'General Comment') by the Covenant's expert supervisory body, the Committee on Economic, Social and Cultural Rights, which had received considerable attention in the UN Economic and Social Council, the Commission on Human Rights and the General Assembly.[16] The Convention on the Rights of the Child (CRC),[17] which, by 1991, had achieved (rapidly) near universal ratification, contains similar provisions: e.g. 'States Parties undertake to promote and encourage international cooperation with a view to achieving progressively the full realisation of the rights [to health]' (Article 24(4)). CRC also, at Article 38, stipulates that '[I]n accordance with their obligations under international humanitarian law to protect the civilian population in armed conflict, States Parties shall take all feasible measures to ensure protection and care of children who are affected by an armed conflict'.[18]

A number of reasons may be adduced for the absence of reference to human rights in the humanitarian discourse of the time. In the first place, it was perceived by some humanitarian actors that humanitarianism was well served by the guidance offered by international humanitarian law (IHL) and such bodies of law as refugee law.[19] Other legal references were not perceived to be necessary, particularly those, such as human rights, which primarily address the relationship between states and their peoples, and thus are not immediately seen to be relevant to programmes of international cooperation (notwithstanding the treaty provisions cited above). Furthermore, it does not appear that there was much sense of the practical relevance of human rights for humanitarian action – for instance, human rights law was sometimes considered to be targeted at times of peace and relative stability – not

---

[16]   Committee on Economic, Social and Cultural Rights, General Comment No. 2: International Technical Assistance Measures (Article 22 of the Covenant), UN Doc. E/1990/23 (1990); see P. Alston, 'The Committee on Economic, Social and Cultural Rights', in P. Alston (ed.), *The United Nations and Human Rights* (Oxford: Clarendon Press, 1992), footnote 130, p. 495.

[17]   Convention on the Rights of the Child, adopted 20 Nov. 1989, G.A. res. 44/25, UN GAOR, 44th Sess., Supp. No. 49, UN Doc. A/44/49 (1989) (entered into force 2 Sept. 1990).

[18]   See, writing in 1999, M. Santos-Pais, 'A Vision for Children: the Convention on the Rights of the Child', in Y. Danieli *et al.* (eds), *The Universal Declaration of Human Rights: Fifty Years and Beyond* (New York: Baywood Publishing, 1998), pp. 131–144.

[19]   See, for instance, ICRC, 'The Movement and Refugees', 25th International Conference of the Red Cross, Geneva, 23 to 31 October 1986, Resolution 17, available at http://www.icrc. org/Web/Eng/siteeng0.nsf/iwpList141/C64E92901DE3E198C1256B6600592A29.

relevant to emergency situations.[20] In any case, it was not then obvious what human rights law had to say to what was perceived as the core of humanitarianism – the delivery of 'assistance', and all the less so when that assistance was in the context of 'natural' disasters.[21]

It must also be noted that human rights actors simply did not acknowledge the relationship between the sectors. Thus, the General Comment of the Committee on Economic, Social and Cultural Rights, referred to above, focuses its attention exclusively on those aspects of international cooperation relating to human development, and human rights leaders were later to admit that the various issues simply had not been on their radar.[22] Also, as of 1991, the UN had yet to establish a high level human rights leadership post (the position of high commissioner for human rights not being filled until 1994), thus potentially depriving the drafting of the resolution of a human rights advocacy voice. Finally, it can be observed that, as of 1991, there was as yet no visibility of human rights field officers in humanitarian environments, with the first deployment of a human rights field operation having occurred just that year.[23]

Before concluding an examination of the situation as of 1991 it can be suggested that, for all the explicit ignoring of human rights, some of its principles were already implicitly informing discourse. For instance, resolution 46/181's provisions indicating the primary duty on the part of states to meet the humanitarian needs of their people ('[E]ach State has the responsibility) – can easily be derived from the obligations on states contained in international legal instruments such as the Covenant on Economic, Social and Cultural Rights. Human rights considerations may also underlie the resolution's formulation, whereby international assistance 'should' be provided with the consent of the affected country, rather than it 'must' be so provided – thus adopting that understanding of state sovereignty which sees it as tempered by considerations of the welfare of its people.[24]

Historical Review 2: The Subsequent Ten Years

The 1990s were marked by conflict after conflict resulting in massive suffering of civilian populations and humanitarian emergencies, such as in, to recall just a few locations, former Yugoslavia, Rwanda, Chechnya, Sierra Leone, East Timor and Angola. In response to the scale of these catastrophes, international capacity

---

[20] See D. Paul, *Protection in Practice: Field-level Strategies for Protecting Civilians from Deliberate Harm*, Humanitarian Relief Network (London: Overseas Development Institute, 1999), p. 3.

[21] See, for instance, B. Ramcharan, 'Strategies for the International Protection of Human Rights in the 1990s', *Human Rights Quarterly* vol. 13, no. 2 (1991), pp. 155–169.

[22] K. Roth, 'Defending Economic, Social and Cultural Rights', *Human Rights Quarterly* vol. 26, no. 1 (2004), pp. 72–73.

[23] See chapter 1 by M. O'Flaherty in the present volume.

[24] See, E. Tsui and T. Myint-U, 'The Institutional Response', in *The Humanitarian Decade* vol. 2 p. 9.

to deliver humanitarian response grew exponentially, with a myriad of active non-governmental organisations, UN agencies and donor states.[25] In marked contrast to many earlier conflicts, the wars of the period, given their commonly internal nature, often overwhelmed their victims at their home locations or forced them into internal displacement rather than to safety across international frontiers. What movement across borders did occur often resulted in replacing one high risk location with another. One consequence of the changing nature of the impact of conflict was that a great deal of humanitarian work came to be undertaken within the conflict zones themselves. This change in the locus of humanitarian attention rapidly clarified some profoundly important issues.[26] In the first instance, it created situations where humanitarian workers witnessed – sometimes were the first to witness – the conflict-related perpetration of human rights abuses, often at great risk to themselves. They also observed how their programming could actually sustain a conflict, such as by the feeding of combatants or the manipulation of programming by the various factions. Such experiences led to a widespread view that delivery of assistance in and of itself was inadequate and that humanitarianism must identify and address the patterns of abuse that precipitated and fed conflict.[27] Thus originated a trend in humanitarianism that has commonly come to be referred to as 'new humanitarianism'.[28]

Patterns of abuse and of responses thereto can be considered and addressed from numerous vantage points and disciplines. Thus, in the 1990s, humanitarian actions attracted conflict resolution and conflict management models, such as the 'Do No Harm' approach, championed by Mary B. Anderson.[29] Another element of the 'new humanitarianism' approaches is that of human rights. By the mid-1990s, prominent NGOs such as *Médecins Sans Frontières* (MSF) were increasingly exploring the human rights perspectives.[30] The adoption, in 1994, of the 'Code of Conduct for the International Red Cross and Red Crescent Movement and NGOs in Disaster Relief', also created a space in which it became possible to identify a high, albeit not comprehensive, degree of mutuality between humanitarianism's core principles and those of human rights.[31] NGO efforts were mirrored by those of some UN

---

[25]   See M. Bowden, 'Foreword', in *The Humanitarian Decade* vol. 2, pp. vii–x.

[26]   For a review of the situation, the issues and the literature, see N. Stockton, 'The Changing Nature of Humanitarian Crises', in *The Humanitarian Decade* vol. 2, pp. 15–38.

[27]   See Weiss, *Military-Civilian Interaction*, chapter 1.

[28]   C. Short, 'Principles for a New Humanitarianism', lecture at European Union, European Commission Humanitarian Aid (ECHO)/Overseas Development Institute Conferences (London, 1998).

[29]   M. B. Anderson, *Do No Harm: Supporting Local Capacities for Peace Through Aid* (Cambridge: Local Capacities for Peace Project, Collaborative for Development Action, 1996).

[30]   See paper by F. Heyster, *Médecins Sans Frontières Temoignage: From Public Abstinence to Mission Statement* (December 1999), on file with the present author.

[31]   International Committee of the Red Cross, 'The Code of Conduct for the International Red Cross and Red Crescent Movement and NGOs in Disaster Relief' (1994), available at http://www.icrc.org/Web/Eng/siteeng0.nsf/html/57JMNB?OpenDocument; by 2004, the 'Code of Conduct' had been adopted by 280 humanitarian organisations.

agencies. The United Nations Children's Fund (UNICEF) was notable in this regard as it endeavoured to integrate an organisational commitment to the rights of the child into all aspects of its work.[32] In 1997, the UN secretary-general was calling for cross-cutting attention to human rights across all the activities of the UN.[33] His call was reinforced and supported by the then newly-appointed UN High Commissioner for Human Rights, Mary Robinson,[34] albeit it was not until the new millennium that her office devoted resources to address issues of human rights and humanitarianism.

Various explanations have been identified for humanitarianism's discovery of human rights. For some organisations it was a matter of expediency – human rights norms and mechanisms, by being called into service for advocacy and to compel changes of behaviour, could serve the goals of humanitarianism.[35] In such cases it has been suggested that the focus of humanitarian attention was principally on issues of civil and political rights and on international accountability and justice.[36] For other organisations, the attraction of human rights had also to do with the manner in which it identified the human as a subject endowed with rights rather than as a beneficiary of largesse – it being considered that this human rights approach could render humanitarian work more respectful of its 'beneficiaries' and, ultimately, more sustainable.[37]

The discussion of the role of human rights was very much centred on issues of protection – how a human rights approach could better contribute to the safety of the victims of conflict-related humanitarian emergencies. In a series of workshops organised by the ICRC, attempts were made to define the protection function.[38] It was concluded that protection, 'encompass[es] all activities aimed at ensuring full respect for the rights of the individual in accordance with the letter and the spirit of the relevant bodies of law, i.e. human rights law, IHL and refugee law. Human rights and humanitarian organisations must conduct these activities in an impartial manner (not on the basis of race, national or ethnic origin, language or gender)'.[39] The definition describes a protection activity as an activity which, 'prevents or puts a stop to a specific pattern of abuse and/or alleviates its immediate effects (responsive action); restores people's dignity and ensures adequate living conditions through

---

[32] See 'Realizing Rights, Getting Results', available at http://www.unicef.org/rightsresults/index.html.

[33] Report of the Secretary-General, Renewing the United Nations: A Programme for Reform, UN Doc. A/51/950 (1997).

[34] M. Robinson, 'Realising Human Rights: Take Hold of it Boldly and Duly', Oxford University Romanes Lecture (11 November 1997), available at http://www.unhchr.ch/huricane/huricane.nsf/view01/9C0D6698ABCB7A4BC125662E00352F81?opendocument.

[35] F. Heyster, *Médecins Sans Frontières Temoignage*.

[36] See UNICEF note, *A Human Rights-based Approach to Programming in Humanitarian Crises: Is UNICEF up to the Challenge* (September 2003), on file with the present author.

[37] M. Santos-Pais, 'A Vision for Children' : the Convention on the Rights of the Child', in *The Universal Declaration of Human Rights: Fifty Years and Beyond*.

[38] ICRC, *Strengthening Protection in War: A Search for Professional Standards* (ICRC: Geneva, 2001).

[39] *Ibid.*, p. 19.

reparation, restitutions and rehabilitation (remedial action); fosters an environment conducive to respect for the rights of individuals in accordance with the relevant bodies of law (environment building)'.[40] Debate tended to concentrate on the plight of certain categories of people in need of protection, notably internally displaced persons[41] and children.[42] An important feature of the discourse was the assumption, consistent with the outcome of the ICRC workshops, that while human rights had a role in contributing to the development of protection strategies it was but one legal source, with refugee and IHL and practice being of equal significance. This approach is reflected in guidance material generated in the period, notably the UN 'Guiding Principles on Internal Displacement';[43] and it also underlay the establishment by the UN Inter-Agency Standing Committee (IASC) of its reference group on human rights and humanitarian action, which was mandated to address the impact for humanitarian work of all three of the bodies of law and practice.[44] The tri-sourced model of protection is also reflected in the outcome of the ICRC protection workshops that were already referred to.

The extent to which discourse in the period under review focused on protection is noteworthy. It seems to reflect the then widely held assumption that human rights actually had only to do with this aspect of humanitarian action and that it had little to offer for enhanced delivery of 'assistance'.[45] Various commentators of the time did refer to assistance in the context of rights-related approaches but principally in terms of how it might be better undertaken with a view to the enhancement of protection.[46] While there is nothing objectionable in a focus on protection, it did have the consequence of facilitating the overlooking of the

---

[40]   *Ibid.*, pp. 20–24.

[41]   See F. Deng, Comprehensive Study Prepared by Mr. Francis M. Deng, Representative of the Secretary-General on the Human Rights Issues Related to Internally Displaced Persons, UN. Doc E/CN.4/1993/35 (1993); and F. Deng, *Internally Displaced Persons Compilation and Analysis of Legal Norms* (Geneva: Office of the United Nations High Commissioner for Human Rights (OHCHR), United Nations, 1998).

[42]   See G. Machel, Promotion and Protection of the Rights of Children: Impact of Armed Conflict on Children, UN Doc. A/51/306 (1996).

[43]   Guiding Principles on Internal Displacement, UN Doc. E/CN.4/1998/53/Add.2 (1998).

[44]   See IASC, 'Frequently Asked Questions on International Humanitarian, Human Rights and Refugee Law' (2004), available at http://www.humanitarianinfo.org/iasc/publications.asp.

[45]   H. Slim has written that, 'in the 1990s, the term, "protection", was picked up and expanded to the point at which it now [2002] is: becoming the umbrella term of choice to describe all humanitarian action' – H. Slim, 'Protecting Civilians: Putting the Individual at the Humanitarian Centre', in *The Humanitarian Decade* vol. 2, p. 159. That may be so, but a review of the literature of the time makes clear that human rights was commonly perceived only to apply to those parts of the protection framework other than those concerned with assistance issues.

[46]   See, for example, J. Darcy, *Human Rights and International Legal Standards: What do Relief Workers Need to Know* (London: Relief and Rehabilitation Network, 1997); and M. Frohardt, D. Paul and L. Minear, *Protecting Human Rights: The Challenge to Humanitarian*

broader potential role of human rights in changing assistance methodologies.[47] In general, it may also be that it reflected the biased attention to civil and political human rights to the disregard of economic, social and cultural rights, which was noted earlier.[48]

The extensive reflections in the 1990s on the relationship between human rights and humanitarian action were mirrored by experimentation in the field, as is well reflected in an IASC authorised compendium of field practices, *Growing the Sheltering Tree* (2001).[49] A notable aspect of this experimentation was the extent to which it was undertaken in partnership between humanitarian and human rights operations. From the outset of their co-deployment they engaged with each other, usually on the basis of expediency in terms of their respective goals, and often without the benefit of any institutional guidance. In the early days, such as during the war in Bosnia and Herzegovina, cooperation tended to be limited to modest exchanges of information on abuses and in support of such humanitarian activities as the return of displaced persons.[50] Later in the decade the partnerships grew rather sophisticated. In Sierra Leone, for instance, human rights and humanitarian organisations developed an integrated information exchange system and undertook joint programming for release and care for abductees.[51] The partnership there grew to be so valued that when, in 1999, there was a UN move to dismantle its human rights operation, it was the spirited protest of local and international humanitarian groups that helped see the plan reversed.[52] Sierra Leone also provided the context for a discrete but effective advocacy partnership between two major humanitarian and human rights NGOs.[53] In Angola, the UN human rights operation benefited

---

Organisations, Occasional Paper no. 35 (Providence: Watson Institute for International Studies, 1999).

[47]   For an exception to his approach, see the thoughtful 'non-paper' produced by UNICEF in 1998, *Strategies towards a Human Rights Approach: A Step by Step Process of Integrating Human Rights and Humanitarian Action*, on file with the present author, which develops a model of rights-based programming.

[48]   See UNICEF note, *A Human Rights-based Approach to Programming in Humanitarian Crises: Is UNICEF up to the Challenge*.

[49]   IASC, *Growing the Sheltering Tree* (Geneva: UNICEF on behalf of the IASC, 2002), available at http://www.unicef.org/publications/index_4397.html.

[50]   See chapter 15 by M. O'Flaherty in the present volume.

[51]   See M. O'Flaherty, 'The Role of the Human Rights Community in the Sierra Leone Peace Process', *Human Rights Quarterly* vol. 26, no. 1 (2004), pp. 29–62.

[52]   *Ibid.*

[53]   Information known to the present author but retained at request of personnel of one of the involved organisations.

from significant funding arrangements entered into with humanitarian donors and NGOs.[54] Afghanistan also provided a rich vein of experience.[55]

The growing attention to human rights was not without its critics.[56] In the first place it was suggested that the ability of a human rights approach to bring added value had yet to be demonstrated. For instance, commentators pointed to the limitations inherent in the systems of human rights advocacy and enforcement – such as the largely voluntary methods of international human rights supervision. The point was also frequently made that the drawing of attention to human rights abuses by humanitarian organisations put their programmes and their personnel at risk.[57] Issues of principle were raised, for instance concerning the perceived clash between the understanding of humanitarian neutrality and the forms of witnessing, reporting and condemnation that seemed to be inherent in the human rights approach.

At least some of the criticism did not go unanswered. Many human rights actors shared the views regarding the weakness of the international human rights system but perceived these as challenges to be overcome[58] – in affirmation of their optimism they could eventually point to such developments as the appointment of the high commissioner for human rights in 1994 and the adoption of the Statute for the International Criminal Court in 1998.[59] With regard to the putting at risk of humanitarian workers, ample field experiences provided examples of divisions of labour between human rights and humanitarian actors, which served to protect programmes and staff.[60] And, the ICRC workshops, referred to above, went to lengths to identify a formal compatibility between human rights and humanitarian principles (identifying the former as among the sources for the latter), although it has to be said that none of the arguments for the compatibility of the humanitarian principle of neutrality with the human rights principle of accountability are particularly compelling.[61]

---

[54]   See chapter 16 by T. Howland in the present volume.

[55]   N. Niland, 'Rights, Rhetoric and Reality: A Snapshot from Afghanistan', in *The UN, Human Rights and Post-conflict Situations*, pp. 322–346.

[56]   Regarding this paragraph, see, in general, *Médecins sans Frontières*-Holland, *Final Report*, Conference on the Cooperation between Humanitarian Organisations and Human Rights Organisations, Amsterdam, The Netherlands (9 February 1996).

[57]   W. G. O'Neill, *A Humanitarian Practitioner's Guide to International Human Rights Law*, Occasional Paper no. 34 (Providence: Watson Institute for International Studies, 1999).

[58]   See, for example, M. Robinson, 'Human Rights at the Dawn of the 21st Century', speech given at the Interregional meeting organised by the Council of Europe in advance of the World Conference on Human Rights, Strasbourg, 28–30 January 1993, re-printed in *Human Rights Quarterly* vol. 15, no. 4 (1993), pp. 629–639.

[59]   Rome Statute of the International Criminal Court, UN Doc. A/Conf.183/9 (1998) UNTS 90 (entered into force 1 July 2002).

[60]   IASC, *Growing the Sheltering Tree*, pp. 28–35.

[61]   For an argument regarding a dilution of humanitarian principles during the 1990s see, N. Stockton, 'The Changing Nature of Humanitarian Crises', in *The Humanitarian Decade* vol. 2.

In general, very little attention seems to have been paid during the period to the implications of some core issues of legal doctrine.[62] One of these, already mentioned, is that of the treaty-based obligations on states to provide humanitarian assistance. Another concerns the nature of human rights treaty obligations. These fall on states and not on individuals, NGOs or others. Accordingly, to what extent can obligation, responsibility and a right to intervene be imputed to humanitarian actors? In addition, what relevance can a body of law, which identifies the state as duty bearer, have to emergency contexts in which the state may, in fact, be powerless? Still more concerns relate to the triple legal source of the protection concept and indeed of the entire rights-based approach to humanitarianism. For instance, what practice guidance can be deduced from the interplay of human rights and IHL when their relationship is often unclear?[63] Also, since it is by no means universally accepted among scholars that refugee law and IHL can be considered to confer rights on individuals,[64] what are the legal implications of their foundational significance, including for purposes of identifying rights and duty bearers?

Historical Review 3: The Situation in 2005

The challenges to and the responses of humanitarianism through the 1990s and into the new millennium were such that, by 2005, commentators were observing that the sector's form and identity had changed beyond recognition.[65] It is to this state of humanitarianism that this chapter now turns.

Perhaps most notable of human rights-related developments in humanitarianism in the new millennium has been the widespread emergence of models of human-rights based humanitarian assistance or programming – addressing both protection and assistance, and relevant to any form of humanitarian situation, be it 'natural' or man-made.[66] This was visible within the 'Sphere Project'.[67] Sphere is an initiative of a consortium of NGOs and the Red Cross and Red Crescent Movement, based on the core beliefs that 'all possible steps should be taken to alleviate human

---

[62] By way of exception, see an internal note on rights-based programming by UNICEF, 1998, on file with the present author.

[63] O'Neill, *A Humanitarian Practitioner's Guide to International Human Rights Law*, pp. 58 ff.

[64] H. Slim, 'Not Philanthropy but Rights: The Proper Politicisation of Humanitarian Philosophy,' *International Journal of Human Rights* vol. 6, issue 2 (2002), pp. 1–22.

[65] See, Overseas Development Institute, 'What is Humanitarianism Anyway?', Humanitarian Policy Group Research Proposal (January 2004) available at http://www.odi.org.uk/hpg/papers/wiha.pdf; and A. Stoddard, 'Humanitarian NGOs' : Challenges and Trends', in *Humanitarian Assistance and the "Global War on Terror": A Review of Trends and Issues.*

[66] Although the idea that human rights is essentially about protection persists. See, for example, H. Slim and L. E. Eguren, *Humanitarian Protection*, pp. 6–7.

[67] http://www.sphereproject.org.

suffering arising out of calamity and conflict and that those affected by disaster have a right to life with dignity and therefore a right to assistance'. Initiated in 1997, but considerably revised in recent years, it comprises a number of humanitarian practitioners' tools which now include practice guidance on how the rights-based approach can impact assistance programming.[68] Similar approaches can now be detected in the UN humanitarian assistance planning and fundraising framework, the Consolidated Appeal Process (CAP). The Technical Guidelines for the CAP (updated August 2003) state that, '[g]reater efforts should be made to integrate human rights and humanitarian principles in the CAP, in accordance with the Secretary General's Reform to mainstream human rights throughout the UN's work with a view to enhancing its effectiveness and ensuring its principled basis'. The centrality of human rights data gathering and analysis to the CAP process is reflected in the IASC's Assessment Framework and the Assessment Matrix tools, developed in 2003–2004, and which are intended to ensure that the cross-cutting issues of protection, anti-discrimination and participation are addressed throughout. The final section of the Matrix, on assessment of national context identifies as coterminous those elements necessary to avoid/redress humanitarian emergency and those that are necessary for the promotion and protection of human rights (including open democratic institutions, rule of law, free media and so forth). A number of sector-specific rights-based programming tools were also developed, some of which contained sophisticated analysis and helpful guidance for practitioners.[69]

These innovations in humanitarian practice were informed, to some extent, by the ongoing debate regarding issues of human rights-based approaches to development (RBA). RBA refers to efforts to undertake development activities in a manner that serves to promote the human rights of the affected populations.[70] It has multiple origins.[71] One of these is the writings of development scientists who, concerned for human well-being, grew disaffected with prevailing economic models and development strategies such as that of structural adjustment.[72] Another is the manner, described earlier, in which some development/humanitarian agencies perceived a duty on their part to implement law – this particularly having been the case for UNICEF.[73] Prominent

---

[68]   See, for example, The Sphere Project, *Humanitarian Charter and Minimum Standards in Response* 2nd edn (Sphere Project: Geneva, 2004), pp. 28, 319.

[69]   See for instance, J. Asher, *The Right to Health: A Resource Manual for NGOs* (Commonwealth Medical Trust: London, 2004).

[70]   See, H. Slim, 'A Response to Peter Uvin: Making Moral Low Ground, Rights as the Struggle for Justice and the Abolition of Development', *Praxis: International Development Studies Journal* vol. XVII (2002).

[71]   See M. Darrow and T. Amparo, 'Power, Capture and Conflict: A Call for Human Rights Accountability in Development Cooperation', *Human Rights Quarterly* vol. 27, no. 2 (2005).

[72]   See C. Johnson and D. Start, *Rights, Claims and Capture: Understanding the Politics of Pro-Poor Policy*, Overseas Development Institute, Working Paper 145 (2001).

[73]   UNICEF note, *A Human Rights-based Approach to Programming in Humanitarian Crises: Is UNICEF up to the Challenge.*

theories of the nature of poverty also contributed greatly to the first stirrings of RBA. In particular, Amartya Sen's capability approach[74] to poverty laid the foundations for an analysis that would highlight the extent to which poverty is caused by, and may be understood as, a failure to enjoy certain human rights.[75]

Out of roots such as these a wide range of academic, policy and practical initiatives emerged.[76] Through the 1990s and into the present decade, rights-based approaches to development had taken shape in a disparate and sometimes inconsistent manner not unlike the process within humanitarianism. Some approaches considered human rights to be no more than one of a range of tools to be applied or disregarded according to particular circumstances,[77] whereas others treated human rights as a non-negotiable normative framework for development work.[78] Some core perceptions did however inform almost all approaches, notably the principle of non-discrimination and the recognition that a principal purpose of development is the empowerment of the most marginalised members of society.

Recent years have seen a considerable degree of further clarification of the core principles of RBA, or at least the development of one more or less articulated school thereof. This school is that of RBA as understood by the UN. Individual UN agencies, especially UNICEF and the United Nations Development Programme (UNDP) had been at the forefront of early RBA developments[79] and the UN high commissioner for human rights had made the matter a priority issue for her office.[80] The UN actors had also sought, from the late 1990s and within the framework of the United Nations Development Group,[81] to identify core aspects of RBA that might inform their coordinated action – a process that was spurred on by the various UN reform initiatives of the UN secretary-general[82] as well as the linkages between human rights

---

[74] A. Sen, *Inequality Reexamined* (Cambridge: Harvard University Press, 1992); and A. Sen, *Development as Freedom* (New York: Knopf, 1999).

[75] OHCHR, *Human Rights and Poverty Reduction* (Geneva, 2004).

[76] See M. Darrow and T. Amparo, 'Power, Capture and Conflict'.

[77] For an example of an instrumental use of the human rights approach see, World Bank, *Engendering Development: Through Gender Equality in Rights, Resources and Voice* (Washington, DC: World Bank, 2001).

[78] For instance, U. Jonsson, *Human Rights Approach to Development Programming* (Nairobi: UNICEF 2003).

[79] See UNDP, *Integrating Human Rights with Sustainable Human Development* (New York, 1998).

[80] See, for example, the OHCHR presentation, 'Human Rights in Development', (2000): available at http://www.undg.org/search.cfm?by=keywords&q=human%20rights&page=2&num=10&sort=Score&view=basic&archives=0.

[81] See the materials at http://www.undg.org/search.cfm?by=keywords&q=human+rights&opt=any&section=1&page=1&archives=1&detailed=&basic=&num=10&sort=postdate.

[82] Reports of the Secretary-General, Renewing the United Nations: A Programme for Reform, An Agenda for Further Change, UN Doc. A/57/387 (2002), In Larger Freedom: Towards Development, Security and Human Rights for All, UN Doc. A/59/2005 (2005).

and development that were contained in the Millennium Development Goals.[83] The process of reflection led, in May 2003, to a common UN position on RBA, contained in what is known as the 'Statement of Common Understanding', adopted at Stamford, Connecticut, USA (the 'Stamford Statement').[84] The 'Stamford Statement' asserts that all programmes of development cooperation, policies and technical assistance should further the realisation of human rights as laid down in the Universal Declaration of Human Rights (UDHR) and other international human rights instruments and that, '[h]uman rights standards contained in, and principles derived from, the UDHR and other international human rights instruments guide all development cooperation and programming in all sectors and in all phases of the programming process ... Development cooperation contributes to the development of the capacity of "duty-bearers"[85] to meet their obligations and/or of "rights-holders" to claim their rights'. The Statement identifies a number of elements, which it considers as:

> necessary, specific and unique to a human-rights based approach:
>
> a) Assessment and analysis in order to identify the human rights claims of rights holders and the corresponding human rights obligations of duty-bearers as well as the immediate, underlying and structural causes of the non-realisation of rights.
>
> b) Programmes assess the capacity of rights holders to claim their rights and of duty bearers to fulfil their obligations. They then develop strategies to build these capacities.
>
> c) Programmes monitor and evaluate both outcomes and processes guided by human rights standards and principles.
>
> d) Programming is informed by the recommendations of international human rights bodies and mechanisms.

Also of interest for an understanding of the insinuation of RBA in humanitarian practice is the initiative of the high commissioner for human rights to issue a set of guidelines, *A Human Rights Approach to Poverty Reduction Strategies*.[86] These, in following Sen's capability approach, propose that the combating of poverty, including extreme poverty, must, at a minimum, promote the rights to food, health,

---

[83]   United Nations Millennium Declaration, UN Doc. A/RES/55/2 (2000); see also, World Summit Outcome, UN Doc. A/60/L.1 (2005), at 119–131.

[84]   Report of the Second Interagency Workshop on Implementing a Human Rights-Based Approach in the Context of UN Reform, Stamford, Connecticut, 5–7 May 2003, available at www.undg.org/documents/4128–Human_Rights_Workshop_Stamford_Final_Report.doc

[85]   In RBA discourse the terms 'duty-bearer' and 'obligation', when applied outside the context of the state tend to refer to roles and responsibilities relevant to the effective implementation of rights rather than to any form of formal legal responsibility. See, for example, Jonsson, *Human Rights Approach to Development Programming*, chapter 3. See, also, M. O'Flaherty, Address to: 'Our Rights, Our Future Human Rights Based Approaches in Ireland, Amnesty International Conference', Dublin, 27 September 2005, available at http://www.amnesty.ie/user/content/view/full/4648.

[86]   OHCHR, *A Human Rights Approach to Poverty Reduction Strategies* (Geneva: OHCHR, 2002), available at http://www.ohchr.org/english/issues/poverty/guidelines.htm.

education, decent work, adequate housing, personal security, the right to appear in public without shame, equal access to justice and the enjoyment of political rights and freedoms. The guidelines also cite and locate the imperatives that rights-based efforts overcome poverty, ensure participation of the poor, avoid and tackle all manner of discrimination, ensure accountability and serve ultimately for the empowerment of the poor.[87]

This cross-fertilisation from the development to the humanitarian sector is being stimulated by a number of factors. For UN actors it emerged from the consistent policy-level commitment to 'mainstream' human rights approaches throughout the system. More generally, it has been facilitated by the fact that so many of the major NGO and UN humanitarian actors are also prominent in the development field. It seems to be occurring without much attention being addressed to some practice differences between emergency and development responses, such as, for instance, regarding the possibly differing role of the state in emergency and more stable environments, and concerning the particular protection considerations in times of crisis.[88]

Another significant feature of the contemporary situation is the increasingly strong emphasis placed on the protection responsibilities of UN humanitarian actors. This impetus, already visible in the late 1990s, is prompted by those protection considerations discussed earlier. It may also be related to a desire of the Security Council to forge progress for human welfare around issues upon which the Council's membership may easily find consensus.[89] And it has been argued by some UN insiders that the UN debate has much to do with inter-agency rivalries and with a quest of its humanitarian coordination office, the United Nations Office for the Coordination of Humanitarian Affairs (OCHA), to forge a substantive role for itself.[90] Whatever the reasons, the situations of women, children and civilians affected by armed conflict have become standing items on the Security Council's agenda, and there have been many specific practice implications in the field. For instance, in December 2004, the IASC issued a 'Statement of Commitment on Action to Address Gender Based Violence in Emergencies', containing an extensive list of specific monitoring, reporting, protection and accountability actions to be undertaken.[91] Since 2000, child protection advisers have been appointed to a number of peace

---

[87]   For a discussion of the guidelines see, M. Nowak, 'A Human Rights Approach to Poverty', in M. Scheinen and M. Suksi (eds), *Human Rights in Development Yearbook 2002* (Leiden: Martinus Nijhof, 2005).

[88]   See J. Macrae, 'Defining the Boundaries: International Security and Humanitarian Engagement in the post Cold War World', in *The Humanitarian Decade* vol. 2, pp. 112–117.

[89]   See H. Slim, 'Protecting Civilians: Putting the Individual at the Humanitarian Centre', in *The Humanitarian Decade* vol. 2, pp. 155–158.

[90]   Interviews conducted by the present author with UN personnel in Geneva and New York, 2004 and 2005.

[91]   IASC, 'Statement of Commitment on Action to Address Gender Based Violence in Emergencies', available at http://www.humanitarianinfo.org/iasc/publications.asp.

missions.[92] More recently, the practice has begun of the deployment of 'protection officers' side by side with human rights officers and others within UN integrated peace missions, and managed by the missions' senior humanitarian officer.[93] While such deployments may not be appropriate or wise (concern is frequently expressed that the establishment of functions overlapping those of existing field teams, such as those of UNICEF and human rights field operations, may serve to compromise rather than enhance the UN's protection efforts[94]), they do certainly highlight the need for the putting in place of clear humanitarian policy and methodological tools for the undertaking of human rights-related work.

Humanitarian field experimentation has continued to occur and efforts to integrate human rights approaches are often innovative. For instance, there was a vigorous engagement with a number of transitional justice frameworks. Thus, in Sierra Leone, UNICEF engaged directly with the Truth and Reconciliation Commission and produced and disseminated a children's version of the commission's final report.[95] Also in Sierra Leone, a number of humanitarian workers gave evidence for the prosecution at that country's Special Court.[96] Human rights-based programming initiatives have been equally novel. By way of illustration, one humanitarian NGO, Action Aid developed programmes for peacebuilding in Burundi and to tackle the root causes of extreme poverty in Bolangir, India.[97]

Another feature of the contemporary situation is the increasingly prominent role being played by the Office of the High Commissioner for Human Rights (OHCHR), which assumed the chair of the IASC Task Force in 2000.[98] In 2002, OHCHR, in response to reform proposals of the secretary-general, initiated an ambitious plan, known as 'Action 2', to insert human rights skills and resources in all UN country teams, including those in emergency environments, with a view to those teams paying

---

[92]   Report of the Secretary-General, Children and Armed Conflict, UN Doc. A/58/546 S/2003/1053 (2003), at 5.

[93]   See United Nations and Partners, *2005 Work Plan for the Sudan* (Khartoum: OCHA, 2005).

[94]   See comments made by UN Deputy High Commissioner for Human Rights M. Khan-Williams', at the 'Retreat for UN Humanitarian Coordinators', 'Session 2: Responding to the Crisis of Protection', 17 March 2005, a record of which is on file with the present author.

[95]   UNICEF, National Forum for Human Rights and United Nations Assistance Mission in Sierra Leone/Human Rights, *Children and The Truth and Reconciliation Commission for Sierra Leone: Recommendations for Policies and Procedures for Addressing and Involving Children in the Truth and Reconciliation Commission* (2001), available at http://www.unicef. org/emerg/files/SierraLeone-TRCReport.pdf.

[96]   On the risks and the legal aspects of the limitations for such cooperation see, K. Mackintosh, 'How Far can Humanitarian Organisations Control Co-operation with International Tribunals?', *Journal of Humanitarian Assistance* (May 2005), available at http:// www.jha.ac/articles/a175.pdf.

[97]   See Action Aid, *Global Progress Report 2003*, available at http://www.actionaid.org/ wps/content/documents/GlobalProgressReport2003_1832005_112717.pdf.

[98]   On behalf of OHCHR, the present author chaired the Task Force from 2000 to 2002.

priority attention to the development of strong national human rights protection capacities.[99] This seems to be a welcome development given the primary role of the state in human rights law and for its implementation, and it may serve as something of a corrective to some of those less legally explicable expressions of human rights, which identify human rights duty bearers in a promiscuous manner.[100] In 2005, OHCHR, in its *Plan of Action*, reiterated its commitment to Action 2 while also expressing its determination to continue supporting an integration of human rights in humanitarian action and to itself become much more active at the field level.[101]

The ongoing formulation of draft guidelines on human rights for UN humanitarian coordinators is an expression of the new commitment of OHCHR. These guidelines,[102] commissioned by OHCHR, will provide the first more or less comprehensive assistance on the issues for the heads of UN humanitarian teams in the field. The draft addresses all forms of humanitarian environment, be they man-made or otherwise. Particular attention is paid to the applicability of human rights to both programming (assistance) and protection activities. It is proposed that the principles underlying the human rights system can be held equally to apply for humanitarian work, and it is noted that 'it is widely accepted that a human-rights related approach to programming places emphasis both on outcomes and the process by which outcomes are achieved. Participation, local ownership, capacity development and sustainability are essential characteristics of a human-rights related approach'.[103] The guidelines suggest that this is a context in which to locate human rights-based protection work: '[R]ights-related programming, given its "holistic" approach to the situation and to the status of the rights-holder, reinforces the importance of humanitarian agencies engaging in protection activities'.[104] In this context some suggested misconceptions regarding human rights-related humanitarian work are addressed. For instance, the idea is countered that the rights-related approach leads the humanitarian inevitably into confrontation with authorities – it is suggested that human rights-based dialogue with authorities is sometimes welcomed[105] and that, in any case, there are many opportunities for division of advocacy labours among the humanitarian and human rights communities, thus diminishing the risk of adverse impacts on particular programmes. Subsequent sections of the guidelines provide concrete assistance to humanitarian coordinators for the gathering and assessment of human rights-related information and for the application of this information. The

---

[99] Report of the Secretary-General', Strengthening the United Nations: An Agenda for Further Change, at 51.

[100] For instance, see Jonsson, *Human Rights Approaches to Development Programming*, pp. 20–23.

[101] The United Nations High Commissioner for Human Rights, *The OHCHR Plan of Action: Protection and Empowerment* (Geneva: OHCHR, 2005), pp. 24–25.

[102] The initial draft was written for OHCHR by the present author and the references to it are based on a file copy.

[103] *Ibid.*, at section 4.

[104] *Ibid.*

[105] ICRC, *Strengthening Protection in War*, pp. 106–107.

text on human rights monitoring, analysis, reporting and intervention emphasises the complexity of these tasks and generally draws on experience gathered in the context of the work of human rights monitors. The guidelines conclude with suggestions regarding the forms of human rights partnership and coordination systems that humanitarian coordinators can put in place, with strong emphasis placed on the role of human rights field operations.

There remain areas of legal uncertainty.[106] Some of these, at least with regard to the responsibilities of UN actors, received attention in Nigel White and Dirk Klaasen's 2005 edited volume, *The UN, Human Rights and Post-conflict Situations*.[107] They concluded that, 'there is still a lack of clarity about the application of human rights law to UN activities, including the post-conflict phase, since the UN is not a State and therefore not a party to any of the human rights treaties … This shows the pressing need for the formal recognition by the UN's political organs of the applicability of human rights standards preferably within a constitutional framework'.[108] The responsibility of a state to permit the delivery of humanitarian assistance has also been examined[109] as have at least some aspects of the relationship between human rights law and IHL.[110] And some light has been shed on issues of the right or obligation to intervene for delivery of humanitarian assistance, although the policy debate around these matters primarily concentrated on the distinct context of military intervention.[111]

In conclusion, it is necessary to turn to an ongoing debate regarding the very fundamentals of humanitarianism – with some commentators considering the sector to be in a state of 'crisis'[112] and in need of profound reform. The relevant critics take as their starting point such phenomena as the privatisation of aid, the delivery of aid directly by military forces and the subordination of humanitarian assistance to some political or military objective, including objectives within the so-called 'war

---

[106] For related expressions of concern see, *Sphere Project Evaluation*, January 2004, at section III, available at http://www.sphereproject.org/about/ext_eva/sphere_eval_fin.pdf.

[107] See footnote 4.

[108] N. D. White, 'Towards a Strategy for Human Rights Protection in Post-conflict Situations', in *The UN, Human Rights and Post-conflict Situations*, p. 463. See also K. Kenny, 'UN Accountability for its Human Rights Impact: Implementation through Participation', in the same volume, pp. 438–462.

[109] See, for instance, J. Dungel, 'A Right to Humanitarian Assistance in Internal Armed Conflicts Respecting Sovereignty, Neutrality and Legitimacy: Practical Proposals to Practical Problems', *Journal of Humanitarian Assistance* (May 2004), http://www.jha.ac/articles/a133.htm.

[110] See, for instance, H.-J. Heintze, 'On the Relationship between Human Rights Law Protection and International Humanitarian Law', *International Review of the Red Cross* vol. 86, no. 856 (December 2004), pp. 789–814.

[111] The literature is voluminous. Regarding policy proposals see, *inter alia*, International Commission on Intervention and State Sovereignty, *The Responsibility to Protect* (Ottawa: International Development Research Centre, 2001) and Report of the Secretary-General, *In Larger Freedom*.

[112] D. Rieff, *A Bed for the Night*, p. 24.

on terror'.[113] From experience in Afghanistan, Iraq and elsewhere it is argued that humanitarianism has been gravely undermined by its association with the activities and objectives of combatants and occupying forces/authorities. Many commentators also have in mind the UN integrated missions, wherein all UN action, including its humanitarian component, is intended to be subsumed within what is ultimately a political operation with political goals. At least one senior commentator identifies the pursuit of human rights as being an inherently political activity and therefore to be avoided. Writing in 2004, Nicolas de Torrente, executive director of MSF, wrote:

> [A] number of NGOs have embraced the idea of enhancing the relevance of their relief work by placing it within a broader framework of resolving conflict and promoting human rights. The availability of donor funding for [such] 'coherence'-based activities has also played a key role in bringing about this change ... The 'coherence' agenda challenges the essence of humanitarian action as a neutral and impartial endeavour. At its core, it implies that aid may be selectively allocated to certain groups of victims, or withheld from others, depending on their political usefulness, instead of being allocated according to, and proportionate to, needs alone.[114]

It is not difficult to sympathise with much of de Torrente's general concern. However, his argument fails to acknowledge the political component in all responses to crisis – it is inconceivable to consider any human rights or humanitarian action that will not have consequences for a given political situation. It is not this unavoidable aspect of the actions which is at issue, but rather the challenge of ensuring that the actions are consistently implemented on the basis of the applicable laws and principles. In this regard, it may be recalled that human rights law has at its core such principles as universality, indivisibility and non-discrimination. Perhaps, then, the issue is one of how best to protect the actions of both humanitarian and human rights actors from forces that seek to draw them away from their ethical/legal bases (this point is at least valid as regards human rights – an examination of the question of the degree to which humanitarianism, given its extent and the diversity of its actors and its self-understandings, lacks or is incapable of articulating such a shared ethical base is beyond the scope of this chapter[115]). In this regard, Antonio Donini, writing specifically on the issue of UN integrated missions, suggests that UN humanitarian and human rights staff might best be taken out of the 'political UN', whereby, '[h]umanitarianism and human rights would thus have their own neutral space separate from the integrated mission'.[116]

---

[113] L. Minear, 'The Political Context of Humanitarian Action: Some Reflections', in *The Humanitarian Decade* vol. 2, p. 104.

[114] de Torrente, 'Humanitarian Action Under Attack', p. 26. For a response to his article, see P. O'Brien, 'Politicized Humanitarianism: A Response to Nicholas de Torrente', *Harvard Human Rights Journal* vol. 17 (2004), 31–39; see also D. Rieff, *A Bed for the Night*.

[115] See P. Walker, 'What Does it Mean to be a Professional Humanitarian'.

[116] A. Donini, 'The Forest and the Trees: The Evolving Nature of Coordination', in *The Humanitarian Decade* vol. 2, p. 140. See also the comment of then Secretary-General of MSF Rafael Vila San Juan, speaking in 2002, about a need 'to disentangle humanitarian assistance

The Possibilities for Partnership between Human Rights Field Operations and Humanitarian Actors

This review has demonstrated the increasingly widespread recognition of a role of human rights in humanitarianism, albeit in a context of ongoing resistance and desire on the part of some for a return to earlier, simpler days. It has also taken note of the extent to which there have been, and are, many instances of partnerships between human rights and humanitarian operations, as well as of the development of the relevant guidance materials.

Before specifically examining partnerships in the field, it is worthwhile to briefly to dwel on the partnership potential on the broad sectoral levels. In the first place, there is a striking similarity between the quests for professional coherence in both of the sectors. For instance, as seen in the writing of Peter Walker,[117] the challenges to the identification of the parameters of a professional role for humanitarian workers are very similar to those for human rights actors,[118] and it is likely that the respective findings, including those of the present volume, will be mutually useful. The potential for such benefit has already been demonstrated in the context of a number of workshops which brought the two sectors together in recent years.[119] Equally, humanitarianism's reflection on its relationship to political goals is no less important for human rights organisations. In this regard, the findings of the various humanitarian assessments of UN integrated missions are of great interest and relevance.[120] Finally, and more generally, the sheer scale of humanitarianism is such that it will always be able to devote vastly greater resources to processes of self-reflection and reform than ever will those organisations that deploy human rights field operations. As a result, and taking account of the multiple commonalities and similarities, it seems inevitable that the human rights actors will be the principal beneficiaries from the inter-sectoral exchange and support.

---

from politics, by reclaiming humanitarian space, and the core principles of impartiality and independence', address to Panel Discussion on the 10th Anniversary of General Assembly resolution 46/182, 17 July 2002, reported in *The Humanitarian Decade* vol. 1, 24.

[117] P. Walker, 'What Does it Mean to be a Professional Humanitarian'.

[118] See M. O'Flaherty, 'Human Rights Monitoring and Armed Conflict: Challenges for the UN', *Disarmament Forum* no. 3 (2004), 47–58.

[119] For instance, the two workshops co-hosted by OHCHR and International Council of Voluntary Agencies in Geneva in 2001 and 2004, see http://www.icva.ch/cgi-bin/member/browse.pl?doc=doc00000237; see also the report of a 2002 workshop on issues of ethics in humanitarian and human rights organisations, in D. A. Bell and J. A. Carens, 'The Ethical Dilemmas of Humanitarian and Human Rights NGOs: Reflections on a Dialogue between Practitioners and Theorists', *Human Rights Quarterly* vol. 26, no. 2 (2004), 300–329.

[120] See, especially, E. B. Eide, A. T. Kaspersen *et al.*, *Report on Integrated Missions: Practical Perspectives and Recommendations*, Independent Study for the Expanded UN ECHA Core Group (May 2005).

Turning to the narrower range of partnership possibilities in the field, it is useful, based on the analysis in the present chapter, first to distinguish some five approaches to human rights by humanitarian actors, each with its own implications for partnership, while recalling that, notwithstanding which of these approaches may apply, it is likely that diverse understandings of human rights-based or human rights-related approaches will be encountered. The five are:

- The 'rights-based' term approach – in which case there should be a congruity of goals that should facilitate sturdy partnerships and which may range across all the work areas of the human rights field operation. Rights-based approaches have been adopted by some UN agencies as well as by a number of humanitarian NGOs. It is important to keep in mind, though, that such an approach is adopted voluntarily by an organisation, with nothing like the normative consequences which arise for states. Furthermore, given its voluntary nature, the term 'rights-based approach' has varying meanings in the humanitarian world. In this regard, it should be recalled that it often refers to an approach that is rooted in three bodies of law – international humanitarian, refugee and human rights – and that there is no shared understanding of the practical implications of this tri-sourcing.
- The rights as a tool approach – here the partnership will be an opportunistic one in the sense that a humanitarian actor may recognise the utility of human rights to serve what it may see as a distinct humanitarian goal. In such cases, the humanitarian interest is most likely in issues of civil and political rights, advocacy and regarding forms of justice and accountability.
- The absence of a policy approach. There remain very many humanitarian organisations that have as yet to identify a specific policy approach regarding human rights. Partnership may well be possible with them in cases where an accidental coincidence of goals and interest may be identified or on the basis of the initiative of individuals within the organisations.
- The wary coexistence approach. It is quite possible that a human rights field operation may coexist with a humanitarian field mission, which either addresses human rights opportunistically or has embraced some form of right-based approach, but which is wary of too close a partnership with the human rights operation. This could, for instance, be the case when the human rights field operation is part of a UN integrated mission. In such cases it is likely that some form of cooperation may be established on the basis of clearly elaborated terms of engagement. In any case, it is important to ensure that a difficult relationship does not foster unhelpful competition or otherwise undermine shared human rights goals.
- The anti-human rights approach. Such an approach, precluding all possibilities of partnership, may be theoretically possible; but it is likely to be extremely rarely, if ever, encountered.

Within the context of any of these approaches, and from the point of view of the human rights field operation, some partnership principles may be proposed:

1. The possibilities for partnership that should be considered range across much of the spectrum of the work areas of a human rights field operation. To adapt the list found in chapter 1 of the present volume, these can be loosely identified as monitoring, reporting, advocacy and intervention, capacity building (including in the programmes of humanitarian and development contexts), support to peace processes and transitional justice and in-mission sensitisation.

2. Partnerships must be constructed on the understanding that the human rights field operation does not in any sense 'own' the human rights agenda. Humanitarian operations may legitimately undertake very many of the activities that might have, in the past, been the domain of a human rights field operation, such as, for instance, human rights reporting and advocacy. However, effective partnerships will be built on sound assessment of comparative strengths, and of efficient and appropriate divisions of labour.

3. The partnerships should be contexts for mutual learning. A humanitarian organisation, given the long tradition of humanitarianism and its extensive ongoing processes of self-reflection, will almost always have much to teach the human rights operation, including in terms of strategies for human rights-based programming. The human rights field operation, for its part, should also be able to guide a partnership in terms of the nature and the application of human rights law and related good practice.

4. Partnerships should be based on mutual respect and full consideration for respective principles and operating guidelines. Thus, for instance, when human rights-sensitive information is shared by a humanitarian organisation, the conditions for such sharing must be scrupulously respected.

5. Occasions will arise where each partner should appropriately locate its activities within the planning and fundraising framework of the other. For instance, there are opportunities for human rights field operations to do planning and seek funds within the context of the CAP.

6. There is already a considerable corpus of experience for the undertaking of partnerships, which is chronicled extensively. It is important to take stock of this experience with a view to promoting good practice.

7. Partnerships will, however, often require innovative and experimental approaches. These should be thoroughly monitored, evaluated and publicised,whereby they can contribute to the development of doctrine and methodologies.

Concluding Comment

As in the case of human rights field operations themselves, the story of human rights-related humanitarian action is a short one, marked by a rapid development of practice and related discourse. From the outset, the practice has been marked by forms of partnership in the field between human rights and humanitarian operations. Inevitably, experience has indicated doctrinal and practical concerns and challenges. Perhaps today, more than at any other time, the very fundamentals are under threat, with some critics calling for a total expunging of human rights from humanitarianism. For all of the risks associated with such questioning of fundamentals, the current debate allows the context for a comprehensive review of the nature and the implications of rights-related approaches and for confronting the issues of law, principle and policy that arise. On this basis, it is likely that a far firmer base may be established for clear and effective partnerships between the sectors in the field.

Chapter 10

Protection: The United Nations Children's Fund Experience

Karin Landgren[1]

Introduction

The United Nations Children's Fund's (UNICEF) role in conflict and post-conflict situations has evolved rapidly in the 15 years between 1990 and 2005, particularly in respect of child protection. The bulk of UNICEF's work is carried out through five-year country programmes negotiated with the host government. While UNICEF started life as the United Nations International Children's Emergency Fund, and does strengthen support to field staff during crises, the agency does not operate through extraordinary 'field operations' that are the subject of this volume.[2] Its country offices, covering some 160 countries and territories, are permanently operational, and represent a significant resource for international protection.

The agency's expanding role in child protection in unstable situations reflects heightened international awareness of the many ways children's rights are violated in times of conflict,[3] as well as an amplified international treaty regime for their protection. Increasingly, although still incompletely, there is recognition that functioning child protection systems contribute to furthering national development, democracy and security.[4] UNICEF bases its programmatic and advocacy strategies on frameworks for both child protection and emergency response, which are discussed further below. In addition, the agency continues to develop child protection indicators and expand its role in monitoring and reporting on child rights in conflict.

UNICEF's child protection work since 1990 falls naturally into three rough chapters. Before 1995, UNICEF's protection efforts in complex emergencies

---

[1]   The author would like to express appreciation to colleagues who provided feedback on early drafts: Una McCauley, Manuel Fontaine, Rebecca Symington, Pamela Shifman and Alexandra Yuster. The views expressed herein are the author's, and do not necessarily represent those of the United Nations Children's Fund.

[2]   With the outbreak of war in the former Yugoslavia, however, UNICEF established new offices there.

[3]   See G. Machel, Report on the Impact of Armed Conflict on Children, UN Doc. A/51/306 (1996).

[4]   UNICEF, *The State of the World's Children 2006* (Oxford: Oxford University Press, 2005).

– notably in Rwanda and the former Yugoslavia, but stretching back to the 1980s – emphasised the provision of essential services to war-affected children, including the negotiation of 'Days of Tranquility' for humanitarian access. In the second chapter, between 1995 and 2001, UNICEF asserted greater responsibility for the protection of children, during conflict, from violence, exploitation and abuse, and began to organise itself accordingly. And in the third chapter, from 2002, UNICEF identified both child protection and emergency response as agency priorities, adopting organising frameworks for both to promote a more systematised approach.

One of these, the 'Protective Environment Framework' (2002), provides a consistent approach to protection across countries, translating the programmatic content of child protection into concrete activities and measurable results, both preventive and responsive.[5] This Framework was also intended to bridge the gap between traditional development activities and approaches, on the one hand, and human rights-driven protection from violence, exploitation and abuse, on the other. With the 'Core Commitments for Children in Emergencies' (2000, revised 2004, see below), UNICEF spelled out its systematic response to protection in the immediate aftermath of emergencies.

This overview will examine the three recent chapters in UNICEF's development as a protection agency, devoting most of its span to the period since 2002. It will expand on the principal aspects of UNICEF's protection response to children in crises, as this aspect of UNICEF's work corresponds most closely to the 'field operations' which are the subject of the present volume. The fact that UNICEF is at work before, during and after a natural disaster or conflict allows it to play a pivotal role in linking humanitarian assistance and protection to long-term programmes.

According to UNICEF's 'Mission Statement',[6] the agency is guided by the Convention on the Rights of the Child[7] (CRC) and 'insists that the survival, protection and development of children are universal development imperatives that are integral to human progress'. The Mission Statement underlines UNICEF's commitment to 'ensuring special protection for the most disadvantaged children – victims of war, disasters, extreme poverty, all forms of violence and exploitation and those with disabilities'.[8]

UNICEF uses 'child protection' to refer specifically to prevention of and response to violence, exploitation and abuse, and to services for the recovery and social reintegration of child victims. In the agency's programmatic work, child protection also includes issues and situations that are not inherently violations of human rights, generally those that heighten children's risk of being subjected to harm such as separation from caregivers, disability and contact with the justice system.

---

[5]   See UNICEF, *Child Protection: Progress Analysis and Achievements in 2003*, Medium-Term Strategic Plan 2002–2005, Programme Division, at 5.

[6]   See http://www.unicef.org/crc/index.html.

[7]   Convention on the Rights of the Child, adopted 20 Nov. 1989, G.A. res. 44/25, UN GAOR, 44th Sess., Supp. No. 49, UN Doc. A/44/49 (1989) (entered into force 2 Sept. 1990).

[8]   http://www.unicef.org/about/who/index_mission.html.

The definition of child protection as actions which strengthen children's safety and recovery from violence, exploitation and abuse differs from the scope attributed to 'protection' by other protection-mandated agencies of the United Nations (UN).[9] Elsewhere, the term may encompass all activities aimed at ensuring full respect for the rights of the individual, often in circumstances where this is not being ensured by the government. However, as the UN has recognised that *all* its activities should be directed towards the protection and promotion of human rights,[10] it appears inconsistent to give such efforts a separate rubric. UNICEF programmes to support the right to education (in or out of emergencies), for example, are called 'education' programmes – not 'protection' programmes. Strengthening children's right to protection against violence, exploitation and abuse is but one aspect of programming for human rights.

UNICEF's Experience to 1994

As far back as 1953, the General Assembly referred to 'the role that the United Nations Children's Emergency Fund plays in the whole international programme for the protection of the child'.[11] UNICEF's longstanding response to children in conflict was oriented towards their care, consistent with its traditional focus on the health of infants, young children and their mothers. This approach also predated the adoption of significant international child rights commitments. UNICEF's work on protection against violence, exploitation and abuse, and its emphasis on the role of adolescents, blossomed some years after the adoption of the Convention on the Rights of the Child.

Throughout the 1980s, UNICEF projects addressed 'children in especially difficult circumstances' (CEDC). These included support to non-governmental organisations (NGOs) working with street children and children with disabilities. UNICEF's Executive Board adopted a policy on CEDC in April 1986,[12] reaffirming UNICEF's mandate and responsibilities for the child as a whole. This policy recommended that UNICEF 'promote, where necessary, in Government, professional groups and private sectors, enhanced awareness concerning children in especially difficult circumstances

---

[9] Elsewhere, the term is used variously to describe (a) action to protect *some* of the rights of *some* particularly beleaguered groups (refugees or internally displaced persons, for example), or (b) particular actions – principally advocacy and legislative – in support of the rights of the population as a whole. In 1996–1999, a Protection Workshop under the auspices of the ICRC defined protection as '…all activities aimed at obtaining full respect for the rights of the individual in accordance with human rights, humanitarian and refugee law', cited in Inter-Agency Standing Committee (IASC), *Growing the Sheltering Tree: Protecting Rights Through Humanitarian Action* (Geneva: UNICEF, 2002), p. 11.

[10] See Report of the Secretary-General, In Larger Freedom: Towards Development, Security and Human Rights for All, UN Doc. A/59/2005 (2005) at 16.

[11] See Resolutions adopted by the General Assembly at its Eighth Session during the period from 15 September to 9 December 1953, UN GAOR, 8th Session, Supp. No. 17, UN Doc. A/2630 (1953), at 802.

[12] UNICEF Executive Board resolutions E/ICEF/1986/CRP 33 and CRP 37 of 30 April 1986.

and of the need for preventive and rehabilitative action for them', and that support for such children be integrated into existing UNICEF-supported programmes. It also called on UNICEF to work closely with other relevant international agencies on this issue.

The 1989 CRC would bring dramatic changes in the scope of UNICEF's work, although this impact would not be felt for some years. Beginning in 1985, however, UNICEF identified a more assertive role in situations of conflict, promoting and organising 'Days of Tranquility' during which ceasefires and access were secured, providing a brief lull from violence, and allowing children to be vaccinated. That year in El Salvador, some 250,000 children were vaccinated on three separate 'Days of Tranquility' – by International Committee of the Red Cross (ICRC) teams in contested areas, and by civilians elsewhere.[13] Subsequent 'Days of Tranquility' have been held in Sri Lanka, Sudan, Tajikistan and Afghanistan, among other countries, negotiated by UNICEF and the World Health Organization.[14]

UNICEF was a founding partner in Operation Lifeline Sudan (OLS).[15] The OLS-UNICEF southern sector office was established in 1989 to provide humanitarian assistance in areas under the control of non-state armed groups, principally the Sudanese People's Liberation Movement/Army (SPLM/A). The office was initially created in response to widely-publicised famine conditions in southern Sudan in 1988, a time when UNICEF did not yet have a presence in the area. OLS-UNICEF negotiated with the government and non-state actors to obtain humanitarian access and the provision of essential services. Subsequently, 'ground rules' for the security of operations in southern Sudan were agreed among all parties, and expanded to reflect human rights standards.

A significant bookend to this period, and a curtain-raiser to the next, was UNICEF's work with separated, unaccompanied and detained minors in the Great Lakes region of Africa following the Rwanda genocide of April 1994. Concerned with the fate of separated and unaccompanied children, the Office of the United Nations High Commissioner for Refugees (UNHCR), UNICEF and the ICRC issued joint guidelines on the evacuation of children from the region, drawing on similar guidance issued by UNICEF and UNHCR for the former Yugoslavia in 1992.[16] These partners, along with the International Federation of Red Cross and Red Crescent Societies, further agreed to pool on a central database standardised information on unaccompanied children as well as parents seeking missing children. The database was managed by the ICRC in Nairobi.[17] Important ground was being laid for the wide-ranging inter-agency and NGO networks that would, in the years after 2000,

---

[13]   *UNICEF Children in Especially Difficult Circumstances*, policy review paper for the 1986 Executive Board, E/ICEF/1986/L.3 (December 1985), pp. 14–15.

[14]   A list of countries with documented humanitarian ceasefires, including for immunisation purposes, can be found at http://www.who.int/hac/techguidance/hbp/cease_fires/en/.

[15]   See http://www.un.org/av/photo/subjects/sudan.htm.

[16]   'UNHCR, UNICEF, ICRC, Evacuation of Children from Conflict Areas: Considerations and Guidelines' (Geneva: UNHCR and UNICEF, 1992).

[17]   IASC, *Growing the Sheltering Tree*, p. 164.

produce extensive joint guidance on child protection and work in a coordinated fashion not only in situations of armed conflict but also following the Southeast Asian tsunami of December 2004 and the South Asia earthquake of October 2005.

1995 to 2001

UNICEF's focus on children and armed conflict continued: children and war was the topic of the flagship *State of the World's Children* (1996) issued in December 1995, which included an 'Anti-War Agenda'.[18] Ms Graça Machel had been appointed by the UN secretary-general to undertake a study on the impact of armed conflict on children,[19] and by 1995–96, UNICEF was heavily involved in the consultations and preparation of her 'Report on the Impact of Armed Conflict on Children',[20] which was presented to, and endorsed by, the General Assembly in November 1996. Its ten principal recommendations pertain to peace and security, the monitoring and reporting of child rights violations, health and psycho-social well-being, education, the needs of adolescents, gender-based violence, internally displaced children, child soldiers and landmines.[21] Following this report, in 1997 the UN secretary-general appointed a special representative on children in (later *and*) armed conflict.[22]

The bulk of international law on children's rights was adopted during this period, addressing many of the issues that form the core of UNICEF child protection work: violence, exploitation, abuse, conflict with the law and loss of parental care. International conventions from this period cover the worst forms of child labour, transnational organised crime including trafficking, war crimes against children, the use of children in armed conflict and the trafficking, sale and sexual exploitation of children. The Optional Protocol to the CRC on involvement of children in armed conflict[23] has been particularly valuable in expanding the agreed protection of children from recruitment and use in hostilities.

In 1996, UNICEF's Executive Board adopted a new child protection policy, replacing its 1986 policy on children in especially difficult circumstances.[24] It explicitly moves beyond the notion of 'children in especially difficult circumstances' as noting categories of children in need of additional services, and 'To define children by the circumstances that have negatively affected them is to characterize them as

---

[18] UNICEF, *The State of the World's Children 1996* (Oxford: Oxford University Press, December 1995).

[19] Pursuant to General Assembly resolution 48/157 (1994), UN Doc. A/RES/48/157 (1994).

[20] See G. Machel, Report on the Impact of Armed Conflict on Children.

[21] *Ibid.*, at 62, 90, 110, 126, 135, 165, 183, 203, 240.

[22] See General Assembly resolution 51/77(1997), UN Doc. A/RES/51/77 (1997), at 7.

[23] See General Assembly resolution 54/263 (2000), UN Doc. A/RES/54/263 (2000).

[24] UNICEF, A Review of UNICEF Policies and Strategies on Child Protection, UN Doc. E/ICEF/1996/14 (1996).

deviant from social norms instead of recognizing that they are victims of socially deficient structures and policies'.[25]

The same year, UNICEF also adopted its mission statement, under which it is guided by the CRC.[26] Despite the mission statement and the new child protection policy, many senior UNICEF staff still viewed child protection issues as too sensitive to address. One senior staff member reflected on UNICEF's discomfort with a role defined by human rights:

> Many in the organization were convinced that human rights and development were not a good mix. The normative processes of treaty bodies and the stark divisions created by the cold war between civil and political rights, and economic, social and cultural rights had convinced UNICEF that its programmes of cooperation should best be kept separate from the polarized world of human rights … In UNICEF's view, at the time, its involvement in politically charged activities such as the drafting of a human rights treaty could compromise the organization's tradition of impartiality and jeopardize its ability to work for needy children everywhere and with all sides in a conflict.[27]

Nonetheless, this mission statement gave impetus to child protection. So did parallel developments raising the profile of human security and the protection of civilians, among them the 1995 publication *Our Global Neighbourhood* by the Commission on Global Governance,[28] the campaign to ban the use of landmines,[29] the Human Security Network[30] (established in 1999) and the report of the International Commission on Intervention and State Sovereignty, *The Responsibility to Protect*.[31] With the attention in the Security Council on the protection of civilians, these helped gain political space for child protection in programming and advocacy.

UNICEF's programmatic work on children in armed conflict continued apace. Between 1995 and 1996, separate but identical 'Agreements on Ground Rules' were signed by OLS-UNICEF southern sector and representatives of the SPLM/A, South Sudan Independence Movement (SSIM/A) and SPLM-United.[32] The purpose of the Ground Rules was to establish minimal acceptable standards of conduct for OLS-UNICEF southern sector and the relief wings of the rebel movements. They make reference to and express support for human rights and humanitarian obligations,

---

[25]   *Ibid.*, at 3 and 9.

[26]   See footnote 6.

[27]   M. Newman-Williams, 'How Things Changed', *UN Chronicle* (Summer 1999), available at http://www.findarticles.com/p/articles/mi_m1309/is_2_36/ai_57590302#continue.

[28]   Commission on Global Governance, *Our Global Neighbourhood* (Oxford: Oxford University Press, 1995).

[29]   See http://www.icbl.org/.

[30]   See http://www.humansecuritynetwork.org/.

[31]   International Commission on Intervention and State Sovereignty, *The Responsibility to Protect* (Ottawa: International Development Research Centre, 2001).

[32]   Available at http://www.reliefweb.int/rw/rwb.nsf/db900SID/EVIU-6E7E22?Open Document.

including the CRC and the Geneva Conventions.[33] UNICEF provided training on the Ground Rules to the various rebel factions, local community leaders and humanitarian workers.

A workshop convened by UNICEF, other UN agencies and NGOs in Cape Town in April 1997 drew up a definition of 'child soldiers' and identified a range of promising practices for their demilitarisation, demobilisation and reintegration. In 1998, the organisation appointed its first chief of child protection, and later that year convened a meeting of all its representatives serving in conflict-affected countries. That meeting, held in Martigny, Switzerland generated a commitment to develop greater capacity within UNICEF to respond more systematically and efficiently to crises and chronic instability. An important outcome was the first formulation of a minimum set of 'Core Corporate Commitments' (CCCs) identifying UNICEF's initial response to the protection and care of children and women in emergencies.[34] The CCCs were approved by UNICEF's Executive Board in 2000.

In February 1999, UNICEF's executive director addressed the Security Council at its first open briefing on the protection of civilians, calling for an end to the recruitment and use of children in hostilities, increased protection for humanitarian assistance and personnel, support for action against landmines, protection of children from the effects of sanctions, and specific provisions for children in peacebuilding efforts.[35] She also called for an end to impunity for war crimes against children, and early warning and preventive action in support of children. Between August 1999 and July 2005, the Security Council adopted six landmark resolutions on the protection of children in armed conflict.[36] In the first of these, resolution 1261, the Security Council called for 'personnel involved in UN peacemaking, peacekeeping and peace-building activities to have appropriate training on the protection, rights and welfare of children'; in resolution 1314 it 'reaffirmed its readiness to continue to include, where appropriate, child protection advisers in future peacekeeping

---

[33] Geneva Convention for the Amelioration of the Condition of the Wounded and Sick in Armed Forces in the Field of August 12, 1949, 75 UNTS (1950), 31; Geneva Convention for the Amelioration of the Condition of Wounded, Sick and Shipwrecked Members of Armed Forces at Sea of August 12, 1949, 75 UNTS (1950), 85; Geneva Convention Relative to the Treatment of Prisoners of War of August 12, 1949, 75 UNTS (1950), 135; Geneva Convention Relative to the Protection of Civilian Persons in Time of War of August 12, 1949, 75 UNTS (1950), 286.

[34] UNICEF, *Core Corporate Commitments in Emergencies*, available at http://www.unicef.org/emerg/files/CCC_Booklet_EAPRO.pdf.

[35] See UN Security Council, 54th Year, 3977th Meeting, Friday, 12 February 1999, New York, UN Doc. S/PV.3977 (1999), at 5–8.

[36] See Security Council resolution 1261 (1999), UN Doc. S/RES/1261 (1999); Security Council resolution 1314 (2000), UN Doc. S/RES/1314 (2000); Security Council resolution 1379 (2001), UN Doc. S/RES/1379 (2001); Security Council resolution 1460 (2003), UN Doc. S/RES/1460 (2003); Security Council resolution 1539 (2004), UN Doc. S/RES/1539 (2004); and Security Council resolution 1612 (2005), UN Doc. S/RES/1612 (2005).

operations'. The first such adviser posts were quickly established within missions in Sierra Leone, the Democratic Republic of Congo and East Timor.

The massive and widespread use of rape and other sexual violence in wartime, including its deliberate infliction for population displacement and social disintegration, had come to the forefront of public attention during the conflict in the former Yugoslavia. By 1995, UNHCR had published the first guidelines on this issue, prompted in part by former Yugoslavia and Rwanda, but also by the sexual violence inflicted on Somali refugee women in Kenya.[37] For UNICEF, the problem of gender-based violence struck several chords: up to half the victims were children, and UNICEF was also encouraging attention to the commercial sexual exploitation of children, a problem governments had become readier to acknowledge and confront. In 1996, UNICEF, the government of Sweden, and the NGO ECPAT (End Child Prostitution, Child Pornography and Trafficking of Children for Sexual Purposes) co-convened the First World Congress on the Commercial Sexual Exploitation of Children. A Second World Congress was held in Yokohama in 2001, convened by the same partners and the government of Japan.[38]

Reports that sexual exploitation and abuse were occurring at the hands of peacekeepers and humanitarian workers had emerged in the 1990s. The sex industry that had grown up in Phnom Penh to coincide with the United Nations Transitional Administration in Cambodia (1992–1993) was no secret, nor was the one in Mozambique during the UN Operation in Mozambique (1992–1994). Sexual exploitation of women and children by peacekeepers and humanitarian workers was not taken seriously before a UNHCR/Save the Children report on abuses in Sierra Leone, Liberia and Guinea was made public in early 2002, revealing the widespread exchange of sex for money or gifts, with the victims mainly girls between 13 and 18.[39] Children orphaned or separated from one or both parents were the most vulnerable.[40] The trafficking of women and girls for sexual exploitation has also been observed in cash-rich, regulation-poor post-war environments: in Bosnia, officials were found to be taking part in the trafficking as well as patronising the brothels.[41]

---

[37]   UNHCR, *Sexual Violence against Refugees: Guidelines on Prevention and Response*, 1 March 1995, revised 1 May 2003 as *Sexual and Gender-Based Violence against Refugees, Returnees and Internally Displaced Persons: Guidelines for Prevention and Response* (Geneva: UNHCR, 2003).

[38]   For more, see http://www.csecworldcongress.org/en/.

[39]   UNHCR/Save the Children, *Sexual Violence and Exploitation: The Experience of Refugee Children in Guinea, Liberia and Sierra Leone*, available at http://www.reliefweb. int/rw/rwb.nsf/AllDocsByUNID/6010f9ed3c651c93c1256b6d00560fca.

[40]   See http://www.irinnews.org/report.asp?ReportID=23126&SelectRegion=West_Afri ca&SelectCountry=GUINEA-LIBERIA-SIERRA_LEONE.

[41]   See 'Testimony before the Senate Committee on Foreign Relations Subcommittee on Near Eastern and South Asian Affairs, by Regan E. Ralph, Executive Director, Women's Rights Division, Human Rights Watch' (22 February 2000), available at http://www.hrw.org/backgrounder/wrd/trafficking.htm.

Child Protection as a UNICEF Priority, 2002–2005

In late 2001, child protection became a priority area of UNICEF's work, one of five set by UNICEF's Executive Board for the period 2002–2005.[42] Through this placement in the front ranks of UNICEF's work, the content of child protection work through a range of changing conditions has become well understood.

As a development agency, UNICEF is routinely present and engaged in programmes at field level before, during and after crises; these programmes are expected to support children's right to protection from violence, exploitation and abuse under all conditions, not only as an exceptional response to unusual circumstances such as conflict. In non-emergency conditions, the agency supports governments to strengthen the protective environment for children through systemic changes, an approach described in more detail below. In emergencies, UNICEF also supports short- and medium-term interventions, which may substitute for an absent or over-stretched authority.

The 'Protective Environment Framework' encouraged a shift in UNICEF's child protection programmes. It expressed protection in terms of the broad and common factors that determine whether or not children are likely to be protected, including the existence of appropriate legislation and its implementation, the prevailing customs and attitudes, and the availability of essential social support and other services. From a tradition of small projects that were primarily responsive and palliative, it emphasised, instead the systemic changes needed to allow children to grow up assured of greater safety. This perspective also promoted the integration of child protection onto broader human rights, governance and development agendas.

Strengthening protective factors and reducing vulnerabilities can be discerned as far back as a policy review paper prepared for UNICEF's 1986 Executive Board, which noted that:

> ... UNICEF faces significant opportunities to champion development strategies that reach the poor and effectively reduce their vulnerability. In this situation, it is well served by its standing policy favouring interventions with long term developmental effects – such as supporting innovations and services that can continue long after the period of crisis ... UNICEF is especially well positioned to help reinforce the capacity of families and communities to reduce their own vulnerability and the consequent threat to their children.[43]

In practice, however, most UNICEF country programmes venturing into this area did so through support for services targeting affected children, an approach also identified in the 1986 policy review paper.

The Protective Environment Framework[44] identifies eight broad elements as instrumental to child protection – whatever the country, its level of development

---

[42]   See http://www.unicef.at/shop/dbdocs/mtsp-en.pdf for an overview of the priorities.

[43]   UNICEF, A Review of UNICEF Policies and Strategies on Child Protection, at 17.

[44]   An extended discussion can be found in K. Landgren, 'The Protective Environment: Development Support for Child Protection', *Human Rights Quarterly* vol. 27, no. 1 (2005), 214–248.

or the prevalent human rights violations. *Government commitment and capacity*, the first element, can include ratification of international child rights conventions, adequate budgetary provision for child protection, and public prioritising of protection issues, for example. *Legislation and enforcement*, the second, would entail the incorporation of relevant international standards, the prosecution of violators, the police and judiciary functioning without interference, child-friendly and confidential redress and other mechanisms, the non-criminalisation of victims, and so on. *Protective Culture and Customs*, the third element, must consider the impact of discrimination faced by women and girls, violence as a component of masculine identity, harsh childcare and other traditional practices, and the manner in which disputes are settled, among many other issues; the central importance of this element in child protection reflects the reality of continuing harm to children through acts that have widespread *social* acceptance, regardless of the legislation in place.

The fourth element, *Open Discussion*, encompasses the engagement of civil society and the media in child protection, and the acknowledgement of harmful and exploitative incidents and practices at community and national level and to a degree where young people are able to raise such issues at home, at school and with each other. The fifth element, closely related, is that of *Children's Lifeskills, Knowledge and Participation*. Here, children are helped to acquire information that they need, as well as problem-solving and negotiating skills; they are encouraged to form views and express them, and listened to when they do so. As part of the sixth element, the *Capacity of Families and Communities*, parents and other caregivers observe protective childrearing practices; families are supported with childcare needs; and communities support and monitor the protection of children. Armed conflict presents an obvious threat to the protective functioning of many of these elements; other challenges include the prevailing demographic balance – namely, that there are enough adults able to look after and protect children. Demographic imbalances are created not only through conflict and displacement, but also through disease, notably HIV/AIDS.

Social protection – services and cash transfers that support vulnerable families and children –strengthen the capacity of families and communities, and of children themselves; it is part of the seventh element of the protective environment, *Essential Services*, encompassing both basic services needed by all and targetted services for those in need. Among these services would be the provision of education to all children, including refugees (with teachers trained, present and working, and classrooms safe and supportive), the non-discriminatory provision of healthcare, including for children in the sex industry and juvenile detainees, and the availability of social workers, shelters and hotlines. Finally, the eighth element, *Monitoring, Reporting, and Oversight*, requires that data be systematically collected, transparently reported and used by policy-makers, that independent observers have access to children in traditionally marginalised groups, and that civic review be encouraged and respected.

These illustrations of the elements of child protection are not exhaustive, and each country will analyse its own situation to identify where child protection gaps or failures are occurring. In practice, those gaps should be addressed in a coherent framework. Good examples include strengthening national child protection systems through improved policy, legislation and implementation capacity, or working with the media in ways that contribute to more open discussion, to better monitoring and to changing unprotective traditions. All of the elements included in the protective environment approach can be strengthened through the work of UN agencies, bilaterals and non-governmental organisations.

Crises bring increased violence and abuse, both direct and indirect. The direct violence of armed conflict includes killing and landmines. The indirect consequences include an upsurge in domestic violence and sexual exploitation, often fuelled by the increased availability of small arms. These do not cease when the conflict ends. A study by the Overseas Development Institute found the proliferation of small arms the greatest post-war threat to civilian security in Burundi, with some 80% of households in Bujumbura and in the larger provinces possessing small arms: the weaponry exacerbates widespread rape as well as contributing to the dispossession of widows from their land.[45] Institutions, from government down to community structures, fail to function protectively, and transgressors are no longer held accountable for their acts. A lack of food, fuel and water can push women and girls into transactional or survival sex, as can inadequate parental or foster care.

An approach that strives to reinforce systemic national, societal and familial protective factors and attenuate non-protective ones might seem ill-suited to emergencies. Nonetheless, the principal interventions UNICEF undertakes in crises hew closely to the elements of the protective environment: one element, essential services, is a mainstay of humanitarian response. UNICEF's statement of *Core Commitments in Emergencies*[46] identifies the priority child protection actions as follows:

First Six to Eight Weeks

1. Conduct a rapid assessment of the situation of children and women. Within the appropriate mechanisms, monitor, advocate against, report and communicate on severe, systematic abuse, violence and exploitation.

2. Assist in the prevention of separation and facilitate the identification, registration and medical screening of separated children, particularly those under five years of age and adolescent girls.

3. Ensure that family-tracing systems are implemented with appropriate care and protection facilities.

4. Prevent sexual abuse and exploitation of children and women by:

(i) monitoring, reporting and advocating against instances of sexual violence by military forces, state actors, armed groups and others;

---

[45] E. B. Rackley, 'Armed Violence against Women in Burundi', *Humanitarian Exchange* no. 31 (September 2005), 34–36.

[46] UNICEF, *Core Commitments for Children in Emergencies*, June 2004 (revised March 2005), 10–13, available at http://www.unicef.org/publications/index_21835.html.

(ii) provide post-rape health and psychosocial care and support.[47]

Internally, with regard to humanitarian workers and staff:

(i) undertake and promote humanitarian activities in a manner that minimises opportunities for sexual exploitation and abuse;

(iii) ensure that all UNICEF staff and partners sign the Code of Conduct and are aware of appropriate mechanisms for reporting breaches of its six core principles.

Beyond Initial Response

5. Within established mechanisms, support the establishment of initial monitoring systems, including on severe or systematic abuse, violence and exploitation.

6. In cases where children are separated from caregivers, or at risk of being separated, expand support directly and through partners to:

(i) assist in preventing the separation of children from their caregivers;

(ii) facilitate the identification, registration and medical screening of separated children, particularly those under five and adolescent girls;

(iii) facilitate the registration of all parents and caregivers who have lost their children;

(iv) provide support for the care and protection of separated children, including shelter;

(vi) support partners involved in tracing and reunification and provide tracing equipment as required.

7. Provide support for the care and protection of orphans and other vulnerable children.

8. Support the establishment of safe environments for children and women, including child-friendly spaces, and integrate psychosocial support in education and protection responses.

9. In cases of armed conflict and in accordance with international legal standards, directly and through partners:

(i) monitor, report on and advocate against the recruitment and use of children in any capacity during armed conflicts;

(ii) seek commitments from parties to refrain from recruiting and using children; and

(iii) negotiate the release of children who were recruited and introduce demobilisation and reintegration programmes.

10. Within established mechanisms, monitor, report on and advocate against the use of landmines and other indiscriminate weapons by both state and non-state actors. Coordinate mine-risk education.

---

[47] Reference should be made to the Declaration of Commitment on HIV/AIDS, See UN Doc. A/RES/S-26/2 following (2001) at 58–64.

The critical role of families in child protection is here reflected in preventing separation from a child's caregivers. The importance of monitoring and reporting on violence, exploitation and abuse is reflected at several points in the Core Commitments. Actions to hold perpetrators accountable – from insistence that UNICEF staff and partners sign the 'Code of Conduct' against sexual exploitation and abuse, to the establishment of post-conflict criminal tribunals and enquiries – reflect the importance of government commitment, and legislation and its enforcement.

UNICEF does not take on the Core Commitments alone, but coordinates and contributes to them, drawing on a growing store of standards and guidance on the issues discussed below, which it has helped formulate through existing child protection networks of UN, intergovernmental and non-governmental agencies.

Programming for Children in Conflict and Crisis

This review of UNICEF's child protection programming priorities and experience in the contexts of conflict and disaster will address six aspects: unaccompanied and separated children, psychosocial support, protection from gender-related violence, demobilisation and reintegration of child soldiers and prevention of recruitment, children and justice, and monitoring and reporting.

Unaccompanied and Separated Children

In January 2004, 'Inter-agency Guiding Principles on Unaccompanied and Separated Children'[48] were issued jointly by UNICEF, the ICRC, the International Rescue Committee, Save the Children UK, UNHCR and World Vision International – partners that had set up a working group on unaccompanied and separated children in 1995. Noting the particular vulnerability of children separated from parents or other caregivers, this short and accessible publication discusses preventing separation and preserving family unity; tracing and family reunification; and interim and durable care arrangements. The guidelines, as well as the close working relationships established between agencies, have enabled common positions to be taken on child protection issues at the peak of crises, notably the Southeast Asian tsunami of December 2004.

---

[48] 'Inter-agency Guiding Principles on Unaccompanied and Separated Children', issued by the International Committee of the Red Cross, January 2004, on behalf of ICRC, the International Rescue Committee, Save the Children (UK), UNICEF, UNHCR and World Vision International.

The 'Guiding Principles' give priority to preventing the separation of children from their families wherever possible. Preventive actions can be as simple as making sure children know their full names and where they come from, and giving children name tags in the event of displacement. Agencies themselves are expected to review their support for services in the light of preventing family separation – knowing for example, that establishing orphanages or long-term centres for children risks encouraging the placement there of children who might otherwise have remained with their families. It is incumbent on relief workers to keep under review changes that could provoke further separations, including threats to food or physical security. Instinctive protective reactions, moreover, are not always the right ones: history is dotted with unhappy examples of separated children evacuated from war zones.[49] Any evacuation of children demands close safeguards.

As a longer-term measure, the registration of all children at birth creates a record of identity and family relationships that can facilitate subsequent tracing. At the onset of an emergency, separated children are to be identified and registered, with as much documentation as possible to facilitate the tracing of relatives. Many tracing methodologies exist: the paramount concern in all is that neither the child nor relatives be endangered by them, as can happen where family members who stayed behind are identified as the relatives of a refugee. Tracing can be complicated at the best of times, let alone in the midst of conflict, and until tracing efforts are exhausted, nothing should be done to compromise a child's prospects of family reunification, such as adoption or a change of name.

Psychosocial Support

In conflicts and disasters, children may experience terror, separation, extreme disruption, a loss of nurturing, displacement, violence and more. UNICEF and partners working in this field produced guidance in 2006 on how best to help children cope and minimise their distress.[50]

The term 'psychosocial' describes intertwined psychological (internal) and social (external) factors. Psychosocial programming aims to restore as much sense of normalcy for the child as possible. Building on the work of the International Save the Children Alliance, UNICEF convened workshops in 1997 and 1998 to develop guiding principles for psychosocial programming. These principles emphasise respect for local culture, community-based approaches and children's participation.[51] Local authorities, communities, parents and children should all be

---

[49]   See E. M. Ressler, N. Boothby and D. Steinbock, *Unaccompanied Children: Care and Protection in Wars, Natural Disasters and Refugee Movements* (Oxford: Oxford University Press, 1988).

[50]   IASC, 'Guidelines on Mental Health and Psychosocial Support', (forthcoming).

[51]   G. Machel, *The Impact of Armed Conflict on Children: A Review of Progress since the 1996 United Nations Report on the Impact of Armed Conflict on Children* (London: Hurst & Co., 2001), pp. 84–87.

engaged in the planning and implementation of community-based psychosocial support. Initiatives that promote resilience and coping in children, and respond to unmet psychological and social needs,[52] are preferred over approaches that focus on the traumatic event or events, particularly in the first few months. The post-traumatic stress disorder approach taken in the past often entailed training local specialists in methods believed to de-sensitise the child to the experience, including through 'debriefing' or otherwise reliving the event(s) in question. UNICEF has moved away from this approach, which may not respond to the continuing deprivation and risk faced by children in conflict and disaster, and which also tends to be labour-intensive and costly. The psychosocial model recognises that stress symptoms affect most people who experience traumatic events, and that continued stress and mental health problems can be reduced if protective factors around the child are strengthened. These include helping caregivers to play *their* role in supporting the child.

UNICEF has taken the position that psychosocial support need not await the end of conflict or hostilities, and that an understanding of psychosocial impact should always be factored in to operational interventions such as the provision of education, shelter and food aid. One practice which has been found effective for promoting psychosocial well-being is establishing 'child-friendly spaces' – protected sites providing respite from the surrounding chaos and offering services, including schooling and recreation. These spaces also foster young people's participation in community life. The peer-to-peer 'Return to Happiness' programme began in Mozambique in 1992. Adolescent girls and boys, supervised by teachers, were trained in 'play therapy' – ways of cultivating trust and hope in younger children through games, art, puppetry, songs and story-telling. It was later replicated in Colombia for conflict-affected communities (1996); Venezuela after the mudslide (1999); Timor Leste after the civil war (2000); and Ecuador following a volcanic eruption (2001).[53] UNICEF has helped establish child-friendly spaces in different forms in Albania, Liberia, Turkey, Angola, Guinea, the North Caucasus and India, in the aftermath of natural disasters as well as in armed conflict.[54]

The protection and healing provided by families and caretakers themselves should not be underestimated. Several months after the December 2004 tsunami, focus groups were conducted in Banda Aceh with some 250 parents and caretakers in the hardest-hit communities. The groups were asked about changes in their children's attitudes and behaviours. Parents and caregivers appeared very aware of their children's well-being. Very few serious problems, and no serious mental health problems, were found. Changes reported in most children included a fear of the ocean, of sleeping alone, and of entering homes alone; rather than pathologise these

---

[52] See discussion in E. M. Ressler, J. M. Tortorici and A. Marcelino, *Children in War: A Guide to the Provision of Services* (New York: UNICEF, 1993), p. 166.

[53] Information provided by Ms Saudamini Siegrist, UNICEF Innocenti Research Centre, Florence.

[54] More on UNICEF's work in these countries is available at http://www.unicef.org/infobycountry/index.html.

reactions, agencies were encouraged to continue to focus on rebuilding attachments and social support, with plenty of structured activities.[55]

Children who have experienced conflict are not alone in needing psychosocial support. The lessons learned from psychosocial support efforts in emergencies are now being applied to a host of other situations, including in respect of children who have been trafficked, abused, institutionalised or detained unnecessarily or under harsh conditions, subjected to child marriage or other harmful practices, orphaned, or stigmatised by disability, AIDS or other factors. Adopting a psychosocial approach does not exclude the fact that some children may need individual interventions, including professional mental health intervention, in the longer run.

Protection from Gender-based Violence

Sexual violence and abuse in conflict or as a means of conflict is carried out primarily against women and girls, by men. Occasionally, such violence is performed by men against men and boys, as during the war in the former Yugoslavia. More rarely, sexual abuse by women against male prisoners comes to light as an interrogation technique.[56] Sexual abuse has been a hallmark of conflicts, including, in World War Two, the use of Korean and other 'comfort women' by the Japanese military, and the mass rapes by Soviet forces during the liberation of Berlin.

The massive and widespread rapes in the former Yugoslavia and in Rwanda (where over a quarter of a million women are believed to have been raped) generated both outrage and action. The International Criminal Tribunals of the Former Yugoslavia and Rwanda prosecuted crimes of sexual and gender violence as crimes against humanity and genocide for the first time. They upheld convictions of rape and other forms of sexual violence as instruments of genocide (*Akayesu*[57]), crimes against humanity (*Akayesu*,[58] *Kunarac*[59]) and war crimes (*Čelebići,*[60] *Furundžija*[61]), among other findings.[62] The use of children as sexual slaves or concubines fell within

---

[55]   Private communication to the author.

[56]   See http://www.cbsnews.com/stories/2005/01/27/national/main669845.shtml,   27 January 2005.

[57]   *Prosecutor v. Jean-Paul Akayesu*, Judgement, Case No. ICTR-96-4-T, Chamber 1, 2 September 1998.

[58]   *Ibid.*

[59]   *Prosecutor v. Dragoljub Kunarac et al*, Judgement, Case No. IT-96-23-T & IT-96-23/1-T, Trial Chamber, 22 February 2001.

[60]   *Prosecutor v. Zejnil Delalić et al*, Judgement, Case No. IT-96-21-T, Trial Chamber II, 16 November 1998.

[61]   *Prosecutor v. Anto Furundžija*, Judgement, Case No. IT-95-17/1-T, Trial Chamber II, 10 December 1998.

[62]   See E. Rehn and E. J. Sirleaf, *Women, War and Peace: The Independent Experts' Assessment* (New York: UNIFEM/UNFPA, 2002).

the 1997 definition of child soldiers,[63] and the 1998 Rome Statute establishing the International Criminal Court included rape as a crime against humanity.[64]

Programmatic work to prevent and respond to sexual violence has also developed, but it is frequently hampered; where rapes form part of the tactics of a war, as in Sudan, it has proved impossible to undertake prevention piecemeal. In Darfur, *Medécins sans Frontières* reported treating 500 survivors of sexual violence in just four months of 2005, with girls as young as seven and eight having been raped.[65] Speaking to the Security Council in 2005, the UN emergency relief coordinator noted that the impact of these abhorrent acts was compounded by the actions of the Sudanese government:

> Not only do the Sudanese authorities fail to provide effective physical protection, they inhibit access to treatment. Victims are publicly castigated and some have been imprisoned. Unmarried pregnant women have been treated as criminals, arrested and subjected to brutal treatment by police thus becoming victims yet again. Both survivors of sexual violence and NGO staff providing assistance are harassed and intimidated by the authorities.[66]

Preventing and responding to gender-based violence is difficult even where it occurs without the overt or tacit support of the authorities. Since the mid-1990s, humanitarian workers have become more aware of the protection aspects of 'technical' camp management and relief issues, including women and girls' exposure to risk through insufficient or distant water and firewood, poor placement and lighting of latrines, insensitive layout of camps and weak perimeter protection, as well as automatic designation of males as heads of family for the purposes of representation and receipt of food. But it has proved more difficult to address the imbalances of money and power, and the absence of oversight and accountability mechanisms, that contribute to the sexual exploitation of children by peacekeepers, humanitarian workers and local officials.

In 2002, an inter-agency task force on sexual exploitation and abuse outlined recommendations for preventing sexual exploitation and abuse in humanitarian crises. The following year, the UN secretary-general issued a bulletin to all staff on special measures for protection from sexual exploitation and sexual abuse to publicise the standards of conduct expected not only of UN staff but also individuals and organisations entering into cooperative arrangements with the UN. It prohibits

---

[63] See 'Cape Town Principles' and 'Best Practices', adopted at the symposium on the prevention of recruitment of children into the armed forces and on demobilization and social reintegration of child soldiers in Africa (27–30 April 1997) at http://www.unicef.org/emerg/files/Cape_Town_Principles.pdf.

[64] Rome Statute of the International Criminal Court, UN Doc. A/CONF.183/9 (1998), Article 7.

[65] Human Rights Watch, *Sexual Violence and its Consequences among Displaced Persons in Darfur and Chad*, Briefing Paper (12 April 2005).

[66] Statement to Security Council, 21 June 2005, see UN Doc. SC/8420, press release, 21 June 2005.

sex with children under the age of 18. In 2005, application of the 'Code of Conduct' was extended to UN peacekeeping troops.[67]

There are many examples of programmes to assist victims of sexual exploitation and violence.[68] In the first year of a UNICEF project in the Democratic Republic of Congo, over 10,000 women and children who had been subjected to sexual violence received assistance, including food and non-food items, counselling, and family mediation where survivors of rape had been rejected by their husbands, parents or community. In Goma, UNICEF has supported two hospitals that provide rape victims with medical and surgical care, voluntary and confidential counselling, and treatment for sexually transmitted infections, including HIV. Between April and September 2003, one of the hospitals registered 973 female victims of sexual violence, aged between seven and 80, and performed over 150 operations for fistula.[69] While political attention remains focused on sexual violence by military, militia and humanitarian actors, shocking levels of sexual violence are often taking place within families and communities in conflict contexts, and protection-mandated agencies should also consider this whenever discussing and addressing sexual violence.

Recruitment, Demobilisation and Reintegration of Children Associated with Armed Groups and Forces

The Graça Machel report[70] brought worldwide attention to the existence of child soldiers, whose numbers have been estimated at between 200,000 and 300,000.[71] Four years earlier, in 1992, a general discussion day organised by the Committee on the Rights of the Child had recommended an optional protocol to the Convention to raise to 18 the minimum age of recruitment.[72] Under the CRC, state parties are to observe applicable international humanitarian law in respect of children[73] and to refrain from recruiting children below the age of 15.[74] State parties are also enjoined to take all feasible measures to ensure that children under-15 do not participate in

---

[67]　See Report of the Special Committee on Peacekeeping Operations and its Working Group on the 2005 resumed session, UN Doc. A/59/19/Add.1 (2005), at 8–9, endorsed by General Assembly resolution of 30 June 2005, Comprehensive Review of a Strategy to Eliminate Future Sexual Exploitation and Abuse in United Nations Peacekeeping Operations, UN Doc. A/RES/59/300 (2005).

[68]　For more on these and other examples see http://www.unicef.org/infobycountry/index. html.

[69]　UNICEF *The Impact of Conflict on Women and Girls in West and Central Africa and the UNICEF Response* (2005) available at http://www.unicef.org/publications/index_25262.html.

[70]　See G. Machel, Report on the Impact of Armed Conflict on Children.

[71]　See http://www.unicef.org/crc/index_30203.html.

[72]　'Committee on the Rights of the Child, Report on the Second Session, UN Doc. CRC/C/10 (1992), at 75.

[73]　Article 38(1).

[74]　Article 38(3).

hostilities.[75] The use of the lower age limit of 15 appeared inconsistent with the Convention's definition of children as being under the age of 18.[76]

The Machel report supported an optional protocol to the CRC to raise the age of recruitment and participation in hostilities to 18 years for both government and non-government forces.[77] The issue was a controversial one, despite other instruments enhancing the protection of children from other harmful forms of labour. The International Labour Organization (ILO) Minimum Age Convention of 1973 had made eighteen 'the minimum age for admission to employment or work which by its nature or the circumstances in which it is carried out is likely to jeopardise the health, safety or morals of young persons'.[78] While that Convention did not include armed conflicts within its scope, the 1999 ILO Worst Forms of Child Labour Convention outlawed the forced or compulsory recruitment or use of children under 18 in armed conflict.[79] The Optional Protocol to the CRC on the involvement of children in armed conflict refers explicitly to the prohibition of recruitment and use of children by armed groups – and to states' responsibility for all feasible measures to prevent it.[80] Although negotiations on the Optional Protocol failed to establish a 'straight 18' ban for both voluntary and compulsory recruitment by states, this Protocol raised the earlier standards set by international law.

In April 1997, a symposium on child soldiers organised by UNICEF and the NGO Sub-Group on Refugee Children and Children in Armed Conflict adopted the 'Cape Town Principles on the Prevention of Recruitment of Children into the Armed Forces and Demobilization and Social Reintegration of Child Soldiers in Africa'. These include the following definition of child soldiers:

> Any person under 18 years of age who is part of any kind of regular or irregular armed force or armed group in any capacity, including, but not limited to: cooks; porters; messengers; and anyone accompanying such groups other than purely family members. The definition includes girls and boys recruited for sexual purposes and for forced marriages. It does not, therefore, only refer to a child who is carrying or has carried arms.[81]

This definition is important and often overlooked: children abducted or conscripted by rebel and government forces alike perform a range of actions, only some of which involve weaponry, and child soldier demobilisation exercises have failed when limited to children carrying a weapon. Former child soldiers should be separated from their former military command structure as soon as possible. These should

---

[75] Article 38(2).
[76] Article 1.
[77] G. Machel, Report on the Impact of Armed Conflict on Children, at 62.
[78] ILO, C138, 1973, Article 3(1).
[79] ILO, C182, 1999, Articles 2 and 3.
[80] General Assembly resolution 54/263 (2001), Optional Protocols to the Convention on the Rights of the Child on the Involvement of Children in Armed Conflict and on the Sale of Children, Child Prostitution and Child Pornography, UN Doc. A/RES/54/263 (2001), Article 4.
[81] See footnote 63.

not be a sub-set of adult demobilisation programmes. Disentangling children from their lives as soldiers, in which they have been forced to commit and to experience human rights abuses, is exceptionally complicated, placing severe demands not only on them but also on their families and societies, who tend to shun them – whether they have taken part in atrocities or borne babies out of wedlock. Recently, the terminology of 'children associated with armed groups and forces' has begun to replace 'child soldiers'.

Child soldier reintegration initiatives supported by UNICEF are taking place all over the world, including in Afghanistan, Colombia, Sri Lanka, Sudan, Somalia, the Democratic Republic of Congo, Burundi and Uganda.[82] In Afghanistan, for example, the work of demobilisation and reintegration began with assessment visits to 26 of the country's 32 provinces, by UNICEF child protection staff with the support of United Nations Assistance Mission in Afghanistan political affairs officers.[83] They collected information through meetings with traditional leaders, interviews with over 100 child soldiers, focus group discussions and existing military information. The lack of birth registration complicated determinations of age.

The assessment visits led UNICEF and partners to put the number of child soldiers in Afghanistan at approximately 8000: all males, predominantly from poor families. Their activities included cleaning and storing weapons, acting as messengers and porters, enforcing 'vice and virtue norms' under the Taliban, cleaning the barracks and cooking. On the front lines, they were used as combatants, spies, trench- and grave-diggers, and porters. They were subjected to violence and abuse. Most had joined local armed groups, who demanded a son from each household and taxed those who could not supply one. For some, joining conferred power or status, in a situation where neither work nor education were available. Some parents sent their children to fight for ideological reasons; in other cases they accompanied older siblings.

Unusually, most child soldiers remained in regular contact with their families, which made their demobilisation and reintegration easier. No interim care centres were set up: instead, mobile demobilisation teams worked with local *shuras* (councils of elders) to facilitate demobilisations and inform families and communities of what to expect, and district-level verification committees were set up to identify and register child soldiers. Community meetings were held to reinforce, among other things, good *tarbia*.[84]

---

[82]   For more on these and other examples see http://www.unicef.org/infobycountry/index.html.

[83]   Information in these paragraphs on child soldier demobilisation in Afghanistan comes from an undated UNICEF draft report, on file with the present author.

[84]   *Tarbia* refers to the quality of manners and relationships, and is regarded as an essential quality. Good *tarbia* includes good and clean language, respect for elders and parents, bodily cleanliness and hospitality. An extended discussion of the importance of *tarbia* can be found in *The Children of Kabul* by UNICEF and Save the Children (June 2003) at http://www.savethechildren.org/publications/children_of_kabul.pdf.

A child soldier who leaves his or her command structure generally has few skills and a strong need to reconnect with family and friends or join a new community. Support in Afghanistan included skills training and tool kits, as well as small enterprise grants, recreational activities and peer support, informal education and lifeskills. In some situations, demobilised child soldiers are helped to live independently. In northern Uganda, where an estimated 20,000 children have been abducted by the Lord's Resistance Army,[85] UNICEF supports reception centres run by partners. Here, family tracing takes place and children who have escaped or been released receive basic medical attention, HIV-prevention education, and counselling. They are also given basic commodity kits of blankets, basins, jerry-cans and mattresses: Many children, especially adolescent mothers, do not return to their former homes when they leave the centres.

UNICEF advocates against cash assistance to child soldiers as part of demobilisation efforts. Apart from appearing to reward their *metier*, the cash is coveted by former commanders, who may still wield influence over the children, and places the children at risk. Children may also take the cash and offer themselves for re-recruitment.

In Sri Lanka, UNICEF undertook wide-ranging consultations in 1997–98 on a 'Call to Action' declaring children as 'Zones of Peace' – language that had been used in the Machel report. At that moment the conflict in Sri Lanka, having begun (or recrudesced) in 1983, affected an estimated 900,000 children – through large-scale displacement (some 380,000), disruption of health and school services, an increase in communicable diseases, and, of course, violence, both direct and indirect, including the death of family members, maiming by landmines and the pervasive climate of fear and intimidation. In 2002, UNICEF established a database to document all claims, which number several thousand, of child recruitment by the Liberation Tigers of Tamil Eelam (LTTE) armed group. Parents or relatives of children thought to have been recruited were helped to register this information at the five UNICEF offices located in territory controlled by the LTTE. UNICEF maintains a steady stream of advocacy and engagement with both the government and the LTTE, which has repeatedly made commitments to end its recruitment of child soldiers; a few months after an 'Action Plan' on children affected by war was signed by the LTTE and the government in 2003, the LTTE released 49 children and promptly recruited 23 others. In mid-2005, the database of recruited children contained over 4,811 unresolved cases.

Justice for Children

UNICEF has had a lengthy engagement in juvenile justice issues, originally centred in its Latin American offices. Its involvement in transitional justice issues relating

---

[85]   Most are boys between the ages of 13 and 16, but many girls are also taken. Periodically, small numbers of abducted children are released; there is no reliable count of how many have been released, have otherwise returned or have died.

to children began in the aftermath of the Rwanda genocide, when thousands of children were among those detained under brutal conditions. The focus of UNICEF's subsequent efforts, however, has been to support accountability mechanisms for crimes against children during conflict, child-friendly procedures within transitional justice mechanisms,[86] and appropriate juvenile justice frameworks thereafter.

In rapid developments since the mid-1990s, children have been involved as victims and witnesses before truth commissions,[87] mixed tribunals and traditional justice mechanisms. Children have not been indicted by international or mixed tribunals, and the Rome Statute limits prosecutions to persons over 18. This has not been the case within traditional justice mechanisms, such as *gacaca* in Rwanda. Dilemmas arise for UNICEF and other organisations faced with promoting accountability for crimes against children, on the one hand, and respect for the best interests of the child, including reintegration and preservation of confidentiality, on the other.

The Special Court for Sierra Leone offers an interesting example. During the decade-long conflict in Sierra Leone, many thousands of children were deliberately abducted, forcibly recruited, made to kill or maim others, raped, mutilated and otherwise abused. The prosecutor had determined that children would be treated as victims of war crimes and not as perpetrators, and provision had to be made for child witnesses before the Court. The Victims and Witnesses Section of the Court was responsible for all protection and assistance, including medical and rehabilitative support, to witnesses, and worked closely with child protection agencies including UNICEF in devising child-friendly procedures. The Special Court for Sierra Leone became the first court to find the recruitment or use of children under 15 in hostilities a war crime under customary international law.[88]

The Sierra Leone parliament asked the Truth and Reconciliation Commission (TRC – a non-judicial mechanism, established in February 2000) to implement special procedures to work with both child victims and child perpetrators of abuses. UNICEF worked with other UN agencies and the 'Child Protection Network' – the government and national and international NGOs – to develop child-friendly procedures, including the training of statement-takers on child protection, keeping the identities of children confidential and the organisation of closed sessions and special hearings for children. Statement-taking at community level was an important activity, with close to 200 children interviewed and their statements taken, in their own communities. Children were interviewed by one TRC statement taker, with the support of a child protection worker. The TRC and child protection agencies agreed formally through the 'Framework for Cooperation' to work together on these measures and procedures, in line with their respective mandates and roles. According

---

[86]   This section draws on background papers prepared for an expert discussion on transitional justice and children, held at Innocenti Research Centre, Florence, 10–12 November 2005.

[87]   Including those in South Africa, Sierra Leone, Peru and Timor Leste.

[88]   *Prosecutor v. Sam Hinga Norman*, Decision on Preliminary Motion Based on Lack of Jurisdiction, Case No. SCLS-2003-14-AR72(E), Appeals Chamber, 31 May 2004.

to staff involved in the process, the agreed procedures were not closely adhered to and many inconsistencies occurred. Nonetheless, the Framework was groundbreaking in establishing norms for the involvement of children in the process.[89]

Invariably, a post-conflict challenge is how best to provide children and adolescents with opportunities, guidance and support – and protection – to participate in a meaningful way. In Sierra Leone, UNICEF helped organise thematic hearings on children and, working with children's groups, prepared a child-friendly version of the Commission's report. Over 100 children took part in the process, 15 of them closely. Children from all over Sierra Leone took part in a Children's National Assembly in Freetown in December 2003, and discussed the child-friendly version of the report of the Truth and Reconciliation Commission.[90]

During conflicts, national judicial systems may have been destroyed or incapacitated; their rebuilding requires the rebuilding of both capacity and trust that they will function with integrity. Absent functioning court systems, children may remain in custody without trial for months or even years. When deprived of their liberty, some groups of children, including former child soldiers, face serious risks of ill treatment, abuse, torture and extended periods of detention. In addition to the daily risk of violence at the hands of other detainees and prison staff, including the acute threat of sexual violence, they may be subjected to discriminatory application of criminal procedures and penalties.

Monitoring and Reporting

UNICEF has monitored children recruited as soldiers in Sri Lanka and in northern Uganda. Since 2001, the annual secretary-general's report to the Security Council on children and armed conflict has included information on grave violations of children's rights, annexing information on offending parties.[91] By Security Council resolution 1612, the secretary-general was asked to implement a monitoring and reporting mechanism (MRM) for six egregious child rights violations in situations on the Council's agenda, and also to apply it to other situations of armed conflict.[92]

The MRM is to monitor the following violations against children: killing or maiming; recruitment or use in conflict; abduction; rape or other grave sexual violence; denial of humanitarian access; and attacks against schools or hospitals. At country level this is to take place through 'child protection networks' under the overall responsibility of the UN resident coordinator, humanitarian coordinator or

---

[89]   Information provided by Ms Saudamini Siegrist, UNICEF Innocenti Research Centre, Florence.

[90]   UNICEF, National Forum for Human Rights and United Nations Assistance Mission in Sierra Leone, *Recommendations for Policies and Procedures for Addressing and Involving Children in the Truth and Reconciliation Commission* (June 2001), available at http://www.sierra-leone.org/trc-documents.html.

[91]   As requested by Security Council resolution 1379 (2001), UN Doc. S/RES/1379 (2001), at 10–11.

[92]   See Security Council resolution 1612 (2005), UN Doc. S/RES/1612 (2005) at 2.

special representative of the secretary-general. Parties to conflict in five countries on the Council's agenda are named as violators in connection with the recruitment and use of children by armed groups: these are Burundi, Côte d'Ivoire, Democratic Republic of Congo, Somalia and Sudan. The first phase of monitoring and reporting may include additional countries where monitoring work is ongoing or which have already been named in reports to the Council. Ultimately a system of monitoring and reporting, to be credible, will need to cover all countries in conflict.

The monitoring and reporting mechanism is intended to help step up international response to human rights violations, not solely as an information system. While an important political step in child protection, it has raised ethical issues: the imperative that agencies act on the violations they report, for example, and the issue of whether monitoring and reporting will create a backlash, forcing the shutdown of other important activities, such as vaccinations.

Conclusion

The fact that the protection from violence, exploitation and abuse provided to children today holds the keys to tomorrow's human capital, development, democracy and security may sound like a truism. But it has yet to be understood and reflected in national development planning, and its appearance on the Security Council's agenda, while highly significant, remains 'seasonal' – linked to the presentation of the secretary-general's annual report on children and armed conflict. The importance of addressing child protection in humanitarian logistics and support services, when laying the groundwork for institutions of security and justice, and in responding to disease pandemics still awaits full acknowledgement. UNICEF is one actor whose multifaceted country programmes, and whose continuity of presence in the field, can reinforce global understanding of the long-term importance of better child protection.

Chapter 11

Protection: The Office of the United Nations High Commissioner for Refugees Experience

Maria Stavropoulou[1]

This chapter traces the origins of the Office of the United Nations High Commissioner for Refugees (UNHCR) protection work and the principles that have shaped its presence in the field over the past several decades. Basing itself on the provisions of the 1951 Convention relating to the Status of Refugees (Refugee Convention)[2] and the UNHCR statute,[3] which are few in comparison to the plethora of international human rights instruments, UNHCR has developed a relatively concrete set of protection tasks and functions, aiming at satisfying the basic needs and human rights of a refugee. In turn, these functions require that staff entrusted primarily with protection work demonstrate certain skills, in large part acquired through training provided by UNHCR itself. The above are outlined in this chapter, in recognition of the fact that UNHCR 'protection' work is largely 'human rights' work, and hence can inform significantly the types of human rights field work described elsewhere in the present volume.

The Mandate of UNHCR to 'Protect'

The origins of UNHCR's protection mandate are found in the pioneering work of Fridtjof Nansen, who is regarded as the founding father of the international system of refugee protection.[4] In the aftermath of World War I, Nansen, who believed in

[1] The views expressed in the present chapter are those of the author and do not necessarily represent those of the Office of the United Nations High Commissioner for Refugees. The author is very grateful to Corinne Lewis, Karen Farkas and Bart Leerschool for their comments and suggestions.
[2] Convention relating to the Status of Refugees, signed 28 July 1951, 189 UNTS 150 (entered into force 22 April 1954).
[3] Statute of the Office of the United Nations High Commissioner for Refugees, UN Doc. A/RES/428 (V) (1950).
[4] UNHCR, *The State of the World's Refugees: The Challenge of Protection* (London: Penguin Books, 1993), p. 4.

the opportunities that the newly established League of Nations presented for world peace and stability, was entrusted with four huge humanitarian operations. These included the repatriation of half a million prisoners of war, the organisation of a massive relief operation to stem famine in Russia, the provision of travel documents to refugees and stateless persons[5] so they could travel, and the management of the Greek–Turkish population exchange in the early 1920s. In 1921, in order to provide for the coordination of relief efforts, the League of Nations appointed Nansen as the first high commissioner for refugees.

While in Nansen's days international human rights texts did not exist, at least not in the general fashion they are understood and applied at present, Nansen's operations would undeniably qualify today as activities aiming at safeguarding specific human rights (for instance, the right to return to one's own country, the right to life, the right to food and an adequate standard of living, and the right to physical security). At the same time it is important to note that, in its early stages of development, international protection was not afforded to refugees on an individual basis, but rather through a group or category approach (such as Russians who did not enjoy the protection of the USSR, Armenians, Assyrians and Assyro-Chaldeans, Germans who did not enjoy the protection of the emerging Nazi government of the late 1930s, and others).[6] By the time UNHCR was created in 1950, the group approach had been abandoned in favour of a general definition of a 'refugee', which, however, was based on more precise criteria as to the nature of 'acceptable refugeehood'.

UNHCR was established by the General Assembly of the United Nations (UN) to 'provide international protection' and seek 'permanent solutions for the problem of refugees'. The UNHCR Statute specifically defines the groups and individuals for whom the high commissioner is competent.[7] These include refugees covered by earlier instruments and arrangements, but also persons who are outside their country of origin because of a well-founded fear of persecution by reason of race, religion, nationality, membership of a particular social group or political opinion.[8] As Goodwin-Gill notes, the refugee definition in the Statute remains a critical point of departure in determining who is entitled to the protection and assistance of UNHCR, since it is the lack of protection by their own governments which distinguishes

---

[5]   It is interesting to note that one of the first forms refugee protection took, at the initiative of Nansen, was the provision of internationally recognised travel documents, which became known as the 'Nansen passports'. One of most acute problems refugees face is the lack of national passports, proving, *inter alia*, that they avail themselves of the protection of their country of origin. Consequently, an immediate step to redress this was (and is) the issuance of an internationally recognised travel document, the most visible manifestation of 'international protection'. Today, the provision of travel documents is enshrined in Article 28 of the 1951 Refugee Convention. See A. Grahl-Madsen, *Commentary on the Refugee Convention 1951* (Geneva: UNHCR, 1997), p. 117 *et seq*.

[6]   G. S. Goodwin-Gill, *The Refugee in International Law* , 2nd edn (Oxford: Clarendon Paperbacks, 1996), pp. 4–6.

[7]   Paragraph 6 of the Statute of the Office of the United Nations High Commissioner for Refugees.

[8]   For the full definition see paragraph 6A, *ibid*.

refugees from ordinary aliens.[9] In other words, international protection is the means through which a human being can be shielded from 'persecution',[10] which today is widely interpreted to mean human rights violations that have reached a certain threshold of intensity or seriousness.[11]

In attempting to address this gap in national protection,[12] UNHCR and the international community will aim generally to protect the refugee's basic human rights,[13] including the rights to life, liberty and the security of the person.

The Content of 'International Protection'

The Statute specifically provides how the high commissioner is to provide for the protection of refugees.[14] This includes promoting the conclusion of international conventions for the protection of refugees, and supervising their application; promoting with governments the execution of measures to improve the situation of refugees, assisting governmental and private efforts to promote 'assimilation' within national communities or repatriation; promoting the admission of refugees, obtaining from governments information concerning the number and conditions of refugees and the laws and regulations concerning them and establishing contact with private organisations dealing with refugee questions. The Statute provides that the work of the high commissioner will be of an 'entirely non-political character'. It is to be 'humanitarian and social'.

The essential elements of international protection include at least the following:

(i)   admission to safety;
(ii) exemption from forcible return to a country of danger;
(iii) non-discrimination; and
(iv) assistance for survival.[15]

'Protection activities' may focus on specific issues peculiar to the refugee: for example, ensuring that no refugee is returned to a country in which he or she will

---

[9]   Goodwin-Gill, *The Refugee in International Law*, p. 8.

[10]   See also UNHCR, *The State of the World's Refugees*, p. 11.

[11]   J. Hathaway, *The Law of Refugee Status*, (Toronto: Butterworths, 1991). For a critique see D. J. Steinbock, 'The Refugee Definition as Law: Issues of Interpretation', in F. Nicholson and P. Twomey (eds), *Refugee Rights and Realities* (Cambridge: Cambridge University Press, 1999), p. 31.

[12]   Goodwin-Gill, *The Refugee in International Law*, p. 8.

[13]   Few would argue today that UNHCR's protection work is fundamentally that of protecting human rights rather than humans as such. Refugee human rights are those found in all international human rights instruments as well as those distinct ones guaranteed in the Refugee Convention.

[14]   Paragraph 8 of the Statute of the Office of the United Nations High Commissioner for Refugees, including a full list of responsibilities of the high commissioner.

[15]   UNHCR, *The State of the World's Refugees*, p. 5.

be in danger; ensuring that asylum seekers have access to an informed procedure and that every refugee is recognised as such, that asylum is granted, that expulsion is prevented, and that travel and identity documents are issued.[16] Interventions with governments, to ensure the above, are the norm, although UNHCR is not limited in working with non-governmental organisations (NGOs) and any other actor useful in refugee protection. More recently UNHCR's indirect or promotional activities include the development of laws benefiting refugees, the promotion of international instruments, training, dissemination and promotion of refugee law, and engagement with the entire spectrum of international and regional human rights instruments and bodies.[17]

Interestingly, UNHCR has an express supervisory responsibility over the implementation of the Refugee Convention. According to Article 35, contracting states undertake to cooperate with UNHCR in the exercise of its functions and facilitate, in particular, its duty of supervising the application of the provisions of the Convention.[18] In addition they must submit information and statistical data, as per paragraph 2 of the same Article, in order to enable UNHCR to 'make reports to the competent organs of the United Nations'. This information will concern the condition of refugees, the 'implementations' of the Convention, and laws, regulations and decrees which concern refugees. The high commissioners are also entitled to present views to the General Assembly and the Economic and Social Council and their subsidiary bodies.[19]

Having said this, it is also important to note that the foundation for UNHCR's ability to carry out international protection is the cooperation of states; where such cooperation is either lacking or limited, UNHCR is restricted in carrying out its protection activities and supervisory responsibility.

UNHCR activities closely resemble current work of human rights organisations, in so far as monitoring, reporting, advocacy and the promotion of instruments are concerned. Even the constant tension between operations on the one hand and

---

[16]   Goodwin-Gill, *The Refugee in International Law*, p. 8.

[17]   As Walter Kälin notes, international protection has 'evolved from a surrogate for consular and diplomatic protection … into a broader concept that includes protection not only of rights provided for by the 1951 Convention and the 1967 Protocol but also of refugees' human rights in general'. See W. Kälin, 'Supervising the 1951 Convention Relation to the Status of Refugees: Article 35 and Beyond', in E. Feller, V. Türk and F. Nicholson (eds), *Refugee Protection in International Law* (Cambridge: Cambridge University Press, 2003), p. 619. Concerning the increasing interaction between human rights and refugee issues, see for example, M. Stavropoulou, 'Displacement and Human Rights: Reflections on UN Practice', in *Human Rights Quarterly* vol. 20, no. 3 (1998), 515–554. See also B. Gorlick, 'Refugee Protection in Troubled Times', in N. Steiner *et al.* (eds), *Problems of Protection* (London: Routledge, 2003), p. 87–95.

[18]   See also Grahl-Madsen, *Commentary on the Refugee Convention 1951*, p. 254, who notes that the obligation to cooperate extends to all of the functions of the high commissioner's office, irrespective of their legal basis.

[19]   Paragraph 11 of the Statute of the Office of the United Nations High Commissioner for Refugees.

monitoring and reporting ('supervisory responsibilities')[20] on the other, frequently also found in the human rights field operations and amply described in other parts of the present volume, have been a reality in UNHCR's field work for decades.[21]

Nevertheless, there is a limit to the parallels that can be drawn between action by the international community to protect the rights of refugees on the one hand, and the rights of other individuals on the other. UNHCR's 'protection' function, based on the Refugee Convention and the UNHCR Statute, is a *substitute* for the normal safeguards (read human rights) expected to be provided by one's own government ('diplomatic protection' in its strict sense, or otherwise, and in a broader fashion, 'international protection'[22]). In other words, and depending on a given situation, UNHCR operations can be of quite a wide range, including the actual provision of shelter, medical facilities and education, identity documents and status determination,[23] to a degree rarely if ever met in human rights operations. In addition, UNHCR's protection role in a given refugee situation ends only with the attainment of durable solutions[24] (which take the form either of voluntary repatriation, local integration and ultimately full citizenship in the host country, or resettlement in a third country), a quest without parallel in human rights field operations.

UNHCR Protection Work in the Field

A feature that sets apart UNHCR operations from human rights field operations is the fact that in most UNHCR field work the provision of humanitarian assistance (in the form of arranging for food rations, clean water, tents or fences or de-mining) goes hand in hand with 'protection' activities *stricto sensu* (and which include registration, refugee status determination, interventions to avert *refoulement*, to mention a few examples). In fact, for decades a clear division of functions existed in UNHCR between 'assistance' on the one hand and 'protection' on the other, which was reflected in the structure of the Office. To some extent this continues to be the case today, with a Department of Operations and a Department of International Protection remaining two distinct pillars in the work of UNHCR.[25] However, it is

---

[20] V. Türk, 'UNHCR's Supervisory Responsibility', *Revue Quebecoise de Droit International* vol. 14, no. 1 (2001), 138.

[21] See also footnote 37 and accompanying text.

[22] See footnote 17.

[23] See, for example, UNHCR, *Global Report 2004* (Geneva: UNHCR, 2005).

[24] UNHCR, Note on International Protection, UN Doc. A/AC.96/830, (1994) at 8.

[25] Protection work in the field is guided by headquarters, and in particular the Department of International Protection (DIP), recently restructured and renamed Division of International Protection Services (DIPS). Through the decades DIP has maintained a relatively independent status *vis-à-vis* the regional bureaux, and has enjoyed much respect for its work in enhancing and promoting the development of international law. See V. Türk, 'The Role of UNHCR in the Development of International Law', in R*efugee Rights and Realities*, p. 153. A special division in DIPS, namely the Solutions and Operations Support Section, has been created to provide support to UNHCR's field operations in terms of protection, to provide also

also no longer contested that the dividing line between 'assistance' and 'protection' work, which has always been vague at best, today no longer exists. Already in 1994, the 'Note on International Protection' pointed out that concrete practical measures are equally important 'tools' of protection as are legal and diplomatic measures.[26] The 'Note' further observed that presence in the field and unhindered access to refugees by UNHCR 'have proved to be "tools" of crucial importance which are an indispensable complement to protection activities in the legal and political domains'. It is arguable that in many cases the provision of humanitarian assistance, especially on a large scale, is actually the most important leverage available for the provision of protection.

Monitoring

One of the main tasks of field offices, which is closely linked to UNHCR's supervisory responsibility, is that of monitoring the situation of refugees and other persons of concern to UNHCR.[27] The purpose of monitoring is to provide feedback to governments and other stakeholders, and may include the entire range of entitlements a refugee has by virtue of international refugee and human rights law (such as access to a safe territory, access to an asylum procedure, access to means of survival, the standards implemented in national legislation relating to refugee status determination, equal rights in terms of social security).

In July 2002, UNHCR's Department of International Protection issued a 'Checklist' for designing protection strategies and measuring progress. While primarily designed to enhance the actual delivery of international protection, including the measurement of signs of progress in their implementation, the 'Checklist' also greatly facilitates monitoring the situation itself.[28] It is divided into four different chapters, dealing with the well-being of refugees in emergencies and camps, ensuring proper treatment in individual asylum systems, broadening and implementing durable solutions and building a legal framework in partnership with civil society. For instance, then, in connection with the first 'goal' ('emergencies and camps'), and concerning the adequacy of responses to mass influx situations, one

---

protection oversight and to be the interface with the 'operations' of UNHCR. In 2006 the post of assistant high commissioner for protection was created to enhance further the Office's protection profile, DOS was also restructured and renamed Division of Operational Support.

[26]   UNHCR, Note on International Protection, at 14.

[27]   Persons 'of concern' may include returnees, internally displaced persons, stateless persons and local communities hosting refugees or who are themselves in danger of being displaced. In recent years DIP (and UNHCR as a whole) has been criticised by various commentators for their policies in situations of 'in-country protection', such as in the former Yugoslavia and Rwanda. See, for example, G. S. Goodwin-Gill, 'Refugee Identity and Protection's Fading Prospect', in *Refugee Rights and Realities*, p. 220 *et seq.*

[28]   See UNHCR, 'Designing Protection Strategies and Measuring Progress: Checklist for UNHCR Staff', UNHCR/IOM/43/2002, UNHCR/FOM/41/2002 (26 July 2002) (internal – Checklist external).

of the indicators reads: 'Women have safe access to water and fuel without being exposed to security risks. These and other services are available at a closer distance than before'.[29] Particular attention is paid throughout the 'Checklist' to the situation of women, children and the elderly.

UNHCR is not limited to monitoring the delivery of international protection by governments. On the contrary, it often works with, and *ipso facto* monitors, the conduct of other actors, be it rebel groups or *de facto* authorities in control of territories or international or regional operations.[30]

In terms of monitoring capacities, the sheer number of UNHCR staff will determine its monitoring coverage. Hence, actual presence at the borders, where an influx or refugee movement is taking place, is crucial in most refugee situations. It is frequently the case, however, that UNHCR has to depend on formal and informal networks of NGOs, civil society, local journalists or lawyers to fill its 'gaps' in terms of information gathering, due to staffing shortages.

One of the most important indicators in all situations when it comes to 'protection' is the extent to which UNHCR has access to refugees. Access is a pre-condition for monitoring the situation and of ensuring that information made available by others is accurate and reflective of the actual situation. UNHCR, however, is not always allowed to have effective access to its beneficiaries.

Reporting

As mentioned above, UNHCR is mandated to report on its activities and on the situation of refugees every year to the General Assembly and the UNHCR Executive Committee. It issues a *Global Report*, as well as a 'Note on International Protection', both of which give a 'picture' of the overall situation of refugees in the world and the most acute problems. However, UNHCR is also frequently asked to provide information to governments, international and regional human rights bodies and international tribunals, human rights NGOs as well as national institutions for human rights protection (e.g. ombudsmen). The degree of formality and detail of this reporting greatly depends on each situation as well as on the mandate of those requesting it; in general, however, UNHCR is often turned to as an authoritative voice and an objective monitor by third parties seeking information on a particular refugee situation.

Field offices write every year an Annual Protection Report, an internal document describing the evolving situation in the country to which they are accredited. This report is supposed to form the basis for planning operations in the following years, in a manner that will address the identified protection concerns. Annual Protection Reports cover the entire range of a refugee's rights in a host country, from registration and provision of documents to access to education and possibilities of local integration and, in addition to the 'Checklist' mentioned above, provide a guide

---

[29]   *Ibid.*, p. 29.
[30]   See, for example, UNHCR, *Global Report 2004*, chapter on Somalia at p. 223, and on Sri Lanka at p. 382.

for protection staff as concerns the types of information they are supposed to collect and analyse.

While UNHCR reports regularly to its supervisory bodies and they are mandated to adopt resolutions on specific situations, the actual effectiveness of these is uncertain. At the same time, the annual protection reports, which contain detailed information, are internal documents that are not made available to third parties.

Intervention and Advocacy

UNHCR works in partnership with governments and NGOs to find solutions for concrete problems that refugees may face in a country. Interventions usually take the form of quiet diplomacy, whether on specific cases or issues, including oral and written interventions. Much depends on what is the most effective form of advocacy in a particular culture. Cultures where matter-of-fact working relations work better, or where diplomatic protocol prescribes so, written interventions may be routinely required. On the other hand, if informal relations work better, such as in the Mediterranean cultures, whereas formal correspondence rarely produces results, the emphasis will be placed on such oral communication, and written interventions will be reserved for matters of utmost importance.

The same applies to methods of advocacy. Where the 'stakeholders' are few and specific, and well ingrained in refugee issues, advocacy work may be more effective through letters, issuance of memoranda, *amicus curiae* briefs to courts and routine high level communication with NGOs. Where, on the other hand, the who-knows-who approach is the one that works, informal channels of communication with judges, members of parliament and public officials might be the only possible and effective means of operating. Each operation has to invest time and energy in exploring which working methods are most efficient, and there is certainly no blue-print for this.

As concerns the use of the media and of international pressure, field operations need to assess if, when and how to use them. Some governments or actors are sensitive to international or media criticism, others are not. In some countries the media may not be free enough so as to be worth investing in, in order to exercise any pressure; in others, use of the media may make eminent sense in even routine issues. In general, however, UNHCR has made great strides in recent years in using the media, not only for advocacy purposes, but more generally also in publicising the plight of refugees and sensitising the local and international civil society. While concerns still remain as to whether UNHCR adequately 'exploits' the immense possibilities presented by the timely use of the media, unquestionably the organisation is no longer as cautious as it was even a decade ago.

UNHCR is entitled to intervene on behalf of individual refugees ('individual cases') where necessary, to ensure their protection and welfare, and this is not perceived with the same suspicion as when international human rights bodies intervene on behalf of an individual victim of a human rights violation.[31] The degree

---

[31]   W. Kälin, 'Supervising the 1951 Convention Relation to the Status of Refugees', in *Refugee Protection in International Law*, p. 623.

to which a UNHCR representation will intervene in individual cases depends greatly on the situation at hand. In some situations UNHCR itself will carry out individual refugee status determination,[32] while in others it will reserve involvement only in emergencies or in precedent-setting cases being heard in court. The stage of development of local protection capacities is of crucial importance; however, for UNHCR it may also be a difficult decision whether to intervene in an individual case and decide in favour of a 'quick-fix' solution, or whether to push for resolution through local capacities, such as the justice system, which may in the long-term have greater impact (in the form, for instance, of developed jurisprudence).

In some cases it may be appropriate to use the media to present a particular individual story, not only in an effort to identify a solution, but more importantly in order to highlight a more general problem. The use of the media in such, and in other, cases, however, frequently requires specialist professionals who can turn legal concerns to stories, and who can judge the timeliness and appropriateness of interventions with the media. UNHCR has invested time and effort in elaborating a public information strategy, including the use of the internet; while it still has a long way to go, it would appear, to the present author at least, that it is much advanced in comparison to human rights field operations.[33]

Having said the above, it is also important to note that in the absence of some form of international enforcement machinery as regards respect for refugee law, UNHCR's advocacy efforts and interventions may not have the desired effectiveness at all times.

Capacity Building

An area of UNHCR field work not unlike the Office of the UN High Commissioner for Human Rights' (OHCHR) 'advisory services and technical cooperation' relates to work that can be collectively described as 'capacity building', even though it encompasses very varied activities. Among them one can distinguish four different types:

(i)   development of a legal framework,
(ii) development of an institutional framework,
(iii) networking and empowerment of local NGO and civil society actors, and
(iv) provision of training to both government officials and NGO staff.

The development of a legal framework usually starts with advocacy towards accession to the international refugee instruments, then continues with the promulgation

---

[32]   See, for example, UNHCR, *Global Report 2004*, chapter on Turkey at p. 444.

[33]   For instance, the Office of the United Nations High Commissioner for Human Rights website, in comparison to the OHCHR site, employs a less legalistic approach, investing in 'human interest stories'. See www.ohchr.org, www.unhcr.ch.

of national laws in implementation of the Refugee Convention. [34] These laws, in their turn, normally implement a national refugee status determination procedure, and define the rights that refugees and asylum seekers will have (or not), and their obligations. UNHCR has developed unique expertise in the design of asylum laws and systems, and offices are usually invited to comment on draft laws impacting on refugees, if not provide first drafts themselves altogether. The same applies to other categories of persons 'of concern' to UNHCR, in particular stateless persons and procedures to determine the status of statelessness and the acquisition of nationality. [35] Even when UNHCR provides its legal expertise in a cooperative fashion, however, problems may arise where the outcome of this cooperation in the end is one with which UNHCR does not agree; hence, offices frequently have to tread a thin line to ensure that their cooperation will not be used as an 'excuse' for a disputed result.

The development of local, national and regional institutional frameworks is no less important, since it is common understanding that the best laws are not worth much if appropriate agencies are not in place to enforce them. No models of institutional frameworks exist, since this will greatly depend on government structures, priorities and judicial systems. In general, however, UNHCR encourages specialised structures (such as a specific ministry or commissioner) within a government rather than a splintering of responsibilities, or at least 'focal point' agencies and interlocutors. Furthermore, UNHCR greatly values state actors with a certain degree of independence, such as the judiciary, parliamentarians and ombudsmen. It being impossible, once again, to generalise, it is important to stress once more that a proper analysis of 'stakeholders' is necessary before embarking on any particular path of advocacy for institutional reforms.

In addition to the above, UNHCR places much value in enhancing the role of local civil societies and empowering NGO actors, in particular, to work with refugees and carry out advocacy work on their behalf. In recognition of this a large international conference was held in 1994 in Oslo to bring together 'partners in action' for the protection of refugees; following this PARinAC (UNHCR-NGO Partnership in Action) conference, UNHCR, together with a few international NGOs, published a 'Field Guide for NGOs', which contains practical advice for on-the-ground interventions. [36] At the field level, furthermore, UNHCR often finds that it has a role to play in bringing together NGOs, or bringing them together with

---

[34] One of the most important divisions of DIPS is the Protection Operation and Legal Advice section. In addition to developing global legal standards and interpreting law and policies in the area of forced displacement, the section also provides concrete guidance on doctrinal issues, promotes the use of human rights law to the protection of persons of concern to UNHCR, and liaises between UNHCR and other human rights bodies and institutions.

[35] See UNHCR, *The State of the World's Refugees: Fifty Years of Humanitarian Action* (Oxford: Oxford University Press, 2000), p. 189.

[36] See UNHCR and NGO partners, *Protecting Refugees: A Field Guide for NGOs* (Geneva: UNHCR, 1999), available at http://www.icva.ch/files/protectionfieldguide.pdf. For more manuals and guidelines for partners see link www.unhcr.ch/cgi-bin/texis/vtx/partners?id=3bdeb7123.

government authorities; or it provides advocacy lines and strategies that can be used by NGOs on their own, or working among themselves, to improve the situation of refugees. In many field locations, UNHCR invests heavily in coordination meetings and creation of advocacy networks and platforms. Involvement of other influential actors may be part of this networking with NGOs, especially international NGOs, international and regional human rights bodies and mechanisms, and national human rights institutions. Nevertheless, UNHCR and many NGOs do not have the same mandates or methods of work and there may be limits to comprehensive, streamlined and genuine cooperation.

Finally, UNHCR provides training and legal and other technical advice to government and NGOs.[37] The situation at hand determines the content of such training, which may be of a very general nature (and focuses on the difference between an undocumented migrant and an asylum seeker and the principle of *non-refoulement*), or may be very specialised (e.g. the use of the European Court of Human Rights in disputed asylum cases). Over the last decade, the provision of training with international and local actors has increased, in recognition of the fact that refugee protection must be mainstreamed into the work of international and local actors that can secure the rights of refugees. At the same time, training on UNHCR principles may be very sensitive where the local legal framework is at odds with those principles. In such cases it may be difficult to conduct training that does not 'betray' UNHCR principles but is not seen as irrelevant to those being trained either. Provision of training and other capacity-building measures must also not provide an alibi for insufficient monitoring, reporting and advocacy activities.

UNHCR Field Presence and Capacity

UNHCR offices in the field are responsible for implementing protection and assistance policies and strategies in the area under their respective jurisdiction.[38] Usually an office will consist of international and national staff. UNHCR presence in the field can take various forms, such as regional representations (covering more than one country), country representations, sub-offices, field offices and other types

---

[37]   Within DIPS, the Protection Capacity Section (PCS) has the primary responsibility for promoting refugee law with external partners. It coordinates the printing of UNHCR refugee law publications and other training tools and organises international and regional refugee law courses. PCS also coordinates initiatives aiming to improve refugee status determination procedures, including by providing advice and operational support to relevant national authorities. Another section, the Protection Information Section, provides UNHCR staff, governments, the judiciary, researchers and refugee law practitioners with pertinent country of origin information.

[38]   UNHCR, *UNHCR Manual*, chapter 2, 'Organisational Structure and Responsibilities' (Updated September 2004) (Geneva: UNHCR, 2004), p. 74. Guidance on how 'protection' is to be delivered can be found, *inter alia*, in UNHCR, 'Designing Protection Strategies and Measuring Progress: Checklist for UNHCR Staff'.

of presence. A country-level office may have sub-offices or field offices in a country and may have over a hundred staff. It may however also be small and consist of only a few staff. In exceptional cases there may be an office staffed only by national staff or an honorary representative. Country-level representatives report normally to the regional bureau at headquarters, although other reporting lines may also be possible (e.g. to a special envoy of the high commissioner, in complex humanitarian emergencies).

In principle, international staff rotate every few years; there may also be exceptions, however, in cases of emergency missions, where UNHCR presence may expand or shrink very rapidly. It is generally considered that international staff 'bring' with them not only varied international experience, but also neutrality, impartiality and less susceptibility to local or government pressures. In other words, international staff are seen in many situations as less prone to local sensitivities or corruption. On the other hand, without the valuable local experience and expertise, not to mention networking possibilities that local staff often have, international staff may be unable to operate. Hence, most UNHCR offices employ a mix of international and national staff. This, on balance, seems to work, since it is a system that, despite the enormous hurdles[39] it presents both for international and local staff, has been maintained for decades.

Development of 'Protection Competencies'

There is great variety in what can be described as 'protection work' and it depends greatly on the conditions refugees find themselves in, the geo-political situation of a given country and the precise role of the UNHCR office. Hence, protection officers may find themselves doing 'a little bit of everything' or doing highly specialised refugee status determination or legal work. The skills required also depend on the profile of every protection post. Generally, however, professional staff in protection functions (both international and national) tend to have legal or similar backgrounds, and may be required to demonstrate or acquire, *inter alia*, the following 'competencies',[40] or abilities.

- Understanding the legal and political issues that impact on the area of operation and using this to develop an approach to protection activities that is realistic and sensitive to the operational context.
- Establishing networks of trust with communities of refugees and influential contacts within the relevant authorities and other actors.

---

[39] International staff are required to rotate according to a strict system; personal circumstances rarely play a role in the posting system. For local staff the corresponding difficulties emanate from having to adjust to sometimes rapidly changing managers, hence priorities and management styles, as well as the inevitable stagnation resulting from limited career opportunities within the 'national staff' category.

[40] UNHCR, Career Management System, CMS Information: Competencies and Typical Jobs, Annexes I, II and III.

- Monitoring significant legal activities, practices and approaches and initiating and promoting initiatives for favourable refugee-related legislation/practices.
- Monitoring and analysing relevant political, security and human rights developments.
- Monitoring the security and safety of refugees to ensure admission, prevent *refoulement*, arbitrary arrest and detention, etc.
- In consultation with other colleagues, monitoring and overseeing through field visits all aspects of protection, including provision of basic human needs.
- Coordinating with others to identify rapidly vulnerable groups and individuals, women and children.
- Conducting eligibility interviews in a thorough yet compassionate manner [sic].
- Providing principled and accurate advice and positions on refugee law and policy to a range of individuals within and external to UNHCR.
- Assessing the needs for capacity building at government and NGO level and developing initiatives that will have an overall impact on protection standards at country level.
- Building a network of contacts to promote refugee law and related human rights/humanitarian law.
- Planning, organising and designing training activities tailored to meet the needs of different audiences.

In addition, however, protection staff may also be involved, quite heavily at times, in programme issues impacting on refugee protection, or external relations, whether relations with donors or with the media. UNHCR has compiled over the years 'standard job descriptions' for its protection staff, to ensure consistency of some degree despite the very varied demands of each position.

Unlike perhaps human rights field operations, it is recognised within UNHCR that 'protection' is not only the responsibility of a few specialised lawyers, but also of all UNHCR staff and, in particular, social services staff, programme officers, field officers, but also managers at all levels.

UNHCR Induction Courses and Protection Learning Programmes

In the past ten to fifteen years UNHCR has developed different training programmes for its staff, including modules on different aspects of 'protection work'. Some of them are designed for protection officers, while others are for all UNHCR staff, in recognition of the fact that every individual staff member's work has as its ultimate goal the protection of refugees. Three learning programmes are currently offered: the protection learning programme, which is designed for all staff and aims at fostering a common understanding of UNHCR's protection mandate and principles of international refugee and human rights law; two thematic learning programmes on armed conflict and broader migration movements, for senior managers, designed to enhance their capacity to respond to complex protection situations; and a resettlement learning programme. Other *ad hoc* programmes are also occasionally delivered, such as train-the-trainers programmes, supposed to help protection officers acquire training skills, special legal seminars on European Union laws, sexual and gender-based violence issues, the protection of refugee children and resettlement.[41] An operations management learning programme, designed for managers, contains elements of protection and field work, as does also training for handling emergency situations.[42] UNHCR staff are, furthermore, obliged to undergo training in basic security issues, and staff accepting to participate in the so-called 'emergency roster' undergo an intensive two-week training course which includes simulation exercises of real emergencies, including security emergencies.

The Theory and Reality of Protection Work in the Field

Working with UNHCR can be very rewarding at the professional and personal level. The organisation boasts two Nobel peace prizes, and scores of dedicated, highly competent staff, including, in particular, protection staff. Nevertheless, as with many UN and other agencies, lack of adequate resources can be so acute at times as to be debilitating; especially in the area of protection, it seems that there are never enough staff to carry out monitoring and interventions in the field. In addition, weaknesses in accountability and performance appraisal systems, as well as a relative sense of impunity, have resulted on occasion in corruption, sexual harassment and abuse of refugees or harassment of staff.[43] In an effort to recall some of the basic ethics and principles that guide the work of UNHCR, a 'Code of Conduct' has been developed and signed by all staff members, interns and others working for UNHCR.[44] UNHCR offices are required to adopt 'standard operating procedures', which determine how refugees or complaints are received and addressed.

The 'Code of Conduct' and other instructions and guidelines, added to the production of 'protection training materials' and 'protection guidelines' regularly being issued, can be frustrating for many staff, who find themselves too overworked to include a learning angle into their daily work. Learning opportunities, especially if not actively supported by managers, may thus not be observed, integrated into actual working methods or not followed through. High turnover of senior managers and pressure from governments and donors often result in a proliferation of new

---

[41]   Handbooks for these activities have also been developed and are being updated every few years, such as the *Resettlement Handbook*, the *Registration Handbook*, the *Repatriation Handbook* etc. Other training materials available include modules on international protection, on refugee status determination, on interviewing and interpreting, and on human rights. See http://www.unhcr.org.

[42]   See for instance, UNHCR, *Handbook for Emergencies*, 2nd edn (2000), available at http://www.unhcr.ch/cgi-bin/texis/vtx/publ/opendoc.pdf?tbl=PUBL&id=3bb2fa26b.

[43]   Appropriately, two of the new management learning programme modules offered by the UNHCR staff administration section for managers focus on accountability, and recall the UN and UNHCR instructions on these issues, with an emphasis on sanctions.

[44]   UNHCR, *Code of Conduct and Explanatory Notes* (Geneva: UNHCR, 2004).

policies or initiatives, without adequate time being given to consolidate them. In such cases field staff may disregard them altogether as too ephemeral or irrelevant to their situation.

The accountability of the organisation also has been questioned at times.[45] Efforts to strengthen performance appraisal procedures continue to be hampered by not being sufficiently prioritised, less than diligently carried out, and not always reflecting reality. Or they may not play the role they are supposed to in postings decisions, where other external factors, such as geographical distribution, may be more influential.

One of the most serious deficiencies in the accountability chain has resulted in insufficient security considerations. UNHCR and many other agencies active in human rights and humanitarian operations operate today in increasingly hostile environments. The inviolability of international organisations, especially the UN, but even the International Committee of the Red Cross, is no longer a given in the context of civil conflicts and situations of general unrest. This sad reality is sharply driven home to the thousands of humanitarian workers each time a 'security incident' takes place, such as the August 2003 bombing of the UN headquarters in Baghdad (during which one of the highest level UN humanitarian and human rights officials, the late Sergio Vieira de Mello, was killed), hostage takings and shootings, not to mention routine harassment by military and militias. Security awareness, hence, has become a must for every UNHCR staff member, while security measures are now being implemented in every operation, often at the expense of unhindered access to, and by, refugees and other persons of concern.

Finally, UNHCR operations frequently face financial and political challenges. The worst are large scale protracted refugee situations, 'forgotten emergencies' or emergencies that have not been picked up by the international media, where under-funding and the absence of durable solutions limits severely the possibility of addressing even the most acute human needs. In such cases, protection work can be very demoralising, and staff may have to resort to professional counselling and administrative measures available to relieve stress accumulated during serving in hardship posts.[46]

---

[45]   See, for example, UNHCR, Evaluation and Policy Analysis Unit, *The State of UNHCR's Organizational Culture* (Geneva: UNHCR, 2005).

[46]   Such counselling can be provided by staff welfare officers (specialised staff). Staff working in hardship posts are entitled to longer periods of leave or mandatory absence from their duty station. A revised policy was issued in August 2001: *Managing Stress in Humanitarian Emergencies*.

Chapter 12

Protection: The International Committee of the Red Cross Experience

Alain Aeschlimann

Introduction

In a volume on human rights field operations, inclusion of a chapter on the International Committee of the Red Cross (ICRC), whose history and *raison d'être* are interlinked with protection, seems particularly relevant.

At a time where the United Nations (UN) is going through a process of reforms, and where new approaches, particularly by clusters, are discussed and tested, protection is also increasingly on the agenda of various actors, agencies and non-governmental organisations (NGOs). The presence in the field of more organisations dealing with protection offers opportunities to improve protection of individuals. It also creates a real risk of overlapping and a sense of confusion for all those involved, whether for the authorities and non-state actors, for the victims, for the public and for humanitarian or human rights organisations themselves.

Consequently, discussion between all concerned, in particular mandated organisations and non-mandated organisations, is crucial. This includes considering and assessing what exists, what is working well and where possible gaps lie, and identifying the issues in need of improvement. Keeping in mind the interest of the victims and affected persons, the priority must be to cover protection needs more fully, to develop complementarity[1] between all actors and organisations involved, and to avoid duplication of efforts, contradictory messages and mere competition. This means in particular identifying the strengths and weaknesses of each organisation and maintaining a regular and open dialogue, while being aware of the respective specificities and missions of each one.

Today more than ever before, consultation between all those involved is an ethical, legal and operational necessity, imposed by people's right to enjoy maximum protection. Being mainly field oriented with longstanding experience in protection and a clear mandate, ICRC strongly wishes to be part of this dialogue, as an integral element of the general protection framework.

---

[1] The 'protection matrix' mentioned in footnote 10 is a useful tool to define and develop such a complementarity.

This chapter first puts protection in a more global context. It then describes ICRC's mandate and the modalities and specificities of its action in the field of protection. Finally, it addresses some of the challenges ICRC faces in its protection work and ends with comments on ICRC relations with human rights field operations.

General Considerations Regarding Protection

The prime responsibility in providing solutions, as well as directly providing protection to individuals, falls unequivocally upon the respective governments, authorities and other bodies that control a given territory, including armed groups or international forces. Protection efforts in particular by human rights and humanitarian organisations can have no meaningful impact without a corresponding political will from the concerned authorities and/or arms carriers and, often, from the community of states.[2]

Humanitarian efforts therefore mainly aim at having 'those in charge' take up their responsibilities. They can never be a substitute for political action. Consequently, deploying in the field more human rights or protection officers or ICRC delegates, or any other humanitarian workers, will not be *the* solution or the panacea.

Proper respect for the rule of law and human dignity lies in the existence of an environment conducive to protection, the existence of which is the result of a combination of efforts.

Such an environment includes, in a given context, adhesion to the relevant international treaties, adoption of national laws and regulations, establishment of reliable institutions, internal control and review mechanisms and information about compulsory norms and prohibited practices, particularly through education. Military personnel and those involved in law enforcement activities must benefit from training programmes as well as from enough material, financial and human resources. When abuses occur, the justice system must be able to act to sanction such behaviours and avoid impunity. It must also ensure that the victims receive assistance and compensation.

Such a favourable environment, even if it does exist, remains potentially unstable. It may be undermined at any time by unforeseen events such as armed conflict, terrorist attacks, emerging social tensions or simply changes in attitudes. Thus, the risk of abuse is constant. Openness to scrutiny and to development of institutions and good practices helps to prevent and eliminate abuses, and consequently contributes

---

[2]   In particular, states party to the Geneva Conventions have a responsibility to 'respect and ensure respect for the ... Convention in all circumstances' (Article 1 common to the four 1949 Geneva Conventions), which may be exerted individually or collectively. See Geneva Convention I for the Amelioration of the Condition of Wounded and Sick Armed Forces in the Field, 12 August 1949, 75 UNTS (1950), 31; Geneva Convention II for the Amelioration of the Condition of Wounded, Sick and Shipwrecked Members of Armed Forces at Sea, 12 August 1949, 75 UNTS (1950), 85; Geneva Convention III Relative to the Treatment of Prisoners of War, 12 August 1949, 75 UNTS (1950), 135; Geneva Convention IV Relative to the Protection of Civilian Persons in Time of War, 12 August 1949, 75 UNTS (1950), 287.

to building, maintaining and strengthening a favourable environment. In this process, regulatory mechanisms, which may be either internal or external, play a key role.

Internal regulatory mechanisms act inside the country and are specific to the society in which they work. They include the independent media, ombudspersons, national human rights commissions, various citizens' rights groups, lawyers, an independent judicial system, the traditional role of elders in certain societies, etc. External regulatory mechanisms act at the level of the international community, mainly by bringing diplomatic and economic pressure to bear on the authorities and/or arms carriers concerned. They include the international media, international tribunals, other governments, international humanitarian organisations (UN agencies and NGOs) and international human rights bodies or organisations.[3]

Diverse and complementary action by all these mechanisms is required. This includes political incentives or pressure, measures aimed at fostering development, justice and cooperation, promotion of human rights and/or international humanitarian law (IHL) or the organising of training programmes for law enforcement personnel. Some actors denounce violations and abuses perpetrated by states and arms carriers, while others give priority to monitoring activities. Finally, numerous organisations are involved in assistance activities to victims and other affected persons.

Although external by nature, ICRC shares features with internal regulatory mechanisms, mainly by virtue of its independence, its day-to-day presence on the ground, its contacts with all relevant authorities and its marked preference for confidential dialogue. Consequently, it acts as a substitute for internal regulatory mechanisms by intervening mainly in crisis situations, when internal regulatory mechanisms are in general dysfunctional, obstructed or do not or no longer exist.

In a given context, an analysis of the different components of this global protection environment and an early identification of the problems and gaps is a prerequisite for any action in the field of protection. This includes assessing which regulatory mechanisms are effectively operating and the roles and specificities of each one.

The following definition for protection activities was drawn during a series of workshops organised by ICRC with humanitarian and human rights NGOs and UN agencies from 1996 to 2000: 'all activities aimed at ensuring full respect for the rights of the individual in accordance with the letter and the spirit of the relevant bodies of law, i.e. human rights law, international humanitarian law and refugee law'.[4] This is the broadest definition that may be given to protection.

---

[3]   Either UN bodies established by treaties, such as the Committee Against Torture or the Human Rights Committee; or mechanisms established by resolutions of the UN Human Rights Council, such as the special rapporteur on torture and other cruel, inhuman or degrading treatment or punishment, or the special rapporteur on extrajudicial, summary or arbitrary executions; or the Office of the United Nations High Commissioner for Human Rights; or regional mechanisms, such as the European Committee for the Prevention of Torture, the Inter-American Commission on Human Rights, or the African Commission on Human and People's Rights); or NGOs.

[4]   See ICRC, *Strengthening Protection in War: A Search for Professional Standards* (Geneva: ICRC, 2001).

Conversely, within ICRC, protection *stricto sensu* encompasses those activities aimed at preventing and/or putting an end to and/or avoiding the recurrence of the violations of the obligations of the authorities/arms carriers or the rights of individuals in accordance with the letter and the spirit of IHL and other fundamental protective norms in situations of violence. These activities seek to affect the causes of abuses, not their consequences.[5]

ICRC Mandate and Bases for its Action

At the centre of ICRC's action are the individuals, the persons at risk and those affected by armed conflicts and other situations of violence. As an organisation driven by the realities on the ground, ICRC has strived throughout its existence to adapt its operational response to the specificities of each context, the existing environment and the evolving nature of armed violence, and of the parties to a conflict and other arms carriers.

Since its founding in 1863, ICRC has combined legal work and operational activities, asserting additionally that protection and assistance are two interlocking aspects of those operational activities. The work of ICRC is therefore equally rights based and needs oriented: it combines activities centred on the causes of violations and abuses (preventing and putting an end to human suffering) and on their consequences (alleviating human suffering). In other words, ICRC operations include protection and assistance activities based on a solid legal frame of reference, which has proven to be pertinent through ICRC's long experience in the midst of armed conflicts and other situations of violence.

ICRC action has also been firmly guided by the fundamental principles of the Red Cross and Red Crescent Movement – among others, the principles of humanity, impartiality, neutrality and independence.[6]

A number of tasks were specifically assigned to ICRC by the Geneva Conventions of 1949 and their Additional Protocols of 1977.[7] The complete scope of ICRC's

---

[5]   Activities which primarily aim at giving aid to cover material, physical or psychological needs of victims and other affected persons are assistance activities.

[6]   See, in particular, J. Pictet, *The Fundamental Principles of the Red Cross: Commentary* (Geneva: ICRC, 1979).

[7]   Beside specific rights and tasks in international armed conflicts (in particular access to prisoners of war, civilian internees and other persons deprived of their liberty and to any other protected person; right to be notified of the detention, internment or death of protected persons in the hands of the adverse party; right to receive application from protected civilians; operation of the Central Tracing Agency; ability to facilitate the exchange of family news by and for protected persons; role of transmission of information with regard to missing persons; etc), see also Article 9 common to the 1st, 2nd and 3rd Geneva Conventions and Article 10 of the 4th Geneva Convention ('The provisions of the present Convention constitute no obstacle to the humanitarian activities which the International Committee of the Red Cross or any other impartial humanitarian organization may, subject to the consent of the Parties to the conflict concerned, undertake for the protection of [respectively] wounded and sick,

mandate is defined by the International Red Cross and Red Crescent Movement,[8] which include, among others:

1. to work for the faithful application of IHL;
2. to endeavour at all times – as a neutral institution whose humanitarian work is carried out particularly in time of international and other armed conflict or internal strife – to ensure the protection of and assistance to military and civilian victims of such events and of their direct results;
3. to work for the understanding and dissemination of knowledge of IHL and to prepare any development thereof; and
4. to take any humanitarian initiative which comes within its role as a specifically neutral and independent institution and intermediary.

These Statutes were approved by the International Conference of the Red Cross and Red Crescent, which also integrates all the states parties to the Geneva Conventions, providing special recognition by the international community of ICRC's mandate. ICRC remains mandate bound to act in favour of all the persons affected by armed conflict and violence, and cannot therefore delegate or forgo some or all of its activities in their favour.

As shown above, the history and the identity of ICRC are closely linked to IHL. However, ICRC has also integrated in its legal frame of reference the fundamental rights of individuals under human rights law.

Keen to maintain a strict independence in the manner in which it fulfils its mandate, ICRC deploys its activities based on its own qualification of a given situation, as well as an evaluation of the humanitarian consequences resulting from this situation.

Such an evaluation includes the identified needs and the patterns of abuse, their importance, the urgency to address them and the effective involvement of other actors and organisations. This enables ICRC to determine its priorities in a given context. Objectives are then defined, on the basis of which an operational strategy is established, taking into account the political will of the concerned authorities or non-state actors, the security concerns and other constraints.

---

shipwrecked, prisoners of war, civilian persons and for their relief') and Article 3 common to the four Geneva Conventions ('An impartial humanitarian body, such as the ICRC, may offer its services to the Parties to the conflict'). See Protocol Additional to the Geneva Conventions of 12 August 1949, and Relating to the Protection of Victims of International Armed Conflicts, 8 June 1977, 1125 UNTS 3 and Protocol Additional to the Geneva Conventions of 12 August 1949, and Relating to the Protection of Victims of Non-International Armed Conflicts, 8 June 1977, 1125 UNTS 609.

[8]   Article 5 paragraph 2 and 3 of the 1986 Statutes of the International Red Cross and Red Crescent Movement.

The strategy is built on a combination of modes of action which comprise: persuasion of the authorities or non-state actors, support to them, direct services or substitution, mobilisation of third parties and, exceptionally, public denunciation.[9]

The strategy defined enables ICRC to act at the appropriate level of intervention (responsive action, remedial action and environment building).[10]

---

[9] The modes of action can be defined as follows:

- persuasion or promotion of a sense of responsibility: convincing the authorities/ arms carriers to take action themselves to prevent or stop an abuse or violation or to help the victims thereof;
- support: direct or indirect cooperation with the authorities/arms carriers by giving them the means and/or capacities to fulfil their legal obligations;
- substitution: acting in lieu of the defaulting authorities/arms carriers to stop an abuse or violation or help the victims thereof;
- mobilisation: generating the interest and external influence of other entities (states, NGOs, institutions of civil society, international or regional organisations, etc) to obtain support enabling an abuse or violation to be prevented or stopped or to elicit encouragement or help for the authorities/arms carriers in fulfilling their legal responsibilities and obligations;
- denunciation: publicising the existence of abuse and violations so as to exert pressure on the authorities and compel them to take action to stop an abuse or violation or to help the victims thereof.

For definitions, see, in particular: P. Bonard, *Modes of Action Used by Humanitarian Players: Criteria for Operational Complementarity* (Geneva: ICRC, 1999); ICRC, *Strengthening Protection in War*, pp. 29–33; H. Slim and A. Bonwick, *Protection: An ALNAP Guide for Humanitarian Organisations* (London: Overseas Development Institute, 2005).

[10] See definitions in ICRC, *Strengthening Protection in War*, pp. 21–24:

- 'Responsive action': any activity undertaken in the context of an emerging or established pattern of abuse to prevent its recurrence, put a stop to it, and/or alleviate its immediate effects.
- 'Remedial action': action taken to restore people's dignity and ensure adequate living conditions subsequent to a pattern of abuse.
- 'Environment-building': efforts fostering a social, cultural, institutional and legal environment conducive to respect for the rights of the individual.

The following so called 'protection matrix' is commonly used in ICRC operations to define and visualise the activities it is carrying out or plans to carry out as well or, by including activities by other organisations and actors, to identify gaps and the best complementarity of efforts between all concerned.

	Denunciation	Mobilisation	Persuasion	Support	Substitution
Responsive Action					
Remedial Action					
Environment Building					

ICRC Protection Activities *Stricto Sensu*

Background and Developments in the Nature of ICRC Activities

In general terms, ICRC protection activities can be divided between activities in favour of persons deprived of freedom and activities in favour of the civilian population and other persons not or no longer taking part in hostilities or acts of violence (referred to within ICRC as 'protection of the civilian population').

In history, ICRC protection activities initially focused on visits and other activities in favour of persons deprived of their freedom, such as prisoners of war, civilian internees, persons detained for security reasons. The first visits took place as early as 1870 during the Franco-Prussian War, and ICRC's action behind bars remains until now a significant feature of its endeavours.[11] One of the first protective measures devised by ICRC was to take the identity of these persons deprived of freedom and considered at risk and to give them the possibility to transmit news to their relatives.

In the aftermath of the Spanish Civil War and the Second World War, it became obvious that the highest price in conflict had been paid by the civilian population, hence, the insistence on reinforced protection which was ultimately bestowed upon them by the 1949 Geneva Conventions and their Additional Protocols of 1977. These facts implied that ICRC, which had previously carried out activities of protection of the civilian population in a broad manner, had to adapt its working methods and redirect its priorities in order to be able to reach the more vulnerable groups of victims.

The 1967 Six Days War and its aftermath, the conflict in Lebanon and the conflicts in Latin America in the 1980s marked a significant evolution in the development of ICRC activities of protection of the civilian population and its adoption of an increasingly rigorous policy and methodology. In the late 1980s, ICRC moved towards more systematic monitoring and a practice of representations with regard to the use of means and methods of combat.

Within the last 15 years, ICRC has increasingly developed environment-building activities, such as advice to governments on national measures for the implementation of IHL or the promotion of the knowledge of IHL and other fundamental norms protecting the human being and their integration within military and law enforcement forces training and doctrine.

In 2005, ICRC carried out visits to persons deprived of liberty in some 2,400 places of detention in more than 80 countries. It also carried out protection activities for the civilian population in about half of these.

---

[11] For a recent description of these activities, see A. Aeschlimann, 'Protection of Detainees: ICRC Action Behind Bars', *International Review of the Red Cross* vol. 87, no. 857 (2005), 83.

Characteristics of ICRC's Protection Approach

ICRC's approach comprises several particular features. Some are shared by other actors and organisations, while others are specific to ICRC. However, all these characteristics combined give ICRC's interventions their added value and make the institution unique. These characteristics include proximity with the affected persons, confidential dialogue, non-political and independent action, individual follow-up, flexibility and rapid deployment combined with long-term commitments.

Proximity with the Persons Affected by Armed Conflict and other Situations of Violence

Being operationally involved in crisis situations (international armed conflicts, internal armed conflicts, internal disturbances and other situations of internal violence, transition periods), ICRC does not in principle comment or act on events if, for whatever reason, it has not visited the area where those events occurred or has not acquired firsthand knowledge of the situation. As a rule, ICRC always tries to establish a presence on the ground, as close as possible to the persons affected by armed conflict and violence. This direct presence enables ICRC to acquire sufficient knowledge of the situation, to be in close proximity both with the affected persons and with the authorities or non-state actors, to maintain a permanent dialogue with all concerned, and to intervene very rapidly on the ground in the acute phase of a crisis.

Direct contact with detainees or civilians who have suffered abuses or have directly witnessed them is crucial for ICRC as it will generally base its representations only on accounts given by them. In principle, it will not use those given by others, whether NGOs or any other group or institution, nor will it base its actions on second-hand accounts. It is not by lack of trust that ICRC does so, but is directly related to its priority, when required, to assist the persons affected in parallel to its protection efforts.

In addition, this proximity with those affected is a guarantee for ICRC to be as objective as possible and to be credible in its dialogue with the concerned authorities or non-state actors. ICRC delegates have often succeeded in convincing authorities to take action because they had been on the spot and could give detailed information on the events. However, ICRC will often welcome information provided by others in order to identify areas of concern to follow-up on or to confirm its own findings.

The implementation of assistance programmes in given areas also contributes to fostering this proximity.

Dialogue – Confidentiality

The cornerstone of ICRC's approach is dialogue, both with the persons affected and the authorities and non-state actors.

Based on its findings in the field, ICRC engages in a confidential bilateral dialogue with all authorities, warring parties and armed groups, at whatever level, in order to report on the humanitarian consequences of the violations of IHL and other fundamental norms protecting individuals. These contacts also provide an opportunity to recall the applicable rules, formulate proposals for solutions and thus obtain compliance with the law and ease the plight of the affected persons.

The construction of a network characterised by a close, structured and professional relationship with all parties to a conflict or arms carriers promotes trust and acceptance. This trust, nurtured by frequent meetings between ICRC and the authorities or non-state actors, is established and developed based, among other things, on the confidential nature of ICRC's work. It is a long and patient task, which includes devising new ways of reaching the potential perpetrators of violence or those who control them. In crisis situations, dysfunctional chains of command often require all echelons of the civil and, if need be, military hierarchy to be contacted, informed and convinced of the soundness of ICRC's recommendations.

Confidentiality is a working method and a strategic choice, but not an end in itself. It allows ICRC to address what are generally very sensitive issues with complete independence and free of any pressure of public opinion, the media or political organisations. It allows quicker and facilitated access to those in need. By accepting the working methods of ICRC and its presence, the authorities agree to enter into discussions on sensitive issues and, in a way, undertake to dealing with them in good faith.

The confidential nature of ICRC's work is endorsed and confirmed in international law by the recognition of its right to refrain from providing evidence to court. A Trial Chamber of the International Criminal Tribunal for the former Yugoslavia ruled in 1999 (case Prosecutor v. Simić *et al.*[12]) that as a matter of customary international law, ICRC enjoys an absolute privilege to withhold confidential information. This privilege was reiterated in the International Criminal Court (ICC) Rules of Procedure and Evidence (Rule 73 covering privileged communications and information[13]).

---

[12] *Prosecutor v. Blagoje Simić, Milan Simić, Miroslav Tadić, Stevan Todorović and Simo Zarić* (IT-95-9), Decision on the Prosecution Motion under Rule 73 for a Ruling Concerning the Testimony of a Witness, Trial Chamber, 27 July 1999.

[13] See Sub-rule 4:

'The Court shall regard as privileged, and consequently not subject to disclosure, including by way of testimony of any present or past official or employee of the International Committee of the Red Cross (ICRC), any information, documents or other evidence which it came into the possession of in the course, or as a consequence of, the performance by ICRC of its functions under the Statutes of the International Red Cross and Red Crescent Movement, unless:

(a)   After consultations undertaken pursuant to sub-rule 6, ICRC does not object in writing to such disclosure, or otherwise has waived this privilege; or

(b)   Such information, documents or other evidence is contained in public statements and documents of ICRC.'

See International Criminal Court, Rules of Procedure and Evidence, UN Doc. PCNICC/2000/1/Add.1 (2000), at 38–39.

When its confidential representations and efforts have no impact or when the authorities do not abide by the agreed procedures, ICRC may decide to publicise its concerns.[14] ICRC decides to make public representations or appeals only when strict conditions are met and when it is convinced that derogating from its customary reserve in this way will benefit the persons affected and not harm them. Before this, it may prefer to make discreet interventions to third parties known to have an influence on one or another of the parties to the conflict or arms carriers.

A Strictly Humanitarian, Non-political and Independent Approach

In contexts of conflict or acute tension, a strictly humanitarian, non-political and independent approach is particularly relevant. It is directly related to the nature of ICRC as a specifically neutral and independent institution and intermediary, its strict respect of the above-mentioned Red Cross and Red Crescent principles and its precise objective of improving the situation of persons affected.

ICRC recently renewed its calls for recognition of the merits of neutral and independent humanitarian action and for the need to protect this action as a whole from any risks arising from the involvement of the military in humanitarian activities and from a possible misunderstanding that all pursue the same political objectives. Such calls were related to the new forms of reaction to crisis which appeared in several contexts in recent years, particularly under the form of UN or other international missions integrating military, political and humanitarian aspects. The inherent merits of such integrated missions must be recognised, particularly insofar as they promote a coordinated dialogue among all those involved in reconstruction work. However, such missions also comprise risks for humanitarian action. Misperceptions, misunderstandings, confusion with other actors can rapidly destroy the capital of trust which humanitarian action enjoys and which ICRC tirelessly endeavours to build, and consequently endanger such an action.

ICRC's specific nature as a neutral and independent institution and intermediary was instrumental in securing its access to detainees held by various international forces, whether of a peacekeeping, peacemaking or peace-enforcement nature. Its action in favour of such detainees would not have had the same credibility without ICRC's independence from governments and the United Nations system. This concerned mainly the UN Operation in Somalia,[15] the Stabilization Force in

---

[14]   Conditions for such denunciations of specific violations are: (1) the existence of large-scale and repeated violations; (2) ICRC delegates have directly witnessed such violations, or their existence and extent and respective data have been established by means of reliable and verifiable sources; (3) ICRC's confidential approaches to end these violations have had no impact or results; (4) a public statement by ICRC would be conducive to the interests of the persons concerned. *Cf.* 'Action by the International Committee of the Red Cross in the Event of Violations of International Humanitarian Law or of Other Fundamental Rules Protecting Persons in Situations of Violence', *International Review of the Red Cross* vol. 87, no. 858 (2005), 393–400.

[15]   See Security Council resolution 751 (1992), UN Doc. S/RES/751 (1992).

Bosnia and Herzegovina,[16] the United Nations Mission in Kosovo,[17] the Kosovo Force,[18] the International Force for East Timor[19] and the United Nations Transitional Administration in East Timor.[20] ICRC is also visiting persons held by international tribunals (International Criminal Tribunal for former Yugoslavia, International Criminal Tribunal for Rwanda, Special Court for Sierra Leone and the ICC).

ICRC often exercises humanitarian good offices and mediation on the basis of its position as a neutral and independent intermediary. It accumulated for example extensive experience in supervising the release of persons deprived of liberty and organising their repatriation or return home.

Concern for the Individuals and Individual Follow-up

ICRC's vocation is to attend above all to the individuals, their problems and needs. Consequently, the individuals, mainly the persons affected, their interests and the respect for their will lie at the centre of its action. In general, ICRC puts more emphasis on the individual protection of the persons, when necessary, than, for example, on the ill-functioning of the detention system as a whole. ICRC also assesses whether its actions may have any negative consequences for the persons it strives to protect. In case of reprisals by the authorities or non-state actors against individuals after an ICRC action or representation, ICRC will immediately react and engage the relevant actors. In extreme cases, if ICRC comes to the conclusion that there is a risk that the authorities or the non-state actors take retaliatory measures against a victim or a witness of abuse who came to report to its staff, it may decide to abstain from using the available information.

ICRC's focus on the individual is reflected by individual monitoring, throughout their time in captivity, of persons deprived of their freedom whom ICRC deems to be at risk. Concretely, ICRC registers the identity of such detainees and enters them into a database. ICRC then regularly follows up on those detainees and checks whether they are still present or to where they were transferred, and whether or how their situation has changed. The information is ultimately stored at ICRC headquarters. The same applies to persons affected outside situations of detention.

ICRC's priority on and concern for the individual is complemented by efforts to identify patterns of violations and to develop efforts to prevent and put an end to such abuses. In detention-related activities, ICRC may also adopt, depending on the circumstances and the attitude of the authorities, a structural approach that focuses on improving the way the places of detention are run, reducing structural

---

[16] See Agreement on the Military Aspects of the Peace Settlement, Annex 1A to the General Framework Agreement for Peace in Bosnia and Herzegovina, Attachment to UN Doc. A/50/790-S/1995/999 (30 November 1995).

[17] See Security Council resolution 1244 (1999), UN Doc. S/RES/1244 (1999).

[18] See Military Technical Agreement, http://www.nato.int/kfor/kfor/documents/mta.htm.

[19] See Security Council resolution 1264 (1999), UN Doc. S/RES/1264 (1999).

[20] See Security Council resolution 1272 (1999), UN Doc. S/RES/1272 (1999).

shortcomings and dysfunctions and enabling systems and behaviours to be reformed in the long term.

Flexibility and Rapid Deployment in Emergencies

Owing to the evolving nature of armed conflicts and the variety of situations in which it has to intervene, ICRC has always been permeated by a realistic and pragmatic view. Firmness on its principles and its mandate, leading to predictability with regard to its areas and modes of intervention, are combined with constant operational adjustments to the local reality and environment, and to the problems identified and their causes.

Due to the nature of armed conflicts, their often unexpected occurrence and the sudden magnitude of the humanitarian needs they generate, ICRC developed a capacity to react and intervene within a very short time. This implies, in particular, early negotiations with the authorities and/or non-states actors, contingency planning, quick deployment of material and logistics means, and availability of staff with specific skills on very short notice.

Although it has traditionally focused on urgent needs, often with a life threatening character, ICRC is nowadays addressing a large variety of needs, depending on the situation.

An Adapted and Integrated Approach: from Monitoring to Assistance

ICRC adopts a holistic approach integrating a large spectrum of activities with the focus on making the relevant authorities aware of their responsibilities. ICRC has at its disposal a broad range of means, skills and competencies that are mobilised according to its objectives and operational strategies in a given context. The best response or responses are defined following an analysis of the situation, its characteristics and dynamics, as well as the policies, practices and available resources of the authorities and/or non-state actors. This is complemented by proper knowledge of the problems and abuses based on ICRC's findings on the ground.

Through its protection activities, ICRC's priority is to persuade the responsible authorities and non-state actors to respect the fundamental rights of the individuals. It does so through confidential bilateral written or oral representations, on some occasions through discreet interventions to third parties or, in exceptional cases, through public communication. It may also engage in other forms of activities, which include technical advice and cooperation for the improvement of national laws and regulations; efforts to improve the knowledge of the content of IHL and other fundamental rules; the establishment of specialised education and training for law enforcement personnel, such as police and security forces and the military or for prison officials; increased presence in a given area; accompaniment; the evacuation of vulnerable persons; mine risks education; the registering of vulnerable persons; the restoring of family links through the exchange of family news; inquiries into the fate and whereabouts of missing persons and the search for them; reunion of dispersed families; assistance aimed at reducing risk exposure; and liaising with and between warring parties on specific humanitarian issues or the evacuation of persons.

In addition, ICRC provides, when necessary, a variety of direct services and material aid aimed at mitigating the consequences of abuses, mainly in the field of economic security, water and habitat as well as health services. It does so directly, often in cooperation with the local National Red Cross or Red Crescent Society, or by supporting the competent authorities and existing structures.

Mid to Long-term Commitment in a Given Context

In addition to being able to react and intervene within a very short time, ICRC commits itself to act in the mid to long-term, as long as the situation continues to require its intervention or as long as there are remaining needs related to the conflict or other situation of violence.

The financing system of ICRC, which is not based on projects and earmarked funding, and its rather sound financial situation to date facilitate such mid to long-term commitments.

Professionalism and the Role of Training

In order to be relevant, to formulate recommendations adapted to the various contexts and to take appropriate action, ICRC makes a point of being professional in its approach.

Professionalism is reached through standardised working guidelines, recruitment of professionals and proper training.

Thanks to its longstanding experience, ICRC has formalised policies and guidance, starting mainly in the 1980s, now covering a very large number of domains. Some are purely internal directives while others were made public[21] and are also referred to by other organisations.

---

[21] See in particular 'Action by the International Committee of the Red Cross in the event of violations of international humanitarian law or of other fundamental rules protecting persons in situations of violence', *International Review or the Red Cross*, no. 858 (2005); M. Harrof-Tavel, 'Action Taken by the International Committee of the Red Cross in Situations of Internal Violence', *International Review of the Red Cross*, no. 294 (1993), 204; ICRC, *Strengthening Protection in War: A Search for Professional Standards*; *Addressing the Needs of Women affected by Armed Conflicts: An ICRC Guidance Document* (Geneva: ICRC, 2004); *The Missing and their Families: Summary of the Conclusions Arising from Events Held Prior to the International Conference of Governmental and Non-Governmental Experts (19–21 February 2003)* (Geneva: ICRC, 2003); *Interagency Guiding Principles on Unaccompanied and Separated Children* (Geneva: ICRC, 2004); *Restoring Family links: A Guide for National Red Cross and Red Crescent Societies* (Geneva: ICRC, 2000); P.G. Nembrini, *Water, Sanitation, Hygiene and Habitat in Prisons* (Geneva: ICRC, 2005); D. Maher, M. Grzemska, *et al.*, *Guidelines for the Control of Tuberculosis in Prison* (Geneva, World Health Organization,

Additionally, ICRC recruits and includes in its teams experts for specific types of activities, such as doctors experienced in matters relating to detention, and experts in specific fields such as water, sanitation and habitat, nutrition, agriculture, psychology or legal issues.

As protection as such was not a topic taught in universities or professional schools, nor could professionals be transferred from other organisations, at least until recently, ICRC had to rely on its own training system to ensure professionalism. In addition, ICRC was faced with a high turnover among its field expatriate staff due to work under demanding circumstances, in stressful security environments and frustration due to the often limited short-term visible impact of protection work. As such, ICRC developed a training system to provide an opportunity to transmit knowledge and develop skills to adapt in the situations where it operates. Training also aims at ensuring coherence in analysis and action, and consequently predictability, despite the variety of contexts in which ICRC is present.

Training in protection is a complex topic as it includes, in addition to technical knowledge (law, security management, report writing, etc), behavioural issues (for example how to speak with and show empathy to a victim, how to identify a traumatised person, how to negotiate with authorities,[22] how to integrate and adapt to cultural aspects) and ethical aspects (how to carry out activities, how to avoid putting the persons affected at risk, etc).

Every international staff member working with ICRC attends a four-week integration course with a significant focus on protection. Personnel who have acquired sufficient experience and who specialise in the field of protection attend a course for protection coordinators, which aims at improving their knowledge on various issues and offers additional tools for them to conduct analyses and to develop protection strategies and actions. Medium-level and senior staff also attend a course on law and protection and may benefit from a series of courses on different issues such as management, security and stress, communication, etc. In addition, individual opportunities for further training are sometimes proposed to some personnel, such as short-term courses organised by other institutions, additional academic studies, internships in or secondment to other institutions or organisations. Ultimately, experience, on the spot training, as well as coaching and support by more senior staff play a key role.

Between 2000 and 2003, ICRC organised in Geneva protection seminars for interested staff from NGOs and UN agencies. Such seminars have been conducted at the regional level since 2005.

1998); C. de Roover, *To Serve and Protect: Human Rights and Humanitarian Law for Police and Security Force* (Geneva: ICRC, 1998); ICRC, *The Law of Armed Conflict: Teaching File for Instructors* (Geneva: ICRC, 2002).

[22]   See, in particular, D. Mancini-Griffoli and A. Picot, *Humanitarian Negotiation: A Handbook for Securing Access, Assistance and Protection for Civilians in Armed Conflict*, Centre for Humanitarian Dialogue (London: Royal United Services Institute for Defence and Security Studies, 2005).

Specific Challenges

Protection work, as conceived and carried out by ICRC, faces numerous challenges, such as security constraints, the quality of the information collected and analyses made, difficulties in assessing the parameters of military operations and evaluating protection activities, to mention only a few.

Security Constraints

Without a sufficient level of security for the persons affected or witnesses of abuses, and for the humanitarian staff, no meaningful protection action can be considered by ICRC. In many areas, security constraints are increasing and sometimes hampering access and effective protection activities. This is notably due to the nature of conflicts, the increased weight of criminal interests and the rejection by some groups of any humanitarian presence or compliance with the provisions of IHL and other fundamental norms. In addition, the merging of military, humanitarian and political mandates, the increased will to instrumentalise humanitarian activities and the difficulties to ensure the perception of an independent and neutral humanitarian action have also effects on security.

Quality of Information and Analysis

ICRC bases its work and representations on allegations, mainly from victims and witnesses. The veracity of these allegations has to be assessed and crosschecked in each case. Exaggerations and rumours are a permanent risk which professionalism and rigor seek to minimise. ICRC is not a judicial or investigative body. It does not have the mission or the means to prove that abuses were perpetrated. With the consent of the persons concerned, it brings what are alleged facts to the knowledge of the authorities, together with its own observations and conclusions. The aim is to make the relevant authorities aware of their responsibilities. It is then upon these authorities to conduct their own enquiry and, if the information reported by ICRC is confirmed, to take all necessary steps, whether organisational, administrative, disciplinary or even penal.

Difficulty in Assessing the Legality of the Conduct of Military Operations

Analysing whether military operations and hostilities were conducted in a way consistent with IHL has proved extremely difficult. For security reasons, ICRC staff are rarely on the spot during such operations and have therefore to make such an analysis only after the events. In addition to legal expertise, military knowledge is needed. Assessing the legality of an attack cannot be exclusively based on its consequences in humanitarian terms but needs also often to take account of other considerations. One major parameter consists of establishing whether the required precautionary measures were taken before and at the time of launching the attack, based on the information the military commander had at his disposal when ordering the attack. It is only the concerned military force which has all this information. Consequently, ICRC is careful before drawing conclusions that violations occurred, except in obvious cases. Sometimes ICRC has to limit itself to transmit allegations from affected persons and to request the relevant authorities or non-state actors to examine the existence of the various parameters related to the legality of the actions.

Difficulty of Evaluating Protection Activities

Evaluating protection activities often proves to be an arduous task. Many elements internal to ICRC may have an impact on the quality of its action, such as the quality of the information collected by ICRC personnel, the quality and quantity of representations made to the authorities or the identification of the authorities most relevant to take adequate measures. A series of external factors may contribute to an evolution with regard to respect for the rights of the individuals, including changes in the field of politics or military operations, changes on the ground such as movements of populations or economic variations, or action by other actors dealing with protection. Defining indicators to assess one's own action and its impact is therefore often very challenging.

Relations of ICRC with Human Right Field Operations

ICRC has followed the evolution of human rights field operations, since their advent, as it has been working in the majority of contexts where they were deployed. This is part of ICRC's endeavour to ensure complementarity and to coordinate activities with other organisations.

ICRC has repeatedly stressed its willingness to coordinate with others while insisting on the fact that the need to preserve its neutrality and independence prevents it from being formally coordinated by other agencies or bound in advance to a specific sectoral approach. ICRC is genuinely committed to developing operationally efficient complementarity in the best interest of the affected persons. This requires sustained dialogue with key partners at the bilateral and multilateral levels. Throughout, ICRC consistently respects its own working procedures and principles, in particular confidentiality. In all processes, ICRC priority is action oriented and reality based.

As the Office of the United Nations High Commissioner for Human Rights (OHCHR) is extending its field presence through human rights field operations, dialogue and coordination will no doubt intensify. It is obvious that the final objectives of human rights field operations and ICRC are close. ICRC has *a priori* a positive attitude towards the intervention of other bodies as it aims at improving the impact of humanitarian action in the widest sense, at increasing awareness of the plight of the affected persons and at ensuring that international standards are respected. However, it is important to remain attentive to the risk of too many actors becoming involved as well as the application of different standards. Complementarity between ICRC and human rights field operations has to be developed on the basis of elements such as the qualification of the situation concerned, the need to have an independent and neutral intermediary involved, respective mandates and capacities, the areas and types of respective activities, the ways of action, the period and duration of intervention and the body of law concerned.

The characteristics of ICRC's approach have been outlined above. In its interaction with human rights field operations, ICRC has been confronted with a huge variety of mandates and activities. The challenge for ICRC has been to adapt to the specificity of each operation. ICRC has had difficulties understanding the logic behind various forms of operations and following the various types of activities concretely carried out. An improved predictability of the situations where such operations take place and the activities carried out would definitely be helpful and greatly facilitate the identification of complementarity in concrete cases.

ICRC acknowledges that human rights field operations are generically characterised by some features that may complement ICRC's approach. These features are mainly:

- the expertise in human rights law and the very large (and nearly unlimited) scope of areas of concern, including civil, political, economic, social and cultural rights. In comparison, except mainly in cases of occupation of territories, ICRC generally focuses on violations of the safety, physical and psychological integrity, dignity and the basic welfare of individuals;
- the regular use of public communication, thus keeping the international community aware of the problems and generating pressure to establish and maintain an environment conducive to protection;
- the link with the human rights system and mechanisms, in particular special procedures, treaty bodies and the Human Rights Council;
- the close relations with states as members of the UN and the role played in regard to political decisions, in particular decisions from the United Nations General Assembly and Security Council;
- upholding the rule of law with a focus on issues such as the legality of detention and the administration of justice;
- the possibility to cooperate with or rehabilitate the justice system, to carry out investigation and collect evidence of violations and to submit collected evidence to court or other bodies.

At the same time, depending on the situation and the activities carried out by the human rights field operation, notably in case of an integrated mission or when acting as a component of a peace operation under Chapter VII of the United Nations Charter,[23] global political considerations may curb the functions of human right field

---

[23] Charter of the United Nations, 59 Stat. 1031, T.S. 993, 3 Bevans 1153 (entered into force 24 October 1945).

officers. Some months ago, the deterioration of relations between ONUCI (United Nations Operation in Côte d'Ivoire)[24] and a party to the conflict directly affected the possibilities of action for the human rights component. The same applies for example in the Democratic Republic of Congo, where clashes rose between MONUC (United Nations Mission in the Democratic Republic of Congo)[25] and one of the armed groups present.

The challenge for ICRC is to have its specificity continue to be perceived and acknowledged by the various parties to a conflict and arms carriers. Its priority and the sense of its mission are to work with all parties in a given context. Blurring of mandates and ways of operating and possible misunderstanding that all are part of a more global political agenda may hamper the fragile trust and acceptance by all parties and arms carriers. Consequently, ICRC has to find a balance between maintaining the perception of its specific nature, promoting dialogue and coordination with human rights field operations and respecting the confidentiality it is committed to. There is no doubt that access became sometimes difficult or even impossible in some areas for security reasons as various parties or arms carriers were not making any distinction between the different organisations involved and, as a priority, wished to avoid the presence of any potential external witness.

ICRC has so far identified some 25 contexts where ICRC delegates and human rights field officers have interacted in one way or another. The minimum interaction identified includes mere courtesy discussion and exchange of views on generic activities carried out (as in the Central African Republic, Sierra Leone or the Palestinian territories). This increases as far as real attempts to agree on a type of sharing of tasks and set out practical methods of coordination (including avoiding a simultaneous presence in places of detention) and consultation (as in Rwanda, Bosnia and Herzegovina and Nepal). In between, there is a large range of situations with periodic meetings in which matters of common interest are discussed (as in Afghanistan; Liberia; Guinea-Bissau; Côte d'Ivoire; Democratic Republic of Congo; Burundi; Darfur, Sudan; Ethiopia/Eritrea and Colombia). With regard to sharing information on specific violations of IHL or other fundamental rules collected by its staff or detailed individual documented cases, ICRC has a restrictive approach in accordance with its policy of confidentiality. In general terms, ICRC delegates may only communicate the extent of humanitarian needs assessed in certain areas by ICRC teams. As human rights field officers are not subject to such restrictions, they may transmit to ICRC all information at their disposal. Where appropriate, ICRC provides informal expert advice on international humanitarian law.

A case in point is the human rights field operation which developed in Rwanda after the genocide, between 1994 and 1999, and included more than 100 observers at any one time.[26] Considering the limited size of the country, this huge number

---

[24]   See Security Council resolution 1479 (2003), UN Doc. S/RES/1479 (2003).

[25]   See Security Council resolution 1258 (1999), UN Doc. S/RES/1258 (1999).

[26]   See I. Martin, 'After Genocide: The UN Human Rights Field Operation in Rwanda', in A. Henkin (ed.) *Honoring Human Rights* (The Hague: Kluwer Law International, 2000).

of observers had an effect on the work of ICRC, which was also carrying out a large action with a focus on detention issues (including the provision of a significant amount of life saving assistance and other direct services in prisons, in particular food and medicines). In fact, ICRC was frequently reproached by the authorities, the inmates and the population in general regarding human rights field officers' behaviour. To improve complementarity and avoid duplication in their activities for persons deprived of liberty, ICRC and OHCHR issued, at field level, joint guidelines for their respective staff. These guidelines specified the material and psychological conditions of detention and the treatment of persons deprived of liberty as ICRC's focus and judicial guarantees and the administration of justice as the focus of OHCHR. They also outlined the registration of the identity of the detainees by ICRC and its individual follow-up of their movements throughout places of detention until the end of their detention time, while stressing human rights monitors' monthly fact-finding missions in prisons to record observations regarding respect for international human rights standards.

Protection coordination meetings have recently been organised in some countries between various organisations at field level within different frameworks. This trend will be reinforced with the cluster approach the UN system is promoting and implementing in various contexts. ICRC, which insisted on not being formally part of the cluster approach to keep with its neutral and independent identity, tries to concentrate its participation as an observer to coordination meetings that bring added value to work on the ground without merely adding a bureaucratic layer. Within the limits imposed by confidentiality, ICRC is consequently taking part in a selected way. The decision to participate is primarily based on an analysis of whether such participation might jeopardise the confidence that the authorities and non-state actors have in ICRC.

In the future, it has to be seen how human rights field operations develop, how much predictability can exist and how the best possible complementarity can be worked out at general and local levels.

Chapter 13

Protection: A Non-governmental Organisation Experience, Peace Brigades International

Liam Mahony[1]

Introduction

> I can say with certainty that the fact that we are alive today is mainly because of Peace Brigades' work.
>
> (Luis Perez Casas, Lawyer's Collective 'Jose Alvear Restrepo,' Bogotá, Colombia)

'International protective accompaniment' is the physical accompaniment by international personnel of activists, organisations or communities who are threatened with politically-motivated attacks. Peace Brigades International (PBI) has been developing this tactic since the mid-1980s, sending hundreds of volunteers into different conflict scenarios around the world. This chapter describes and analyses the protective dynamic of accompaniment, and is complemented by a previous lengthier publication: *Side-by-Side: Protecting and Encouraging Threatened Activists with Unarmed International Accompaniment.*[2]

PBI currently sustains a presence of about 80 people working in several conflicts, responding to requests for accompaniment from all kinds of threatened civil society organisations and communities. Accompaniment can take many forms. Some threatened activists receive 24 hours-a-day accompaniment. For others the presence is more sporadic. Sometimes team members spend all day on the premises of an office of a threatened organisation. Sometimes they live in threatened rural villages in conflict zones.

This accompaniment service has three simultaneous and mutually-reinforcing impacts. The international presence *protects threatened activists* by raising the stakes of any attacks against them. It *encourages civil society activism* by allowing threatened organisations more space and confidence to operate and by building links of solidarity with the international community. And it *strengthens the international*

---

[1] The views and analysis of this document are based largely on experiences of PBI, but are entirely the responsibility of the author.

[2] New Tactics in Human Rights Project, Center for Victims of Torture (Minneapolis, 2004), available at http://www.newtactics.org.

movement for peace and human rights by giving accompaniment volunteers a powerful first-hand experience, which becomes a sustained source of inspiration to themselves and others upon their return to their home country.

This chapter will analyse how protective accompaniment works, based on the substantial experience of PBI in Colombia, Indonesia, Mexico, Guatemala, Haiti, Sri Lanka and El Salvador. Since the early 1990s, numerous other organisations have also provided protective international accompaniment in other settings, modifying the approach according to their particular identity and mission. For the sake of focus and space, the analysis in the present chapter will be limited to PBI.

What is Protective Accompaniment?

The accompaniment volunteer[3] is literally the embodiment of international human rights concern, a compelling and visible reminder to those using violence that it will not go unnoticed. The volunteers act essentially as unarmed bodyguards, often spending 24 hours a day with human rights workers, union leaders, peasant groups and other popular organisations that face mortal danger from death squads, state forces or possibly other abusers. The premise of accompaniment is that there will be an international response to whatever violence the volunteer witnesses. Behind such a response lies the implied threat of diplomatic and economic pressure – pressure that the sponsors of such violence prefer to avoid.

Victims of human rights abuse are frequently those attempting to organise social change movements that question their society's powerful elites. An international presence at their side can be a source of hope to these activists. It assures them that they are not alone, that their work is important, and that their suffering will not go unnoticed by the outside world. Thus, the volunteer's presence not only protects, but also encourages, the growth of civil society activism in repressive situations.

Accompaniment is a service to key local protagonists in struggles for justice, non-violence and human rights. These local activists are the ones building civil society from the ground up while facing deadly and daily risks. Some of the people being protected are extraordinary leaders – courageous and charismatic activists, lawyers or non-governmental organisation (NGO) leaders. Others are average citizens thrust into extraordinary circumstances by the trauma of events around them. Whether they are lawyers, women's groups, peasant organisations, labour unions, internally-displaced populations or community organisations, they are all struggling to defend their basic human rights and dignity.

Since PBI's first accompaniment began in Guatemala in the early 1980s, thousands of people have been protected. Hundreds of organisations and activists have felt the security and encouragement to expand their work, to persevere despite

---

[3]   For simplicity the author will use the short-hand term 'volunteer' when referring to the personnel doing accompaniment, as the majority of organisations providing accompaniment do so with volunteers. The tactic could of course also be carried out by paid personnel, so this terminology should not be considered exclusive of that option.

the risks. And volunteers have travelled from all over the world to participate in this service.

In the course of two decades of experience not a single activist receiving one-on-one PBI accompaniment has ever been killed. In only two situations has a deadly attack occurred against a community while PBI sustained a presence there. And not a single PBI volunteer has been killed. Accompaniment has proved to be very effective protection, even in situations where the overall human rights situation was deteriorating and where death squads seemed impervious to external pressure.

Peace Brigades began offering accompaniment in Guatemala in 1984. It expanded to El Salvador (1987–1992) and Sri Lanka (1989–1998). As of 2006, PBI has over 40 people in Colombia (since 1994), 15 more in Indonesia, eight in Mexico and a team of nine in Guatemala.[4]

Accompaniment has three primary impacts:

- Protection of threatened activists and organisations,
- Encouragement of individuals and civil society movements, and
- Building a global movement for peace and human rights.

Protection: Deterring Attacks against Civil Society Leaders, Groups and Communities

International accompaniment can succeed in deterring attacks because the decision-makers behind these attacks seldom want a bad international image. They do not want the world to know about what they are doing. They do not want diplomats making them uncomfortable mentioning human rights problems in their meetings. They do not want to read in the international press that they are being called monsters or criminals. They will avoid all that if they can.

The decision-makers may be high level government officials, high level military officials, lower-level officials, private elite businessmen (local or international) with influence or private enforcement capacity, or non-state armed group leadership. In every case, the accompaniment functions by increasing the perceived political costs of ordering an attack in front of these international witnesses – witnesses whose sponsor organisations are committed to making such attacks as costly as possible.

The direct perpetrators of attacks might be soldiers, police, paramilitary organisations, guerrillas or hired assassins, among others. In each case, the accompaniment strategy requires a thorough analysis of the chain of command between the perpetrator and the higher-level decision-maker. We should not assume that the thugs who pull the trigger are unaffected by international presence. No one wants an unexpected witness around when they are carrying out a crime. On the one hand the volunteer's presence may have a moral influence on individual perpetrators. On the other it also introduces an uncertainty factor – the attacker does not know what the consequences of this witness will be, so unless he has explicit orders that

---

[4]   For more on this work see http://www.peacebrigades.org/.

take the accompaniment into account, he is likely to restrain himself rather than risk getting in trouble with his superiors.

Accompaniment Protection and the Line of Command

To appreciate the added value of accompaniment as protection, consider first the more traditional model of international human rights pressure. Although systemic human rights abuses require the collaboration of a variety of actors at different levels in the line of command, international pressure is usually only directed at the decision-makers at the top, urging them to stop abuses. And at the bottom, the international community sometimes offers a variety of kinds of support to threatened activists themselves.

But international human rights pressure is now a decades-old practice, and states have developed very nimble counter-measures to prevent this pressure from having its desired impact. They have learned to *deflect* pressure using propaganda to destroy the credibility of the accusing organisation or the targeted activists, such as labelling them terrorists. By such labelling states gain international support from allies for their policies. States also develop *buffer* mechanisms to absorb and co-opt human rights pressure without overt denials, including the creation of state agencies to deal with the human rights community. The existence of such institutions allows the state to acknowledge a problem and claim it is taking all possible measures. *Smokescreens* are another very effective counter-measure, allowing the decision-maker to argue that it is not responsible for the abuses, even though it admits they occur. A common and devastatingly effective smokescreen is the use of paramilitary or death squad operations secretly under military control. In other cases, justifications such as 'lack of discipline' or 'loose cannons' distance the high-level decision-makers from the abuses. Smokescreens give both the state and its international allies a level of *plausible deniability* when faced with accusations.

A good accompaniment strategy can address these counter-measures to some extent, both complementing and augmenting traditional external pressure in the following ways:

- The accompaniment volunteer is directly visible to potential direct perpetrators, a unique impact among international efforts.
- PBI extends the pressure throughout the chain of command, by meeting with all different levels of the military and civilian hierarchy, on both national and local levels. Without this, there is no assurance that the 'message' of international pressure is transmitted through the different levels. In these meetings, PBI diplomatically ensures that every echelon of the decision-making system is aware of the presence and of its link to the international community. This process increases accountability, to some extent combating the smokescreens.
- The accompaniment vastly strengthens the international support felt by the threatened activists.

- The 'first-hand witness' effect strengthens the credibility of the local activists, their organisations, and the overall international effort to protect them. As a constant reminder that there is a still a problem, it also confronts the state's *buffer* strategies, as it is harder for the state to claim it is solving the problem by itself.
- The presence of volunteers from many countries 'in the line of fire' engages their embassies and home governments more forcefully in human rights protection, strengthening the overall pressure on top decision-makers.
- When an attack or harassment happens despite PBI's presence, PBI's global emergency alert network immediately responds, with both high level and grassroots pressure, reminding decision-makers that they cannot allow such 'mistakes'.

Case Study: Colectivo de Abogados, Colombia

For many years PBI has been accompanying lawyers from the Bogotá-based Lawyers Collective (*Colectivo de Abogados José Alvear Restrepo*), one of the largest and most threatened professional human rights organisations in Colombia. This accompaniment sometimes involves around-the-clock escorting, with volunteers from the PBI team taking turns with individual lawyers of the collective. This individual accompaniment involves being constantly ready to move at someone else's schedule, with the discretion to stay 'out of their business' while maintaining visibility. Threats and attacks against human rights defenders in Colombia have been so merciless that they can affect every aspect of daily life.

> Wherever Alirio travels, be it from home to work, to court, or to meetings around the city, he moves in a bullet proof car, wears a bullet-proof jacket and has a constant PBI presence at his side … One day we parked in the underground car park of the thirty-storey building in which his office is located. 'Do you mind if we walk up rather than take the lift?' he asked. 'It's just that I never get any exercise these days – it's simply too risky for me to go to the gym or the park.' (James Savage, PBI Volunteer from the UK)

Encouraging Civil Society in the Face of Repression

In situations of widespread political repression or terror, activists are not asking for accompaniment merely to confront a personal fear or an immediate threat. They are confronting systemic policies of violence that can frighten whole populations into political paralysis. Deliberate political use of terror is as old as war itself. In recent history, however, advances in the sciences of weaponry, information control, mass media and psychology have facilitated the exercise of mass-scale terror with a previously inconceivable efficiency. Social control is achieved by efficiently manipulating diverse individual responses to danger and fear. The goal of state terror is to keep people isolated from each other. Civilian organisations are a threat to overcoming that isolation: any organising is empowering and, as such, confronts and questions the terror system.

Terror is very efficient: you do not need to kill everyone if you can paralyse the majority by only directly attacking a minority. It is the audience that counts, with each victim advertising the state's power to others. Torture, short of death, is an especially effective tool for encouraging collective paralysis. Human rights abuse is thus often a rational choice made by strategic thinkers. The techniques have been developed through a long history of military psychological operations. To policymakers, terror may seem no more immoral than other strategic choices in a war against an enemy. And, as with other military or strategic policies, strategists study the successes and failures of others, perfecting the tools.

> There are always people on the street corners spying on us to watch our movements. So when they see that internationals are physically entering our offices, this helps us tremendously. (Aura Elena Farfan, Guatemalan Families of the Disappeared)

Nevertheless, even the most organised state terror system cannot watch everyone, nor kill anyone at any time it pleases. Surveillance is expensive and labour-intensive. Processing and interpreting all the data from surveillance is even more demanding, and intelligence planners frequently have more data than they can effectively analyse. The state's omnipotence is never so complete, but it wants people to think so, since this belief prompts a self-regulation of political activity.

The desired impact of repression, threats and intimidation is to diminish the range of action for civil society groups. People feel they have fewer tactical choices for public action that will not result in retaliation. They may fear travelling outside the major cities. Their organisations suffer diminished participation – membership drops. And activists often suffer serious mental health problems resulting from the stress of constant insecurity.

By providing encouragement to these activists and organisations, protective accompaniment reduces the fear, reduces the stress and promotes increased participation and organising. Activists and groups begin to choose tactics and actions they would otherwise fear to try. They travel where they would otherwise fear to go. New members join their organisations who might otherwise stay away in fear. The sense of isolation that was inspired by fear is broken by international solidarity.

Case Study: Communities Resisting War in Rural Colombia

The Colombian conflict has spawned the worst human rights situation in the Western hemisphere, with thousands of political murders annually and over two million internally displaced people. In the rural regions of Urabá and Chocó, several communities of displaced peasants have initiated a daring strategy in the face of armed conflict and repeated expulsions from their land. With the support and solidarity of national and international NGOs they are creating communities with a special commitment to resist *any* collaboration with any of the several armed parties that terrorise the region, which include the military, multiple guerrilla organisations, and the most brutal of all: paramilitary associations who collaborate with the army. Some communities are called 'peace communities', others 'communities in resistance'. One, along the Cacarica River, calls itself a 'Community of Self-determination, Dignity, and Life' (which we will refer to simply as 'Cacarica').

The essence of the strategies of these communities is to create a sense of unity and a disciplined approach to all the armed parties, and to back this up with national and international strategies of solidarity and pressure in order to defend their right to a space free from military, paramilitary or guerrilla harassment. Peace Brigades International has provided steady accompaniment in two of these communities for several years – San José de Apartadó and Cacarica. The boundary sign outside the 'San José de Apartadó Peace Community' reads:

The community
* freely participates in community tasks
* says no to injustice and impunity
* doesn't participate in the war, whether directly or indirectly, nor carries arms
* doesn't manipulate or give information to any of the warring parties

The communities have faced a constant barrage of attacks and harassment of different sorts, from across the armed spectrum – but mostly from paramilitary groups aligned with the army and the economic elites of the country. Paramilitaries have murdered many community members, and when terror did not succeed in scaring the residents out of their peace strategy, the paramilitaries turned to economic strangulation, blockading access routes. This harassment has been backed up by a concerted public relations smear campaign by the army against the communities, labelling them 'terrorists'.

In Cacarica, PBI has a small hut where volunteers stay. Volunteers can get there only by boat, and they spend several days to a week at a time in the community before rotating out, returning to their home base in the nearby city of Turbo when replaced by other volunteers. They stay abreast of all political developments in the region and in the community. Volunteers have satellite phones, with which they can immediately alert the rest of the organisation about any attack on the community. On these phones they also have the home and mobile numbers of local police and military commanders, of diplomatic allies and other authorities who will also be alerted the moment anything happens requiring a rapid response.

If a paramilitary incursion should occur, for instance, PBI volunteers will be able to alert the international community, literally within minutes. PBI's team in Bogotá can immediately contact key governmental and military officials as well as allies in the diplomatic community to generate a rapid response. They will also immediately contact PBI's offices around the world, and generate a strategic response on an international level if necessary. On numerous occasions PBI has been able to put national and international pressure on the local military to react even while paramilitaries were still carrying out their attacks or harassment.

The war in this region has been intense, and it is an area nearly completely controlled by right-wing paramilitaries who have been unrelenting in their persecution of the communities. So it is somewhat difficult to measure the protective impact of the presence. However, the fact that physical attacks against residents reduced after the first years, and the paramilitaries turned to more subtle economic tactics could be a sign of the impact of PBI's presence and the generally high level of international solidarity the communities received.

The harassment has also extended to PBI. In fact, in 2003 and 2004, high level military officials and Colombian President Álvaro Uribe himself issued a series of controversial statements alleging links between these communities, their international accompaniment and guerrilla 'terrorists'. President Uribe asserted, 'I reiterate to the police, if these [foreign human rights observers] continue to obstruct justice, put them in prison. If they have to be deported, deport them'.[5] PBI organised a substantial defensive international response demanding the retraction of these accusations and insisting that the government assure the security of the international presence. The response included letters to Uribe from the United States Congress, a delegation of embassy officials to the region, supportive articles in Colombian newspapers, special meetings between diplomatic officers and government officials, of support for PBI from United Kingdom Government Minister Bill Rammell, as well as the French ambassador, a public communiqué by the European Union, a public expression of concern by the Inter-American Commission of Human Rights and more, sending a clear message of international concern about the importance of the PBI presence in the region.

PBI volunteers are considered almost members of the community. The residents feel a strong sense of solidarity from and towards PBI, who they see as showing a steadfast commitment to their struggle for dignity. They have expressed on numerous occasions how much encouragement they get from PBI's presence, and how it strengthens them to carry on. The volunteers who have had the opportunity to live in Cacarica and San José de Apartadó have been changed forever by the experience. They will never forget the dedication, the creativity, the humility and the courage of the people in these communities who are standing up, non-violently, to some of the most vicious paramilitary groups in the world. And the volunteers are bringing this inspiration with them when they go back to their home country.

Encouragement, Protection and Political Space[6]

The concept of 'political space' is crucial to understanding how the incremental protection and encouragement provided by accompaniment interact with each other. Each actor in a complex conflict situation, whether a soldier or a human rights

---

[5]   Speech given by President Álvaro Uribe on 27 May 2004 at San José de Apartadó, Colombia. ['Es muy claro: le reitero la sugerencia al DAS y a la Policía, respetuosa, de que si estas personas vuelven a obstruir la justicia, los metan a la cárcel y si hay que deportarlos, se deportan'.]
[6]   The analysis of this section is drawn from L. Mahony and L. E. Eguren, *Unarmed Bodyguards: International Accompaniment for the Protection of Human Rights* (West Hartford: Kumarian Press, 1997).

activist, perceives a broad array of possible political actions and associates a certain cost/benefit analysis or set of consequences with each action. The actor perceives some consequences as acceptable, some not acceptable, thereby defining the limits of a distinct political space (see Figure 1).

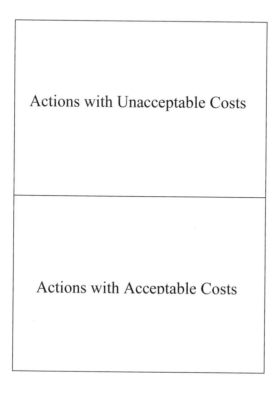

Figure 1   Each actor's political space

Accompaniment alters this mapping of political space for a threatened human rights activist (see Figure 2). It shifts the borderline upward, expanding the space of political action available to the activist. The middle ground is made up of actions that will no longer be attacked in an unbearable fashion. There are still actions which will provoke unacceptable consequences, even with accompaniment.

The notion of 'acceptable' consequences can be fluid over time, and will vary greatly among individuals or organisations. For some, torture or death of a family member might be the most unbearable consequence. For others a threshold might be crossed at the first threats. An organisation might be willing to risk the death of a member, but not the annihilation of the whole group.

Accompaniment tends to limit, or shrink, the aggressor's options for violent or repressive action – which we will call 'impunity space' (see Figure 3). Again, there will still be actions whose consequences are acceptable. As with the activist, so with the aggressor: The concept of 'acceptable' is fluid and variable. One government official might be extremely savvy and sensitive to international criticism, while an independent death-squad leader might be more immune.

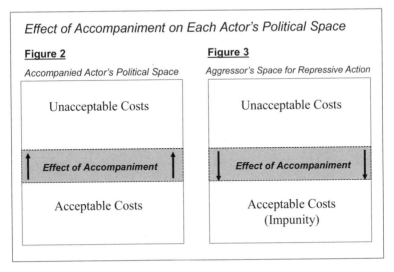

Figure 2
Effect of accompaniment on each actor's political space: Accompanied actor's political space

Figure 3
Effect of accompaniment on each actor's political space: Aggressor's space for repressive action

Accompaniment is effective, in both Figures 2 and 3, in the grey zone. If the aggressor's ability to attack has been significantly limited, the presence is real protection. If the activists can carry out significant political activities that otherwise they would have avoided, then that accompaniment has encouraged the strengthening and growth of a non-violent civil society.

But no one knows where the borders are! This is the critical complication, which requires an expansion of our analysis. All actors are guessing about the possible repercussions of their actions, and they are all making mistakes. A dictator might not have attacked a certain organisation if he had known that this would attract greater diplomatic support to the organisation and increase its international profile and credibility. Meanwhile, the activists are also making mistakes: a young factory worker may think it would be dangerous to be an outspoken union leader. But she figures the odds are more in her favour if she is just a quiet rank-and-file member. Then she is dead. At the factory next door, everyone is too scared to even talk about unionising. Yet maybe there would be no repercussions at all. They do not know. Nobody knows. Everyone learns by trial and error, and the errors are costly.

People base their decisions on their own perceptions and projections of what consequences they might suffer. These projections might be based on substantial historical or political analysis; on simple prejudices; on an emotional reaction to a past trauma; or any number of other psychological factors. Graphically, this uncertainty and the consequences on the impact of accompaniment are shown in Figures 4 through 7.

In space A (Figure 4), the activist unknowingly walks into danger and suffers the consequences. In space B, fear has been instilled so effectively that the activist is inhibited from taking actions which are in fact relatively safe. In situations of state terrorism, this space can be huge: nearly all political or social action is feared; only passivity appears to have acceptable consequences. The darker shaded grey area, then, is really the only political space that is truly 'available' to the activist. Space A is too dangerous, and space B has been eliminated in the activist's own mind.

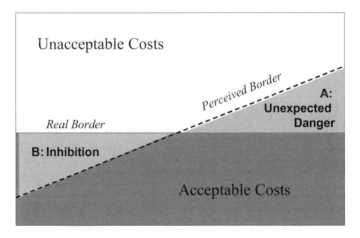

Figure 4   Activist's political space: Reality and perception

Accompaniment expands this available space by pushing both the 'real' and 'perceived' borders upwards (see Figure 5). The actions in the dark grey shaded area are now available to the activists, but for a variety of reasons. Actions in B2, for instance, were not dangerous in the first place: the activist has simply overcome internalised inhibitions. Accompaniment in this case functions as encouragement and not protection. Actions in A3 are now safer, but since the activists never saw them as unacceptably dangerous, the accompaniment here is serving as pure protection, and not encouragement. In area F both encouragement and protection are acting together: the activist is encouraged to take new action which was previously too dangerous, and is now protected.

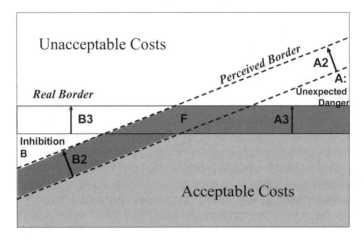

Figure 5   Activist's political space and effect of accompaniment

There is still fear: area B still exists with accompaniment. In fact, area B3 consists of additional actions that are now relatively safe, but the activist still does not trust in this safety. Finally, area A2 represents the accompaniment nightmare: the activist believes these actions to be safer now, but in fact they are not. The activist may walk confidently because of the encouraging international presence.

The aggressor faces many different types of consequences for repressive action. Some are local, such as increased unrest if the aggressor is a state, or increased group loyalty or solidarity amongst the victims. International pressure is just one factor. Other perceived benefits might outweigh the costs. Getting rid of a troublesome activist, for instance, might seem worth a short-term embarrassment. Thus, 'unacceptable costs', refers to the net effect of all these factors. Again, in Figure 6, only the actions in the darker grey area are truly available 'impunity space'.

Protective accompaniment purports to deter violence and shrink this space (see Figure 7) by moving both lines downward, eliminating the dark grey zone from the available space for repressive action. In the case of the activist, we distinguished between protection and encouragement; with the aggressor we speak of discouragement and deterrence. The aggressor is discouraged from acting in area D2, even though the real costs are acceptable. He overestimates the power of accompaniment and becomes even more overcautious. In area G, we come the closest to real deterrence: The accompaniment has raised the costs of repression; the aggressor recognises this and holds back.

Sometimes, accompaniment helps the aggressor avoid mistakes. Thus, actions in area C2 are blunders with or without accompaniment, but the aggressor did not recognise them as such until the accompaniment was present. While discouraging the aggressor's 'mistake', accompaniment is protecting the intended target. From the standpoint of the activist, after all, repression by mistake is no less damaging.

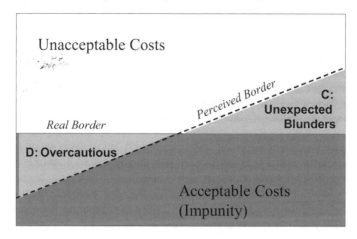

Figure 6 Activist's political space: Reality and perception

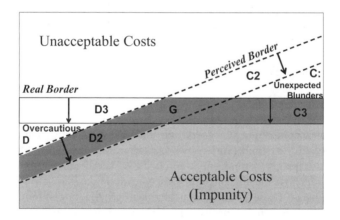

Figure 7 Aggressor's repressive space and effect of accompaniment

Finally, returning to Figure 7, the aggressor might commit a repressive act (area C3), and suffer unacceptable consequences because of accompaniment. In the immediate event, accompaniment has failed to deter, but over the course of time, such events should change the aggressor's perception of the available space. If the aggressor learns from mistakes, the 'perceived' line should move closer to the real line. The accompaniment thus discourages future aggression. And the more severe the political cost, the greater the credibility and success of future accompaniment.

Volunteers Building a Global Movement

I had thought for a number of years doing accompaniment work would be the highest expression of solidarity with other people. To potentially put yourself at risk so another person could continue to their human rights work ... doing that was enacting a dream and that's a pretty powerful thing to do. The whole time there was some part of me that was just incredibly content and happy about being there despite of the challenges and difficulties I encountered. (John Krone, PBI Mexico project volunteer)

PBI encourages volunteers from all over the world to get actively involved in peace and human rights work. The organisation has chapters in 15 countries around the world doing outreach and recruitment of volunteers, and building up networks of political pressure in each of their countries. Eighty or so people each spend a year or more working on PBI teams in conflict zones in urban and rural areas. These volunteers are from many countries and of many ages, with a minimum threshold of 25 years old.

On a given day in the life of a PBI accompaniment volunteer, s/he might spend some of it meeting with a human rights defender to discuss risks and plans for future accompaniment, or escorting them to a meeting or on a trip or patiently sitting and waiting outside an office while the activist is doing their daily routine. S/he might have a meeting with representatives from the military, the government, the diplomatic community or other NGOs in the country. S/he might spend it involved in an emergency activation of the organisation's international support network. Or it might be a day for writing reports, taking care of administrative duties or cleaning the house.

Training for Accompaniment

PBI and other accompaniment organisations have been training volunteers for this service for over 20 years, and a variety of models have been developed. PBI's trainings are highly participatory: volunteers go through a series of exercises and role-plays to help them visualise the challenge they are considering and to help trainers gauge their preparedness. These trainings consider such criteria as commitment to non-violence and human rights, capacity for intensive political analysis, understanding of the country of the project, cautious judgement, patience and humility, ability to work in a team under high stress and more.[7]

---

[7]   More detail on the criteria for selection of volunteers for different PBI projects can be found on the organisation's website: http://www.peacebrigades.org; Also Training for Change, a Philadelphia-based NGO created by veteran trainer George Lakey, has developed a comprehensive manual on training for this kind of service, encompassing a variety of techniques developed over the years. The manual draws from a wide variety of training experiences, including some techniques from PBI trainings. It is a highly recommended resource for those considering training for accompaniment work: *Opening Space for Democracy: Third-Party Nonviolent Intervention. Curriculum and Trainers Manual*, by D. Hunter and G. Lakey, available from Training for Change, peacelearn@igc.org; http://www.TrainingForChange. org.

Coming Home

Each volunteer comes home with a story to tell, and often with an intense drive to continue serving the cause of human rights. They may be driven to keep abreast of the situations of the groups they had the privilege to accompany. After doing accompaniment, human rights abuses can no longer be seen as far away statistics: those people are your friends and they have given you something deeply important in your life.

Returned volunteers often also get more deeply involved in working in their own communities for justice, peace and human rights. Each of them is a resource in their own community, a person with a unique first-hand experience from which others can learn and be inspired. In fact, it is quite common for returned accompaniment volunteers to make substantial changes in their life plans and careers in order to sustain greater life-long commitment to service.

The expansion of a global movement for peace and human rights is a vital consequence of accompaniment in the field. The protection and encouragement that local activists can get from accompaniment is directly correlated to the strength of the global network of solidarity that cares about them. Accompaniment volunteers not only represent this network on the ground – they also strengthen it when they get home.

Spreading the Accompaniment Tactic

PBI is constantly receiving and exploring new requests for accompaniment. Based on lessons learned from its many projects over the years, PBI has developed explicit criteria and procedures for diagnosing requests and deciding to set up new projects. Protective accompaniment is also being used widely now by other NGOs. Each of these organisations has their own identity and mandate, different from PBI, and they adapt the accompaniment into their broader missions.

The 'Guatemala Accompaniment Project', for instance, is fielded by NISGUA (the National Organization in Solidarity with the People of Guatemala, Washington, DC). The accompaniment their eight to ten volunteers offer is part of a broader advocacy mandate. NISGUA develops 'Sister Communities' in North America who sponsor volunteers to live in their counterpart community in Guatemala, focusing on communities of returned refugees and communities who are actively pursuing genocide cases against former military leaders. NISGUA is actively involved in offering political and other support for the political initiatives of these communities, and the sister community relationships strengthen the NISGUA constituency for political lobbying of the United States government to change its policies with respect to Guatemala.

The 'Non-violent Peace Force' has a team of about 25 volunteers spread between a half-dozen locations in Sri Lanka. They are accompanying villages in all regions of the country during a delicate ceasefire and negotiation process between the Liberation Tigers of Tamil Eelam and the Sri Lankan government. This is the Peace

Force's first field presence, but they have created a broad network of support around the world for the ambitious long-range goal of creating the capacity to run multiple large-scale non-violent field missions around the world.

The Peace Force has only been in the field a short time, but they spent years in preparation before launching their Sri Lanka pilot project, studying the lessons of other accompaniment groups to try to maximise the protection and encouragement impact while avoiding as much as possible the learning-curve pitfalls that can hurt any first effort. The Peace Force is also approaching the global movement-building objective in a different way than previous accompaniment initiatives: they have created a modified coalition structure – an organisational membership model through which dozens of organisations around the world from both northern and southern countries can 'join' their organisation. Member organisations are expected to offer political support, recruitment and resources, and can participate in Peace Force decision-making processes.

The 'Christian Peacemaker Teams' (CPT), a United States-based project of the Mennonite, Brethren and Quaker churches, has had a long-term presence of volunteers in Hebron, Palestine since the mid-1990s.[8] Volunteers do school accompaniment, they document the human rights situation and they carry out non-violence trainings. They make regular visits to Palestinian families involved in the 'Campaign for Secure Dwellings', and offer solidarity to victims of home demolitions. CPT joins with Palestinians and Israeli peace groups to develop action campaigns that expose the human reality of the Israeli occupation. CPT's accompaniment is spiritually-based and also involves creating inter-religious solidarity among Christians, Muslims and Jews.

The 'Ecumenical Accompaniment Project in Palestine and Israel' (EAPPI) is a project of the Geneva-based World Council of Churches, hosted by Christian and Orthodox Palestinian churches. EAPPI is part of broader program of solidarity and global advocacy of the World Council focused on the objective of ending the occupation. Since starting in August 2002, EAPPI has sent over 60 accompaniers from 30 churches in eight countries.

Discussion: Factors Affecting the Protection Function

Accompaniment cannot protect a targeted person in all situations. There are certain prerequisites and conditions that affect the potential protective impact. First of all, there must be *a clear source of threat*. You cannot strategise or leverage pressure on decision-makers behind abuses unless you know who to target. And this is not always so simple. Threats are often anonymous. Conflict dynamics can be complex, with more than two or three violent parties. An organisation or activist may have enemies in more than one place. There is often a tendency to oversimplify

---

[8]   CPT also managed a long-term project in Haiti, starting in 1993, and currently sustains presences in Colombia and Iraq as well. They have also implemented shorter-term projects and delegations in Chechnya and other conflicts.

conflicts, assuming that one party is always the bad guy, and anonymous threats can be too easily attributed to the party that appears to be most likely. Alternatively, there are cases where people operating within highly charged political situations might nevertheless be receiving threats that are not explicitly politically motivated. Communities sometimes have long-standing conflicts, which even precede the wars around them. An accompaniment organisation needs to have a highly developed capacity for conflict analysis, and a trustworthy network of advisors who know the history of the conflicts around them and can help parse out the sources of threats.

It is possible, of course, to choose to operate in situations where you cannot get enough information about the threats. An organisation might take a calculated risk, and 'hope' that whoever is responsible will be less likely to attack in the presence of witnesses. This does certainly happen, in part because it is both psychologically and politically extremely difficult to say 'no' to a person or group in need. Under such circumstances, though, an organisation should have clear criteria about security risks and uncertainty levels. It is also essential to be transparent with the groups being accompanied: if you are going in only on hope and commitment with high uncertainty about the sources of the threats, this should temper claims of protection.

Assuming, however, that you can identify the source with a reasonable level of certainty, you next need to be sure that the leadership making decisions about these threats or abuses has some sensitivity to international pressure, and you need to try to gauge *how much*. There is almost always *some* sensitivity, and there is never *total* sensitivity. Even the most vicious and apparently autonomous armed actor in today's world is dependent on some kind of external support or alliance, be it political, military or economic. And the most apparently sensitive government in the world can have enemies it is willing to suffer serious political costs to remove. Gauging this sensitivity requires not only a good domestic analysis of the conflict, but also a capacity for analysing trans-national linkages and external points of leverage.

If you identify a source of threat, and sensitivity to pressure, the next questions are: *Does your accompaniment organisation have the capacity to leverage such pressure? And can you be sure that the abusing party knows that you can do it?* This is where having a strong network of high-level contacts on both an international and national level is quite crucial. Having contacts and allies in governments internationally gives an accompaniment organisation the capacity to create pressure on a high level. Having contacts (even unfriendly ones) inside the government and military on the ground ensures that they know that your organisation has this leverage. By extension, the protection of accompaniment is increased the more the organisation is able to make its presence and function known all the way down the chain of command from decision-maker to perpetrator.

Factors Affecting the Encouragement Function

No activist or group is going to want accompaniment unless they are already committed to risk some level of public organising. If they have made that choice, then in order for them to benefit from the potential confidence boost of accompaniment, they need to understand fully how accompaniment works. It is vital that those who are accompanied recognise the power of accompaniment to protect them, but that they *do not overestimate it!* The encouraging impact of accompaniment must be realistic – if not it can provoke excessive risk-taking and backfire.

An accompaniment organisation also needs to take cultural or social factors into account. There may be taboos or social costs associated with proximity to foreigners in certain situations. There may be situations where the gender of the volunteer or the accompanied person is a relevant factor as to whether the accompaniment will create a situation of trust or one of discomfort. Accompaniment volunteers need a high degree of cultural sensitivity.

Trust is the magic word in situations of conflict and insecurity. Threatened groups function with high levels of fear and suspicion. They may be facing governments who infiltrate and spy on them. Suspicion is a rational consequence of war and repression. Your local partners must not only *want* the accompaniment, they need to believe that your organisation and the individuals in it are trustworthy. Gaining people's trust often first happens through a step-by-step process of word-of-mouth contact: individuals and groups are more willing to start trusting you if they know that someone else they trust also trusts you. So it is quite important to move slowly and make contacts with organisations through contacts with whom you already have good relationships.

Accompaniment volunteers have to sustain that trust by showing a high degree of self-discipline, sensitivity and humility. Loose lips sink ships, as the saying goes. An accompaniment organisation with volunteers who are nosy, rash, unable to maintain in confidence what they overhear or are too intrusive into the lives or politics of those they accompany, will not be trusted. And *if you are not sufficiently trusted, there is no encouraging impact.* On the contrary, mistrust causes a heightened sense of insecurity.

Intensive accompaniment is personally and socially stressful for threatened people. It is an intrusion in their lives. Accompaniment volunteers should not expect close friendships with those they accompany. They should not expect to be included in their social or political life. It may happen. But such inclusion may also be a serious burden to the accompanied activist, adding stress and diminishing the empowering impact of the presence.

Factors Affecting the Objective of Building the Movement

The strength of an organisation's global network is a direct factor in the level of protection and solidarity it can offer, and an accompaniment organisation needs to make choices with a long-term perspective of strengthening that network.

However, the multiple objectives of accompaniment can make these choices difficult. Consider for instance the selection of volunteers. One set of criteria might maximise the service that can be provided 'on the ground': things like self-discipline over curiosity and risk-taking; patience, humility, capacity to go with the flow of the decisions of those you accompany, high level of political analysis, a smooth capacity to work in a team under stress. When you look at what might maximise the 'movement-building' objective for volunteers upon their return, there are additional criteria: initiative to do local organising, outgoing capacity to publicise the work, public speaking, media skills, fundraising skills, etc. If you are lucky, you find a match for all these criteria in each volunteer. But the practical reality is that every organisation faces a limited recruitment pool and must make hard choices. If you do not pay enough attention to 'on the ground' skills, costly and dangerous mistakes may be made that will affect people's immediate safety as well as the longer-term reputation of the organisation. And if you do not pay enough attention to recruiting and developing movement-building skills, your organisation will lose crucial opportunities to grow and strengthen its international protective network of support.

Another dilemma has to do with the relationship between the scale of a presence – the number of volunteers – and the selection criteria. There is always a desire to provide a high quality service, by setting the strictest possible selection criteria for field workers/volunteers. But the impact on building a global movement is increased if there are more field staff passing through a project and returning home to share their experience and participate in movement-building and advocacy. Similarly, the same quality-of-service pressure tends to encourage longer stays in the field by volunteers. Longer stays take advantage of accumulated experience, and offer our clients greater comfort and familiarity with the volunteers. But with shorter stays, more field volunteers would be returning home to do advocacy and movement-building. If a project sustains 20 people on the ground, the number of volunteers returning home to do movement-building is inversely proportional to the length of stay. Some organisations have chosen to address this dilemma by having long-term teams while also allowing for the possibility of much shorter volunteer stays (of a few months or less), or by organising a programme of 'delegations' whereby many people can spend short stays of two or three weeks in the field, gaining a brief experience that can still provide an important resource for building grassroots support when they return home.

The reason this kind of work has such powerful movement-building potential is because the field experience changes people's lives, and it is very inspiring to hear about it. People with significant accompaniment experience are 'experts', but also personal models that others admire. They have a lot to offer.

Large-scale Institution 'Presence as Protection'

What PBI's work has demonstrated is that the very fact of being present can have protective power if used correctly. Some successful human rights monitoring operations in United Nations peace missions have shown this on a larger scale. Larger scale efforts might go beyond protection of individuals or groups and actually have a pacifying impact on the dynamics of a conflict. The Office of the United Nations High

Commissioner for Human Rights has overseen large-scale monitoring operations, although it may have much greater potential for such work. Other intergovernmental bodies, such as the Organization for Security and Co-operation in Europe (in Bosnia and Kosovo)[9] or the Organization of American States (in Haiti) have also implemented large unarmed presences. In addition, *ad hoc* intergovernmental coalitions have set up large monitoring presences, for example in Sri Lanka (Sri Lanka Monitoring Mission), Palestine (Temporary International Presence in Hebron) and the Joint Monitoring Mission in the Nuba Mountains, Sudan.[10]

The Geneva-based Centre for Humanitarian Dialogue has recently completed a systematic research project on these experiences, resulting in a manual *Proactive Presence: Field strategies for civilian protection*, which forms part of a longer-term advocacy programme to persuade major international government organisations to significantly increase their projection of unarmed monitoring operations into conflict zones as a means of protecting civilians.[11]

'Presence as Protection' Within Other Kinds of Field Missions

It is also possible to integrate the protective and encouragement functions of accompaniment into other kinds of organisational work in conflict zones. Humanitarian relief operations, international medical organisations, educational workers or any number of intergovernmental agencies, and religious workers or missionaries are all present in zones of conflict. Their primary mission may not be 'protection' but very often their mandate might *allow* for a protection function, or they may find themselves forced into security situations in which protection of local people is their paramount challenge.

Many other groups can also provide protection by their presence, even while carrying out other tasks. But the impact of such a presence, both in terms of protection and encouragement, can be amplified if these organisations take conscious steps to do so.

For instance, a relief or development operation may have a certain sector of the population it serves. Threatened civil society groups may not be their direct partners, yet they will often be in close proximity to such groups. If such international groups make the effort to stay aware of the political threats facing different groups around them, they can go out of their way to make contact now and then with these threatened groups and individuals, offering what solidarity they can. They can pass information

---

9   See chapter 18 by S. Ringgaard-Pedersen and A. Lyth in the present volume.

10   For more background on this idea, see L. Mahony, 'Unarmed Monitoring and Human Rights Field Presences: Civilian Protection and Conflict Protection', *The Journal of Humanitarian Assistance* (2003), http://www.jha.ac/articles/a122.htm.

11   See L. Mahony, *Proactive Presence: Field strategies for civilian protection* (Geneva: Centre for Humanitarian Dialogue, 2006). Copies are available from the Centre for Humanitarian Dialogue, and a PDF version of the manual is available and can be found at http://www.hdcentre.org.

to the outside world about these situations of danger and put local groups in contact with potential supporters outside the conflict.

Most international operations in a conflict zone also have some level of contact with authorities, the military or other armed groups. Often this contact is for the purpose of securing access or passage. At other times such contact is unplanned, such as at roadblocks and the like. In any case, all international staff of groups working in conflict zones could benefit from some training in political sensitivity and diplomacy in order to make the most of such contacts with potentially abusive parties. Those who commit human rights abuses need to be reminded frequently that the international community is paying attention to their behaviour. Such reminders can be polite, they can be indirect, they can come in many forms. Every organisation talking to a local commander or thug has the opportunity not only to get agreement to get their particular resources through to their projects, but also to send other more subtle messages that will sustain awareness on the part of the abusers that these international groups are also concerned about *all* the civilians around them, and not merely their direct partners.

If more international organisations working in conflict zones added the objective of civilian protection to their mandates, other opportunities would arise for maximising the protective impact of their presence. There are often people in organisations on the ground who want to take more deliberate steps to respond to political threats against civilians around them, but feel that their institutional mandate prevents them from doing anything so 'political'. The more these institutions embrace the uncertainty and risk of working in conflict zones, and the moral necessity of a protection commitment, the more such committed staff will be enabled to take useful steps to help local groups in peril – including groups who may not be their direct partners.

Accompaniment groups and others who already have experience trying to implement a protection mandate may be able to offer training to help other groups' personnel develop the necessary habits and discourse to maximise the protective impact of their important presence on the ground.

Conclusion

New conflicts continue to erupt, and new requests for accompaniment arise all over the world. But despite the rapid growth of the human rights movement in recent decades, most new accompaniment requests go unanswered. The international community has thus far been unable to marshal effectively the necessary resources and commitment to meet the needs.

Accompaniment extends the boundaries of the 'international community' beyond governments, beyond the United Nations, beyond the established humanitarian agencies. Accompaniment has helped connect grassroots efforts for justice and human rights around the world with these larger international structures. The volunteers are a living bridge between threatened local activists and the outside world, and also between their own home communities and the reality of the global struggle for peace and human rights.

These links may help to overcome the seemingly impossible challenge of human rights protection. In the final analysis, the international community's response to human rights abuse is not a question of resources but one of hope and empowerment.

Accompaniment volunteers experience a rare privilege of standing at the side of some of the world's most courageous and committed activists. This courage injects immeasurable energy into the international community's efforts.

A request for human rights protection should never fall on deaf ears. The international community needs to redefine what is possible. We can take the lead from these threatened activists who are asking for support. They do the impossible every day.[12]

---

[12] See further: Peace Brigades International: http://www.peacebrigades.org. Addresses for each national chapter also can be found on this website; Christian Peacemaker Teams: http://www.cpt.org; Ecumenical Accompaniment Project in Palestine and Israel: http://www.eappi.org; Guatemala Accompaniment Project: http://www.nisgua.org; Nonviolent Peace Force: http://www.nonviolentpeaceforce.org; Training for Change: http://www.trainingforchange.org.

Chapter 14

Case Study: The United Nations Human Rights Field Operation in East Timor

Patrick Burgess

Introduction

Background

Following the 'Carnation Revolution' in 1974 the Portuguese government decided to release all its colonial holdings, including East Timor. Political parties hastily formed in East Timor, and related competition led to instability, which quickly escalated to a civil war involving serious violations committed by all sides. Ten days after the Fretilin party declared victory and independence, the Indonesian military forces mounted a full-scale invasion of the territory, on 10 December 1975. The 24 year military occupation which followed was characterised by the local population's continued resistance and claims to independence, and gross human rights violations, the majority of which were committed by members of the Indonesian security forces, who targeted those who were affiliated with the independence movement. It is estimated that between 120,000 and 200,000 East Timorese died as a result of the conflict.[1]

In 1998, student reaction to military violence in Jakarta led to the overthrow of the Soeharto military dictatorship. On 27 January 1999, interim-President Habibie, declared that the ongoing debate over East Timor should be settled by giving the local population an opportunity to vote for independence or to remain part of Indonesia in a United Nations-run ballot. The preparation and conduct of the ballot, between May and September 1999, was marked by violations committed by members of the Indonesian security forces and the East Timorese militia groups which they had created and controlled, targeting pro-independence supporters in order to intimidate them to vote to remain part of Indonesia.[2] On 4 September 1999, 78.5% of East Timorese voters chose the independence option. The result was followed by three weeks of massive payback destruction and violence by Indonesian forces

---

[1] *Report of the East Timor Commission for Reception, Truth and Reconciliation* (CAVR Report, 31 October 2005), 'Part 1: Introduction', available at http://www.ictj.org/cavr.report. asp.

[2] *Ibid.*, 'Part 8: Accountability and Responsibility'.

and Timorese pro-Jakarta militias. More than 60,000 houses were burned, 75% of infrastructure destroyed, almost all movable property, motor vehicles etc, looted and transported over the border into Indonesia. An estimated 1,500 civilians were killed, 500,000 East Timorese were displaced, and there was widespread commission of rape, assault and other violations.[3]

During this period, the Indonesian government refused to allow international peacekeepers to intervene. Finally, following the direct intervention by United States President Bill Clinton, Jakarta requested international assistance. The International Force for East Timor (INTERFET), led by Australia, was quickly deployed. Following their arrival on 20 September 1999, the Indonesian security forces and East Timorese militia groups who had been responsible for the violations quickly evacuated over the border into Indonesian West Timor.[4]

The Establishment of United Nations Transitional Administration in East Timor

United Nations (UN) Security Council resolution 1272 (1999) established the United Nations Transitional Administration in East Timor (UNTAET) on 25 October 1999, giving it a mandate to 'exercise all legislative and executive authority, including the administration of justice'. The mandate included the power to provide security and maintain law and order, ensure the delivery of humanitarian and development assistance, establish an effective administration, support capacity building in preparation for self-government, and assist in establishing the necessary conditions for sustainable development.[5]

The mission was authorised to include up to 8,950 peacekeeping troops, 1,640 civilian police (CIVPOL) and an unspecified number of other international staff. It was to be organised under three 'pillars': humanitarian, military and governance/ public administration. Two deputy special representatives would be responsible for the humanitarian and governance/public administration pillars, with the special representative of the secretary-general and transitional administrator (SRSG) having ultimate authority over all matters within the territory. Within the Office of the Special Representative of the Secretary-General and Transitional Administrator

---

3   See *Report of the International Commission of Inquiry on East Timor to the Secretary-General*, UN Doc. A/54/726, S/2000/59 (2000), at 121–141 and Indonesian Commission of Investigation into Human Rights Violations (KPP-HAM), Report on the Investigation of Human Rights Violations in East Timor (January 2000), chapter 3, available at http://www. jsmp.minihub.org/Reports/KPP%20Ham.htm.

4   See *CAVR Report*, 'Part 8: Accountability and Responsibility' and I. Martin, *Self-Determination in East Timor: The United Nations, the Ballot, and International Intervention*, International Peace Academy Occasional Papers (Boulder: Lynne Reinner, 2001), J. G. Taylor, *East Timor: The Price of Freedom* (London: Zed Press, 2000).

5   Security Council resolution 1272 (1999), UN Doc. S/RES/1272 (1999). See also A. Devereux, 'Searching for Clarity: A Case Study of UNTAET's Application of International Human Rights Norms', in N. D. White and D. Klaasen (eds), *The UN, Human Rights and Post-conflict Situations* (Manchester: Manchester University Press, 2005), pp. 293–321.

there were advisors on political, constitutional, legal, human rights and electoral affairs, and public information.[6]

Sowing Seeds of Future Problems: Lack of Sufficient Planning

Owing to the unexpected levels of violence and destruction surrounding the ballot there was little opportunity for the UN Mission in East Timor (UNAMET) mission to undertake a thorough planning process for the mission that would follow it. The planning for UNTAET began late, and took place in New York, far from the sources of local knowledge in East Timor, and with little consultation with local actors.

The plans for UNTAET included a Human Rights Unit (HRU) of the SRSG's office, which comprised only a small team of human rights field officers whose role focused mainly on training. In addition, district administrators were to lead governance teams, including a human rights field officer, in each of the 13 districts of East Timor, but the nature of their work and their reporting lines were unclear.[7]

The Legal, Judicial Affairs and Constitutional Affairs sections, and the later-established Serious Crimes Unit and Office of the General Prosecutor were all divisions within UNTAET whose mandates and responsibilities overlapped with that of the HRU. In addition the Office of the United Nations High Commissioner for Refugees (UNHCR), the United Nations Children's Fund (UNICEF) and other agencies were programming in rights-related areas. Many of the early difficulties which the HRU faced were directly related to inadequate planning and the lack of a clear understanding of what the unit's work should be and how its responsibilities interacted with those of other sections of the mission.

UNTAET Human Rights Unit

Recruitment of Staff

As UNTAET followed closely on the Bosnia and Kosovo missions, the personnel section of the UN Department of Peacekeeping Operations (DPKO) struggled to recruit and deploy thousands of 'experts' who could assist with the transition to an independent government. Many of those who were hurriedly recruited had few qualifications or experiences that were directly relevant to their positions.

The leadership of the East Timorese resistance, civil society representatives and local leaders initially held high hopes for the assistance the UN would provide. However, their experiences with inexperienced staff quickly led to frustration and

---

[6]   See Security Council resolution 1272 (1999), UN Doc. S/RES/1272 (1999); and Report of the Secretary-General on the Situation in East Timor, UN Doc. S/1999/1024 (1999), at 25.

[7]   Report of the Secretary-General on the Situation in East Timor, (1999), at 25.

dissatisfaction.[8] The ability of only a small percentage of UN workers to communicate with the local population and scarcity of interpreters compounded this problem.

The fact that East Timor had been a major international human rights issue for 24 years meant that there was a group of human rights activists who had a deep understanding of the complex issues, had developed relationships with former members of the resistance and local non-governmental organisations (NGOs), and could speak the language. Gradually, a number of these individuals were recruited to work in the HRU. Some were also recruited to work in other sections, particularly Political Affairs. The deeper experience and understanding of local issues, credibility and contact with local actors made a significant contribution to the general work of the mission. However, it was also to complicate the relationships with other sections, whose policies and decisions had not been based on close consultation with local actors.

Getting Started

At the time of the arrival of the first director of the HRU in late November 1999, the unit consisted only of three members, one of whom was an investigator on a short-term consultancy. During the first months it worked from a small office near that of the SRSG. However, as the unit became more involved in forensic investigations it moved to a building on the edge of Dili that had sufficient space for a morgue and freezer for recovered bodies. Although this facilitated independence and removed the unit from much of the distraction of mission politics it also served to separate the HRU from other sections that limited its effectiveness. With hindsight, a better choice would have been to maintain its physical presence close to that of other substantive sections, in order to facilitate the flow of information, encourage networking and increase the level of human rights input in policy deliberations.

The 1999 violence had destroyed the entire commercial sector in East Timor. All equipment, vehicles, furniture and even food had to be sourced elsewhere and transported into the territory by air and sea. As initial equipment, vehicles, furniture etc, became available it tended to be retained by sections of the mission that were themselves involved in the supply line or close to it. It was extremely difficult for the HRU to obtain the resources necessary to work effectively. In particular, vehicles were unavailable for field work, and computers and printers, when available, had to be shared. The physical separation of the unit from the rest of the mission contributed to this problem, as did the fact that the administrative staff in charge of resources had little understanding of what a human rights section did and its relative importance to the mission.

---

[8]   See the East Timor section of International Policy Institute, *A Case for Change: A Review of Peace Operations* (King's College London, 2003).

Investigation of Past Crimes

The INTERFET international peacekeeping force, led by Australia, was deployed from nearby Darwin to East Timor on 20 September 1999, immediately following the agreement of the government of Indonesia to the intervention of peacekeepers. INTERFET forces arrested and detained a number of East Timorese militia members in the days after their arrival, the remainder quickly fled over the border into Indonesian West Timor. They also took statements from witnesses and began to gather some forensic evidence relating to crimes committed.

The HRU also began to undertake some investigations into past crimes. This included enlisting the assistance of forensic experts and being involved in the exhumation of bodies and their subsequent forensic examination.

By this time CIVPOL had begun to be deployed in East Timor. However, few of these officers had any knowledge of the events in East Timor and, with interpreters in drastically short supply, had limited means of communicating with witnesses. Investigations by CIVPOL in relation to past crimes was slow to commence and were, in their early stages, significantly less professional than those conducted by the Australian military investigators of INTERFET.[9]

Local actors were, justifiably, anxious that a slow start by the UN investigations would diminish the likelihood of successful prosecutions due to deterioration of available physical evidence and reduce the ability of witnesses to accurately recall events. Representatives of various local and international NGOs were increasingly moving around the country, interviewing victims and witnesses, in a relatively *ad hoc* and un-coordinated manner.

Owing to a lack of coordination, victims were repeatedly interviewed by a variety of investigators from different institutions. The interviews were often conducted by individuals who, although well-motivated, had little professional training, and were recorded in a variety of independent formats that could not be easily correlated.

Ironically, multiple statements collected with the purpose of assisting prosecution not only risked re-traumatising victims but could also potentially hinder successful prosecution of offenders. According to the Indonesian criminal code, which remained in force,[10] only statements taken by police were admissible as evidence in a prosecution case produced in court. However, statements collected by non-police investigators could later be used by defence counsel in cross examination, to support an argument that multiple different accounts given by the same witness demonstrated a lack of ability to recall past events accurately. In fact, a witness may have given a similar account to all investigators, but they had each recorded it differently.

---

[9]   S. Jones, 'East Timor: The Troubled Path to Independence', in A. Henkin (ed.), *Honoring Human Rights Under International Mandates: Lessons From Bosnia, Kosovo, and East Timor* (Washington, DC: Aspen Institute, 2003).

[10]   UNTAET Regulation No. 1999/1 of November 27, 1999 provided that the pre-existing Indonesian law should continue to apply in East Timor except where it was inconsistent with international human rights principles or was amended by UNTAET Regulation.

Although inadmissible in court, the witness accounts gathered by civil society investigators could have provided an extremely useful information base for police investigators. The statements taken, if coordinated and accurately recorded, could have indicated to police investigators which witnesses should be re-interviewed and which did not need to be approached again. Unfortunately, because of a lack of coordination and an inability of the CIVPOL investigators to communicate with local civil society actors, the vast majority of victim and witness accounts collected in the aftermath of the violence were not used in any way in the subsequent investigation and prosecutions.

The Serious Crimes Investigation Unit

The investigation and prosecution of those responsible for mass violations committed in East Timor should have been a relatively straightforward process, at least in relation to those perpetrators who remained in the jurisdiction. Unlike many other transitional contexts, the government actors and security forces personnel responsible for planning and executing the systematic violence were no longer present. Thousands of eyewitnesses were available and willing to give evidence, with little to fear from any retribution for doing so. There were no significant elements within the investigating or prosecuting authorities that were compromised or struggling with mixed motivations in relation to their work or goals. The UN held total control over all aspects of the government, police and prosecutorial authorities.

Despite this favourable context for prosecutions, managerial incompetence and rivalries between different sections of the UNTAET mission severely reduced the effectiveness of the investigative process during the initial two years of the mission.

In March 2000, the Special Representative of the Secretary-General and Transitional Administrator, the late Sergio Viera de Mello, issued a written directive that the 'majority' of CIVPOL investigators were to be transferred to a new unit, the Serious Crimes Investigations Unit (SCIU), which was to be headed up by the director of the Human Rights Unit. Despite the terms of the directive, by June not a single CIVPOL officer had been transferred to the SCIU. Senior commanders within CIVPOL made it clear that they did not agree with the directive from the SRSG, and found ways to delay its implementation.

The deadlock reached crisis level in June, when a meeting involving the HRU, Judicial Affairs and CIVPOL sections of the mission was organised to seek a solution. CIVPOL commanders stated that they were unable to supply the 'majority' of their investigators to the SCIU but agreed to provide 23 investigators. Although this was far from satisfactory, and fell short of the terms of the SRSG's directive, it was seen as a positive break of the deadlock. At least now the SCIU could begin its work.

However, a significant proportion of those transferred were, in fact, not investigators at all. Others were officers who were viewed as incompetent by their peers. Although the mission had supplied computers and vehicles to CIVPOL according to the number of officers, no vehicles or computers were transferred to the

SCIU with the officers, leaving them practically unable to undertake investigations. Meanwhile evidence deteriorated and the frustration of East Timorese counterparts over the lack of progress increased. Despite these difficulties the SCIU scrambled for resources, a small number of dedicated officers joined the unit and it was able to commence its work.

On 6 June 2000, a new Office of the General Prosecutor was established.[11] The SCIU was transferred from the HRU to this section, as it was logical that both investigations and prosecutions were closely coordinated. Although at this time the director of the HRU agreed to the logic of the transfer, subsequent events raised the question of whether it would have been more effective to maintain the Office under the direction of the HRU.

In the remainder of 2000 and throughout 2001 the Serious Crimes Unit (SCU), as it was now called, was the subject of a continuous series of highly-publicised complaints and scandals. A steady stream of experienced prosecutors and investigators resigned, citing nepotism and a serious lack of professionalism and management skills by those who were directing the unit. After several reports in the international media, an independent expert was hired to undertake an assessment of the SCU, producing a report that was highly critical of the unit's management.[12]

The problems persisted until, eventually, the deputy prosecutor general and the chief of the SCU left the mission and were replaced. The appointment of a new, highly professional deputy prosecutor general in 2001 began the transformation of the section into an effective operation. For the first time since the unit's inception two years previously, cases were managed effectively and the number of indictments issued increased significantly.

With hindsight, the deep knowledge of the history of the human rights violations, contacts and credibility with local actors, and capacity to speak local languages, which was available to the HRU, could have made a significant contribution to the investigation of past crimes. An arrangement should have been pursued whereby the HRU continued to play an important role alongside the investigators and prosecutors of the Serious Crimes Unit.

The Serious Crimes Unit and the Special Panels of the Dili District Court were mandated to investigate and try 'serious crimes' until June 2005. At the completion of the mandate, 87 accused persons had been tried. However, those who were subject to this process were all 'smaller fish' – East Timorese members of militia groups. Those responsible for the planning and implementation of the coordinated programme of mass violations remained out of reach of the East Timorese courts, over the border in Indonesia. In total, over 300 indictments were issued by the Special Panels, the vast majority involved individuals who are believed to be in Indonesian West Timor.

---

[11] On the Organization of the Public Prosecution Service in East Timor, UNTAET/REG/2000/16 of 6 June 2000.

[12] Unpublished report of consultant M. Fisk on file with present author.

The Accountability Process in Indonesia

In late 1999 investigations by the Indonesian Human Rights Commission, the UN International Commission of Inquiry into the East Timor (ICIET) violations and a combined investigation of a number of special rapporteurs concluded that the Indonesian military had been primarily responsible for the violations.[13] The ICIET recommended the establishment of an *ad hoc* international criminal tribunal, similar to those established to deal with violations in the former Yugoslavia and Rwanda. However, following strong commitments to bring those responsible to account by the Indonesian government it was decided that Indonesia should first be given the chance to prosecute those within its jurisdiction, whilst the Serious Crimes process in East Timor would target those accused who were physically within the territory.[14]

An *ad hoc* tribunal was established within the Indonesian court system, with a mandate to try those responsible for crimes against humanity committed in four of the 13 districts of East Timor in April and September 1999.[15] This limited temporal and geographical mandate restricted the ability to prosecute for the coordinated programme of violence, which took place across the entire territory between January and October 1999. In January 2002, 18 individuals, including a number of senior military officers, the former chief of police and the former governor, were indicted on charges of crimes against humanity, and trials began in March 2002. The ensuing process has been widely referred to as a 'farce' in which indictments were poorly drafted, insufficient evidence to convict was produced by the prosecution, and the courtrooms were filled with armed and uniformed military personnel.[16] At the time of writing, the only one of the 18 persons indicted who had not been acquitted was Eurico Gutteres, an East Timorese militia leader who remained free, on bail, whilst awaiting an appeal against his conviction for crimes against humanity.

The HRU closely monitored this process, advising both the United Nations Office of the High Commissioner for Human Rights (OHCHR) and the SRSG on developments, and attending high-level meetings in Dili and Jakarta. In addition,

---

[13]   KPP-Ham, *Report on the Investigation of Human Rights Violations in East Timor*; Report of the International Commission of Inquiry on East Timor to the Secretary-General and Report on the Joint Mission to East Timor Undertaken by the Special Rapporteur of the Commission on Human Rights on Extrajudicial, Summary or Arbitrary Executions, the Special Rapporteur of the Commission on the Question of Torture and the Special Rapporteur of the Commission on Violence against Women, Its Causes and Consequences, UN Doc. A/54/660 (1999).

[14]   Letter dated 26 January 2000 from the Minister for Foreign Affairs to the Secretary-General, UN Doc A/54/727, S/2000/65, (2000); Resolution adopted by the UN Human Rights Commission Special Session on East Timor, UN Doc. E/CN.4/S-4/L.1/Rev.1 (1999), at 5–6.

[15]   The *ad hoc* tribunal was established under Indonesian Law No. 26/2000.

[16]   See D. Cohen *Intended to Fail: The Trials before the Ad Hoc Human Rights Court in Jakarta* (August 2003); International Center for Transitional Justice, *Justice for Timor Leste: The Way Forward* (14 April 2004); and Amnesty International and Judicial System Monitoring Programme, *Justice for Timor-Leste: The Way Forward* (AI Index: ASA 21/006/2004).

officers of the HRU accompanied East Timorese witnesses who gave evidence in the Jakarta court, although it had been promised there was no effective system of protection for these victims and witnesses. They were abused and threatened by members of the Indonesian military and former East Timorese militia both inside and outside the court, until eventually no further witnesses agreed to participate. Following this, a small number of witnesses gave evidence from East Timor through video-link. This too was discontinued, although if there was sufficient will for witnesses to give evidence it could have provided a solution to the difficulties surrounding East Timorese witnesses providing evidence in Jakarta.

On 6 April 2000, a memorandum of understanding (MOU) was signed by the Indonesian attorney general and the SRSG of UNTAET. The terms of the MOU included an agreement to share evidence and for both parties to 'transfer to each other all persons whom the competent authorities of the requesting Party are prosecuting for a criminal offence or whom these parties want for the purposes of serving a sentence'.[17]

In accordance with the document, the SCU prepared evidence and witnesses in the five major cases that were being investigated by the Indonesian attorney general's office. In July–August 2000, an Indonesian team arrived in Dili, where it proceeded to examine the witnesses and evidence prepared by the SCU over a three week intensive programme. Later, the government of Indonesia was to distance itself from the MOU, declaring the attorney general had no right to sign it without the prior agreement of parliament, and on this basis refused to provide information or witness statements to the UNTAET investigators.

Expansion of the Role of the HRU

During the early stages of the mission some critics believed that the HRU was placing too much emphasis on past violations rather than dealing with current issues. The transfer of responsibility for dealing with past crimes allowed the HRU to expand and broaden the scope of its work. Through a participatory workshop involving all members of the unit it developed a strategic plan that was based on the work of four teams: legal, monitoring, training and reconciliation. After significant advocacy and participation in the mission's budget process, the number of staff of the unit was expanded to approximately 60 – including some unfilled posts 'borrowed' from other sections allocated budgets – half of whom were internationals.

Delays in Recruitment

The recruitment of additional personnel brought into focus difficulties arising from the relationship between DPKO and OHCHR in relation to the recruitment of human rights field officers for DPKO missions. An MOU between the two agencies

---

17   Memorandum of Understanding Regarding Co-Operation in Legal, Judicial and Human Rights Related Matters, signed on behalf of UNTAET and the Attorney-General of the Republic of Indonesia (6 April 2000), section 9.

stipulated that the director of DPKO field mission human rights sections should be approved by OHCHR and that there should be 'consultation' on the recruitment of other staff.

The meaning of 'consultation' in the MOU was interpreted to mean that all UNTAET human rights field officer recruits must be first approved by OHCHR. In fact all of the names proposed by the HRU in Dili were eventually approved by Geneva, but the approval mechanism added an average of between three to five months to their recruitment, leaving their positions unfilled in the interim. These bureaucratic delays directly resulted in a major reduction in the ability of the HRU to deliver human rights services.

The Importance of Adding Value

The reputation and status of the HRU, in the eyes of other sections of the mission was extremely important in the context of UNTAET work. Other units, such as the Political, Constitutional, Judicial Affairs, Electoral and Legal Affairs sections, included lawyers with some degree of expertise in human rights issues, and some who considered themselves to be human rights experts. All sections of the mission faced an overload of work and were seeking streamlined means to achieve their goals. The inclusion of the HRU in issues involving other sections could not be forced due to an obligation to consult or be included.

The HRU could only significantly contribute to the policies of the mission if it could add value to the expertise that was available to other sections. Some of the staff who were initially deployed to serve in the HRU did not perform well, which negatively affected the status of the section within the mission. It seems that their recruitment had been based on having served in previous missions, irrespective of the quality of their performance in those previous positions. The new wave of recruitment of human rights field officers, many of whom had local languages and specifically relevant experience, quickly served to remedy this problem. In addition, a policy was accepted that all district officers who did not have a local language should, on arrival, begin an intensive course of study in the Tetum, with a stated expectation that they would be fluent in that language when the time came to recommend extensions of their contracts after six months.

The balancing act between the need to be included to be effective and the duty to fearlessly report violations was extremely challenging. In some situations, months of painstaking bridge-building was quickly lost by over-zealous activism of members of the HRU who were former staff members of international NGOs, unaccustomed to working within UN or government structures. Although well-motivated, they sometimes tended to be disproportionately negative and critical of activities and policies of the mission. On the other hand, there was a tendency of some officers with lengthy UN experience to be overly accepting of the failures and limitations of the mission and its personnel. The HRU included a balance of 'new faces' and veterans of other missions. Despite some difficulties, in general the energy and idealism of the new recruits helped to limit a tendency to complacency of some of the UN veterans. The veterans, on the other hand, contributed a higher degree of pragmatism, and a recognition of the importance of working in partnership with other parts of the mission in order to be effective. An important lesson learned is the need to recognise the different qualities brought through differing backgrounds and the need to maintain a successful balance of enthusiasm, energy and experience.

Capacity building was considered to be the major determinant in recruiting national staff for the unit. Unlike other sections, the HRU made a specific policy decision not to recruit national staff who had significant human rights experience through previous work experience with local NGOs. Although recruiting experienced staff would have made the work of the HRU easier it would have drained the capacity of the local civil society actors, rather than assist them. Instead, inexperienced personnel were hired, and an intensive training programme was provided for them. This policy proved to be very successful, and on the later downsizing of the office national staff who had completed the training programmes were quickly hired by government departments, NGOs and international agencies.

District Human Rights Officers

One international human rights field officer, paired with a national staff member, was deployed into each of the 13 districts. As part of the district teams they reported to both the district administrator and the director of the HRU, which created some confusion and at times conflict. Reports of district human rights officers (DHROs) were, on some occasions, edited and censored by district administrators. District teams often did not include a full complement of staff and some human rights field officers were asked to undertake other duties, either instead of, or in addition to, those relating to human rights. As the mission progressed, a number of the DHROs were placed into vacant positions as acting district administrators, or their deputies, despite the fact that these positions were significantly more senior. Although the local language skills and competence of the DHROs enabled them to generally fill the more senior roles successfully, the focus of their work shifted away from human rights to more general concerns, and it was not possible for the HRU to recruit new officers to replace them in the interim, despite the fact that the acting positions sometimes continued for many months.

The HRU's strategic plan set out a number of 'core' goals and activities that each DHRO was expected to undertake. These included monitoring and producing regular reports, protection of vulnerable returnees, training local human rights trainers, establishing a small local human rights organisation focused around these trainers in each district, and writing a narrative summary of the 1999 violence, with attached lists of victims and reported perpetrators, as available from pre-existing sources. In addition to these 'core' activities, each DHRO could propose other 'elective' activities relevant to particular districts. These included support for human rights education, survivor's groups, reconciliation initiatives and human rights promotion through local sporting or cultural events around human rights themes.

The 1999 DHRO reports provided the only systematic survey of the 1999 events across all districts, including the death toll, based on case files of approximately 1,400 victims. The reports were provided to an OHCHR-supported consultant,

Geoffrey Robinson, who used the information and other available data to produce a 300-page report on crimes against humanity committed in 1999.[18] OHCHR did not release the report to the public, but provided it as a submission of OHCHR to the East Timor Commission for Reception, Truth and Reconciliation.

The small district-based human rights resource centres established by DHROs proved to be popular and useful during the first one to two years of operation. However, as donor funding became more difficult to secure for ongoing operations they began to gradually experience difficulties. By the end of 2002 only a few remained productive, and by 2004 all had closed. Despite the failure of the goal to maintain these small centres permanently, the programme served to provide a human rights focus across the entire territory and to provide local expertise where little had previously existed. In many cases the individuals trained by the HRU took up other district-based positions in which they were able to use the knowledge gained.

Protection

The East Timorese political leadership clearly wanted all of the estimated 250,000 refugees in Indonesian West Timor to return to East Timor as soon as possible, regardless of their past political affiliation or participation on crimes. Returnees were delivered to the border by representatives of UNHCR and the International Organization for Migration and, after a short time in transit facilities, transported to their villages. A small proportion of these returnees had been involved directly in the violence of 1999. At that time, backed by the strong Indonesian military presence, they had attacked members of their own communities. Returning without their protectors brought a significant likelihood that they would be 'paid back' for these actions.

The HRU believed that the protection of particularly vulnerable returnees was of critical importance, as a few cases of payback could easily escalate into a situation of widespread community violence and renewed divisions between factions. DHROs began a programme of identifying those at risk prior to their return, and meeting with the receiving communities to determine if it was safe for particular individuals to return, and work out ways in which at-risk returnees could safely be reintegrated. Although this work could technically have been seen as within the mandate of UNHCR, the field presence of the international and national human rights officers in each district provided a broader capacity to provide assistance. In the districts where UNHCR maintained international field officers the work was carried out jointly. This programme of protecting vulnerable returnees made a significant contribution to maintaining peace in the fragile post-conflict situation.

---

[18]   G. Robinson, *East Timor 1999 Crimes Against Humanity*, consultant's report for the OHCHR (July 2003), provided as a submission from OHCHR to the CAVR.

Legal

The role of the legal team of the HRU included monitoring and reporting on the development of the courts and judicial system, drafting and reviewing of proposed legislation concerning human rights issues, providing assistance to the development of the constitution, preparation for the ratification of core human rights treaties on independence, participating in inquiries and investigations conducted by the mission, and assisting the establishment of the East Timor Commission for Reception, Truth and Reconciliation (CAVR).

A number of these roles intersected with those of other sections of the mission. The drafting of legislation, particularly, involved a significant amount of cooperative effort and at times conflict between competing points of view. A decision had been made to maintain Indonesian laws as applicable law, except where it violated international human rights standards, or was specifically replaced by newly drafted UNTAET Regulations.[19] Problems arose because the UNTAET mission did not recruit specialist parliamentary draft-persons. Drafting laws is a highly technical skill, requiring years of training and practical experience. Despite this, UNTAET recruited lawyers to fulfil a range of general legal duties relevant to the mission, some of them relatively junior, and almost all with little or no previous experience drafting legislation. In attempting to compose laws on a range of subjects they would often refer to the examples provided by similar legislation in their own country. As the drafters were drawn from a wide range of nationalities, with both common and civil law systems, the result was an inconsistent collection of new laws, of widely varying quality. Some of the human rights lawyers who were recruited early in the mission did not have sufficient expertise to add value to this process, and their continuing insistence on being included produced some antagonism from other sections. This improved significantly when more senior, expert human rights lawyers were recruited.

On a number of occasions the legal officers of the HRU found themselves in the frustrating position of objecting to draft legislation that contained significant provisions, but which were in violation of international human rights standards or which would clearly lead to future problems. For example, draft legislation proposed the establishment of a police service and legal aid commission that were not independent from their political masters, the drafters defending this arrangement on the basis that it was similar to that in their own countries.

Treaties

With the assistance of a technical cooperation project funded by OHCHR, the HRU facilitated the preparation of necessary steps for the ratification of the core human rights treaties by the independent government of East Timor from the first days of

---

[19]   On the Authority of the Transitional Administration in East Timor, UNTAET/REG/1999/1 of 27 November 1999.

independence. Although this required a significant amount of additional work, the result guaranteed the new government's commitment to international human rights standards from its inception, before political rivalries and divisions could produce obstacles.

Elections

On 30 August 2001, national elections were held to choose representatives of the Constituent Assembly, whose task was to draft the constitution. It was decided that the representatives elected would also become the first Parliament, thereby saving the cost and effort required for two separate elections. Although this appeared to be a pragmatic solution at the time it was not without cost. In effect, the arrangement allowed those individuals elected to draft a regime of powers that they themselves would exercise as the first parliament and, in the case of the Fretilin party (whose elected members constituted a large majority of the Constituent Assembly) as the first government.

The HRU was not included in the component of the mission that would monitor the elections, and it was only after vigorous advocacy that it was agreed that they could monitor, but their work should be specifically limited to human rights violations and not include procedural irregularities, etc. The East Timorese held grave fears that the election would be marred by mass violence, as had their former experience, in 1999. However, the election was an outstanding success, with 91% of the population voluntarily participating, and no major violence or violations reported.

Following the elections, a draft report written by a HRU legal officer, in which minor irregularities were emphasised and the major overall achievements hardly considered, was poorly received by the SRSG and other sections of the mission, who felt that the HRU was taking an un-balanced position that did not appreciate the enormous effort of those involved and the excellent goal achieved. The director, who was on leave at the time, later amended the report, but once again the status of the unit and its associated level of inclusion and effectiveness were damaged.

This situation served as a reminder that human rights field work must always strive to be balanced. In field operations where the obstacles and problems are almost overwhelming, positive achievements need to be celebrated, as they nourish sagging morale. Human rights components may always measure the performance of others only against the highest international standards, but if so the measurement will, by definition, always be negative. Care needs to be taken also to include consideration of the complex reality of the context, and include appreciation, and – where warranted – celebration, of efforts which, even though they fall short of the highest international standards, exceed what might reasonably be expected to be achieved.

The Constitution

Although it was recognised by the mission that the process of drafting the East Timorese constitution could only be considered valid if it included extensive consultation with the population, no concrete steps were taken to implement such consultation until it was too late to do so effectively. In the final weeks before the drafting process began, meetings were hastily arranged in each district. However the initial draft was heavily influenced by the Fretilin political party's direction, with little recognition of comments made by community groups and individuals during the last-minute round of consultations.

The first draft fell far short of international standards on many human rights-related issues. The HRU was not formally invited to participate directly in the constitutional process, but managed to have significant input on rights-related provisions by recruiting a human rights constitutional expert and working directly with those involved in the drafting process. It did this through hosting discussion groups, producing written inputs on problematic sections and providing advice. Some other agencies also provided experts who worked around the fringes of the process to provide information to the members of the Constituent Assembly.

At the end of the drafting process, approximately 25 sections that had been identified by as problematic by the HRU had been removed or amended to include greater recognition of human rights principles. The final draft, although not perfect, was a vast improvement on the earlier one, and provided an acceptable level of recognition and protection of fundamental human rights.[20]

Justice

The development, or lack thereof, of the capacity to deliver justice in East Timor was widely considered to be the most significant failure of the mission. The HRU played only a peripheral, largely monitoring role in the justice sector, due to the existence of the Judicial Affairs section. With hindsight, the significant capacity of the HRU could have made a bigger contribution to the justice sector, if an arrangement to facilitate it had been agreed upon with the Judicial Affairs section.

Early in the life of the UNTAET mission a decision was taken to appoint only East Timorese judges, with the exception of the two Special Panels, which had jurisdiction to hear cases, including crimes against humanity, genocide and other 'international crimes' related to the violence in 1999.[21] The Special Panels (and the superior Court of Appeal) were to consist of two international judges sitting together with one East Timorese judge. All other cases, criminal or civil, were to be heard by East Timorese judges.

The decision to appoint East Timorese judges was taken largely on the advice of international staff who had served in the Kosovo mission where a similar policy had worked with relative success. However, the Kosovo and East Timor contexts were extremely different. The local lawyers appointed as judges in Kosovo included a number of highly educated and experienced practitioners, including former judges.

---

[20] See Constitution of the Democratic Republic of East Timor, Titles I, II and III, available at http://www.etan.org/etanpdf/pdf2/constfnen.pdf.

[21] On the Establishment of Panels with Exclusive Jurisdiction Over Serious Criminal Offences, UNTAET/REG/2000/15 of 6 June 2000.

In contrast there were less than a hundred East Timorese who had law degrees (almost all from Indonesian universities) and only a handful with any practical experience in the courts at all. The expectation that these well-motivated but inexperienced lawyers could quickly learn how to judge complex cases was unfounded. It quickly contributed to an unmanageable backlog of cases, overcrowded prison facilities and illegal detentions as the judges were unable to process remand hearings within the required time periods.

In theory, the UN was to hire mentors for the East Timorese judges, who would guide them through a learning process. However, the East Timorese judges expressed increasing discontent, complaining that without a common language they could not communicate, and that the mentors were not highly motivated. When a civil society group with a monitoring mandate printed the salary scale of the UN professionals the judges became even more discontent, claiming that they undertook the bulk of the work whilst the mentors received 20 times their salaries. As time passed, a number of the Timorese judges rejected the assistance of the mentors totally.

Language became a key issue in the justice sector. Eventually, the constitution would provide for two official languages, Portuguese and Tetum, and two working languages, Indonesian and English. Despite the fact that less than 10% of the population spoke Portuguese it was adopted as the language to be used in the courts. This provided serious issues concerning access to justice and the ability of judges and lawyers to work in a language they did not understand. In addition, the senior East Timorese officials in the Judicial Affairs section refused to allow the judges and lawyers to be trained in any language other than Portuguese, which resulted in wasting much of the valuable opportunity for education.

The HRU managed to conduct one of the few training programmes for judges, which was delivered in the Indonesian language. In 2001, renowned jurists from Australia and Indonesia and the UN special rapporteur on the independence of the judiciary conducted an extremely successful week-long human rights training for East Timorese judges.

The problem in relation to training and mentoring was not limited to judges. It was common for the prosecutors and public defenders to be mentored by UN lawyers who had little or no previous criminal law experience. The court administration suffered from similar problems, as well as a chronic lack of resources. Two years after the commencement of the mission the judges had not been supplied with copies of the applicable law. Public defenders had no access to vehicles and consequently could not make field visits to view crime scenes and interview witnesses even in complex trials for crimes against humanity.[22]

There was also a serious disparity between the resources and competence of UN prosecutors and defence counsel who appeared before the Special Panels. The prosecutors had vehicles and resources, working as party of highly-resourced teams.

---

[22]   Judicial System Monitoring Programme, *Justice in Practice: Human Rights in Court Administration*, JSMP Thematic Report No. 1 (November 2001), available at http://www.jsmp.minihub.org/Reports/JSMP1.pdf.

Some had significant experience in the International Criminal Tribunal for the former Yugoslavia and International Criminal Tribunal for Rwanda. The international defence counsel representing East Timorese charged with crimes against humanity, however, included several lawyers who had not appeared in any criminal cases at all before coming to East Timor. They therefore had no hope of understanding the complexities and strategies involved in conducting a rigorous defence of their clients.[23]

Transitional Justice and Reconciliation

Following a workshop on transitional justice, the National Counsel of Timorese Resistance passed a unanimous resolution, at their National Congress in August 2000 that there should be a truth and reconciliation commission established to assist in dealing with the legacy of past human rights violations. A request for assistance was made to the Special Representative of the Secretary-General and Transitional Administrator, the late Sergio Viera de Mello. Consequently, at a meeting between the SRSG and the directors of the Judicial Affairs, Serious Crimes and Human Rights sections it was decided that the HRU should take the lead in taking the necessary steps to establish such a commission.[24] A steering committee was formed that included 11 representatives of East Timorese civil society groups as well as UNTAET staff from both the HRU and the Political section, and UNHCR. The steering committee was chaired by the director of the HRU.

The HRU provided significant resources to the steering committee in order to facilitate the eventual establishment of CAVR. It provided the secretariat, district officers facilitated consultations and legal staff worked on drafting the regulation establishing the Commission. It also organised and participated in meetings involving rival East Timorese factions in Bali and Indonesian West Timor, and provided significant assistance in the early days after the establishment of the Commission, before it had recruited its own staff.

The role of the HRU in the creation of the CAVR was unusual, in that such transitional justice mechanisms had not been previously been interpreted as part of the mandate of a peacekeeping operation. UNTAET, which was both the mission and the government, had a mandate to establish all institutions considered necessary, so the limit of its authority was not in issue. However, the role of the HRU in developing and later supporting the CAVR squarely raised the question of whether reconciliation is within the mandate of peacekeeping missions.

---

[23]   D. Cohen, *Seeking Justice on the Cheap: Is the East Timor Tribunal Really a Model for the Future?*, Asia Pacific Issues, Analysis from the East-West Centre, No. 61 (August 2002). See also Crisis Group, *Indonesia: The Implications of the Timor Trials*, Asia Briefing no. 16 (8 May 2002); Amnesty International, *East Timor: Justice Past, Present and Future* (AI Index: ASA 57/001/2001); and Human Rights Watch, *Trial Welcome but Justice Still Elusive in East Timor* (26 January 2001).

[24]   On the Establishment of a Commission for Reception, Truth and Reconciliation in East Timor, UNTAET/REG/2001/10 of 13 July 2001.

In East Timor, as in many other similar contexts, the issue of reconciliation was directly related to the maintenance of peace. The prospect of continuing peace was unlikely without reconciliation between groups and individuals who had been in conflict. The reconciliation work of other peacekeeping missions had often been limited to political events, particularly organising and hosting meetings and negotiations between the leaders of rival groups. The CAVR's mandate provided it with much broader functions to investigate and report on past human rights violations and undertake a variety of grass-roots programmes whose goals were to promote reconciliation and assist in restoring the dignity of victims.[25] These included major national public hearings focusing on particular themes of the past conflict, district and sub-district public hearings for victims, participatory mapping exercises which recorded local histories of human rights violations, healing workshops for victims, and Community Reconciliation Procedures (CRP), which directly followed up the protection role that had been filled by UNTAET's district human rights officers.

The CRP programme[26] provided an alternative mechanism for dealing with perpetrators of past politically motivated 'lesser' crimes (not including murder, rape or torture). Instead of being investigated and prosecuted these 'lesser' offenders could provide a statement to the CAVR that included admission of their wrongdoing. The statement was then forwarded to the Office of the General Prosecutor, which considered whether it was suitable to proceed by CRP. If approved, a village-based hearing was arranged, presided over by a five-person panel chaired by a CAVR regional commissioner. At the hearing the perpetrators were required to make a public confession and apology. Victims and community members were free to comment, provide questions, and participate in finding a solution. Eventually an agreement was brokered whereby the perpetrator could voluntarily agree to undertake certain community service and/or reparations in order to be accepted back into his or her community. This agreement was recorded and forwarded to the relevant district court. On completion of the agreed acts the perpetrator received automatic immunity from future criminal or civil liability for all actions dealt with by the CRP.

By the completion of its field programmes in April 2004, approximately 1,500 cases of these relatively 'minor' perpetrators had been completed.[27] The earlier protection work of the HRU, and the follow-on CRP programme made a significant contribution to avoiding the 'payback' violence targeting returnees who had been involved in the 1999 violations. Only a very small number of revenge attacks were reported.

The passage of time in a context of peace was a relatively new phenomenon for the East Timorese. Anger and sensitivity gradually receded, making the explosion into violence less likely and providing opportunity for the deeper, long-term work on reconciliation and development to proceed. The CRP programme also helped the infant judicial system by absorbing a significant number of cases that would

---

[25]   See *CAVR Report*, 'Part 2: The Mandate of the Commission'.
[26]   *Ibid*, 'Part 9: Community Reconciliation'.
[27]   *Ibid*.

otherwise have remained to be dealt with by the already grossly overburdened police, prosecutors, judges and court administration.

Human Rights Violations by UN Personnel

In general, reported violations by UNTAET personnel whilst on mission were fewer than other comparable missions. This may be due to a strong initial position taken by the SRSG in implementing the policy that mission personnel who committed serious crimes outside of their working hours and duties should be investigated and prosecuted in the local judicial system. Despite this, there were a number of disturbing examples where mission personnel were not held to account.[28] A UN professional was charged over an incident in which a local resident had been killed by the vehicle he was driving whilst drunk. However, after a period spent in a local prison awaiting trial the individual managed to leave the country whilst on bail, notwithstanding that his passport had been impounded and held by a component of the UNTAET mission. A Jordanian peacekeeper who was charged with the rape of a local woman also managed to leave the country, whilst on bail awaiting trial. Such incidents contributed to the criticism and lack of confidence in the integrity of the mission by local partners and the general population.

Role of OHCHR

The lack of an UNTAET budget line that could provide funds for human rights activities created significant problems for the HRU. Those who compiled the budget did not include a consideration of the many types of human rights programmes that are useful in a peacekeeping context, but which require materials other than those available to other 'standard' mission components. Budget lines for training materials, tools for forensic investigations, copies of human rights instruments, expert consultants to assist on particular themes and human rights promotional materials such as books, pamphlets, posters, t-shirts, etc, were not included in the UNTAET mission budget. Consequently, there was initially no way that the unit could effectively undertake these kinds of activities.

The role of OHCHR in providing technical assistance was extremely useful as it helped to fill this gap of available resources. The range of the projects that could be included was also very flexible, which allowed the HRU to tailor the proposal to the specific needs in the field. In this way both the DPKO mission and OHCHR benefited. OHCHR was able to take advantage of the HRU personnel who were already on the ground, to assist in delivering its programmes, without having to incur the expense of funding these personnel. The UNTAET mission benefited by being able to deliver programmes without having to provide the materials and additional consultant services. Some of the programmes were also assisted by the direct participation of OHCHR Geneva staff.

---

[28]   A. Devereux, 'Searching for Clarity: A Case Study of UNTAET's Application of International Human Rights Norms', pp. 318–321.

Programmes completed through the OHCHR technical assistance project included:

- the training of district human rights trainers who then worked to promote human rights principles across the territory;
- the training of both international and national human rights field officers by expert staff from the OHCHR office in Geneva;
- the training of East Timorese police by international experts;
- the provision of a consultant to assist in developing and standardising human rights databases of local civil society groups and the HRU;
- the provision of a full time consultant to assist in preparation for the ratification of core human rights treaties;
- the provision of copies of international human rights instruments; and,
- the support of human rights promotional activities designed to be effective in the East Timorese context. These included design and production of t-shirts displaying the core principles of the Universal Declaration of Human Rights in the Tetum language, development and distribution of colourful comic books of stories reflecting the core provisions of human rights treaties (in Indonesian, Tetum and English), human rights promotion through theatre, music, sporting and cultural events.

Although the technical support programme was eventually successful, approval from the Geneva office was subject to extensive delays of up to one year before the proposed projects could be commenced. These delays resulted in the loss of a significant portion of the potential human rights programming, which could have been completed. The delay was so long for the first year's programme that the projects could not be implemented in that year.

The relationship between OHCHR and the HRU also added significant work for the staff of the unit. As part of a peacekeeping mission, the HRU was obliged to provide written drafts for inclusion in the mission reports to the secretary-general, Security Council and General Assembly, and for other thematic reports being prepared by various sections of the UN Secretariat. In addition, the HRU was expected to complete reports and advice for OHCHR, as required for the Commission on Human Rights sessions and other needs.[29] The HRU also assisted in hosting a range of visits and missions to East Timor, which added to the already overwhelming demands on the unit's personnel.

---

[29] See, for example, Interim Report of the United Nations High Commissioner for Human Rights on the Situation of Human Rights in Timor-Leste, UN Doc. A/57/466 (2002); Report of the United Nations High Commissioner for Human Rights on the Situation of Human Rights in Timor-Leste, UN Doc. E/CN.4/2001/37 (2001); and Report of the Representative of the Secretary-General on Internally Displaced Persons, Mr Francis M. Deng, to the Commission on Human Rights in accordance with Commission Resolution 1999/S-4/1 of 27 September 1999, UN Doc. E/CN.4/2000/83/Add.3 (2000).

The HRU was fortunate to host the then High Commissioner for Human Rights, Mary Robinson, during two visits to East Timor.[30] These visits were highly significant for the local population as the high commissioner was recognised as having been one of very few high profile advocates for the rights of the East Timorese people during the difficult years. East Timorese civil society groups also expressed support for the decision of the high commissioner to withdraw her association and support for the *ad hoc* tribunal in Jakarta due to fundamental flaws in its mandate.

In 2000, the high commissioner accompanied a UNTAET human rights field officer to a meeting of women victims in Suai district. Mrs Robinson took a small baby who was the result of militia rape in her arms, telling the women that the baby was a specially-blessed child, and should always be especially loved and respected. When the high commissioner asked its name the mother smiled and said 'Mary'. The young child, renamed Mary Robinson, then five years old, made a visit with her mother to one of the CAVR public hearings on gender-based violence in 2005.

Transition to UNMISET

The UNTAET mission's mandate was completed when the UN secretary-general handed over authority for the territory to the independent government on 20 May 2002. Unlike the early stages of UNTAET, the role of a human rights section in the successor (UN Mission in Support of East Timor) UNMISET mission was closely considered during the planning process. Initially it was proposed to have a very small component of three human rights experts, which would advise the SRSG on human rights issues. However, it was argued by the HRU, with eventual success, that the work of a substantial human rights section was integral to security issues, and therefore a core component of the mission. A significant section with 15 international positions, including district human rights officers, was eventually approved. As part of the negotiations to approve the inclusion of DHROs in the mission budget it was agreed that they would be expected to fill a broader role, including reporting not only on human rights issues but also political and other developments. Although this arrangement provided some difficulties it was an essential reason for the inclusion of the DHROs in the budget. The HRU was also authorised to maintain teams to train police and military, advise on legal issues relating to rights, and to assist reconciliation.[31]

By including in UNMISET's staffing table two relatively senior human rights officers whose work would focus on reconciliation and supporting the CAVR, DPKO accepted the direct relationship between reconciliation and peacekeeping. The two officers, who had extensive local contacts and credibility, played a central role in the work of the CAVR, as the major reconciliation initiative in the country. Their work not only assisted in settling past issues and therefore diminishing the likelihood of

---

[30]   See Report of the United Nations High commissioner for Human Rights on the Situation of Human Rights in Timor-Leste (2001), at 4–7.

[31]   Security Council resolution 1410 (2002), UN Doc. S/RES/1410 (2002).

renewed violence, but also provided a valuable link between the UNMISET mission and the various stakeholders involved in reconciliation programmes.

Lessons Learned

1. The planning exercise for the UNTAET mission did not anticipate the wide needs the mission would have for human rights expertise. It is important that the planning teams for future missions include relatively senior members with significant human rights field experience. Human rights experts who do not have wide field experience cannot be expected to anticipate the variety of roles a human rights presence may fulfil and the complex ways in which a mission may develop. The planning of the UNTAET mission included insufficient consultation with local actors, which led to a variety of serious problems later in the mission.

2. The role and responsibilities of the human rights component of the mission need to be clearly defined. This will assist in dealing with the overlap with other sections. If human rights field officers are part of multi-disciplinary district teams, their reporting and responsibility lines should be clear. Arrangements that include dual reporting or responsibility are unsatisfactory unless it is also made clear which of the lines of authority has precedence.

3. In the present author's opinion, unsatisfactory recruitment was responsible for the majority of problems faced by the mission in general, and caused difficulties for the human rights section in its early days. Experience in previous missions was a significant criterion for hiring many UN staff, notwithstanding that the individual had performed poorly in previous missions. Leaving positions unfilled through bureaucratic delays directly reduces the potential for achieving human rights goals, places additional stress on staff who must cover the work of those yet to be recruited and leads to other sections of the mission taking over responsibilities that could better be undertaken by human rights experts. Recruitment of human rights field officers must be based on recognition that experts situated at headquarters have access to far less information about the context and needs of the mission than those in the field. Selection should therefore be the responsibility of the senior officer in the field with strictly enforced short time limits imposed on overview mechanisms.

4. There must be early consideration of the needs a human rights field operation has for project equipment and expenses. This should include the capacity to recruit specialist short-term consultants for specific needs. The availability of funds for these needs should be included in mission budgets, with some flexibility to account for unforeseen needs.

5. Staff operating at headquarters level need to be mindful that field operation personnel will be facing an overwhelming workload, and that extra reporting or other requirements will directly detract from the work they can achieve in the field. Requests for additional work done should therefore be kept to those

Chapter 15

Case Study: The United Nations Human Rights Field Operation in Sierra Leone[1]

Michael O'Flaherty[2]

The Sierra Leone human rights community has played a high-profile role in the country's long and troubled peace process. This chapter seeks both to describe and to assess that role and takes account of, *inter alia*, the activities of non-governmental organisations (NGOs) and the United Nations (UN) human rights programme. The period chosen for review, 1998 to 2000, covers the most significant stages of the peace process: from the return to Sierra Leone of its elected government in early 1998, through the phase of the Lomé peace negotiations/agreement, to the adoption of the Abuja Agreement in November 2000. The chapter concludes that the human rights community can take credit for a substantial contribution to the peacebuilding process. Failures on the part of the human rights actors to achieve peace process related goals are also identified and analysed.

Overview of the Situation, 1998–2000

January 1998 to January 1999: Return of the Government to the Rebel Incursion into Freetown

In February 1998, the Economic Commission of West African States Monitoring Group (ECOMOG), the Nigerian-led West African military intervention force, succeeded in ejecting a military/rebel junta regime, the Armed Forces Revolutionary Council (AFRC) that had joined forces with the armed opposition Revolutionary United Front (RUF), from Freetown and much of west and southern Sierra Leone. In March, the elected civilian government of President Ahmad Tejan Kabbah returned from its exile in Guinea. Over the course of the following weeks the diplomatic community also came back to Freetown and international humanitarian programming was re-invigorated. The period also saw the return of a UN special envoy as well as the deployment of World Bank and other international assistance.

---

[1]   This chapter was first published under the title of 'Sierra Leone's Peace Process: The Role of the Human Rights Community', in *Human Rights Quarterly* vol. 26, no. 1 (2004).
[2]   Much gratitude is expressed to those who commented on drafts of this text, especially to Tessa Kordeczka, Corrine Dufka and Richard Bennett.

The mood of the period was optimistic, at least among the Freetown elites. Although the rebels were still active, particularly in the north and parts of the east, it was widely considered to be only a matter of time before they would be overcome by the ECOMOG forces under their lauded commander, Brigadier General Khobe. Sierra Leone was apparently entering a post-conflict reconstruction phase in which the focus would be on the consolidation of peace and restoration of normality. This belief prompted initiation of an ambitious programme for disarmament, demobilisation and reintegration of former combatants and the establishment of a small UN mission, the United Nations Observer Mission in Sierra Leone (UNOMSIL),[3] in which the only military element was a modest team of unarmed officer-level observers. The government, confident in its stability, also embarked on the large-scale process of bringing the junta civilian and military leadership before courts to be tried for the capital offence of treason. The rebel leader, Foday Sankoh, who had been in custody in Nigeria from March 1997 to July 1998 and subsequently in Freetown, was also to be tried on similar charges. Lower ranking junta officials were obliged to submit to a vetting process to determine their loyalty to the state.

The optimism was misplaced and soon dissipated. The rebels continued to wield considerable force. They controlled the principal diamond fields and were in receipt of assistance from Liberia. ECOMOG, for its part, were hampered by the lack of the resources necessary to achieve sustained superiority and it was widely reported that it was suffering heavy losses. Its Sierra Leonean co-fighters were the traditional hunter militia, comprised principally of the Kamajor group, known as the Civilian Defense Force or CDF. Although vicious in battle, the CDF could not be considered a disciplined military body. The remaining months of 1998 saw a pattern of rebel successes, reversing earlier ECOMOG gains, and the fighting came ever closer to Freetown itself.

The continued instability and fighting,[4] including the deliberate targeting and terrorising of civilians, exacerbated country wide human suffering. There was ongoing displacement of civilians and high levels of malnutrition and disease. The social and physical infrastructure was destroyed with no opportunity to begin its repair. Throughout 1998 rebel forces perpetrated summary execution, amputation, mutilation and other forms of torture, as well as abduction and rape. Typically, they looted and destroyed houses in combat areas. The CDF were also responsible for serious human rights abuses, for instance, ethnically motivated killing of non-combatants as well as the execution and maltreatment of prisoners. There were persistent reports of unacceptable behaviour by ECOMOG elements, including illegal detention, torture and ill-treatment of combatants during surrender or capture.

---

3   See Security Council resolution 1181 (1998), UN Doc. S/RES/1181 (1998), at 6–7.

4   See First Report of the Secretary-General on the United Nations Observer Mission in Sierra Leone, UN Doc. S/1998/750 (1998); Second Report of the Secretary-General on the United Nations Observer Mission in Sierra Leone, UN Doc. S/1998/960 (1998); Third Report of the Secretary-General on the United Nations Observer Mission in Sierra Leone, UN Doc. S/1998/1176 (1998).

In the closing months of the year the treason trials that had by and large respected international standards of due process were coming to a close, with most of the civilian defendants found guilty and sentenced to death – although all of the convictions remained subject to consideration by an appeal court. Most of the military defendants were also convicted in a court martial, without right to appeal. Despite condemnation of the military trial process by the UN and others, as well as reminders from the rebels that they would exact revenge for any executions, 24 of the defendants were killed semi-publicly (in a quarry close to Freetown), with photographs of the scene published in local newspapers.[5]

By December 1998 the rebels were close to Freetown, and notwithstanding repeated protestations to the contrary by the government, the UN chief military observer and others, it became clear that an attack on the city was likely. Already floundering, international reconstruction and humanitarian programmes came to a halt and many foreigners and some Sierra Leoneans evacuated. By the last days of December the CDF were deployed for the first time in the capital's streets, much augmented by local volunteers, and there were repeated instances of vigilante killings of suspected rebel sympathisers.

Early on the morning of 6 January 1999, the rebels, principally comprising former army elements as well as RUF, attacked and occupied the eastern part of the city without difficulty. By mid-morning their advance was halted in the city centre and the remaining UN staff were successfully evacuated. The government remained in the ECOMOG-controlled western suburbs. During the course of the following week or so, Freetown experienced an unprecedented savaging.[6] It is estimated that some 5,000 Freetown residents and combatants were killed and thousands more were abducted.[7] There were hundreds of incidences of mutilation and amputation of limbs. At least half of the housing stock was destroyed, as well as historic landmarks, government buildings and such symbolic targets as the Nigerian High Commission, the UNOMSIL offices and the central prison (which was emptied). Many of the rebel fighters were children, among whom drug use was common. ECOMOG and government forces also perpetrated grave human rights abuses, such as the summary execution of scores of suspected rebel sympathisers and aerial attacks on civilian targets.[8]

---

[5]   Most Freetown newspapers carried photographs of the executions during the following week. See, for example, editions of *Herald Guardian*; *The African Champion*.

[6]   See Fourth Report of the Secretary-General on the United Nations Observer Mission in Sierra Leone, UN Doc. S/1999/20 (1999); Fifth Report of the Secretary-General on the United Nations Observer Mission in Sierra Leone, UN Doc. S/1999/237 (1999).

[7]   Internal report of UNOMSIL by M. O'Flaherty, *Report of Human Rights Assessment Mission to Freetown 25 January and 1 to 4 February 1999*, subsequently made public by Special Representative of the Secretary-General Francis Okelo (on file with the present author). See also Fifth Report of the Secretary-General on the United Nations Observer Mission in Sierra Leone (1999), at 2.

[8]   M. O'Flaherty, *Report of Human Rights Assessment Mission*.

January 1999 to July 1999: Repulsion of the Rebels from Freetown to the Lomé Agreement

The rebels were unable to maintain their hold in Freetown and they were quickly pushed eastwards out of the centre in heavy fighting that further devastated the city's hinterland. Perpetration of atrocities by rebels also persisted. ECOMOG, under a new commander, appeared to be gaining the upper hand in the countryside and it took significant steps to impose discipline within its ranks. Meanwhile, the UN, diplomats, and a large number of the Sierra Leone elite awaited the possibility of safe return in Conakry, Guinea, where they established useful information exchange arrangements and debated next steps for the country. Most of these evacuees had returned to Freetown by March or April.

In the period from January to April 1999, Sierra Leone political discourse, in sharp contrast to the situation for much of 1998, generally assumed that an end to fighting would require an accommodation with the rebels and that the route ahead was that of the 'twin-track', of parallel military and diplomatic efforts.[9] There was a perception that the rebels were strong and resilient and that ECOMOG would never have the capacity to definitely eradicate them country wide. Furthermore, the elected civilian politicians who were about to assume control in Nigeria had made clear that they would take their soldiers home sooner rather than later, despite the fact that Sierra Leone had not yet developed a new army of its own. There was no sense at the time that any other international peacekeeping force, such as of the UN, was likely to be established. And nearly all parts of the international political community encouraged the seeking of an arrangement with the rebels, with the United Kingdom going so far as to demand this in return for its military aid.[10] Sierra Leoneans themselves were utterly exhausted of war and desperate for peace and stability.

The mood was captured in the proceedings of a national consultative conference which took place in Freetown in April. Attended by the political leadership, traditional leaders (such as the paramount chiefs), civil society representatives (such as non-governmental organisations and professional and trade associations), and even with a message from Foday Sankoh, it proposed terms for a peace settlement broadly based on the provisions of the unimplemented 1996 Abidjan Peace Agreement.[11] In return for a cessation of hostilities and recognition by the rebels of the legitimacy of the government, it suggested limited power-sharing in the lead up to national

---

[9]   Fifth Report of the Secretary-General on the United Nations Observer Mission in Sierra Leone, (1999), at 15.

[10]   P. Penfold, UK High Commissioner, Address at the April 1999 National Consultative Conference, reported in National Commission for Democracy and Human Rights, *The Road to Peace: Report of the National Consultative Conference on the Peace Process in Sierra Leone* (April 1999).

[11]   See National Consultative Conference on the Peace Process, *Summary of Consensus* (12 April 1999), available at http://www.sierra-leone.org/nccpp041299.

elections, conferring of amnesty on combatants and establishment of a truth and reconciliation commission (see further below).[12]

Within weeks of the conference, the government and the UN had facilitated a meeting of the RUF in Lomé, Togo, at which the RUF was expected to develop its strategy for a peace process. Sankoh, who until then had remained in custody having been sentenced to death, was allowed to attend. By mid-May, the RUF had submitted its proposals for a peace agreement, and the government, although objecting to a number of the provisions (such as for a joint transitional government), replied in a conciliatory manner. On the basis of this exchange, peace talks got underway in Lomé on 25 May. The government delegation contained both politicians and representatives of civil society. Civil society groups also visited the talks on a number of occasions. There was a mediation committee of observers comprising member states of the Economic Commission of West African States (ECOWAS), Committee of Seven on Sierra Leone, the ECOWAS Secretariat, the Commonwealth, Organization of African Unity (OAU), UN and the governments of Libya, the United Kingdom and the United States.

Early in the talks the parties agreed to a ceasefire, the release of all 'prisoners of war and non-combatants', and unhindered delivery of humanitarian assistance.[13] The Lomé Peace Agreement[14] itself was signed on 7 July. It gave the RUF a place in government and made Sankoh the head of a commission tasked to oversee the state's mineral resources. It provided for the establishment of a national electoral commission, a commission to review the state constitution, a new human rights commission (a form of one was already in existence), and a truth and reconciliation commission. It also contained a number of other specific provisions dealing with, for instance, issues of human rights. An amnesty was conferred on 'combatants and collaborators in respect of anything done by them in pursuit of their objectives'.[15] Sankoh received an absolute pardon. The UN representative, on instruction from the secretary-general, appended a handwritten disclaimer to his signature to the agreement stating that the UN did not recognise the effect of the amnesty as regards such international crimes as crimes against humanity.[16]

While the agreement was being negotiated, Mary Robinson, the UN High Commissioner for Human Rights, had visited Freetown and drawn attention to the acute levels of human rights abuse and the need for justice and accountability.

---

[12]   See Penfold, *Road to Peace*.

[13]   Peace Agreement Between the Government of Sierra Leone and the Revolutionary United Front (RUF) of Sierra Leone, 7 July 1999, Sierra Leone-RUF, Annex III–IV, available at http://www.usip.org/library/pa/sl/sierra_leone_07071999_toc.

[14]   See *ibid*. See also the Sixth Progress Report of the Secretary-General on UNOMSIL, UN Doc. S/1999/645 (1999).

[15]   Peace Agreement, Article IX.

[16]   See I. Martin, 'Justice and Reconciliation: Responsibilities and Dilemmas of Peacemakers and Peacebuilders' (November 2000), available at http://www.ciaonet.org/wps/mai05/mai05.pdf (this paper was presented to a November 2000 Aspen Institute meeting entitled 'The Legacy of Abuse – Justice and Reconciliation in a New Landscape').

Within the context of the adoption by the UN, the government and civil society of a 'Human Rights Manifesto',[17] she committed her office to, *inter alia*, support the establishment of the truth and reconciliation commission and the new human rights commission. She also initiated a study on how to counter impunity, such as, initially, by means of an international commission of enquiry.

July 1999 to May 2000: Adoption of the Lomé Agreement to the Attacks on the United Nations Assistance Mission in Sierra Leone

The Lomé Agreement contained very short implementation timelines. Almost none of these would be met.[18] The government itself tended to honour its commitments, for example according cabinet seats to the RUF and facilitating the establishment of Sankoh's minerals oversight function. The UN high commissioner for human rights and UNOMSIL also took the necessary action for establishment of the truth and reconciliation commission and a number of Lomé implementation monitoring bodies.

The rebels were much less cooperative. Releases of abductees were slow and rarely spontaneous. Humanitarian access to rebel-held territory involved exhausting negotiation and was sometimes subject to unacceptable conditions. The process of demobilisation of combatants was extremely slow and, in any case, few rebels seemed willing to come forward. Furthermore, fighting continued in many locations and patterns of human rights abuse persisted, albeit at lower levels of intensity (although the humanitarian crisis continued unabated). As early as August a number of UNOMSIL civilian and military personnel, together with journalists and religious workers, were abducted by rebels close to Freetown and only released after strenuous diplomatic efforts. Rebel actions came to demonstrate considerable disunity within their ranks. In particular, ex-army elements were clearly operating distinctly from the RUF. Even within the RUF itself splits were evident and Sankoh was shown to lack total control.

The situation in Sierra Leone continued to slide throughout 1999 and into 2000.[19] Rebel obstruction and disregard for the peace agreement was exacerbated by the phased withdrawal of ECOMOG and the failure of the UN to deploy a sturdy peacekeeping force in good time. The new UN mission, United Nations Mission in Sierra Leone (UNAMSIL), was only established in October 1999, with the first armed troops not arriving until 29 November. During May 2000, the lightly armed, under-manned, and poorly-led UNAMSIL forces came under rebel attack in a number

---

[17]   A copy of the Manifesto is on file with the present author.

[18]   See Seventh Report of the Secretary-General on the United Nations Observer Mission in Sierra Leone, UN Doc. S/1999/836 (1999); Eighth Report of the Secretary-General on the United Nations Mission in Sierra Leone, UN Doc. S/1999/1003 (1999); First Report of the Secretary-General on the United Nations Observer Mission in Sierra Leone, UN Doc. S/1999/1223 (1999).

[19]   *Ibid.* See also Second Report of the Secretary-General on the United Nations Mission in Sierra Leone, UN Doc. S/2000/13 (2000); Fourth Report of the Secretary-General on the United Nations Mission in Sierra Leone, UN Doc. S/2000/455 (2000).

of locations. By the middle of that month 352 of them had been abducted and 11 peacekeepers had been killed. At the same time, with fears of another rebel incursion to Freetown, there were evacuations of UN representatives and other foreigners. The situation began to stabilise only with the deployment of British armed forces who secured the international airport and the city.[20]

May 2000 to November 2000: Re-establishment of Control to the Abuja Agreement

The humiliating events of May 2000 led to some fundamental changes of approach by the government and the UN.[21] Sankoh and other senior RUF personalities were taken into custody. The government requested UN assistance for the establishment of an international court to try the top RUF leadership. UNAMSIL was reconfigured whereby it would have sturdy terms of engagement as a Chapter VII peace-enforcement mission, and it became the largest UN peacekeeping mission in the world.[22]

The UN Security Council visited Sierra Leone in October, as did the UN secretary-general in December. The visits underscored the high importance for the UN of salvaging its peacekeeping reputation through succeeding in Sierra Leone. Meanwhile, the United Kingdom significantly enhanced its programme of training a new Sierra Leone army.

---

[20] See Fifth Report of the Secretary-General on the UN Mission in Sierra Leone, UN Doc. S/2000/751 (2000); Sixth Report of the Secretary-General on the United Nations Mission in Sierra Leone, UN Doc. S/2000/832 (2000).

[21] *Ibid.* See also Seventh Report of the Secretary-General on the United Nations Mission in Sierra Leone, UN Doc. S/2000/1055 (2000); Eighth Report of the Secretary-General on the United Nations Mission in Sierra Leone, UN Doc. S/2000/1199 (2000).

[22] Pursuant to the provisions of Chapter VII of the United Nations Charter, the Security Council may determine the existence of any threat to the peace, breach of the peace or act of aggression and may make recommendations, or decide what measures shall be taken by United Nations Member States in accordance with Articles 41 and 42 of the Charter, to maintain or restore international peace and security. According to Security Council resolution 1289 (2000) of 7 February 2000, the mandate has been revised to include the following tasks: to provide security at key locations and government buildings, in particular in Freetown, important intersections and major airports, including Lungi airport; to facilitate the free flow of people, goods and humanitarian assistance along specified thoroughfares; to provide security in and at all sites of the disarmament, demobilisation and reintegration programme; to coordinate with and assist the Sierra Leone law enforcement authorities in the discharge of their responsibilities; to guard weapons, ammunition and other military equipment collected from ex-combatants, and to assist in their subsequent disposal or destruction. The Council authorised UNAMSIL to take the necessary action to fulfil those additional tasks, and affirmed that, in the discharge of its mandate, UNAMSIL may take the necessary action to ensure the security and freedom of movement of its personnel and, within its capabilities and areas of deployment, to afford protection to civilians under imminent threat of physical violence, taking into account the responsibilities of the government of Sierra Leone.

It took some months before any significant country-wide improvement could be observed. In July the situation was still being described by the UN as resembling civil war,[23] although that month saw the decimation by British forces of the previously dangerous group of former soldiers lodged in the Occra hills near Freetown. The period was also marked by a flare up of fighting and instability on the Guinean and Liberian borders, with related population displacement into Sierra Leone. The Guinea incidents were instigated by RUF and Liberian elements[24] and raised fears of the Sierra Leone conflict escalating into a regional war.

In November, following intense UN and ECOWAS diplomacy, the RUF agreed to a ceasefire, and to the Abuja Agreement, that included a commitment to returning to the provisions of the Lomé Agreement such as disarmament and demobilisation.[25] This was a key turning point. With hindsight it can be seen as the seminal moment at which a process of definitive consolidation of peace got underway. The closing months of 2000 also saw the clarification between the UN Secretariat and the government of Sierra Leone in the form of a 'special court' to try those with the greatest responsibility for conflict-related crimes.[26] This court would exist side-by side with the Truth and Reconciliation Commission, efforts for the establishment of which were re-invigorated by the Office of the UN High Commissioner for Human Rights (OHCHR) in November. Already, the possible forms of relationship between the two institutions had begun to elicit great discussion and concern in civil society.[27]

The Human Rights Community, 1998–2000

The Sierra Leone Groups

Since the mid-1990s, Sierra Leone has been fortunate to have an energetic human rights NGO community, led by such skilled and courageous leaders as Joseph Rahall, Isaac Lappia, Helen Bash Taqui and Frank Kargbo. The NGOs varied greatly in size and skill, including, for instance, the extremely well-endowed and organised Campaign for Good Governance, a national section of Amnesty International, Church-supported groups such as Caritas, and some tiny but intrepid bodies such as Prison Watch. The organisations had limited operating capacity outside the western

---

[23]   See Fifth Report of the Secretary-General on the United Nations Mission in Sierra Leone (2000), at 5–6.

[24]   See Seventh Report (2000).

[25]   See Eighth Report of the Secretary-General on the United Nations Mission in Sierra Leone, at 2.

[26]   See Report of the Secretary-General on the Establishment of a Special Court for Sierra Leone, UN Doc. S/2000/915 (2000). The Statute of the Special Court for Sierra Leone, is available at www.sc-sl.org.

[27]   The fascinating and generally important process of clarification of the relationship between the two institutions is beyond the temporal scope of this chapter.

province (and next to none in rebel controlled areas). A loose coalition of the NGOs, the National Forum for Human Rights, was established with the encouragement of the United States Embassy in 1996. By 1998 the Forum had 18 member organisations. It operated effectively as a clearing house for information and as an umbrella body. In 2000, with the assistance of the UNAMSIL Human Rights Section, it received international donor funding that permitted it to establish a permanent secretariat.

A number of NGOs and church-related groups that would not describe themselves as human rights organisations also played an important role in the sector. Prominent among these was the Inter-Religious Council, which brought together the Christian and Muslim leadership and many of the groups active in the humanitarian sector. In addition, occasionally the Sierra Leone Bar Association took positions on issues of human rights.

Throughout the period there existed a government-established human rights body, the National Commission for Democracy and Human Rights (NCDHR), which was generously funded by the United Nations Development Programme (UNDP). It was led for most of the period under review by the highly effective Kadie Sesay. The NCDHR failed to meet the UN standards for independent national human rights institutions, as set out in the Paris Principles,[28] and was never wholly trusted by the NGO community. It did, however, engage in human rights awareness raising and, in 1998, established a number of human rights monitoring committees. In 1999 the government also appointed an ombudsperson, who, largely unfunded, made no discernible impact in terms of promotion and protection of human rights.

The United Nations

The first UN human rights presence in Sierra Leone took the form of the deployment, in April 1998, of a human rights advisor to the office of the UN special envoy (this title was subsequently changed to 'special representative'), recruited by the Department of Peacekeeping Operations (DPKO) but in receipt of substantive backstopping from OHCHR. On 13 July 1998, Security Council resolution 1181 (1998) established UNOMSIL. Its mandate dictated that close attention be paid to issues of human rights:

> [UNOMSIL is mandated to] report on violations of international law and human rights in Sierra Leone and, in consultation with the relevant United Nations agencies, to assist the government of Sierra Leone in its efforts to address the country's human rights needs.[29]

To implement the mandate, the UNOMSIL/UNAMSIL Human Rights Section concentrated on three areas: monitoring the human rights situation, reporting thereon both internally and publicly with associated advocacy initiatives, and providing

---

[28]   See United Nations High Commission for Human Rights, Fact Sheet No. 19, *National Institutions for the Promotion and Protection of Human Rights* (Geneva: UN, 1993), available at http://www.unhchr.ch/html/menu6/2/fs19.

[29]   See footnote 3.

technical cooperation to civil society and the government. It was also involved in the Lomé peace negotiations and the efforts for implementation of the agreement. These activities are discussed further below.

The UNOMSIL Human Rights Section initially comprised five human rights officers. For most of the period until the end of 1998 they were augmented by trial observers provided by the International Bar Association.[30] In January 1999, following the rebel incursion to Freetown, UNOMSIL was temporarily evacuated to Conakry, Guinea. The entire UN mission was downsized and it was proposed by the local mission management effectively to dismantle the human rights team, since, as it was erroneously argued, even after return to Freetown the team would not be able to operate because of the ongoing emergency conditions. However, following strong representations by the team itself, as well as on many levels in the UN, and the diplomatic and NGO communities, the team survived, albeit reduced to two. During the period in Conakry, this duo facilitated the establishment and activities of the Sierra Leone Human Rights Committee (see below), undertook short investigation trips to Sierra Leone, developed relations with the refugee community and continued to provide detailed situation reports. UNOMSIL returned to Freetown on 30 March 1999, and by July 1999 its Human Rights Section had been restored to its former full complement. Following the Lomé Peace Agreement, the Security Council, by resolution 1260 (1999), increased the number of international human rights officers to 14.[31] However, due to the exceedingly slow, cumbersome and inefficient OHCHR/DPKO recruitment procedures, it was not until 2001 that the figure was fully attained.

OHCHR, as well as supporting the UNOMSIL/UNAMSIL human rights team, was also directly engaged in Sierra Leone. During 1998 its activities were mainly of a technical cooperation nature, through the funding of the programme of the World Conference for Religion and Peace and facilitation of the activities of the International Bar Association. During that year and beyond, it also facilitated a number of advocacy interventions of the high commissioner for human rights, rapporteurs of the UN Commission on Human Rights and the UN Human Rights Committee. OHCHR engagement intensified following the visit to Freetown of the high commissioner in June 1999, the signing of the Human Rights Manifesto, and the adoption of the Lomé Agreement.

The capacity of the UN to undertake human rights protection and capacity-building activities was enhanced by the protection programmes of the United Nations Children's Fund (UNICEF) and the Office of the United Nations High Commissioner for Refugees, the activities of a UN humanitarian coordination unit (Office for the Coordination of Humanitarian Affairs (OCHA)), as well as of an International Committee of the Red Cross (ICRC) delegation (which was absent from Sierra Leone in the first part of 1999 due to serious misunderstandings with the government). The UN special representative of the secretary-general on children and armed conflict (SRSGCAC) also intervened in Sierra Leone on a number of occasions, including in the context of the Lomé negotiations.

---

[30]   See R. Field, 'Mission Impossible', COUNSEL (October 1998).
[31]   Security Council resolution 1260 (1999), UN Doc. S/RES/1260 (1999), at 6.

International NGOs

A number of international human rights NGOs were active during the period under review. Amnesty International has a long record of reporting on and advocating regarding the situation in Sierra Leone, issuing reports of high calibre, as well as urgent appeals and other forms of intervention.[32] It also provided steady support to its national section. In 1999, Human Rights Watch located a staff member on a permanent basis in Sierra Leone. Its frequent reports and other interventions attracted considerable notice.[33] Article XIX was engaged throughout the period, paying particular attention to the truth and reconciliation process in close collaboration with a local NGO, Forum of Conscience. In 1998, with OHCHR funds, the World Conference for Religion and Peace commenced a wide-ranging programme of human rights capacity building and institutional support with the Sierra Leone Inter-religious Council. The support provided to UNOMSIL by the International Bar Association has already been mentioned. In late 1999, on the invitation of OHCHR/UNAMSIL, the International Human Rights Law Group began a programme of support for the Truth and Reconciliation Commission. The Group subsequently established its own activities in Sierra Leone. Other human rights capacity-building NGOs, such as International Service for Human Rights, provided training and international experience for national human rights advocates. At the end of 2000, No Peace without Justice developed a programme of support to the government for the establishment of the Special Court. International Alert and the International Crisis Group, both of which had been very active regarding Sierra Leone prior to the 1997 coup, played no apparent role during the period under review.

A number of international humanitarian organisations took an interest in issues of human rights. Foremost among these was *Médecins Sans Frontières* (MSF). In April–May 1998, MSF alerted the UN to the scale of the rebel atrocities against civilians, thus helping ensure the initiation of the UN human rights programme. Many other international NGOs were to become active in one way or another in the promotion of human rights, including World Vision, Concern, Goal, Oxfam (UK) and Save the Children (UK).

Human Rights Coordination

As already described, national NGO coordination was undertaken primarily by means of the National Forum for Human Rights. This body was not, however, intended to be, nor was it, capable of ensuring wider coordination of governmental, non-governmental, national and international actors. The UN human rights programme, from the outset, sought to facilitate this coordination by, for instance, providing

---

[32]   See, for example, its excellent report on the situation in 1998, Amnesty International, *Sierra Leone 1998 – a Year of Atrocities Against Civilians* (1 November 1998), available at http://www.web.amnesty.org/library/index/engafr510221998.

[33]   See Human Rights Watch, 'Rebel Atrocities against Civilians in Sierra Leone' (15 May 1999), press release available at http://www.hrw.org/press/1999/may/s10517.

opportunities for NGOs, government and national and internationals to meet. In January 1999, the UN institutionalised this coordination framework by establishing a national Human Rights Committee, which brought together all of these sectors in a horizontal structure focused on information exchange. The Committee also developed a context in which to develop common advocacy positions (such as on the issue of combating impunity) and was a channel for the national human rights community to engage with all aspects of the UN programme in Sierra Leone. The Committee took on specific monitoring and reporting functions after Lomé, which are discussed below.

During the period under review the Human Rights Committee can be considered to have functioned well. However, its role was not always supported by certain stronger members, such as the NCDHR, which occasionally seemed to perceive itself as being in competition with the NGOs, and some participants from international human rights NGOs, who to a certain extent used the Committee as an information source but did not otherwise contribute to its activities.

The Human Rights Community and the Peace Process

There are no tidy dates whereby the beginning and end of Sierra Leone's conflict can be located. The fighting persisted in various levels of intensity and with varying geographical scope throughout 1998–2000 and one could not absolutely identify distinct times of peace and of conflict. It is not therefore possible to categorise efforts of the human rights community in any neat linear and chronological line of three phases: an in-conflict phase of peace-related activities, a peace negotiation phase and a post-agreement phase.

That stated, human rights actors did undertake activities relating to all three such situations – the difference being that, given the ebbs and flows of the fighting, they tended to undertake elements of each simultaneously or in reaction to immediately prevailing circumstances. What is more, in all phases or situations, including in the darkest moments of the fighting, the human rights community retained a palpable sense that it was building foundations for sustainable peace. Accordingly the present chapter categorises its discussion as follows: (a) human rights community efforts to address the ongoing conflict; (b) human rights community contributions to the peace negotiations; and (c) human rights community efforts for implementation of the peace agreement.

Human Rights Community Efforts to Address the Ongoing Conflict

Those human rights efforts undertaken regarding the conflict and which have most direct relevance for the attainment of a lasting peace can be categorised as follows.

Activities for the empowerment of human rights civil society   It was obvious in Sierra Leone that the ability of the human rights community to effectively carry out activities for peace would turn on its strength, skills, and capacity to access and influence decision-makers. With this in mind it consciously implemented empowerment activities which persisted throughout 1998–2000. Reference has already been made to the role of the National Forum for Human Rights and the pivotal function of the Human Rights Committee. These bodies gave a vehicle and a voice to the human rights community.

There was also an effort made throughout the period for the delivery of conflict-related human rights skills, such as for monitoring and reporting activities. The training lead was taken by the UN human rights team, which delivered its first training programme for Freetown-based activists in July 1998 and gathered together 80 human rights workers from across the country for major training in November of that year. Subsequently, a number of NGOs implemented targeted trainings across the country, including in rebel controlled areas during periods of limited access.

Training was not limited to the group of self-identified human rights organisations. It was also offered to actors who had a potential role in performing monitoring, reporting or other rights-based work. For instance, religious leaders had an important role in promoting human rights through the churches and the mosques both in government and rebel controlled areas – the UN facilitated a human rights training programme for them under the auspices of the Inter-Religious Council. The humanitarian community was also a potentially significant partner, especially for the monitoring of the situation in the countryside (as well as for promoting rights-based methodologies by means of its approach to programming) and the UN devoted resources to delivering advice and participating on an ongoing basis in humanitarian planning and operational forums.

Still another aspect of empowerment activities was the manner in which the members of the human rights community were able to intervene to support each other in handling moments of crisis. This solidarity was most tested at the time of the rebel incursion into Freetown in January 1999. The UN offered to evacuate those of the leadership who wished to leave, and a small number took up the offer. Amnesty International also made funds available for evacuation of those other members of the human rights community who were believed to be at particular risk. The National Forum for Human Rights was able to gather most of the others and take them into hiding, and, despite being exposed to extreme risk, they survived. A few weeks later it was the turn of the national NGOs to support their international counterparts: when the UN mission sought to effectively dismantle its human rights team, the NGO community was vociferous in its objections and was paid heed to.[34]

Ensuring the Widespread International Reporting of the Conflict from a Human Rights Perspective

Addressing the human rights abuses of the conflict and ensuring that attention be paid to peace strategies required that the plight of civilian victims be effectively reported, both directly to key decision-makers and to the public.

---

[34]   Local NGOs made a number of oral interventions with UNOMSIL management. Written appeals were sent by international NGOs, including Amnesty International.

The reporting of the human rights situation was undertaken at the international and national levels and in a variety of guises, by both the UN and the NGOs. Effective reporting initially required a country-wide capacity to gather the information skilfully. This posed great challenges in Sierra Leone, where the UN human rights team was tiny and the human rights community had limited capacity outside the western area. Reference has already been made to a number of initiatives to overcome these shortcomings, such as the various training efforts, as well as to the attempts to draw humanitarian workers and others into some form of monitoring activities.

By and large these efforts had some success, whereby, for instance, some parts of the humanitarian community became significant providers of information. In addition, the centralised nature of the country meant that information from government-controlled areas tended eventually to reach Freetown. Information from deep within rebel controlled areas was more difficult to obtain, at least prior to the slight opening up of access that came with the Lomé Agreement. Before this access, a certain amount of information could be obtained from meeting with refugees in Guinea and from internally displaced persons (IDPs). Also, some of the activists who had received the UN human rights training in 1998 subsequently found themselves in rebel-controlled areas and were able, very occasionally, to transmit situation reports. For instance, a small group of former trainees, at high risk to themselves, maintained a chronicle of the human rights situation in a provincial town during the period when it was entirely closed off from the outside world by its rebel controllers.[35]

The principal UN public reporting tool was the report of the secretary-general on UNOMSIL/UNAMSIL to the Security Council, which was typically issued once every two to three months. This invariably contained a section detailing the human rights situation. It also contained human rights commentary in its various other sections (such as those addressing political, military and humanitarian issues). Although the human rights section of these reports was always rather short (perhaps two out of a total of 12 pages), it more or less accurately conveyed the situation at any given time and was effective in drawing the human rights situation to the attention of the Security Council. The UN reports were much less successful in drawing wide public attention due to the UN's weakness in ensuring wide and effective dissemination of its publications. A number of UN reports were also submitted to the Commission on Human Rights as reports of the high commissioner for human rights. These afforded a greater scope to discuss matters in detail. However, they tended to be published with data already in the public domain and they too suffered from the UN's poor public dissemination abilities.

---

[35] A report, written in hand in a school notebook, eventually found its way to the UNOMSIL Human Rights Section.

The UN also submitted highly detailed weekly and monthly internal reports to headquarters in New York as well as to the high commissioner for human rights. The reports to New York were used systematically in closed briefings to the Security Council. They were made available to the Sierra Leone government and the diplomatic community in Freetown. Only very rarely, however, did they get public dissemination. Somebody at UN headquarters apparently leaked one such report, on the situation in Freetown in January 1999, to the *New York Times*. One of this report's findings was that ECOMOG forces had been responsible for summary executions and other human rights abuses.[36] The leak led to widespread publicity and resulted in successful international pressure on Nigeria to address the problem – which it did almost immediately, at least to the extent of reining in its forces, withdrawing some ECOMOG officers, changing its high command, and establishing a joint military-civilian liaison board. The present author is not aware, however, that any judicial steps were ever instigated against the perpetrators.

In 1999 the UN began to issue a redacted version of its internal human rights reports in the form of a public newsletter, which was distributed in Sierra Leone as well as in the wider international human rights community.

Two international NGOs, Amnesty International and Human Rights Watch, took the lead in undertaking independent international reporting of the situation. Although these reports appeared somewhat sporadically and did not purport to provide comprehensive coverage, they were always authoritative and detailed. They received wide distribution and complemented the UN public reporting very well in that they were much more expansive. They also benefited greatly from the far superior public dissemination skills and capacities of the NGOs (inevitably though, the NGO reports raised the ire of UN human rights staff who frequently read in them details that they had already themselves covered, perhaps months before, in the reports to the Security Council and which had elicited next to no public notice at the time).

It can be concluded that the international reporting of the situation by the Sierra Leone human rights community was effective. It is clear that the UN reports had an impact on the Security Council. A correlation can be drawn between references to human rights in these reports and the Council's own outputs, such as the president's statements and resolutions, which increasingly came to describe and define the situation in Sierra Leone as being one of fundamental human rights abuse. The NGO reports for their part deserve the credit for attracting wide international public interest. The UN and NGO reports together, notwithstanding their shortcomings, succeeded in defining international perceptions of the conflict and in ensuring that human rights considerations would be required to inform the peace process.

---

[36]   See *Report of Human Rights Assessment Mission to Freetown*; and J. Miller, 'UN Monitors Accuse Sierra Leone Peacekeepers of Killings', *New York Times*, 12 February 1999, A-12.

Undertaking Human Rights Advocacy and Interventions

The tit-for-tat nature of much war-time violence can feed the conflict and drive the prospect of peace even further away. It is thus relevant to examine briefly the role of the human rights community in seeking to break such abusive patterns during the periods of conflict.

The most consistent form of advocacy, the simple act of ensuring ongoing public reporting of the situation, has already been examined. This reporting was also occasionally supported by highly-targeted appeals deliberately intended to bring pressure on the combatants. These sometimes had a discernable impact on at least the reported levels of human rights abuse in the country. For instance, on 17 June 1998, the head of UNICEF, Carol Bellamy, OCHA, Sergio Viera de Mello, and the High Commissioner for Human Rights, Mary Robinson, issued a strongly worded joint statement describing the acts of the rebels as 'outrageous violations of human rights ... and grave breaches of international humanitarian law'.[37] They called for judicial accountability for such abuses. The statement got wide publicity and was conveyed throughout Sierra Leone by means of the *BBC World Service*. During subsequent weeks, clinics reported a palpable, albeit short-lived, drop in the rates of admission of victims of amputation and other forms of mutilation. Although similar reactions could be observed on other such occasions, no particularly systematic study has ever been attempted to measure or predict the correlation between such actions and levels/patterns of abuse.

The human rights community also intervened directly with the parties. This was, inevitably, easiest to undertake with the government. There were, for instance, frequent interventions throughout the period under review regarding the recruitment of child combatants within the CDF. Human rights activists considered that these tended to have an immediate, if not particularly lasting, impact. The UN had more success in its interventions regarding the 1998 civilian treason trials that it had closely monitored. In almost every instance when it complained about the judicial process or the conditions of detention of the prisoners, the government reacted constructively. UN monitoring also encouraged the government to assiduously respect the rights of appeal of convicted people, as a result of which they avoided the hasty executions that were being called for by much of the Freetown media.[38] The UN and NGOs had no such success in their efforts to ensure a fair trial of military personnel subject to trial by court martial, probably because they were perceived to be junta ringleaders and it was felt that their swift punishment would allay public anger. However, the UN's strident efforts[39] to protest the sentences of death probably influenced the

---

[37]   Press Release, United Nations, Crisis in Sierra Leone Highlights Urgent Need for an International Criminal Court (June 1998), press release, UN Doc. HR/98/40 (1998).

[38]   All of the civilians subsequently escaped from prison at the time of the rebel incursion into Freetown.

[39]   Including appeals by the UN secretary-general, the high commissioner for human rights, the UN Human Rights Committee and Amnesty International.

government decision to spare the lives of a small number of the condemned. Another example of a UN intervention, this time successful, was an urgent telephoned appeal to President Kabbah seeking to calm the dangerous mood on the streets of Freetown on 26 December 1998, when a crowd had lynched two alleged rebels and was rampaging through the city centre. Within the hour, the Minister for Information, Julius Spencer, was successfully pleading on national radio for people to go home and not to take the law in their own hands.

There were also direct interventions with the rebel forces. Religious-based human rights actors had some success in making specific requests, such as those regarding the situation of individual abductees or for limited humanitarian access. The UN also frequently attempted to engage with the rebels. For instance, on 21 February 1999, following a meeting with RUF leaders, the rebels announced that they would, 'take punitive measures against any members who would violate human rights' and that they 'condemn all human rights violations and atrocities including amputations, mutilations, maiming, rape, etc., perpetrated against the civilian population'.[40] The most conspicuous UN effort was the delivery to the RUF leadership at their Lomé meeting in May 1999 of an *Aide Mémoire*,[41] which stated the various human rights and humanitarian law provisions related to the patterns of abuse which they perpetrated. The note also drew attention to the international criminal law consequences of these abuses. The rebels accepted the note saying that they previously had not been aware of the legal consequences of their acts and that they would abide by its provisions (!). For a subsequent period the note was delivered to rebel leaders whenever UN human rights staff encountered them. While there is no evidence that the *Aide Mémoire* had any significant impact on actual behaviour, it in itself, with the manner of its acceptance, did remove from the rebels the excuse that they had often employed: that their noble cause justified their deeds, or the often repeated denial that they were responsible for the abuse of civilians.[42] It may also have evidentiary value for any future criminal prosecutions.

Establishing Building Blocks for Future Accountability for Human Rights Abuses

Throughout 1998–2000 the human rights community sought to put in place elements necessary to ensure that some form of accountability might eventually occur for the human rights abuses that had taken place. First, it remained preoccupied with recording the situation as it unfolded: not only to assist individual criminal trials,

---

[40]   UN and RUF Joint Communiqué, on file with the present author.

[41]   A copy of the *Aide Mémoire* is on file with the present author.

[42]   For an exposition of RUF thinking see, *RUF, Footpaths to Democracy – Towards a New Sierra Leone*, vol. 1, (1995) (on file with the present author). The back cover of this publication states: 'Each generation has the onerous task to judge the performance of its institutions, particularly the government. The African people of Sierra Leone evaluated the performance of the [government] and the consensus was that in order to save the nation from its perennial political, social and economic predicament, the entrenched system could only be changed by armed uprising of the people imbued with a clear ideology.'

but also to establish an historical account that might combat tendencies towards myth-making or those subsequent distortions of the truth that could fuel hatred and prejudice.

The UN, and other, public reporting was clearly intended to serve this purpose. The authors of the UN internal human rights reports also had in mind the value of these texts as detailed, if incomplete, documents of record that might at an appropriate time be placed in the public domain. UN reports, however, only covered the period since the appointment of the UN human rights advisor in April 1998, and, with the exception of some excellent material published by Amnesty International, there was a dearth of recorded information regarding the period of brutal junta control (May 1997 to January 1998). Throughout 1998 the UN human rights team, recognising that it clearly did not itself have the resources, sought financial assistance to undertake a modest chronicling exercise regarding the junta period. The efforts were unsuccessful, at least partly because of reluctance on the part of many donors to recognise the worth of the exercise. In any case, the evacuations of January 1999 and subsequent developments, such as the discussion of establishment of a truth commission, overtook the proposal and it was not pursued further.

Cautious donor responses also impeded efforts by the National Forum for Human Rights during 1998–1999 to set up a central human rights information clearing system and database. Funding was eventually received in 2000 but the information system as originally conceived never came into being, partly due to the shifting priorities in response to the volatile situation throughout that year.

The other major contribution by the human rights community to ensure eventual accountability was its sustained effort to keep alive discussion of the eventual establishment of some form of formal accountability and reconciliation mechanism. The discussion first emerged in an un-focused manner in 1998, largely in reaction to repeated, inconsistent and unclear government offers of amnesty to rebels who would lay down their arms. The credibility of the offers was never clear and, in any case, there appeared to be no public appetite for generosity to the rebels.

By the time of the rebel incursion into Freetown the situation had dramatically altered, with more and more voices calling for a settlement with the rebels. The UN human rights team responded to the real possibility of the granting of impunity by expressing its concern to the government in the person of the attorney general and minister for justice. It initiated an internal reflection, involving OHCHR, on strategies to ensure accountability of, at least, the principal offenders and how to best support the eventual establishment of a sturdy truth and reconciliation commission.

The United Nations also requested that the human rights community, in the framework of the Human Rights Committee, meeting first in Conakry and, from March in Freetown, develop proposals on the matter. The Committee called for the establishment of a 'Truth, Justice and Reconciliation Commission' at some future time in the context of a peace agreement. The concept was spelled out in a statement of 1 March 1999 delivered to President Kabbah and signed by representatives of 22 Sierra Leone human rights groups, that stated:

The Human Rights Community is of the view that while it is important to look forward to the future rather than the past during this critical peace process, the disturbing cycle of impunity in Sierra Leone will not be broken unless there is some form of censure or punishment to some perpetrators of gross abuses of human rights in the country. Accordingly, therefore, the Human Rights Community proposes the creation of a Truth, Justice and Reconciliation Commission in Sierra Leone which will, inter-alia, enable the country to cope with the aftermath of the crisis by hearing the truth directly from perpetrators of gross human rights violations, help survivors of violations cope with their trauma, and recommend judicial prosecutions for some of the worst perpetrators of the violations.[43]

It was also suggested that the commission be established with the participation and widespread consultation of civil society and both the governmental and rebel participants in the conflict, and the UN was requested, 'to provide guidance on the functioning of truth commissions and similar post-conflict structures in other countries'.[44]

The fate of these and other proposals is discussed below in the context of an examination of the role played by the human rights community in the peace process itself which can be said to have gotten underway in March/April 1999.

The Human Rights Community and the Peace Negotiations Preparations for Lomé

The 1 March meeting with President Kabbah can be seen as the initial formal engagement of the human rights community with what would become known as the Lomé peace process. At that meeting an agenda for peace was spelled out.[45] As well as calling for accountability in the manner described above, the human rights leadership also proposed:

a) That it, and other parts of civil society, be allowed to play an active role in the peace process;

b) That any peace agreement contain clear provisions for the protection and promotion of human rights; and

c) That a peace agreement not provide for power-sharing with rebels prior to a general election.

Just five weeks later, at the behest of the government, the NCDHR convened the national consultative conference on the peace process, intended to build national consensus around broad negotiating parameters for future peace talks.[46] The human rights community played an active part in the conference and convened its own

---

[43] A copy of the statement is on file with the present author.

[44] *Ibid.*

[45] *Ibid.*

[46] See Penfold, *The Road to Peace: Report of the National Consultative Conference on the Peace Process in Sierra Leone.*

working group. It also heavily influenced the proceedings by ensuring the inclusion of standard discussion items in the taskings for all of the conference's 19 working groups, such as the possible role of a truth and reconciliation commission, the manner in which a peace agreement should address the plight of abductees and the possible role of a reparation fund for victims of human rights abuse.

In its own report to the plenary,[47] the human rights working group largely reflected the positions that had been stated to the president, with the addition of a call for a peace agreement, including a provision for the release of all abductees. The group also endorsed the idea that a reparation fund should be established for victims of gross human rights violations, funded by the government and donors. The one significant deviation from the proposals put to the president was a disagreement regarding whether there could be any role for an amnesty in a peace agreement.[48]

Ultimately, the conference conclusions,[49] although reflecting to a great extent the elements of the unimplemented 1996 Abidjan Peace Agreement, endorsed many of the proposals, including the call for a role for civil society in the peace process, the need for peace negotiations to address the plight of abductees, opposition to power-sharing before elections, the establishment of a reparation fund for victims and the establishment of a commission to be termed, a 'truth and reconciliation commission' – thus the term 'justice' disappeared. The conclusions further proposed that the establishment of the commission should be accompanied by an amnesty for combatants.[50] The conclusions were described as a 'conference consensus' although a number of participants complained privately that, with regard to the amnesty provision, they had been bullied into acquiescing in an outcome insisted upon by the government and its international supporters. Notwithstanding, the human rights community could depart from the conference satisfied that it had introduced or encouraged the introduction of a number of issues that would become agenda items for the peace talks themselves.

The weeks following the conference were ones of intense activity for the human rights community. Within the framework of the Human Rights Committee and with the support of the UN human rights team, it hammered out positions on the various aspects of the peace process. The community was encouraged by the unexpected announcement by the president on 27 April that a new Human Rights Commission would be established by statute, which would conform to international standards and would wield considerable powers. The UN immediately promised its full support for this initiative. Another surprise in those weeks was the extension of an invitation by the government to the UN High Commissioner for Human Rights, Mary Robinson, to visit the country. In agreeing, she said that one of the primary purposes of her visit would be to support the peace process.[51]

---

[47]   *Ibid.*, pp. 100–103.

[48]   *Ibid.*, p. 100.

[49]   *Ibid.*, pp. 36–39.

[50]   *Ibid.*, 36.

[51]   Former UN High Commissioner for Human Rights Mary Robinson, Address at the ceremony of signing of the Human Rights Manifesto (24 June 1999) (on file with the present

The Human Rights Community at Lomé

The peace talks commenced on 26 May and, in conformity with the conclusions of the April conference, the leadership of the human rights community was invited to participate in an observer status, while the NCDHR chair, Kadie Sesay, was appointed as a negotiator. The leader of the government delegation was Solomon Berewa, the attorney general and minister for justice, who had a record of maintaining close and generally constructive contact with the UN human rights team. UN human rights officers were also to be present throughout as part of the UN observer team, and UN humanitarian officers participated from time to time. The negotiations were organised within the framework of a number of drafting committees, one of which was designated, 'the committee for humanitarian, human rights and socio-economic issues'. This committee was co-chaired by Kadie Sesay. While the committee was tasked with addressing a range of human rights and related issues, it was precluded from dealing with all aspects of the amnesty discussions, which were instead assigned to a political committee.

Proceedings got off to a good start with a sideline agreement by the parties for the release of all abductees and the removal of obstructions to the delivery of humanitarian assistance. Both of these issues had been the focus of hard lobbying by the human rights and humanitarian observers. The agreement on humanitarian access, in particular, was a result of the intensive efforts of the UN humanitarian coordinator.

With these immediate issues duly addressed, the principal negotiations got underway in earnest. There were a number of draft texts on the table, principally of the government and the OAU. These, by and large, reflected elements of the conclusions of the April conference, including many proposals that had been launched first by the human rights community. Although technically confidential, it was possible to obtain copies of the drafts, and the UN and NGO observers had the opportunity to prepare commentaries. The drafting committee proved amenable to receiving these comments and a number of them came to be reflected directly in the final texts.

The following are the principal human rights elements of the peace agreement, together with an indication of the extent of influence exerted by human rights observers present in Lomé.

Article XV accords freedom of movement and guarantees for security of UNOMSIL human rights officers. This was inserted at the behest of UN human rights observers.[52]

Article XXII provides for the return and reintegration of refugees and IDPs. At the request of the UN observers it is stipulated that such return must be 'voluntary'.[53]

Article XXIV, using wording identical to a provision of the 1996 Abidjan Peace Agreement, affirms the importance of 'the basic civil and political liberties' as

---

author).
[52]   Peace Agreement, Article XV.
[53]   *Ibid.*, Article XXII.

contained in Sierra Leone law and international human rights instruments. The human rights observers, while welcoming the thrust of this provision, were unsuccessful in extending it to cover also economic, social and cultural rights.[54]

There is a provision for establishment of an independent human rights commission and for national programmes of human rights education and awareness raising (Article XXV). The UN observers were able to adjust the language of the provision whereby it provided the basis for establishment of a commission in conformity with international best practice; they also encouraged the drafters to include the provision whereby the high commissioner for human rights and others might render technical cooperation.[55]

Article XXVI stipulates the establishment of a truth and reconciliation commission, 'to address impunity, break the cycle of violence, provide a forum for both the victims and perpetrators of human rights violations to tell their story, get a clear picture of the past in order to facilitate genuine healing and reconciliation'. The Commission would also be tasked to address the rehabilitation of victims. Article XXVI was fashioned to substitute for judicial accountability, and the language used, for instance regarding the addressing of impunity, was directly influenced by human rights lobbying. However, efforts to insert the word 'justice' in the title of the commission, as per the original pre-April conference discussions, were unsuccessful.[56]

Article XXVII, on humanitarian access, and Article XXI, on release of prisoners and abductees, have been addressed above.[57] Article XXIX stipulates that there shall be a programme for rehabilitation of war victims.[58]

Article XXX provides that special attention be paid to the needs of child combatants and that resources be mobilised in this regard, including through the SRSGCAC, UNICEF and other agencies. The agreement's preamble also refers specifically to the needs of children and the central importance of adherence to the Convention on the Rights of the Child.[59] These provisions were inserted on the suggestion of SRSGCAC and child protection bodies.[60]

The committee with responsibility for drafting the terms of the amnesty was not amenable to the lobbying efforts of the human rights community. A number of attempts were made, however, to moderate the scope of the proposed sweeping provision. In particular, UN senior observer Francis Okelo, the special representative of the secretary-general, was advised by his human rights team to seek amendments to the draft provision whereby it did not extend to international crimes and that its application in any individual case be dependent on full cooperation with the Truth and Reconciliation Commission. He was further encouraged at the time of the talks

---

54   *Ibid.*, Article XXIV.
55   *Ibid.*, Article XXV.
56   *Ibid.*, Article XXVI.
57   *Ibid.*, Article XXVII.
58   *Ibid.*, Article XXIX.
59   Convention on the Rights of the Child, adopted 20 Nov. 1989, GA res. 44/25, UN GAOR, 44th Sess., Supp. No.49, Un Doc. A/44/49 (1989) (entered into force 2 Sept. 1990).
60   Peace Agreement., Article XXX.

to take a strong position on the issuance of guidelines by the secretary-general regarding UN involvement in peace talks that set limits on the extent to which the UN could associate itself with amnesty provisions.

These efforts were unsuccessful, and Article IX provides for the pardoning of Foday Sankoh and the granting of, 'absolute and free pardon and reprieve to all combatants and collaborators in respect of anything done by them in pursuit of their objectives, up to the signing of the present Agreement'. The UN secretary-general immediately instructed Okelo to disassociate the organisation from the provision by appending to his signature as witness to the agreement the words, 'the United Nations holds the understanding that the amnesty and pardon in Article IX of the agreement shall not apply to international crimes of genocide, crimes against humanity, war crimes and other serious violations of international humanitarian law'.[61]

Meanwhile, as the peace talks were underway from 24–25 June, Mary Robinson visited Freetown and repeatedly urged that peace without justice would be unacceptable. She discussed with the government and others the possibility that either in the peace agreement or in parallel, and notwithstanding the discussion in Lomé of an amnesty, that an international commission of inquiry be envisaged as a first step towards ensuring some form of future accountability. The suggestion aroused some interest and a concept of such an inquiry was put to Solomon Berewa and others at the negotiations by the UN human rights team. The negotiators did not choose to take it up, although a number of government negotiators did express interest in re-opening the issue at some time in the future. Mary Robinson also took the opportunity to reconfirm her commitment to provide all possible support of her office for the establishment of the National Human Rights Commission and the Truth and Reconciliation Commission. The commitment is enshrined in the Human Rights Manifesto.

The Manifesto also provided the UN with an opportunity to have the government commit to, and elaborate details of, some of the human rights proposals that were emerging in the peace negotiations. Thus, the Manifesto commits the government to 'inclusion in all peace settlement agreements of strong human rights components, including the establishment or re-enforcement of relevant national institutions and provisions for the monitoring of respect for human rights by governmental and nongovernmental organisations'. It also binds the government to the establishment of a human rights commission, 'which will be in compliance with the international standards'.[62]

Human Rights Community Efforts for Implementation of the Peace Agreement

With the conclusion of the Lomé Agreement, the human rights community's role in its implementation came to assume a fourfold dimension.

---

[61]   See Seventh Report of the Secretary-General on the United Nations Mission in Sierra Leone (2000), at 34.

[62]   A copy of the Manifesto is on file with the present author. See also *ibid.*

Establishment of Monitoring Systems

Although the Lomé Agreement provided for a number of monitoring/implementation bodies, it had no provision regarding the supervision of the implementation of its human rights provisions. The Human Rights Committee, recognising this gap and borrowing heavily from similar initiatives[63] following Bosnia and Herzegovina's Dayton/Paris Peace Agreement, established a tracking mechanism. The Committee undertook to make periodic assessments on the status of the key human rights agreements as well as to document steps taken, programmes initiated or achievements made in each thematic area. Findings were to be published in an 'Implementation Bulletin'. The thematic areas were identified as: establishment of institutions and mechanisms; release of abductees; specific issues related to children; promotion of the voluntary return of refugees and IDPs; promotion of economic, social and cultural rights, including the issue of humanitarian assessment; promotion of civil and political rights and constitutional review; and, sensitisation of the community regarding the human rights provisions of the agreement.

The Bulletin was prepared on behalf of the Committee by the UN human rights team, based on information provided by the Committee membership. It was disseminated to all stakeholders, to the media, international human rights groups and to UN headquarters. About four editions of the Bulletin appeared in 1999 and a similar number in the first part of 2000, but it slipped into abeyance with the incidents of May 2000. In the preceding months it had been experiencing the difficulty that there was so little implementation to report. Its real period of usefulness was in the months immediately following the adoption of the agreement, when it constituted the only reporting device of its type and served both to raise awareness of, and clarify, key implementation issues. For instance, it helped maintain attention to the plight of abductees, a voiceless community often overlooked.

Establishment of Certain of the Institutions Provided for under the Agreement

Under the terms of the Human Rights Manifesto, the high commissioner for human rights had committed to support the establishment of the Human Rights Commission and the Truth and Reconciliation Commission. She made good her commitment by already confirming her offer of assistance in a letter to President Kabbah on the day following the Lomé signing. During what remained of 1999 the assistance took the form of deployment of experts to assist the UN human rights team in providing the technical support for the design of the institutions.

UN efforts for the establishment of the Truth and Reconciliation Commission were closely coordinated with a sub-group of the Human Rights Committee that,

---

[63]   See M. O'Flaherty and G. Gisvold (eds), *Post-War Protection of Human Rights in Bosnia and Herzegovina*, International Studies in Human Rights vol. 53 (The Hague: Martinus Nijhoff, 1998); M. O'Flaherty, 'International Human Rights Operations in Bosnia and Herzegovina', in A. Henkin (ed.), *Honoring Human Rights* (The Hague: Kluwer Law International, 2000).

with NCDHR, facilitated a set of national consultations on how the commission should look in practice. It was this UN/civil society partnership that ultimately provided the elements for a draft statute which the UN put before the government. The government accepted the draft with little change and it was adopted into law on 22 February 2000.[64] The statute, drawing on extensive consultations, as well as emerging international 'best practice', proposed a study commission comprising both national and international commissioners, with subpoena powers and authorisation to review the period since 1991. The Commission would be empowered to make binding recommendations to government regarding ensuring an impartial historical record, preventing the repetition of the violations of abuses suffered, addressing impunity, responding to the needs of victims and promoting healing and reconciliation.

With the adoption of the statute, the high commissioner, availing herself of generous UK funding, began implementing a pre-establishment phase for the Commission, consisting of the development of a national public awareness campaign and commissioning studies that would assist the Commission in its work. Not much had been achieved, however, by the time of the May 2000 incidents and, at the request of the UK, the programme was suspended pending clarification of the situation. Only in September of that year did efforts resume with a visit by an OHCHR technical mission.[65] The process of preparing for establishment of the Commission got underway properly following a national conference in November that issued a strong declaration calling for establishment of the Commission side by side with a 'Special Court'.[66]

UN efforts for the establishment of the Human Rights Commission also proceeded, but with little output in the period under review. A number of OHCHR missions were undertaken and work began on the drafting of a statute for consideration by the government. However, the human rights community in Sierra Leone, by and large, was concentrated on efforts for the establishment of the Truth and Reconciliation Commission, and the UN human rights team resources were stretched to their limits. In any case, what momentum there had been was lost for the remainder of 2000 following the May incidents.

Efforts for the Release of Abductees

Implementation of the agreement struck at Lomé, for release of what it termed, 'prisoners of war and non-combatants', was to be facilitated by a UN committee with NGO and ICRC participation. The human rights community was represented in the committee through, among others, the UN human rights team, UNICEF child protection staff, and a representative of the National Forum for Human Rights. The committee saw its work as comprising advocacy for release, care for released

---

[64]   Truth and Reconciliation Act 2000 (2000), available at http://www.sierra-leone.org/trcact2000.

[65]   Mission led by the present author.

[66]   Declaration on file with the present author.

persons and the maintenance of a database on abductees. It also inevitably took on an analysis role.

The range of tasks of the committee gave it a novel dimension, bringing together the classic human rights community with humanitarian colleagues, and dealing with everything from negotiation with rebel commanders to construction of camps. A clear division of labour emerged, in which the human rights specialists, especially the UN human rights and child protection teams, took the lead in negotiating with the rebels. Negotiation teams visited rebel camps at about five locations during the closing months of 1999 and succeeded in gaining the release of several hundred abductees, almost all of them children. On one occasion, a negotiator was held captive for a number of days and the generally declining security situation rendered visits such as these increasingly difficult to implement. It also quickly became clear that it would prove exceptionally difficult to secure the release of adolescent and adult women, all of whom had been claimed as 'wives' of the combatants, and many of whom knew of no other life. And it became obvious that the incidence of sexual abuse of women abductees was at 100%.

With the deteriorating post-Lomé situation, the efforts for the release of abductees grew less and less successful. In addition, a certain ratio of releases occurred spontaneously and without the intervention or knowledge of the Committee (and therefore without its being able to offer the housing and medical support that it had put in place). The efforts did, however, as has been noted, keep the issue on the political agenda. The committee's efforts also provided the data and analysis whereby the plight of war-related sexual abuse was highlighted.

Maintenance of Attention to the Issue of Accountability

The international human rights community expressed outrage with the amnesty provision in the Lomé Agreement. Its denunciation was expressed, for instance, in the form of condemnatory statements by Human Rights Watch and Amnesty International.[67] There were calls for the establishment by the UN of an international commission of enquiry. This proposal had already been introduced by the high commissioner for human rights during her visit to Freetown and she undertook to keep it alive, but in a way not disruptive of implementation of the peace agreement. Her vision of such a commission was described in the secretary-general's report to the Security Council of 30 July 1999:

> [T]he Security Council may wish to consider ... the establishment in due course of a commission of enquiry, as recommended to the government of Sierra Leone by the High Commissioner for Human Rights. Such a commission would investigate and assess human rights and humanitarian law violations and abuses perpetrated by all parties since the commencement of the conflict in 1991.[68]

---

[67] See Amnesty International, *Sierra Leone: Ending Impunity – An Opportunity Not To Be Missed* (26 July 2000), available at http://web.amnesty.org/library/index/engafr510602000.

[68] Seventh Report of the Secretary-General on the United Nations Observer Mission in Sierra Leone (1999), at 47.

In order to keep the proposal alive she requested that a senior Kenyan lawyer, Bethuel Kipligat, develop modalities for the operation of such a commission side by side with a truth and reconciliation process. He had not yet reported at the time of the May 2000 incidents and, in any case, events overtook his task with the subsequent developments regarding the Special Court.

In the meantime, UN human rights reporting of the ongoing situation continued, as did that of the NGO community. Through the closing months of 1999 and into 2000, in the context of increasing levels of violence, combatants were repeatedly reminded in meetings, press statements, UN reports and the media, that the amnesty provision had no effect regarding international crimes and that, in any case, it did not even purport to apply to actions committed following the signing of the Lomé Agreement. Human rights activists also met with the newly-appointed head of the Sierra Leone police, former senior UK police officer Keith Biddle, requesting that contemporaneous incidents of human rights abuses be investigated and treated as criminal matters. He agreed. Police efforts, however, were greatly constrained by limited capacity, as well as by very partial deployment in the provinces with none at all in rebel-controlled areas.

The climate regarding issues of accountability was to change utterly with the incidents of May 2000. The government reacted to them on 12 June by requesting that the UN secretary-general establish a 'special court', to try the RUF leadership, that would be established under Security Council authority and would enforce both international and domestic Sierra Leonean law. During July, the human rights community convened a number of meetings on the issue at which some common positions were developed. In the first place it was felt that the personal jurisdiction, targeting just the RUF, was unacceptably narrow. Secondly, it was considered that the court should be entirely internationalised, without the involvement of Sierra Leone judges or its laws. It was also agreed that the court should exist side by side with the Truth and Reconciliation Commission. Finally, it was argued that the amnesty provision of the Lomé Agreement should be considered null and void.

These views were conveyed to relevant parts of the UN system, notably the Office of Legal Affairs (which at least at that time appeared to have limited experience of engagement with civil society actors), as well as to the government. There was general agreement regarding all but the proposals for complete internationalisation of the court. International human rights NGOs, such as Human Rights Watch, in their advocacy had also conceded the possibility that the court have a mixed national/international character.

On 14 August, the Security Council proposed establishment of a Special Court to 'prosecute persons who bear the greatest responsibility' for perpetration of 'crimes against humanity, war crimes and other gross abuses of international humanitarian and Sierra Leonean law'.[69] It was left to the secretary-general to propose the various details to the Council for its subsequent consideration. These views were

---

[69]   Security Council resolution 1315 (2000), UN Doc. S/RES/1315 (2000), at 2.

contained in a report to the Council, dated 4 October,[70] that had benefited from extensive consultation on the ground, including with the Human Rights Committee membership. The proposals in the report were broadly welcomed by the human rights community, notwithstanding some concerns regarding the formulation of the personal and temporal jurisdiction, worries over the part-national nature of the court, the manner in which it might choose to prosecute children, and the eventual relationship with the Truth and Reconciliation Commission. These would all be matters to be extensively addressed subsequent to the period under review in the present analysis.

Conclusion

By the end of 2000, Sierra Leone had achieved a fragile peace, slowly and incrementally won over a period that saw at least one step back for every advance achieved. Credit for the peacebuilding process must go to multiple national and international actors. Among them, the human rights community made an important contribution.

This chapter has sought to identify and analyse this contribution across the range of various sectors and over the entire period under review. The story told is not just one of successes and achievements. Attention is also drawn to a number of failures on the part of the human rights actors to achieve peace process-related goals. It is also possible to discern a number of overarching factors and considerations that, to a significant extent, determined this performance.

In the first place, the many human rights actors could legitimately be described as a single community, well-coordinated and capable of working in concert with each other. This was a result both of the strong and open leadership within a number of the organisations and the existence of key coordination mechanisms, above all the National Forum for Human Rights and the Human Rights Committee. The wide membership of the Committee, including NGOs, the UN, humanitarian organisations and others was also critical to its success. Within the context of these coordination arrangements, the human rights community succeeded in both articulating and programmatically implementing a sophisticated vision of a human rights contribution to peacemaking.

There were limits, however, to both the structures and the scope of the vision. The community was never entirely cohesive and was hampered by the less than enthusiastic participation of such major bodies as the NCDHR. Furthermore, at critical moments the community failed to speak with one voice on fundamental issues – as was the case regarding justice and accountability at the time of the April 1999 national consultative conference.

Second, the presence of a UN human rights team in Sierra Leone was critically important. Its reporting on the situation directly impacted the UN understanding

---

[70]   Report of the Secretary-General on the Establishment of a Special Court for Sierra Leone.

of, and response to, the situation in Sierra Leone. The team's location within the peacekeeping mission context also permitted it to have high-level access to government, rebel leadership and the peace negotiations. The UN's strong attachment to the local NGO community greatly enhanced the latter's status and influence within political circles. The UN also undertook significant skills transfer and repeatedly encouraged the human rights groups to address issues related to the peace process. UN human rights efforts on the ground were significantly augmented by the engagement of OHCHR – without the support of which it is unlikely that the Truth and Reconciliation Commission would ever have been established.

The UN human rights engagement was not an unqualified success. This chapter has referred repeatedly to the under-resourcing of the programme and the consequent inability to address the range of challenges. The problem of lack of human resources was compounded by the flawed procedures for recruitment of human rights field officers. In addition, the occasionally fraught relationships with the peacekeeping mission leadership, such as during the downsizing of the mission in January 1999, had a debilitating effect.

Third, the international human rights NGOs played an important role. Support provided by Amnesty International to its local section sustained and encouraged the high quality leadership within the local NGO community. Amnesty International also drew international attention to Sierra Leone during 1998, a role that it subsequently came to share with Human Rights Watch, which took the important initiative of opening a country office. Peace-related human rights advocacy was also both undertaken and creatively supported by such humanitarian organisations as MSF. International NGOs, in addition, provided significant and necessary technical assistance, for instance in the establishment of the Truth and Reconciliation Commission.

Finally, the successes of the human rights community were at least in part thanks to the relatively open attitude of the government, which repeatedly gave civil society, and its human rights component, opportunities to present their positions and even to influence the peace negotiation process. Such cooperation, of course, had its limits. There were many instances of the government acting directly contrary to the recommendations of the human rights community as well as being itself responsible for serious violations of human rights.

It can be concluded that the successes and failures of the Sierra Leone human rights community were determined by multiple factors, both under and beyond the community's own control. Any attempt at definitive assessment of their achievements must take full account of these considerations. Whatever lessons there are to be learned can usefully be applied for all those engaged in the peacemaking process.

Chapter 16

Case Study: The United Nations Human Rights Field Operation in Angola[1]

Todd Howland[2]

Introduction

The use of non-traditional mechanisms by the Security Council of the United Nations (UN) in achieving peace between the Angolan government and the National Union for the Total Independence of Angola (UNITA) rebels in early 2002 is noteworthy. The two main contributions to the peace process were a field presence, mainly focusing on human rights work, and sanctions against the rebel movement. After close to 30 years of conflict with international actors on occasion acting to augment war and occasionally acting to contribute to peace, the traditional UN peacekeeping operations had been tried. The last of the peacekeeping missions began winding down in 1998 as the Angolan government and UNITA went to war again. Many saw this as evidence of yet another failed UN attempt to achieve peace.

Stung by what appeared to be a good deal of money and political capital being spent as well as a major opportunity for peace lost, the Security Council moved to sanction UNITA and to keep a beachhead in the country.[3] Oddly, but theoretically appropriate, this beachhead came in the form of the Human Rights Division (HRD) of the failed peacekeeping operation. HRD went from a marginal entity within the peacekeeping operation, to becoming the main component of the Security Council's *in situ* contribution to peace. While it would be incorrect to negate the contributions of the various UN attempts to facilitate peace in Angola, it would also be a grave error to fail to examine the lessons that can be gleaned for the UN as a whole from the Angola experience. This is especially true given that many of the Security Council members, UN staff, and other UN member states did not see human rights work as

---

[1] This chapter was first published under the title of 'UN Human Rights Field Presence as Proactive Instrument of Peace and Social Change: Lessons from Angola', in *Human Rights Quarterly* vol. 26, no. 1 (2004).

[2] This assessment is an analysis largely based on the experiences of the present author who worked for the Human Rights Division of the peacekeeping and peacebuilding missions of the United Nations in Angola from August 1998 to November 2001. As a result, this chapter provides a critical and unique insider's view of the human rights field operation model as realised in Angola.

[3] Interviews with members of the diplomatic community, in Luanda (1998–2000).

working to create peace in Angola, but simply maintaining a UN field presence to avoid the label of a complete failure.[4] Interestingly, the Angolan government would only agree to HRD remaining because it was disgusted by what it perceived was a complete failure of the UN troops and police to prevent UNITA from rearming.[5] While a country at war rarely agrees to a human rights operation, it is possible the Angolans saw some value in the government capacity-building work HRD had been doing with the justice system. Additionally they may have perceived HRD as so small and ineffective as to not be a major threat, or that HRD was the least of the evils the Security Council wanted to impose on it. Regardless, HRD was not well understood or supported by New York headquarters, which normally saw its procedures and departmental and/or individual power as more important than maximising the potential substantive contribution on the ground.[6]

The Angola experience highlights the utility of human rights field operations to possible successful UN interventions in complex conflicts and should – over time – reinforce the key role of human rights in peacebuilding and peacekeeping efforts. The purpose of the present chapter is to contribute to the understanding of the current limits and present potential of UN human rights field operations. It does this by examining HRD of the United Nations Office in Angola (UNOA).[7] While this chapter touches on the legal context, human rights situation, and HRD's programmatic activities, its focus is on the lessons to be learned from HRD's effort to implement a strategy that would stimulate an effective response to those human rights violations on the ground and contribute to building an environment conducive for peace.

International Legal Context

There has been a UN peacekeeping or peacebuilding mission on the ground in Angola since 1988.[8] UN human rights work was not part of the first missions. Its inclusion followed general organisational developments, such as the secretary-general's report:

---

⁴   Interviews with departing MONUA staff and DPKO staff, in New York (1998–2000).

⁵   Interviews with Angolan government officials (1998–2000).

⁶   Interviews with members of the diplomatic community, in Luanda (1998–2000).

⁷   On 15 August 2002, the UN Security Council established the United Nations Mission in Angola (UNMA) as a follow-on mission to the United Nations Office in Angola (UNOA). This mission has, as one of its main functions, the assistance of the Angolan government in 'the [p]rotection and [p]romotion of Human Rights and in building institutions to consolidate peace and enhance the rule of law'; see Security Council resolution 1433 (2002), UN Doc. S/RES/1433 (2002).

⁸   United Nations Verification Mission in Angola I (UNAVEM I), 20 December 1988–29 May 1991; UNAVEM II, 30 May 1991–7 February 1995; UNAVEM III, 8 February 1995–30 June 1997; United Nations Observer Mission in Angola (MONUA), 1 July 1997–February 1999 (except HRD, which continued its operational activities during the liquidation of UNOA); the Office of the United Nations in Angola (UNOA), 15 October 1999–14 August 2002; United Nations Mission in Angola (UNMA), 15 August 2002–30 April 2003.

'An Agenda for Peace Preventive Diplomacy, Peacemaking and Peace-keeping';[9] the Vienna Declaration and Programme for Action of the World Conference on Human Rights;[10] the creation of the Office of the United Nations High Commissioner for Human Rights (OHCHR);[11] and the secretary-general's report 'Renewing the United Nations: A Programme for Reform'.[12] These institutional developments, combined with unique factors on the ground, eventually led to the first peacebuilding mission where human rights has played a dominant role.[13]

No concrete mention of human rights can be found in the Security Council resolutions and/or reports of the secretary-general for United Nations Verification Mission in Angola (UNAVEM) I or II. The Bicesse Peace Accord from 31 May 1991 has one general reference to human rights.[14] The 1997 Lusaka Protocol contains a number of rhetorical and general commitments to respect human rights law, but lists very few structural changes or specific actions to be taken by the parties to achieve that respect.[15] The UN was given a role to monitor and verify the work of the new Angolan National Police force to ensure it was acting in accord with the rule of law.[16] Most of the first peacekeeping or peacebuilding missions where a UN human rights component was included had extensive chapters or clearly articulated provisions on human rights in the relevant peace accords. Thus, it is not surprising that Angola's original human rights presence was rather small, for its work was not clearly perceived by many in the UN as being directly linked to the success of the peace process. In fact, the human rights presence was critical to how peace was built.

In the resolution establishing UNAVEM III, the Security Council welcomed 'the Secretary-General's intention to include human rights specialists in the political component of UNAVEM III to observe the implementation of the provisions related to national reconciliation'.[17] Six months later, the Security Council authorised the

---

[9]   Report of the Secretary-General, An Agenda for Peace: Preventive Diplomacy, Peacemaking and Peace-keeping: Report of the Secretary-General Pursuant to the statement adopted by the Summit Meeting of the Security Council on 31 January 1992, UN Doc. A/47/277–S/2411 (1992).

[10]   Vienna Declaration and Programme of Action, UN Doc. A/CONF.157/23 (1993).

[11]   High Commissioner for the Promotion and Protection of All Human Rights, UN Doc. A/RES/48/141 (1993).

[12]   Report of the Secretary-General, Renewing the United Nations: A Programme for Reform, UN Doc. A/51/950 (1997).

[13]   Some observers believe the special representative of the secretary-general (SRSG) at that time was especially interested in human rights and greatly facilitated the application of these institutional developments to the process in Angola. Other observers were concerned that the SRSG's approach to human rights violations was not effective.

[14]   Bicesse Peace Accord, Lisbon, Portugal, signed 31 May 1991.

[15]   Lusaka Protocol, Lusaka, Namibia, signed 15 November 1994 (entered into force 15 November 1994), available at http://www.angola.org/politics/p_lusaka.

[16]   E. Colthoff, *UN Human Rights Work in Angola* (unpublished manuscript, on file with present author).

[17]   See Security Council resolution 976 (1995), UN Doc. S/RES/976 (1995), at 8.

strengthening of the Human Rights Unit (HRU).[18] In successive resolutions it called on the parties to respect human rights, but never specifically defined how the HRU was to contribute to this.[19] The reports of the secretary-general to the Security Council on the situation in Angola provide a bit more information about the early human rights work of the UN in Angola. According to these reports a small sub-unit was created in July 1995 'to deal with human rights issues and observe implementation of the relevant provisions of the Lusaka Protocol ... [and] contribute to the civil education campaign and help to build confidence in the peace process'.[20] At the end of 1995, the HRU and Civilian Police were reported to have been 'monitoring and, as necessary, investigating human rights violations'.[21]

The human rights work done in UNAVEM III began with political affairs officers being assigned to cover the area. While remaining part of the Political Affairs Division, the Human Rights Unit was created in February 1995 and a chief appointed.[22] All the HRU staff members were political affairs officers until May 1996 when a few 'seconded' human rights officers/specialists from the European Parliamentarians for Africa were integrated into the peacekeeping mission.[23]

After the early human rights work of UNAVEM III was severely criticised,[24] it was decided to increase the staff numbers and create the Human Rights Division separate from Political Affairs.[25] Subsequent authority for human rights work was derived from Security Council resolution 1118 (1997) of 30 June 1997 that created the United Nations Observer Mission for Angola (MONUA).[26] Although it made no specific mention of human rights, the resolution incorporated into the work of MONUA work similar to what was already being done by stating that 'MONUA will

---

[18]   The Security Council stated its concern at the report of human rights violations, and recognised 'the contribution human rights monitors can make in building confidence in the peace process'. See Security Council resolution 1008 (1995), UN Doc. S/RES/1008(1995).

[19]   Security Council resolution 1055 (1996), UN Doc. S/RES/ (1996); Security Council resolution 1064 (1996), UN Doc. S/RES/1064 (1996); Security Council resolution 1075 (1996), UN Doc. S/RES/1075 (1996); Security Council resolution 1087 (1996), UN Doc. S/RES/1087 (1996).

[20]   Report of the Secretary-General on the United Nations Angola Verification Mission (UNAVEM III), UN Doc. S/1995/588 (1995), at 22.

[21]   Report of the Secretary-General on the United Nations Angola Verification Mission (UNAVEM III), UN Doc. S/1995/1012 (1995), at 23.

[22]   Interviews with MONUA staff of the Political Affairs Division (1998).

[23]   Interviews with the original active human rights staff (1998).

[24]   Internal Report, I. Martin, *Report on the Human Rights Activities of UNAVEM III and Proposals for an Enhanced Programme* (2 February 1997) (copy on file with present author).

[25]   Plans existed to expand staff number to 58, permit the staff to now investigate human rights abuses, and initiate appropriate actions through the Joint Commission. See Report of the Secretary-General on the United Nations Angola Verification Mission (UNAVEM III), UN Doc. S/1997/115 (1997).

[26]   See Security Council resolution 1118 (1997), UN Doc. S/RES/1118 (1997).

assume responsibility for all components and assets of the UNAVEM III remaining in Angola'.[27]

Another 13 Security Council resolutions were passed over the next 18 months (two more by the end of 1997 and 11 in 1998), only two of which indirectly dealt with the issue of human rights. Both resolutions incorporated human rights through their call for MONUA to contribute to improving the respect for the rule of law in Angola.[28] This apparent lack of interest in human rights could be considered a shift by the Security Council given its early statements related to UNAVEM III.[29] Nonetheless, the secretary-general validated the human rights work being done by MONUA by including it in his report to the Security Council.[30] The implicit rather than explicit inclusion of human rights in the resolution upon which MONUA was based allowed HRD to operate with a broad mandate and to respond with flexibility to the needs on the ground. There were neither expressed limits nor direct support for the UN human rights work emanating from the Security Council at this point.

The importance of the human rights component of MONUA was underscored by Security Council resolution 1229 (1999) of 26 February 1999.[31] The resolution is historic in that it decided 'that the human rights component of MONUA will continue its current activities during the liquidation period'.[32] This was the first time that UN human rights work was mentioned in a Security Council resolution related to Angola or any country as the principle tool on the ground to be used to create conditions for peace.[33] It is important to point out that in the same resolution the Security Council formally ended its peacekeeping mission.[34]

At the time of MONUA, HRD had staff posted in the provinces. As MONUA closed, so did the provincial offices. HRD was dependent on the larger peacekeeping mission for air and vehicle transport, for office space and supplies, for communications – basically everything. Thus, HRD provincial staff were forced back to Luanda as the logistical support for its presence in the provinces evaporated as MONUA liquidated

---

[27]   *Ibid.* There was no specific demand for the deployment of human rights field officers in the Lusaka Protocol. The deployment of human rights field officers was consistent with a policy change made by the UN Secretariat to include human rights components in all peacekeeping and peacebuilding missions and with the personal desire of the then SRSG in Angola.

[28]   See Security Council resolution 1202 (1998), UN Doc. S/RES/1202 (1998) and Security Council resolution 1213 (1998), UN Doc. S/RES/1213 (1998).

[29]   See Reports at footnotes 20 and 21.

[30]   Report of the Secretary-General on the United Nations Observer Mission in Angola (MONUA), UN Doc. S/1998/17 (1998).

[31]   See Security Council resolution 1229 (1999), UN Doc. S/RES/1229 (1999).

[32]   *Ibid.*, at 2.

[33]   *Ibid.* Normally, the human rights component is part of the larger mission. By authorising the continuation of on-the-ground human rights activities as everyone else was told to liquidate, the Security Council implicitly made HRD the most important part of the operation.

[34]   *Ibid.*

or shutdown. While the Security Council had passed its resolution, no discussion at UN headquarters actually defined what, in the wake of the liquidation of MONUA, would be required to support HRD.[35] The assumption appeared to be that HRD would close shop once the last MONUA staffers left Angola. Only one provincial office remained open in addition to the headquarters in Luanda. This office remained open on borrowed time and favours. The local staff person began 'squatting' in another UN office using a vehicle that had been given to another UN agency operating in that province. Doing something mandated by the Security Council suddenly required enormous energy, creativity and a bit of sleight of hand with the local MONUA administration.

Later that year, the Security Council built on its previous foundation when it passed resolution 1268 (1999) of 15 October 1999, which created the United Nations Office in Angola (UNOA) as a peacebuilding mission.[36] This resolution was consistent with '[t]he United Nations Agenda for Peace of 1992 [which] proposed "peacebuilding" as a way of preventing the resumption of civil conflicts but did not dispense a patent medicine for doing so'.[37] The resolution's language was broad. The resolution states UNOA is to work 'with a view to exploring effective measures for restoring peace, assisting the Angolan people in the area of capacity building, humanitarian assistance, the promotion of human rights, and coordinating other activities'.[38] The resolution established UNOA with 30 international substantive staff

---

[35] While the resolution authorised that the human rights component of MONUA continue its activities, the larger, blue-helmeted component was withdrawing. Along with that withdrawal came the removal of logistic support for human rights activities. For example, DPKO, the unit charged with providing support to the peacekeeping mission, had no interest and felt no obligation under the Security Council resolution to support the human rights component if it interfered with closing the larger operation. The failure of the human rights component and OHCHR to keep the provincial offices open, even with the explicit support of the resolution, demonstrated the human rights component's relatively weak position within the UN system.

[36] See Security Council resolution 1268 (1999), UN Doc. S/RES/1268 (1999).

[37] The UN has not been widely successful with these efforts for a number of reasons. R. Wedgewood and H. K. Jacobsen, 'Symposium: State Reconstruction After a Civil Conflict', *American Journal of International Law* vol. 95, no. 1 (2001), citing An Agenda for Peace: Preventive Diplomacy, Peacemaking and Peace-keeping: Report of the Secretary-General Pursuant to the Statement Adopted by the Summit Meeting of the Secretary Council on 31 January 1992. See generally, A. Clapham and M. Henry, 'Peacekeeping and Human Rights in Africa and Europe', in A. Henkin (ed.) *Honoring Human Rights* (The Hague: Kluwer Law International, 2000); T. Howland, 'Mirage, Magic, or Mixed Bag? The United Nations High Commissioner for Human Rights Field Operations in Rwanda', *Human Rights Quarterly* vol. 21, no. 1 (1999).

[38] Some observers have criticised the mandate for failing expressly to support human rights monitoring activities, while others have argued that a full spectrum of field methods can be used consistently with the mandate provided. See footnote 36.

members.[39] HRD is the largest component with 12 international staff members.[40] Thus, the UNOA came to be the first peacebuilding or peacekeeping mission where human rights has played a dominant role.

UN Human Rights Field Work

It must be noted that human rights fieldwork is new within the UN 'toolbox'. While the UN has been in existence for over half a century, it has less than 10 years of experience in organising and deploying UN human rights field operations. What these deployments can and should do is still hotly debated. While lessons can be derived from previous operations and related fields of work, each presence has its own unique legal and operational context. There is no one approach that works in all situations. Thus, HRD's efforts to develop appropriate field methods took place in the context of this debate and as part of the experimentation and innovation that drives this developing area of work.[41]

There are a number of unresolved issues regarding the relation of the OHCHR to UN human rights field presences that are part of peacekeeping or peacebuilding missions. The Department of Peacekeeping Operations (DPKO) ran MONUA. DPKO has a memorandum of understanding with OHCHR that delegates responsibility to OHCHR for recruitment and for providing substantive guidance. OHCHR did recruit personnel. There was a dual reporting line, with one to the special representative of the secretary-general (SRSG) in Angola who reported to the secretary-general through DPKO in New York, and the other to the high commissioner for human rights in Geneva. The Department of Political Affairs (DPA) ran UNOA. DPA has no memorandum of understanding with OHCHR and in a number of DPA missions the role of OHCHR is not significant, either substantively or in recruiting human rights personnel. In relation to UNOA, OHCHR has asserted its role in recruitment.[42]

---

[39] *Ibid.*

[40] It should be noted that technically HRD may have been misnamed. Normally a Division is headed by a D1, a section by a P5 and a Unit by a P4. HRD has never been headed by a D1, but has only been headed at the P5 level. Nonetheless, components are designated given their relative importance within a peacekeeping operation or within the institution. Thus, the move to Division for human rights gave it more status and importance in the time of MONUA. Considering human rights have even more status in UNOA, it seemed inappropriate to rename it a Section. This is especially true considering HRD is known by the public and partners as such.

[41] OHCHR recently began a process to analyse and systematise developments in human rights field work. HRD's work was, by and large, not included in this process even though it is the first peacebuilding mission where human rights is the largest component. Apparently, OHCHR did not have the capacity to provide this kind of substantive support.

[42] The United Nations Mission to Haiti was run by DPA. In discussions with DPA staff members in 2001 who had done the hiring for the United Nations Mission to Haiti, all hiring decisions for human rights staff were made by DPA. There was minimal, and at times, no contact with OHCHR related to hiring. In Angola, OHCHR had been involved in hiring of

Other than OHCHR's yearly meeting in Geneva, where the directors of all UN human rights field operations would meet for a few days to discuss developing field methodologies and to compare notes, there was limited substantive input. While there was frequent contact with Geneva, much of the time was focused on addressing informational needs or efforts to straighten administrative glitches.[43] The New York office of OHCHR was often contacted and provided assistance with administrative and budget-related issues, indicating that most decisions affecting HRD take place in New York (e.g. budget and staffing numbers). The only visit from Geneva OHCHR during the author's more than three-year tenure in Angola was financed by the HRD-Trócaire programme. This was the first visit from anyone from Geneva or New York OHCHR to Angola for a number of years, and it was done in the context of a workshop on a specific topic.[44]

HRD's vision and programme of activities developed without any formal or substantive input from New York (either DPKO nor later DPA) or OHCHR. This absence of input does not reflect a realisation of the importance of decentralisation in decision-making. Instead, New York shapes HRD through mandate and budget questions, while OHCHR's influence is felt through recruitment.

It is important to point out that many HRD staff members had previous UN human rights field or other related experience. Thus, they brought many lessons learned to Angola. This contributed enormously to the development of HRD's effectiveness and strategic approach to programme design and implementation.

National Context

Angola is a state party to a number of human rights-related instruments, including the Covenant of Civil and Political Rights; the Covenant on Social, Economic and Cultural Rights; the Convention on the Rights of the Child; the Convention on the Elimination of All Forms of Discrimination Against Women; the Convention on the Elimination of All Forms of Racial Discrimination; and the African Convention on Human and People's Rights.[45] It has ratified the Geneva Conventions of 1949 and its

---

staff for the previous DPKO run mission and asserted its continuing role in this process, even though there was no MOU requiring this and no history of involvement in DPA human rights hiring decision.

[43]   For example, the loss by OHCHR in Geneva of voluntary contributions for HRD's work in Angola is a good example. It took hours of work by Angola and Geneva-based staff to locate this money and even more to operationalise it.

[44]   An officer from OHCHR Regional Office in South Africa visited in 2000. It was mainly informational. There is still no clarity or consistency as to how these regional offices are run by OHCHR and how they relate programmatically or administratively to larger field operations run by DPA or DPKO. Discussions have taken place mainly because of informal ongoing contact between personnel of both types of offices.

[45]   International Covenant on Civil and Political Rights, adopted 19 Dec. 1966, G.A. res. 2200 (XXI), UN GAOR, 21st Sess., Supp. No. 16, UN Doc. A/6316 (1966), 999 UNTS 171 (entered into force 23 Mar. 1976); International Covenant on Economic, Social and

Protocol I.[46] It has signed but not yet ratified the Ottawa Convention on Anti-Personnel Mines and the Rome Statute of the International Criminal Court.[47] Thirty-four of 166 Articles of the Angolan Constitution deal with human rights-related issues.[48] Article 21 of the Constitution integrates the Universal Declaration of Human Rights into Angolan law.[49] Despite the human rights oriented constitutional framework and its numerous treaty obligations, Angola's reporting to UN human rights treaty bodies has been virtually non-existent and many of its laws are not in strict conformity with its constitution.[50] The Bicesse Accord's focus is on a winner-take-all election. The Lusaka Protocol's focus is on power sharing.[51] Neither document places human rights as a central theme, nor gives much importance to the creation of institutions needed to achieve sustainable peace by promoting respect of human rights. The transformative potential of human rights has been overlooked by the negotiating parties in favour of issues relating directly to the division of power and mechanisms for demobilisation.

Historically, neither the MPLA government nor the rebel movement UNITA have actively invoked human rights as one of their main purposes for existence and struggle. While each movement has within its programme aspects that relate to human rights, for example the struggle for independence from colonial rule, neither

---

Cultural Rights, adopted 19 Dec. 1966, G.A. res. 2200 (XXI), UN GAOR, 21st Sess., Supp. No. 16, UN Doc. A/6316 (1966), 993 UNTS 3 (entered into force 3 Jan. 1976); Convention on the Rights of the Child, adopted 20 Nov. 1989, G.A. res. 44/25, UN GAOR, 44th Sess., Supp. No. 49, UN Doc. A/44/49 (1989) (entered into force 2 Sept. 1990); Convention on the Elimination of All Forms of Discrimination Against Women, adopted 18 Dec. 1979, G.A. res. 34/ 180, UN GAOR, 34th Sess., Supp. No. 46, UN Doc. A/34/46 (1980) (entered into force 3 Sept. 1981), 1249 UNTS 13; International Convention on the Elimination of All Forms of Racial Discrimination, adopted 21 Dec. 1965, 660 UNTS 195 (entered into force 4 Jan. 1969); African Charter on Human and Peoples' Rights, adopted 27 June 1981, OAU Doc. CAB/LEG/67/3 Rev. 5 (entered into force 21 Oct. 1986).

[46]   Geneva Convention for the Amelioration of the Condition of the Wounded and Sick in Armed Forces in the Field of August 12, 1949, 75 UNTS (1950), 31; Geneva Convention for the Amelioration of the Condition of Wounded, Sick and Shipwrecked Members of Armed Forces at Sea of August 12, 1949, 75 UNTS (1950), 85; Geneva Convention Relative to the Treatment of Prisoners of War of August 12, 1949, 75 UNTS (1950), 135; Geneva Convention Relative to the Protection of Civilian Persons in Time of War of August 12, 1949, 75 UNTS (1950), 286; Protocol Additional to the Geneva Conventions of 12 August 1949, and Relating to the Protection of Victims of International Armed Conflicts (Protocol I), 1125 UNTS (1979), 3.

[47]   Convention on the Prohibition of the Use, Stockpiling, Production and Transfer of Anti-Personnel Mines and on their Destruction, G.A. res. 52/38, UN GAOR, 52nd Sess. (1998); Rome Statute of the International Criminal Court, UN Doc. A/CONF.183/9 (1998) UNTS 90 (entered into force 1 July 2002).

[48]   Angolan Constitution Articles 1–2, 4, 9, 18, 20–30, 32–44, 46–50.

[49]   *Ibid.*, Article 21.

[50]   For example, Angola has a penal code dated from 1888, and a criminal procedure code dated from 1926.

[51]   Bicesse Peace Accord, footnote 14; Lusaka Protocol, footnote 15.

has defined its struggle as a human rights struggle. Other parties or movements in Angola can be similarly characterised. Recently, all parties in Angola have added human rights rhetoric to their platforms.[52]

Human rights claims are traditionally those that citizens can legitimately make upon their governments. The rights of citizens are understood as 'correlatives' of duties that governments have.[53] That is, the rights citizens have to certain protections are equivalent to the duties that those citizens' governments have to ensure those protections. Given this understanding of human rights, it makes sense that human rights have not been at the centre of social and political movements in Angola. Angolan citizens do not have a history of participation in political decisions affecting them, nor have they demanded respect for their rights. It is critical that Angolan citizens know their rights and how to exercise them.

This lack of a human rights culture is largely the result of the overall lack of formal education in Angola.[54] Exacerbating this is a substantial lack of institutions and practices that would provide practical education in human rights concepts, laws and infrastructures to those with limited education opportunities. For example, 95% of Angolan municipalities lack functioning municipal courts.[55] Coping with extensive and serious problems in public health, education and water and sanitation systems has become the norm, where those who can afford to simply create their own 'system', while the majority have no access to drinkable water. Furthermore, the lack of municipal or local elections creates a society in which participation in government decisions is virtually non-existent and government representatives and functionaries are not perceived to be in the service of the people. While those with a higher level of education have a greater understanding regarding their rights, even their use of rights is rare. Contributing to this phenomenon is the fear or memories of political repression and scepticism regarding the present functioning of institutions.[56]

Most international aid to Angola has been in the form of humanitarian assistance, which does not consider the transformative potential of such aid. Some in the Angolan

---

[52] Interviews with various leading academics on Angola (1998–2001).

[53] On the idea that a right is a correlative of a duty, see W. N. Hohfeld, 'Some Fundamental Legal Conceptions as Applied in Judicial Reasoning', *Yale Law Journal* vol. 23 (1913). See also J. J. Thomson, *The Realm of Rights* (Cambridge: Harvard University Press, 1990), pp. 61–78.

[54] If people have not been educated of their rights, they likely will not know of the legal and administrative structures where they would complain about violations. Thus, it is difficult to imagine a human rights culture developing without formal education.

[55] Internal Study, Human Rights Division (2001).

[56] See generally, Angola Instituto de Pesquisa Económica e Social, Inquerito ao Conhecimento, *Exercício e Defensa dos Direitos Humanos na Província da Luanda* (Luanda 2000/2001) in cooperation with the Prosecutor General's Office, Trócaire, and the Human Rights Division (hereinafter HR Survey). The public opinion poll interviewed 1,511 Luandans in order to provide a statistically valid sample for Luanda. Certain conclusions from this data gathered only in Luanda can be extrapolated to all Angolans, but these conclusions are not necessarily statistically valid.

government and many in the population are not clear regarding the government's ultimate and primary responsibility for providing for people in need, and fulfilling the basic rights of its citizens. There are many international NGOs operating in Angola, most in the humanitarian arena.[57] Aid providers are not influential in Angola as they are in many developing countries. The amount of aid brought into Angola through bilateral or multilateral efforts is insignificant relative to revenues generated through private sector activity (e.g. multinational corporations).

Angola is no longer an ideological battleground. For most international actors Angola is a place to make money. In light of the importance of the private sector, embassies consider business interests in relation to all positions they take. Any human rights and peacebuilding effort needs to recognise the importance of the private sector. In Angola it is especially critical given the amount of money generated.[58] Nonetheless, it is important to note that the amount of money flowing from these private sector revenues into human rights-related state and government institutions is relatively very low.

While it can be argued that a country with such large revenues does not need international support, aid is largely focused in the area of humanitarian assistance, which has an extremely small or, perhaps, even negative transformative potential (e.g. the creation of dependence and distortions regarding the relation of state to citizen). Areas that are not well supported through the present state budget but which do have a large transformative potential, for example justice-related institutions, are open and have asked for international support. The lack of serious donor attention to this area is noteworthy.[59]

Regardless of how one analyses the human rights situation in Angola, listing the human rights abuses present there does little to explain why these abuses are taking place and how they can be stopped. Such a list would merely show that the situation is grim. Angola has an historic and infamous reputation for human rights violations; however, most of the recent violations stem from systemic dysfunctionalities. Angola, at present, is not ruled by a government that elaborates and implements plans

---

[57] HRD worked with the UN Office of the Humanitarian Coordinator to give seminars to the international NGOs operating in Angola. HRD had direct and extensive contacts with many of the international NGOs operating in Angola.

[58] HRD's attempt to integrate a human rights approach into the work of the multinationals, specifically related to the oil sector, has been insufficient. It is easier to treat these companies as just another donor, rather than attempt to organise them to support certain fundamental ideas or changes in society, e.g. creating a fully functioning justice system. While HRD's survey containing questions related to oil company compliance with human rights obligations and contacts with the Ministry of Petroleum was interesting, HRD has not managed to follow this research to a productive end.

[59] Some embassies have recognised the transformative potential of work in the justice sector. Their respective capitals, however, are more comfortable giving humanitarian assistance and even resist providing assistance in the human rights and justice area. The Dutch are a noteworthy example: they were instrumental in advocating that HRD remain in Angola, but The Hague desired to limit assistance just to the humanitarian area.

to eliminate or neutralise perceived or real political opposition. The government has not used its extremely large natural resource base to create a fully functional infrastructure that would serve to strengthen the whole spectrum of human rights.

The present human rights situation is the result of a convergence of historical and contemporary factors and interests that need to be isolated and understood before improvement can be facilitated and/or obtained. For too long, human rights were somehow considered something that would improve automatically once peace was achieved. It is important to note that this idea has had many adherents. Over time, HRD has helped to influence this widely held notion, and government and military officials have noted a growing understanding that respect for human rights can help to create the conditions needed for a sustainable peace.[60] Ignoring pending human rights issues will only result in continued social turmoil.

Lessons to be Learned

Human Rights as Vehicle to Facilitate Peace and Positive Social Change

Many people still conceive of human rights field officers (HRFOs) as monitors or observers who report on a problem or violation, and others – usually the parties to a peace accord – then take action to rectify it.[61] The Angola experience, however, highlights another type of human rights field officer (HRFO), one who is a proactive social change agent. Her or his role is to understand the situation and its many dysfunctionalities and to motivate domestic actors to minimise or end the violations.

The HRFOs work to augment the state's capacity to respect human rights (supply) and increase the citizens' proaction to ensure their rights are respected (demand).[62] HRD invests in social capital. It recognises it is in Angola to stimulate internal processes for positive social change, and understands that these processes can originate in government or civil society but progress can only be achieved by making advances on both fronts. Without demand from civil society, rights will not be realised. Without increased capacity of the state to respond appropriately, demand will not produce the desired change. Demand, in turn, can produce movement for creating greater capacity of the state to respond. While HRD is a social change agent,

---

[60]   The UN, and especially HRD, has contributed to this change in discourse and understanding. See for example, T. Howland, 'Human Rights and Peace', Address at the 'Pro Peace Conference' (18–21 July 2000).

[61]   The role of human rights field presences has, at times, been limited to monitoring or observation. See for example, Amnesty International, *Peacekeeping and Human Rights* (1994); International Human Rights Trust, *Toward a Human Rights Partnership for Effective Field Work* (1998).

[62]   The use of the terms supply and demand to encapsulate the twofold work of HRD may have first been used in conversation by Mario Aduata of the Angolan Institute for Economic and Social Research.

it cannot produce social change in Angola unilaterally. It requires trust between partners, and the inculcation by state and civil society actors to take effective and sustainable action to create long term positive social change. It requires sufficient capacity building to ensure partners can effectively continue this work upon HRD's departure. It must be understood by all parties that HRD is merely a temporary catalytic actor, not a permanent solution/presence.

The mission statement for HRD stated that it 'exists to facilitate incremental measurable positive change in the human rights situation in Angola'.[63] This rather broad mission statement was created based upon the UNOA mandate, the UN Charter,[64] and the various human rights treaties to which Angola is a state party. Specifically, 'the HRD works to facilitate a change in perspective from human rights work being seen as a clandestine activity to a normal vehicle for positive and incremental social change'.[65]

Government buy-in to the process of improving human rights is essential. Due to Angola's history of colonialism and its subsequent one-party state, there is little experience with a sovereign citizenry despite the introduction of multiparty democracy in 1991. Government, and especially the ruling party, needs to see human rights-related reforms as a means of opening society gradually and permitting officials and entities to benefit as well as the base (i.e. being re-elected because of having passed popular reforms).

The work done by HRD related to the right to liberty is an example of the analysis needed to begin developing an effective response to human rights violations. Here, HRD identified over 20 contributing causes. HRD's response included six projects with the government and state authorities, eight projects with civil society and targeted advocacy to change the policy of five entities.

Certainly, violation of the right to liberty is not the most frequent or egregious violation being committed in Angola; however, it has been positively addressed using HRD's approach. It demonstrates that government, state and civil society actors are open, can improve their human rights-related work, and strategic and timely interventions from the international community can provide concrete contributions.

Supply – Work with Government

The objective for human rights interventionists is to improve the situations they encounter, rather than simply denouncing them. Nonetheless, for most human rights activists, working with a government is heresy. Thus, it is not surprising that HRD's work was controversial. Some observers have lauded HRD's work with the Angolan government as a creative cooperation that opened opportunities for change

---

[63] Internal Strategy Paper by M. de Sousa, Director of the Angola Institute for Research, Human Rights Division Programme for 2001 (2000).

[64] Charter of the United Nations, 59 Stat. 1031, T.S. 993, 3 BEvans 1153 (entered into force 24 October 1945).

[65] See footnote 60.

previously unavailable in Angola. Others, however, worry that the support provided to the Angolan government by HRD is nothing more than a costly legitimisation of the present widespread violations.[66]

HRD has developed a series of ongoing human rights projects in Angola with government and state partners:

- case tracking systems with the prosecutors, police, prisons and courts, designed to provide a means to improve respect for liberty and due process rights;
- professional and human rights training for police, prison officials, prosecutors and judges, designed to improve the capacity for respect of human rights within the justice system;
- municipal justice project, designed to extend and improve access to and delivery of justice by increasing the number of municipalities served by a functioning justice system through training and infrastructure support;
- support of the 9th Commission of National Assembly to improve its capacity to respond to citizen complaints of human rights violations;
- support of Ministry of Foreign Relations in its production of useful and fact-based reports to treaty bodies;
- support of the Supreme Court to make its decisions available to the public thereby augmenting rule of law in Angola;
- support of the Angolan Army to implement a human rights educational project designed to reach all soldiers and to reinforce the willingness and ability of citizens to complain about violations committed by soldiers;
- and human rights awareness efforts with the Ministry of Justice and national radio.

Moving from a relationship of suspicion and hostility between the government and the UN to one of trust, especially using human rights as the vehicle, defies conventional wisdom. However, this is exactly what was done by HRD. Its work greatly repaired frayed UN-Angola relations following the failure of the Lusaka peace process and the government's perception that the UN peacekeepers had failed to prevent UNITA from rearming. The experience of Angola supports the work of a group of scholars that have attempted to elevate the importance of understanding people and personal dynamics as opposed to traditional theories, which focus on institutions devoid of people.[67]

According to some observers, HRD's proactive work with the Angolan government goes against development practices because HRD goes 'too far' in becoming an active partner (for example, facilitating project implementation).

---

[66]   See for example, M. Picken, *Summary Report for the Swedish Embassy on Programs and Strategies in the Area of Human Rights and the Administration of Justice in Angola*, (April 2001) (on file with present author).

[67]   See, for example, D. Kennedy, 'International Refugee Protection', *Human Rights Quarterly* vol. 8, no. 1 (1986); D. Kennedy, 'Spring Break', *Texas Law Review* vol. 63 (1985).

Curiously, though, some of these same observers feel HRD did not go far enough to protect rights and to enforce laws. HRD does not play a more robust role akin to the one played in UN missions where the UN is a governing body.[68] HRD does not take over government functions, as certain people would argue is appropriate (even if unrealistic), but plays a role in stimulating change and making that change happen. It does this by maximising the political 'space' it is allotted in which to act, as well as the limited resources it has.

Demand – Civil Society

Efforts to have civil society actors, such as local NGOs, other UN entities, international NGOs and the private sector,[69] contribute to the demands for quantitative and qualitative improvements in human rights are still in their infancy. Many governments, including Angola, were concerned over resources flowing to civil society. This is not unusual, given the United Nations is comprised of member states and UN entities like the UNDP that typically work almost exclusively with state actors. The recognition that civil society has an important role in improving dysfunctional societies and gaining acceptance for related initiatives, even in the context of an ongoing civil war, is no small feat.

HRD has developed a comprehensive catalogue of ongoing human rights projects with civil society and private sector partners:

- lawyers taking and litigating human rights cases (*Maos Livres* and *Pronto Socorro Juridico*);
- community-based human rights counsellors (many working out of churches and providing information about the full spectrum of human rights and support to resolve/respond to civil, political, economic, social or cultural rights violations);
- legal support for those who have been detained (e.g. Bar Association's work in police holding cells);
- radio shows featuring human rights issues (e.g. Get-up-Stand-up and *Maos Livres*);
- production of human rights awareness material as well as street and radio theatre by various NGOs;

---

[68]   It is important to point out that some observers see HRD as going too far in its project work with government, but not far enough as an international enforcer of human rights. See for example, Picken, *Summary Report for the Swedish Embassy on Programs and Strategies in the Area of Human Rights and the Administration of Justice in Angola*.

[69]   Many issues, such as a functioning justice system, should be of interest to all levels of the private sector. The private sector and especially multinational corporations, have enormous influence in Angola. The transformative potential of projects in this area is extremely high. However, because the probability of success and immediate impact may be low, support for human rights may not be seen as consistent with increased short-term profitability. Further attention, investment, persistence and creativity will be needed to produce desirable results.

- extension of private radio signals to the entire country;
- integration of human rights or a rights-based perspective into the work of UN and international non-governmental organisations (INGOs);
- study of the perspective of oil companies regarding their role in the human rights situation;
- public opinion poll of how the Angolans view the oil companies' contribution to improving the state of human rights (the goal being that the oil companies add their support for improvements in the human rights situation, by, for example, enhancing the Angolan justice system).

Work in the area of government institutions needed to ensure respect for human rights (e.g. increasing the number of municipal courts), and civil society demand for the respect of these rights (e.g. more community-based advocates) is interdependent. Work can be done in isolation on either the 'supply' or 'demand' side, but improvement in one area fuels improvement in the other demonstrating the synergy present in HRD's programme.

Strategic Vision Maximises Impact

The goal is a measurable improvement in the human rights situation.[70] HRD's attempts to look at the many contributing factors present in human rights violations resulting from civil war, the Cold War, the lack of formal education, inadequate salaries and colonial history giving way to the one party state does not diminish the responsibility of the state for the violations. It is difficult to imagine how sustainable improvement in the human rights situation can be achieved in Angola without a quantitative and qualitative change in the institutions needed to protect human rights. Thus, the HRD needed to facilitate positive change in those institutions to contribute concretely to measurably improving the human rights situation and thereby maximise its impact.

Developing Measures of Change

While quantifying and digitising human rights violations has developed over time with the efforts of institutions, like HURIDOCS (International Human Rights Information and Documentation Systems)[71] and the American Association for the Advancement of Science, the application of social science methods to the human

---

[70]   For example, it is important to see the link between the growth of corruption and the failed peace process of Bicesse. Too much emphasis was placed on the election and dismantling of repressive institutions and not nearly enough on creating the institutions necessary for checks and balances and the protection of the rights of citizens. Strong institutions existed for maintenance of order during the one-party state. While repressive in character, the military courts did check corruption and abuses that were not sanctioned by the state. The civil institutions that took over this role were not present in much of the country and did not enjoy much credibility or stature.

[71]   See http://www.huridocs.org/.

rights area has been slow in developing. In order to better define their objectives and desired outcomes, efforts are being made to integrate development tools into human rights projects. This work is still in the experimental phase.[72] Adding to the difficulty is that Angola is a data-poor country. Basic statistics are not easy to find, and, even when found, they are not always reliable. Angola has not regularly reported to human rights treaty bodies and the data it has submitted has not been systematically collected.[73]

HRD's work in this area can be divided into three spheres. First, it has created measurable indicators for the success of individual projects. This process is not yet complete. Second, HRD is working to have the UN system use a common set of indicators in order to measure the success of the UN work in Angola. A limited set of statistical benchmarks could squarely place the UN's work in Angola into a human rights framework. HRD has advocated that the UN collect and monitor this rather small set of statistics, which would help to demonstrate whether the UN advocacy and project-based work is making a tangible difference in people's lives. These statistics have most often been used by the UN country team in efforts to create a Common Country Assessment (CCA) and in early efforts at creating a UN Development Assistance Framework (UNDAF). The CCA was not officially produced, so this work remains on the drawing board. Even so, many UN agencies work either individually or in cooperation with Angolan government entities to produce statistics and estimates regarding the level of respect for a number of socio-economic rights (e.g. education, health, access to drinkable water and sanitation).

Third, and most important, are the efforts by HRD to help the Angolan government and civil society create useful measures for keeping their 'fingers on the pulse' of the current human rights situation and determining the extent to which human rights interventions are positively impacting the situation. For example, HRD has supported various case-tracking projects with the judiciary, prosecutors' office, police investigators and prisons. These computerised systems provide a means for the relevant authorities to know who has been detained, for how long, for what reason and where in the legal system the case is situated. These systems individually and collectively provide useful baseline information regarding liberty and access to justice-related rights. They provide a means by which 'superior' authorities can control the quality of work of the personnel 'below' them (e.g. the respect for legal procedures and time limits). Furthermore, the case-tracking systems provide a means to measure change over time. Thus, these projects provide a means to evaluate the impact of not only policy directions from higher authorities regarding specific violations, but also the effectiveness of capacity-building work, such

---

[72] See for example, T. Howland, 'Learning to Make Proactive Human Rights Interventions Effective: The Carter Center and Ethiopia's Office of the Special Prosecutor', *Wisconsin Journal of International Law* vol. 18 (2000).

[73] HRD held a seminar for the Angolan government in 1999 on reporting to treaty bodies. The seminar focused on evaluating past reports and identifying areas for improvement. Part of the problem was lack of timely reporting.

as training. This system can also measure the impact of salary changes and other political changes, such as an amnesty law, on specific human rights violations, such as arbitrary detentions.

Another important example of work done in this area was the survey of 1,511 Luandans in 2000 regarding their views on human rights: what human rights are, whether they know how to use them and whether they in fact do so. This precedent-setting quantitative work, was combined with the qualitative results of 14 focus groups addressing these three questions. The survey was carried out by the Angolan Research Institute (a civil society organisation) in cooperation with the Prosecutor General's Office and HRD.[74] The survey revealed that 47.5% of the Luandan population do not understand the legal nature of rights and how rights can be used to improve their own well-being.[75]

One final example is HRD's work to computerise the complaints of human rights violations received by the Ninth Commission of the National Assembly and to assist them to produce an annual report indicating the number and type of complaints received, where the complaints were referred and whether the case was resolved.

Action is Needed

Expansion to the provinces – an unrealised potential The Angola government, which is responsible for widespread human rights violations, has recognised HRD's work in various settings, such as the Third Committee of the General Assembly,[76] and has invited HRD to establish an office in every province.[77] For HRD, these developments indicate that the government may be beginning to recognise its very serious human rights problems and is taking steps toward improving the situation. It was also a major political victory for HRD, indicating that its strategy to engage and build trust had produced more space for it to operate. This may be one of the few examples in UN history where an expansion of its human rights presence took place during the continuation, and perhaps even increase, in armed conflict.

Unfortunately, local administrative officials and New York headquarters were reticent to provide HRD with the support it needed to expand its efforts to the

---

[74]   The same people will not be surveyed periodically, but a random sample will be taken. The survey itself can also be seen as an awareness tool for those surveyed and for those who will benefit from the report (e.g. media coverage of its findings). See Martin, *Report on the Human Rights Activities of UNAVEM III and Proposals for an Enhanced Programme.*

[75]   *Ibid.*

[76]   The government of Angola has cited the work of HRD as precedent setting in a statement made in the Third Committee of the UN General Assembly on 27 October 2000, indicating that 'the partnership between the Human Rights Division and the Government can be seen as a great triumph [and encouraged] other countries to multiply this experience of cooperation'.

[77]   This, for certain individuals, is proof positive that HRD must be absolutely useless in the country, considering the number and character of daily abuses in Angola and how counter-intuitive it is for a traditional human rights advocate to receive such an invitation.

provinces. Even after a clear statement from the Angolan government, the UN did not want to act. This was especially frustrating given statements made by members of the Security Council, other UN entities and NGOs about the need for HRD to be operating in the provinces. The representative of the secretary-general on internally displaced persons stated: 'Although the Representative is aware of resource constraints, he nonetheless recommends that serious consideration be given to expanding the Human Rights Division's capacity and presence throughout the country'.[78] The report of the Inter-Agency Network on Internal Displacement during its visit to Angola also stated: 'HRD/UNOA [should] urgently pursue the implementation of its plan to strengthen its presence and activities at provincial level'.[79]

In early 2001, HRD attempted to move forward with the expansion without full administrative support. Some HRFOs were angry about the lack of perceived political support for the expansion, as they were being asked to travel to the provinces without proper radios, communications or vehicle support. Efforts were made to obtain such support from the same UN entities and INGOs who had been vocal about the need for HRD to expand to the provinces.

Much time and motivation was lost because of the lack of clarity by a few HRFOs as to whether UNOA and UN headquarters actually supported the extension. It is important to note that the member states and the government looked to HRD regarding implementation of the provincial expansion and held it accountable for not moving quickly enough. HRD's expansion was tied to support from the Field Administration and Logistics Division (FALD)/UNOA administration. FALD does not feel that same accountability because it looks more to its internal regulations and procedures than to the substantive mandate for direction.

In an attempt to move forward while recognising that international staff numbers were going to remain limited and support from FALD would not be obtained immediately, HRD turned to voluntary contributions from donors and began employing national HRFOs and housing them with other UN entities or NGOs already operating in the field. The national HRFOs were to be recruited locally and would support HRD to:

1. Collect baseline information regarding the current human rights situation in the provinces (in order to help measure the impact of HRD's and others' efforts).
2. Help to create mechanisms the community could utilise to exercise their rights.

---

[78] Report of the Representative of the Secretary-General on Internally Displaced Persons, Mr. Francis Deng, Submitted Pursuant to Commission on Human Rights Resolution 2000/53, UN Doc. E/CN.4/2001/5/Add.5 (2001), at 99.

[79] The Network visit was led by Dennis McNamara working for the UN Office on Humanitarian Coordination. Report of the Senior Inter-Agency Network on Internal Displacement, Mission to Angola 12–17 March 2001, UN Office for the Coordination of Humanitarian Affairs, available at http://www.reliefweb.int/idp/docs/reports/Angolamarch2001iarep.pdf.

3. Link this community work with the national capacity-building work already being done with the courts, prosecutors, prisons, police and Angolan Army.
4. Attempt to have UN entities and INGOs work from a human rights-based perspective to ensure that the relation between state and citizen is clarified and to include an advocacy component in every project.[80]

The representative of the secretary-general (RSG) attempted to rearrange internal resources in order to provide funds for national HRFOs to staff the provincial offices, but even here difficulties arose.[81] The project was being implemented when the present author left Angola, but was shelved following the author's departure pending official support from New York headquarters. In the end, this support would have been forthcoming if the experiment had moved forward with local personnel and support from embassies and other UN entities or NGOs. Waiting for UN headquarters when the mandate exists is the easy way out, but it does not maximise the field operation's potential. In this case, the expansion would have been extremely useful, given the lacunae created by the absence of HRD in the provinces when the war ended in early 2002.

Obtaining and Disbursing Funds – Regular Budget (Accessed Contributions)

Interestingly, the main problem faced by HRD relating to money was not actually getting it, but finding an acceptable way to disburse it. A Security-Council based operation theoretically has access to assessed contributions (regular budget support). UNOA was a Security Council-based operation. Regardless of the 'Brahimi Report', which clearly criticises Security Council mandates without budgets,[82] there were

---

[80] This task recognises the limits of having one person per province and creates a multiplier effect by teaming with INGOs already working in the area. Further, it provides a means for HRD to work more intensely in the area of socioeconomic rights, given many of the INGOs work in this area as well.

[81] This problem highlights how far UN practice is from important recommendations for reform. 'Effective peace-building requires active engagement with the local parties, and that engagement should be multidimensional in nature. First, all peace operations should be given the capacity to make a demonstrable difference in the lives of the people in their mission area, relatively early in the life of the mission. The head of mission should have authority to apply a small percentage of mission funds to 'quick impact projects' aimed at real improvements in quality of life'. Report of the Panel on United Nations Peace Operations (Brahimi Report), UN Doc. A/55/305-S/2000/809 (2000), at 37.

[82] 'Less than complete Council commitment to peace implementation ... offers encouragement to spoilers'. That has also been said regarding support for human rights components within peace missions. 'The human rights components within peace operations have not always received the political support and administrative support they require, however, nor are their functions always clearly understood by other components'. While in Angola the role of human rights was much more clearly understood, some in New York seemed not to understand the Security Council directive nor the need to support UNOA's proposed budget. *Ibid*, at 56 and 41.

other factors at work that prevented HRD from obtaining full support from the regular budget. Some governments feel the use of the regular budget process should be limited and voluntary contributions should be used more often.[83] Historically, DPA and DPKO/FALD have been the only entities within the UN system to have access to assessed peacekeeping contributions. Funding the UNOA budget in accord with the Security Council resolution would be perceived by certain individuals and entities as giving OHCHR access to assessed funding for its activities, a precedent for which there is resistance.

The role of human rights work is also changing as UN human rights field methods develop and human rights components are added to peacekeeping and peacebuilding missions that are not clearly grounded in a peace accord. Notably, the UNOA mandate calls on HRD to perform capacity building, which implicates project funds. In an unprecedented move, the UN attempted to provide partial funding for HRD activities in 2001 through the regular budget, but anything directly labelled human rights activities in the UNOA budget was cut. Activities more akin to what administrative and political people in New York saw as normal peacekeeping expenses squeaked by, resulting in some human rights project activity being paid for by assessed contributions.

The UN needs to budget for human rights personnel and projects as part of the regular yearly budget from accessed contributions. Until that happens, voluntary contributions will be needed. Typically, HRD did not have significant difficulties raising money through embassies and foreign ministries. Of course, this significant investment of time could have been redirected to substantive work had the UN provided project money in the regular budget. Nonetheless, the interaction with the embassies often helped to sharpen and improve project ideas.

Obtaining and Disbursing Funds – Voluntary Contributions

HRD better linked its programme planning for 2001 with various budget processes: the UN Consolidated Appeal Process (CAP), individual donor cycles, OHCHR Annual Appeal and the regular budget process for UNOA. HRD's programme for 2001 was used as the basis for its submission to all four processes.

1. The CAP, which attracts voluntary contributions, has proved to be a useful tool in that it helps stimulate interest in the programme, especially in the capitals of the donor countries.
2. Individual donor contact may proceed, follow, or be separate from the CAP process. Both relate to voluntary contributions. A few donors have even expressed the importance of creating two-year programmes and moving away from the CAP, while others have indicated the CAP is an essential mechanism to supporting HRD.[84]

---

[83] Discussion with various members of diplomatic corps (1998–2000). The US is among those countries that would like to limit the regular budget process. This is an ideological position that makes reforming and improving the UN mission difficult to achieve.

[84] Interviews with diplomatic representatives in Angola (1998–2001).

3. While HRD provided OHCHR with its programme for 2001, it did not appear in OHCHR's Annual Appeal for voluntary contributions.[85]

The donor base has grown to include Norway, the UN (through accessed contributions), The Netherlands, Italy, Finland, Canada, Sweden, Congo Brazzaville, Ireland, Germany and the United States. Each donor has a different approach and different needs. A good deal of time is spent with donors, making HRD more like a typical UN agency than a Security Council operation. It is important to note that the donors have provided useful political and technical support, which probably would not be as easily obtained if they had not invested in HRD.

Need for Efficient, Decentralised and Appropriate Funding Disbursement Mechanism – Trócaire (an Irish NGO)

It is precisely the lack of a means to operationalise donor funds that led to the partnership with Trócaire. Although HRD had potential Angolan partners, projects and donors, it had no means to receive and disperse funds. MONUA administrative and political hierarchy were not interested in any new projects, as they felt the end of the mission was approaching. This made HRD presence unstable, given it had limited administrative support. Trócaire originally saw the partnership as a means of creatively contributing to the UN human rights capacity in Angola at a critical juncture. Trócaire took the rhetoric of the secretary-general and the high commissioner for human rights seriously regarding the need for the UN to team with NGOs in order for it to respond in a timely fashion to the challenges and opportunities on the ground. It was a precedent-setting alliance. Trócaire provided a mechanism to receive donors' funds, disburse them to partners and report to donors.

The first HRD-Trócaire project collaboration started at the end of 1998. These *ad hoc* collaborations grew into a joint programme. The programme demonstrated through action that HRD and Trócaire were interested in working with the government to improve the human rights situation. HRD-Trócaire cooperation began at the same time as momentum for MONUA's ouster from the country was growing. The HRD-Trócaire programme was conceptualised and mainly implemented at a time that it was unclear whether the Angolan government would accept a continued UN Security Council-based presence or a field office of OHCHR.

---

[85] It appears OHCHR had not yet created a policy of how it relates to DPKO and DPA field missions with a human rights component, even though some of the requests for these human rights components were included in its Annual Appeal. The decision was related to the fact that HRD wanted OHCHR's assistance to raise funds, but wanted these funds to flow through DPA rather than Geneva. Thus, HRD's proposal was that OHCHR would participate in raising funds over which it had no direct control, but could maintain indirect influence through contributing to field methods. OHCHR was not comfortable with this supporting role, but did help raise funds for DPA/DPKO missions when it had more direct control over the use of the funds (e.g. the funds would flow through its Technical Cooperation procedures).

When the programme was less than one year old, the new Trócaire leadership already began to show its reticence to continue the joint programme established in April 1999. While donors were ready to invest more in the programme, Trócaire did not want to take on more money or commit itself to a long period of cooperation.[86] Regardless of some of the complications and stress caused during the HRD-Trócaire partnership, Trócaire's assistance allowed HRD to become a proactive player in the human rights situation in Angola. The end of the Trócaire partnership signalled the need to find another mechanism to receive, disperse and report to donors regarding the use of their funds.

Need for Efficient, Decentralised and Appropriate Funding Disbursement Mechanism – OHCHR

The 2000 UN CAP had indicated donations for HRD should be provided through OHCHR. Money deposited in December 1999 was not operationalised until October 2000. OHCHR literally lost a donation that was sent to it and it took many hours of work by both Geneva and HRD to find it. Once the money was located, OHCHR decided that a new mechanism was needed to operationalise it, and a trust fund was established out of DPA in New York.[87]

Need for Efficient, Decentralised and Appropriate Funding Disbursement Mechanism – Trust Fund

Finally a mechanism to receive donor money was located: 'The UN Trust Fund in Support of Special Missions and Other Activities Related to Preventive Diplomacy and Peacemaking' managed by DPA. While many had said trust funds are slow, do not use modern project methods,[88] and charge high fees, there were basically no other realistic options. In many ways the Trust Fund's real or perceived imperfections were irrelevant, due to HRD's needs and the lack of immediately available alternative options.

DPA and the Trust Fund mechanism saved HRD and UNOA from losing credibility, and increased confidence by providing a means to continue to fund its project-based work. DPA was open to the idea of HRD using the Trust Fund, as it

---

[86] Interviews with donors to the joint program and Trocaire representatives (1999–2000).

[87] It should be mentioned that OHCHR is not yet comfortable with decentralised fundraising and is not yet willing or capable to play a supportive or complementary role for efforts made in the field. It prefers centralised fundraising, perhaps to maximise its control. This centralised method differs from how most UN agencies presently function. OHCHR was thus eliminated as a possible mechanism.

[88] Trust funds appear to demand that the use of all money is planned well in advance. While planning is appropriate and needed, often realities and opportunities on the ground change or shift. Trust funds do not have the flexibility to respond timely, thus locking one into specifics that may not maximise the contribution at that point in time.

recognised that HRD's work was consistent with its own peacebuilding goals. The Trust Fund is technically managed in New York. It authorises spending in accord with UN financial regulations. UNOA's administrative staff are utilised to facilitate Trust Fund spending and for financial reporting.

The Trust Fund mechanism appeared to solve many problems: it provided HRD with a means to receive donor support and gave it access to the extensive and experienced administrative staff in UNOA in the areas of finance, procurement and personnel, to name a few.[89]

Conclusion

There were no celebrations in New York or Geneva feting HRD and its contribution to achieving peace in Angola. In fact, what may exist is denial and consternation due to the fact that a handful of marginalised human rights field officers actually helped create the conditions for peace in Angola, therefore further undermining traditional thinking and powerful institutions within the UN.

HRD made a modest contribution to establishing the environment for peace in Angola. This contribution needs to be understood and its experience used to improve overall UN effectiveness. While this contribution could have been much greater had it had the critically-needed support necessary to carry out its mandate, HRD was successful enough to give pause to those in the UN who have lingering doubts about whether the UN is in fact a human rights organisation. The Angola HRD case clearly demonstrates that the UN conceptual and operational efforts need to emanate from a human rights core.

How lasting peace will be in Angola relates directly to the government's ability to respect the full spectrum of human rights. Angola has the resources to end preventable diseases, to have each child get a decent education and to have a viable court system functioning throughout the country. Thus, the UN and specifically the Security Council should not forget their human rights core simply because the fighting has stopped. A real challenge exists to build the capacity of both Angolan

---

[89]   It should be pointed out that the transition to the Trust Fund and UNOA administration was not as smooth as it could have been. Supporting human rights projects is significantly different from supporting 6,000 blue helmets. The FALD administrators who ran UNOA administration have vast experience in keeping troops supplied and supported. Fitting human rights projects into procedures designed for the purpose of supporting troops, like buying large amounts of canned fish, was not easy. HRD's system was similar to development project management because it relied heavily on grants to and reports from project partners. The experience was a new one not only for HRD, but also for the UNOA administrative staff. It led to a great deal of confusion on the part of HRFOs and administration. It took a good deal of time, patience and experimenting to come up with a means to make a human rights project support fit into an administrative structure designed to support large numbers of blue helmets in the field. It took at least six months of trial and many errors to get the system functional because the procedures are not designed to support project work.

civil society to effectively demand their rights, and the Angolan government to supply the institutions needed to respect these rights. We will know when the task has been completed, for we will see effective advocacy that results in the revenues from the oil, diamonds and other natural resources being actively employed to respect and buttress the rights of all Angolans.

Chapter 17

Case Study: Comparative Aspects of the Human Rights Field Operations in Bosnia and Herzegovina and Guatemala[1]

Milburn Line

Part I: From Massive Violations towards Sustainable Human Rights Protection

As we approach the eighth anniversary of the Dayton peace accords and the seventh anniversary of the Guatemalan peace accords it is important to revisit efforts to implement each agreement and ask how human rights issues have been integrated into each of the respective peace processes.

Both the Bosnian and Guatemalan peace processes are largely viewed as successes given that they ended atrocities and massive human rights violations that marked the conflicts in each place. The two peace agreements were signed[2] with high-profile backing of the international community and significant international resources were dedicated to implementation of the peace accords and reconstruction efforts. But did these peacekeeping missions transcend the immediate goals of ceasing hostilities to ensure that human rights standards and long-term sustainability of the peace process would not be compromised? Could more have been accomplished? Are there trade-offs between human rights standards and ending the violence that leads to human rights violations? The present author's experience indicates that the international organisations charged with ensuring implementation of the peace accords did not use all the management tools available to them. Furthermore, there are specific,

---

[1]   This chapter was first published under the title of 'Managing for Sustainable Human Rights Protection: International Missions in the Peace Processes of Bosnia and Herzegovina and Guatemala', in N. D. White and D. Klaasen (eds), *The UN, Human Rights and Post-conflict Situations* (Manchester: Manchester University Press, 2005).

[2]   The General Framework Agreement for Peace in Bosnia and Herzegovina, known as the Dayton Peace Agreement, was signed in Paris, France 14 December 1995. See General Framework Agreement for Peace in Bosnia and Herzegovina, Attachment to UN Doc. A/50/790-S/1995/999 (1995). The Guatemalan Peace Accords were signed in Guatemala City, Guatemala on 29 December 1996. See Agreement on a Firm and Lasting Peace, Annex II to UN Doc. A/51/796-S/1997/114 (1996).

identifiable issue areas where human rights standards may not have been the primary basis for critical policy decisions even when not necessary to achieve stability.

It is important to note at the outset that the international organisations alone should not be blamed for all of the shortcomings in their respective peace processes. In both cases, the national governments of Bosnia and Herzegovina and Guatemala are largely responsible for lack of substantive implementation of the peace accords they signed. In each case, the various governments (and their armies) involved in the conflicts were largely responsible for the human rights violations that resulted in international peacekeeping interventions. However, it is this unity of experience of massive human rights violations that makes the two processes comparable. In both Bosnia and Herzegovina and Guatemala, the international community was moved by human rights atrocities to commit long term political and economic resources to establishing a durable peace. The relative success of each, and specific examples of failures to take steps necessary to prevent continued or future human rights violations, are discussed below.

Bosnia and Herzegovina

The war in Bosnia and Herzegovina led to the death of an estimated 200,000 people,[3] mainly civilians, as the leaders of three ethno-nationalist political factions implemented policies of ethnic cleansing and even genocide.[4] The Dayton Peace Agreement of 1995 ended the violence even though few were convinced at the time that the ceasefire would be definitive. Perhaps the fundamental contradiction of the peace process in Bosnia and Herzegovina was that the same political parties that waged the war were the ones that signed the peace agreement and were responsible for its implementation. Unfortunately, this may have been the price of peace and a necessary compromise to end the atrocities being committed on all sides against civilians.

The Dayton Peace Agreement, in specific annexes dedicated to the Constitution of Bosnia and Herzegovina (Annex Four), Human Rights (Annex Six) and Refugees and Displaced Persons (Annex Seven),[5] enshrined basic human rights standards including the return of pre-war property and freedom to decide where to live. This

---

[3]   Although no truth commission has documented exact numbers, a 1998 World Bank case study 'Post-Conflict Reconstruction: Bosnia and Herzegovina' states the number as 250,000 deaths resulting from the conflict.

[4]   The International Criminal Tribunal for the Former Yugoslavia issued indictments for the crime of genocide on the territory of Bosnia and Herzegovina against Radovan Karadžić, Ratko Mladić, Duško Sikirica and Goran Jelisić in 1995; Simo Drljača, Milan Kovačević and Milomir Stakić in 1997; Radislav Krstić in 1998; Momcilo Krajišnik in 2000; Biljana Plavšić and Slobodan Milošević in 2001; and Momir Nikolić, Vujadin Popović, Ljubiša Beara and Ljubomir Borovčanin in 2002.

[5]   See footnote 2. See also M. O'Flaherty and G. Gisvold (eds), *Post-War Protection of Human Rights in Bosnia and Herzegovina*, International Studies in Human Rights vol. 53 (The Hague: Kluwer Law International, 1998); and W. Benedek, H. Alefsen, M. O'Flaherty

meant that the roughly two million refugees and displaced persons removed from their homes by ethnic cleansing could, by the standards of the peace accords, return to their pre-war homes regardless of whether the current local political power was of their ethnicity or not. Over the last eight years Bosnia and Herzegovina has largely stabilised, with incidents of violence being relatively rare. One of the main achievements of the international community is that there now exists a generalised freedom of movement between the ethnically-based entities.

However, international community efforts at implementing the human rights standards of the peace accords became increasingly fixated on return of property and reconstruction to the detriment of other issues central to long-term sustainability of the peace process. The organisations charged with implementing the peace process, including the Office of the High Representative (OHR), Organization for Security and Co-operation in Europe (OSCE) and the United Nations (UN), have focused their efforts on return of property to expelled ethnicities, and reconstruction, without dedicating a corresponding amount of attention to other critical elements of the process.

Achieving respect for the rights of individuals regardless of ethnicity as envisaged in Dayton in Bosnia and Herzegovina requires efforts to implement non-discriminatory employment practices; respect for freedom of religious practices; and an education system that does not force adherence to the ideological perspective of any single ethnicity. Almost eight years after Dayton, the international community has not implemented adequate policy initiatives to ensure that these standards are met despite their continual identification by organisations of refugees and displaced persons (even though millions were spent on international staff dedicated to these issues with few results produced).[6]

By not having a pro-active policy to ensure non-discriminatory hiring (and re-hiring) of minorities who have had their property returned in areas from which they were expelled, the returnees have no way to sustain themselves and little hope of finding work. By not aggressively defending rights of religious practice, exemplified in the May 2001 debacle at sites of destroyed mosques in Banja Luka and Trebinje in which mobs impeded reconstruction efforts, the international community allows ethno-nationalists to convince potential returnees that they will not be accepted. And by not having instituted a national policy to guarantee an educational system sensitive to ethnic diversity, minorities will not be able to send their children to local schools.

By concentrating its focus and resources on return of property and reconstruction to the detriment of other key human rights standards, the international community in

---

and E. Sarajlija (eds), *Human Rights in Bosnia and Herzegovina after Dayton: From Theory to Practice* (The Hague: Kluwer Law International, 1999).

   [6]   See *Preventing Minority Return in Bosnia and Herzegovina: The Anatomy of Hate and Fear* (1999); *Bosnia's Refugee Logjam Breaks: Is the International Community Ready* (2000); and *Bosnia: Reshaping the International Machinery* (2001) all published by the Crisis Group, available at http://www.crisisgroup.org.

Bosnia not only compromises its function of standard setting but is actually cementing ethno-nationalist consolidation. Displaced persons/refugees who receive their property in areas controlled by another ethnicity with no prospects for employment, religious practice or education will invariably give up and sell their property to other displaced persons/refugees seeking to stay in their own ethnic enclave.

Guatemala

The 36-year conflict in Guatemala that ended with the peace accords of December 1996 was also noted for massive human rights violations, including genocide, perpetrated mainly by state security forces against Mayan indigenous populations in the mountainous northwest region of the country. The atrocities resulted in the deaths of some 200,000 people[7] and, as in Bosnia and Herzegovina, inspired worldwide condemnation. The lead agency of international community efforts to end the conflict, the United Nations Verification Mission in Guatemala (MINUGUA), began its first two years of operations as a human rights verification mission.[8]

Despite the centrality of human rights violations in the conflict, the peace process in Guatemala also contained a fundamental contradiction: the truth commission – the Commission for Historical Clarification (HCC) – did not have the power to refer cases to the courts or even name those found responsible for violations. This added to the legacy of impunity for human rights violations and contributed to the continued inertia in the courts regarding cases of human rights violations, and facilitated the continued presence of notorious human rights violators in government. The most obvious example is a former dictator and army general accused of genocide, Efraín Ríos Montt, now president of the Congress. However, this may have been another necessary compromise to end the conflict. Human rights violators associated with the army or state would not have agreed to a peace accord that allowed their identification and eventual prosecution.

What is not a necessary compromise is the low-profile attitude adopted by MINUGUA in verifying compliance with the provisions of the peace accords. In March 2001, the mission announced rescheduling of key provisions of the accords instead of denouncing the Guatemalan government's failure to comply with important commitments to reduce the army and dissolve the Presidential General Staff (*Estado Mayor Presidencial*), the secret security agency cited as a principal source of systematic human rights violations. Parts of the official report of the secretary-general of the UN read as if written as a parody:

- 'The ceremony at which the rescheduled implementation timetable for

---

[7]   Commission for Historical Clarification, *Guatemala: Memory of Silence Tz'inil na'tab'al*, Conclusions and Recommendations (1999), para. 2.

[8]   See L. Franco and J. Kotler, 'Combining Institution Building and Human Rights Verification in Guatemala: The Challenge of Buying in Without Selling Out', in A. Henkin (ed.), *Honoring Human Rights* (The Hague: Kluwer Law International, 2000).

2000–2004 was signed and presented took place on 12 December 2000. The President of the Republic, the *President of the Congress*, and the President of the judiciary signed as honorary witnesses and stated that full implementation of the new timetable, through the combined efforts of the State and civil society, would give considerable impetus to Guatemala's democratic development. I am encouraged by this *renewed commitment to peace, this time expressed by the national authorities at the highest level* and reiterated on 14 January 2001 by the President of the Republic in a speech marking the end of his first year in government'.

- 'There had been a gradual reduction in the budget for the armed forces, but this trend was reversed in the 2000 financial year. *The Mission found that while the budget for 2000 should have been 981 million quetzales, 1,225.4 million were actually spent. The budget allocation for 2001 is in line with the agreed reduction and the Mission hopes that 2001 will not see a repetition of the budget transfers or increases which in 2000 breached the commitment to a reduction'*.

- 'The commitment to replace the Presidential General Staff was rescheduled for the first half of 2003. *Unfortunately, the new timetable for 2000–2004 did not envisage any intermediate action that might reflect gradual progress on this commitment'*. [9]

While the final observations at least mention the necessity of political will by the current government to reverse the stagnation of the peace accords, the language of the report and actions of the mission were anything but vigorous. It is possible that the General Assembly of the United Nations is not aware of the identity of the president of the Congress honoured in the report, but this reality is not lost on the people of Guatemala. Most importantly, MINUGUA's failure to protest non-compliance with the peace accords means that it is left to local organisations of civil society and human rights, already decimated in the previous era of repression directed against them by the state. By abandoning civil society MINUGUA has contributed to the continued polarisation of Guatemalan society that impedes long-term reconciliation. [10]

Some Preliminary Conclusions and Recommendations

Massive violations of human rights, including genocide, were characteristic of the conflicts in both Bosnia and Herzegovina and Guatemala. Therefore, it is logical that ensuring the sustainable protection of human rights and achieving some measure of

---

[9]   Report of the Secretary-General, United Nations Verification Mission in Guatemala, UN Doc. A/55/973 (2001), at 78 (italics added).

[10]   It is worth noting that further military spending continued to overspend the amount stipulated in the peace accords, by 26% in 2000 and 45% in 2001 as cited in *Prensa Libre*, 18 May 2002.

justice would be fundamental elements of the strategy of the international community to go beyond merely preventing further conflict and establishing a lasting peace. The following are institutions/actions designed to fulfil key steps of the peace processes in both places.

Key Steps	Bosnia and Herzegovina	Guatemala
(1) Prevent recurrence of violence/war	• Presence of North Atlantic Treaty Organization (NATO) troops	• Demobilise guerrillas and reduce army
(2) Articulate human rights standards	• Dayton Peace Accords (11/95)	• Peace Accords (12/96)
(3) Implement policies to achieve justice	• International Criminal Tribunal for the Former Yugoslavia (Hague)	• Commission for Historical Clarification (HCC)
(4) Plant foundation for sustainable, peaceful future	• Implementation of Peace Accords (via the Office of the High Representative and other international organisations including OSCE and UN)	• Implementation of Peace Accords (verified by MINUGUA)

In both cases, efforts at conflict management were relatively successful – the level of violent confrontation was reduced and daily life stabilised. In addition, the architecture of both processes was sound: human rights and fundamental freedoms were enshrined in both peace agreements.

As noted, both processes also contained flaws that compromised prospects for justice. However, a peace accord acceptable to the warring parties, the ethnic cleansers negotiating Dayton or a weak truth commission in Guatemala, may have been necessary to achieve short-term stability.

What are not acceptable trade-offs in the justice versus stability continuum are compromises affecting the long-term sustainability of these processes. In both our examples, international organisations failed to exercise the kind of robust management needed to set standards that will establish enduring respect for human rights. In Bosnia and Herzegovina, the international community could have implemented policies on fair employment, freedom of religion and education in addition to their efforts for return of property and reconstruction. In Guatemala, MINUGUA could have protested lack of compliance with the peace accords vigorously or organised economic incentives for compliance in coordination with the donor community.

By failing to address the universe of human rights issues, these missions not only compromised their standard-setting functions but undermined long-term prospects for their respective peace processes. In Bosnia, this means the consolidation of ethnic cleansing. In Guatemala, delays in implementation mean the government continues to be dominated by human rights violators and the army consumes levels of resources similar to the period of armed conflict.

So why would missions not act more vigorously? After all, it is their own credibility at stake. Perhaps, as missions institutionalise themselves after conflict there is less perceived need for robust action and strategic planning as there is less danger of immediate violence. Missions begin to deal with their natural interlocutors, in these cases members of governments implicated in human rights violations, and the human rights agenda becomes less a priority than the appearance of stability both amongst implementing agencies and vis-à-vis the structures that define their mandates.

But this is not long-term stability. Human rights standards in post-conflict situations are imported values that cause resistance from the warring parties. Much of the institutional machinery of peace processes is external (i.e. NATO, the International Tribunal for the Former Yugoslavia (ICTY), OHR, OSCE, MINUGUA, HCC). The challenge for peacekeeping missions is creating local ownership of human rights protection. Neither Bosnia and Herzegovina nor Guatemala has developed effective judicial systems to ensure respect for human rights. In fact, one could argue that the efforts of the ICTY and MINUGUA have weakened local institutions charged with such tasks (for example, the ICTY taking the pressure off local judicial action to prosecute human rights violations in BiH, and MINUGUA substituting the functions of the Office of the Human Rights Ombudsperson as discussed below).

From the weaknesses identified in the preliminary examples reviewed in Part I of this chapter, three management recommendations emerge for improving future efforts:

1. *Long-term strategic planning.* The missions reviewed appear to manage often on an *ad hoc* basis, reacting to crises and attempting to take advantage of temporally defined windows of opportunity. Multi-year strategic planning, including the development of indicators and an eventual exit strategy, could help ensure that critical human rights issues were addressed.

2. *Accountability of international organisations.* The missions reviewed here have a limited amount of management oversight, and what they do have is not always the most appropriate for implementing human rights standards. The Peace Implementation Council, in the case of OHR, and the General Assembly of the UN for MINUGUA and the United Nations Mission to Bosnia, often have short attention spans and may be more interested in short-term stability than long-term standards. Broader review and higher accountability of missions within the hierarchy of international organisations, by the human rights community (including non-governmental organisations (NGOs)), and amongst local experts/populations in host countries might improve management practices.

3. *Local ownership of justice processes.* Missions should incorporate an articulated strategy for handover to local institutions to accompany their operations (an obvious potential indicator would be prosecution of human rights violators in local courts).

Part II of this chapter explores illustrative examples of how application of these three principles could contribute to managing for sustainable human rights protection.

Before entering into further examples, however, it is worth reiterating that both of these peace processes originated in response to massive human rights violations. Therefore, the final analysis of their efforts should include sustainable human rights protection as a fundamental criterion for evaluation. As missions become institutionalised day-to-day relations with their interlocutors and the appearance of stability often transcend the issues of human rights protection that brought them into existence. Weakened application of justice principles may be necessary to achieve a peace agreement that stops human rights violations. However, continued compromise for the sake of short-term stability once human rights standards have been incorporated into formal accords undermines the possibility of sustained peace. Unfortunately, the people of Bosnia and Herzegovina and Guatemala are still a long way from achieving lasting protection of their rights. By not aggressively defending the entire gamut of human rights standards, international missions may leave the door open for the same abuses to spiral into the pattern of violations that began the cycle.

Part II: Illustrative Examples of Managing for Sustainable Human Rights Protection

The following are discussions designed to illustrate the specifics of each of the recommendations. The examples, divided into primary examples with more detail and secondary examples with basic highlights, are selected to demonstrate coherence with issues discussed in the present chapter. The examples are not exhaustive: a limited number of issue areas are discussed and the actual process of developing these recommendations to assist in management decisions would need to be much broader in scope and require budgetary resources to accomplish their objectives.

Long-term Strategic Planning

The missions reviewed appear to manage often on an *ad hoc* basis reacting to crises and attempting to take advantage of temporally-defined windows of opportunity. Multi-year strategic planning, including the development of indicators and an eventual exit strategy, could help ensure that critical human rights issues were addressed.

Strategic planning, a basic tool which, in the present author's experience is not done in any participatory fashion if done at all, should be conducted in public to promote transparency of the mission's efforts. Most international interventions take place in insecure environments in which perceptions about the motivations of the international community may be questioned by the public and concepts of law and human rights may not necessarily be understood or accepted.

This lack of a common understanding, if not the presence of open suspicion, regarding international community objectives, is often a significant impediment to the implementation of peace accords. UN officials and human rights specialists tend to understand law as emancipatory: rights that protect the individual and communities against abuses by the state or state agents such as the army. However, the historical reality of many Guatemalans and Bosnians is of law exercised as a form of social control and repression. Bridging this gap may be essential to creating realistic understanding and expectations regarding attempts to implement peace accords.

Such obstacles might be mediated by transparent planning that includes mission managers, local civil society representatives, local and international experts and, to the extent possible, relevant local authorities. A participatory and publicly articulated strategic plan would increase local understanding of international community objectives; identify key impediments to implementation of the peace accords; and potentially develop public support for the objectives of the international community as seen in the following examples.

Primary Example: Bosnia and Herzegovina

The Dayton Peace Agreement, in Annex 7: Agreement on Refugees and Displaced Persons, Chapter 1: Protections; Article 1:1, establishes that 'All refugees and displaced persons have the right freely to return to their homes of origin'. Article 2: Creation of Suitable Conditions for Return commits the Parties to 'undertake to create in their territories the political, economic and social conditions conducive to the voluntary return and harmonious reintegration of refugees and displaced persons, without preference for any particular group'.

If a strategic planning exercise had been done at the beginning of major international support for minority return in December 1998, following a pledge of the high representative to facilitate 120,000 minority returns in 1999, the multiplicity of issue areas needed to be addressed to provide durable solutions to returning minorities would have been evident. Instead, over the next years the international community focused most of its energies on reconstruction, return of property, and eventually judicial reform.

General Issue Areas Regarding Minority Return Prioritised by the International Community

Year	1996	1997	1998	1999	2000	2001
Goals	Stabilise warring parties	Implement elections; Freedom of movement	Reconstruction for returning refugees	Reconstruction for returning refugees	Return of property; Reconstruction for refugees	Return of property; Judicial reform

As discussed, strategic planning would have identified broader relevant issue areas.

Hypothetical Strategic Planning for Key Elements Affecting Minority Return

Issues	1999	2000	2001	2002
Security	Train/monitor local police regarding minority rights	Judicial reform Monitor local police	Hand-over to local authorities	Phase-out international oversight
Property	Establish legal framework	Implement plan to return property law	Ensure local management of property return	Phase-out international oversight
Reconstruction	Begin process in strategic rural areas	Continued reconstruction	Continued reconstruction	Phase-out international support
Employment	Establish legal framework	Implement employment policy	Monitor compliance	Hand-over to local authorities
Education	Establish joint curriculum	Implement joint curriculum	Monitor compliance	Phase-out international support
Religious Practice	Create ecumenical task force	Key initiatives (mosques in RS)[11]	Monitor compliance	Phase-out international support

Planning could have also defined key interlocutors to support minority return.

Key Interlocutors (In Addition to Organisations of Refugees and Displaced Persons)

Issues	Interlocutors
Security	NATO Stabilisation Force (SFOR), International Police Task Force (IPTF), local police, judiciary, local authorities
Property	Legal framework, judiciary
Reconstruction	International donors, municipalities (registration and engineering)
Employment	Legal framework, judiciary
Education	Education ministries, international organisations
Religious practice	Religious congregations, local authorities, local police, NATO, IPTF

---

[11]   As of July 2002, reconstruction of the Ferhadija Mosque, a United Nations Educational, Scientific and Cultural Organization Cultural Heritage Monument, in Banja Luka (capital of the Bosnian Serb entity) detonated in 1993 despite not being near any war-related activity, continued to be blocked by bureaucratic impediments regarding permits from a local ministry despite a decision of the Bosnia and Herzegovina Human Rights Chamber in 1999 ordering issuance of the permits.

Strategic planning could have resulted in more detailed analysis of the implementation steps necessary to engage all interlocutors, including regular liaison with the principal stakeholders: refugees and displaced persons (see the following section on Accountability). An investment in planning at the beginning of the process might have ensured a more integrated approach that would have strengthened the possibilities for long-term sustainability of minority return.

Secondary Example: Guatemala

In 1997, benchmark indicators could have been developed for the timetable for implementation of the peace accords. The timetable could have also posited sanctions for non-compliance.

Some Key Elements of the Peace Accords Chronogram: Transformed into an Exit Strategy

Year	1997	1998	1999	2000
Army	Reduce budget and staff	Define new military doctrine	Close military bases	Evaluate compliance
EMP	Reduce budget and staff	Install security for President	Disarticulate EMP	Evaluate security – intelligence
Guerrillas	Surrender arms	Train for sustainability	Incorporate into civilian life	Evaluate/Define future support

By preparing a *publicly* announced exit strategy, MINUGUA might have avoided postponement of the original timetable for implementation of the peace accords or, at least, would have been able to justify its continued presence along established standards for compliance. By anticipating the contingency of non-compliance the mission could have coordinated timely sanctions by the international community that might have prevented rescheduling. In the end, a framework of economic incentives for compliance was not articulated by MINUGUA but by international donors in the meeting of the 'Consultative Group' finally in February 2002.

Accountability of International Organisations

International missions appear to exist in a management accountability void where key stakeholders may or may not be consulted or taken into consideration. Member states of the UN are ultimately responsible for these interventions, but may not be able to effectively conduct oversight at a level of detail critical to ensuring sustainable human rights protection.

One possible solution would be to integrate mechanisms such as evaluations or reviews at the local and national level to ensure some measure of accountability regarding principal stakeholders. These could be linked to the strategic planning process discussed previously. The aforementioned combination of mission management, local civil society representatives, local and international experts and relevant national/local authorities could conduct yearly reviews and evaluations of strategic plans with recommendations for future steps.

Further accountability mechanisms could include evaluations and/or reviews by other relevant UN agencies. For example, a specific technical assistance role of the Office of the United Nations High Commissioner for Human Rights could include a review of ongoing missions regarding sustainable human rights protection – especially for missions that were instituted as a response to massive human rights violations.

Missions should also not disregard the expertise developed internally amongst their own staff. In the present author's experience, field officers are rarely consulted regarding mission policy decisions despite often being the staff members most cognisant of local sensitivities and windows of opportunity. Internal evaluations, based on the local knowledge and participation of field officers, could provide mission managers with better data for policy decisions.

Both local and external reviews and evaluations should be publicised in order to increase public understanding of the peace process. In the following examples, increasing mechanisms of local accountability could have led to international interventions being more responsive to the subtleties of the local human rights situation and more likely to produce lasting results.

Primary Example: Guatemala

The Agreement on Identity and Rights of Indigenous Peoples, signed on 31 March 1995,[12] was a key element in the peace accords for addressing the situation of indigenous people, who constitute the majority of the population. However, over the next seven years MINUGUA did not developed a framework for verification of the rights articulated in the Agreement.[13]

The mission has verified multilingual access to justice and respect for traditional indigenous dress, and issued a report updating lack of compliance with the peace accords regarding indigenous peoples, which describes ethnic discrimination as 'de facto apartheid'. But the United Nations Verification Mission in Guatemala has not developed a verification tool that could serve as a basis for future analysis of respect for the range of rights recognised in the Agreement. Beyond raising fundamental questions regarding the management accountability of the mission – who is responsible when a mission simply does not develop tools to fulfil important functions? – this issue also represents a significant lost opportunity for Guatemalans.

Indigenous rights is a sensitive issue in Guatemala given the historical exclusion of indigenous populations from national discourse and decision-making; the repression aimed at indigenous populations during the 36-year conflict; and apartheid-like fears of indigenous political power among the *Ladino* (Spanish origin) minority. Thus, failure to develop a conceptual framework has contributed to the subject of

---

[12]   Available at http://www.usip.org/library/pa/guatemala/guat_950331.html.

[13]   Statement of the resident representative of the UN in Guatemala in a presentation on 12 July 2002.

indigenous rights continuing to be a source of contention in the peace process. The case of customary (Indigenous or Mayan) law is illustrative. Much has been written about the utility of indigenous conceptions of justice but very little has been done to develop procedures to ensure that customary law practices compliment the formal legal system.[14] By not addressing this issue in operational terms, an opportunity to reduce the level of conflict impeding implementation of the peace accords was lost. Instead, lack of progress has further polarised the debate on customary law between the judiciary and indigenous organisations.

A public process could have been initiated as a multi-year task force of civil society, indigenous and state representatives, including the judiciary in the case of customary law, to formulate policy. This could have produced significant results for the peace process and increased the perception that MINUGUA was responding to stakeholder concerns through conceptual leadership on a critical issue. Fortunately, a process similar to the one proposed here was initiated by the Office of the United Nations High Commissioner for Human Rights in April 2002. Even though eight years late, operationalising the standards of the Agreement on Indigenous Peoples is still fundamental for sustainable human rights protection.[15]

Secondary Example: Bosnia and Herzegovina

Yearly reviews and/or evaluations of efforts to support minority return with the participation of the returning refugees and minorities themselves would have revealed a number of impediments that were treated as political issues or as separate from the process of minority return. For example, anti-minority return political initiatives disguised as security threats in Drvar (violence between 1998 and 2000) and Prnjavor (grenade attacks against minority returnees from 1999–2000) would have been identified as minority rights issues and addressed in a more integral fashion instead of subject to limited and ineffective responses.

Local Ownership of Justice Processes

Missions should incorporate an articulated strategy for hand-over to local institutions to accompany their operations (an obvious potential indicator would be prosecution of human rights violators in local courts).

As noted, most of the infrastructure of international interventions is external (i.e. truth commissions, international criminal tribunals). A principal challenge for

---

[14]   *Defensoría Maya* has published several studies, including '*RI QETAMB'AL CHE RI SUK'B'ANIK*: Experiences in the Application and Administration of Indigenous Justice' (1999) and '*S'UK'B'ANIK*: Administration of Mayan Law' (2000). However, apart from local efforts such as a diploma course in Cobán developed by the local campus of the University of San Carlos, no formal mechanism for integrating the two justice concepts has been developed.

[15]   A press release by the indigenous groups, including *Defensoría Maya*, on 31 March 2003 denounced lack of progress and continuing importance of implementing the Agreement on Indigenous Peoples.

international missions is to bridge the gap between civil society and the state, laying the groundwork for consensus (as opposed to confrontational) efforts to prevent violations and promote respect for human rights standards. To accomplish this, international missions should promote local ownership of human rights issues by planning for hand-over at the beginning of their mandates, again, with representatives of civil society and local authorities, and publicly announce their intentions.

Primary Example: Guatemala

The Comprehensive Agreement on Human Rights signed by the government of Guatemala and the *Unidad Revolucionaria Nacional Guatemalteca* on 29 March 1994[16] defines the terms of reference for establishing MINUGUA. Section X, 'International Verification by the United Nations', Item 16: 'Cooperation and support for national institutions for the protection of human rights' delineates support of the United Nations Mission to the Guatemalan Human Rights Ombudsperson ('*Procurador de Derechos Humanos*' which is translated into English as 'Counsel for Human Rights') in sub-clauses (a), (b) and (c):

> Comprehensive Agreement on Human Rights X. 16. 'The parties agree in acknowledging that international verification must contribute to strengthening the permanent constitutional mechanisms and other national governmental and non-governmental entities for the protection of human rights. In order to support them, the *international verification mission shall be empowered to*:
>
> (a) Cooperate with national institutions and entities, as necessary, for the effective protection and promotion of human rights and, in particular sponsor technical cooperation programmes and carry out institution-building activities;
> (b) Offer its support to the judiciary and its auxiliary organs, the Public Prosecutor's Office, the Counsel for Human Rights, and the Presidential Human Rights Committee in order to contribute to the development and strengthening of national institutions for the protection of human rights and due legal process;
> (c) Promote the international financial and technical cooperation required to strengthen the capacity of the Counsel for Human Rights and that of other national institutions and entities to carry out their functions in respect of human rights.'

The constitutional mandate of the Office of the Human Rights Ombudsperson, in Chapter V of the Guatemalan Constitution, is similar to that of the verification functions of the UN mission. Logically, the Comprehensive Agreement envisions collaboration between the two organisms in the verification, public identification and resolution of human rights issues. However, a review of the 12 human rights reports issued by MINUGUA since its inception reveals very little effort by the mission to fulfil these strengthening functions beyond the initial years of the mission's existence. At the early stages, MINUGUA evidently accomplished some degree of donor coordination for 'Institutional Building' and developed a technical cooperation

---

[16]   See footnote 2.

agreement through the United Nations Development Programme (UNDP) in 1995 to develop investigative capacity and conduct training within the Office of the Human Rights Ombudsperson.

However, starting in 1997,[17] the institutional building efforts described previously, including the efforts at donor coordination and the agreement with UNDP, are not mentioned further. Except for a vague reference to continued technical assistance for the Office of the Ombudsperson,[18] the sections on 'Commitment to strengthening institutions for the protection of human rights' in ensuing reports only discuss the budgetary deficiencies that impede the Office of the Ombudsperson from fulfilling its mandate.

MINUGUA's efforts to strengthen the Office of the Human Rights Ombudsperson are divided into two periods to reflect the initial mandate prior to the signing of the peace accords and the period afterwards.

Potential Institutional Strengthening Goals for Office of the Human Rights Ombudsperson

Year	1995	1996
Goals	Joint Human Rights Verification Initiatives	Shared Technical Capacity for Human Rights Verification

As noted, MINUGUA did initiate technical assistance and donor coordination in 1995. After 1997, there appears to have been virtually no structured cooperation evidenced in mission reports. Collaboration with the Office of the Ombudsperson was made more difficult due to the management practices of the actual person who functioned as ombudsperson between 1997 and 2002. However, by preparing a hand-over management tool early on, MINUGUA would have been able to point out specific failures by the ombudsperson to comply with elements of the joint plan instead of simply ceasing communications between the two organisms. In addition, continued coordination of international donor agencies might have proved very helpful in preventing non-compliance with the timetable for the peace accords discussed previously.

Potential Institutional Strengthening Goals for Office of the Human Rights Ombudsperson

Year	1997	1998	1999	2000
Goals	Definition of Institutional Strengthening Plan	Training Aspects of Hand-over Plan	Implement joint verification aspects of plan	Donor coordination for institutional sustainability and material aspects of plan (transfer material)

---

[17]   Seventh Report on Human Rights of the United Nations Verification Mission in Guatemala, Annex to UN Doc. A/52/330 (1997).

[18]   *Ibid.*

In June 2002, the mission initiated a process to define hand-over of its verification functions and technical capabilities to the Office of the Human Rights Ombudsperson. However, a long-term hand-over framework would have offered the possibility of more consolidated institutional strengthening, as envisioned in the Comprehensive Agreement on Human Rights, instead of attempting to transfer functions in the last year and a half of the mission's presence.

Secondary Example: Bosnia and Herzegovina

In 1999 the high representative began to discuss the idea of 'ownership' of the Dayton peace process to ensure that the entity governments took responsibility for implementation of the peace accords. But missions should define in operational terms how this can be accomplished. Reform of the judiciary, which did not reach significant implementation until 2001 with the High Judiciary Commission, is illustrative of problems of ownership of standards of impartiality.

Local ownership of problems within the judiciary could have been developed as an integral part of the policies for supporting minority return discussed in the first example in Part II as eventually the courts will be responsible for upholding the human rights standards necessary for minorities to coexist in the ethnic enclaves. A specific framework could have been developed for judicial reform in the context of minority rights, including definition of indicators of success.

Potential Goals and Success Indicators for Reform of the Judiciary

Year	1999	2000	2001	2002
Goals	Definition of judicial reform initiative	Implementation of judicial reform	Training and over-sight	Hand-over
Sample success indicators	Agreements with entities. Legal framework for implementation	Integration of multi-ethnic judiciaries	Prosecution of local crimes against minorities	Assessment of protection of minority rights

Developing a framework could have ensured that judicial reform efforts complemented the larger issue of protection of minority rights. Instead, criteria to ensure multi-ethnic representation in the judiciary, absolutely essential for the protection of minorities returning to areas controlled by a dominant ethnicity that monopolises the judiciary, were not included in the final package of reforms. By separating judicial reform from other substantive processes of implementation of the peace accords, the Office of the High Representative made 'ownership' by local authorities less likely.[19]

---

[19] The most recent report of Amnesty International (2002) finds the 'judiciary ... remained largely incapable of conducting proceedings for war crimes and human rights

Conclusion

The Dayton peace accords and the Guatemalan peace accords have been shown to be illustrative of trade-offs between achieving justice and putting an end to violence and massive human rights violations. Even within this context, the analysis shows that international organisations charged with ensuring the implementation of these accords did not use all the tools available to them and that there are specific, identifiable issues where human rights standards were not the primary basis for policy decision, even when this was not necessary in order to achieve stability. In Bosnia, the efforts of the international community to reintegrate populations expelled during the ethnic cleansing became increasingly fixated on the return of property and reconstruction, to the detriment of the gamut of human rights issues faced by these returnees, including discrimination in the workplace, in schools and in the practice of religions. In Guatemala, the UN mission agreed to vague delays in key elements in the timetable for implementation of the peace accords, thus compromising possibilities for long-term protection of human rights and ensuring the continued polarisation of Guatemalan society.

In both cases, compromises to human rights standards were necessary to end the violence. In Bosnia, this meant negotiating the peace agreements with the authors of ethnic cleansing. In Guatemala, the compromise was a weak truth commission with no powers to prosecute human rights violations. However, these may have been necessary trade-offs in order to cease hostilities. But in both cases prospects for long-term sustainability of the peace processes were compromised by the peacekeeping missions' failures to ensure broad standard-setting and compliance with the entire range of human rights issues envisioned in the peace agreements. From the above discussion, three suggestions have emerged for managing future efforts – long-term strategic planning; the accountability of international organisations; and local ownership of justice process.

---

violations committed during and after the war. In the few trials that were conducted, there were consistent indications that courts were not impartial and independent …'.

Chapter 18

The Human Rights Field Operations of the Organization for Security and Co-operation in Europe

Susanne Ringgaard-Pedersen and Annette Lyth

Introduction[1]

The Organization for Security and Co-operation in Europe (OSCE) was one of the first international security organisations to recognise human rights as an integral part of security.[2] When the Helsinki Final Act was adopted in 1975,[3] it marked the first occasion that the 'human dimension' of security – in essence, human rights principles – was included as an explicit element of a regional security framework on the same basis as politico-military and economic issues.[4] The Helsinki Final Act recognises human rights as 'an essential factor for the peace, justice and well-being necessary to ensure the development of friendly relations and co-operation' among states.[5]

The Helsinki Final Act constitutes a milestone in the history of human rights protection. For the first time, human rights principles were included as an explicit

---

[1]   The opinions expressed in this chapter are those of the present authors and do not necessarily reflect the views of the Organization for Security and Co-operation in Europe and the Office for Democratic Institutions and Human Rights (ODIHR).

[2]   For more on the origins of the OSCE and its early history see D. C. Thomas, *The Helsinki Effect: International Norms, Human Rights, and the Demise of Communism*, (Princeton: Princeton University Press, 2001). More on secondary literature on the OSCE and its commitments can be found through the Centre for OSCE Research in Hamburg, Germany.

[3]   The Final Act of the Conference on Security and Cooperation in Europe, 1 August 1975, ILM vol. 14, 1292.

[4]   The text of the Helsinki Final Act and other OSCE documents are available in full on the OSCE website at http://www.osce.org. Documents containing OSCE human dimension commitments have been compiled both thematically and chronologically in *OSCE Human Dimension Commitments,* vols I and II (Warsaw: OSCE/ODIHR, 2005), which is also available electronically on the ODIHR website at http://www.osce.org/odihr and is searchable by issue or by document. All OSCE documents and commitments referred to in this guide can be found in these sources.

[5]   Helsinki Final Act, 1 (VII).

and integral element of a regional security framework. Human rights as an integral part of security are therefore now a well established and unassailable principle in the OSCE region. The principles included in the Helsinki Final Act were later expanded and reinforced in numerous follow-up agreements, including OSCE summits and ministerial meetings. The documents agreed upon at these meetings established human rights as a central element of the work of the organisation. At the most recent OSCE Summit (Istanbul, 1999), for example, the heads of government signed the Charter for European Security,[6] which states: 'We reaffirm that respect for human rights and fundamental freedoms, democracy and the rule of law is at the core of the OSCE's comprehensive concept of security'.

Furthermore, all OSCE participating states have accepted that implementation of OSCE human rights commitments is a matter of direct and legitimate concern to all participating states and is not an internal affair.[7] OSCE participating states are thus not in a position to avoid discussions about human rights problems or to assert that raising human rights concerns constitutes interference in internal affairs.

Politically Binding Commitments

The OSCE process is essentially a political process that does not create legally-binding norms and principles. Unlike many other human rights documents, OSCE human dimension commitments are politically, rather than legally, binding. This is an important distinction, since it limits the legal enforceability of OSCE standards. However, this should not be mistaken as indicating that the commitments lack binding force. The distinction is between legal and political and not between binding and non-binding.[8] This means that OSCE commitments are more than a simple declaration of will or good intention; they constitute a political commitment to comply with these standards. OSCE commitments are adopted by consensus among all participating states and are politically binding. This means that they are immediately binding on all OSCE participating states, which is different from the United Nations (UN), for example, where standards must first be signed and ratified before they enter into force. This allows the OSCE to react quickly to new needs. For example, when allegations of human rights violations with regard to minorities increased at the beginning of the 1990s, it was the OSCE that reacted first and drafted a comprehensive set of standards in the field of minority protection. Later, these political standards served

---

[6]   See OSCE, Charter for European Security, *Istanbul Document 1999* (January 2000), p. 1.

[7]   Charter for European Security, p. 2.

[8]   For more on the discussion of the nature of OSCE commitments see E. Manton, 'The OSCE Human Dimension Process and the Process of Customary International Law Formation', LL.M. Thesis, republished as 'The OSCE Human Dimension Process and the Process of Customary International Law Formation', in *Institut für Friedensforschung und Sicherheitspolitik* (ed.), *OSCE Yearbook 2005* (Baden-Baden: Institute for Peace Research and Security Policy at the University of Hamburg, 2006).

as basis for the legally-binding Council of Europe Framework Convention on the Protection of National Minorities.[9]

The OSCE Comprehensive Approach to Security: The OSCE Human Rights Framework

The OSCE characterises its approach to regional security as both comprehensive and cooperative.[10] The OSCE approach to security goes well beyond military security and confidence and security-building measures. With initiatives, workshops and training projects, it tries to dispel deep-rooted mistrust, to renew civil dialogue and to encourage the spirit of cooperation. The philosophy is that the various elements that make up peaceful, stable and democratic societies are inter-linked.[11]

The comprehensive security concept is comprised of three dimensions:

1. The 'human dimension' is used to describe the set of standards and activities related to human rights and fundamental freedoms, democracy, elections, tolerance and the rule of law, as well as national minorities, human contacts and international humanitarian law.[12] The main institutions involved in the human dimension are the Office for Democratic Institutions and Human Rights (ODIHR) in Warsaw, the Representative for the Freedom of Media in Vienna and the High Commissioner for National Minorities in The Hague.
2. The 'politico-military dimension' includes confidence and security-building measures through regional security agreements and treaties. The main body in this dimension is the Forum for Security Co-operation which meets every week in Vienna.
3. The 'economic-environmental dimension' includes monitoring of economic and environmental developments and joint projects. The main actor is the Economic and Environmental Co-ordinator, a section within the OSCE Secretariat in Vienna.

---

[9]   Council of Europe, H (1995) 010, Strasbourg, February 1995.

[10]   Comprehensive in that OSCE seeks to deal with an unusually wide range of security-related issues, including preventive diplomacy, politico-military confidence- and security-building measures, arms control, human rights, democratisation, election monitoring and steps to strengthen both economic and environmental security. Cooperative in the sense that OSCE is broadly inclusive in nature: it is not directed against any country; all participating states have equal status; and its decisions are based on consensus.

[11]   See http://www.osce.si/izjave-govori-2005-04-26-zda-govor-zbogar.htm.

[12]   For more details on what constitutes the human dimension, see *OSCE Human Dimension Commitments: Chronological Compilation*, available at http://www.osce.org/odihr/item_11_16238.html. For more on the human dimension in general see J. Binder, *The Human Dimension of the OSCE: From Recommendation to Implementation* (Vienna: Studienreihe des Ludwig Boltzmann Instituts für Menschenrechte, 2001).

As indicated above, the OSCE standards in this field of human dimension cover a wider area than traditional human rights law. In international human rights treaties, individual (or group) rights are formulated, and the state party is obligated to respect and/or guarantee those rights. How to implement these obligations, however, is most often left to the discretion of states. The OSCE human dimension goes further in linking human rights with the institutional and political system of a state. In essence, OSCE states have agreed through their human dimension commitments that pluralistic democracy based on the rule of law is the only system of government suitable to guarantee human rights effectively.

This explains why the OSCE human dimension has been described as a common pan-European public order (*ordre public*). In other words, the OSCE is not simply an organisation of 55 participating states, but a 'community of values'. This linkage is also reflected in its strong commitment to the rule of law and in the way it is formulated as a concept based on the dignity of the human person and a system of rights through law/legal structures.

The OSCE is equipped with a variety of mechanisms, structures and activities aimed at the effective implementation of human dimension commitments. The human dimension is fully integrated into the OSCE political consultation process and in the work of the decision-making bodies and the OSCE field missions. Since 1994, representatives of the participating states have conducted a regular dialogue on the human dimension – including on cases of non-implementation of human dimension commitments – within its Permanent Council.

The OSCE chairman-in-office may inform the Permanent Council of cases of alleged non-implementation on the basis of information received by OSCE bodies such as ODIHR and the field missions. Any participating state may raise in the Permanent Council general concerns or specific cases of human rights violations. The heads of OSCE institutions and field operations report regularly to the Permanent Council and often include human rights issues, including individual cases, in their reports.

The annual Human Dimension Implementation Meeting, Supplementary Human Dimension Meetings and Human Dimension Seminars provide additional fora in which participating states, non-governmental organisations (NGOs) and OSCE bodies can raise human rights concerns and individual cases in any of the 55 participating states.

Beyond formal meetings, the chairman-in-office can, and does, make direct interventions. In some instances, these are confidential diplomatic appeals to governments but, in particularly serious instances, they may be public statements. Heads of institutions and field operations frequently intervene confidentially or publicly in particular cases. In addition, the OSCE has created a number of special procedures, such as the Moscow Mechanism[13] and new measures adopted at the

---

[13]   The Moscow Mechanism, set forth in the Document of the Moscow Meeting of the Conference of the Human Dimension of the CSCE of 4 October 1991, and later streamlined through the Document of the Fourth Meeting of the CSCE Council (Rome) on 1 December

Istanbul Summit,[14] under which participating states can take action in response to serious human rights violations, but these have rarely been put to use.

Unlike some other human rights treaties, for example, the European Convention on Human Rights,[15] the OSCE's basic texts do not provide for a court or other individual petition body to enforce the implementation of OSCE commitments. This reflects the political character of the OSCE and the intention not to duplicate existing mechanisms.

Human Rights in OSCE Field Operations[16]

OSCE's comprehensive approach to security and its specific commitments create a context for the work of all OSCE field operations. It is within this context that OSCE field operations carry out their mandates to assist host governments in solving specific problems and in meeting their commitments. All OSCE missions implicitly have a human rights mandate, but one that is an integrated part of a broad mission mandate encompassing all three dimensions of the OSCE security concept.

The practice of long-term field missions, entrusted with tasks of early warning and conflict prevention, whether to prevent looming potential conflicts or to stop further escalation of already existing conflicts, emerged in 1992. The first missions were sent to areas where the greatest dangers of spillover of the Yugoslav conflict were seen: Kosovo, Sandjak and Vojvodina. This was followed the same year by missions to the former-Yugoslav Republic of Macedonia and to Georgia, and in 1993 by missions to Estonia and Moldova.[17]

The turning point for OSCE was the opening of the first large mission in the former Yugoslavia, the Mission to Bosnia and Herzegovina, in December 1995. The next major phase in the development of OSCE field missions came in the aftermath of the Kosovo crisis and the rapid establishment in 1998–1999 of the largest OSCE field activity to date, the Kosovo Verification Mission (KVM).

OSCE missions are generally regarded as being at the front line of the Organization's work, as important tools for implementing the Organization's

---

1993, establishes a formal mechanism for sending missions of experts and rapporteurs to participating states in response to human rights violations. For more information, see http://www.osce.org/odihr/human_rights/moscow_mechanism.

[14] Paragraph 36 of the Charter for European Security adopted in Istanbul in 1999 includes a number of procedures to ensure compliance with commitments, including dispatching delegations to provide advice or representatives for fact-finding missions, or convening reinforced Permanent Council meetings.

[15] European Convention for the on Human Rights, Convention for the Protection of Human Rights and Fundamental Freedoms, 213 UNTS 222 (entered into force 3 September 1953).

[16] For the purposes of the present chapter and for ease of language, the term 'field operation' is used interchangeably with 'field mission' and 'field presence'.

[17] Centre for OSCE Research (CORE), *The Culture of Dialog: The OSCE Acquis 30 Years after Helsinki*, Institute for Peace Research and Security Policy, University of Hamburg, pp. 22–23.

objectives in countries facing transition challenges. The concrete tasks of a mission as well as its composition are described in the mandate, which is based on an agreement between the Permanent Council and the host country and is renewed every year. The chairman-in-office will typically lead discussions in the Permanent Council. The secretary general can provide analytical support to the chairman-in-office in this process. Missions are led by a head of mission, appointed by the OSCE chairman-in-office.

OSCE missions vary in aim, size and scope. The mandates[18] as well as tools and instruments to implement them vary accordingly. While some missions do not have explicit human dimension mandates, others refer to all three dimensions. In large missions with an extended network of field offices, it is often possible to monitor general trends in the human rights situation, to investigate individual incidents and to react systematically to allegations. Small field operations will necessarily be more limited in how they can react.

The following field operations have explicit mandates to work with promotion, monitoring and protection of human rights: OSCE Mission in Georgia, OSCE Mission to Moldova, OSCE Mission to Bosnia and Herzegovina, OSCE Mission to Croatia, OSCE Mission in Kosovo, OSCE Mission to Serbia and Montenegro and OSCE Presence in Albania.

For the OSCE Centre in Almaty, the OSCE Centre in Ashgabat, the OSCE Centre in Bishkek, the OSCE Centre in Dushanbe, the OSCE Office in Yerevan, and the OSCE Office in Baku, the mandate states that these field operations should promote the implementation of principles and commitments in all OSCE dimensions including the human aspects of security and stability. Even though it is not spelled out as clearly as in the mandate for missions in South Eastern Europe, this nevertheless gives the Centres a basis to work with human rights as it is a significant part of the commitments in the human dimension. Even vaguer is the mandate for the OSCE Centre in Tashkent which merely states that the Centre there should '... promote implementation of OSCE principles and commitments ...'. In this case the mandate to work with human rights must be seen as implicit in the task to promote OSCE commitments. Moreover, human rights work should be subsumed in the early warning and conflict prevention aspects of those field operations.

The mandate for the OSCE office in Minsk does not mention human rights at all, but states that the Centre should assist the Belarusian government in promoting institution building, consolidate the rule of law and develop relations with civil society.

In Ukraine, OSCE has an office and a project coordinator, with a mandate to carry out projects in all dimensions, including with human rights, but without any mandate to monitor or protect.

Currently, OSCE has the following field operations:[19]

---

[18]   All mandates for OSCE missions are listed before.

[19]   For more information on the OSCE field operation see the *Survey of OSCE Long-Term Missions and other OSCE Field Activities* by the OCSE Conflict Prevention Center, available

- OSCE Presence in Albania[20]
- OSCE Mission to Bosnia and Herzegovina[21]
- OSCE Mission to Croatia[22]
- OSCE Mission to Serbia and Montenegro[23]
- OSCE Mission in Kosovo[24]
- OSCE Spillover Monitor Mission to Skopje[25]
- OSCE Office in Minsk[26]
- OSCE Mission to Moldova[27]
- OSCE Project Co-ordinator in Ukraine[28]
- OSCE Office in Baku[29]
- OSCE Mission to Georgia[30]
- OSCE Office in Yerevan[31]
- Personal Representative of the Chairman-in-Office on the Conflict Dealt with by the OSCE Minsk Conference[32]
- OSCE Centre in Almaty[33]
- OSCE Centre in Ashgabad[34]
- OSCE Centre in Bishkek[35]
- OSCE Centre in Tashkent[36]

---

at http://www.osce.org/documents/sg/2004/05/3242_en.pdf.

[20] Permanent Council Decision No. 588, Mandate of the OSCE Presence in Albania, OSCE Doc. PC.DEC/588 (2003).

[21] See Agreement on Human Rights, Annex 6 to General Framework Agreement for Peace in Bosnia and Herzegovina, Attachment to UN Doc. A/50/790-S/1995/999 (30 November 1995).

[22] Permanent Council Decision No. 112, OSCE Doc. PC.DEC/112 (1996).

[23] Permanent Council Decision No. 401, Establishment of the OSCE Mission to the Federal Republic of Yugoslavia, OSCE Doc. PC.DEC/401 (2001).

[24] Permanent Council Decision No. 305, OSCE Doc. PC.DEC/305 (1999).

[25] Mandate, Articles of Understanding Concerning CSCE Spillover Monitor Mission to Skopje, available at http://www.osce.org/documents/mms/1992/09/520_en.pdf.

[26] Permanent Council Decision No. 526, OSCE Office in Minsk, OSCE Doc. PC.DEC/526 (2002).

[27] CSCE Mission to the Republic of Moldova, CSCE/19-CSO/Journal No. 3, Annex 3 (1993).

[28] Permanent Council Decision No. 295, OSCE Doc. PC.DEC/295 (1999).

[29] Permanent Council Decision No. 318, OSCE Doc. PC.DEC/318 (1999).

[30] Permanent Council Decision No. 575, Extension of the Mandate of the OSCE Mission to Georgia, OSCE Doc. PC.DEC/575 (2003).

[31] Permanent Council Decision No. 314, OSCE Doc. PC.DEC/314 (1999).

[32] Permanent Council See http://www.osce.org/item/13668.html.

[33] Permanent Council Decision No. 243, OSCE Doc. PC.DEC/243 (1998).

[34] Permanent Council Decision No. 244, OSCE Doc. PC.DEC/244 (1998).

[35] Permanent Council Decision No. 245, OSCE Doc. PC.DEC/245 (1998).

[36] Permanent Council Decision No. 397, OSCE Centre in Tashkent, OSCE Doc. PC.DEC/397 (2000).

368 *The Human Rights Field Operation*

- OSCE Centre in Dushanbe[37]

The OSCE has previously had the following field operations:

- OSCE Missions of Long Duration in Kosovo, Sandjak and Vojvodina[38]
- OSCE Representative to the Joint Committee on the Skrunda Radar Station[39]
- OSCE Mission to Ukraine[40]
- OSCE Mission to Estonia[41]
- OSCE Mission to Latvia[42]
- OSCE Advisory and Monitoring Group in Belarus[43]
- OSCE Assistance Group to Chechnya[44]

OSCE Human Rights Field Officers[45]

Recruitment and Staff Training

OSCE field staff members are generally seconded by OSCE participating states who in almost all cases second nationals of their own country. There have been a few cases where states that are partners for cooperation with the OSCE have seconded staff to the field missions (Japan and Korea). Interested applicants have to submit their documents directly to their ministry of foreign affairs (the OSCE participating state) which then decides whether a candidate will be proposed for assignments with OSCE. The OSCE mission makes the final selection from a number of short-listed candidates. OSCE promotes itself as a non-career organisation which simply means that staff are hired on a limited appointment for a specific position. Currently, the period for maximum continuous length of service to OSCE is seven years in a single field mission and ten years in total. As with other staff, the length of service of the human rights field officer depends on the policies of the seconding state, but the standard contract for a secondee is six months.

Because missions vary so much in size and mandate, a human rights professional seconded to OSCE may face a range of tasks depending on the mission in question. The experience of working as one human rights field officer among 200 others in

---

[37] Permanent Council Decision No. 500/Corrected Reissue*, Mandate of the OSCE Centre in Dushanbe, OSCE Doc. PC.DEC/500/Corr.1 (2002).

[38] See 15th CSO Meeting, 14 August 1992, Journal No. 2, Annex 1.

[39] See http://www.osce.org/item/15752.html.

[40] See 27th CSO Meeting, 15 June 1994, Journal No. 3, Decision (c).

[41] See 18th CSO Meeting, 13 December 1992, Journal No. 3, Annex 2.

[42] See 23rd CSO Meeting, 23 September 1993, Journal No. 3, Annex 3.

[43] Permanent Council Decision No. 185, OSCE Doc. PC.DEC/185 (1997).

[44] Permanent Council Decision No. 35, OSCE Doc. PC.DEC/35 (1995).

[45] For more information on OSCE field staff in general see A. Legutke, *Working in OSCE Field Missions: Recruitment, Selection, Preparation, Working and Employment Conditions of OSCE Seconded Personnel* (Hamburg: CORE, November 2003).

one of the larger missions in South Eastern Europe will differ significantly from being the sole international human-dimension officer in an OSCE field presence in a Central Asian country. When seconded to a small mission in Central Asia, the staff member is seconded in a broad human-dimension capacity covering the entire spectrum of the OSCE human dimension as relevant to the host country and the general situation in the region. This obviously makes recruitment to OSCE Centres in Central Asia particularly challenging since one international secondee will have to handle complex issues related to elections, rule-of-law development, human rights, national minorities, freedom of the media, etc.

When seconded to a large mission such as the ones currently deployed in South Eastern Europe, a staff member may be recruited in a much more specialised capacity, such as a rule-of-law officer, capacity-building officer, or human rights field officer (HRFO) in a structure where the human dimension is typically addressed by the three or four specialised departments of elections, democratisation, human rights and/or rule of law. However, as there is no standard OSCE field operation neither is there any standard human rights field officer.

A human rights professional coming to work for OSCE for the first time will have to participate in a general induction course covering the three dimensions, administration and security.

Many new staff members in OSCE field missions are unfamiliar with OSCE and its character as a political organisation, and law graduates can find it difficult to work with standards of a political rather then legal character. In response to this, ODIHR started a general training programme in the human dimension in 2004 which is offered to OSCE field staff four times a year. This training course includes sessions explaining the historical background of OSCE, its political nature and how to work with the implementation of OSCE commitments in practice. This course also provides participants with an in-depth understanding of the OSCE human dimension. However, ODIHR has recognised the need to offer more specialised human rights courses to strengthen the understanding of OSCE specificities in working with human rights issues and to continually provide human rights/human-dimension officers with the tools to address the human rights issues they face in whichever mission they serve.

The human rights field officer can find guidance in OSCE handbooks.[46] However, there is no obligation for the field missions to follow any particular format or procedure when making inquiries into alleged human rights violations. It is often left to the individual human rights department or HRFO to draft mission-specific procedures. The ultimate responsibility, however, lies with the head of mission, who reports to OSCE's chairman-in-office. This absence of procedures ensures a flexibility that allows the organisation to respond quickly and adequately to a changing context. A good example of this is when the KVM was evacuated from Kosovo and instead was

---

[46] See, for example, OSCE, *Individual Human Rights Complaints: A Handbook for OSCE Field Personnel*, (Warsaw: ODIHR, 2003); OSCE, *Preventing Torture: A Handbook for OSCE Field Staff*, (Warsaw: ODIHR, 1999).

quickly adjusted to respond to the needs of the refugees in Macedonia and Albania.[47] This meant that parts of the Mission were involved in humanitarian issues, while others interviewed refugees and documented stories of human rights violations. The latter activity was done in cooperation with the International Criminal Tribunal for the former Yugoslavia.

Monitoring

The core functions of OSCE field operations include such activities as human rights monitoring, making inquiries with government officials, collecting publicly available information, receiving testimonies from individuals, making interventions with public officials and with other relevant organisations on the ground, and writing reports. This is done with the general purposes of engaging the host government in a dialogue on issues of concern; of informing the OSCE Secretariat and relevant institutions about the situation on the ground; of informing OSCE participating states through the chairman-in-office; and of providing a basis for interventions.

When OSCE field staff monitor the human rights situation in any given host country, they first of all measure it against OSCE standards. However, as OSCE is a regional organisation under Chapter VIII of the UN Charter,[48] it operates within the larger context of the UN. Therefore, field staff often refer to relevant human rights obligations under the UN when monitoring and making interventions. Similarly, where applicable, OSCE missions refer to obligations under other regional or sub-regional arrangements.

Individual Complaints[49]

Some OSCE field missions receive and work with individual human rights complaints. Some missions have introduced designated office hours during which a competent HRFO is present and available to receive complaints. Some field missions have also developed a standardised form to document alleged human rights violations. Some field missions, such as for example Armenia and Macedonia have developed databases that help them keep track of the individual complaints. Although there is no common database module for individual cases, the missions have informally exchanged experience and prototypes.

---

[47] For more on the KVM, see OSCE/ODIHR, *As Seen, As Told: An Analysis of the Human Rights Findings of the OSCE Kosovo Verification Mission October 1998 to June 1999*, (Warsaw: OSCE/ODIHR 1999), available at http://www.osce.org/documents/mik/1999/11/1620_en.pdf.

[48] Charter of the United Nations, 59 Stat. 1031, T.S. 993, 3 Bevans 1153 (entered into force 24 October 1945).

[49] For more information on the guidelines on how OSCE missions should deal with individual human rights complaints, see *Individual Human Rights Complaints: A Handbook for OSCE Field Personnel*, (Warsaw: OSCE/ODIHR 2003), available in English and Russian at http://www.osce.org/odihr/item_11_13594.html.

The most elaborated database can be found in the Spillover Mission in Skopje. The basis for every case is a 'Case Summary Form' but any development in a case is carefully noted in a 'Case Contact Form' through which every contact with the victim, authorities or others is noted. This greatly facilitates the institutional memory and makes it possible for a new mission member to quickly get on top of the open cases. The information collected in these forms is fed into a closed- and open-case database.

Other missions do not receive individuals directly but instead they make effort to encourage individuals to make use of national systems if that is possible and appropriate. The presence in Albania, for example, has a policy of referring all persons who approach them with complaints of human rights violations to the national ombudsman. The OSCE Mission in Kosovo has produced a manual on remedies in which different options in the national system are set out and which is given to individuals who approach the missions with complaints.

Although OSCE does not have any formal procedures for the submission of allegations of human rights violations, the organisation uses the same criteria for taking up individual cases as would apply for the submission of cases to any international body. In general, individuals alleging human rights violations are expected to seek a remedy through established domestic means before seeking international assistance. Before becoming involved, the HRFO has to consider whether complainants have attempted to resolve their problem through national means, such as courts, ombudsman offices or other avenues. However, if circumstances in the host country are such that effective and timely domestic remedies are either not available or seem unlikely, or if the allegation is sufficiently grave or urgent, missions can become involved even when domestic remedies have not been pursued.

If the complaint has possible merit but the mission makes a preliminary determination that it is not in a position to become involved, the HRFO should be prepared to offer the complainant suggestions about how he or she might pursue a remedy. This advice could include referring the complainant to appropriate government offices, courts or other groups that deal with human rights issues. It is a good practice for missions to develop and regularly update a handout on how to pursue domestic remedies and on local resources that might be available to help complainants.

If the mission decides to pursue the case further, the next step is to decide how to proceed. In some cases, the complaint may be so compelling and urgent that the mission decides to take action immediately on the basis of the information initially provided.

In many instances the mission may wish to obtain further information before taking action. In general, only large OSCE field operations will be equipped to carry out human rights investigations or inquiries. However, even small missions may initiate inquiries if they are presented with serious individual complaints.

If the mission determines that an inquiry is merited, the next step should be to pursue an inquiry to collect evidence and verify information concerning the alleged violation as well as the response of the authorities including the military, police and the judicial system, where relevant. Such information may be gathered through a more thorough interview with the complainant or by obtaining more information from witnesses and others who may have knowledge of the alleged incident, by checking with independent sources, and through inquiries with the authorities.

However, it is always important that HRFOs keep in mind that any inquiry they undertake is in the nature of fact-finding, not judicial or prosecutorial. Only in very rare occasions have OSCE field mission been involved in gathering evidence for criminal prosecution. They should be careful not to interfere with any official inquiry that may be underway or take any steps that could compromise evidence.

If an investigation establishes that no human rights violation has occurred, the case can be closed, meaning that the mission will not continue to work on the case. If the investigations or inquiries establish the likelihood that there has been a human rights violation, the mission should report its conclusions to the Permanent Council through the chairman-in-office and make recommendations for further action. In either instance, depending on the particularities of the case, it must be determined how pieces of evidence, confidential documents, etc, collected during the investigation should be treated.

Except in rare instances, it is customary and necessary to approach the authorities to inquire whether they can provide clarification or corroboration with regard to the allegation. An exception might be if it is justified to expect that making such an inquiry would further endanger a victim or community.

OSCE field operations have many options for reacting to, and following up, individual complaints of human rights violations. The options range from referring the complainant to domestic government or other offices or NGOs that might help resolve the complaint to pursuing the complaint through a variety of OSCE diplomatic or other channels. In some instances, it might be appropriate for the OSCE to refer a complaint to another international organisation or at least to ensure that the individual lodging the complaint is aware of the appeals options available through other international organisations.

Interventions

An important part of the work of an OSCE HRFO is to follow up on the information collected though the monitoring activities and make interventions as required. Any action by field missions would, as standard OSCE practice, be carried out in a way that tries to elicit a positive and cooperative response from the authorities. The comprehensive approach of the organisation to security should manifest itself in any intervention made by a field operation, whereby the mission exhibits a full understanding of the security situation of the host country. The mission's purpose of intervening in an alleged violation of human rights is not to publicly criticise the authorities (although this may be done in some circumstances), but to resolve the issue.

As a general rule, the first stage will be to make inquiries with the relevant government authorities about the case. The head of mission or other relevant mission officer will determine which authorities to contact, at what level and in what form. If a mission decides to proceed, one obvious option is to raise the case again with government officials at a higher level. As the level of concern and the level of the government officials approached rises, it becomes necessary to involve staff of the mission with corresponding levels of responsibility, up to, in some cases, the head of mission. The intervention of the head of mission may be required when the human rights violations are particularly serious and/or when the violations may have been committed or sanctioned by a high level government official. If a case remains unresolved after a mission has raised it at as high a level as it can – usually ministerial level or above – the mission still has other options available to it for showing concern. These are described below.

The HRFO is expected to have regular contacts with local authorities. It is important to prepare for possible interventions by developing contacts with key officials of the civil administration, military, police, prosecutor's office and other offices to which the mission may wish to appeal for assistance on an individual case. Interventions with government officials can be made either in written form or directly in person. The setting for an oral *démarche* may also be selected: while it would usually be made in the context of a formal office call, it is not unusual for OSCE officials to raise human rights concerns with especially close or trusted contacts in a less formal setting.

Other options for follow up include:

- Monitoring trials;
- Visiting prisons or individuals in detention;
- Visiting refugee camps or camps for internally displaced persons;
- Visiting shelters for victims of domestic violence or victims of trafficking;
- Visiting treatment centres for victims of torture;
- Visiting offices of media outlets, political parties, religious groups, NGOs or others that may be suffering harassment or human rights violations;
- Meeting with individual members of such groups and/or including such persons on guest lists for mission functions;
- Monitoring rallies of political parties or candidates;
- Developing small-scale assistance projects to benefit specific NGOs, minority groups or others that may be suffering discrimination or other violations.

This list is not exhaustive. Local circumstances and the nature of an individual complaint may dictate the extent to which any particular step is likely to be helpful in a specific case.

Reporting

Reporting is one of the standard functions of OSCE field operations. The OSCE Secretariat has issued general guidance on reporting, which is available to all OSCE field personnel and should be followed. Field missions report to all participating states (the Permanent Council) through the OSCE chairman-in-office and supported by the OSCE Secretariat's Conflict Prevention Centre. There is a system in place for sharing these reports with partner organisations both in the host country and at Secretariat level. Confidential reports on individual human rights cases can be submitted by field missions to the chairman-in-office and to the institutions of OSCE.

The extent to which reports deal with human rights issues depends on the mission's mandate and staffing pattern, as well as the circumstances in the country. Field operations have a number of options for reporting, including their regular periodic reports, spot reports and oral reports of the head of mission before the Permanent Council. Large missions will also have an internal reporting system, with field offices reporting to the mission's headquarters.

If a particular issue or individual complaint is especially grave or significant, it may merit a more detailed report. Alternately, the chairman-in-office, the Secretariat, or an institution may request that the mission provide more information on a case, for example, in the context of an upcoming visit to the country by a senior OSCE official.

Training/Capacity-building Projects

Project implementation has increasingly become part of OSCE's field activities, alongside the Organization's traditional diplomatic efforts, its monitoring and reporting tasks and its advisory role to state structures and civil society. Staff in the field and in institutions will, to one degree or another, be involved in developing and implementing projects during their period of service with OSCE.

The OSCE and its institutions have developed increasing expertise in implementing specific types of technical-assistance projects to assist in strengthening human rights protection. Examples of such projects include:

- Revising national legislation to conform with international human rights standards;
- Improving election systems;
- Advancing equality and non-discrimination;
- Protecting the human rights of victims of trafficking;
- Promoting religious freedom;
- Training and capacity building for NGOs involved in monitoring and redressing human rights violations;
- Providing human rights training for police, border guards, prosecutors and judges;
- Promoting reform of prisons and other places of detention;
- Developing better practices for ensuring the rights of internally displaced persons;
- Establishing legal clinics; and
- Developing ombudsman institutions.

Projects are always implemented with the agreement of the host government. The human rights priorities addressed through projects are generated first of all by the needs of the host country as expressed by its authorities, secondly through general priorities of OSCE participating states as expressed through the expanding body of human dimension documents. For such projects to be successful, however, the government must be committed to change and must be prepared to cooperate with implementation.

Role of Institutions

Another option field operations may consider for following up on individual complaints of human rights violations is to raise the issue with other OSCE bodies. These bodies may be able to take further action, or, in some instances, just raising the issue may be enough to draw the government's attention and prompt a response. It would be at the discretion of the mission how and when to raise any issue with any relevant OSCE institution.

The institutions are an especially good resource for the smaller missions where a single staff member covers the entire spectrum of the human dimension. Typically, such a staff member will have expertise in one aspect of the human dimension but in order to respond to situations that fall outside of his or her expertise, the institutions play a pivotal role in providing the necessary guidance and advice.

Case Study: Kosovo Verification Mission

On 16 October 1998, the mandate of the KVM was established in the 'Agreement on the OSCE Kosovo Verification Mission'[50] between the OSCE and the former Republic of Yugoslavia (FRY). Under the terms of the Agreement KVM was responsible for verifying that all parties in Kosovo complied with UN Security Council resolution 1199[51] and with the ceasefire.

Human rights (the human dimension) was not part of the KVM mandate but the mission set the precedence for the now generally accepted view that human rights protection and promotion is implicit in all of OSCE missions.

By late December there were approximately 400 international personnel and 250 local staff at KVM.[52] Because recruitment for KVM initially focused on those with military and police backgrounds, there were only 11 staff members in the Human Rights Division at the end of December.[53] By the end of January 1999, however,

---

[50] Available at http://www.balkan-archive.org.yu/politics/kosovo/documents/agreement 101698.html.

[51] Security Council resolution 1199 (1998), UN Doc. S/RES/1199 (1998).

[52] OSCE-KVM, Human Rights Division (HQ), 'Daily Report 29 December 1998' (internal document).

[53] OSCE-KVM, Human Rights Division (HQ), 'Weekly Report 11–18 December' and 'Weekly Report 19–27 December 1998' (internal document).

HRFOs were present in all five regional centres and most field offices.[54] When the KVM evacuated on 24 March, there were approximately 75 staff members in the Human Rights Division (ten in headquarters and the rest deployed in the regional and field offices).

Although it was extremely difficult to plan a long-term human rights strategy in a state of armed conflict, the Human Rights Division identified core human rights tasks and priorities. The immediate core tasks included monitoring/documenting the conduct of armed forces, police, investigative judges, allegations of humanitarian law violations (this took on a higher priority after the International Criminal Tribunal for the former Yugoslavia (ICTY) was prevented from entering Kosovo) and intervening with FRY and Serbian security forces and the Kosovo Liberation Army (UCK) on individual cases. In terms of prioritising which allegations of human rights violations would be investigated, the Human Rights Division focused on the right to life, right to liberty, rights related to detention and fair trials and issues relating to missing persons.

The KVM Human Rights Division adopted a methodology consisting of:

1. *Documentation*: The sheer number of allegations of human rights violations received by KVM rendered it impossible to investigate them all thoroughly. Thus, accurate documentation became an essential component of the division. Standardised forms were used for incident reports, victim/witness statements and missing-person reports, and a related database was developed to index the information collected. Complaints from witnesses or victims of alleged human rights or humanitarian law violations were given priority. In such cases the HRFOs sought supporting documentation from, for example, medical authorities, and corroborating statements from other witnesses, etc. Videotapes and photographs of crime scenes and killing sites were made, as well as of the victims, to assist in identification. HRFOs monitored official investigations and at times documented those investigations (e.g. post-mortem examinations were documented by KVM when allegations of humanitarian law violations were made).

2. *Independent and impartial investigation*: The Human Rights Division conducted investigations and interventions with local authorities. Senior KVM staff allowed the Human Rights Division to access information and draw independent conclusions based on the information uncovered. The Human Rights Division always had direct access to the head of mission, which further facilitated the 'need to know basis' that was the foundation for independent investigations.

   Impartiality is at the heart of human rights work, and it was imperative to the Human Rights Division that it was seen as impartial. The Human Rights Division consciously and persistently investigated allegations of human rights abuses committed by UCK and Serb authorities.

3. *Reporting*: Reports by the Human Rights Division served four basic functions:

---

[54]   OSCE-KVM, Human Rights Division (HQ), 'Weekly Report 24-29 January' (internal document).

(i)   to inform OSCE senior staff and others about the situation on the ground;
(ii) to discourage authorities whose actions were being monitored and verified from committing violations;
(iii) to inform governments, policymakers and OSCE participating states; and
(iv) to provide a basis for interventions.

The various types of reports utilised by the Human Rights Division were 'incident reports', initially 'daily reports', 'weekly reports', 'monthly reports' and 'special reports'.

Incident reports were prepared: (i) when human rights complaints/abuses were brought to the attention of the regional centres; (ii) when verifiers were asked to investigate human rights complaints; (iii) when KVM representatives intervened in a human rights matter; and (iv) on other matters which a HRFO judged to be of sufficient importance to bring to the immediate attention of KVM headquarters.

The senior HRFOs at the five regional centres were responsible for preparing weekly reports. Weekly reports from the regional centres were collated and summarised in a consolidated headquarters weekly report to the head of mission and the OSCE Secretariat.

Monthly reports were envisaged in order to identify and analyse trends in human rights. For example, attention would be given to identifying systematic patterns of discriminatory treatment of minority groups.

KVM Human Rights Division also set up a comprehensive human rights database with the capacity to record and track all reported violations in Kosovo.

4. *Confidentiality and security*: KVM Human Rights Division operated with strict security and confidentiality safeguards. Incident reports, reports on missing persons and so on, were safely stored, with access restricted to international staff on a 'need to know basis'. When reports were submitted from the field to headquarters, all names were eliminated and a reference numbering system was used.

The security of photos, negatives, videotapes and so on was ensured through log books, and all materials were kept in safes at headquarters. HRFOs were instructed to attach their original notes to the files and they were not allowed to keep extra copies or to distribute them outside KVM. Information regarding ongoing human rights investigations was restricted, and relations with the media were centralised through the KVM spokesperson.

In the days prior to the KVM's withdrawal on 20 March 1999, the Human Rights Division initiated strict procedures for the handling, evacuation and destruction of human rights information. All victim/witness statements, complaints, documents relating to investigations, computer disks, hard drives and physical evidence were collected by the five senior human rights officers for their areas of responsibility and were evacuated. Any related documentation that was not evacuated was either shredded or burned before KVM left Kosovo. All of the human rights data were then collected from the senior human rights officers and centralised by the director of the Human Rights Division immediately after the evacuation. KVM Human Rights Division's files and archives were subsequently transported to OSCE/ODIHR in Warsaw for safekeeping and analysis.

Conclusions

The role of the HRFO in the OSCE context has developed from the first field missions of the early 1990s through a period of expansion. However, as transition countries in the OSCE region consolidate and move closer to other regional and sub-regional bodies for cooperation, the need for large, post-conflict OSCE field missions has diminished. Unfortunately, the presence of an OSCE mission has come to be seen in some places more as an indicator of democratic deficiencies and less as a constructive cooperative tool for efficiently moving towards democratisation and gaining sustainable international legitimacy. As field missions are, by nature, temporary, in the long term field missions will eventually be scaled down or closed, while it is not at all given that new ones will be established. This means that the focus may increasingly shift from the HRFO deployed to a field station to the human rights desk officer, based in OSCE institutions, who will from time to time be deployed on short missions with specific tasks, such as trial monitoring, technical assistance, training or the collection of information on reported human rights violations, etc.

The more immediate challenges for OSCE human rights field work are twofold. The first concerns the challenges of smaller missions where human rights work is sometimes sidelined either because the human dimension officer does not have the necessary expertise or because the mission is concerned about repercussions from the host country when dealing with human rights issues in a mission that is dependent on a yearly renewal of its mandate. In addition, apart from the political oversight through the chairman-in-office and the Permanent Council there is no system in place in OSCE for ensuring that a field mission actually carries out its human dimension mandate; otherwise this is entirely at the discretion of the head of mission. OSCE Permanent Council decisions may to some degree dictate priorities to the head of mission, but there is no doubt that they enjoy extensive autonomy to implement these and generally set mission priorities. With regard to the small centres and offices of OSCE in certain regions, it can be questioned whether it is possible at all to be effective with only one person covering the entire spectrum of the human dimension. On the contrary, raising expectations without any will or capacity to fulfil them can be rather harmful, both for the individuals concerned and for the reputation of the Organization.

The current debate within the Organization over the merits of a project-driven approach versus focusing on core mandate functions, such as monitoring and reporting on the implementation of OSCE commitments, constitutes the second main challenge for future OSCE human rights field work. OSCE is a regional security organisation with a comparative advantage in its comprehensive approach to security, early warning and conflict prevention. The strength of OSCE human rights field work has historically been within core mandate functions, such as human rights monitoring, conducted in the context of early warning, conflict prevention, conflict management and post-conflict rehabilitation. The challenge lies in maintaining this aspect of OSCE field work while conducting technical assistance for rule-of-law development and human rights capacity-building projects where appropriate.

The above case study on the KVM's human rights activities illustrates the enormous potential in OSCE for effective human rights field work. Similarly, other missions have carried out important human rights field work, some of them resulting in significant changes in host governments' attitudes and practices. Given the vast experience within the Organization in human rights field work, not enough has been done to preserve this institutional memory and draw lessons learned from this work, and even less in terms of developing common OSCE mission guidelines or standard operating procedures for the human dimension and human rights field work. ODIHR, as the main institution of OSCE in the human dimension, is called upon to play an active role in this regard.

Chapter 19

Compendium of Resources Regarding Human Rights Field Operations of Intergovernmental Organisations

Kevin Turner[1]

Introduction

This chapter is a compendium of official documents regarding the establishment and operation of human rights field operations. It also lists selected English-language commentary materials on field operations. For the purpose of the chapter, a human rights field operation is understood to be a sustained deployment of unarmed civilian personnel mandated by an intergovernmental organisation to, *inter alia*, develop and enhance local human rights protection and capacities, typically in a conflict or post-conflict situation. Field operations are listed chronologically starting from 1991. Mandates subsequent to the establishing mandate are included only where the human rights functions of the operation were altered significantly.

El Salvador

Official Documents

> United Nations Observer Mission in El Salvador (July 1991 – April 1995).

Agreement on Human Rights, Annex to UN Doc. A/44/971-S/21541 (16 August 1990).
Security Council resolution 693 (1991), UN Doc. S/RES/693 (20 May 1991).
Security Council resolution 729 (1992), UN Doc. S/RES/729 (14 January 1992).
First report of the Director of the Human Rights Division, Appendix to UN Doc. A/45/1055-S/23037 (16 September 1991).
Report of the Director of the Human Rights Division, Annex to UN Doc. A/46/658-S/23222 (15 November 1991).
Note by the Secretary-General, Corrigendum, UN Doc. A/46/658/Corr.1-S/23222/Corr.1 (29 November 1991).

---

[1]   The author is grateful for the research assistance of Rosarie Tucci.

Report of the Director of the Human Rights Division, Annex to UN Doc. A/46/876-S23580 (19 February 1992).

Report of the Director of the Human Rights Division, Annex to UN Doc. A/46/935-S/24066 (5 June 1992).

Report of the Director of the Human Rights Division, Annex to UN Doc. A/46/955-S/24375 (12 August 1992).

Report of the Director of the Human Rights Division of the United Nations Observer Mission in El Salvador up to 31 January 1993, Annex to UN Doc. A/47/912-S/25521 (5 April 1993).

Report of the Director of the Human Rights Division of the United Nations Observer Mission in El Salvador up to 30 April 1993, Annex to UN Doc. A/47/968-S/26033 (2 July 1993).

Report of the Director of the Human Rights Division of the United Nations Observer Mission in El Salvador up to 31 July 1993, Annex to UN Doc. A/47/1012-S/26416 (15 September 1993).

Addendum to the Report of the Director of the Human Rights Division of the United Nations Observer Mission in El Salvador up to 31 July 1993, Annex to UN Doc. A/47/1012/Add.1-S/26416/Add.1 (27 October 1993).

Ninth report of the Director of the Human Rights Division of the United Nations Observer Mission in El Salvador, Annex to UN Doc. A/49/59-S/1994/47 (18 January 1994).

Tenth report of the Director of the Human Rights Division of the United Nations Observer Mission in El Salvador, Annex to UN Doc. A/49/116-S/1994/385 (5 April 1994).

Eleventh report of the Director of the Human Rights Division of the United Nations Observer Mission in El Salvador, Annex to UN Doc. A/48/281-S/1994/286 (28 July 1994).

Twelfth report of the Director of the Human Rights Division of the United Nations Observer Mission in El Salvador, Annex to UN Doc. A/49/585-S/1994/1220 (31 October 1994).

Thirteenth report of the Director of the Human Rights Division of the United Nations Observer Mission in El Salvador, Annex to UN Doc. A/49/888-S/1995/281 (18 April 1995).

Commentary

Acuna, T., *The United Nations Mission in El Salvador: A Humanitarian Law Perspective* (The Hague: Kluwer Law International, 1995).

Bar-Yaacov, N. 'Diplomacy and Human Rights: The Role of Human Rights on Conflict Resolution in El Salvador and Haiti', *Fletcher Forum of World Affairs* vol. 19, no. 2 (1995).

Boutros-Ghali, B., 'Introduction', *The United Nations and El Salvador 1990-1995* The United Nations Blue Book Series, vol. IV (New York: Department of Public Information, United Nations, 1995).

Brody, R., 'The United Nations and Human Rights in El Salvador's "Negotiated Revolution"', *Harvard Human Rights Journal* vol. 8 (1995).

Burgerman, S. D., 'Building the Peace by Mandating Reform: United Nations-Mediated Human Rights Agreements in El Salvador and Guatemala', *Latin American Perspectives* vol. 27, no. 3 (2000).

Doyle, M. *et al.* (eds), *Keeping the Peace: Multi-Dimensional UN Operations in Cambodia and El Salvador* (Cambridge: Cambridge University Press, 1997).

García-Sayán, D., 'The Experience of ONUSAL in El Salvador', in A. Henkin (ed.), *Honoring Human Rights* (The Hague: Kluwer Law International, 2000).

García-Sayán, D., 'Human Rights and Peacekeeping Operations', *University of Richmond Law Review* vol. 29 (1994–1995).

Holiday, D. and Stanley, W., 'Peace Mission Strategy and Domestic Actors: UN Mediation, Verification and Institution-building in El Salvador', *International Peacekeeping* vol. 4, no. 2 (1997).

Johnstone, I., *Rights and Reconciliation: UN Strategies in El Salvador* (Boulder: Lynne Rienner, 1995).

Katayanagi, M., *Human Rights Functions of United Nations Peacekeeping Operations*, International Studies in Human Rights vol. 73 (The Hague: Kluwer Law International, 2002).

Kircher, I., 'The Human Rights Work of the United Nations Observer Mission in El Salvador', *Netherlands Quarterly of Human Rights* vol. 10, no. 3 (1992).

Lawyers Committee for Human Rights, *Improvising History: A Critical Evaluation of the UN Observer Mission in El Salvador* (New York, 1995).

O'Neill, W. G., 'Human Rights Field Operations: A New Protection Tool', in B. G. Ramcharan (ed.), *Human Rights Protection in the Field*, International Studies in Human Rights vol. 87, (Leiden: Martinus Nijhoff, 2006).

Whitfield, T., 'Staying the Course in El Salvador', in *Honoring Human Rights*.

Cambodia

Official Documents

United Nations Transitional Authority in Cambodia (February 1992 – September 1993).

Centre for Human Rights/Office of the United Nations High Commissioner for Human Rights (OHCHR) office in Cambodia (February 1993).

Final Act of the Paris Agreement on Cambodia, UN Doc. A/46/608-S/23177 (30 October 1991).

Security Council resolution 745 (1992), UN Doc. S/RES/745 (28 February 1992).

Report of the Secretary-General, Situation in Cambodia, UN Doc. E/CN.4/1993/19 (14 January 1993).

Commission on Human Rights resolution 1993/6 (1993), Situation of human rights in Cambodia, UN Doc. E/CN.4/RES/1993/6 (19 February 1993).

Economic and Social Council resolution 1993/254 (1993), Situation of human rights in Cambodia, UN Doc. E/1993/254 (28 July 1993).

Situation of human rights in Cambodia, UN Doc. A/48/762 (7 January 1994).

Report of the Special Representative of the Secretary-General, Mr. Michael Kirby, on the situation of human rights in Cambodia submitted pursuant to Commission on Human Rights Resolution 1993/6, UN Doc. E/CN.4/1994/73/Add.1 (21 February 1994).

Report of the Secretary-General, Role of the United Nations Centre for Human Rights in assisting the Government of the People of Cambodia in the promotion and protection of human rights, UN Doc. A/49/635/Add.1 (3 November 1994).

Report of the Secretary-General, Role of the United Nations Centre for Human Rights in assisting the Government of the People of Cambodia in the promotion and protection of Human Rights, UN Doc. A/50/681/Add.1 (26 October 1995).

Report of the Secretary-General, Advisory services in the field of human rights, UN Doc. E/CN.4/1995/89 (19 January 1995).

Situation of Human Rights in Cambodia, Report of the Special Representative of the Secretary-General for Human Rights in Cambodia, Mr Michael Kirby, submitted in accordance with Commission resolution 1994/61, UN Doc. E/CN.4/1995/87 (24 January 1995).

Report of the Secretary-General, Role of the United Nations Centre for Human Rights in assisting the Government of the People of Cambodia in the promotion and protection of human rights, UN Doc. E/CN.4/1996/92 (2 February 1996).

Report of the Secretary-General, Role of the United Nations Centre for Human Rights in assisting the Government of the People of Cambodia in the promotion and protection of human rights, UN Doc. A/51/552 (24 October 1996).

Report of the Secretary-General, Situation of human rights in Cambodia, UN Doc. A/52/489 (17 October 1997).

Report of the Secretary-General, Role of the United Nations Centre for Human Rights in assisting the Government of the People of Cambodia in the promotion and protection of human rights, UN Doc. E/CN.4/1997/84 (31 January 1997).

Report of the Secretary-General, Role of the United Nations Centre for Human Rights in assisting the Government of the People of Cambodia in the promotion and protection of human rights, UN Doc. E/CN.4/1998/94 (11 February 1998).

Report of the Secretary-General, Situation of human rights in Cambodia, UN Doc. A/53/400 (17 September 1998).

Report of the Secretary-General, Role of the Office of the United Nations High Commissioner for Human Rights in assisting the Government and People of Cambodia in the promotion and protection of human rights, UN Doc. E/CN.4/1999/100 (3 February 1999).

Report of the Secretary-General, Situation of human rights in Cambodia, UN Doc. A/54/353 (20 September 1999).

Report of the Secretary-General, Role of the Office of the United Nations High Commissioner for Human Rights in assisting the Government and People of Cambodia in the promotion and protection of human rights, UN Doc. E/CN.4/2000/108 (14 January 2000).

Report of the Secretary-General, Situation of human rights in Cambodia, UN Doc. A/55/291 (11 August 2000).

Report of the Secretary-General submitted in accordance with Commission Resolution 2000/79, Role and achievements of the Office of the United Nations High Commissioner for Human Rights in assisting the Government and People of Cambodia in the promotion and protection of human rights, UN Doc. E/CN.4/2001/102 (9 January 2001).

Report of the Secretary-General, Role and achievements of the Office of the United Nations High Commissioner for Human Rights in assisting the Government and People of Cambodia in the promotion and protection of human rights, UN Doc. A/56/230 (31 July 2001).

Report of the Secretary-General, Role and achievements of the Office of the United Nations High Commissioner for Human Rights in assisting the Government and People of Cambodia in the promotion and protection of human rights, UN Doc. E/CN.4/2002/117 (27 December 2001).

Report of the Secretary-General, Role and achievements of the Office of the United Nations High Commissioner for Human Rights in assisting the Government and People of Cambodia in the promotion and protection of human rights, UN Doc. A/57/277 (6 August 2002).

Report of the Secretary-General, Role and achievements of the Office of the United Nations High Commissioner for Human Rights in assisting the Government and People of Cambodia in the promotion and protection of human rights, UN Doc. E/CN.4/2003/113 (9 January 2003).

Report of the Secretary-General, Role and achievements of the Office of the United Nations High Commissioner for Human Rights in assisting the Government and People of Cambodia in the promotion and protection of human rights, UN Doc. A/58/268 (8 August 2003).

Report of the Secretary-General, Role and achievements of the Office of the United Nations High Commissioner for Human Rights in assisting the Government and People of Cambodia in the promotion and protection of human rights, UN Doc. E/CN.4/2004/104 (16 January 2004).

Report of the Secretary-General, Role and achievements of the Office of the United Nations High Commissioner for Human Rights in assisting the Government and People of Cambodia in the promotion and protection of human rights, UN Doc. E/CN.4/2005/111 (23 December 2004).

Report of the Secretary-General, Role and achievements of the Office of the United Nations High Commissioner for Human Rights in assisting the Government and People of Cambodia in the promotion and protection of human rights, UN Doc. E/CN.4/2006/105 (24 January 2006).

Commentary

Adams, B., 'UN Human Rights Work in Cambodia: Efforts to Preserve the Jewel in the Peacekeeping Crown', in *Honoring Human Rights*.

Ashley, D. 'The Nature and Causes of Human Rights Violations in Battambang Province', in S. Heder and J. Ledgerwood (eds), *Propaganda, Politics, and Violence in Cambodia, Democratic Transition under United Nations Peacekeeping*, (London: M. E. Sharpe, 1996).

Boutros-Ghali, B., 'Introduction', *The United Nations and Cambodia 1991-1995* The United Nations Blue Book Series vol. II (New York: Department of Public Information, United Nations, 1995).

Chopra, J., 'The United Nations Authority in Cambodia', Occasional Paper 15 (Providence: Watson Institute, 1994).

Criswell, D., 'Durable Consent and a Strong Transitional Peacekeeping Plan: The Success of UNTAET in Light of the Lessons Learned in Cambodia', *Pacific Rim Law and Policy Journal* (June 2002).

Katayanagi, M., *Human Rights Functions of United Nations Peacekeeping Operations*.

Lee, C.M. and Metrikas, M., 'Holding a Fragile Peace: The Military and Civilian Components of UNTAC', Doyle, M. *et al.* (eds), *Keeping the Peace: Multi-Dimensional UN Operations in Cambodia and El Salvador* (Cambridge: Cambridge University Press, 1997).

Doyle, M., *UN Peacekeeping in Cambodia: UNTAC's Civil Mandate* (Boulder: Lynne Rienner, 1995).

Duffy, T., 'UNTAC's Mission in Cambodia: Prospects for Democracy and Human Rights, *Asian Affairs* vol. 20 (Winter 1994).

Heininger, J., *Peacekeeping in Transition: The United Nations in Cambodia* (New York: Twentieth Century Foundation, 1994).

Hughes, C., 'UNTAC in Cambodia: The Impact on Human Rights', Occasional Paper Issue 92 (Institute of Southeast Asian Studies, 1996).

Hughes, C., 'Human Rights out of Context (or, Translating the Universal Declaration into Khmer)', in N. D. White and D. Klaasen (eds), *The UN, Human Rights and Post-conflict Situations* (Manchester: Manchester University Press, 2005).

Kirby, M., 'Human Rights, the United Nations and Cambodia', *Australian Quarterly* vol. 67, no. 4 (1995).

O'Neill, W. G., 'Human Rights Field Operations: A New Protection Tool', in *Human Rights Protection in the Field*.

McNamara, D., 'UN Human Rights Activities in Cambodia: In an Evaluation', *Honoring Human Rights*.

Ramcharan, B. G. 'The Protection Methods of Human Rights Field Offices', in *Human Rights Protection in the Field*.

Haiti

Official Documents

| International Civilian Mission in Haiti (February 1993 – January 2000). |

| United Nations Stabilisation Mission in Haiti (April 2004). |

Letter dated 8 January 1993 from the Secretary-General to the President of Haiti on the situation of democracy and human rights in Haiti, Annex I to UN Doc. A/47/908 (24 March 1993).

Resolution adopted by the General Assembly, UN Doc. A/RES/47/20B (20 April 1993).

Interim report of the International Civilian Mission to Haiti for the period 9 February – 31 May 1993, Annex to UN Doc. A/47/960 (3 June 1993).

Report of the International Civilian Mission to Haiti, Annex to UN Doc. A/48/532 (25 October 1993).

Supplementary report of the International Civilian Mission to Haiti, Annex to UN Doc. A/48/532/Add.1 (18 November 1993).

Report of the Secretary-General, The situation of democracy and human rights in Haiti, UN Doc. A/48/931 (29 April 1994).

Report of the International Civilian Mission to Haiti, Annex to UN Doc. A/48/532/Add.3 (27 July 1994).

Report of the Secretary-General, The situation of democracy and human rights in Haiti, UN Doc. A/49/926 (29 June 1995).

Report of the Secretary-General, The situation of democracy and human rights in Haiti, UN Doc. A/50/548 (12 October 1995).

Report of the Secretary-General, The situation of democracy and human rights in Haiti, UN Doc. A/50/861 (25 January 1996).

Report of the Secretary-General, The situation of democracy and human rights in Haiti, UN Doc. A/50/861/Add.1 (15 February 1996).

Report of the Secretary-General, The situation of democracy and human rights in Haiti, UN Doc. A/50/861/Add.2 (13 August 1996).

Report of the Secretary-General, The situation of democracy and human rights in Haiti, UN Doc. A/51/703 (2 December 1996).

Report of the Secretary-General, The situation of democracy and human rights in Haiti, UN Doc. A/51/935 (26 June 1997).

Report of the Secretary-General, The situation of democracy and human rights in Haiti, UN Doc. A/52/687 (18 November 1997).

Report of the Secretary-General, The situation of democracy and human rights in Haiti, UN Doc. A/52/986 (20 July 1998).

Report of the Secretary-General, The situation of democracy and human rights in Haiti, UN Doc. A/53/564 (18 November 1998).

Report of the Secretary-General, The situation of democracy and human rights in Haiti, UN Doc. A/53/950 (10 May 1999).

Report of the Secretary-General, The situation of democracy and human rights in Haiti, UN Doc. A/54/625 (22 November 1999).

International Civilian Mission in Haiti, Three Years of Defending Human Rights, September 1995.

International Civilian Mission in Haiti, Activities Report, October 1995.[2]

International Civilian Mission in Haiti, Activities Report, November 1995.

International Civilian Mission in Haiti, Activities Report, 1 December 1995 – 7 February 1996.

International Civilian Mission in Haiti, Activities Report, 8 February 1996 – 31 March 1996.

International Civilian Mission in Haiti, Activities Report, April 1996.

International Civilian Mission in Haiti, Activities Report, May 1996.

International Civilian Mission in Haiti, Activities Report, June 1996.

International Civilian Mission in Haiti, Activities Report, July 1996.

Haiti: Human Rights and Rehabilitation of Victims, December 1996.

International Civilian Mission in Haiti, Coordination, Analysis and Reports Unit, Human Rights Review, October–December 1998.[3]

International Civilian Mission in Haiti, Coordination, Analysis and Reports Unit, Human Rights Review, January–March 1999.

International Civilian Mission in Haiti, Coordination, Analysis and Reports Unit, Human Rights Review, April–June 1999.

International Civilian Mission in Haiti, Coordination, Analysis and Reports Unit, Human Rights Review, July–September 1999.

International Civilian Mission in Haiti, Coordination, Analysis and Reports Unit, Human Rights Review, October–December 1999.

Security Council resolution 1542 (2004), UN Doc. S/RES/1542 (30 April 2004).

Security Council resolution 1608 (2005), UN Doc. S/RES/1608 (22 June 2005).

Commentary

Bar-Yaacov, N. 'Diplomacy and Human Rights: The Role of Human Rights on Conflict Resolution in El Salvador and Haiti', *Fletcher Forum of World Affairs* vol. 19, no. 2 (1995).

Granderson, C., 'Institutionalizing Peace: The Haiti Experience', in *Honoring Human Rights*.

Khouri-Padova, L., 'Haiti: Lessons Learned', Discussion Paper (DPKO Best Practices Unit, March 2004).

Lawyers Committee for Human Rights, *Haiti: Learning the Hard Way* (New York, 1995).

---

[2]   All International Civilian Mission in Haiti 'Activity Reports' are available at http://www.un.org/rights/micivih/histen.htm#rapports.

[3]   All Coordination, Analysis and Reports Unit documents are available at http://www.un.org/rights/micivih/observen.htm.

Maguire, R., Balutansky, E., Fomerand, J., Minear, L., O'Neill, W. G, Weiss, T. and Zaidi, S. 'Haiti Held Hostage: International Responses to the Quest for Nationhood 1986–1996', Occasional Paper 23 (Providence: Watson Institute, 1996).

Martin, I., 'Paper versus Steel: the First Phase of the International Civilian Mission in Haiti', in *Honoring Human Rights*.

O'Neill, W. G., 'Human Rights Monitoring vs. Political Expediency: The Experience of the OAS/UN Mission in Haiti', *Harvard Human Rights Journal* vol. 8 (1995).

O'Neill, W. G., 'Human Rights Field Operations: A New Protection Tool', in *Human Rights Protection in the Field*.

Abkhazia (Georgia)

Official Documents

Organization for Security and Co-operation in Europe (OSCE) Mission to Georgia (March 1994).

Expansion of the Mandate of the OSCE Mission to Georgia, Permanent Committee of the CSCE Journal No.14/Revised, Annex 1 (29 March 1994).

United Nations Observer Mission in Georgia (December 1996).

Programme for the protection and promotion of human rights in Abkhazia, Annex 1 to Report of the Secretary-General concerning the situation in Abkhazia, UN Doc. S/1996/284 (15 April 1996).

Security Council resolution 1077 (1996), UN Doc. S/RES/1077 (22 October 1996).

Report of the Secretary-General on the situation in Abkhazia, Georgia, UN Doc. S/1997/47 (20 January 1997).

Report of the Secretary-General on the situation in Abkhazia, Georgia, UN Doc. S/1997/340 (25 April 1997).

Report of the Secretary-General on the situation in Abkhazia, Georgia, UN Doc. S/1997/558 (18 July 1997).

Report of the Secretary-General on the situation in Abkhazia, Georgia, UN Doc. S/1997/827 (28 October 1997).

Report of the Secretary-General on the situation in Abkhazia, Georgia, UN Doc. S/1998/51 (19 January 1998).

Report of the Secretary-General on the situation in Abkhazia, Georgia, UN Doc. S/1998/375 (11 May 1998).

Report of the Secretary-General on the situation in Abkhazia, Georgia, UN Doc. S/1999/60 (20 January 1999).

Report of the Secretary-General on the situation in Abkhazia, Georgia, UN Doc. S/1999/460 (21 April 1999).

Report of the Secretary-General on the situation in Abkhazia, Georgia, UN Doc. S/2000/1023 (25 October 2000).

Report of the Secretary-General on the situation in Abkhazia, Georgia, UN Doc. S/2001/401 (24 April 2001).

Report of the Secretary-General on the situation in Abkhazia, Georgia, UN Doc. S/2001/713 (19 July 2001).

Report of the Secretary-General on the situation in Abkhazia, Georgia, UN Doc. S/2001/1008 (24 October 2001).

Report of the Secretary-General on the situation in Abkhazia, Georgia, UN Doc. S/2002/88 (18 January 2001).

Report of the Secretary-General on the situation in Abkhazia, Georgia, UN Doc. S/2002/469 (19 April 2002).

Report of the Secretary-General on the situation in Abkhazia, Georgia, UN Doc. S/2002/742 (10 July 2002).

Report of the Secretary-General on the situation in Abkhazia, Georgia, UN Doc. S/2002/1141 (14 October 2002).

Report of the Secretary-General on the situation in Abkhazia, Georgia, UN Doc. S/2003/39 (13 January 2003).

Report of the Secretary-General on the situation in Abkhazia, Georgia, UN Doc. S/2003/412 (9 April 2003).

Report of the Secretary-General on the situation in Abkhazia, Georgia, UN Doc. S/2003/751 (23 July 2003).

Report of the Secretary-General on the situation in Abkhazia, Georgia, UN Doc. S/2003/1019 (6 October 2003).

Report of the Secretary-General on the situation in Abkhazia, Georgia, UN Doc. S/2004/26 (13 January 2004).

Report of the Secretary-General on the situation in Abkhazia, Georgia, UN Doc. S/2004/315 (20 April 2004).

Report of the Secretary-General on the situation in Abkhazia, Georgia, UN Doc. S/2004/570 (14 July 2004).

Report of the Secretary-General on the situation in Abkhazia, Georgia, UN Doc. S/2004/822 (14 October 2004).

Report of the Secretary-General on the situation in Abkhazia, Georgia, UN Doc. S/2005/32 (12 January 2005).

Report of the Secretary-General on the situation in Abkhazia, Georgia, UN Doc. S/2005/269 (22 April 2005).

Report of the Secretary-General on the situation in Abkhazia, Georgia, UN Doc. S/2005/433 (13 July 2005).

Report of the Secretary-General on the situation in Abkhazia, Georgia, UN Doc. S/2005/657 (18 October 2005).

Report of the Secretary-General on the situation in Abkhazia, Georgia, UN Doc. S/2006/19 (12 January 2006).

Report of the Secretary-General on the situation in Abkhazia, Georgia, UN Doc. S/2006/173 (20 March 2006).

Commentary

Clapham, A. and Martin, F., 'Smaller Missions Bigger Problems', in *Honoring Human Rights*.

Guatemala

Official Documents

> United Nations Verification Mission in Guatemala (September 1994 – December 2004).

> OHCHR Field Operation in Guatemala (January 2005).

Comprehensive Agreement on Human Rights, Annex I to UN Doc. A/48/928-S/1994/448 (19 April 1994).

Agreement on the establishment of the Commission to clarify past human rights violations and acts of violence that have caused the Guatemalan population to suffer, Annex II to UN Doc. A/48/954-S/1994/751 (1 July 1994).

Establishment of a human rights verification mission in Guatemala, UN Doc. A/48/985 (18 August 1994).

General Assembly resolution 48/267 (1994), UN Doc. A/RES/48/267 (28 September 1994).

Report of the members of the Secretary-General's mission to Guatemala, Mr Alberto Díaz Uribe, Mr Diego García-Sayan and Mr Yvon Le Bot, on the evolution of the situation of human rights in Guatemala in the light of the implementation of the peace agreements, submitted in accordance with Commission on Human Rights resolution 1997/51, UN Doc. E/CN.4/1998/93 (13 February 1998).

Report of the Director of the United Nations Mission for the Verification of Human Rights and of compliance with the commitments of the Comprehensive Agreement on Human Rights in Guatemala, Annex to UN Doc. A/49/856 (1 March 1995).

Second report of the Director of the United Nations Mission for the Verification of Human Rights and of compliance with the commitments of the Comprehensive Agreement on Human Rights in Guatemala, Annex to UN Doc. A/49/929 (29 June 1995).

Third report of the Director of the United Nations Mission for the Verification of Human Rights and of compliance with the commitments of the Comprehensive Agreement on Human Rights in Guatemala, Annex to UN Doc. A/50/482 (12 October 1995).

Fourth report on human rights of the United Nations Verification Mission in Guatemala, Annex to UN Doc. A/50/878 (24 February 1996).

Fifth report on human rights of the United Nations Verification Mission in Guatemala, Annex to UN Doc. A/51/1006 (19 July 1996).

Sixth report on human rights of the United Nations Verification Mission in Guatemala, Annex to UN Doc. A/51/790 (31 January 1997).

Seventh report on human rights of the United Nations Verification Mission in Guatemala, Annex to UN Doc. A/52/330 (10 September 1997).

Eighth report on human rights of the United Nations Verification Mission in Guatemala, Annex to UN Doc. A/52/946 (15 June 1998).

Ninth report on human rights of the United Nations Verification Mission in Guatemala, Annex to UN Doc. A/53/853 (10 March 1999).

Tenth report on human rights of the United Nations Verification Mission in Guatemala, Annex to UN Doc. A/54/688 (21 December 1999).

Eleventh report on human rights of the United Nations Verification Mission in Guatemala, Annex to UN Doc. A/55/174 (26 July 2000).

Twelfth report on human rights of the United Nations Verification Mission in Guatemala, Annex to UN Doc. A/56/273 (8 August 2001).

Thirteenth report on human rights of the United Nations Verification Mission in Guatemala, Annex to UN Doc. A/57/336 (22 August 2002).

Report of the Secretary-General, United Nations Verification Mission in Guatemala: A renewal of mandate, UN Doc. A/57/584 (1 November 2002).

Report of the Secretary-General, United Nations Verification Mission in Guatemala: A renewal of mandate, UN Doc. A/58/262 (8 August 2003).

Fourteenth report on Human Rights of the United Nations Verification Mission in Guatemala, Annex to UN Doc. A/58/566 (10 November 2003).

Report of the Secretary-General, United Nations Verification Mission in Guatemala, UN Doc. A/59/746 (18 March 2005).

Agreement on the establishment of an Office of the United Nations High Commissioner for Human Rights in Guatemala (10 January 2005).

Report of the United Nations High Commissioner for Human Rights on the situation of human rights in Guatemala, UN Doc. E/CN.4/2006/10/Add.1 (1 February 2006).

Commentary

Burgerman, S. D., 'Building the Peace by Mandating Reform: United Nations-Mediated Human Rights Agreements in El Salvador and Guatemala', *Latin American Perspectives* vol. 27, no. 3 (2000).

Franco, L. and Kotler, J., 'Combining Institution Building and Human Rights Verification in Guatemala: The Challenge of Buying in Without Selling Out', in *Honoring Human Rights*.

Lawyers Committee for Human Rights, Abandoning the Victims: The UN Advisory Services Program in Guatemala (New York, 1990).

Louise, C., 'MINUGUA's Peace-building Mandate in Western Guatemala', *International Peacekeeping* vol. 4, no. 2 (1997).

Line, M., 'Managing for Sustainable Human Rights Protection: International Missions in the Peace Processes of Bosnia and Herzegovina and Guatemala', in *The UN, Human Rights and Post-conflict Situations*.

Line, M. 'Case Study: Comparative Aspects of the Human Rights Field Operations in Bosnia-Herzegovina and Guatemala', chapter 17 in the present volume.

O'Neill, W. G., 'Human Rights Field Operations: A New Protection Tool', in *Human Rights Protection in the Field*.

Smeets, M., 'The United Nations Mission for the Verification of Human Rights in Guatemala', *Netherlands Quarterly of Human Rights* vol. 15, no. 4 (1997).

Rwanda

Official Documents

Human Rights Field Operation in Rwanda (September 1994 – July 1998).

Report on the situation of human rights in Rwanda submitted by Mr René Degni-Ségui, Special Rapporteur, under paragraph 20 of resolution S-3/1 of 25 May 1994, UN Doc. E/CN.4/1995/12 (12 August 1994).

Report on the situation of human rights in Rwanda submitted by Mr René Degni-Ségui, Special Rapporteur, under paragraph 20 of resolution S-3/1 of 25 May 1994, UN Doc. E/CN.4/1996/7 (28 June 1995).

Report of the United Nations High Commissioner for Human Rights on the human rights field operation in Rwanda, Annex to UN Doc. A/50/743 (13 November 1995).

Report of the United Nations High Commissioner for Human Rights on the activities of the human rights field operation in Rwanda submitted pursuant to General Assembly resolution 50/200, UN Doc. E/CN.4/1996/111 (2 April 1996).

Report of the United Nations High Commissioner for Human Rights on the human rights field operation in Rwanda, Annex to UN Doc. A/51/478 (10 October 1996).

Report of the High Commissioner for Human Rights on the activities of the human rights field operation in Rwanda (HRFOR), UN Doc. E/CN.4/1997/52 (17 March 1997).

Report of the United Nations High Commissioner for Human Rights on the human rights field operation in Rwanda, Annex to UN Doc. A/52/486 (16 October 1997).

Report of the United Nations High Commissioner for Human Rights on the human rights field operation in Rwanda, Annex to UN Doc. A/53/367 (11 September 1998).

Report of the United Nations High Commissioner for Human Rights, Human rights field operation in Rwanda, UN Doc. E/CN.4/1998/61 (19 February 1998).

Commentary

Clarance, W., 'The Human Rights Field Operation in Rwanda: Protective Practice Evolves on the Ground', *International Peacekeeping* vol. 2, no. 3 (1995).

Clarance, W., 'Field Strategy for the Protection of Human Rights', *International Journal of Refugee Law* vol. 9, no. 2 (1997).

Howland, T., 'The Killing of United Nations Human Rights Workers: A Call for an Appropriate UN Response', *Human Rights Tribune* vol. 5, nos. 1 and 2 (1998).

Howland, T., 'Mirage, Magic or Mixed Bag? The United Nations High Commissioner for Human Rights' Field Operation in Rwanda', *Human Rights Quarterly* vol. 21, no. 1 (1999).

Katayanagi, M., *Human Rights Functions of United Nations Peacekeeping Operations.*

Krug, H. N., 'Genocide in Rwanda: Lessons Learned and Future Challenges to the UN Human Rights System', *Nordic Journal of International Law* vol. 67, no. 2 (1998).

Martin, I., 'After Genocide: The UN Human Rights Field Operation in Rwanda', in *Honoring Human Rights.*

O'Neill, W. G., 'Human Rights Field Operations: A New Protection Tool', in *Human Rights Protection in the Field.*

von Meijenfeldt, R., *At the Frontline for Human Rights*, Final Report and Evaluation of European Union Participation in the Human Rights Field Operation in Rwanda, (October 1995).

Angola

Official Documents

United Nations Angola Verification Mission III (February 1995–June 1997).[4]

United Nations Observer Mission in Angola (June 1997–February 1999).

United Nations Mission in Angola (August 2002–February 2003).

OHCHR Field Operation in Angola (February 2003).

Security Council resolution 976 (1995), UN Doc. S/RES/976 (8 February 1995).

Security Council resolution 1008 (1995), UN Doc. S/RES/1008 (7 August 1995).

Report of the Secretary-General on the United Nations Angola Verification Mission, UN Doc. S/1995/588 (17 July 1995).

---

[4]   UNAVEM established January 1989, human rights functions added to mandate in February 1995.

Report of the Secretary-General on the United Nations Angola Verification Mission, UN Doc. S/1995/842 (4 October 1995).

Report of the Secretary-General on the United Nations Angola Verification Mission, UN Doc. S/1995/1012 (7 December 1995).

Report of the Secretary-General on the United Nations Angola Verification Mission, UN Doc. S/1996/75 (31 January 1996).

Report of the Secretary-General on the United Nations Angola Verification Mission, UN Doc. S/1996/171 (6 March 1996).

Report of the Secretary-General on the United Nations Angola Verification Mission, UN Doc. S/1996/248 (4 April 1996).

Report of the Secretary-General on the United Nations Angola Verification Mission, UN Doc. S/1996/328 (30 April 1996).

Report of the Secretary-General on the United Nations Angola Verification Mission, UN Doc. S/1996/503 (27 June 1996).

Progress report of the Secretary-General on the United Nations Angola Verification Mission, UN Doc. S/1996/827 (4 October 1996).

Progress report of the Secretary-General on the United Nations Angola Verification Mission, UN Doc. S/1996/1000 (2 December 1996).

Report of the Secretary-General on the United Nations Angola Verification Mission, UN Doc. S/1997/115 (7 February 1997).

Progress report of the Secretary-General on the United Nations Angola Verification Mission, UN Doc. S/1997/438 (5 June 1997).

Security Council resolution 1008 (1995), UN Doc. S/RES/1008 (7 August 1995).

Security Council resolution 1118 (1997), UN Doc. S/RES/1118 (30 June 1997).

Security Council resolution 1213 (1998), UN Doc. S/RES/1213 (3 December 1998).

Security Council resolution 1229 (1999), UN Doc. S/RES/1229 (26 February 1999).

Security Council resolution 1433 (2002), UN Doc. S/RES/1433 (15 August 2002).

Progress report of the Secretary-General on the United Nations Observer Mission in Angola, UN Doc. S/1997/640 (13 August 1997).

Report of the Secretary-General on the United Nations Observer Mission in Angola, UN Doc. S/1997/807 (17 October 1997).

Report of the Secretary-General on the United Nations Observer Mission in Angola, UN Doc. S/1998/17 (12 January 1998).

Report of the Secretary-General on the United Nations Observer Mission in Angola, UN Doc. S/1998/236 (13 March 1998).

Report of the Secretary-General on the United Nations Observer Mission in Angola, UN Doc. S/1998/333 (16 April 1998).

Report of the Secretary-General on the United Nations Observer Mission in Angola, UN Doc. S/1998/723 (7 August 1998).

Report of the Secretary-General on the United Nations Observer Mission in Angola, UN Doc. S/1998/838 (7 September 1998).

Report of the Secretary-General on the United Nations Observer Mission in Angola, UN Doc. S/1998/931 (8 October 1998).

Report of the Secretary-General on the United Nations Observer Mission in Angola, UN Doc. S/1998/1110 (23 November 1998).

Report of the Secretary-General on the United Nations Observer Mission in Angola, UN Doc. S/1999/49 (17 January 1999).

Report of the Secretary-General on the United Nations Observer Mission in Angola, UN Doc. S/1999/202 (24 February 1999).

Interim report of the Secretary-General on the United Nations Mission in Angola, UN Doc. S/2002/1353 (12 December 2002).

Report of the Secretary-General on the United Nations Mission in Angola, UN Doc. S/2003/158 (10 February 2003).

Commentary

Clapham, A. and Martin, F., 'Smaller Missions Bigger Problems', in *Honoring Human Rights.*

Howland, T., 'UN Human Rights Field Presences as Proactive Instruments of Peace and Social Change: Lessons from Angola', *Human Rights Quarterly* vol. 26, no. 1 (2004).

Howland, T., 'Case Study: The United Nations Human Rights Field Operation in Angola', chapter 16 in the present volume.

Burundi

Official Documents

OHCHR Field Operation in Burundi (November 1995).

United Nations Operation in Burundi (May 2004).

Agreement on the establishment of an Office of the United Nations High Commissioner for Human Rights in Burundi (November 1995).

Report of the Secretary-General on the situation in Burundi, UN Doc. S/1996/335 (3 May 1996).

Report of the Secretary-General on the situation in Burundi, UN Doc. S/1996/660 (15 August 1996).

Report of the Secretary-General on the situation in Burundi, UN Doc. S/1996/887 (29 October 1996).

Report of the Secretary-General on the situation in Burundi, UN Doc. S/1997/547 (15 July 1997).

Report on the situation of human rights in Burundi submitted by the Special Rapporteur, Mrs Marie-Thérèse A. Keita Bocoum, in accordance with Commission Resolution 2000/20, UN Doc. E/CN.4/2001/44 (19 March 2001).

Interim report of the Special Rapporteur of the Commission on Human Rights on the human rights situation in Burundi, Annex to UN Doc. A/56/479 (17 October 2001).

Report on the situation of human rights in Burundi submitted by the Special Rapporteur, Mrs Marie-Thérèse A. Keita Bocoum, in accordance with Commission resolution 2001/21, UN Doc. E/CN.4/2002/49 (7 March 2002).

Report on the situation of human rights in Burundi submitted by the Special Rapporteur, Mrs Marie-Thérèse A. Keita Bocoum, in accordance with Commission resolution 2002/12, UN Doc. E/CN.4/2003/45 (25 January 2003).

Situation of human rights in Burundi, UN Doc. A/58/448 (20 October 2003).

Report on the situation of human rights in Burundi submitted by the Special Rapporteur, Mrs Marie-Thérèse A. Keita Bocoum, in accordance with Commission resolution 2003/16, UN Doc. E/CN.4/2004/35 (19 March 2004).

Security Council resolution 1545 (2004), UN Doc. S/RES/1545 (21 May 2004).

First report of the Secretary-General on the United Nations Operation in Burundi, UN Doc. S/2004/682 (24 August 2004).

Second report of the Secretary-General on the United Nations Operation in Burundi, UN Doc. S/2004/902 (15 November 2004).

Report on the human rights situation in Burundi submitted by the Independent Expert, Akich Okola, UN Doc. E/CN.4/2005/118 (1 February 2005).

Third report of the Secretary-General on the United Nations Operation in Burundi, UN Doc. S/2005/149 (2 March 2005).

Fourth report of the Secretary-General on the United Nations Operation in Burundi, UN Doc. S/2005/328 (17 May 2005).

Report on the human rights situation in Burundi submitted by the Independent Expert, Akich Okola, Annex to UN Doc. A/60/354 (14 September 2005).

Fifth report of the Secretary-General on the United Nations Operation in Burundi, UN Doc. S/2005/728 (21 November 2005).

Report of the Independent Expert on the human rights situation in Burundi, Akich Okola, UN Doc. E/CN.4/2006/109 (23 December 2005).

Sixth report of the Secretary-General on the United Nations Operation in Burundi, UN Doc. S/2006/163 (14 March 2006).

Commentary

Clapham, A. and Martin, F., 'Smaller Missions Bigger Problems', in *Honoring Human Rights*.

Liberia

Official Documents

> United Nations Observer Mission in Liberia (November 1995–September 1997).[5]

> United Nations Mission in Liberia (September 2003).

Security Council resolution 1020 (1995), UN Doc. S/RES/1020 (10 November 1995).

Fourteenth progress report of the Secretary-General on the United Nations Observer Mission in Liberia, UN Doc. S/1995/1042 (18 December 1995).

Fifteenth progress report of the Secretary-General on the United Nations Observer Mission in Liberia, UN Doc. S/1996/47 (23 January 1996).

Sixteenth progress report of the Secretary-General on the United Nations Observer Mission in Liberia, UN Doc. S/1996/232 (1 April 1996).

Seventeenth progress report of the Secretary-General on the United Nations Observer Mission in Liberia, UN Doc. S/1996/362 (21 May 1996).

Nineteenth progress report of the Secretary-General on the United Nations Observer Mission in Liberia, UN Doc. S/1996/858 (17 October 1996).

Twentieth progress report of the Secretary-General on the United Nations Observer Mission in Liberia, UN Doc. S/1996/962 (19 November 1996).

Twenty-first progress report of the Secretary-General on the United Nations Observer Mission in Liberia, UN Doc. S/1997/90 (29 January 1997).

Twenty-second progress report of the Secretary-General on the United Nations Observer Mission in Liberia, UN Doc. S/1997/237 (19 March 1997).

Twenty-third progress report of the Secretary-General on the United Nations Observer Mission in Liberia, UN Doc. S/1997/478 (19 June 1997).

Twenty-fourth progress report of the Secretary-General on the United Nations Observer Mission in Liberia, UN Doc. S/1997/643 (13 August 1997).

Final report of the Secretary-General on the United Nations Observer Mission in Liberia, UN Doc. S/1997/712 (12 September 1997).

Situation of human rights and fundamental freedoms in Liberia, UN Doc. E/CN.4/2004/5 (12 August 2003).

Comprehensive Peace Agreement between the Government of Liberia and the Liberians United for Reconciliation and Democracy and the Movement for Democracy in Liberia and Political Parties, Accra, 18 August 2003, Annex to Letter from the Permanent Representative of Ghana to the United Nations Addressed to the President of the Security Council, UN Doc. S/2003/850 (29 August 2003).

---

[5]   United Nations Observer Mission in Liberia established in September 1993, human rights functions added to mandate in November 1995.

Security Council resolution 1509 (2003), UN Doc. S/RES/1509 (19 September 2003).

Report of the Secretary-General to the Security Council on Liberia, UN Doc. S/2003/875 (11 September 2003).

First progress report of the Secretary-General on the United Nations Mission in Liberia, UN Doc. S/2003/1175 (15 December 2003).

Technical cooperation and advisory services in Liberia, Preliminary report of the Independent Expert, Charlotte Abaka, UN Doc. E/CN.4/2004/113 (16 February 2004).

Second progress report of the Secretary-General on the United Nations Mission in Liberia, UN Doc. S/2004/229 (22 March 2004).

Third progress report of the Secretary-General on the United Nations Mission in Liberia, UN Doc. S/2004/430 (26 May 2004).

Fourth progress report of the Secretary-General on the United Nations Mission in Liberia, UN Doc. S/2004/725 (8 September 2004).

Fifth progress report of the Secretary-General on the United Nations Mission in Liberia, UN Doc. S/2004/972 (17 December 2004).

Situation of human rights in Liberia, Report of the Independent Expert on human rights in Liberia, Charlotte Abaka, UN Doc. E/CN.4/2005/119 (6 January 2005).

Sixth progress report of the Secretary-General on the United Nations Mission in Liberia, UN Doc. S/2005/177 (17 March 2005).

Seventh progress report of the Secretary-General on the United Nations Mission in Liberia, UN Doc. S/2005/391 (14 June 2005).

Eighth progress report of the Secretary-General on the United Nations Mission in Liberia, UN Doc. S/2005/560 (1 September 2005).

Ninth progress report of the Secretary-General on the United Nations Mission in Liberia, UN Doc. S/2005/764 (1 December 2005).

Tenth progress report of the Secretary-General on the United Nations Mission in Liberia, UN Doc. S/2006/159 (10 March 2006).

Commentary

Cain, K. L., 'The Rape of Dinah: Human Rights, Civil War in Liberia, and Evil Triumphant', *Human Rights Quarterly* vol. 21, no. 2 (1999).

Clapham, A. and Martin, F., 'Smaller Missions Bigger Problems', in *Honoring Human Rights*.

Nowrojee, B., 'Joining Forces: United Nations and Regional Peacekeeping: Lessons from Liberia', *Harvard Human Rights Journal* vol. 8 (1995).

Former Yugoslavia⁶

Official Documents

> United Nations Mission in Bosnia-Herzegovina (December 1995–December 2002).

> United Nations Confidence Restoration Operation in Croatia (March 1995–January 1996).

> United Nations Transitional Administration for Eastern Slavonia, Baranja and Western Sirmium (January 1996–January 1998).

> United Nations Mission in Kosovo (June 1999).

> OHCHR office in Serbia and Montenegro (March 2003).

Report of the Secretary-General on the International Conference on the Former Yugoslavia, UN Doc. S/24795 (11 November 1992).

Commission on Human Rights resolution 1993/7 (1993), UN Doc. E/CN.4/RES/1993/7 (23 February 1993).

Periodic report on the situation of human rights in the territory of the Former Yugoslavia submitted by Mr Tadeusz Mazowiecki, Special Rapporteur of the Commission on Human Rights, pursuant to paragraph 32 of Commission resolution 1993/7 of 23 February 1993, UN Doc. E/CN.4/1994/3 (5 May 1993).

Second periodic report on the situation of human rights in the territory of the Former Yugoslavia submitted by Mr Tadeusz Mazowiecki, Special Rapporteur of the Commission on Human Rights, pursuant to paragraph 32 of Commission resolution 1993/7 of 23 February 1993, UN Doc. E/CN.4/1994/4 (19 May 1993).

Third periodic report on the situation of human rights in the territory of the Former Yugoslavia submitted by Mr. Tadeusz Mazowiecki, Special Rapporteur of the Commission on Human Rights, pursuant to paragraph 32 of Commission resolution 1993/7 of 23 February 1993, UN Doc. E/CN.4/1994/6 (26 August 1993).

Fourth periodic report on the situation of human rights in the territory of the Former Yugoslavia submitted by Mr Tadeusz Mazowiecki, Special Rapporteur of the Commission on Human Rights, pursuant to paragraph 32 of Commission resolution 1993/7 of 23 February 1993, Mostar: The Cause for Concern, UN Doc. E/CN.4/1994/8 (6 September 1993).

Fifth periodic report on the situation of human rights in the territory of the Former Yugoslavia submitted by Mr Tadeusz Mazowiecki, Special Rapporteur of the Commission on Human Rights, pursuant to paragraph 32 of Commission

---

⁶ Baranja; Bosnia and Herzegovina; Croatia; Eastern Slavonia; Kosovo; Macedonia; Montenegro; Serbia; Western Sirmium.

resolution 1993/7 of 23 February 1993, UN Doc. E/CN.4/1994/47 (17 November 1993).

Sixth periodic report on the situation of human rights in the territory of the Former Yugoslavia submitted by Mr Tadeusz Mazowiecki, Special Rapporteur of the Commission on Human Rights, pursuant to paragraph 32 of Commission resolution 1993/7 of 23 February 1993, UN Doc. E/CN.4/1994/110 (21 February 1994).

Seventh periodic report on the situation of human rights in the territory of the Former Yugoslavia submitted by Mr Tadeusz Mazowiecki, Special Rapporteur of the Commission on Human Rights, pursuant to paragraph 37 of Commission resolution 1993/7 of 9 March 1994, Situation in Gorazde, UN Doc. E/CN.4/1995/4 (10 June 1994).

Eighth periodic report on the situation of human rights in the territory of the Former Yugoslavia submitted by Mr Tadeusz Mazowiecki, Special Rapporteur of the Commission on Human Rights, pursuant to paragraph 37 of Commission resolution 1993/7 of 9 March 1994, UN Doc. E/CN.4/1995/10 (4 August 1994).

Report of the Secretary-General pursuant to resolution 908 (1994), UN Doc. S/1994/1067 (17 September 1994).

Ninth periodic report on the situation of human rights in the territory of the Former Yugoslavia submitted by Mr Tadeusz Mazowiecki, Special Rapporteur of the Commission on Human Rights, pursuant to paragraph 37 of Commission resolution 1993/7 of 9 March 1994 and Economic and Social Council decision 1994/262 of 22 July 1994, UN Doc. A/49/641-S/1994/1252 (4 November 1994).

Report of the Special Rapporteur submitted pursuant to Commission resolution 1994/72, Special Report on the Media, UN Doc. E/CN.4/1995/54 (13 December 1994).

Report of the Secretary-General Submitted pursuant to Security Council resolution 1009, UN Doc. S/1995/730 (23 August 1995).

Tenth periodic report on the situation of human rights in the territory of the Former Yugoslavia submitted by Mr Tadeusz Mazowiecki, Special Rapporteur of the Commission on Human Rights, pursuant to paragraph 37 of Commission Resolution 1994/7 of 9 March 1994, UN Doc. E/CN.4/1995/57 (9 January 1995).

Security Council resolution 981(1995), UN Doc. S/RES/981 (31 March 1995).

Periodic report submitted by Mr Tadeusz Mazowiecki, Special Rapporteur of the Commission on Human Rights, pursuant to paragraph 42 of Commission resolution 1995/89, UN Doc. E/CN.4/1996/3 (21 April 1995).

Periodic report on the situation of human rights in the territory of the Former Yugoslavia submitted by Mr Tadeusz Mazowiecki, Special Rapporteur of the Commission on Human Rights, pursuant to paragraph 42 of Commission resolution 1995/89 of 8 March 1995, UN Doc. E/CN.4/1996/6 (5 July 1995).

Report of the Secretary-General submitted pursuant to Security Council resolution 981, UN Doc. S/1995/650 (3 August 1995).

Final periodic report on the situation of human rights in the territory of the Former Yugoslavia submitted by Mr Tadeusz Mazowiecki, Special Rapporteur of the Commission on Human Rights, pursuant to paragraph 42 of Commission resolution 1995/89, UN Doc. A/50/441-S/1995/801 (28 September 1995).

Report of the Secretary-General, The situation in the occupied territories of Croatia, UN Doc. A/50/648 (18 October 1995).

Report on the situation of human rights in the territory of the Former Yugoslavia submitted by Mrs. Elisabeth Rehn, Special Rapporteur of the Commission on Human Rights, pursuant to Commission to resolution 1995/89 and Economic and Social Council decision 1995/290, Annex to UN Doc. A/50/727-S/1995/933 (7 November 1995).

Basic agreement on the region of Eastern Slavonia, Baranja and Western Sirmium between the Government of the Republic of Croatia and the local Serbian community, Annex to UN Doc. S/1995/951 (12 November 1995).

Report of the Secretary-General, Situation of human rights in Kosovo, UN Doc. A/50/767 (20 November 1995).

Report of the Secretary-General pursuant to Security Council resolutions 981 (1995), 982 (1995) and 983 (1995), UN Doc. S/1995/987 (23 November 1995).

Agreement on Human Rights, Annex 6 to General Framework Agreement for Peace in Bosnia and Herzegovina, Attachment to UN Doc. A/50/790-S/1995/999 (30 November 1995).

Report of the Secretary-General pursuant to Security Council resolution 1026 (1995), UN Doc. S/1995/1031 (13 December 1995).

Report of the Secretary-General pursuant to Security Council resolution 1025, UN Doc. S/1995/1028 (13 December 1995).

Report on the situation of human rights in Croatia pursuant to Security Council resolution 1019, UN Doc. S/1995/1051 (21 December 1995).

Security Council resolution 1088 (1996), UN Doc. S/RES/1088 (12 December 1996).

Further report on the situation of human rights in Croatia pursuant to Security Council resolution 1019, UN Doc. S/1996/109 (14 February 1996).

Report of the Secretary-General on the United Nations Mission in Bosnia and Herzegovina, UN Doc. S/1997/468 (16 June 1997).

Further report on the situation of human rights in Croatia pursuant to Security Council resolution 1019, UN Doc. S/1996/456 (21 June 1996).

Further report on the situation of human rights in Croatia pursuant to Security Council resolution 1019, UN Doc. S/1996/691 (23 August 1996)

Further report on the situation of human rights in Croatia pursuant to Security Council resolution 1019, UN Doc. S/1996/1011 (5 November 1996).

Report of the Secretary-General on the United Nations Mission in Bosnia and Herzegovina, UN Doc. S/1997/694 (8 September 1997).

Report of the Secretary-General, Human rights situation in Kosovo, UN Doc. A/52/502 (17 October 1997).

Report of the Secretary-General on the United Nations Mission in Bosnia and Herzegovina, UN Doc. S/1997/966 (10 December 1997).

Report of the Secretary-General on the United Nations Mission in Bosnia and Herzegovina, UN Doc. S/1998/227 (12 March 1998).

Report of the Secretary-General on the United Nations Mission in Bosnia and Herzegovina, UN Doc. S/1998/491 (10 June 1998).

Report of the Secretary-General on the United Nations Mission in Bosnia and Herzegovina, UN Doc. S/1998/862 (16 September 1998).

Report of the Secretary-General on the United Nations Mission in Bosnia and Herzegovina, UN Doc. S/1998/1174 (16 December 1998).

Report of the Secretary-General on the United Nations Mission in Bosnia and Herzegovina, UN Doc. S/1999/284 (16 March 1999).

Security Council resolution 1244 (1999), UN Doc. S/RES/1244 (10 June 1999).

Report of the Secretary-General on the United Nations Mission in Bosnia and Herzegovina, UN Doc. S/1999/670 (11 June 1999).

Report of the Secretary-General on the United Nations Mission in Bosnia and Herzegovina, UN Doc. S/2000/529 (2 June 2000).

Situation of human rights in the territory of the Former Yugoslavia, UN Doc. E/CN.4/1996/63 (14 March 1996).

Report of the Secretary-General pursuant to resolution 1035 (1995), UN Doc. S/1996/460 (21 June 1996).

Report of the Secretary-General, Situation of human rights in Kosovo, UN Doc. A/51/556 (25 October 1996).

Further report on the situation of human rights in Croatia pursuant to Security Council Resolution 1019, UN Doc. S/1997/195 (5 March 1997).

Situation of human rights in the territory of the Former Yugoslavia, UN Doc. E/CN.4/1998/14 (31 October 1997).

Report of the Secretary-General, Human rights situation in Kosovo, UN Doc. A/53/653 (30 October 1998).

Situation of human rights in the territory of the Former Yugoslavia, UN Doc. E/CN.4/1998/63 (14 January 1998).

Situation of human rights in Bosnia and Herzegovina, Croatia and the Federal Republic of Yugoslavia, UN Doc. A/53/322 (11 September 1998).

Security Council resolution 1037 (1996), UN Doc. S/RES/1037 (15 January 1996).

Situation of human rights in the Former Yugoslavia, UN Doc. E/CN.4/1999/42 (20 January 1999).

Situation of human rights in Kosovo, UN Doc. E/CN.4/RES/1999/2 (13 April 1999).

Report of the High Commissioner for Human Rights on the situation of human rights in Kosovo, Federal Republic of Yugoslavia, UN Doc. E/CN.4/2000/7 (31 May 1999).

Report of the Secretary-General on the United Nations Interim Administration in Kosovo, UN Doc. S/1999/779 (12 July 1999).

Report of the Secretary-General on the United Nations Interim Administration in Kosovo, UN Doc. S/1999/987 (16 September 1999).

Situation of human rights in Bosnia and Herzegovina, the Republic of Croatia and the Federal Republic of Yugoslavia (Serbia and Montenegro), UN Doc. A/54/396-S/1999/1000 (24 September 1999).

Report of the High Commissioner for Human Rights on the situation of human rights in Kosovo, Federal Republic of Yugoslavia, UN Doc. E/CN.4/2000/10 (27 September 1999).

Report of the Secretary-General on the United Nations Interim Administration in Kosovo, UN Doc. S/1999/1250 (23 December 1999).

Situation of human rights in the Former Yugoslavia, UN Doc. E/CN.4/2000/39 (28 December 1999).

Report of the Secretary-General on the United Nations Interim Administration in Kosovo, UN Doc. S/2000/177 (3 March 2000).

Report of the High Commissioner for Human Rights on the situation of human rights in Kosovo, Federal Republic of Yugoslavia, UN Doc. E/CN.4/2000/32 (17 March 2000).

Report of the Secretary-General on the United Nations Interim Administration in Kosovo, UN Doc. S/2000/538 (6 June 2000).

Report of the Secretary-General on the United Nations Interim Administration in Kosovo, UN Doc. S/2000/878 (18 September 2000).

Situation of human rights in Bosnia and Herzegovina, the Republic of Croatia and the Federal Republic of Yugoslavia, UN Doc. A/55/282 (20 October 2000).

Report of the Secretary-General on the United Nations Interim Administration in Kosovo, UN Doc. S/2000/1196 (15 December 2000).

Situation of human rights in the Former Yugoslavia, UN Doc. E/CN.4/2001/47 (29 January 2001).

Agreement on the establishment of an Office of the United Nations High Commissioner for Human Rights in Serbia and Montenegro (18 March 2003).

Office of the United Nations High Commissioner for Human Rights, 'Taking Stock of Human Rights in Bosnia and Herzegovina', Outcome Document (December 2005).

Report of the Secretary-General on the United Nations Interim Administration in Kosovo, UN Doc. S/2006/45 (25 January 2006).

OSCE Mission to Bosnia and Herzegovina (December 1995).

Kosovo Verification Mission (October 1998–March 1999).

OSCE Mission to Serbia and Montenegro (January 2001).

OSCE Mission in Kosovo (July 1999).

OSCE Mission to Croatia (April 1996).

Final Report of the CSCE Mission, No. 14/93 (6 August 1993).

Permanent Council Decision No. 112, OSCE Doc. PC.DEC/112 (18 April 1996).

Permanent Council Decision No. 176, OSCE Doc. PC.DEC/176 (26 June 1997).

Permanent Council Decision No. 305, OSCE Doc. PC.DEC/305 (1 July 1999).

OSCE Mission in Kosovo, Department of Human Rights and Rule of Law Section, Second assessment of the situation of Ethnic Minorities in Kosovo (26 July 1999).

OSCE, Kosovo Verification Mission, *Human Rights: As seen, As told*, vol. I (5 November 1999).

OSCE, Kosovo Verification Mission, *Human Rights: As seen, As told*, vol. II (5 November 1999).

OSCE Mission in Kosovo, Department of Human Rights and Rule of Law Section, Report 1: Material needs of emergency judicial system (7 November 1999).

OSCE Mission in Kosovo, Department of Human Rights and Rule of Law Section, Report 2: Development of the Kosovo judicial system (17 December 1999).

OSCE Mission in Kosovo, Department of Human Rights and Rule of Law Section, Assessment of the situation of ethnic minorities in Kosovo (15 February 2000).

OSCE Mission in Kosovo, Department of Human Rights and Rule of Law Section, Report 3: Expiration of detention periods for current detainees (8 March 2000).

OSCE Mission in Kosovo, Department of Human Rights and Rule of Law Section, Report 4: Expiration of detention periods for current detainees (18 March 2000).

OSCE Mission in Kosovo, Department of Human Rights and Rule of Law Section, Report 5: The treatment of minorities by the judicial system (13 April 2000).

OSCE Mission in Kosovo, Department of Human Rights and Rule of Law Section, Report 6: The unlawfulness of regulation 1999/26 (29 April 2000).

OSCE Mission in Kosovo, Department of Human Rights and Rule of Law Section, Report 7: Access to effective council – Stage 1 (23 May 2000).

OSCE Mission in Kosovo, Department of Human Rights and Rule of Law Section, Update on the situation of ethnic minorities in Kosovo (10 June 2000).

OSCE Mission in Kosovo, Department of Human Rights and Rule of Law Section, Report 8: Access to effective council – Stage 2 (20 July 2000).

OSCE Mission in Kosovo, Department of Human Rights and Rule of Law Section, Review 1: The criminal justice system in Kosovo, February – July 2000 (10 August 2000).

OSCE Mission in Kosovo, Department of Human Rights and Rule of Law Section, Assessment of the situation of ethnic minorities in Kosovo (10 October 2000).

Establishment of the OSCE Mission to the Federal Republic of Yugoslavia, Decision No. 401 of 11 January 2001 adopted by the Permanent Council of the Organization for Security and Co-operation in Europe, OSCE Doc. PC.DEC/401 (11 January 2001).

OSCE Mission in Kosovo, Department of Human Rights and Rule of Law Section, Combating trafficking in Kosovo (5 June 2001).

OSCE Mission in Kosovo, Department of Human Rights and Rule of Law Section, Strategy for Justice (28 July 2001).

OSCE Mission in Kosovo, Department of Human Rights and Rule of Law Section, Review 2: The criminal justice system in Kosovo, September 2000 – February 2001 (28 July 2001).

OSCE Mission in Kosovo, Department of Human Rights and Rule of Law Section,

Assessment of the situation of ethnic minorities in Kosovo (28 July 2001).

OSCE Mission in Kosovo, Department of Human Rights and Rule of Law Section, Assessment of the situation of ethnic minorities in Kosovo (1 October 2001).

OSCE Mission in Kosovo, Department of Human Rights and Rule of Law Section, Review 3: The criminal justice system in Kosovo, March 2001 – August 2001 (8 November 2001).

OSCE Mission in Kosovo, Department of Human Rights and Rule of Law Section, Property rights in Kosovo (13 January 2002).

OSCE Mission in Kosovo, Department of Human Rights and Rule of Law Section, Report 9: Administration of justice (15 March 2002).

OSCE Mission to Bosnia and Herzegovina, Access of Roma to education and health services in Tuzla Canton, Federation of Bosnia and Herzegovina, December 2001 – January 2002 (2 April 2002).

OSCE Mission in Kosovo, Department of Human Rights and Rule of Law Section, Review 4: The criminal justice system in Kosovo, September 2001 – February 2002 (29 April 2002).

OSCE Mission in Kosovo, Department of Human Rights and Rule of Law Section, Ninth assessment of the situation of ethnic minorities in Kosovo (27 May 2002).

OSCE Mission in Kosovo, Department of Human Rights and Rule of Law Section, Tenth assessment of the situation of ethnic minorities in Kosovo (12 March 2003).

OSCE Mission in Kosovo, Department of Human Rights and Rule of Law Section, Review 5: The criminal justice system in Kosovo, March 2002 – April 2003 (20 May 2003).

OSCE Mission in Croatia, The ombudsman institution in Croatia: An expert analysis (6 June 2003).

OSCE Mission in Kosovo, Department of Human Rights and Rule of Law Section, Property rights in Kosovo, 2002 – 2003 (30 June 2003).

OSCE Mission to Bosnia and Herzegovina, Fair employment project report 2002 (21 July 2003).

OSCE Mission to Bosnia and Herzegovina, Trial monitoring report the implementation of the new criminal procedure code in courts in Bosnia and Herzegovina (17 December 2004).

OSCE Mission in Kosovo, Department of Human Rights and Rule of Law Section, Human rights challenges following the March riots (25 March 2004).

OSCE Mission in Kosovo, Department of Human Rights and Rule of Law Section, Review of the criminal justice system: The administration of justice in the municipal courts (30 March 2004).

OSCE Mission in Kosovo, Department of Human Rights and Rule of Law Section, Legal System Monitoring Section, Review of the criminal justice system: Crime, justice and punishment (14 December 2004).

OSCE Mission to Bosnia and Herzegovina, Report on Roma informal settlements in Bosnia and Herzegovina (8 April 2005).

OSCE Mission in Kosovo, Department of Human Rights and Rule of Law Section,

Implementation of assembly laws by the Executive Branch of the provisional institutions of self-government (18 January 2005).

OSCE Mission in Kosovo, Department of Human Rights and Rule of Law Section, Legal System Monitoring Section, Kosovo: The response of the legal system to the March 2004 riots (2 December 2005).

OSCE Mission in Kosovo, Department of Human Rights and Rule of Law Section, Implementation of Kosovo assembly laws, Report II (15 December 2005).

OSCE Mission to Bosnia and Herzegovina, Report on the Roma civil registration information campaign (17 January 2006).

OSCE Mission to Bosnia and Herzegovina, Plea agreements in Bosnia and Herzegovina: Practices before the courts and their compliance with international human rights standards (9 February 2006).

Commentary

Benedek, W., Alefsen, H., O'Flaherty, M. and Sarajlija, E. (eds), *Human Rights in Bosnia and Herzegovina after Dayton: From Theory to Practice* (The Hague: Kluwer Law International, 1999).

Betts, W. *et al.*, 'The Post-Conflict Transitional Administration of Kosovo and the Lessons-Learned in Efforts to Establish a Judiciary and Rule of Law', *Michigan Journal of International Law* vol. 22 (2001).

Brand, M., 'Effective human rights protection when the UN 'becomes the state': lessons from UNMIK', in *The UN, Human Rights and Post-conflict Situations*.

Cordone, C., 'Bosnia and Herzegovina: The Creeping Protectorate' in A. Henkin (ed.), *Honoring Human Rights under International Mandates: Lessons from Bosnia, Kosovo, and East Timor* (Washington, DC: Aspen Institute, 2003).

European Commission for Democracy through Law, 'Report on the Implementation of the Constitutional Law on Human Rights and Freedoms and on the Rights of Ethnic Communities and Minorities in the Republic of Croatia' (Venice, May 1996).

Gavigan P., 'Proposal for a Human Rights Mandate for an International Post-Conflict Mission to the Former Yugoslavia Republic of Macedonia' in *Honoring Human Rights under International Mandates*.

International Policy Institute, *A Case for Change: A Review of Peace Operations* (King's College London, 2003).

Jonas, N. 'UNMIK and the Ombudsperson Institution in Kosovo: Human Rights Protection in a UN Surrogate State', *Netherlands Quarterly of Human Rights* vol. 22, no. 3 (2004).

Kenny, K., 'Formal and Informal Innovations in the UN Protection of Human Rights: The Special Rapporteur on the former Yugoslavia', *Austrian Journal of Public and International Law* vol. 48 (1995).

Katayanagi, M., *Human Rights Functions of United Nations Peacekeeping Operations*.

Line, M., 'Managing for Sustainable Human Rights Protection: International Missions in the Peace Processes of Bosnia and Herzegovina and Guatemala', in *The UN, Human Rights and Post-conflict Situations*.

Line, M., 'Case Study: Comparative Aspects of the Human Rights Field Operations in Bosnia and Herzegovina and Guatemala', chapter 17 in the present volume.

Marshall, D. and Inglis, S., 'The Disempowerment of Human Rights-Based Justice in the United Nations Mission in Kosovo', *Harvard Human Rights Journal* vol. 16 (2003).

Mertus, J., 'Improving International Peacebuilding Efforts: The Example of Human Rights Culture in Kosovo', *Global Governance* vol. 10, no. 3 (2004).

Minear, L., Clark, J., Cohen, R., Gallagher, D., Guest, I. and Weiss, T., 'Humanitarian Action in the Former Yugoslavia: The UN's Role, 1991–1993', Occasional Paper 18 (Providence: Watson Institute, 1994).

Ocran, T. M., 'How Blessed Were the UN Peacekeepers in Former Yugoslavia?: The Involvement of UNPROFOR and Other UN Bodies in Humanitarian Activities and Human Rights Issues in Croatia 1992–1996', *Wisconsin International Law Journal* vol. 18, no. 1 (2000).

O'Flaherty, M. and Gisvold, G. (eds), *Post-war Protection of Human Rights in Bosnia and Herzegovina* (The Hague: Martinus Nijhoff, 1998).

OHCHR Staff, 'The OHCHR Kosovo Emergency Operation: Lessons Learned', in *Human Rights Protection in the Field*.

O'Neill, W. G., 'Human Rights Field Operations: A New Protection Tool', in *Human Rights Protection in the Field*.

O'Neill, W. G., *Kosovo: An Unfinished Peace* (Boulder: Lynne Rienner, 2001).

O'Neill, W. G., 'Kosovo: Unexpected Barriers to Building Peace and Security' in *Honoring Human Rights under International Mandates*.

Ramcharan, B. G., 'The Protection Methods of Human Rights Field Offices', in *Human Rights Protection in the Field*.

Reka, B., *UNMIK as an International Governance in Post-war Kosovo: NATO's Intervention, UN Administration and Kosovar Aspirations* (Skopje: Logos, 2003).

Rosas, A. and Timo, L., 'OSCE Long-Term Missions' in M. Bothe, N. Ronzitti and A. Rosas (eds) *The OSCE in the Maintenance of Peace and Security: Conflict Prevention, Crisis Management and Peaceful Settlement of Disputes* (The Hague: Kluwer Law International, 1997).

Strohmeyer, H., 'Collapse and Reconstruction of a Judicial System: The United Nations Missions in Kosovo and East Timor', *American Journal of International Law* vol. 95, no. 1 (2001).

Strohmeyer, H., 'Making Multilateral Interventions Work: The UN and the Creation of Transitional Justice Systems in Kosovo and East Timor', *Fletcher Forum of World Affairs* vol. 25 no. 2 (2001).

Ward, B., 'The Failure to Protect Minorities in Post-War Kosovo', *Helsinki Monitor 2000* no.1.

Democratic Republic of Congo

Official Documents

> OHCHR Field Operation in Democratic Republic of Congo (August 1996).

> United Nations Organization Mission in the Democratic Republic of Congo (February 2000).

Agreement on the establishment of an Office of the United Nations High Commissioner for Human Rights in Democratic Republic of the Congo (21 August 1996).

Report on the situation of human rights in Zaire, Prepared by the Special Rapporteur, Mr Roberto Garretón, in accordance with Commission resolution 1996/77, UN Doc. E/CN.4/1997/6 (1 January 1997).

Report on the situation of human rights in Zaire, Prepared by the Special Rapporteur, Mr Roberto Garretón, in accordance with Commission resolution 1996/77/Add.2 UN Doc. E/CN.4/1997/6/Add.2 (2 April 1997).

Report on the situation of human rights in the Democratic Republic of Congo (formerly Zaire), submitted by the Special Rapporteur, Mr Roberto Garretón, in accordance with Commission resolution 1997/58, UN Doc. E/CN.4/1998/65 (30 January 1998).

Report of the Secretary-General on the United Nations Organization Mission in the Democratic Republic of the Congo, UN Doc. S/2000/30 (17 January 2000).

Security Council resolution 1291 (2000), UN Doc. S/RES/1291 (24 February 2000).

Second report of the Secretary-General on the United Nations Organization Mission in the Democratic Republic of the Congo, UN Doc. S/2000/330 (18 April 2000).

Third report of the Secretary-General on the United Nations Organization Mission in the Democratic Republic of the Congo, UN Doc. S/2000/566 (12 June 2000).

Fourth report of the Secretary-General on the United Nations Organization Mission in the Democratic Republic of the Congo, UN Doc. S/2000/888 (21 September 2000).

Fifth report of the Secretary-General on the United Nations Organization Mission in the Democratic Republic of the Congo, UN Doc. S/2000/1156 (6 December 2000).

Sixth report of the Secretary-General on the United Nations Organization Mission in the Democratic Republic of the Congo, UN Doc. S/2001/128 (12 February 2001).

Seventh report of the Secretary-General on the United Nations Organization Mission in the Democratic Republic of the Congo, UN Doc. S/2001/373 (17 April 2001).

Eighth report of the Secretary-General on the United Nations Organization Mission in the Democratic Republic of the Congo, UN Doc. S/2001/572 (8 June 2001).

Ninth report of the Secretary-General on the United Nations Organization Mission in the Democratic Republic of the Congo, UN Doc. S/2001/970 (12 October 2001).

Tenth report of the Secretary-General General on the United Nations Organization

Mission in the Democratic Republic of the Congo, UN Doc. S/2002/169 (15 February 2002).

Eleventh report of the Secretary-General General on the United Nations Organization Mission in the Democratic Republic of the Congo, UN Doc. S/2002/621 (5 June 2002).

Twelfth report of the Secretary-General General on the United Nations Organization Mission in the Democratic Republic of the Congo, UN Doc. S/2002/1180 (18 October 2002).

Thirteenth report of the Secretary-General General on the United Nations Organization Mission in the Democratic Republic of the Congo, UN Doc. S/2003/211 (21 February 2003).

Report of the United Nations High Commissioner for Human Rights to the Security Council on the situation of human rights in the Democratic Republic of the Congo, UN Doc. S/2003/216 (24 February 2003).

Second special report of the Secretary-General on the United Nations Organization Mission in the Democratic Republic of the Congo, UN Doc. S/2003/566 (27 May 2003).

Fourteenth report of the Secretary-General General on the United Nations Organization Mission in the Democratic Republic of the Congo, UN Doc. S/2003/1098 (17 November 2003).

Fifteenth report of the Secretary-General General on the United Nations Organization Mission in the Democratic Republic of the Congo, UN Doc. S/2004/251 (25 March 2004).

Third special report of the Secretary-General on the United Nations Organization Mission in the Democratic Republic of the Congo, UN Doc. S/2004/650 (16 August 2004).

Update on other aspects of the activities of the United Nations Organization Mission in the Democratic Republic of Congo, Annex I to Third special report of the Secretary-General on the United Nations Organization Mission in the Democratic Republic of the Congo, UN Doc. S/2004/650 (16 August 2004).

Security Council resolution 1565 (2004), UN Doc. S/RES/1565 (1 October 2004)

Sixteenth report of the Secretary-General General on the United Nations Organization Mission in the Democratic Republic of the Congo, UN Doc. S/2004/1034 (31 December 2004).

Seventeenth report of the Secretary-General General on the United Nations Organization Mission in the Democratic Republic of the Congo, UN Doc. S/2005/167 (15 March 2005).

Special report on elections in the Democratic Republic of the Congo, UN Doc. S/2005/320 (26 May 2005).

Eighteenth report of the Secretary-General General on the United Nations Organization Mission in the Democratic Republic of the Congo, UN Doc. S/2005/506 (2 August 2005).

Nineteenth report of the Secretary-General General on the United Nations Organization Mission in the Democratic Republic of the Congo, UN Doc. S/2005/603 (26 September 2005).

Twentieth report of the Secretary-General on the United Nations Organization Mission in the Democratic Republic of the Congo, UN Doc. S/2005/832 (28 December 2005).

Colombia

Official Documents

OHCHR Field Operation in Colombia (January 1997).

Agreement on the establishment of an Office of the United Nations High Commissioner for Human Rights in Colombia (Geneva, 29 November 1996), Annex to Report of the United Nations High Commissioner for Human Rights in Colombia, UN Doc. E/CN.4/1997/11 (24 January 1997).

Action by the Colombian Government for the establishment of an Office of the United Nations High Commissioner for Human Rights, Annex to UN Doc. E/CN.4/1997/128 (25 March 1997).

Report of the United Nations High Commissioner for Human Rights in Colombia, UN Doc. E/CN.4/1997/11 (24 January 1997).

Report by the United Nations High Commissioner for Human Rights, UN Doc. E/CN.4/1998/16 (9 March 1998).

Report of the United Nations High Commissioner for Human Rights on the Office in Colombia, UN Doc. E/CN.4/1999/8 (16 March 1999).

Report of the United Nations High Commissioner for Human Rights on the Office in Colombia, UN Doc. E/CN.4/2000/11 (9 March 2000).

Report of the United Nations High Commissioner for Human Rights on the human rights situation in Colombia, UN Doc. E/CN.4/2001/15 (8 February 2001).

Report of the United Nations High Commissioner for Human Rights on the human rights situation in Colombia, UN Doc. E/CN.4/2002/17 (2 February 2002).

Report of the United Nations High Commissioner for Human Rights on the human rights situation in Colombia, UN Doc. E/CN.4/2003/13 (24 February 2003).

Report of the United Nations High Commissioner for Human Rights on the human rights situation in Colombia, UN Doc. E/CN.4/2004/13 (17 February 2004).

Report of the United Nations High Commissioner for Human Rights on the human rights situation in Colombia, UN Doc. E/CN.4/2005/10 (28 February 2005).

Report of the United Nations High Commissioner for Human Rights on the situation of human rights in Colombia, UN Doc. E/CN.4/2006/9 (6 February 2006).

Commentary

Clapham, A. and Martin, F., 'Smaller Missions Bigger Problems', in *Honoring Human Rights*.

Ramcharan, B. G., 'The Protection Methods of Human Rights Field Offices', in *Human Rights Protection in the Field*.

OHCHR Staff, 'Protecting Human Rights in a Situation of Humanitarian Crisis: The Case of Colombia', in *Human Rights Protection in the Field*.

Sierra Leone

Official Documents

> United Nations Observer Mission in Sierra Leone (July 1998 – October 1999).

> United Nations Assistance Mission in Sierra Leone (October 1999 – December 2005).

> United Nations Integrated Office in Sierra Leone (January 2006).

Security Council resolution 1181 (1998), UN Doc. S/RES/1181 (13 July 1998).
First progress report of the Secretary-General on the United Nations Observer Mission in Sierra Leone, UN Doc. S/1998/750 (12 August 1998).
Second progress report of the Secretary-General on the United Nations Observer Mission in Sierra Leone, UN Doc. S/1998/960 (16 October 1998).
Third progress report of the Secretary-General on the United Nations Observer Mission in Sierra Leone, UN Doc. S/1998/1176 (16 December 1998).
Fourth progress report of the Secretary-General on the United Nations Observer Mission in Sierra Leone, UN Doc. S/1999/20 (7 January 1999).
Fifth progress report of the Secretary-General on the United Nations Observer Mission in Sierra Leone, UN Doc. S/1999/237 (4 March 1999).
Sixth progress report of the Secretary-General on the United Nations Observer Mission in Sierra Leone, UN Doc. S/1999/645 (4 June 1999).
Peace agreement between the Government of Sierra Leone and the Revolutionary United Front of Sierra Leone, Annex to UN Doc. S/1999/777 (12 July 1999).
Seventh progress report of the Secretary-General on the United Nations Observer Mission in Sierra Leone, UN Doc. S/1999/836 (11 August 1999).
Security Council resolution 1260 (1999), UN Doc. S/RES/1260 (20 August 1999).
Eighth progress report of the Secretary-General on the United Nations Observer Mission in Sierra Leone, UN Doc. S/1999/1003 (23 September 1999).
Security Council resolution 1270 (1999), UN Doc. S/RES/1270 (22 October 1999).
First report on the United Nations Mission in Sierra Leone (UNAMSIL), UN Doc. S/1999/1223 (6 December 1999).
Report of the United Nations High Commissioner for Human Rights, UN Doc. A/55/36 (1 January 2000).
Second report of the Secretary-General pursuant to Security Council resolution 1270 (1999) on the United Nations Mission in Sierra Leone, UN Doc. S/2000/13 (11 January 2000).
Third report of the Secretary-General on the United Nations Mission in Sierra Leone, UN Doc. S/2000/186 (7 March 2000).

Fourth report of the Secretary-General on the United Nations Mission in Sierra Leone, UN Doc. S/2000/455 (19 May 2000).

Fifth report of the Secretary-General on the United Nations Mission in Sierra Leone, UN Doc. S/2000/751 (31 July 2000).

Sixth report of the Secretary-General on the United Nations Mission in Sierra Leone, UN Doc. S/2000/832 (24 August 2000).

Seventh report of the Secretary-General on the United Nations Mission in Sierra Leone, UN Doc. S/2000/1055 (7 November 2000).

Eighth report of the Secretary-General on the United Nations Mission in Sierra Leone, UN Doc. S/2000/1199 (15 December 2000).

Ninth report of the Secretary-General on the United Nations Mission in Sierra Leone, UN Doc. S/2001/228 (14 March 2001).

Tenth report of the Secretary-General on the United Nations Mission in Sierra Leone, UN Doc. S/2001/627 (25 June 2001).

Report of the United Nations High Commissioner for Human Rights on the human rights situation in Sierra Leone, UN Doc. A/56/281 (9 August 2001).

Eleventh report of the Secretary-General on the United Nations Mission in Sierra Leone, UN Doc. S/2001/857 (7 September 2001).

Twelfth report of the Secretary-General on the United Nations Mission in Sierra Leone, UN Doc. S/2001/1195 (12 December 2001).

Thirteenth report of the Secretary-General on the United Nations Mission in Sierra Leone, UN Doc. S/2002/267 (13 March 2002).

Fourteenth report of the Secretary-General on the United Nations Mission in Sierra Leone, UN Doc. S/2002/ 679 (19 June 2002).

Report of the United Nations High Commissioner for Human Rights on assistance to Sierra Leone in the field of human rights, UN Doc.A/57/284 (7 August 2002).

Fifteenth report of the Secretary-General on the United Nations Mission in Sierra Leone, UN Doc. S/2002/987 (5 September 2002).

Sixteenth report of the Secretary-General on the United Nations Mission in Sierra Leone, UN Doc. S/2002/1417 (23 December 2002).

Seventeenth report of the Secretary-General on the United Nations Mission in Sierra Leone, UN Doc. S/2003/321 (18 March 2003).

Eighteenth report of the Secretary-General on the United Nations Mission in Sierra Leone, UN Doc. S/2003/863 (25 June 2003).

Nineteenth report of the Secretary-General on the United Nations Mission in Sierra Leone, UN Doc. S/2003/863 (5 September 2003).

Report of the United Nations High Commissioner for Human Rights on assistance to Sierra Leone in the field of human rights, UN Doc.A/58/379 (18 September 2003).

Twentieth report of the Secretary-General on the United Nations Mission in Sierra Leone, UN Doc. S/2003/1201 (23 December 2003).

Twenty-first report of the Secretary-General on the United Nations Mission in Sierra Leone, UN Doc. S/2004/228 (19 March 2004).

Twenty-second report of the Secretary-General on the United Nations Mission in Sierra Leone, UN Doc. S/2004/536 (6 July 2004).

Twenty-third report of the Secretary-General on the United Nations Mission in Sierra Leone, UN Doc. S/2004/724 (8 September 2004).

Report of the United Nations High Commissioner for Human Rights on assistance to Sierra Leone in the field of human rights, UN Doc.A/59/340 (9 September 2004).

Twenty-fourth report of the Secretary-General on the United Nations Mission in Sierra Leone, UN Doc. S/2004/965 (7 December 2004).

Report of the High Commissioner for Human Rights, Situation of human rights in Sierra Leone, UN Doc. E/CN.4/2005/113 (2 February 2005).

Twenty-fifth report of the Secretary-General on the United Nations Mission in Sierra Leone, UN Doc. S/2005/273 (26 April 2005).

Report of the United Nations High Commissioner for Human Rights on assistance to Sierra Leone in the field of human rights, UN Doc.A/60/349 (18 August 2005).

Security Council resolution 1620 (2005), UN Doc. S/RES/1620 (31 August 2005).

Twenty-sixth report of the Secretary-General on the United Nations Mission in Sierra Leone, UN Doc. S/2005/596 (13 September 2005).

Twenty-seventh report of the Secretary-General on the United Nations Mission in Sierra Leone, UN Doc. S/2005/777 (7 December 2005).

Report of the High Commissioner for Human Rights, Assistance to Sierra Leone in the field of human rights, UN Doc. E/CN.4/2006/106 (15 February 2006).

Commentary

International Policy Institute, *A Case for Change: A Review of Peace Operations*, (King's College London, 2003).

Juma, L., 'The Human Rights Approach to Peace in Sierra Leone: The Analysis of the Peace Process and Human Rights Enforcement in a Civil War Situation', *Denver Journal of International Law and Policy* vol. 30, no. 3 (2003).

O'Flaherty, M., 'Sierra Leone's Peace Process: The Role of the Human Rights Community', *Human Rights Quarterly* vol. 26, no. 1 (2004).

O'Flaherty, M., 'Case Study: The United Nations Human Rights Field Operation in Sierra Leone', chapter 15 in the present volume.

Ramcharan, B. G. 'The Protection Methods of Human Rights Field Offices', in *Human Rights Protection in the Field*.

Guinea-Bissau

Official Documents

> United Nations Post-conflict Peace-Building Support Office in Guinea-Bissau
> (April 1999).

Letter dated 26 February 1999 from the Secretary-General addressed to the President of the Security Council, UN Doc. S/1999/232 (3 March 1999).

Security Council resolution 1233 (1999), UN Doc. S/RES/1233 (6 April 1999).

Report of the Secretary-General on developments in Guinea-Bissau and the activities of the United Nations Peace-Building Support Office in that country, UN Doc. S/1999/1015 (29 September 1999).

Report of the Secretary-General on developments in Guinea-Bissau and the activities of the United Nations Peace-Building Support Office in that country, UN Doc. S/1999/1276 (23 December 1999).

Report of the Secretary-General on developments in Guinea-Bissau, UN Doc. S/2000/250 (24 March 2000).

Report of the Secretary-General on developments in Guinea-Bissau and the activities of the United Nations Peace-Building Support Office in that country, UN Doc. S/2000/632 (28 June 2000).

Report of the Secretary-General on developments in Guinea-Bissau and the activities of the United Nations Peace-Building Support Office in that country, UN Doc. S/2000/920 (29 September 2000).

Report of the Secretary-General on developments in Guinea-Bissau and the activities of the United Nations Peace-Building Support Office in that country, UN Doc. S/2001/237 (16 March 2001).

Report of the Secretary-General on developments in Guinea-Bissau and the activities of the United Nations Peace-Building Support Office in that country, UN Doc. S/2001/622 (22 June 2001).

Report of the Secretary-General on developments in Guinea-Bissau and the activities of the United Nations Peace-Building Support Office in that country, UN Doc. S/2001/915 (27 September 2001).

Report of the Secretary-General on developments in Guinea-Bissau and the activities of the United Nations Peace-Building Support Office in that country, UN Doc. S/2001/1211 (14 December 2001).

Report of the Secretary-General on developments in Guinea-Bissau and the activities of the United Nations Peace-Building Support Office in that country, UN Doc. S/2002/312 (26 March 2002).

Report of the Secretary-General on developments in Guinea-Bissau and the activities of the United Nations Peace-Building Support Office in that country, UN Doc. S/2002/662 (13 June 2002).

Report of the Secretary-General on developments in Guinea-Bissau and the activities of the United Nations Peace-Building Support Office in that country, UN Doc. S/2002/1367 (13 December 2002).

Report of the Secretary-General on developments in Guinea-Bissau and the activities of the United Nations Peace-Building Support Office in that country, UN Doc. S/2003/621 (9 June 2003).

Report of the Secretary-General on developments in Guinea-Bissau and the activities of the United Nations Peace-Building Support Office in that country, UN Doc. S/2003/1157 (5 December 2003).

Report of the Secretary-General on developments in Guinea-Bissau and the activities of the United Nations Peace-Building Support Office in that country, UN Doc. S/2004/456 (4 June 2004).

Report of the Secretary-General on developments in Guinea-Bissau and the activities of the United Nations Peace-Building Support Office in that country, UN Doc. S/2004/969 (15 December 2004).

Security Council resolution 1580 (2004), UN Doc. S/RES/1580 (22 December 2004).

Report of the Secretary-General on developments in Guinea-Bissau and the activities of the United Nations Peace-Building Support Office in that country, UN Doc. S/2005/174 (16 March 2005).

Report of the Secretary-General on developments in Guinea-Bissau and the activities of the United Nations Peace-Building Support Office in that country, UN Doc. S/2005/380 (10 June 2005).

Report of the Secretary-General on developments in Guinea-Bissau and the activities of the United Nations Peace-Building Support Office in that country, UN Doc. S/2005/575 (12 September 2005).

Report of the Secretary-General on developments in Guinea-Bissau and the activities of the United Nations Peace-Building Support Office in that country, UN Doc. S/2005/752 (2 December 2005).

Report of the Secretary-General on developments in Guinea-Bissau and the activities of the United Nations Peace-Building Support Office in that country, UN Doc. S/2006/162 (14 March 2006).

Timor-Leste

Official Documents

United Nations Transitional Administration in East Timor (October 1999 – May 2002).

United Nations Mission in Support of East Timor (May 2002 – May 2005).

United Nations Office in Timor-Leste (May 2005).

Security Council resolution, UN Doc. S/RES/1272 (25 October 1999).

Report of the United Nations High Commissioner for Human Rights, UN Doc. A/55/36 (1 January 2000).

Report of the United Nations High Commissioner for Human Rights on the situation of human rights in East Timor submitted to the Commission on Human Rights at its fourth special session, Annex to UN Doc. E/CN.4/2000/44 (24 March 2000).

Report of the High Commissioner for Human Rights, Situation of human rights in East Timor, UN Doc. E/CN.4/2000/27 (29 March 2000).

Report of the Secretary-General on the United Nations Transitional Administration in East Timor, UN Doc. S/2000/738 (26 July 2000).

Report of the United Nations High Commissioner for Human Rights on the situation of human rights in Timor-Leste, UN Doc. E/CN.4/2001/37 (6 February 2001).

Progress report of the Secretary-General on the United Nations Transitional Administration in East Timor, UN Doc. S/2001/719 (24 July 2001).

Interim report of the United Nations High Commissioner for Human Rights on the Situation of Human Rights in East Timor, UN Doc. A/56/337 (6 September 2001).

Report of the United Nations High Commissioner for Human Rights on the situation of human rights in East Timor, UN Doc. E/CN.4/2002/39 (1 March 2002).

Report of the Secretary-General on the United Nations Transitional Administration in East Timor, UN Doc. S/2002/432 (12 April 2002).

Security Council resolution 1410 (2002), UN Doc. S/RES/1410 (17 May 2002).

Report of the United Nations High Commissioner for Human Rights, UN Doc. A/57/36(Supp) (9 October 2002).

Report of the United Nations High Commissioner for Human Rights, Situation of human rights in Timor-Leste, UN Doc. E/CN.4/2003/37 (4 March 2003).

Report of the United Nations High Commissioner for Human Rights on the situation of human rights in Timor-Leste, UN Doc. E/CN.4/2004/107 (19 January 2004).

Report of the Secretary-General on the United Nations Mission in Support of East Timor, UN Doc. S/2004/333 (29 April 2004).

Report of the United Nations High Commissioner for Human Rights on technical cooperation in the field of human rights in Timor-Leste, UN Doc. E/CN.4/2005/115 (22 March 2005).

Security Council resolution 1599 (2005), UN Doc. S/RES/1599 (28 April 2005).

Progress report of the Secretary-General on the United Nations Office in Timor-Leste, UN Doc. S/2005/533 (18 August 2005).

Commentary

Bongiorno, C. 'A Culture of Impunity: Applying International Human Rights Law to the United Nations in East Timor', *Columbia Human Rights Law Review* vol. 33, no. 3 (2002).

Burgess, P. 'Case Study: The United Nations Human Rights Field Operation in East Timor', chapter 14 in the present volume.

Criswell, D., 'Durable Consent and a Strong Transitional Peacekeeping Plan: The Success of UNTAET in Light of the Lessons Learned in Cambodia', *Pacific Rim Law and Policy Journal*, June 2002.

Devereux, A., 'Searching for Clarity: A Case Study of UNTAET's Application of International Human Rights Norms', in *The UN, Human Rights and Post-conflict Situations*.

Jones, S., 'Human Rights and Peacekeeping in East Timor', in *Honoring Human Rights under International Mandates*.

International Policy Institute, *A Case for Change: A Review of Peace Operations*, (King's College London, 2003).

Ishizuka, K., 'Peacekeeping in East Timor: The Experience of UNMISET', *International Peacekeeping* vol. 10, no. 3 (2003).

Klabbers, J., 'Redemption Song? Human Rights versus Community-Building in East Timor', *Leiden Journal of International Law* vol. 16, no. 2 (2003).

Kondoch, B., 'The United Nations Administration of East Timor', *Journal of Conflict and Security Law* vol. 6, no. 2 (2001).

Martin, I., *Self-Determination in East Timor: The United Nations, the Ballot, and International Intervention* (Boulder: Lynne Rienner, 2001).

Orient Foundation, *The Legacy and Lessons of the United Nations Transitional Administration in East Timor* (28 June 2002).

Ramcharan, B. G. 'The Protection Methods of Human Rights Field Offices', in *Human Rights Protection in the Field*.

Rodrigues, G., 'States, National Interest and Human Rights: Some Thoughts on the UN Process Leading up to UNTAET', in M. Almeida (ed.), *Nationbuilding in East Timor* (Canadian Peacekeeping Press, 2001).

Smith, M. G. and Dee, M., *Peacekeeping in East Timor: The Path to Independence* (Boulder: Lynne Rienner, 2002).

Strohmeyer, H., 'Collapse and Reconstruction of a Judicial System: The United Nations Missions in Kosovo and East Timor', *American Journal of International Law* vol. 95, no. 1 (January 2001).

Strohmeyer, H., 'Making Multilateral Interventions Work: The UN and the Creation of Transitional Justice Systems in Kosovo and East Timor', *Fletcher Forum of World Affairs* vol. 25, no. 2 (2001).

Sudan

Official Documents

OHCHR Field Operation in Sudan (March 2000).

United Nations Mission in Sudan (March 2005).

Agreement between the High Commissioner for Human Rights and the Government of Sudan (March 2000).

Situation of human rights in Sudan, Report of the Special Rapporteur, Gerhart Baum, submitted in accordance with Commission resolution 2002/16, UN Doc. E/CN.4/2003/42 (6 January 2003).

Security Council resolution 1564 (2004), UN Doc. S/RES/1564 (18 September 2004).

Security Council resolution 1574 (2004), UN Doc. S/RES/1574 (19 November 2004).

Report of the Secretary-General on the Sudan, UN Doc. S/2005/57 (31 January 2005).

Report of the Secretary-General on the Sudan pursuant to paragraphs 6, 13 and 16 of Security Council resolution 1566 (2004), paragraph 15 of resolution 1564 (2004) and paragraph 17 of 1574 (2004), UN Doc. S/2005/140, (4 March 2005).

Security Council resolution 1590 (2005), UN Doc. S/RES/1590 (24 March 2005).

Report of the Secretary-General on Sudan, UN Doc. S/2005/411 (23 June 2005).

Report of the Secretary-General on Sudan, UN Doc. S/2005/579 (12 September 2005).

Report of the Secretary-General on Sudan, UN Doc. S/2005/821 (21 December 2005).

Report of the Special Rapporteur on the human rights situation in Sudan, Sima Samar, UN Doc. E/CN.4/2006/111 (11 January 2006).

Second periodic report of the United Nations High Commissioner for Human Rights on the human rights situation in Sudan (27 January 2006).

Report of the Secretary-General on Sudan, UN Doc. S/2006/160 (14 March 2006).

Eritrea / Ethiopia

Official Documents

> United Nations Mission in Ethiopia and Eritrea (July 2000).

Agreement between the Government of the State of Eritrea and the Government of the Federal Democratic Republic of Ethiopia, Annex to UN Doc. S/2000/1183-A/55/686 (12 December 2000).

Security Council resolution 1320 (2000), UN Doc. S/RES/1320 (15 September 2000).

Progress report of the Secretary-General on Ethiopia and Eritrea, UN Doc. S/2001/608 (19 June 2001).

Report of the Secretary-General on Ethiopia and Eritrea, UN Doc. S/2001/843 (5 September 2001).

Progress report of the Secretary-General on Ethiopia and Eritrea, UN Doc. S/2001/1194 (13 December 2001).

Progress report of the Secretary-General on Ethiopia and Eritrea, UN Doc. S/2002/245 (8 March 2002).

Progress report of the Secretary-General on Ethiopia and Eritrea, UN Doc. S/2002/977 (30 August 2002).

Progress report of the Secretary-General on Ethiopia and Eritrea, UN Doc. S/2002/1393 (20 December 2002).

Progress report of the Secretary-General on Ethiopia and Eritrea, UN Doc. S/2003/257 (6 March 2003).

Progress report of the Secretary-General on Ethiopia and Eritrea, UN Doc. S/2003/665 (23 June 2003).

Progress report of the Secretary-General on Ethiopia and Eritrea, UN Doc. S/2003/858 (4 September 2003).

Progress report of the Secretary-General on Ethiopia and Eritrea, UN Doc. S/2004/180 (5 March 2004).

Progress report of the Secretary-General on Ethiopia and Eritrea, UN Doc. S/2004/543 (7 July 2004).

Progress report of the Secretary-General on Ethiopia and Eritrea, UN Doc. S/2004/708 (2 September 2004).

Progress report of the Secretary-General on Ethiopia and Eritrea, UN Doc. S/2004/973 (16 December 2004).

Report of the Secretary-General on Ethiopia and Eritrea, UN Doc. S/2005/142 (7 March 2005).

Report of the Secretary-General on Ethiopia and Eritrea, UN Doc. S/2005/400 (20 June 2005).

Report of the Secretary-General on Ethiopia and Eritrea, UN Doc. S/2005/553 (30 August 2005).

Report of the Secretary-General on Ethiopia and Eritrea, UN Doc. S/2006/1 (3 January 2006).

Report of the Secretary-General on Ethiopia and Eritrea, UN Doc. S/2006/140 (6 March 2006).

Afghanistan

Official Documents

United Nations Assistance Mission in Afghanistan (March 2002).

Agreement on provisional arrangements in Afghanistan pending the re-establishment of permanent Government institutions, with four annexes, signed Petersberg, Germany, 5 December 2001, Annex II, Role of the United Nations during the interim period, UN Doc. S/2001/1154 (5 December 2001).

Security Council resolution 1383 (2001), UN Doc. S/RES/1383 (6 December 2001).

Security Council resolution 1401 (2002), UN Doc. S/RES/1401 (28 March 2002).

Interim report of the Special Rapporteur of the Commission on Human Rights on the situation of human rights in Afghanistan, UN Doc. A/57/309 (13 August 2002).

Report of the United Nations High Commissioner for Human Rights, UN Doc. A/57/36 (9 October 2002).

Report of the Secretary-General, The situation in Afghanistan and its implications for international peace and security, UN Doc. A/57/487-S/2002/1173 (21 October 2002).

Report of the Secretary-General, The situation in Afghanistan and its implications for peace and security: Emergency international assistance for peace, normalcy and reconstruction in war-stricken Afghanistan, UN Doc. A/58/616 (3 December 2003).

Report of the Secretary-General, The situation in Afghanistan and its implications for international peace and security, UN Doc. S/2003/1212 (30 December 2003).

Report of the Secretary-General, The situation in Afghanistan and its implications for international peace and security, UN Doc. A/57/762-S/2003/333 (20 March 2003).

Report of the Secretary-General, The situation in Afghanistan and its implications for international peace and security, UN Doc. A/58/742-S/2004/230 (19 March 2004).

Report of the Secretary-General, The situation in Afghanistan and its implications for international peace and security, UN Doc. A/58/868-S/2004/634 (12 August 2004).

Report of the independent expert of the Commission on Human Rights on the human rights situation in Afghanistan, UN Doc. A/59/370 (21 September 2004).

Report of the Secretary-General, The situation in Afghanistan and its implications for peace and security: Emergency international assistance for peace, normalcy and reconstruction in war-stricken Afghanistan, UN Doc. A/59/581-S/2004/925 (26 November 2004).

Report of the independent expert on the situation of human rights in Afghanistan, M. Cherif Bassiouni, UN Doc. E/CN.4/2005/122 (11March 2005).

Report of the Secretary-General, The situation in Afghanistan and its implications for peace and security: Emergency international assistance for peace, normalcy and reconstruction in war-stricken Afghanistan, UN Doc. A/59/744-S/2005/183 (18 March 2005).

Report of the Secretary-General, The situation in Afghanistan and its implications for peace and security: Emergency international assistance for peace, normalcy and reconstruction in war-stricken Afghanistan, UN Doc. A/60/224-S/2005/525 (12 August 2005).

Report of the High Commissioner for Human Rights on the situation of human rights in Afghanistan and on the achievements of technical assistance in the field of human rights, UN Doc. A/60/343 (9 September 2005).

Report of the Special Rapporteur on violence against women, its causes and consequences, Yakin Ertük, integration of the human rights of women and a gender perspective, UN Doc. E/CN.4/2006/61/Add.5 (15 February 2006).

Report of the High Commissioner for Human Rights on the situation of human rights in Afghanistan and on the achievements of technical assistance in the field of human rights, UN Doc. E/CN.4/2006/108 (3 March 2006).

Commentary

Bosi, T. D., 'Post-Conflict Reconstruction: The United Nations' Involvement in Afghanistan', *New York Law School Journal of Human Rights* vol. 19, no. 4/6 (2003).

Chesterman, S., *Tiptoeing Through Afghanistan: The Future of UN State-Building*, International Peace Academy (September 2002).

International Policy Institute, *A Case for Change: A Review of Peace Operations* (King's College London, 2003).

Niland, N., 'Rights, Rhetoric and Reality: A Snapshot from Afghanistan' in *The UN, Human Rights and Post-conflict Situations*.

Niland, N., 'The Marginalization of Human Rights in Afghanistan', in A. Donini, (ed). *Nation-Building Unraveled?: Aid, Peace and Justice in Afghanistan* (Bloomfield: Kumarian Press, 2003).

Côte d'Ivoire

Official Documents

United Nations Mission in Côte d'Ivoire (May 2003 – April 2004).

United Nations Operation in Côte d'Ivoire (April 2004).

Security Council resolution 1479 (2003), UN Doc. S/RES/1479 (13 May 2003).

First report of the Secretary-General on the United Nations Mission in Côte d'Ivoire, UN Doc. S/2003/801 (8 August 2003).

Second report of the Secretary-General on the United Nations Mission in Côte d'Ivoire, UN Doc. S/2003/1069 (4 November 2003).

Report of the Secretary-General on the United Nations Mission in Côte d'Ivoire submitted pursuant to Security Council resolution 1514 (2003) of 13 November 2003, UN Doc. S/2004/3 (6 January 2004).

Security Council resolution 1528 (2004), UN Doc. S/RES/1528 (27 February 2004).

First report of the Secretary-General on the United Nations Operation in Côte d'Ivoire, UN Doc. S/2004/443 (2 June 2004).

Second report of the Secretary-General on the United Nations Operation in Côte d'Ivoire, UN Doc. S/2004/697 (27 August 2004).

Third progress report of the Secretary-General on the United Nations Operation in Côte d'Ivoire, UN Doc. S/2004/962 (9 December 2004).

Fourth progress report of the Secretary-General on the United Nations Operation in Côte d'Ivoire, UN Doc. S/2005/186 (18 March 2005).

Fifth progress report of the Secretary-General on the United Nations Operation in Côte d'Ivoire, UN Doc. S/2005/398 (17 June 2005).

Sixth progress report of the Secretary-General on the United Nations Operation in Côte d'Ivoire, UN Doc. S/2005/604 (26 September 2005).

Seventh progress report of the Secretary-General on the United Nations Operation in Côte d'Ivoire, UN Doc. S/2006/2 (3 January 2006).

Eighth report of the Secretary-General on the United Nations Operation in Côte d'Ivoire, UN Doc. S/2006/222 (11 April 2006).

Albania

Official Documents

OSCE Presence in Albania (December 2003).

Permanent Council Decision No. 588, Mandate of the OSCE Presence in Albania, OSCE Doc. PC.DEC/588 (18 December 2003).

Semi-annual OSCE report on activities in Albania (June 2003).

OSCE Presence in Albania, Rule of Law/Human Rights Department, Pre-trial Detention Situation Survey (August 2003).

OSCE Presence in Albania, Legal sector report for Albania (2004).

Semi-annual OSCE report on activities in Albania (February 2004).

OSCE Presence in Albania, Rule of Law and Human Rights Department, Interim report on fair trial development project, October 2003 – July 2004 (September 2004).

Semi-annual OSCE report on activities in Albania (September 2004).

Iraq

Official Documents

United Nations Assistance Mission in Iraq (June 2004).

Security Council resolution 1546 (2004), UN Doc. S/RES/1546 (8 June 2004).

Report of the Secretary-General pursuant to paragraph 24 of resolution 1483 (2003) and paragraph 12 of resolution 1511 (2003), UN Doc. 2004/625 (5 August 2004).

Report of the Secretary-General pursuant to paragraph 30 of resolution 1546 (2004), UN Doc. S/2004/710 (3 September 2004).

Report of the Secretary-General pursuant to paragraph 30 of resolution 1546 (2004), UN Doc. S/2004/959 (8 December 2004).

Report of the Secretary-General pursuant to paragraph 30 of resolution 1546 (2004), UN Doc. S/2005/141 (7 March 2005).

Report of the Secretary-General pursuant to paragraph 30 of resolution 1546 (2004), UN Doc. S/2005/373 (7 June 2005)

United Nations Assistance Mission in Iraq, Human Rights Office, 'Human Rights Report, 1 July – 31 August 2005'.[7]

United Nations Assistance Mission in Iraq, Human Rights Office, 'Human Rights Report, 1 September – 31 October 2005'.

Report of the Secretary-General pursuant to paragraph 30 of resolution 1546 (2004), UN Doc. S/2005/585 (7 September 2005).

United Nations Assistance Mission in Iraq, Human Rights Office, 'Human Rights Report, 1 November – 31 December 2005'.

United Nations Assistance Mission in Iraq, Human Rights Office, 'Human Rights Report, 1 January – 28 February 2006'.

Nepal

Official Documents

OHCHR Field Operation in Nepal (April 2005).

Agreement on the establishment of an Office of the United Nations High Commissioner for Human Rights in Nepal (10 April 2005).[8]

Office of the High Commissioner for Human Rights, Nepal, Attacks against public transportation in Chitwan and Kabhrepalanchok Districts, Investigation Report (18 August 2005).

Report of the United Nations High Commissioner for Human Rights on the human rights situation and the activities of her Office, including technical cooperation, in Nepal, UN Doc. A/60/359 (16 September 2005).

Office of the High Commissioner for Human Rights, Nepal, Investigations of violations of international humanitarian law in the context of attacks and clashes between the Communist Party of Nepal (Maoist) and Government Security Forces, Findings and Recommendations (January – March 2006).

Report of the United Nations High Commissioner for Human Rights on the human rights situation and the activities of her Office, including technical cooperation, in Nepal, UN Doc. E/CN.4/2006/17 (16 February 2006).

Office of the High Commissioner for Human Rights, Nepal, Report of investigation into arbitrary detention, torture and disappearances at Maharajgunj RNA barracks, Kathmandu, in 2003 – 2004 (26 May 2006).

---

[7]   All United Nations Assistance Mission in Iraq 'Human Rights Reports' available at http://www.uniraq.org/aboutus/HR.asp.

[8]   Agreement available at http://nepal.ohchr.org/mandate.htm.

Uganda

Official Documents

> OHCHR Field Operation in Uganda (June 2005).

Agreement on the establishment of an Office of the United Nations High Commissioner for Human Rights in Uganda (June 2005).
Report on the work of the Office of the High Commissioner for Human Rights in Uganda, Annex to UN Doc. E/CN.4/2006/10/Add.2 (2 March 2006).

Human Rights Field Operations Generally

Official Documents

Comprehensive review of the whole question of peacekeeping operations in all their respects: Report of the panel on UN peace operations, UN Doc. A/55/305-S/2000/809 (21 August 2000).
Report of the United Nations High Commissioner for Human Rights: Building a partnership for human rights, UN Doc. E/CN.4/1997/98 (24 February 1997).
Report of the United Nations High Commissioner for Human Rights, UN Doc. A/54/36(Supp) (1 January 1999).
Report of the Secretary-General, Advisory services and technical cooperation in human rights, UN Doc. E/CN.4/1999/99 (5 February 1999).
OHCHR field presences/operations, Annex II to UN Doc. E/CN.4/1999/9 (2 March 1999).
Report of the United Nations High Commissioner for Human Rights, UN Doc. A/59/36 (4 October 2004).
OSCE, Survey of Long-Term Missions and Other OSCE Field Activities, OSCE Conflict Prevention Centre, SEC.INF/33/05 (26 August 2005).

Commentary

Amnesty International, *Peace-keeping and Human Rights* (London, January 1994).
Clapham, A. and Martin, F., 'Peacekeeping and Human Rights in Africa and Europe', in *Honoring Human Rights*.
Gaer, F., 'Human Rights NGOs in UN Peace Operations', *International Peacekeeping* vol. 10, no. 1 (2003).
Gallagher, A., 'United Nations Human Rights Field Operations', in R. Hanski and M. Suski (eds), *An Introduction to the International Protection of Human Rights* (Turku: Institute for Human Rights, Åbo Akademi, 1997).
García-Sayán, D., 'Human Rights and Peacekeeping Operations', *University of Richmond Law Review* vol. 29 (1994–1995).

Hannum, H., 'Human Rights in Conflict Resolution: The Role of the Office of the High Commissioner for Human Rights in UN Peacemaking and Peacebuilding', *Human Rights Quarterly* vol. 28, no. 1 (2006).

Human Rights Watch, *The Lost Agenda: Human Rights and UN Field Operations* (June 1993).

International Policy Institute, *A Case for Change: A Review of Peace Operations* (King's College London, 2003).

Katayanagi, M., *Human Rights Functions of United Nations Peacekeeping Operations* (The Hague: Kluwer Law International, 2002).

Kenny, K., *Human Rights Field Operations* (Ireland: Human Rights Trust, 2000).

Kenny, K., 'When Needs Are Rights: An Overview of UN Efforts to Integrate Human Rights in Humanitarian Action', Occasional Paper 38 (Providence: Watson Institute, 2000).

Little, D., 'Protecting Human Rights During and After Conflict: The Role of the United Nations', *Tulsa Journal of Comparative and International Law* vol. 4 (Fall 1996).

Martin, I., 'Human Rights Monitoring and Institution-Building in Post-Conflict Societies: The Role of Human Rights Field Operations', paper delivered to USAID Conference, 'Promoting Democracy, Human Rights and Reintegration', October 30–31, 1997.

Martin, I., 'A New Frontier: The Early Experience and Future of International Human Rights Field Operations', *Netherlands Quarterly of Human Rights* vol. 16, no. 2 (1998).

O'Flaherty, M. 'Future Protection of Human Rights in Post-Conflict Societies: the Role of the United Nations', *Human Rights Law Review* vol. 3, no. 1 (2003).

O'Flaherty, M. 'Human Rights Monitoring and Armed Conflict, Challenges for the UN', *Disarmament Forum* no. 3 (2004).

OHCHR Staff, 'Protection in the Field: Human Rights Perspectives', in *Human Rights Protection in the Field.*

Select Bibliography

Acuna, T., *The United Nations Mission in El Salvador: A Humanitarian Law Perspective* (The Hague: Kluwer Law International, 1995).

Adams, B., 'UN Human Rights Work in Cambodia: Efforts to Preserve the Jewel in the Peacekeeping Crown', in A. Henkin (ed.), *Honoring Human Rights – From Peace to Justice: Recommendations to the International Community* (Washington, DC: Aspen Institute, 1998).

Aeschlimann, A., 'Protection of Detainees: ICRC Action Behind Bars', *International Review of the Red Cross* vol. 87, no. 857 (2005).

Alfredsson, G. (ed.), *International Human Rights Monitoring Mechanisms: Essays in Honour of Jakob Th. Möller* (The Hague: Martinus Nijhoff, 2001).

Almeida, M. (ed.), *Nationbuilding in East Timor* (Canadian Peacekeeping Press 2001).

Alston, P., *The United Nations and Human Rights* (Oxford: Clarendon Press, 1992).

Alston, P. (ed.), *Non-State Actors and Human Right* (Oxford: Oxford University Press, 2005).

Amerasinghe, C. F., *Principles of the Institutional Law of International Organizations* (Cambridge: Cambridge University Press, 2005).

Anderson, M. B., *Do No Harm: Supporting Local Capacities for Peace Through Aid* (Cambridge: Local Capacities for Peace Project, Collaborative for Development Action, 1996).

Anderson, M. B., *Do No Harm: How Aid can Support Peace – or War* (Boulder: Lynne Rienner, 1998).

Annan, K., 'UN Peacekeeping Operations and Cooperation with NATO', *NATO Review* 5 (1993), pp. 3–7.

Annan, K., 'Strengthening United Nations Action in the Field of Human Rights: Prospects and Priorities', *Harvard Human Rights Journal* vol. 10 (1997), 1–9.

Anonymous, 'Human Rights in Peace Negotiations', *Human Rights Quarterly* vol. 18, no. 2 (1996), 249–258.

Arbour, L., *The OHCHR Plan of Action: Protection and Empowerment* (Geneva: OHCHR, May 2005).

Asher, J., *The Right to Health: A Resource Manual for NGOs* (London: Commonwealth Medical Trust, 2004).

Ashley, D., 'The Nature and Causes of Human Rights Violations in Battambang Province', in S. Heder and J. Ledgerwood (eds), *Propaganda, Politics, and Violence in Cambodia, Democratic Transition under United Nations Peacekeeping*, (London: M. E. Sharpe, 1996).

Aust, A., *Modern Treaty Law and Practice* (Cambridge: Cambridge University Press, 2000).

Bar-Yaacov, N., 'Diplomacy and Human Rights: The Role of Human Rights on Conflict Resolution in El Salvador and Haiti', *Fletcher Forum of World Affairs* vol. 19, no. 2 (1995).

Bayefsky, A. F., *The UN Human Rights Treaty System: Universality at the Crossroads* (The Hague: Kluwer Law International, 2001).

Beauchamp, T. L. *et al.* (eds), *Principles of Biomedical Ethics*, 5th edn (Oxford: Oxford University Press, 2001).

Bell, C., *Peace Agreements and Human Rights* (Oxford: Oxford University Press, 2000).

Bell, D. A., J. H Carens, 'The Ethical Dilemmas of Humanitarian and Human Rights NGOs: Reflections on a Dialogue between Practitioners and Theorists', *Human Rights Quarterly* vol. 26, no. 2 (1996), 300–329.

Benedek, W., *et al.* (eds), *Human Rights in Bosnia and Herzegovina after Dayton: From Theory to Practice* (The Hague: Kluwer Law International, 1999).

Betts, W. *et al.*, 'The Post-Conflict Transitional Administration of Kosovo and the Lessons-Learned in Efforts to Establish a Judiciary and Rule of Law', *Michigan Journal of International Law* vol. 22 (2001), 371–389.

Binder, J., *The Human Dimension of the OSCE: From Recommendation to Implementation* (Wien: Studienreihe des Ludwig Boltzmann Instituts fur Menschenrechte, 2001).

Bloed, A. (ed.), *Monitoring Human Rights in Europe: Comparing International Procedures and Mechanisms* (Dordrecht: Martinus Nijhoff, 1993).

Bosi, T. D., 'Post-Conflict Reconstruction: The United Nations' Involvement in Afghanistan', *New York Law School Journal of Human Rights* vol. 19, no. 4/6 (2003).

Bothe, M. *et al.* (eds), *The OSCE in the Maintenance of Peace and Security* (The Hague: Kluwer Law International, 1997).

Boutros-Ghali, B., 'Human Rights: The Common Language of Humanity', in *World Conference on Human Rights: The Vienna Declaration and Programme of Action* (New York: United Nations, 1993).

Boutros-Ghali, B., 'Introduction', The United Nations Blue Book Series vol. IV, *The United Nations and El Salvador 1990–1995* (New York: Department of Public Information, United Nations, 1995).

Bonard, P., *Modes of Action Used by Humanitarian Players: Criteria for Operational Complementarity* (Geneva: ICRC, 1999).

Bongiorno, C., 'A Culture of Impunity: Applying International Human Rights Law to the United Nations in East Timor', *Columbia Human Rights Law Review* vol. 33, no. 3 (2002).

Bowden, M., 'Foreword', in *The Humanitarian Decade* vol. 2 (New York: OCHA, 2004).

Bracken, P. J. *et al.* (eds), *Rethinking the Trauma of War* (New York: Free Association Books, 1998).

Brand, M., 'Effective Human Rights Protection When the UN Becomes the State: lessons from UNMIK', in N. D. White and Klaasen, D. (eds), *The UN, Human Rights and Post-Conflict Situations* (Manchester: Manchester University Press, 2005).

Brody, R., 'The United Nations and Human Rights in El Salvador's "Negotiated Revolution"', *Harvard Human Rights Journal* vol. 8 (1995).

Burg, S. L. *et al.* (eds), *The War in Bosnia Herzegovina: Ethnic Conflict and International Intervention* (London: M. E. Sharpe, 2000).

Burgerman, S. D., 'Building the Peace by Mandating Reform: United Nations-Mediated Human Rights Agreements in El Salvador and Guatemala', *Latin American Perspectives* vol. 27, no. 3 (2000).

Cain, K. L., 'The Rape of Dinah: Human Rights, Civil War in Liberia, and Evil Triumphant', *Human Rights Quarterly* vol. 21, no. 2 (1999).

Campbell, C., 'Peace and the Laws of War: The Role of International Humanitarian Law in the Post-Conflict Environment', *International Review of the Red Cross* no. 839 (2000), 627–651.

Carment, D. *et al.* (eds), *Conflict Prevention: Path to Peace or Grand Illusion* (Tokyo: United Nations University, 2003).

Caverzascio, S. G. (ed.), *Strengthening Protection in War: A Search for Professional Standards* (Geneva: ICRC, 2001).

Caverzascio, S. G., *Addressing the Needs of Women Affected by Armed Conflicts: An ICRC Guidance Document* (Geneva: ICRC, 2004).

Chesterman, S., *Tiptoeing Through Afghanistan: The Future of UN State-Building* (International Peace Academy, September 2002).

Chesterman, S. (ed.), *Civilians in War* (Boulder: Lynne Rienner, 2001).

Chesterman, S., *You, the People: The United Nations, Transitional Administration, and State Building* (Oxford: Oxford University Press, 2005).

Chopra, J., *The United Nations Authority in Cambodia*, Occasional Paper 15 (Providence: Watson Institute for International Studies, 1996).

Clapham, A. and M. Henry, 'Peacekeeping and Human Rights in Africa and Europe', in A. Henkin, (ed.) *Honoring Human Rights* (The Hague: Kluwer Law International, 2000).

Clapham, A. and F. Martin 'Smaller Missions Bigger Problems', in A. Henkin (ed.), *Honoring Human Rights: From Peace to Justice* (The Hague: Kluwer Law International, 2000).

Clarance, W., 'The Human Rights Field Operation in Rwanda: Protective Practice Evolves on the Ground', *International Peacekeeping* vol. 2, no. 3 (1995).

Clarance, W., 'Field Strategy for the Protection of Human Rights', *International Journal of Refugee Law* vol. 9, no. 2 (1997).

Cohen, D., 'Seeking Justice on the Cheap: Is the East Timor Tribunal Really a Model for the Future?' *Asia Pacific Issues, Analysis from the East-West Centre* 61 (August 2002).

Cohen, D., *Intended to Fail: The Trials before the Ad Hoc Human Rights Court in Jakarta* (New York: International Center for Transitional Justice, 2003).

Cordone, C., 'Bosnia and Herzegovina: The Creeping Protectorate' in A. Henkin (ed.), *Honoring Human Rights under International Mandates: Lessons from Bosnia, Kosovo, and East Timor* (Washington, DC: Aspen Institute, 2003).

Crawford, J. *et al.* (eds), *The Future of UN Human Rights Treaty Monitoring* (Cambridge: Cambridge University Press, 2000).

Criswell, D., 'Durable Consent and a Strong Transitional Peacekeeping Plan: The Success of UNTAET in Light of the Lessons Learned in Cambodia', *Pacific Rim Law and Policy Journal* (June 2002).

de Beco, G., 'Compliance with International Humanitarian Law by Non-State Actors', *Journal of International Law of Peace and Armed Conflict* vol. 18 (2005), 190–199.

de Roover, C., *To Serve and Protect: Human Rights and Humanitarian Law for Police and Security Force* (Geneva: ICRC, 1998).

de Torrente, N., 'Humanitarian Action Under Attack: Reflections on the Iraq War', *Harvard Human Rights Journal* vol. 17 (2004), 1–30.

de Waal, A., *Famine Crimes: Politics & the Disaster Relief Industry in Africa* (Oxford: James Currey, 1997).

Danieli, Y. *et al.* (eds), *The Universal Declaration of Human Rights: Fifty Years and Beyond* (New York: Baywood Publishing, 1998).

Darcy, J., *Human Rights and International Legal Standards: What do Relief Workers Need to Know* (London: Relief and Rehabilitation Network, 1997).

Darrow, M., T. Amparo, 'Power, Capture and Conflict: A Call for Human Rights Accountability in Development Cooperation', *Human Rights Quarterly* vol. 27, no. 2 (2005), 471–538.

Deng, F., *Internally Displaced Persons Compilation and Analysis of Legal Norms* (Geneva: OHCHR, 1998).

Devereux, A., 'Searching for Clarity: A Case Study of UNTAET's Application of International Human Rights Norms', in N. D. White and D. Klaasen (eds), *The UN, Human Rights and Post-conflict Situations* (Manchester: Manchester University Press, 2005).

Donini, A. (ed.), *Nation-Building Unravelled?: Aid, Peace and Justice in Afghanistan* (Bloomfield: Kumarian Press, 2003).

Donini, A., 'The Forest and the Trees: The Evolving Nature of Coordination', in *The Humanitarian Decade* vol. 2 (New York: OCHA, 2004).

Doyle, M., *UN Peacekeeping in Cambodia: UNTAC's Civil Mandate* (Boulder: Lynne Rienner, 1995).

Doyle, M. *et al.* (eds), *Keeping the Peace: Multi-Dimensional UN Operations in Cambodia and El Salvador* (Cambridge: Cambridge University Press, 1997).

Duffy, T., 'UNTAC's Mission in Cambodia: Prospects for Democracy and Human Rights', *Asian Affairs* vol. 20 (Winter 1994).

Dungel, J., 'A Right to Humanitarian Assistance in Internal Armed Conflicts Respecting Sovereignty, Neutrality and Legitimacy: Practical Proposals to Practical Problems', *Journal of Humanitarian Assistance* (2004).

Eide, E. B. *et al.* (eds), 'Report on Integrated Missions: Practical Perspectives and Recommendations', in *Independent Study for the Expanded UN ECHA Core Group* (New York: UN ECHA, 2005).

Feller, E. *et al.* (eds), *Refugee Protection in International Law* (Cambridge: Cambridge University Press, 2003).

Field, R., 'Mission Impossible', *Counsel* (October 1998).

Forsythe, D. F., 'The United Nations and Human Rights', *Political Science Quarterly* vol. 100 (1985), 249–269.

Franco, L. and Kotler, J., 'Combining Institution Building and Human Rights Verification in Guatemala: The Challenge of Buying in Without Selling Out', in A. Henkin (ed.), *Honoring Human Rights: From Peace to Justice* (The Hague: Kluwer Law International, 2000).

Frohardt, M. (ed.), *Protecting Human Rights: The Challenge to Humanitarian Organisations*, Occasional Paper No. 35 (Providence: Watson Institute for International Studies, 1999).

Gaer, F., 'Human Rights NGOs in UN Peace Operations', *International Peacekeeping* vol. 10, no. 1 (2003).

Gallagher, A., 'United Nations Human Rights Field Operations', in R. Hanski and M. Suski (eds), *An Introduction to the International Protection of Human Rights* (Turku: Institute for Human Rights, Åbo Akademi, 1997).

García-Sayán, D., 'Human Rights and Peacekeeping Operations', *University of Richmond Law Review* vol. 29 (1994–1995).

García-Sayán, D., 'The Experience of ONUSAL in El Salvador', in A. Henkin (ed.), *Honoring Human Rights* (The Hague: Kluwer Law International, 2000).

Gavigan P., 'Proposal for a Human Rights Mandate for an International Post-Conflict Mission to the Former Yugoslavia Republic of Macedonia', in A. Henkin (ed.), *Honoring Human Rights under International Mandates: Lessons from Bosnia, Kosovo, and East Timor* (Washington, DC: Aspen Institute, 2003).

Gert, B., *Morality: A New Justification of the Moral Rules* (Oxford: Oxford University Press, 1988).

Gert, B. *et al.* (eds), *A Return to Fundamentals* (Oxford: Oxford University Press, 1997).

Goodwin-Gill, G. S., *The Refugee in International Law*, 2nd edn (Oxford: Clarendon Paperbacks, 1996).

Goodwin-Gill, G. S., 'Refugee Identity and Protection's Fading Prospect', in F. Nicholson (ed.), *Refugee Rights and Realities* (Cambridge: Cambridge University Press, 1999).

Gorlick, B., 'Refugee Protection in Troubled Times', in N. Steiner *et al.* (eds), *Problems of Protection* (London: Routledge, 2003).

Grahl-Madsen, A., *Commentary on the Refugee Convention 1951* (Geneva: UNHCR, 1997).

Granderson, C., 'Institutionalizing Peace: The Haiti Experience', in A. Henkin (ed.), *Honoring Human Rights* (The Hague: Kluwer Law International, 2000).

Hannum, H., 'Human Rights in Conflict Resolution: The Role of the Office of the High Commissioner for Human Rights in UN Peacemaking and Peacebuilding', *Human Rights Quarterly* vol. 28, no. 1 (2006).

Hanski, R. *et al.* (eds), *An Introduction to the International Protection of Human Rights* (Turku: Institute for Human Rights, Åbo Akademi University, 1997).

Harrof-Tavel, M., 'Action Taken by the International Committee of the Red Cross in Situations of Internal Violence', *International Review of the Red Cross* no. 294 (1993).

Hathaway, J., *The Law of Refugee Status* (Toronto: Butterworths, 1991).

Hayner, P. B., *Unspeakable Truths: Confronting State Terror and Atrocity* (New York: Routledge, 2001).

Heininger, J., *Peacekeeping in Transition: The United Nations in Cambodia* (New York: Twentieth Century Foundation, 1994).

Heintze, H. J., 'On the Relationship between Human Rights Law Protection and International Humanitarian Law', *International Review of the Red Cross* no. 856 (2004), 789–814.

Henkin, A. *Honoring Human Rights and Keeping the Peace: Lessons from El Salvador, cambodia and Haiti* (Washington, DC: Aspen Institute, 1995).

Henkin, A. *Honoring Human Rights – From Peace to Justice: Recommendations to the International Community* (Washington, DC: Aspen Institute, 1998).

Henkin, A. (ed.), *Honoring Human Rights* (The Hague: Kluwer Law International, 2000).

Henkin, A. (ed.), *Honoring Human Rights under International Mandates: Lessons from Bosnia, Kosovo, and East Timor* (Washington, DC: Aspen Institute, 2003).

Heyster, F., *Médecins Sans Frontières Temoignage: From Public Abstinence to Mission Statement* (December 1999).

Holiday, D. and Stanley, W., 'Peace Mission Strategy and Domestic Actors: UN Mediation, Verification and Institution-building in El Salvador', *International Peacekeeping* vol. 4, no. 2 (1997).

Honwana, A. *et al.* (eds), *Makers and Breakers: Children and Youth in Postcolonial Africa* (Trenton: Africa World Press, 2005).

Howland, T., 'The Killing of United Nations Human Rights Workers: A Call for an Appropriate UN Response', *Human Rights Tribune* vol. 5, nos. 1 and 2 (1998).

Howland, T., 'Mirage, Magic or Mixed Bag? The United Nations High Commissioner for Human Rights' Field Operation in Rwanda', *Human Rights Quarterly* vol. 21, no. 1 (1999).

Howland, T., 'UN Human Rights Field Presences as Proactive Instruments of Peace and Social Change: Lessons from Angola', *Human Rights Quarterly* vol. 26, no. 1 (2004), 1–28.

Hughes, C., 'UNTAC in Cambodia: The Impact on Human Rights', Occasional Paper Issue 92 (Institute of Southeast Asian Studies, 1996).

Hughes, C., 'Human Rights out of Context (or, Translating the Universal Declaration into Khmer)', in N. D. White and D. Klaasen (eds), *The UN, Human Rights and Post-conflict Situations* (Manchester: Manchester University Press, 2005).

Hunter, D. H. *et al.* (eds), *Opening Space for Democracy: Third-Party Nonviolent Intervention, Curriculum and Trainers Manual* (Philadelphia: Training for Change, 2004).

Ishizuka, K., 'Peacekeeping in East Timor: The Experience of UNMISET', *International Peacekeeping* vol. 10, no. 3 (2003).

Jarvis Thomson, J., *The Realm of Rights* (Harvard: Harvard University Press, 1990).

Johnstone, I., *Rights and Reconciliation: UN Strategies in El Salvador* (Boulder: Lynne Rienner, 1995).

Jonas, H., *The Imperative of Responsibility: In Search of an Ethics for the Technological Age* (Chicago: University of Chicago Press, 1984).

Jonas, N., 'UNMIK and the Ombudsperson Institution in Kosovo: Human Rights Protection in a UN Surrogate State', *Netherlands Quarterly of Human Rights* vol. 22, no. 3 (2004).

Jones, S., 'Human Rights and Peacekeeping in East Timor', in A Henkin. (ed.), *Honoring Human Rights under International Mandates: Lessons from Bosnia, Kosovo, and East Timor* (Washington, DC: Aspen Institute, 2003).

Jones, S., 'East Timor: The Troubled Path to Independence', in A. Henkin (ed.), *Honoring Human Rights under International Mandates: Lessons from Bosnia, Kosovo, and East Timor* (Washington, DC: Aspen Institute, 2003).

Jonsson, U., *Human Rights Approaches to Development Programming* (Nairobi: UNICEF, 2003).

Jonsson, U., *Human Rights Approach to Development Programming* (New York: UNICEF, 2004).

Juma, L., 'The Human Rights Approach to Peace in Sierra Leone: The Analysis of the Peace Process and Human Rights Enforcement in a Civil War Situation', *Denver Journal of International Law and Policy* vol. 30, no. 3 (2003).

Kälin, W., 'Supervising the 1951 Convention Relation to the Status of Refugees: Article 35 and Beyond', in E. Feller *et al.* (eds), *Refugee Protection in International Law* (Cambridge: Cambridge University Press, 2003).

Katayanagi, M., *Human Rights Functions of United Nations Peacekeeping Operations*, International Studies in Human Rights vol. 73 (The Hague: Kluwer Law International, 2002).

Kelsall, T., 'Truth, Lies, Ritual: Preliminary Reflections on the Truth and Reconciliation Commission in Sierra Leone', *Human Rights Quarterly* vol. 27, no. 2 (2005), 361–391.

Kennedy, D., 'International Refugee Protection', *Human Rights Quarterly* vol. 8, no. 1 (1985).

Kennedy, D., 'Spring Break', *Texas Law Review* vol. 63 (1985), 1377.

Kenny, K., 'Formal and Informal Innovations in the UN Protection of Human Rights: The Special Rapporteur on the Former Yugoslavia', *Austrian Journal of Public and International Law* vol. 48 (1995).

Kenny, K., *Human Rights Field Operations* (Ireland: Human Rights Trust, 2000).

Kenny, K., 'When Needs are Rights: An Overview of UN Efforts to Integrate Human Rights in Humanitarian Action', Occasional Paper 38 (Providence: Watson Institute for International Studies, 2000).

Kenny, K., 'UN Accountability for its Human Rights Impact: Implementation through Participation', in N. D. White and D. Klaasen (eds), *The UN, Human Rights and Post-conflict Situations* (Manchester: Manchester University Press, 2005).

Khouri-Padova, L., 'Haiti: Lessons Learn(ed)', *Discussion Paper* (DPKO Best Practices Unit, March 2004).

Kirby, M., 'Human Rights, the United Nations and Cambodia', *Australian Quarterly* vol. 67, no. 4 (1995).

Kircher, I., 'The Human Rights Work of the United Nations Observer Mission in El Salvador', *Netherlands Quarterly of Human Rights* vol. 10, no. 3 (1992).

Klabbers, J., 'Redemption Song? Human Rights Versus Community-building in East Timor', *Leiden Journal of International Law* vol. 16, no. 2 (2003).

Kondoch, B., 'The United Nations Administration of East Timor', *Journal of Conflict and Security Law* vol. 6, no. 2 (2001), 245–265.

Krug, H. N., 'Genocide in Rwanda: Lessons learned and future challenges to the UN Human Rights System', *Nordic Journal of International Law* vol. 67, no. 2 (1998).

Landgren, K., 'The Protective Environment: Development Support for Child Protection', *Human Rights Quarterly* vol. 27, no. 1 (2005), 214–248.

Lee, C. M. and Metrikas, M., 'Holding a Fragile Peace: The Military and Civilian Components of UNTAC', in M. Doyle *et al.* (eds), *Keeping the Peace: Multi-Dimensional UN Operations in Cambodia and El Salvador* (Cambridge: Cambridge University Press, 1997).

Lee, R. S., 'United Nations Peacekeeping: Development and Prospects', *Cornell International Law Journal* vol. 28 (1995), 619–630.

Line, M., 'Managing for Sustainable Human Rights Protection: International Missions in the Peace Processes of Bosnia and Herzegovina and Guatemala', in N. D. White and D. Klaasen (eds) *The UN, Human Rights and Post-conflict Situations* (Manchester: Manchester University Press, 2005).

Little, D., 'Protecting Human Rights During and After Conflict: The Role of the United Nations', *Tulsa Journal of Comparative and International Law* vol. 4 (Fall, 1996).

Louise, C., 'MINUGUA's Peace-building Mandate in Western Guatemala', *International Peacekeeping* vol. 4, no. 2 (1997).

Lutz, E. *et al.*, 'Human Rights and Conflict Resolution from the Practitioners' Perspective', *The Fletcher Forum of World Affairs* vol. 27, no. 1 (2003).

McNamara, D., 'UN Human Rights Activities in Cambodia: An Evaluation', in A. Henkin (ed.), *Honoring Human Rights* (The Hague: Kluwer Law International, 2000).

Mackintosh, K., 'How Far Can Humanitarian Organisations Control Co-operation with International Tribunals?', *Journal of Humanitarian Assistance* (May 2005).

Machel, G., *The Impact of Armed Conflict on Children: A Review of Progress since the 1996 United Nations Report on the Impact of Armed Conflict on Children* (London: Hurst & Co., 2001).

Macrae, J. *et al.* (eds), 'Humanitarian Assistance and the "Global War on Terror": A Review of the Trends and Issues', *HPG Report* no. 14 (London: Overseas Development Institute, July 2003).

Macrae, J., 'Defining the Boundaries: International Security and Humanitarian Engagement in the post Cold War World', in *The Humanitarian Decade* vol. 2 (New York: OCHA, 2004).

Maguire, R. *et al.*, *Haiti Held Hostage: International Responses to the Quest for Nationhood 1986–1996*, Occasional Paper 23 (Providence: Watson Institute for International Studies, 1996).

Maher, D. *et al.* (eds), *Guidelines for the Control of Tuberculosis in Prison* (Geneva: World Health Organization, 1998).

Mahony, L., 'Unarmed Monitoring and Human Rights Field Presences: Civilian Protection and Conflict Protection', *The Journal of Humanitarian Assistance* (2003).

Mahony, L., *Proactive Presence: Field Strategies for Civilian Protection* (Geneva: Centre for Humanitarian Dialogue, 2006).

Mancini-Griffoli, D. *et al.* (eds), *Humanitarian Negotiation: A Handbook for Securing Access, Assistance and Protection for Civilians in Armed Conflict* (Geneva: Centre for Humanitarian Dialogue, 2004).

Mancini-Griffoli, D. *et al.* (eds), *Humanitarian Negotiation: A Handbook for Securing Access, Assistance and Protection for Civilians in Armed Conflict* (London: RUSI, 2005).

Manton, E., 'The OSCE Human Dimension Process and the Process of Customary International Law Formation', IFSH (ed.), *OSCE Yearbook 2005* (Baden-Baden: Institute for Peace Research and Security Policy at the University of Hamburg, 2006).

Marshall, D., S. Inglis, 'The Disempowerment of Human Rights-Based Justice in the United Nations Mission in Kosovo', *Harvard Human Rights Journal* vol. 16 (2003).

Martin, I., 'Paper versus Steel: The First Phase of the International Civilian Mission in Haiti', in A. Henkin (ed.), *Honoring Human Rights* (The Hague: Kluwer Law International, 2000).

Martin, I., 'After Genocide: The UN Human Rights Field Operation in Rwanda', in A. Henkin (ed.), *Honoring Human Rights* (The Hague: Kluwer Law International, 2000).

Martin, I., 'A New Frontier: The Early Experience and Future of International Human Rights Field Operations', *Netherlands Quarterly of Human Rights* vol. 16, no. 2 (1998).

Martin, I., *Self-Determination in East Timor: The United Nations, the Ballot, and International Intervention* (Boulder: Lynne Rienner, 2001).

Matheson, M. J., 'United Nations Governance of Post-conflict Societies', *American Journal of International Law* vol. 95 (2001), 76–85.

Mertus, J., 'Improving International Peacebuilding Efforts: The Example of Human Rights Culture in Kosovo', *Global Governance* vol. 10, no. 3 (2004).

Minear, L., *Helping People in an Age of Conflict: Toward a New Professionalism in U.S. Voluntary Humanitarian Assistance* (Washington, DC: Interaction, 1988).

Minear, L., 'The Political Context of Humanitarian Action: Some Reflections', in *The Humanitarian Decade* vol. 2 (New York: OCHA, 2004).

Minear, L. *et al.*, 'Humanitarian Action in the Former Yugoslavia: The UN's Role, 1991–1993', Occasional Paper 18 (Providence: Watson Institute for International Studies, 1994).

Minow, M., 'The Hope for Healing: What Can Truth Commissions Do?' R. I. Robert (ed.), *Truth v. Justice: The Morality of Truth Commissions* (Princeton: Princeton University Press, 2001).

Moir, L., *The Law of Internal Armed Conflict* (Cambridge: Cambridge University Press, 2002).

Mokhiber, C. G., 'The United Nations Programme of Technical Cooperation in the Field of Human Rights' in G. Alfredsson (ed.), *International Human Rights Monitoring Mechanisms: Essays in Honour of Jakob Th. Möller* (The Hague: Martinus Nijhoff, 2001).

Moser-Phuangsuwan, Y. *et al.* (eds), *Nonviolent Intervention Across Borders: A Recurrent Vision* (Honolulu: University of Hawaii, 2000).

Nembrini, P. G., *Water, Sanitation, Hygiene and Habitat in Prisons* (Geneva: ICRC, 2005).

Newcomb Hohfeld, W., 'Some Fundamental Legal Conceptions as Applied in Judicial Reasoning', *Yale Law Journal* vol. 23 (1913).

Newman-Williams, M., 'How Things Changed', *UN Chronicle* (Summer 1999).

Nicholson, F. (ed.), *Refugee Rights and Realities* (Cambridge: Cambridge University Press, 1999).

Niland, N., 'The Marginalization of Human Rights in Afghanistan', in A. Donini (ed.), *Nation-Building Unraveled?: Aid, Peace and Justice in Afghanistan* (Bloomfield: Kumarian Press, 2003).

Niland, N., 'Rights, Rhetoric and Reality: A Snapshot from Afghanistan', in N. D. White and D. Klaasen (eds), *The UN, Human Rights and Post-conflict Situations* (Manchester: Manchester University Press, 2005).

Nowak, M., 'Is Bosnia and Herzegovina Ready For Membership in the Council of Europe?' *Human Rights Law Journal* vol. 20 (1999), 285.

Nowak, M., 'A Human Rights Approach to Poverty', in M. Scheinen *et al.* (eds), *Human Rights in Development, 8 Yearbook 2002* (Leiden: Martinus Nijhof, 2002).

Nowak, M., 'Lessons for the International Human Rights Regime from the Yugoslav Experience', in *Collected Courses of the Academy of European Law, Volume VIII/2* (The Hague: Kluwer Law International, 2000).

Nowak, M., *Introduction to the International Human Rights Regime* (Leiden: Martinus Nijhoff, 2003).

Nowrojee, B., 'Joining Forces: United Nations and Regional Peacekeeping: Lessons from Liberia', *Harvard Human Rights Journal* vol. 8 (1995).

O'Brien, P., 'Politicized humanitarianism: A response to Nicholas de Torrente', *Harvard Human Rights Journal* vol. 17 (2004), 31–40.

O'Flaherty, M., 'Treaty Bodies Responding to States of Emergency', in J. Crawford *et al.* (eds), *The Future of UN Human Rights Treaty Monitoring* (Cambridge: Cambridge University Press, 2000).

O'Flaherty, M., 'Future Protection of Human Rights in Post-conflict Societies: The Role of the United Nations', *Human Rights Law Review* vol. 3, no. 1 (2003).

O'Flaherty, M., 'Human Rights Monitoring and Armed Conflict: Challenges for the UN', *Disarmament Forum* no. 3 (2004).

O'Flaherty, M., 'Sierra Leone's Peace Process: The Role of the Human Rights Community', *Human Rights Quarterly* vol. 26, no. 1 (2004).

O'Flaherty, M., 'Future Protection of Human Rights in Post-Conflict Societies', in N. D. White and D. Klaasen (eds), *The UN, Human Rights and Post-conflict Situations* (Manchester: Manchester University Press, 2005).

O'Flaherty, M., 'We Are Failing the Victims of War', in B. G. Ramcharan (ed.), *Human Rights Protection in the Field, International Studies in Human Rights* vol. 87 (Leiden: Martinus Nijhoff, 2006).

O'Flaherty, M. and G. Gisvold (eds), *Post-war Protection of Human Rights in Bosnia and Herzegovina* (The Hague: Martinus Nijhoff, 1998).

O'Neill, W. G., 'Human Rights Monitoring vs. Political Expediency: The Experience of the OAS/UN Mission in Haiti', *Harvard Human Rights Journal* vol. 8 (1995).

O'Neill, W. G., 'A Humanitarian Practitioner's Guide to International Human Rights Law', Occasional Paper No. 34 (Providence: Watson Institute for International Studies, 1999).

O'Neill, W. G., *Kosovo: An Unfinished Peace* (Boulder: Lynne Rienner, 2001).

O'Neill, W. G., 'Gaining Compliance without Force: Human Rights Field Operations', in S. Chesterman (ed.), *Civilians in War* (Boulder: Lynne Rienner, 2001).

O'Neill, W. G., 'Kosovo: Unexpected Barriers to Building Peace and Security', in A. Henkin (ed.), *Honoring Human Rights under International Mandates: Lessons from Bosnia, Kosovo, and East Timor* (Washington, DC: Aspen Institute, 2003).

O'Neill, W. G., 'Human Rights Field Operations: A New Protection Tool', in B. G. Ramcharan (ed.), *Human Rights Protection in the Field*, International Studies in Human Rights vol. 87 (Leiden: Martinus Nijhoff, 2006).

Ocran, T. M., 'How Blessed Were the UN Peacekeepers in Former Yugoslavia?: The Involvement of UNPROFOR and Other UN Bodies in Humanitarian Activities and Human Rights Issues in Croatia 1992–1996', *Wisconsin International Law Journal*, vol. 18, no. 1 (2000).

Oraa, J., *Human Rights in States of Emergency* (Oxford: Clarendon Press, 2004).

Orakhelashvili, A., 'The Post-War Settlement in Iraq: The UN Security Council Resolution 1483 (2003) and General International Law', *Journal of Conflict and Security Law* vol. 8 (2003), 307–314.

Pajic, Z., 'A Critical Appraisal of Human Rights Provisions of the Dayton Constitution of Bosnia and Herzegovina', *Human Rights Quarterly* vol. 20, no. 1 (1998), 125.

Paul, D., *Protection in Practice: Field-level strategies for Protecting Civilians from Deliberate Harm* (London: Overseas Development Institute, Humanitarian Relief Network, 1999).

Rackley, E. B., 'Armed Violence against Women in Burundi', *Humanitarian Exchange* no. 31 (2005), 34–36.

Ramcharan, B. G. (ed.), *International Law and Fact-Finding in the Field of Human Rights* (Leiden: Martinus Nijhoff, 1982).

Ramcharan, B. G., 'Strategies for the International Protection of Human Rights in the 1990s', *Human Rights Quarterly* vol. 13, no. 2 (1991), 155–169.

Ramcharan, B. G. (ed.), *The International Conference on the Former Yugoslavia* (Leiden: Martinus Nijhoff, 1997).

Ramcharan, B. G., *The United Nations High Commissioner for Human Rights: The Challenges of International Protection*, International Studies in Human Rights vol. 71 (The Hague: Kluwer Law International, 2002).

Ramcharan, B. G., 'Human Rights and Conflict Resolution', *Human Rights Law Review* vol. 4, no. 1 (2004).

Ramcharan, B. G. (ed.), *Conflict Prevention in Practice: Essays in Honour of James Sutterlin* (Leiden: Martinus Nijhoff, 2005).

Ramcharan, B. G., *A UN High Commissioner in Defence of Human Rights: No License to Kill or Torture* (Leiden: Martinus Nijhoff, 2005).

Ramcharan, B. G., 'The UN High Commissioner for Human Rights and International Humanitarian Law', Occasional Paper Series, Program on Humanitarian Policy and Conflict Research, Harvard University (2005).

Ramcharan, B. G. (ed.), 'Human Rights Protection in the Field', *International Studies in Human Rights* vol. 87 (Leiden: Martinus Nijhoff, 2006).

Ramcharan, B. G., 'The Protection Methods of Human Rights Field Offices', in B. G. Ramcharan (ed.), *Human Rights Protection in the Field*, International Studies in Human Rights vol. 87 (Leiden: Martinus Nijhoff, 2006).

Ramet, S. P., *Balkan Babel: The Disintegration of Yugoslavia from the Death of Tito to Ethnic War*, 2nd edn (Boulder: Westview, 1996).

Ratner, S. R., 'The Cambodia Settlement Agreements', *American Journal of International Law* vol. 87 (1993), 1–41.

Rehn, E., E. J. Sirleaf (eds), *Women, War and Peace: The Independent Experts' Assessment* vol. 1(UNIFEM/UNFPA, 2002).

Reinisch, A., *International Organizations before National Courts* (Cambridge: Cambridge University Press, 2000).

Reka, B., *UNMIK as an International Governance in Post-war Kosovo: NATO's Intervention, UN Administration and Kosovar Aspirations* (Skopje: Logos, 2003).

Ressler, E. M. *et al.* (eds), *Children in War: A Guide to the Provision of Services* (New York: UNICEF, 1993).

Ressler, E. M. *et al.* (eds), *Unaccompanied Children: Care and Protection in Wars, Natural Disasters and Refugee Movements* (Oxford: Oxford University Press, 1998).

Rieff, D., *A Bed for the Night* (London: Vintage, 2002).

Robert, R. I. (ed.), *Truth v. Justice: The Morality of Truth Commissions* (Princeton: Princeton University Press, 2001).

Rodrigues, G., 'States, National Interest and Human Rights: Some Thoughts on the UN Process Leading up to UNTAET', in M. Almeida (ed.), *Nationbuilding in East Timor* (Canadian Peacekeeping Press 2001).

Rorty, R., 'Human Rights, Rationality, and Sentimentality', in S. Shute (ed.), *On Human Rights: The Oxford Amnesty Lectures 1993* (New York: Basic Books, 1993).

Rosas, A. and Timo, L., 'OSCE Long-Term Missions', in M. Bothe, N. Ronzitti and A. Rosas (eds), *The OSCE in the Maintenance of Peace and Security: Conflict Prevention, Crisis Management and Peaceful Settlement of Disputes* (The Hague: Kluwer Law International, 1997).

Roth, K., 'Defending Economic, Social and Cultural Rights', *Human Rights Quarterly* vol. 26, no. 1 (2004).

Sands, P. *et al.* (eds), *Bowett's Law of International Institutions*, 5th edn (London: Sweet & Maxwell, 2005).

Schabas, W., 'The Relationship Between Truth Commissions and International Courts: The Case of Sierra Leone', *Human Rights Quarterly* vol. 25, no. 3 (2003).

Scheinen, M. *et al.* (eds), *Human Rights in Development, 8 Yearbook 2002* (Leiden: Martinus Nijhof, 2002).

Schermers, H. G. *et al.* (eds), *International Institutional Law: Unity within Diversity*, 4th edn (Leiden: Martinus Nijhoff, 2003).

Sen, A., *Development as Freedom* (New York: Anchor Books, 1999).

Shaw, R., 'Rethinking Truth and Reconciliation Commissions: Lessons from Sierra Leone', *United States Institute of Peace*, Special Report No. 130 (February 2005).

Shute, S. (ed.), *On Human Rights: The Oxford Amnesty Lectures 1993* (New York: Basic Books, 1993).

Skaar, E. *et al.* (eds), *Roads to Reconciliation* (Lanham: Lexington Books, 2005).

Slim, H., 'Not Philanthropy but Rights: The Proper Politicisation of Humanitarian Philosophy', *International Journal of Human Rights* vol. 6, no. 2 (2002).

Slim, H., 'Protecting Civilians: Putting the Individual at the Humanitarian Centre', in *The Humanitarian Decade* vol. 2 (New York: OCHA, 2004).

Slim, H. *et al.*, *Humanitarian Protection* (Pilot Version) (London: ALNAP, 2004).

Slim, H. *et al.*, *Protection: An ALNAP Guide for Humanitarian Organisations* (London: Overseas Development Institute, 2005).

Sloan, J., 'The Dayton Peace Agreement: Human Rights Guarantees and their Implementation', *European Journal of International Law* vol. 7 (1996), 207.

Smeets, M., 'The United Nations Mission for the Verification of Human Rights in Guatemala', *Netherlands Quarterly of Human Rights* vol. 15, no. 4 (1997).

Smith, M. G. and M. Dee, *Peacekeeping in East Timor: The Path to Independence* (Boulder: Lynne Rienner, 2002).

Stavropoulou, M., 'Displacement and Human Rights: Reflections on UN Practice', *Human Rights Quarterly* vol. 20, no. 3 (1998).

Stedman, S. *et al.* (eds), *Ending Civil Wars: The Implementation of Peace Agreements* (Boulder: Lynne Rienner, 2002).

Steinbock, D. J. 'The refugee definition as law: issues of interpretation', in F. Nicholson (ed.), *Refugee Rights and Realities* (Cambridge: Cambridge University Press, 1999).

Steiner, H. J. *et al.* (eds), *International Human Rights in Context: Law, Politics, Morals: Text and Materials*, 2nd edn (Oxford: Oxford University Press).

Steiner, N. *et al.* (eds), *Problems of Protection* (London: Routledge, 2003).

Stockton, N., 'The Changing Nature of Humanitarian Crises', in *The Humanitarian Decade*, vol. 2 (New York: OCHA, 2004).

Stoddard, A., 'Humanitarian NGOs: Challenges and Trends', in J. Macrae *et al.* (eds), 'Humanitarian Assistance and the "Global War on Terror": A Review of the Trends and Issues', *HPG Report* no. 14 (London: Overseas Development Institute, July 2003).

Strohmeyer, H., 'Collapse and Reconstruction of a Judicial System: The United Nations Missions in Kosovo and East Timor', *American Journal of International Law* vol. 95, no. 1 (2001).

Strohmeyer, H., 'Making Multilateral Interventions Work: The UN and the Creation of Transitional Justice Systems in Kosovo and East Timor', *Fletcher Forum of World Affairs* vol. 25, no. 2 (2001).

Taylor, J. G., *East Timor: The Price of Freedom* (London: Zed Press, 2000).

Thomas, D. C., *The Helsinki Effect: International Norms, Human Rights, and the Demise of Communism* (Princeton: Princeton University Press, 2001).

Thoolen, H., 'Early Warning and Prevention', in G. Alfredsson (ed.), *International Human Rights Monitoring Mechanisms: Essays in Honour of Jakob Th. Möller* (The Hague: Martinus Nijhoff, 2001).

Tsui, E. *et al.*, 'The Institutional Response – Creating the Framework in Response to New Challenges', in *The Humanitarian Decade*, vol. 2 (New York: OCHA, 2004).

Türk, V., 'The Role of UNHCR in the Development of International Law', in F. Nicholson (ed.), *Refugee Rights and Realities* (Cambridge: Cambridge University Press, 1999).

Türk, V., 'UNHCR's Supervisory Responsibility', *Revue Quebecoise de Droit International*, vol. 14, no. 1 (2001), 138.

Ulrich, G., 'Optimum Ethical Standards', *Proceedings Seminar on Health Research Ethics in Africa*, republished in *Acta Tropica* vol. 78, no. 1 (Elsevier, January 2001).

von Meijenfeldt, R., 'At the Frontline for Human Rights', Final Report and Evaluation of European Union Participation in the Human Rights Field Operation in Rwanda (October 1995).

Walker, P., 'What Does it Mean to be a Professional Humanitarian', *The Journal of Humanitarian Assistance* (2004).

Ward, B., 'The Failure to Protect Minorities in Post-War Kosovo', *Helsinki Monitor 2000* no.1 (2000).

Wedgewood, R. *et al.*, 'Symposium: State Reconstruction after a Civil Conflict', *American Journal of International Law* vol. 95, no. 1 (2001).

Weiss, T. G., *Military-Civilian Interaction: Humanitarian Crises and the Responsibility to Protect*, 2nd edn (Lanham: Rowman and Littlefield, 2005).

White, N. D., *The UN System: Toward International Justice* (Boulder: Lynne Rienner, 2002).

White, N. D., *The Law of International Organisations*, 2nd edn (Manchester: Manchester University Press, 2005).

White, N. D. and D. Klaasen (eds), *The UN, Human Rights and Post-conflict Situations* (Manchester: Manchester University Press, 2005).

Whitfield, T., 'Staying the Course in El Salvador', in A. Henkin (ed.), *Honoring Human Rights* (The Hague: Kluwer Law International, 2000).

Wieruszewski, R., 'Case Study on the Former Yugoslavia: The International Mechanisms, Their Efficiency and Failures', in A. Bloed (ed.), *Monitoring Human Rights in Europe: Comparing International Procedures and Mechanisms* (Dordecht: Martinus Nijhoff, 1993).

Wilde, R., 'From Danzig to East Timor and Beyond: The Role of International Territorial Administration', *American Journal of International Law* vol. 95 (2001), 583–606.

Wilde, R., 'International Territorial Administration and Human Rights', in N. D. White and D. Klaasen (eds), *The UN, Human Rights and Post-conflict Situations* (Manchester: Manchester University Press, 2005).

Woodward, S. L., *Balkan Tragedy: Chaos and Dissolution after the Cold War.* (Washington, DC: Brookings Institution, 1995).

Ziegler, M. *et al.*, 'From Peace to Governance: Police Reform and the International Community', *Report from November 2001 Conference at the Washington Office on Latin America and John Hopkins School of Advanced Studies* (2001).

Index